Breaking the Engagement

Breaking the Engagement

How China Won & Lost America

DAVID SHAMBAUGH

OXFORD
UNIVERSITY PRESS

OXFORD

UNIVERSITY PRESS

Oxford University Press is a department of the University of Oxford.
It furthers the University's objective of excellence in research, scholarship,
and education by publishing worldwide. Oxford is a registered trade mark of
Oxford University Press in the UK and in certain other countries.

Published in the United States of America by Oxford University Press
198 Madison Avenue, New York, NY 10016, United States of America.

© Oxford University Press 2025

CIP data is on file at the Library of Congress

ISBN 9780197792421

DOI: 10.1093/oso/9780197792421.001.0001

Printed by Marquis, Canada

MIX
Paper | Supporting
responsible forestry
FSC
www.fsc.org   FSC® C103567

Previous Books by David Shambaugh

China's Leaders: From Mao to Now (2021, 2023)
International Relations of Asia (edited, 2008, 2014, 2022)
Where Great Powers Meet: America & China in Southeast Asia (2021)
China & the World (edited, 2020)
The China Reader: Rising Power (edited, 2016)
China's Future (2016)
China Goes Global: The Partial Power (2013)
Tangled Titans: The United States and China (edited, 2012)
Charting China's Future: Domestic & International Challenges (edited, 2011)
China's Communist Party: Atrophy & Adaptation (2008)
China–Europe Relations: Perceptions, Policies, and Prospects (coedited, 2008)
China Watching: Perspectives from Europe, Japan, and the United States (coedited, 2007)
Power Shift: China & Asia's New Dynamics (edited, 2005)
The Odyssey of China's Imperial Art Treasures (coauthored, 2005)
Modernizing China's Military: Progress, Problems, and Prospects (2002)
Making China Policy: Lessons From the Clinton and Bush Administrations (coedited, 2001)
The Modern Chinese State (edited, 2000)
Is China Unstable? (edited, 2000)
The China Reader: The Reform Era (coedited, 1999)
China's Military Faces the Future (coedited, 1999)
Contemporary Taiwan (edited, 1998)
China's Military in Transition (edited, 1997)
China and Europe, 1949–1995 (1996)
Greater China: The Next Superpower? (edited, 1995)
Deng Xiaoping: Portrait of a Chinese Statesman (edited, 1995)
Chinese Foreign Policy: Theory & Practice (coedited, 1994)
American Studies of Contemporary China (edited, 1993)
Beautiful Imperialist: China Perceives America, 1972–1990 (1991)
The Making of a Premier: Zhao Ziyang's Provincial Career (1984)

Dedicated to **Winston Lord**

Distinguished diplomat, strategist, advocate, mentor, friend, and

United States Ambassador to China, 1985–1989

Photo 0.0 Hon. Winston Lord, US Ambassador to China, 1985–1989.
Photo Credit: US Department of State, courtesy of Winston Lord

This book is respectfully dedicated to someone who I hold in the highest esteem: the Honorable Winston Lord. Winston is deserving of this dedication for several reasons: he is one of America's most experienced and accomplished senior diplomats—having served at the very highest level of government in the Nixon, Ford, Reagan, and Clinton administrations, having played an instrumental role in the Nixon–Kissinger opening to China in 1971–1972, and serving as US Ambassador to China from 1985 to 1989. His illustrious career also included serving as President of the Council on Foreign Relations from 1977 to 1985 (when we first met). We have had a running conversation about US–China relations over many years, and he took significant time to read and comment on several portions of this book manuscript. We also share a deep common passion for sports— particularly basketball and football—and we regularly exchange emails about various games, teams, players, and league changes. It is highly unusual for one to make a good new friend later in life—but Win and I have done so, and I deeply appreciate his friendship, advice, and sense of humor. He is a great role model and a Great American.

Contents

List of Photographs

List of Figures

Preface

I like puzzles. Every one of my previous books began with a puzzle—a phenomenon that I was intrigued by but could not easily explain. When I started researching and writing these books—whether the one on China's Communist Party,[1] China's modernizing military,[2] China's America Watchers,[3] China's expanding global role,[4] China's future,[5] China's leadership,[6] China and Southeast Asia,[7] China's imperial art treasures,[8] or other topics—I did not know exactly where I would come out when I embarked. I had informed hunches—although I eschew formulaic hypotheses that many social scientists seem to insist on—but I was not sure where I would come out after I explored the evidence. I am an empirical inductive scholar; I follow and weave together the evidence into a coherent account. I also believe that good writing is about "telling a story." What is the story that the evidence sustains? This volume is no different.

From Engagement to Disengagement

The book is concerned with two basic puzzles. First, why have US–China relations fluctuated so regularly back and forth from amity to enmity over many decades and centuries, and why has it been so difficult to establish a sustainable equilibrium in the relationship? How could the United States and China, after two decades of estrangement and conflict during the 1950s and 1960s suddenly pivot to embrace and engage each other during the 1970s for five decades (through the 2010s)? This period is known as the "era of engagement." The second puzzle is why this American strategy of engagement with China has fractured in recent years (2017–2024) and has been replaced by institutional disengagement, partial economic decoupling, societal suspicions, and strategic competition against China? (Throughout the book I capitalize "Engagement" when it refers to the US government strategy, while I do not capitalize "engagement" when it refers to society-to-society interactions. When it is a mixture of the two, I do not capitalize it.) Is this most recent deterioration a temporary phase in a much longer fluctuating relationship, which will eventually pass and return to more amicable ties? Or is it something more fundamental, secular, and longer-lasting? These are the principal puzzles that motivate this study.

This is therefore principally a study of US foreign policy and the *American* side of the US–China relationship. As the United States is a democracy, its foreign policy must enjoy domestic support to be sustainable. Across eight presidents and their administrations (Nixon to Obama), there existed broad-based support for engagement with China. Not only have the strategy and associated polices been fundamentally challenged and largely withdrawn during the first Trump and Biden administrations, but the broad-based "Engagement Coalition" of US government agencies and domestic actors also concomitantly fractured.

Like the ancient Indian fable of the three blind men feeling the elephant, engagement meant different things and served different purposes for various constituencies in the United States. The beauty of the Engagement strategy was its elasticity, in that it offered something for multiple constituencies across the government and the country, and thus various interest groups became stakeholders in the relationship. Fundamentally, every constituency bought into the premise that direct contact between Americans and their Chinese counterparts was a good thing, the deeper the better; that engagement with the United States would contribute to the modernization and liberalization of China over time, to the integration of the People's Republic of China (PRC) into the (US-led) liberal international order; and that there were both direct and indirect benefits to be gained by the United States from such interactions and integration. China's broader engagement with the world and with the post–World War II international order was also seen as beneficial to American interests. Many European, Asian, and other nations also accepted this strategic logic—as they pursued their own versions of engagement with China.

Despite periodic disruptions in the bilateral relationship (most notably, the Tiananmen massacre of 1989), engagement with China was rarely questioned. While some Democrats felt that engagement was too indulgent of the abuse of human rights and repression inflicted by the Chinese Communist regime on its people, and some Republicans questioned the long-term wisdom of strengthening China's capacities through trade and technology transfer, these naysayers were at the margins of US policy discourse on China—while a strong bipartisan center continually bought into the logic of Engagement. It was axiomatic.

For decades, the US foreign policy establishment produced report after report on the need for continued bilateral engaged cooperation and integration of China internationally into the multilateral institutional order. This was further evidenced by the continually expanding executive-branch bureaucratic interactions with their Chinese government counterparts, deepening state and local ties, the vast proliferation of academic and civil society interactions, ever-broadening trade and commercial relations, as well as considerable tourism, immigration, and inter-societal exchanges. Engagement with China was (rightfully) seen as both necessary and successful.

Then, beginning around 2015–2017, it all came asunder. The fundamental tenets of Engagement began to be questioned toward the end of the Obama administration, and then the Trump administration (2017–2021) broke with the previous eight administrations and largely abandoned the strategy and modalities of Engagement altogether. The Biden administration (2021–2025) continued to pursue a strategy of comprehensive competition toward China and Engagement effectively ended.

What went wrong? Why—after decades of consensus and strong buy-in from multiple constituencies (which became stakeholders)—did the American Engagement strategy and coalition begin to fracture and unravel? And when exactly? Figure 0.1 illustrates that American public opinion of China has dramatically plummeted to the point in 2023 and 2024 (according to the Pew Research Center) where eight of ten Americans (83 and 81 percent respectively) held "unfavorable" views of China. Why has that occurred? Pew's survey of 2024 closely paralleled the findings of 2023, except (as shown in Figure 0.2)

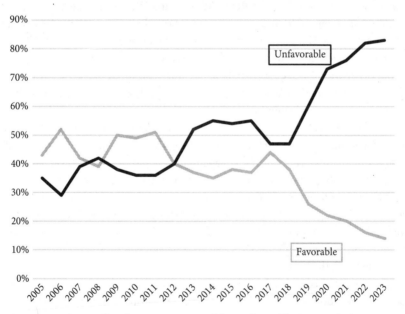

Figure 0.1 Pew Polls of American Favorable/Unfavorable Views of China.

Sources: Pew Research Center (July 2023), "China's Approach to Foreign Policy Gets Largely Negative Reviews in 24-Country Survey," https://www.pewresearch.org/global/2023/07/27/chinas-approach-to-foreign-policy-gets-largely-negative-reviews-in-24-country-survey/; Pew Research Center (January 2024) "Views of China and Xi Jinping": https://www.pewresearch.org/global/2024/07/09/views-of-china-and-xi-jinping/.

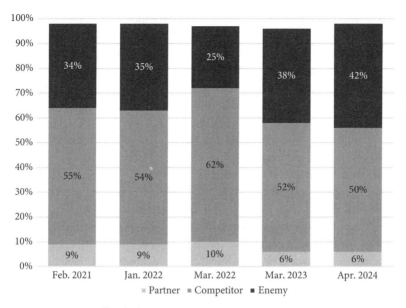

Figure 0.2 Pew Polls of China as Enemy/Competitor/Partner.

Source: Pew Research Center, May 2024, "Americans Remain Critical of China," https://www.pewresearch.org/wp-content/uploads/sites/20/2024/04/pg_2024.05.01_us-views-china_report.pdf.

the finding that those Americans who viewed China as an "enemy" rose to 42 percent among all polled, 50 percent described it as a "competitor," while only 6 percent saw it as a "partner." If there is one thing that Republicans and Democrats seem to agree on, it is that China poses multifaceted challenges and dangers to the United States.

These stark negative perceptions did not emerge overnight—as there has been a consistent secular downward trend for nearly a decade. Moreover, American opinions are mirrored by a similar sharp deterioration in global views of China, where a 35-nation cross-section of publics surveyed in January 2024 indicated that only 35 percent held a favorable view of China while 52 percent held unfavorable views.[9]

Although the progressive deterioration of the US–China relationship began with the Global Financial Crisis (2008–2009)—after which China became progressively disillusioned with the United States while American attempts to forge cooperation with China became increasingly difficult as Beijing became more truculent—the American policy framework of Engagement generally held until the Trump administration. Despite continued official Engagement under Obama, inside and outside of government, the multiple premises of the strategy and benefits began to be questioned privately. Once President Trump took office in 2017, all pretenses of official Engagement were quickly abandoned: bilateral intergovernmental dialogues were abruptly slashed from 98 to 2, his administration was the first ever to publicly label China as a "strategic competitor,"[10] he launched a trade war, and the relationship went into freefall. After entering office in 2021, the Biden administration largely continued the Trump approach (with some substantive modifications but less bombast).[11]

A central argument of this book is that not only did US government policy and strategy toward China change fundamentally during the Trump and Biden administrations—but that the underlying *coalition of constituencies* in American society had much to do with the unraveling of engagement. Strategies and policies emanating from Washington cannot be sustained without domestic buy-in and support. Beginning during the second Obama administration, for their own reasons, each individual constituency which had become stakeholders of the Engagement Coalition with China, individually and progressively became disillusioned with their counterparts in China, were not reaping the benefits expected from their engagement, and became new stakeholders in what I call the new "Counter-China Coalition."

Outline of the Book

Following this Preface, Chapter 1, considers why the US–China relationship has historically had such difficulty establishing an equilibrium, repeatedly fluctuating over the years from amity to enmity. It posits several interrelated explanations to account for the repetitive fluctuation and the most recent deterioration of relations. The asymmetry of power between the two countries has been one factor. Occasional clashing interests is another. But the main explanation for the two-plus centuries of fluctuation, I argue, lies in America's expectations of China and its long-standing "missionary complex" to mold, shape, and change China in modern and liberal directions. This paternalistic impulse has been at the core of the American approach to China since the 1780s. When China generally cooperated with this transformative mission, the two countries generally got along and found some stability in their relationship. However, when China resisted and pushed back against America's attempts to shape it, Americans became frustrated, and disharmony ensued. Chapter 1 then concludes by considering the "Did Engagement Fail ?" debate of 2017–2021—a debate waged among American foreign policy elites in policy journals and newspapers. Some provocatively argued that "Engagement had failed" and thus needed to be abandoned as a guiding government strategy—while others pushed back and defended the benefits of engagement. The critics of engagement generally argued that the policies associated with the Engagement strategy had failed in one of its main intended purposes: to politically liberalize China. The defenders argued that even if this was the case, America and Americans had still considerably benefited from engagement with China and that such benefits were in the broad national interest. Still other participants in the debate—the defenders of Engagement (primarily former US government officials)—argued that the Engagement strategy had *never* intended to liberalize and change China politically.

Section I of the book (Chapter 2) examines what I believe to have been the content and central components of the US Engagement strategy from the 1980s–2010s. To be sure, Engagement evolved over time—but it also included a number of continuous elements. Since there is no secret or master document in the US National Archives that explicitly describes a single Engagement strategy subscribed to by successive administrations, this chapter is my own rendering of what I understood to be the key ideational premises, elements of the Engagement strategy, and goals/tactics of implementing the strategy.

Chapter 3 of Section II examines the genesis of what I call the "Engagement Coalition." I reveal that elements of the coalition had their origins much earlier than the establishment of diplomatic relations in 1979. Most readers and experts likely think that the American Engagement strategy began with President Nixon's bold opening to China in 1972, or with President Jimmy Carter's official diplomatic recognition of the PRC and normalization of US–China diplomatic relations in 1979. In fact, I found that the Engagement Coalition had its origins much earlier. It began soon after China "fell" to the Communists in 1949 while Americans were debating "Who Lost China?" Readers will see that there were advocates for engagement of China both inside the US government (including at very high levels) and in American society at this early juncture.

Actually, the roots of engagement lie in American support for Nationalist China during the Republic of China era (1912–1949), even as far back as the 18th and 19th centuries. Throughout this lengthy period, Americans not only sought to trade with China commercially (after 1784), but to mold and shape it (especially after 1820) religiously, intellectually, socially, economically, and politically. As noted above, Americans have had an over two-centuries-long "missionary complex" to change China. Although this transformational mission and the US–China relationship was halted by the culmination of the communist revolution in 1949 and outbreak of the Korean War in 1950, and by the two subsequent decades of the Cold War, there actually remained advocates for engaging and recognizing the new People's Republic of China throughout the 1950s, 1960s, and 1970s. This chapter illuminates, for the first time, the genesis of this Engagement Coalition, which was stealthily taking shape during the height of the Cold War and Sino-American estrangement. It ends with a discussion of the Richard Nixon and Gerald Ford administrations' attempts to engage with China absent formal diplomatic relations.

Following mutual diplomatic recognition in January 1979, Chapter 4 focuses more directly on the post-normalization period and the successive presidencies of Jimmy Carter, Ronald Reagan, George H. W. Bush, Bill Clinton, George W. Bush, and Barack Obama. It traces what each of these presidents and their senior administration officials specifically said about Engagement with China.

Section III of the book is about the fracturing of the Engagement Coalition in the United States since 2017. Chapter 5 begins by describing the Trump's administration's abrupt abandonment of Engagement and the Biden administration's essential continuation of tough—but smarter—policies to disengage, decouple, derisk, and disrupt China. Chapter 6 is centered on the US national/federal government in Washington, DC. This "Inside the Beltway" chapter examines how the executive branch, Congress, and the national security community (military and intelligence agencies) all came to view China suspiciously and have consequently formed a new Counter-China Coalition. Chapter 7 moves "Outside the Beltway" to examine four key sectors in American society and how they have all contributed to, and been impacted by, the general "disengagement" from China: non-governmental organizations (NGOs), universities, the business community, and states.

Section IV of the book examines the competing visions for a new and workable American China strategy. Chapter 8 delves deeply into the animated Great American China Policy Debate in the United States raging since 2019. The chapter identifies five competing schools of thought in the debate. Chapter 9, the final concluding chapter, summarizes the book's arguments and findings, while also offering the author's own ideas for a future policy of "Assertive Competition and Competitive Coexistence" with China.

Finally, the Appendix turns the tables around by examining how China's "America Watchers" have interpreted the period of engagement and post-engagement. Drawing on a detailed examination of domestic Chinese publications—materials unearthed and mostly examined for the first time—it describes the abysmal and shocking "intelligence failure" of China's supposedly professional America specialists, who completely failed to anticipate or understand the significant shifts occurring in American society, government, and thinking about China during the 2010s. After the fact, they did better in retrospectively explaining the policy changes and their causes, but not beforehand. China's America Watchers were on "engagement autopilot"—they were complacent and never really considered the possibility of a fundamental departure by the United States from its long-standing Engagement approach. The Appendix also asks the basic question: Has there been a "Who Lost America?" debate in Beijing? If not, why not?

Living Engagement and Disengagement

The story told in this book of America's past engagement and now relative disengagement with China also parallels my own personal and professional life over the past half-century. Since the mid-1970s, my own life has been intertwined with China and US–China relations; I am a living example and beneficiary of the engagement policy over a quarter century. I have also become, over the past decade, an example of a "disillusioned former engager" who now believes that the United States needs to *disengage* from and counter China in a variety of ways.[12] China is now America's foremost competitor and rival. Thus, my life and career have experienced the same path that this book describes.

Like many other Americans, I was fascinated watching the live television footage of President Nixon's historic and dramatic visit to China in February 1972. Although I had some direct exposure to Chinese culture while visiting Hong Kong with my parents in 1960 and staying that summer in Taiwan with my older brother who was serving in the US Military Assistance Group (MAG), China itself remained terra incognita for me until President Nixon's famous trip. The year after it, during my sophomore year of college at the University of New Mexico, I signed up for two courses: "The Chinese Revolution and Maoist Thought" taught by a fiery Marxist professor and "Modern Chinese History" taught by a cultural historian of China.

I then took a gap year between my sophomore and junior years (1974–1975), during which I circumnavigated the globe—going over water and land from New York to Nepal (by necessity I had to fly to Thailand, Hong Kong, and Japan, before returning to the United States). While in Hong Kong toward the end of the journey, I happened to meet a British businesswoman who had just come out of "Red China" (it turned out that she had simply been to the Canton Trade Fair). This really intrigued me. So, the next day I took the train up to Hong Kong's border with mainland China. I walked outside the village of Lowu to witness high fences and barbed wire as far as the eye could see (to restrict mainland Chinese from escaping). On the other side of the barbed wire were only rice paddies (today it is the sprawling metropolis of Shenzhen). This further intrigued me: What was really happening on the other side, in the world's most populous nation? Actually, I had some inkling because of the course "The Chinese Revolution and Maoist Thought," in which we had studied the then-unfolding Cultural Revolution (and even tried to replicate some of its practices—like small group self-criticism sessions—in our class). I knew that Chinese society was in great tumult—but it was all hidden behind the barbed wire fences and beyond the rice paddies. So, I became even more puzzled about China.

After returning to the United States, I was seized with the desire to study China and Asia. After a semester, I thus transferred from New Mexico to George Washington University (GW) in Washington, DC, to enroll in the undergraduate East Asian Studies program, studying the Chinese language for the first time (I met my future wife in this class) and concentrating my studies on "Communist China" in GW's well-known (and conservative) Institute for Sino-Soviet Studies. I studied under Professors Franz Michael, Gaston Sigur, Harold C. Hinton, William Johnson, and others. All of them left a deep impact on me.

Then, after graduation, I had a very fortuitous opportunity to work in the US government for two years—first, as an intern and then an intelligence analyst in the China and Southeast Asia divisions of the Department of State's Bureau of Intelligence and Research (INR). One day, there was an inter-agency staff meeting concerning the unfolding Khmer Rouge genocide in Cambodia and escalating tensions on the Cambodian–Vietnamese and Thai–Cambodian borders. By that time, the Indochina analyst position in the Southeast Asia division of INR had come open and I was transferred from the China division to be the full-time Indochina analyst. During the coffee break, I was unexpectedly approached by Michel (Mike) Oksenberg from the White House National Security Council staff. Oksenberg was a well-known academic China expert on leave from the University of Michigan to serve in the White House as Zbigniew Brzezinski's and President Carter's top China specialist (he had formerly been Brzezinski's PhD student at Columbia). At the National Security Council, he was not only in charge of the China policy portfolio, but he also had responsibility for Indochina (which is why he was at the Cambodia meeting). Oksenberg began by asking me how I liked working at the State Department. "It's great," I sheepishly responded, "I have been given new responsibilities, having worked in the China office and now on Indochina." He then suddenly shocked me by saying, "Well, I have heard good things about your work here and I have been reading your reports. How would you like to come over to the National Security Council and be my assistant?" In my astonishment, I splashed the coffee out of my cup (but fortunately did not drop it), as my hands trembled. "Well, of course, I would," was all that I could muster.

As a result, my personal and professional life changed at that moment, as they became entwined with Oksenberg. As it turned out, beginning in October 1977, over the subsequent 14 months at the White House National Security Council, I not only followed developments in Indochina full-time, but Mike also had me work on a variety of China-related issues: intelligence assessments of China's internal and external situation, US export controls (the White House was trying to loosen them), resolving commercial "claims and assets" of nationalized

American companies in China, and several other practical aspects of the policy and legal adjustments necessary should the United States diplomatically recognize the PRC. I was also involved in preparing briefing papers for Dr. Brzezinksi's important visit to Beijing in May 1978 (which broke the ice on normalization), and I was left in charge of the office while the delegation was in Beijing.

Following the Brzezinski trip, during the second half of 1978, I became aware of the delicate highly secret negotiations that the United States was conducting with the Chinese leadership to consummate the normalization of official diplomatic relations (and I kept the secret). Thus, I was among the few not shocked when President Carter addressed the nation on December 15, 1978, stunningly announcing to the world that the United States and China had agreed to establish full and formal diplomatic relations two weeks later on January 1, 1979. I was also on the South Lawn of the White House on the frigid late-January day when President Carter welcomed Chinese leader Deng Xiaoping to commemorate normalization (see Photo 0.1), and I had the honor of meeting Deng on three occasions during his historic state visit (exchanging words in Chinese twice). I

Photo 0.1 Madame Zhuo Lin, Rosalynn Carter, Deng Xiaoping, and Jimmy Carter at the arrival ceremony for the Vice Premier of China, White House, January 29, 1979.

Photo Credit: Jimmy Carter Presidential Library, public domain via Wikimedia Commons was thus literally present at the outset of US–China engagement and had a very minor role in working on some of the policy changes necessary to achieve it. I had been extremely privileged to be a part of the run-up to normalization.

I left the National Security Council at the very end of December 1978 to concentrate full-time on my MA studies at Johns Hopkins School of Advanced International Studies (SAIS), where one of my classmates and friends was Nicholas Burns, America's Ambassador to China (at the time of writing.)

In the spring of 1979, soon after normalization, I visited mainland China for the first time as part of a SAIS faculty–student delegation. Then, in 1980, I was in one of the first groups of American students to study (Chinese language) in China—at Nankai University in Tianjin, returning for further language study at Fudan University in Shanghai in 1983.

These early visits to, and stays in, China afforded my first opportunities to see the country. The cities were drab. Monotony characterized everything. Architecture was largely in socialist block style, modeled on East German and Soviet housing. The tallest building in Beijing was the 15-story Beijing Hotel. People wore the same egalitarian blue communist garb. In the summer, slight variance in dress was permitted—everyone wore white shirts, and some women sported skirts. Bicycles were ubiquitous and people were everywhere! Automobiles were few, public buses and trucks were more frequent, while it was not uncommon to see animals (sheep, horses, camels) on the streets of Beijing after dark. Living quarters were extremely cramped, with generations living together, with little privacy for anyone. No private telephones existed. Shops offered little diversity of goods, and many products required state-issued ration coupons to acquire them. The countryside was more diverse but very poor. Peasants tilled fields with rudimentary hand plows as they had for centuries, while rural villages were dusty with no real commerce.

Beginning about 1982, this all began to change, as the country and the economy began to spring to life and awake from its socialist slumber, the nightmare of the Cultural Revolution, and three decades of stultifying communism.

Before I left the National Security Council, Oksenberg called me into his office one day and stunned me again (as he had two years before that at the State Department coffee break): "How would you like to come out to Michigan and be my PhD student?" Although I was enjoying my studies at SAIS a lot, the chance to go to Ann Arbor and the University of Michigan (then the center of the Sinological universe) was a once-in-a-lifetime opportunity. So, after completing my MA at SAIS in 1980, I enrolled in the PhD program in Political Science at Michigan.

After two years of coursework, passing my doctoral examinations and identifying my PhD dissertation topic, I became a real participant in US–China academic engagement. I was fortunate enough to be selected as one of the

20 American doctoral students sent by the Committee on Scholarly Communication with the People's Republic of China (CSCPRC) of the US National Academy of Sciences to conduct research (and in my case, also to take courses) in the PRC. Moreover, I was the *first* foreign (not just American) student permitted by the Chinese Ministry of Education to study in an international relations department since Soviet students had done so during the 1950s. I spent two years (1983–1985) in the International Politics Department (国政系) at Beijing (Peking) University researching my dissertation on China's America Watchers' perceptions of the United States.[13]

Spending these two years in China was an exceptional opportunity. I traveled by train all around the country, visiting Xinjiang and Tibet and other remote parts of central, south, southwest, and northeast China (see Photo 0.2). I played on Peking University's basketball team (going 56-4 over two years, winning two

Photo 0.2 The author in China, 1985.

Photo Credit: Author's photo, courtesy of Sakhr Faruqi

Beijing city championships and playing in the national tournaments in 1984 and 1985). Some of my best Chinese friends to this day were my teammates then.

During this time, I witnessed President Ronald Reagan's state visit to China in 1984 and experienced the fascination with the United States and the "America fever" (美国热) that was sweeping over urban China. I was also fortunate to have a part-time role as a consultant to the Ford Foundation, which was beginning a series of programs to train Chinese abroad in the fields of law, economics, and international relations (IR). Ford asked me to help assess the state of IR studies in China (I wrote several reports) and in their selection of fellowship candidates to go abroad; I interviewed and helped to select about 200 Chinese "scholars" (some of whom were intelligence analysts) in IR to go to the United States and Europe for advanced university training. This gave me a personal window into how American foundations and NGOs approached and operated in China in those very early days of engagement.

After returning to Ann Arbor in 1985, I buckled down to write my dissertation. After a year of writing while I was contemplating the academic job market, I was fortunate to be hired as a Program Associate of the Asia Program at the Woodrow Wilson International Center for Scholars (The Wilson Center) in Washington. Within months on the job, the Asia Program director abruptly resigned to take a new job—and I was thrust into serving as acting program Director (at the age of 33). This became a baptism-under-fire experience with the policy and diplomatic communities in Washington, DC. I was responsible for designing and convening private and public sessions to discuss China and US–China relations. I also interacted with the Chinese Embassy, including Ambassador Han Xu.

During that year, though, I was invited to apply for the academic position of Lecturer in Chinese Politics at the University of London's School of Orien-tal & African Studies (SOAS). To my pleasant surprise, I was interviewed and selected for the position. Resigning from the Wilson Center position and leav-ing the heady policy environment at a top think tank in Washington, DC, to move across the Atlantic Ocean into a new country and university environment was a difficult decision, but I had spent the previous decade training to be an academic professor—and this was a rare opportunity. Thus, beginning in the fall of 1988, my career took me to England for almost a decade (being promoted from Lecturer to Senior Lecturer to Reader in Chinese Politics).

While I sometimes had regrets for leaving the Washington policy envi-ronment and the United States, living and working in the United Kingdom was in fact a blessing in disguise—as it opened my eyes to how both the British and other Europeans viewed and dealt with China. My five-year posi-tion (1991–1996) as Editor of *The China Quarterly*, then the world's leading scholarly journal on China, afforded ample opportunities to cross the English

Channel to familiarize myself with European Sinology. I made a variety of lasting professional and personal friendships both with academics and government officials, and I have maintained a lasting interest in Europe–China relations ever since (on which I have published quite a bit). These experiences provided another important window into engagement with China. I learned that while not as zealous as Americans, in their own ways the British and continental Europeans were also committed to trying to "shape" China's trajectory internally and externally—primarily through establishing a variety of training programs for Chinese in media, law, academia, governance, and different elements of civil society. My experience also included serving for seven years on the China Exchange Board of the British Academy, where I gained firsthand experience negotiating scholarly exchanges with the Chinese Academy of Sciences and Chinese Academy of Social Sciences (including during the difficult aftermath of June 4, 1989, when I was dispatched on a solo reconnaissance mission to assess the environment for resuming suspended exchanges). I also conceptualized and worked with the European Commission in Brussels to establish the European China Academic Network (ECAN), and served as the inaugural Director. All of this exposure taught me important lessons about "working from within" the Chinese system, as well as within Europe.

In 1996, I was suddenly invited to apply for two open positions at George Washington University (my alma mater). I was interviewed and hired as a Professor of Political Science and International Affairs and Director of the Sigur Center for Asian Studies in the Elliott School of International Affairs at GW. This presented another tough decision, as I was very happy with my personal and professional life in England, but I decided to return to the United States (Elliott School Dean Harry Harding was instrumental in luring me back across the Atlantic, and he has been my mentor, role model, colleague, and good friend ever since).

Thereafter, my participation in the US–China relationship and engagement process resumed. Throughout this 28-year-long period, I have participated in countless conferences and meetings in China (see Photo 0.3), have led or have been a member of numerous delegations to China (although the vast majority of my visits to China were individual), interacting with a wide range of scholars and intellectuals, being a visiting scholar in residence in six different institutes of the Chinese Academy of Social Sciences: the Institute of Marxism–Leninism (马列所), the Institute of American Studies (美国所), the Institute of European Studies (欧洲所), the Institute of Political Science (政治学所), the Institute of World Economics and Politics (世经政所), and the Contemporary China Institute (当代中国所).[14]

Photo 0.3 The author speaking at a conference hosted by the Chinese Communist Party, 2011.
Photo Credit: Author's photo

I visited China for professional purposes at least once a year every year between 1979 and 2015—36 consecutive years of visiting and five years total of living in China. I have met and interviewed Party, government, and military officials at multiple levels—including Chinese Communist Party (CCP) Politburo members and Central Committee Department directors, State Council ministers and vice ministers, People's Liberation Army (PLA) generals, provincial and municipal leaders, and a wide range of academic and civil society actors. I have visited 27 of China's 31 provinces (only missing Inner Mongolia, Guizhou, Ningxia, and Qinghai), and have traveled deep into the interior of the country by rail and road. I have lectured (in English and Chinese) to multiple audiences (including many students, PLA officers, CCP officials, journalists, think-tank analysts, university professors, etc.), and I have given many interviews to Chinese media. My Chinese name (Shen Dawei, 沈大伟) is widely known. I have been feted at banquets in the Great Hall of the People and have met with senior leaders in the Great Hall's cavernous reception rooms. I started studying the Chinese language nearly 50 years ago and I am reasonably fluent. I have many good professional colleagues and a number of close personal Chinese friends. My wife and two sons lived with me in China several times (our younger son, Xander, attended eighth grade at a Beijing international school and we also shared the memorable experience of attending the 2008 Olympic Games together.)

Being based in Washington, DC, has also afforded me an up-close perspective and ringside seat to the evolving US–China relationship. I have witnessed every single Chinese leader's visit to the United States over this period (Deng Xiaoping, Jiang Zemin, Hu Jintao, Xi Jinping) and I was also in Beijing for former presidents Ronald Reagan's and Barack Obama's state visits. I have met every Chinese ambassador to the United States and every American ambassador to China since 1979 (and was twice considered for the ambassadorship myself). I have also regularly been called upon by different administrations (Democratic and Republican alike) and by different parts of the US government for consultations and advice on China policy, intelligence, and strategy. In addition, I have advised a wide range of American universities, philanthropic foundations, banks and companies, think tanks, and other NGOs involved with China.

Beginning during my year as a Fulbright Senior Visiting Scholar in China in 2009–2010, I began to sense that some very troubling underlying dynamics were at work in the country that were cancerous to the US–China relationship. Inside China and the CCP, various negative anti-foreign and anti-American trends were percolating, and there were various signs of tightening of interactions and cooperation with foreigners. After a frustrating experience with the Chinese Academy of Social Sciences (CASS), which did little to help facilitate my ten months of research, I asked the vice president of CASS in charge of their foreign exchanges (外办) why they had been so obstructionist, particularly toward an American who was so well known in China and internationally, who had done so much to advance the US–China relationship, and who had helped CASS itself over many previous years. "Dr. Shambaugh," he slowly and tersely replied, "We no longer feel we need to assist American scholars like we used to in previous years."

As I left Beijing in the summer of 2010, I had a gnawing sense of apprehension about the direction China was heading in and the underlying growing negativity toward the United States percolating inside of the country. When I returned to America, my premonitions and sense of foreboding was matched by a parallel growing shift in the views of China among Washington China experts, largely in response to assertive actions taken by the PRC during the previous year (which became known as China's "Year of Assertiveness"). My sense that a fundamental and qualitative shift in US–China relations was occurring led me to edit a book titled *Tangled Titans: The United States and China*.[15]

Many of the negative trends that I noticed during 2009–2010 continued and intensified after Xi Jinping came to power in 2012. In 2015, I authored a lengthy op-ed article in *The Wall Street Journal's* weekend edition detailing the concerning trends I saw occurring in the CCP, in the Chinese economy and society, and in China's foreign relations. *The Wall Street Journal* chose the catchy—but unfortunate—title "The Coming Crack-Up of China" for the article, which generated considerable international attention.[16] While it was controversial and much discussed around the world, the Chinese authorities were not at all pleased. They did not consider the article analytical—but rather to be an attack on China, on the CCP, and on Xi Jinping. What really troubled them was the headline—"crack-up" translates as *bengkui* (崩溃) in Chinese, the very same term the CCP uses to describe the collapse of the former Soviet Union. The article was thus judged not only to be highly critical of the CCP and its leader, but was understood to be predicting the collapse of the PRC and of the CCP rule itself! This was *not* actually what I argued in the article—I argued that the CCP was reverting to "atrophy" (a progressive deterioration) after a lengthy period of reform and "adaptation."[17] But for the CCP authorities (particularly in the CCP Propaganda Department, as I was subsequently told) it had hit a very raw nerve. In the article, I argued that if the CCP did not rectify many of these negative trends and elements of "atrophy," then it possibly *could* lead to progressive regime decay and/or collapse.

As a consequence, my 35 years of direct and deep personal engagement with China was brought to a screeching halt. In an instant, I went from being an "old friend of China" (老朋友) to being banished. A central directive (中央指示) from the Central Foreign Affairs Office (中央外办) was dispatched to all universities and think tanks in Beijing "not to invite or receive Shen Dawei" (不能邀请, 接待 沈大伟). Fortunately, the directive apparently was not sent to institutions outside of Beijing, or they decided to ignore it, and I thus enjoyed very productive professional visits to Fudan University in Shanghai in 2017 and to Xiamen University in 2019 (as well as to Hong Kong and Macao in 2018 and 2019, respectively).

After more than three decades of consistent—and often high-level—interactions in China, I was suddenly banned! My article and its headline had really hit the insecure nerves and run afoul of the CCP's *apparatchiks* (I was later told that it was specifically the CCP Propaganda Department). When I subsequently visited Henry Kissinger in his Park Avenue office in New York not long after the article was published (see Photo 0.4), he told me in his thick German accent, "Zee Chinese … zay are verrry upset about your article." I am surprised that my case had come up in discussions with someone as high-level as Dr. Kissinger, but it does illustrate the level of officialdom that it had reached.

While I continue to have extremely positive feelings for the Chinese people and my own personal friendships forged over decades, as well as many wonderful memories of my years in China, and I continue to believe in the importance of dialogue between our two countries—my experience with the aftermath of *The Wall Street Journal* article does not at all endear me to the authorities in China.

Photo 0.4 Henry Kissinger and Author.
Photo Credit: Author's photo

Then, in the fall of 2023, the Chinese Embassy in Washington, DC, suddenly invited me to lunch and informed me that I "was welcome to visit China again." This was, of course, good news to hear. It might have been better if the official had apologized for the arbitrary nine-year "invitation ban" that I had been placed under, but that was a bridge too far. I had hoped, over the course of the nine years, that this day would eventually come and that I would again be allowed to visit the country that is the object of my professional life. Soon thereafter, I received my first invitation, but it was not of interest. All along I had believed that the best way to return was as a member of a high-ranking American delegation (so that it would provide "institutional cover" and the Chinese government could see that I was still an actor on the American side of US–China relations). Unfortunately, for these nine years, I had also been frozen out of being included in delegations from organizations like the National Committee on US–China Relations (where I had served as a member of the Board of Directors prior to *The Wall Street Journal* incident), think tanks, and NGOs (perhaps because they feared that the Chinese would not issue me a visa and then the organizations concerned would be put in a difficult position). Nor was I in a position to lead any more delegations and co-organize conferences under the auspices of the China Policy Program at George Washington, which I established in 1998 and with which I had a long track record of joint events with Chinese interlocutors (see Photo 0.3).

Then fortuitously, in the spring of 2024, I was invited to join a very high-level "Track II" delegation to China organized by the Aspen Strategy Group and led by noted Harvard Emeritus Professor Joseph S. Nye. Joe knew my situation, which we discussed over lunch at Stanford while we were both in residence at the Hoover Institution, and he personally extended the invitation. This was the perfect opportunity, and I returned to Beijing for the first time in nine years. I was warmly welcomed by all our official Chinese interlocutors. Now that I had been let out of the proverbial "penalty box," in Chinese political parlance I had been "rehabilitated" (平凡). While it had been a long and unpleasant nine years—which taught me, if nothing else, the capriciousness of the Chinese Leninist system, where "old friends" can become "non-friends" overnight—it was wonderful to be back in Beijing, and I expect to resume visiting China in the future.

My own personal experience of coming full circle from deep personal engagement with China to forced disengagement to modest re-engagement mirrors the broad story about America's relations with China that this book tells.

Chapter 1
Elusive Equilibrium

"So much was invested in a China that would liberalize and play a constructive role in the global commonwealth. Now there is widespread disappointment and frustration."

—Philip Zelikow and Condoleezza Rice[1]

The recent period of strained US–China relations is hardly the first time that Americans have become disenchanted with China and the relationship has deteriorated. A stable equilibrium has long been elusive in the relationship, while fluctuation has been the norm. Even during the four decades when engagement predominantly prevailed (1980s to 2010s), the relationship (and American policy) was periodically hit by exogenous events that temporally impacted it. But each time, after the passage of time and certain steps taken by each government, the relationship resumed and restabilized somewhat—until the next disruption occurred. Such cycles of engagement–estrangement–reengagement have been recurrent in Sino-American relations.

What Explains the Historical Fluctuation in Sino-American Relations?

The recent deterioration and current phase of strained relations can only be understood in the longer historical context of the US–China relationship. It is not new, and is simply the latest downward swing in more than a century of oscillating relations. This repetitive pattern predates Sino-American relations during the Communist era since 1949. It was evident throughout the era of Nationalist China (1912–1949) and dating back to the late-Qing dynasty after the 1780s. So, what causes these repetitive swings in Sino-American relations—from amity to enmity and back again (sometimes referred to as the "love–hate cycle")? Why has it been so difficult to establish and sustain an equilibrium in the relationship? I have puzzled over this oscillation for some time, as I teach my annual graduate course on US–China relations. But observing oscillation is one thing—explaining it is quite another. What has actually caused the relationship to fluctuate so repetitively across 250 years of different types of Chinese governments (imperial, nationalist, communist)? And what have been the principal causes of—and alternative explanations for—the most recent deterioration of relations since 2017?

Both countries and governments bear some responsibility for the cyclical fluctuations. Neither side is blameless. Exogenous shocks also occasionally occur and shake the relationship, to which both sides must respond. There also exist deep structural factors—disparities in relative power and international circumstances—which shape the relationship. Subjective factors such as nationalism, patriotism, race, and interpersonal connections also play roles.

The asymmetry of power between the two countries has certainly been an important factor over time. It is not so much that America has sought to leverage its power over China. It did not need to—China knew it was the weaker party. As such, China was willing to sublimate many of its negative reactions to American actions—because it *needed* the United States: for its economy, for its development, and for its security. But the stronger that China has become over the past decade or so, the less it has been willing to accommodate itself to American desires. The narrowing of the "power gap" has thus definitely affected this dynamic in recent years, as the Chinese communist government feels emboldened and is no longer willing to "play along" with the United States and sublimate itself to American wishes.

Changes in China's behavior over the past decade have certainly also been a contributing factor to the deteriorating relationship, as Chinese leader Xi Jinping has produced extensive changes in his government's domestic and foreign policies—and these policies have directly and negatively threatened and impacted American interests.[2] This is true not only of US government interests, but also of the interests of a wide range of domestic American actors. Xi's strong illiberalism has violated America's moral sensibilities while directly impacting American civil society, academic, business, and governmental actors operating in China. Xi's assertive expansionism abroad has challenged long-standing American alliances and diplomatic, military, and public diplomacy interests worldwide, while Beijing's increasing opposition to the Liberal International Order has dashed hopes that China could be America's partner in global governance (euphemistically known as a "G-2"). Moreover, beginning around 2015, Chinese intelligence agencies, united front, cyber, and propaganda organs deepened their presence and malign "influence activities" *inside* of the United States (and many other countries)—triggering serious counterintelligence concerns.

In short, Xi's rule and policies have undermined the central rationale for engagement: China is no longer moving in a more liberal direction, as it generally had been, however hesitantly, during the rule of Xi's predecessors

Jiang Zemin and Hu Jintao. Xi has become a neo-totalitarian despotic dictator. Beginning in 2010 (two years before Xi Jinping came to power), China's party-state began to noticeably ramp up its repression domestically and assertiveness abroad.[3]

Other factors undercutting the rationale for engagement with China have had to do with changes in the United States. Throughout the 2010s, several systemic changes became apparent in American society, economy, and politics—which collectively undermined the Engagement Coalition's and ordinary Americans' interests.[4] Globalization and outsourcing of manufacturing to China hollowed out many American industries, companies, and whole communities. The resulting unemployment, personal hardships, and real sense of disenfranchisement swept across the country. This became fertile fodder for the political right, and Donald Trump tapped into it. Broader political populism and illiberalism took hold across the land.[5] The religious right joined the political left in viewing Xi Jinping's religious and ethnic repression and human rights abuses as deep moral concerns. Xi's intensified repression has thus undercut a central premise of engagement—to *liberalize China* politically, socially, and economically.

In addition, China's external actions have played a role: its dramatic buildup of military power; its increasing intimidation of democratic Taiwan; its coercive and mercantilist economic policies; its pressure against American allies in Asia and Europe while cultivating Vladimir Putin's Russia and other authoritarian states; its attempts to mobilize (along with Putin's Russia) a broad anti-American worldwide united front; its caustic "wolf warrior" public diplomacy; and its proven attempts to infiltrate and manipulate governments, societies, and institutions worldwide. These aggressive actions by Xi Jinping's China have all contributed to American alienation from China.

For all of these reasons, the core premises of engagement with China have been undermined and the relationship has deteriorated. China has not turned out as the premises and advocates of engagement had expected and is now directly confronting the United States and challenging core American interests and values. Accordingly, "Communist China" has again been demonized from many quarters, and a new bipartisan political consensus has emerged against China across the United States. Chapters 5, 6, 7, and 8 trace this process of estrangement.

All of these factors are no doubt part of the *explananda* for the recent deterioration of the relationship. But, taking a longer perspective, this book offers several other feasible explanations for the recent downturn and historical fluctuations.

First, I would make the perhaps novel argument that one key reason for the repeated swings in the relationship over a very long period of time has been American expectations of China, the transposition of these expectations on to China, and China's reactions to these American expectations. I would thus argue that the overwhelming "driver" in the relationship over time has therefore been America and its historic paternalism and desire to shape China in liberal directions. America has been the independent variable and China the dependent variable. America has long sought to change and liberalize China; this has been constant for two and a half centuries.[6] When China sought to "learn" from America and conformed with American expectations, however imperfectly, the two countries got along; when China stood up for its own interests and pushed back against America, relations soured. Put another way, when Chinese nationalism and sense of exceptionalism resisted American exceptionalism, the relationship deteriorated. When China sublimated its nationalism and acted in a pragmatic manner to take what the Americans could offer to China's nation-building mission while accommodating American preferences, then the two sides have gotten along much better. China *needed* America for its economic and technological modernization, but Chinese government authorities often chafed over the American desire to liberalize China socially, intellectually, and politically.

Second, this book also argues that American strategy and policy toward China over the past half century—which has been characterized by the term "engagement"—was the product of multiple domestic American constituencies (both governmental and non-governmental), all of which bought into—and became stakeholders of—the relationship with China. Collectively, I call these constituencies the Engagement Coalition. They all benefited from relations with China.

Third, ironically and counterintuitively, it can be argued that the demise of the Engagement strategy was in some part the result of its own successes. That is, as different sectors of American society progressively sunk roots in and with China, around 2010 they began to encounter substantially increased Chinese suspicions and resistance to their efforts—whether businesspeople, scholars and educators, NGOs and a variety of civil society actors, government officials, military and national security actors, and journalists. Around this time, American engagement efforts produced stepped-up countermeasures from the Chinese Communist Party security state. The more Americans became involved with their Chinese counterparts, the greater bureaucratic rigidities these Americans encountered—taken together with the Leninist political system, the arbitrariness and corruption, the excessive controls and surveillance, the xenophobia and nationalism, the lack of transparency and predictability (to say nothing of the lack of laws and due processes), and the political paranoia of their Chinese counterparts, these factors collectively alienated Americans of different constituencies. In other words, the more the United States engaged *in* China, the more politically threatening it seemed to the Chinese Communist Party and government, and the more resistance the Chinese side put up to American efforts. The Chinese Communists have *always* been suspicious of, and have tried to limit, the perceived threats posed by the American presence in China to their political system and culture—but beginning around 2010, and after Xi Jinping came to power in 2012, this perception and these countermeasures have increased substantially.

Thus, ironically, instead of forging cooperation and genuine partnerships, engagement often produced the *exact opposite* for Americans: alienation and estrangement. This is a counterintuitive and novel argument. The well-intentioned and benign American presence in China were seen as just the opposite by Chinese authorities, who saw them as subversive and malign. The closer the two sides became, the more their interests and practices clashed. Engagement first drove them together—but then drove them apart.

Again, it was growing American disaffection born out of Chinese resistance that was the main dynamic—China was not conforming to American expectations. There is also an underlying sense of extreme disappointment in America's current disenchantment with China. That is, Americans have long had the idea that their efforts in China were benign, well-meaning, and in *China's* interests! There is a sense of America having been "gamed" and "played" by China—that China was simply accepting the US presence and programs while taking advantage of American largesse to constantly strengthen itself and ultimately resist the United States. No country has contributed more to China's modernization than the United States, yet China has never said "thank you" and has never explicitly recognized all that the US has done to help China modernize. This makes some Americans feel that they have been taken advantage of. If anything, though, it is really reflective of American naïveté and self-indulgence. That is, Americans' sense of their country's "exceptionalism" and their belief that American ways of doing things had universal appeal and applicability and should therefore be (paternalistically) shared with others—all set Americans up for disappointment. America's "victory" in the Cold War over the Soviet Union and other communist states only served to fuel Americans' intoxication with the American Model, Washington Consensus, and "End of History" paradigm. Americans had come to believe that their system was vindicated and invincible. This self-indulgence not only furthered the long-standing mission to liberalize and transform China, but it also led the United States to overlook the fundamental Leninist nature of the Chinese system as well as the very real progress China was making in its technological and military modernization. Looked at this way, it was not only Chinese push-back during the 2010s that alienated Americans trying to engage with China, but Americans should accept some responsibility for perhaps an overly naïve approach to China in the first place (however well-meaning and benignly intended).

Taking the Longer View

Understanding the recent deterioration in the Sino-American relationship thus really requires us to look at it in a much broader context and longer timeframe. Above all, in my view, it requires recognizing the two-and-a-half centuries-long American "missionary complex" to shape and transform China: to help it modernize economically and technologically, to contribute to the development of a liberal society and political system, and to make it a country that did not threaten America or its interests in Asia or the world.

The United States has never been content to just "let China be." To reiterate my core argument, it has always sought to change China, to mold China, and evolve the country in a liberal and "modern" direction. In his pathbreaking and profound 1995 book *China and the American Dream*,[7] sociologist Richard Madsen correctly argued that it was the American "Liberal Myth" that has primarily animated the relationship and undergirded the dramatic expansion of the relationship during the 1980s following the strategic breakthrough of the 1970s. Madsen argued, correctly in my view, that China's "reform and opening" policies under Deng Xiaoping triggered and resurrected a "dormant gene" in "American DNA" to mold and transform China (in a liberal direction).

This transformative tendency had laid dormant in the American body politic and society for three decades following the culmination of the Chinese Communist revolution in 1949, the collapse of America's ally (Chiang Kai-shek's Nationalist regime) on the Chinese mainland, and the subsequent "Who Lost China?" recriminations in Washington. But America's latent "missionary complex" was quickly aroused and resurfaced following the normalization of diplomatic relations in 1979 and Deng Xiaoping's domestic reforms. Deng himself was twice anointed "Man of the Year" by *Time* magazine and the American media was filled with stories about China "going capitalist" during the 1980s. America's historical "missionary complex" had been resurrected.

Madsen's wonderful study traces this decade and phenomenon extremely well. It is one of the very best books ever written about Sino-American relations in my opinion. My book—the one you are now holding—is something of a companion to Madsen's earlier effort.

The repetitive oscillation back-and-forth between cooperation and confrontation in US–China relations over the past centuries is also anchored in a deeper American ambivalence and repeated domestic debates over China policy. This became immediately evident in the first two American diplomatic envoys dispatched to Beijing (then known as Beiping): Anson Burlingame and J. Ross Browne.

Appointed by President Abraham Lincoln, Burlingame served in the Chinese capital from 1862 to 1867 (see Photo 1.1), and he was revered by the Qing court.

Photo 1.1 Anson Burlingame, American Minister to China, 1862–1867.

Photo credit: The Lincoln Collection, Indiana State Museum

Why? Because he indulged and respected Chinese sensitivities and national pride, rather than advocating for special privileges—backed by coercion—then more characteristic of Great Britain and the European powers. In distinct contrast, Burlingame's benign approach was deemed the "cooperative policy."[8] In his definitive study of the pre–1914 era in US–China relations, the late historian Michael Hunt described Burlingame's approach as "patient paternalism."[9] Burlingame's accommodationist approach was epitomized in one speech in New York when he urged, "Let her (China) alone; let her have her own independence; let her develop in her own time and her own way."[10] The Qing Dynasty Court so liked Burlingame that in 1868 (see Photo 1.2) it appointed him to represent China to *all* Western powers, and appointed him to lead a diplomatic mission to America and Europe to negotiate favorable terms for interactions, treaties, and to solicit support for China.[11] In was on this trip that Burlingame died suddenly in February 1870 in St. Petersburg, Russia, while on his global mission to persuade other nations to accept China on its own terms.

Burlingame left his stamp on US–China relations in the form of a document signed in Washington in July 1868, known as the "Burlingame Treaty," which formalized diplomatic relations and conferred on China "most favored nation" trading status. The treaty also unlocked the free flow of Chinese immigration to the United States, which catalyzed the mass exodus of families from the Pearl River delta to California and laborers ("coolies") to work on the

THE HON. ANSON BURLINGAME, AMBASSADOR OF THE CHINESE EMPIRE, WITH THE MEMBERS OF HIS LEGATION.

Photo 1.2   American Minister to China Anson Burlingame with members of the first Chinese governmental delegation to the United States, 1868.

Photo credit: Granger Historical Picture Archive

Transcontinental Railroad, while Article 7 of the treaty opened the door to Chinese students to come to the United States for study.[12] Burlingame thus opened the doors to two pillars of subsequent engagement: immigration and educational exchanges.

Following his death, Burlingame was succeeded by J. Ross Browne as plenipotentiary to China. Appointed by President Andrew Johnson, Browne (see Photo 1.3) only lasted two years in his post (1868–1870). His views of China, and how to approach it, could not have been more different from Burlingame's. The two men's approaches epitomize the polar opposite views that have anchored American China policy ever since. Where Burlingame was indulgent of the Chinese, Browne was indignant, condescending, and racist. He viewed China as a morally degenerate society and the Qing state as weak and corrupt. Instead of Burlingame's benign accommodationist approach, reflecting his idealism of America as a social and cultural reformer, Browne advocated tough diplomatic pressure, moral condemnation, and the threat of force. In contrast to his optimistic and idealistic predecessor, Browne was a skeptic, a pessimist, a satirist, a muckraking journalist but respected author.[13] He had no background and no prior interest in China. His appointment by President Johnson, then undergoing impeachment proceedings by "radical Republicans" in Congress, was an attempt by Johnson to gain support from West Coast political and commercial elites, with whom Browne had influence.[14]

Once he arrived in Beiping, Browne quickly distanced himself from his predecessor's policies and persona. After a little more than three months on the ground, Browne asserted that he saw no evidence of "a more liberal or enlightened policy" on the part of the Chinese authorities, instead concluding that "China is now in a state of demoralization and decay, whatever theorists may say to the contrary."[15] Tolerance and indulgence of Chinese sensitivities were tantamount to appeasement in Browne's view. Only "determined moral pressure" combined with a "vigorous manifestation of power" by Western governments would bring about transformative change in China, Browne counseled the State Department.[16]

These parallel approaches by America's two earliest emissaries to the Middle Kingdom perfectly encapsulate and illustrate the conflicting attitudes and tactics echoed in American debates about China policy in recent years. What both Burlingame and Browne agreed on was the legitimate need to *change* China—on that core premise there was no disagreement. They only disagreed on the tactics. Browne did not believe that the Chinese rulers wanted to reform (in more modern and liberal directions)—he saw China as a degenerate lost cause—whereas Burlingame believed they were genuine reformists, arguing that only by working with Chinese would-be reformers could America bring change to China. Burlingame's argument has been at the heart of the Engagement strategy and

Photo 1.3 J. Ross Browne, American Minister to China, 1868–1870.

Photo credit: Public domain via Wikimedia Commons

advocates since the 1980s—while Browne's advocacy of moral shaming combined with strong deterrent power has typified the arguments of "realists" and "China hawks" in recent American debates (see Chapter 8).

Browne's inclinations and policy advice were short-lived and were quietly repudiated by the succession of subsequent American diplomatic emissaries in Beiping to the end of the 19th century.[17] By the turn of the century, America was becoming a Pacific power, while Japan, Russia, and European states were all expanding their own spheres of influence and establishing colonies and treaty ports across mainland and maritime Asia.

By distinct contrast, the United States was fashioning a more egalitarian and enlightened policy in the region generally and toward China specifically. This formally became known as the "Open Door" policy, as formally stated in Secretary of State John Hay's "Open Door Notes" of 1899–1900.[18] The Notes were sent to China, Japan, Russia, and all European powers, and they advocated for equal opportunity and access by all external actors in trading with China.

The Open Door Notes echoed Anson Burlingame's instincts; they formally cast America's China policy in a benign direction and, in essence, for the US government to be the guarantor of Chinese sovereignty. Not only was America's approach benign, but it importantly provided the framework for multiple sectors of American society to get involved on the ground in China. The late Michael H. Hunt, a leading historian of US–China relations of his generation, aptly labeled this cross-sectoral coalition of American actors as the "Open Door Constituency."[19] In his pathbreaking study *The Making of a Special Relationship: The United States and China to 1914*, Hunt meticulously demonstrated how different sectors of American society all gained an interest and stake in relations with China—American merchants and business, religious missionaries and social reformers, politicians and diplomats, educators, scientists and medical practitioners, and the military.

This pan-American coalition served to undergird the US government's broad approach to China—which lasted through the end of the Qing dynasty in 1911 and throughout the Republic of China's rule of the mainland (1912–1949). Moreover, I would argue that this coalition was the forerunner to what I call in this book the "Engagement Constituency" that undergirded the US approach to China in the 1970s–2010s.

The Recent China Engagement Debate

In recent years, two heated interconnected debates over American China strategy and policy have erupted, mainly inside Washington, DC, but also across the country. The first, which we will consider in this chapter, was over the efficacy of the Engagement strategy itself—with some arguing that it had "failed"; some arguing that it had outlived its purposes; others arguing that it had not provided the benefits and payoffs anticipated; many declaring that engagement was "dead" and needed to be replaced with a whole new China strategy; some arguing that engagement had indeed delivered the goods for the American people (quite literally in the case of trade) and had been a highly beneficial strategy; and yet others arguing that the Engagement strategy was still "alive" and simply needed refurbishment.

This debate began in 2016, continued throughout the Trump administration, and essentially ended by 2021. The second debate is the subject of Chapter 8. It grew out of the first debate and continues as of this writing. This debate is over the future US strategy, policies, and relations with China.

The Critics of Engagement

Presidential candidate Donald Trump was acting as a catalyst of the first debate when he railed on the campaign stump during 2016 about "China raping America." But Trump was hardly the first candidate for president who criticized his predecessor's China policies during the election campaign—indeed it has been almost axiomatic to do so. Recall Bill Clinton's criticism of George H. W. Bush for "coddling dictators from Baghdad to Beijing," or George W. Bush's criticisms of Clinton's pursuit of a "constructive strategic partnership" with China (George W. Bush was the first candidate for president to label China a "strategic competitor").

Once in office post-election, however, such criticisms quickly faded away as the new presidents dropped the rhetoric and "reverted to the mean" in their policies: Engagement. Trump did the same thing. His first year in office was characterized by continuity with the Engagement policy and traditional accoutrements of it: he toned down his anti-China rhetoric, held a "get to know each other" summit with Xi Jinping at his Florida resort, followed by an elaborate "state visit plus" trip by Trump to Beijing. But then things began to go off the rails. A year after entering office, the Trump administration abruptly abandoned any pretenses to the long-standing US Engagement strategy—and began to systematically dismantle the framework that had guided American strategy, policy, and relations with China for a quarter century. The administration also took specific aim at the whole concept of engagement, claiming in its *National Security Strategy of the United States* in 2017,[20]

> For decades, U.S. policy was rooted in the belief that support for China's rise and for its integration into the post-war international order would liberalize China ... These competitions [with Russia and China] require the

United States to rethink the policies of the past two decades—policies based on the assumption that engagement with rivals and their inclusion in international institutions and global commerce would turn them into benign actors and trustworthy partners. For the most part, this premise turned out to be false.

The *National Security Strategy* also explicitly labeled China—for the first time of any US administration—as a "strategic competitor" and "revisionist state." The Trump administration also subsequently published the important document *The United States' Strategic Approach to the People's Republic of China*, which set out in considerable detail the various challenges that China presents to the United States and how America should "prevail in the strategic competition with the PRC."[21]

However, even before the Trump administration changed the rhetoric and launched the first salvos of its trade war and multifaceted attacks on China, the American foreign policy elite and business community were beginning to show signs of discomfort, not only with China but with the long-standing consensus of "engaging" it. Such sentiments had begun to percolate late in President Obama's second term, as China had become a much more truculent and difficult partner. Efforts by the Obama administration to continue to try and "engage" China on a range of issues through a range of bureaucratic mechanisms were producing minimal returns on investment of time and resources.

The opening shot in the "Did Engagement Fail?" debate was fired by two former Obama administration officials in a widely read article, published in 2018 in *Foreign Affairs*, entitled "The China Reckoning: How Beijing Defied American Expectations."[22] In it, Kurt Campbell and Ely Ratner made the case that the long-standing strategy/policy of engagement had failed to deliver the anticipated and widespread American expectations—these expectations being that, as a result of multifaceted engagement with the United States and opening to the world, China would experience two things: political liberalization (in part due to economic marketization) and integration into the liberal international system:

Neither carrots nor sticks have swayed China as predicted. Diplomatic and commercial engagement have not brought political and economic openness. Growth was supposed to bring not just further economic opening but also political liberalization. Neither U.S. military power nor regional balancing has stopped Beijing from seeking to displace core components of the U.S.-led system. And the liberal international order has failed to lure or bind China as powerfully as expected. China has instead pursued its own course, belying a range of American expectations in the process.

Although Campbell and Ratner did not explicitly say that Engagement had "failed," it was implicit and was interpreted this way. The inference was that it had failed because it had not succeeded. What perhaps made the authors' arguments more startling was their admission that the twin expectations I have noted were fallacious in the first place. "The policies built on such expectations have failed to change China in the ways we [the United States] intended or hoped," they admitted, adding, "The record is increasingly clear that Washington once again put too much faith in its power to shape China's trajectory."[23]

Their article was like an erupting volcano—triggering vigorous waves of debates inside the US foreign policy establishment. After it was published, Campbell and Ratner retrospectively argued, "Our objective in writing 'The China Reckoning' was to interrogate the old consensus and spark a debate about the assumptions that have guided US China policy."[24] Spark a debate they certainly did.

The critics of the past Engagement strategy and policies were led by two senior international relations scholars: John Mearsheimer of the University of Chicago and Aaron Friedberg of Princeton University. Both men had long warned of the potential dangers of China's rise. Both had previously anchored their arguments in the belief that China sought absolute "hegemony" over Asia. In his book *The Tragedy of Great Power Politics*, Mearsheimer argued that rising powers first seek dominance over their own territorial regions and that this was a virtual law of international relations.[25] Professor Friedberg explicitly did the same in his appropriately titled book *A Contest for Supremacy: America, China, and the Struggle for Mastery in Asia*.[26] Both professors foresaw that there would be an inevitable clash—of interests if not militaries—between the United States as an Asia-Pacific power and China as an aspiring regional power. Both argued that the only way to possibly avert this inevitability was for the United States (and its allies) to preemptively contain China.

Both scholars returned to the fray in recent years, and participated in the "Did Engagement Fail?" debate, by arguing even more explicitly that engagement had not only been a failure—but that it had been a monstrous and naïve mistake in the first place. In 2022, Mearsheimer claimed in an interview,

> What we foolishly did was pursue a policy of engagement, which was explicitly designed to help China grow more powerful economically. Of course, as China grew economically, it translated that economic might into military might, and the US, as a consequence of this foolish policy of engagement, helped to create a peer competitor ... The US was not only expecting China to grow more powerful—it was purposively helping China to grow more powerful. It was doing this based on the assumption that China would become a democracy over time and therefore would become a responsible stakeholder in

an American-led order. Of course, that didn't happen. China did not become a democracy. And China, in effect, has set out to establish hegemony in Asia and challenge the US around the planet. We now have a new Cold War.[27]

For his part, Friedberg published an entire book critiquing the engagement policy.[28] In *Getting China Wrong*, he carefully dissected the origins, premises, expectations, and rationales of the four-decade-long Engagement strategy of the United States—and he showed how the CCP and the PRC have systematically gone about undermining those expectations. His is an important book that should be carefully read by all who try to understand US engagement of China, American grand strategy, and the future evolution of the US approach to China. While highly critical of engagement, Friedberg does not argue that American policymakers were blind or naïve. He observes, "Engagement was a gamble rather than a blunder. US and Western policymakers cannot be faulted for placing their original bet. Where they erred was in doubling down on it repeatedly and not hedging adequately against the possibility that the wager might not pay off."[29]

Two other neorealist critics of engagement are the former Republican official Robert Blackwill and scholar Ashley Tellis, who joined forces to produce two important Council on Foreign Relations (CFR) reports calling for a new "grand strategy" on China.[30] Their first report (2015) took aim at the errant liberal "end of history" assumptions that the post–Cold War world would be characterized by liberal norms and institutions, which China would have no choice but to accept and assimilate. Their second report (2020) offered 22 specific policy prescriptions for a new and tougher US grand strategy toward China. While forward-looking and policy-prescriptive, both CFR reports were implicitly critical of the general premises of engagement theory and specifically critical of Robert Zoellick's famous call for China to become a "responsible international stakeholder" in global governance.[31]

Another leading international relations scholar who entered the fray and implicitly joined the debate was Harvard University's Graham Allison. I say "implicitly" because Allison did not explicitly criticize the Engagement strategy per se—if anything, for many years and like many other US experts, Allison was a strong supporter of and participant in US–China dialogues that were intended to reduce misperceptions and lower tensions. But in 2017, Allison published a major book with the provocative title *Destined for War*.[32] In it, he surveyed 16 historical cases of rising powers vs. established powers, and he found that 12 of the 16 cases ended in war. This he describes as the "Thucydides' Trap." The implication is that, through decades of engagement with China, the United States had built up its own peer competitor and hence had increased the real dangers of great power war.

Allison's much respected Harvard colleague Joseph Nye also weighed into the "Did Engagement Fail?" debate in an op-ed in 2024, in which he observed, "We can date engagement's last gasp to 2015, when China and the US cooperated in supporting the Paris climate agreement ... engagement was effectively dead by 2016."[33] Yet, at the same time, Nye (like many others) argues that there was no other real alternative to the engagement policy over previous decades: "Looking back now, I still think engagement was realistic, though I plead guilty to having had higher expectations for Chinese behavior than what we have seen from Xi." Nye further observed that, "Underpinning the policy [of engagement] was the prediction, from modernization theory, that economic growth would propel China down the same liberalizing path as other Confucian societies like South Korea and Taiwan." Nye also added, "There were signs that China's rapid economic growth was producing some liberalization, if not democratization."[34]

At the Aspen Security Forum in 2024, former Secretary of State and National Security Advisor Condoleezza Rice (now Director of the Hoover Institution) echoed Professor Nye: "With China we made a bet—that a country that had a fundamentally different political system could be integrated into an international economy of largely democratic capitalist states ... So, it's not that we missed it [with the policy of engagement]. We tried for something that I think was the right policy, but in the final analysis it hasn't worked."[35]

Veteran Sinologist Orville Schell also contributed an important article to the debate. Starkly entitled "The Death of Engagement,"[36] Schell's article trawls through 50 years of US–China relations from 1972 to 2020, and he concludes:

> Engagement failed because of the CCP's deep ambivalence about the way engaging in a truly meaningful way might lead to demands for more reform and change and its ultimate demise. Without political reform and the promise of China transitioning to become more soluble in the existing world order, engagement no longer has a logic for the U.S. Beijing's inability to reform, evolve, and make the bilateral relationship more reciprocal, open and level finally rendered the policy inoperable. Because Xi Jinping viewed just such changes threatening his one-party rule, there came to be an irreconcilable contradiction at the heart of engagement that killed it.[37]

I myself would argue that Xi Jinping put the "nail in the coffin" of engagement with his repressive internal and assertive external policies, but I have argued elsewhere (as I do in this book) that the declining efficacy of engagement began to be evident during President Obama's second term (2012–2016). Thus, in my view, the "end of engagement" has been more of an evolving process than a singular event related to Xi.[38]

Thus, a few years before the controversial article by Campbell and Ratner was published, the debate over American China policy was already percolating. Harry Harding, an eminent and seasoned scholar of US–China relations, captured the early phase of the debate well in his 2015 article "Has U.S. China Policy Failed?"[39] Harding began by noting, "The United States is now immersed in its most intensive debate over China policy in decades—certainly since the Tiananmen Crisis of 1989, and possibly since the first serious discussion of normalizing relations with China in the mid-1960s." He then astutely observed, "Some aspects of the debate are even reminiscent of the first great debate over U.S. strategy toward China—the 'Who Lost China' controversy of the early 1950s." Harding's premonition was correct. The article by Campbell and Ratner, published the following year (2016), exactly echoed the earlier "losing China" debate with their argument that the engagement policy had failed and thus, in essence, China was being "lost" again.

The debate did not shift to the alleged "failures of engagement" until 2016 and the article by Campbell and Ratner, although Harding noted in his article that, "Present policy is widely believed to have failed." What Harding did astutely observe was the growing *dissatisfaction* with China in American policy circles: "The immediate stimulus for the current debate over U.S. China policy is a growing and widespread dissatisfaction with China's evolution both domestically and internationally, especially after the end of the Global Financial Crisis and the emergence of Xi Jinping as China's president and Party general secretary." It was precisely this broad-based groundswell of dissatisfaction that soon morphed into sharper and more focused critiques as exemplified by Campbell and Ratner.

The Defenders of Engagement

The criticisms of US engagement policy came fast and furious in the aftermath of the Campbell–Ratner article, and they put many in the US foreign policy establishment on their back feet. These were individuals who had spent their entire professional careers working to engage China. Now their life's work was under attack, and many individuals were naturally defensive. Once the Trump administration launched its broadsides against China beginning in 2018, the "engagers" became even more defensive but began to push back.

The prestigious policy journal *Foreign Affairs* offered what I call the "wistful engagers" their first prominent platform to retaliate and state their case in a multiauthor response to Campbell and Ratner. Entitled "Did America Get China Wrong? The Engagement Debate," prominent Americans J. Stapleton Roy, Joseph Nye, and Thomas Christensen (with Patricia Kim) debated Campbell and Ratner, Aaron Friedberg, and two Chinese contributors.[40]

Stapleton Roy, who served as Ambassador to China from 1991 to 1995 and is one of the most experienced and eminent experts on China and Asia in the United States, opened by stating that "attacks on the *supposedly failed* [emphasis added] China policy of the past 40 years, such as that by Kurt Campbell and Ely Ratner, are based on the false premise that the policy was meant to remake China in the United States' image." Roy then went on to claim, "Constructive engagement has served U.S. interests well. Since the 1980s, cooperation with China has advanced U.S. national interests in many areas." He closed his contribution by arguing for more of the same: "The wisest approach would be to continue engaging with China while focusing on advancing American interests."[41]

In the longest contribution to the symposium, Tom Christensen, a well-known China scholar and former Deputy Assistant Secretary of State during the George W. Bush administration, then criticized Campbell and Ratner: "Their article misses the mark in fundamental ways, offering an often inaccurate account of U.S. officials' expectations of and strategies towards China, and sweeping the many achievements of past decades under the rug."[42]

For his part, Harvard Professor Emeritus Joseph Nye's contribution to the symposium argued that "Kurt Campbell and Ely Ratner are right to raise questions about the assumptions that have guided U.S. China Policy ... U.S. policy toward China has not been a total failure ... Maybe the United States was not so wrong after all."[43]

Winston Lord, a key official in many administrations' China policies and participant in the original Nixon–Kissinger opening to China in 1971–1972, also weighed into the debate in 2023. When asked in an interview, "Was the policy of engagement with China a strategic failure for the U.S.?" Lord responded, "In a word, no. The process (more than policy) pursued for decades by administrations of both parties was not a failure, as misguided revisionists allege. There was no reasonable alternative. Engagement was not naïve."[44] Lord further added,

> Political liberalization in China was not the principal policy rationale of our policy. Nor was it assumed that it would occur. To be sure, there were hopes that opening China to the world and a growing economy and middle class would stir movement towards loosening of the political system, based on this having taken place in so many other places like Taiwan (with obvious Chinese dimensions), South Korea, Indonesia, Chile, etc. This would be a bonus for engagement but was hardly a *sine qua non*. Moreover, the long-term jury is still out—we have not necessarily seen the end of China's political trajectory.[45]

Another salvo in the defend-engagement counterattack came during the summer of 2019 in the form of an op-ed entitled "China Is Not an Enemy" published in *The Washington Post*, coauthored by five distinguished China specialists

(M. Taylor Fravel, Stapleton Roy, Michael Swaine, Susan Thornton, and Ezra Vogel).[46] The genesis of the op-ed was stimulated more by the then-aggressive rhetoric and moves by the Trump administration than by the Campbell–Ratner article. The anxiety levels among this group were rising in intensity—like blood pressure—with every new Trump administration action against the Xi Jinping regime. Their frustration was due in part to the fact that American media were providing *carte blanche* coverage of the Trump administration's rhetoric and actions—without any "balancing" coverage of countervailing viewpoints. So, this group penned their article, but they also had the idea to convert the op-ed into an "Open Letter" to the Trump administration signed by "more than 200 members of the scholarly, foreign policy, military, and business communities" who said,

> We are members of the scholarly, foreign policy, military, and business communities, overwhelmingly from the United States, including many who have focused on Asia throughout our professional careers. We are deeply concerned about the growing deterioration in U.S. relations with China, which we believe does not serve American or global interests. Although we are very troubled by Beijing's recent behavior, which requires a strong response, we also believe that many U.S. actions are contributing directly to the downward spiral in relations.[47]

The Open Letter is also notable for those noted China specialists who chose *not* to sign on (including myself, Harry Harding, Susan Shirk, Orville Schell, Winston Lord, Evan Medeiros, and many others). The Open Letter stimulated a counter-letter by over 100 former US military members, intelligence officers, and think-tankers entitled "Stay the Course: An Open Letter to President Trump."[48]

Also in 2019, following the dueling Open Letters, Harvard Professor Alastair Iain Johnston published a provocative article in *The Washington Quarterly* entitled "The Failures of the 'Failure of Engagement' with China."[49] Johnston is a well-known and accomplished scholar of Chinese foreign and security policy, who is also known for his contrarian publications. That is, he has a history of selecting topics that have become "conventional wisdom" (sometime memes) and then attempting to puncture them in his own articles. In this instance, he directly took on those who argued that engagement had "failed" by arguing that the empirical evidence from senior US officials (including former presidents) did not sustain what he claimed were the two core propositions of the "failed engagement" crowd—namely (1) "That engagement was designed to create a Chinese commitment to the US-dominated liberal order," and (2) "That engagement was designed to liberalize, even democratize, China's political system."[50]

I would agree that these are two of the main arguments on which the "failed engagement" school rests. Johnston argued that the first assumption is invalid as there is no such thing as a "US-led liberal international order." He argued, contrarily, that there are multiple "orders." This is an intriguing argument, with some justification, as the international "order" is indeed contested—essentially between Western and non-Western preferences. But just because the "US-led order" is not absolutely hegemonic does not invalidate it. It has, after all, been at the core of the United Nations and almost all international institutions, rules, and norms governing international relations since World War II (excepting the Soviet Bloc and Non-Aligned Movement). There is no other alternative "system" that has come anywhere near rivaling the Western/American system.

Moreover, Johnston blithely dismissed the argument about political liberalization/democratization as mere "caricatures." But, in fact, the evidence he cited from Presidents George W. Bush and Bill Clinton, as well as from leading former American officials such as Madeleine Albright, Winston Lord, and Samuel Berger, largely tend to *contradict* Johnston's assertions. They are also a handful of "cherry-picked" quotations from these former officials. As we will see in Chapter 2, expectations of political liberalization were very much at the center of the engagement school's perceptions and hopes across multiple US administrations. Moreover, the Engagement Coalition, as I call it in this book, goes well beyond the US government and very much includes a wide range of NGOs and private-sector American actors—*all* of which sought to bring Liberal (with a capital "L") practices to China. So, Johnston's using only a handful of cherry-picked statements by former US government officials is distorting. Even among US government officials, as I will show multiple examples of in Chapter 2, there was a *consistent* view from Presidents Reagan through Obama that liberalizing China's political system was not only a worthy goal—but that there was even some *inevitability* about it. In essence, every single American president made statements affirming the expectation that a more liberal Chinese economy and society would inexorably lead to a more liberal Chinese polity over time. Indeed, Johnston himself quoted George W. Bush, "Economic freedom creates habits of liberty. And habits of liberty create expectations of democracy."[51]

Another person who weighed in to support continued engagement at the time was, not surprisingly, the president of the National Committee on US–China Relations (NCUSCR), Stephen Orlins.[52] I say "not surprisingly" because there has been no single institution in the United States more deeply involved for a longer period of time in the practice of—and defender of—engagement with China than the NCUSCR. This organization epitomizes engagement with China. In his op-ed of 2018, as the engagement debate raged in the United States, Orlins wrote,

Constructive engagement has not failed. It simply needs to be rebooted to meet challenges that its founders could never have envisaged. We should also acknowledge its successes ... A few years after we engaged with China, American soldiers stopped dying in Asian conflicts ... Trade with China supports 2.6 million American jobs ... Chinese investment directly supports over 150,000 American jobs ... While China is still not the responsible stakeholder we had hoped it would become by now, it has come a long way ... The purpose of constructive engagement was never to make China just like us, but to make China a productive member of the global community.[53]

Some elements of the US business community also weighed into the debate on the side of engagement. One example was the "investment strategist" Andy Rothman—long known for his optimistic and rosy views of the Chinese economy—who offered several reasons why "economic engagement" had benefited the United States.[54]

Many Washington think-tank analysts also joined the defend-engagement chorus. Most were deeply disturbed by the Trump's administration's rhetoric and actions—as such they tended to *blame Washington* for the sharp deterioration of US–China relations. For most, it was not China's fault or actions that had caused the relationship to deteriorate so precipitously, it was America's fault! Although most were careful to include brief criticisms of malign Chinese actions in their publications—lest they be seen as pro-China apologists—the majority *zeitgeist* from the think tanks pinned the blame on the US side.

Some prominent think-tankers also warned against the "dangers of disengagement." For example, Brookings Institution senior fellows Jeffrey Bader and Jonathan Pollack pointed to a wide variety of potentially disruptive and destructive Chinese actions that Beijing could take in retaliation to the new confrontational American posture, also pointing out that the vast majority of American allies were unlikely to go along with the new actions to counter China.[55]

Perhaps the most systematic and extensive defense of engagement came in the scholarly volume appropriately entitled *Engaging China: Fifty Years of Sino-American Relations*.[56] This is an unapologetically explicit pro-engagement volume—the contributors make no pretenses otherwise—but the book would have benefited by including at least one chapter that offered a contrasting and critical assessment of engagement. Only "pro-engagers" were invited to contribute.

One overview chapter by former senior US government intelligence official Thomas Fingar argued that, "Engagement was a response to possibilities and opportunities, not an initiative to change China ... No one conceived of engagement as a return to the halcyon days of yore when Americans (and other Westerners) had a moral obligation to bring enlightenment to the Chinese people."[57] I think Fingar is both partially right and dead wrong. He is of course correct that engagement was a "response to possibilities and opportunities" ("feeling the stones while crossing the river" as the Chinese put it). Of course, engagement was iterative and unfolded over time in a reactive and responsive fashion once normalization of relations in 1979 made direct and broad contact between the two societies possible. How could it not unfold piecemeal as opportunities progressively opened? Nobody argues that the United States followed a Master Plan to transform China. There may have been no Master Plan—but there very much were consistently held *assumptions* about what engagement with America would bring to China (see discussion above and Chapter 2).

In his chapter, Fingar further claimed that, "The greatest mistake of all, according to the critics of engagement, was to believe that engagement would lead to the transformation of the regime in Beijing from authoritarian party-state into American-style democracy."[58] Indeed, many members of the American public could be forgiven for believing that this was precisely what was occurring before their eyes in the spring of 1989 prior to the brutal crackdown on the "pro-democracy movement" in Tiananmen Square. But I think that the way Fingar phrases his counter-critique is distorting. I know of *no* serious American China specialist, former government official, or policy expert who thought or argued that "American-style democracy" was feasible for China or was a realistic policy goal of the United States. A more *liberal* China, *within* a one-party reformist system, yes—an American-style democracy, no. This is an important distinction. The "engagement defenders" thus distort, and do a disservice to, the "engagement failure" school.

The other chapter that robustly defends engagement was by Johns Hopkins Professor Emeritus David M. Lampton—known informally in China as "Dr. Engagement" (Kurt Campbell is known as "Dr. Containment"). Lampton is seen this way for good reason: he not only has had a very distinguished academic career as a specialist in Chinese politics, diplomacy, and US–China relations, but he also directed several key institutions involved in US–China engagement—the Committee on Scholarly Communication with the People's Republic of China, the National Committee on US–China Relations, and the Asia Foundation.[59] For his career-long contributions to US–China engagement, the volume is appropriately dedicated to him. Lampton's chapter is largely a lengthy defense of the history of US engagement with China (although, to be fair, he concludes with some sober observations of what he calls "the gathering storm").[60] Like other engagement defenders, Lampton felt obligated to criticize the Campbell and Ratner article: "In their analysis, Kurt Campbell and Ely Ratner laid down an *inaccurate* starting point of the U.S. inquest by attributing to engagement an overarching goal (making China just like America, democratic) that never was the central rationale for most of its architects and implementers during the forty-five-year run as China policy." Instead, Lampton asserts,

> The foundational thinking was that if the two sides built more robust mutual understanding and if the two society organizations and bureaucratic institutions became more intertwined, the relationship would become more stable, productive, and manageable. The more threads tying down the relationship like Gulliver, the more impediments there would be to systemic disruption.

"Stable, productive, manageable"—this is a statement of goals that probably the vast majority of those in the US government who were involved with making China policy over the decades would readily agree with. That is what professional bureaucrats want and seek: stability, productivity, manageability. Keep the boat afloat and do not rock it, keep the train on the tracks, think about tomorrow, and move relations ahead incrementally. They do not think of themselves as change agents. Diplomats are intrinsically and particularly risk-averse. Businesspeople are similarly risk-averse and seek a stable operating environment above all. They are also myopic: their main goal is to make money. Grow the enterprise and make more money. As we will see in Chapters 2 and 7, other professional sectors—American politicians, academics, intellectuals, policy pundits, NGO members, human rights and environmental activists, journalists, lawyers, religious missionaries, national security personnel—all want change in China. For these groups, stability, productivity (and predictability), and manageability are not the most important goals to pursue in relations with China. Their professional missions involve other ends, and they employ other means.

More than five years after the article by Campbell and Ratner was published, the hornet's nest they provoked and the debate their article triggered has morphed into a broader debate over future China strategy. In Chapter 8, I take a deeper dive into how this debate has played out. While complex and still ongoing, the arguments remain somewhat polarized, with a majority view that accepts the premise that engagement (as previously pursued) did indeed fail to deliver on the anticipated expectations—and therefore that a new paradigm of "competition" is necessary to deal with a domestically illiberal and an internationally revisionist China.[61] This new majority consensus exists across the political spectrum, across the country, and across different constituencies, throughout Congress, and throughout much of the foreign policy elite. I call this new *zeitgeist* the "Counter-China Coalition."

Yet, the situation is not so neat and tidy. Variations of arguments exist within the majority "Counter-China" and minority "Re-Engagement" schools. As I have noted, the long-entrenched Engagement Coalition has by no means surrendered and gone silently into the night—they have fought back against what they see as ill-informed, short-sighted, ideological, neo-McCarthyite perspectives and policies. I explore their counterattack in more detail in Chapter 8.

There are different variants of the minority view. One variant of the current debate argues that engagement "just hasn't succeeded yet."[62] This strain argues that China is not an international pariah state and is not out to usurp either the United States or the global liberal order. The argument goes like this: Domestically in China, just hang in there, the liberal seeds have been planted, they just lay dormant under the soil of Xi Jinping's repressive regime—but, given time, they will blossom. This tendency to wish away Chinese perfidy and continually hope for better days is what author James Mann referred to as "the soothing scenario" in his provocative but prescient 2007 book *The China Fantasy*.[63]

This oversimplified dichotomy of the continuing debate is just the tip of the iceberg—as the debates are complex and carry on with fervor in respected foreign policy journals, in books, in Congress, and elsewhere. The multifaceted challenges that China presents to the United States (and to the world) today are so urgent and complicated that most analysts are now debating *how*—not whether—to push back against China.

I

THE CONTENT OF ENGAGEMENT

Chapter 2
The Strategy and Tactics of Engagement

"Underpinning the policy of engagement was the prediction, from modernization theory, that economic growth would propel China down the same liberalizing path as other Confucian societies like South Korea and Taiwan."

—Joseph S. Nye, Harvard University[1]

"Without political reform and the promise of China transitioning to become more soluble in the existing world order, engagement no longer has a logic for the U.S. Beijing's inability to reform, evolve, and make the bilateral relationship more reciprocal, open and level, rendered the policy inoperable. Because Xi Jinping viewed such changes as threatening his one-party rule, there came to be an irreconcilable contradiction at the heart of engagement that killed it."

—Orville Schell, Center on US–China Relations, Asia Society[2]

"The West has been wrong about China. It was long assumed that capitalism, the emergence of a middle class and the internet would cause China to eventually adopt Western political ideas. But these ideas cannot even begin to take root because the Communist Party has never allowed the intellectual soil needed for them to germinate. And it never will."

—Ai Weiwei, Artist[3]

Discerning and describing the US government's strategy of Engagement with the People's Republic of China is not easy. There is no Master Document to be found in the National Archives (classified or unclassified) that delineates the essential purposes and elements of the strategy to be carried out over time, although different administrations have had their own versions. It is important to note that, as an official term, "engagement" was not used to describe US policy until the administration of George H. W. Bush (1988–1993), and then again during the second Clinton administration (1996–2000). After the term "engagement" formally entered the vocabulary of American China policy during these two presidencies, it began to be used retroactively and retrospectively to describe the US approach to China since the Carter administration and normalization of diplomatic relations in 1979. Yet, as we will see in Chapter 3, some of its antecedents harken back to the "recognition controversy" in 1949–1950,[4] the brief consideration by the Kennedy administration of possibly following in Canada's footsteps to relax some of the strictures on the trade relationship (possibly foreshadowing a diplomatic initiative), and the efforts by some prominent Americans and NGOs during the 1970s to lay the groundwork for full diplomatic relations between the two governments and interactions between the two societies.

But the real impetus for engagement can be found in then presidential candidate Richard Nixon's 1967 article in *Foreign Affairs*, in which he explicitly identified two elements that would become central to the Engagement strategy:[5]

Taking the long view, we simply cannot afford to leave China forever outside of the family of nations, there to nurture its fantasies, cherish its hates and threaten its neighbors. There is no place on this small planet for a billion of its potentially most able people to live in angry isolation ... The world cannot be safe until China changes. Thus, our aim—to the extent we can influence events—should be to *induce change.*

Nixon thus very early and very clearly identified integrating China into the international community and inducing change inside of China as the bases and rationale of his subsequent outreach to Beijing. Four years later, with his dramatic opening of 1971–1972, another rationale was abundantly clear: forging a common cooperative strategic counterweight against the Soviet Union.

When Nixon undertook his dramatic visit to China in 1972 and signed the landmark Shanghai Communiqué, a fourth element was added: professional and people-to-people exchanges. The communiqué stated: "The two sides agreed that it is desirable to broaden the understanding between the two peoples. To this end, they discussed specific areas in such fields as science, technology, culture, sports and journalism, in which people-to-people contacts and exchanges would be mutually beneficial."[6] Winston Lord, who was the principal drafter of the communiqué on the American side told me, "Kissinger made sure that economic, cultural, media, sports, scientific exchanges, etc., were in our draft of the Shanghai Communiqué. When, in October 1971, Zhou Enlai rejected our draft for other reasons, Kissinger had me reintroduce these efforts in our redraft. It was the Chinese who tried to scale these back."[7] This is important because it shows that the China opening by Nixon and Kissinger was not solely motivated by strategic concerns (as is commonly thought).

Thus, before Nixon was even driven from office by the Watergate scandal in August 1974, he had identified four core elements that would endure at the heart of Engagement (until the Tiananmen massacre in 1989): international integration, domestic change, professional and people-to-people exchanges, and strategic coordination/cooperation. The Carter and Reagan administrations inherited these four core premises, and following the normalization of official diplomatic relations in 1979, they broadened and filled them out by instituting and institutionalizing a broad range of agreements, exchanges, and programs between the two countries.

It is thus crucially important to understand (and one of the major points of this book) that the US government was by no means the only actor that pursued an Engagement strategy with China. A broad swath of actors in the American private sector also had their own engagement strategies and activities. Viewed from this perspective, engagement with China was primarily an *interactive* process—where the carrying out of exchanges were seen as ends in themselves. Various American institutional actors and constituencies all pursued formalized relationships and exchanges with their Chinese counterparts—to advance their institutional missions and the issues to which they were professionally dedicated.

In this interpretation of engagement, there is no grand strategy or holistic approach guiding the pursuit of relationships with Chinese counterparts. Rather, they are each pursued on their own intrinsic merits. Companies try to produce or sell goods and services; universities set up exchanges of students and faculty for purposes of education and research; NGOs try to advance their causes; think tanks seek dialogues with Chinese counterparts to try to work together to address global challenges; government agencies sign agreements to exchange personnel and undertake joint work in functional areas; and so on. It is all *process-driven*.

This process- and exchange-driven definition of engagement is one major reason why so many Americans who have been involved with China over the decades bristle over the "engagement failed" narrative discussed in Chapter 1—because they did not think that engagement was intended to change China in the first place. Most of these actors simply thought they were pursuing exchanges for the sake of exchanges. Their aperture on the US–China relationship was, in most cases, very narrow; specific relationships were viewed solely through the prism of each institution's footprint in China.

The other type of engagement that I distinguish in this book and chapter is *Engagement as Strategy*. This is a much more dedicated approach to *shaping and changing China.* This is Grand Strategy: it is purposeful and proactive. This is the kind of engagement discussed by the strategists in government, in think tanks, and in academia.

Thus, engagement with China has very much been a "two-level game"—engagement as *process* and Engagement as *strategy.* This chapter examines both dimensions.

The beauty of the concept of engagement also lies in its elasticity—as it encompasses a wide variety of American actors and interactions with China. The genius of the concept is that it offers different things to different groups and constituencies in the United States—thus offering to everybody a "stake" in the strategy and the relationship. Such "buy-in" and "stakeholderness" are critical to generating bipartisan and broad-gauged public support for government policy. I will consider these various actors that comprised what I call the Engagement Coalition in Chapters 3 and 4—whereas what follows in this chapter is more concerned with this coalition's ideational elements.

Engagement as Strategy

From the Carter through the Obama administrations (1979–2017), Engagement was a *strategy* not a singular policy. Policies (plural) were derivative of the overall strategy. Taken together, a bundle of elements comprised what came to be known as "engagement." To a considerable extent, the strategy was iterative and evolved over time; some of it was purposive and derivative from US government policies, some of it was simply part and parcel of a "normalized" nation-to-nation relationship, while some of it was responsive to initiatives and stimuli from within (and between) both societies.

So, what exactly was the strategy of Engagement between 1979 and 2017? As I have noted, there was no single government document that defined and answered this question. There were many components. However, from the Carter through the Obama administrations, I would identify four central strategies and seven specific tactics of the American engagement strategy. The four core strategies were:

- Modernize China Economically
- Liberalize China Politically
- Socialize China Internationally
- Engagement as Process

In short, the strategies were to modernize, liberalize, socialize, and exchange with China.

Let us briefly elaborate these in turn, before turning to the tactics and spheres for implementing the three strategies.

Modernize China Economically

Contributing to the economic modernization of China—and profiting from it through trade and investment—has been at the heart of the American approach to China since the 360-ton sailing schooner the *Empress of China* docked in Canton (Guangzhou) in 1784. For a century thereafter, the Americans were far more interested in *trading* with China—exchanging a variety of exotic goods in both directions—than in contributing to China's modernization, economic, and technological development. But following the Opium Wars (1840–1842), the Qing dynasty awakened to the cold reality that the Industrial Revolution had transformed Europe, launching Great Britain and the continental powers into an entirely new technological era—while China remained an underdeveloped, agrarian, poverty-stricken nation. As a result, the Qing dynasty reformers Li Hongzhang and Zeng Guofan launched the "Self-Strengthening Movement" (自强运动) in an effort to try and catalyze a parallel Industrial Revolution in China. The movement lasted from 1861 to 1894.

It is from this period onward that the United States adopted the explicit goal to contribute to China's modernization. With the exception of the period between 1950 and 1972, to assist China in this quest has unquestionably been seen to be in American national interests—on the assumed premise that the interests of a modern, industrialized China with modern science and technology would naturally converge with those of a modern America. And there would be money to be made in the process! Moreover, assisting in the economic and technological modernization of China—transforming it from what the Americans saw as an impoverished, agrarian backwater into a modern industrialized country—appealed deeply to the paternalistic Christian ethos of Americans. While thousands of missionaries, educators, and medical workers would flood into China and devote themselves to helping the Chinese people establish basic social services—this effort was all part and parcel of the broader American attempt to help China modernize. This effort would reach its zenith following the ultimate failure of the Self-Strengthening Movement, the collapse of the Qing dynasty, and the birth of the Republic of China in 1912. As noted in the Preface, the mid-decades of the early 20th century from the 1920s through 1940s were the heyday of American attempts to help China modernize. This period and these efforts are best captured well in studies by James C. Thomson, Peter Buck, Mary Brown Bullock, and other scholars.[8] During these years, the United States was responsible for building China's higher educational system, its medical school system, its public health system, its financial system, its legal and law enforcement system, its military system, its democratic political system, and other facets of modern nation-state.

This is not idle history irrelevant to the evolution of American engagement since 1972. It is directly relevant in at least two ways: first, because of the deep paternalistic desire among the American people to help China become "modern"; and second, because of the Chinese desire to "learn" from their American "teachers" and "mentors." This deep dynamic in US–China relations cannot be overstated. It has been at the heart of the Sino-American relationship for at least 150 years.

President Nixon's dramatic opening to China in 1971–1972 was overwhelmingly motivated by strategic factors (including Nixon's desire to bring China into the "family of nations")—but helping China to modernize was not an explicit motivation of Nixon's. Implicitly, however, it was insofar as America's policy toward China since 1950 had been to *impede* China's modernization. The US trade and investment embargoes, the travel ban, the entire Containment policy, and US government bureaucratic missions—were all intended to restrict and impede China's development. When Nixon dramatically went to Beijing in 1972, not a single one of his speeches spoke of America assisting in China's modernization (for its part, China itself did not launch its "four modernizations" program until 1973). It really was not until the Carter and Reagan administrations that assisting China's modernization reemerged as an explicit policy goal of the United States (after a 30-year hiatus). For example, President Carter's chief China adviser on the National Security Council staff, Sinologist Michel Oksenberg, stated unequivocally following the normalization of relations, "To be an attractive partner in bilateral relations, China's modernization effort must be successful."[9]

Thereafter, assisting in China's modernization became both a standard component of engagement and the language used by US officials, businesspeople, and scholars. This was a critical baseline assumption for the United States. Since American and Chinese strategic interests now coincided and China had embarked on the official policies of the "four modernizations" and "reform and opening" in which it was experimenting with all kinds of pseudo-capitalist and pseudo-liberal economic and political policies—then why should it *not* be in American national interests to broadly support China's modernization? As several successive US administrations claimed, a "strong, secure, and prosperous China" was seen to be in America's national interests. Even after the debacle of the "Tiananmen massacre" in 1989, this broad assumption was not challenged, even if the United States no longer perceived it in its interests to assist in China's military modernization.

Liberalize China Politically

The second basic element of the engagement strategy was to liberalize China politically. Notice that I intentionally do not use the terms "democracy" or "democratize." There were really only two brief periods when the "D word" became part of the American engagement lexicon. The first was during and after the "pro-democracy" demonstrations in China during the spring of 1989, and even then it was used in the context of supporting the "democratic aspirations" of the Chinese people. The second was during the 1990s, when China was experimenting with "village-level democratic elections" and some American organizations (most notably the Carter Center in Atlanta and the International Republican Institute) sought to assist in the effort.

Other than these two brief periods, promoting democracy in China has never been a realistic objective for the United States—an ultimate ideal perhaps, but not an actual practical goal. The People's Republic of China (PRC) is a one-party system, and all Americans know it. That has not stopped the Chinese Communist Party (CCP) from defining the PRC political system as one of "socialist democracy" or more recently as a "whole-process people's democracy."

If bringing democracy to China has not been an element of engagement, then how best to characterize the *political* component of American strategy and policies? I have long found the term "liberalize" to be the most apt. It refers to a series of measures concerning the political system and civil society that demonstrate China's move away from "totalitarianism" and "hard authoritarianism" toward a more responsive "soft authoritarian" political system.[10] Of course, in CCP official lexicon the terms "liberalism" (自由主义) and "liberalize" (自由化) both carry very negative connotations. Ever since Mao penned his 1937 essay "On Liberalism" through the Deng Xiaoping and post-Deng eras, these pernicious terms have been the objects of harsh propaganda campaigns and personnel purges.

Moving China's Leninist political system in a more liberal direction, with its accompanying features in civil society, has definitely been a central feature of America's engagement with China over the past five decades. This was not simply wishful thinking. It was premised on "modernization theory" and the examples of a wide range of formerly authoritarian regimes that moved *toward* democracy as they economically developed during the 1970s and 1980s. This premise was then buttressed by the "end of history" paradigm put forth by political scientist Francis Fukuyama following the collapse of communist systems in Eastern Europe and the Soviet Union from 1989–1991.[11]

A number of former senior officials vehemently deny that this was ever a conscious US government strategy or actual policy, yet (as we will see in the next chapter) several successive American presidents have spoken of the desire (even the inevitability) for China's political system to move away from its authoritarian ways in more liberal directions (largely as a result of economic openness). President George H. W. Bush said the following at a White House press conference on June 5, 1989 (one day after the Tiananmen massacre on June 4):

> The budding of democracy, which we have seen in recent weeks, owes much to the relationship we have developed since 1972, and its important at this time to act in a way that will encourage the further development and deepening of the positive elements of that relationship and the process of democratization ... I believe the forces of democracy are so powerful ... I am convinced the forces of democracy are going to overcome these unfortunate events in Tiananmen Square.[12]

President Bush (41) was hardly the only American president to discuss China's political reforms and possible democratization. In 1997, President Bill Clinton said:

> Over time, growing interdependence will have a liberalizing effect on China ... The pragmatic policy of engagement, of expanding our areas of cooperation with China while confronting our differences openly and respectfully, this is the best way to advance our fundamental interests and our values and to promote a more open and free China ... America must stay the course of engagement.[13]

In 2005, President George W. Bush argued, "As China reforms its economy, its leaders are finding that once the door to freedom is opened even a crack, it cannot be closed. As the people of China grow in prosperity, their demands for political freedom will grow as well."[14]

Perhaps it is therefore most accurate to say that both the US government and private-sector NGOs sought to support the Chinese government's political reform efforts. Let us not forget that during the Deng/Zhao Ziyang/Hu Yaobang period from 1978 to 1989, and during the Jiang Zemin–Hu Jintao period roughly from 1996 to 2008, the CCP *was* moving in a variety of politically reformist directions.[15] Thus, it was not so much that American actors foisted a cookie-cutter approach on the Chinese—but it was much more the case that the United States sought to support China's own political reform initiatives, while working to strengthen PRC "capacities" from within through a wide variety of training programs (see the discussion below). Such an approach was commensurate with the long-standing US approach during the Cold War to support nascent political reformers in communist countries.

For its part, the CCP and Chinese government have long understood American efforts to "liberalize" their political system as pure political subversion.

Beginning with John Foster Dulles's famous article in *Foreign Affairs* from 1957, and subsequent Congressional testimony of 1959 calling for the "peaceful evolution" (和平演变) of communist political systems,[16] the Chinese Communist Party has vigilantly been on guard against this "peaceful evolution." As veteran China specialist Orville Schell aptly observed in his article "The Death of Engagement" in 2020, "Where American liberals saw reform and hope, CCP stalwarts saw conspiracy, peril, and 'peaceful evolution,' a toxic cocktail of foreign machinations aimed at undermining the Party's 'dictatorship of the proletariat.'"[17]

Integrate China Internationally

This has been a consistent goal of the United States ever since President Nixon's early call in 1967 to bring China into the "family of nations."[18] This goal had two purposes and several means. The first purpose was to simply reflect reality and give the PRC its due place and voice "at the table" at the United Nations and in a broad range of international intergovernmental organizations. The second goal, though, was to "socialize" China into the rules and norms of the post–World War II global institutional system, which had been established by the United States and victorious Allied powers—thereby both serving to stabilize the system (on the premise that a China outside the system was a destabilizing factor) and to give China a stake in upholding and perpetuating the rules and norms of the system.[19] What kind of rules and norms? *Liberal* rules and norms. Socializing China into the liberal norms of the postwar international system became a central—if implicit—aim of American policy.

This process unfolded gradually since the 1980s. At first, China was extremely inexperienced in international affairs and international organizations, as it literally was just "joining the world,"[20] and it needed to first understand how these institutions functioned. I recall buying books in Beijing bookstores during the early 1980s that literally described how multilateral international organizations functioned in basic procedural terms, e.g., how seating was arranged, how documents were drafted, motions were advanced, voting proceeded, and so on. Beijing was also inherently suspicious of these institutions and saw them as "tools of Western imperialism." It essentially took the decade of the 1980s for Beijing to both overcome its prejudices and to gain the practical experience in these global bodies. Thereafter, it was still not smooth sailing or a linear path of integration, as China has consistently evinced ambivalence about its role in the international institutional order. Nonetheless, as I have described elsewhere, [21] the PRC progressively passed through five distinct phases of integration into the "global governance" system, and China has now become a full member of 130 international intergovernmental organizations as well as of the United Nations and 24 of its specialized agencies; it is a signatory to more than 300 multilateral treaties, and participant in more than 1,000 international non-governmental organizations (NGOs).

Embedded within the international institutional integration approach was a deeper strategy of the United States: to *socialize* the PRC into the post–World War II liberal norms, rules, and laws of the international order (such as the General Agreement on Tariffs and Trade, the United Nations Covenants on Social and Political Rights and other human rights standards, freedom of navigation, nuclear non-proliferation and arms control agreements, and other international treaties). By adhering to these norms, procedures, and regulations, China would thereby further strengthen the order and bring itself into compliance with global standards of conduct. As the most populous nation on earth this was not insignificant. American strategists further recognized the PRC's history and potential to disrupt this global order, thus it was believed that the complex multilayered multilateral institutional order itself would have a constraining and socializing effect on the PRC. This element of the Engagement strategy was practiced—and it worked pretty well—from the early 1980s through the early 2000s.

One key milestone in America's attempts to integrate and socialize China into the international institutional order was Deputy Secretary of State Robert Zoellick's famous speech in 2005, which called on China to become a "responsible [international] stakeholder."[22] The thrust of Zoellick's call was that China had become a formal member of almost all international institutions, but the PRC had not yet fully absorbed—or obeyed—the rules and norms of the system. China was indeed still an ambivalent participant, still suspicious, and still opposed to the norms and mechanisms that adhered to Western liberal principles and interests (but not those of the Global South).

Engagement as Process

For many American actors, engagement with China was simply about the *process* of interacting with China, no matter the specific domain. One could substitute the word "process" with "exchanges." For the US government, it literally meant having exchanges with their Chinese government counterparts—both to advance a cooperative agenda as well as to register American complaints in different policy domains. Thus, *institutionalization* of bureaucratic ties was seen as an end as well a means to advance specific bureaucratic agendas.

For American states and cities, universities and research institutions, engagement meant simply exchanging people and forging cooperation (doing things jointly together). For companies as well as non-governmental actors, it was all about being in China and working with Chinese counterparts to both shape Chinese behavior and pursue American institutional interests. I examine these actors in greater length in Chapter 7.

If these were the four main strategies of the American engagement policy, there have also existed some more specific elements—or tactics of engagement—that have been apparent during the decades of engagement. I discuss these seven derivative tactics in the following sections.

Government-to-Government Institutionalization

Institutionalizing bureaucratic ties between government departments is part and parcel of all bilateral intergovernmental relationships. So, it was quite natural that the US and PRC national governments would try to institutionalize inter-ministerial and inter-agency relationships following the normalization of diplomatic relations in 1979. After all, that was the very meaning of "normalization"—without formal diplomatic relations, formal government agreements were not possible. In the case of American strategy toward China, though, it took on added importance.

As the Carter administration's top official responsible for China policy, Michel Oksenberg (himself an academic expert in Chinese bureaucracy) noted, one of the major challenges of normalizing relations was to turn the bureaucratic "missions" of different US government agencies from the inherently negative and "hostile missions" of three decades (1949–1979) during the Cold War and US–China estrangement and hostilities into new positive missions of cooperation and collaboration.[23] However, the White House could not wave a magic wand to do this. Enormous financial resources and deeply entrenched ideological and bureaucratic dispositions were realities. It was like trying to move an ocean liner in mid-course. Yet Oksenberg had the foresight to realize that the common US–Chinese antagonism toward the Soviet Union, which was the principal rationale for rapprochement, would likely not last forever—and therefore that the relationship needed a stronger and more enduring ballast if it were to be sustainable into the future. "Marrying the two bureaucracies together" was his personal goal and his lasting contribution.[24]

Once diplomatic recognition was achieved on January 1, 1979, then the two sides could proceed to institutionalize the relationship. This is what normalization meant in practice. As Oksenberg himself reflected concerning the final two years (1979–1980) of the Carter administration, "The [next] frenzied two years saw thirty-five treaties, agreements, and protocols signed between American and Chinese government agencies."[25] This included 16 agreements in scientific cooperation alone.[26]

As is intrinsic and endemic to bureaucracy, "mission creep" grew continually as the US–China relationship—and engagement—developed. Not only were formal agreements renewed and some new ones initiated, but government-to-government dialogues continuously sprouted like bamboo shoots in a spring rain. The George W. Bush administration, on the initiative of Treasury Secretary Hank Paulson, initiated a new mechanism called the Strategic Economic Dialogue, and his cabinet counterpart Secretary of State Condoleezza Rice started a Senior Dialogue with her Chinese counterpart. The Obama administration combined these two into one: the Strategic & Economic Dialogue. By the end of the Obama administration, no fewer than 98 (!) bilateral intergovernmental dialogue mechanisms existed.[27] Then came the Trump administration, which found them to be a waste of time and resources, terminating them all! As we will see in Chapter 5, the Biden administration continued the Trump freeze (notwithstanding the creation of some "working groups").

Building Society-to-Society Ties

Michel Oksenberg also foresaw the growth potential for society-to-society relationships to develop. At the time, it was unimaginable that millions of tourists would flow in each direction every year; that several hundred thousand Chinese students would come to study in American universities with (considerably) lesser numbers of Americans studying in China; that millions of Chinese would immigrate to America and serve as personal bridges between the two societies; that thousands of Americans would move to China (largely because of their jobs there); that hundreds of American corporations would set up shop in China, with 9,000 people traveling by air between the two countries *every day* prior to the onset of COVID; and that a variety of cultural organizations would become involved in music, arts, sports, and intellectual exchanges. All kinds of universities, NGOs, foundations and philanthropic entities, and other private-sector American actors established relationships with their Chinese counterparts. In seeing a robust future for such exchanges, Oksenberg also offered some sage words of caution:

> As Sino-American relations flourish, the Chinese will be tempted to cast us in some respects as a model worthy of emulation, be it in how to conduct elections, to run a university, or to undertake a census ... The danger is that the emulative effort will fail, and that the Chinese will attribute the failure not to their own incompetence in implementation but to the inadequacies of the model. Be it the advice offered on factory management or cost accounting or a tax code or how to run an airline—all activities in which Americans are presently engaged—the

Chinese must be discouraged from simply borrowing from another culture and encouraged to build upon indigenous practices.[28]

Paralleling the institutionalized relationship at the level of national governments, a similar process of creating a wide range of "sister" state-to-province and city-to-city ties blossomed. Nanjing/St. Louis and Shanghai/San Francisco established the first pairings after normalization in 1979. By 2013, such "twinnings" had grown to 68 of state-to-province pairings and 169 of city-to-city pairings between the United States and China; by 2022, the former had contracted to 50 while the latter had expanded to 234, according to China's State Council.[29] In Chapter 7, I will explore further the contemporary scope of American states' relationships with China.

These various forms of interconnectivity between American and Chinese societies added further—and very important—ballast to the relationship. They were a central part of engagement. They quite literally personalized the relationship. From the American perspective, these activities were never questioned; they were all seen to be quite normal and desirable, the more the better. Overall, this was true—although, as we will see in Chapters 6 and 7, some of these exchanges began to encounter difficulties and impediments in the 2010s and 2020s. With the advent of COVID and the "lockdowns" in China, it was literally impossible to undertake such exchanges. The radically changed political atmosphere in the United States under President Trump and in China under Xi Jinping contributed further to the attenuation of societal ties.

Creating Civil Society in China

Another key element of America's engagement strategy with China has been to support the growth of civil society actors in the country (including Hong Kong). This was a result of both US government strategy to stimulate the growth of civic actors that could be advocates of political and social reform (a core component of the Engagement strategy), but it also was very much the result of the initiatives taken by a wide variety of American NGOs, foundations, and civic organizations that sought a foothold in China—in order to affect Chinese capacities (see the section "Governance and Capacity Building") and behavior in their areas of work. Thus, there was both a "push" (by the US government) and "pull" impetus to American NGO involvement in China. There was also a "demand" signal coming from Chinese society and NGOs for assistance.

The motivations of American NGOs varied but were largely benign and mostly apolitical, as the vast majority were involved in areas such as environmental protection, climate change, journalism, labor standards, human rights,

local elections and governance, legal reform, public health, women's empower-
ment, poverty alleviation, sustainable development, forest management, renewable energy, fine arts, philanthropy, and many other areas. But, make no mistake,
there was also a conscious desire to use NGO involvement as a means to change
and liberalize Chinese society from the bottom-up. Supporting the growth of
civil society in China in general was seen as a means to empower Chinese
civic actors at the local level, which were autonomous from the party-state, and
thus seen to be a key means to dilute the authoritarian administrative controls
of the Chinese Communist regime. Even if they were tied to the party-state,
American engagement with Chinese government-organized NGOs was seen as
a way to affect change from within. But promoting change was the unmistak-
able goal—i.e., to weaken the iron grip of the Chinese Communist party-state, to
empower society vis-à-vis the regime, and to improve the professional capacities
of institutions and personnel in China.

Political scientists and particularly scholars of democracy have long argued
that civil society—defined as society-organized groups, communities, institutions, networks, and other actors that stand between the individual and
the modern state—is a fundamental feature of democracies and liberal political systems. Voluntary participation by individuals in such civic groups is
also considered to be a criterion. Virtually *all* political systems today permit some civic actors to exist. Even authoritarian political systems (like
China) permit civil society actors to exist and operate (above, but not below,
ground).

The key question about civil society therefore is the *degree of autonomy*
from the state or control and cooptation by the state. Only those countries
and political systems that permit true autonomy for civic groups—groups
which are formed without state involvement and with voluntary individual
participation—can thus be said to have authentic and genuine civil society.
This is why such groups are known as *non-governmental* organizations (NGOs).
Thus, authoritarian systems like China technically do not have a genuine civil
society—because of two factors. First, the Chinese party-state organizes many
such groups in the first place, and these are appropriately known as government-
organized NGOs (GONGOS). This has been a hallmark of the CCP's "united
front" approach to society since 1949. Second, if such groups are somehow
organized at the initiative of a group of individuals in society, they are all now
effectively co-opted and controlled by the party-state. While there is considerable variance among civic actors and NGOs in China, as my colleague Bruce
Dickson has detailed,[30] the Chinese party-state has attempted to control them
(with varying success) over time. In October 1989, in the wake of the massacre on June 4th and the political uprisings against communist rule in Eastern
Europe (the latter triggered by social groups), China's Ministry of Civil Affairs

issued the "Regulations on the Management and Administration of Social Orga-nizations" and required all such groups to register with the ministry in order to operate.

NGOs in China proliferated rapidly during the 1990s and 2000s. As they did, the CCP became increasingly nervous about their subversive political potential—particularly in the wake of the "color revolutions" in former Soviet republics and Eastern Europe, where civic groups had indeed been the well-spring of counter-government resistance. Such groups also had been the recipients of financing and "democracy promotion" training by foreign organizations (such as the National Endowment for Democracy in the United States, but many others in the United Kingdom, Scandinavia, France, Germany, Canada, and Australia).

In Chapter 7, I will explore in greater depth the impact that the international non-governmental organizations (INGO) law, and the general political tight-ening under Xi Jinping, has had on American NGO activities in China. But suffice to note here that it has been one core element of engagement that has been significantly and negatively impacted.

The Power of Trade and Marketizing China's Economy

Another central and critical component of the US Engagement strategy has been the economic and commercial dimension. Ever since 1784, when the United States and China first established trading relations, the "China market" has fig-ured prominently in the dreams, minds—and certainly pocketbooks—of the American business community.

This commercial imagination long focused on selling American goods in China and to the Chinese people. Never was it considered what goods Amer-icans may want to import and buy *from* China. In the wake of normalization in 1979, the senior American diplomat John Negroponte asked his State Depart-ment colleagues, "What are we going to buy from these people?"[31] In 1972, the year that the United States lifted its trade embargo and the two sides began trade relations, the United States imported a mere $32.4 million in goods from China while exporting only $63.5 million in return; fast forward 50 years to 2022, when the United States imported $536.8 billion while exporting $153.8 billion, for a whopping $690.6 billion (total amount of trade, including exports and imports)![32]

This stunning growth in trade, which has been matched by an average of $110 billion in American investment into China annually for several decades, has resulted from multiple stimuli. Certainly Ricardo's "law of comparative advantage" was one. The economic reforms undertaken by successive Chinese administrations from Hua Guofeng to Xi Jinping were definitely a huge factor. At the heart of these reforms has been the overall marketization of—and development of the private sector in—the Chinese economy (despite the continuing prominent role of the state sector). Ever since the 1980s, the American government and corporate sector have seen marketization and privatization as a critical component of the engagement strategy. Moreover, as we will see in the next chapter, successive American presidents have explicitly viewed the marketization of the Chinese economy as a precursor to the liberalization—if not the democratization—of China's polity.

Parallel to the domestic marketization of China's economy, successive US administrations have viewed the integration and compliance of Chinese economic entities with international institutional institutions, standards, and rules as a related element of engagement. This tendency was epitomized by the accession of China into the World Trade Organization in 2001, with the critical support of the US government (Clinton administration) and the American corporate community.

The movement toward marketization, privatization, and internationalization of China's economy has definitely come about as the result of the Chinese government's and society's own reformist initiatives. The impetus came from within. To a large extent, therefore, American and foreign corporate engagement with, presence in, and impact on China was a supplementary and secondary factor to China's own economic reform initiatives. At the same time, this corporate presence and these corporate actors served as agents of change vis-à-vis their Chinese counterparts. Their impact was much broader than transferring technologies, setting up factories, producing goods, and creating supply chains. The American and foreign corporate presence directly impacted and shaped Chinese corporate practices and personnel. This was a form of capacity building in the economic domain.

Governance and Capacity Building

"Capacity building" is a term used to describe efforts by Western governments and private-sector actors to enhance the institutional capacities and train professional personnel in Chinese government and private-sector institutions. The goal was to have them practice public policy and governance in ways that reflected the Western liberal traditions of meritocracy, accountability, transparency, rule by law—and to do so in accordance with international standards of human rights.

Capacity building was another core element of the Engagement strategy—on the assumption that training Chinese government bureaucrats (at national, provincial, and local levels) in the practices and the standards of conduct prevalent in the West would inherently be in Western interests. In addition to government officials, specific capacity training programs have targeted several specific sectors of personnel—including lawyers, judges, prison wardens, customs agents, police and law enforcement personnel, intelligence analysts, budget setters and auditors, journalists, businesspeople, and others. Specific training programs—undertaken both inside China and in foreign countries—targeted all of these groups. American foundations (the Ford Foundation in particular, but also the Asia Foundation, Luce Foundation, and Rockefeller Foundation) played a significant role in funding such programs.

Capacity building was, however, hardly just an American undertaking. In truth, Australian, Canadian, and European governments have all undertaken far more capacity building programs with China and have expended far more financial resources than has the US government. This recognized, American efforts in capacity building have been dominated by private-sector actors and not the government. Even if these other governments contributed more resources than the US government (which was largely constrained from doing so by Congressional funding restrictions), capacity building in China has been a core common element in American, European, Canadian, and Australian strategies toward China over time (until "donor fatigue" began to set in around 2008).[33]

Building the Rule of Law

Supplementary to the aforementioned elements of engagement were (past tense) American efforts to build the rule of law in China. Building a legal system was seen as fundamental to many of these other goals. American and other foreign corporate actors could not be expected to operate in China without a full range of laws to both protect their interests and to provide a predictable operating environment for their investments. This included building the scaffolding of corporate law, commercial law, administrative law, investment law, bankruptcy law, arbitration law, tax law, contract law, mergers and acquisitions law, labor law, international trade law, intellectual property law, competition (anti-trust) law, and corporate governance standards.

This involved a number of different initiatives undertaken by a wide range of American actors: training Chinese students in American law schools; providing clerkship opportunities for Chinese in American law firms; sending American legal specialists and lawyers to teach in Chinese law schools; running short courses on specific topics in China for Chinese lawyers; training Chinese judges; establishing American law firm offices in China; advising on legal aid to local

Chinese local government entities; advising on international human rights law; funding legal research institutions; and other areas.

The Ford Foundation has been instrumental in a broad-gauged law program for four decades.[34] Ford started early (in 1979) by providing its first-ever grant ($200,000) to a Chinese entity at the Law Institute at the Chinese Academy of Social Sciences. This grant was followed by a 12-year program (1983–1995) to train over 200 law students (costing the foundation $4 million) in US law schools. During these years, Ford's largesse was administered by a supervisory group of leading American legal specialists known as the Committee on Legal Educational Exchanges with China (CLEEC).[35] A number of America's leading experts in Chinese law became deeply involved in these programs and in advising Chinese legal institutions: Jerome Cohen, Stanley Lubman, Randall Edwards, Jim Feinerman, Bill Alford, Paul Gewirtz, Ira Belkin, and others. In subsequent years, the next generation of American scholars of Chinese law followed suit and became deeply involved in exchange programs and training: Pitman Potter, Don Clarke, Jamie Horsely, Margaret Lewis, Nicholas Howson, Mark Wu, and others.

Several US government departments contributed funding and administered their own legal development and programs and bilateral dialogues, including the Department of Justice, Department of State, Department of Commerce, Environmental Protection Agency, and Department of Labor. The American Bar Association initiated and administered its own programs.[36]

Educating Chinese Students

From the beginning of post-normalization, Americans have believed in educating the next generations of Chinese students—and China has seen it in its national interests to send millions of its young people, its "best and brightest," to the United States to study (see Figure 2.1). For the American side, admitting large numbers of Chinese students to American universities was first seen in the traditional paternalistic light of helping China modernize—to improve Chinese scientific, technological, medical, economic, and vocational expertise. Chinese students would learn the specifics of science and technology, engineering, medicine, and other "hard sciences"—and then return to China and contribute to modernizing their county.

But it was also very much part of the American strategy to help China liberalize—as it was intended that these students would observe, experience, and absorb the American way of life *and* American democracy. Then it was expected that they would return to China as agents of political change. Thus, training Chinese students in US universities was a self-evident "twofer": contribute to both

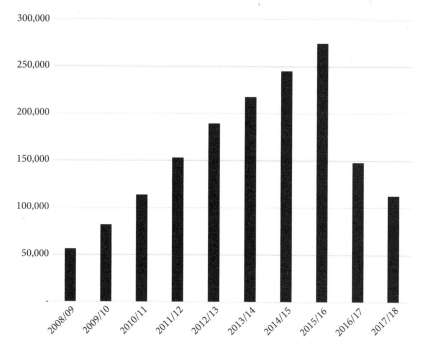

Figure 2.1 Chinese Students Enrolled in American Universities.

Source: United States Department of State, "Nonimmigrant Visa Issuances by Visa Class and Nationality" (2024), https://travel.state.gov/content/dam/visas/Statistics/Non-Immigrant-Statistics/NIVDetailTables/FYs97-23_NIVDetailTable.xlsx.

the modernization and liberalization of China. These dual goals harken back to similar American efforts during the Republic of China (1912–1949 on the mainland).

What American educators had not necessarily anticipated was the considerable positive intellectual contributions that Chinese students would make in university laboratories and (to a much lesser extent) classrooms. The Chinese quickly became the dominant foreign student population in the hard sciences, active collaborators on research projects and coauthors of scientific articles, teaching assistants, and then professors.

As a consequence, what the American government had also not anticipated were the large numbers of students who, upon graduation, would opt to stay in the United States. Indeed, this likely surprised the Chinese government as well, as it had expected these educated graduates to "return to the motherland" (回祖国) to "build the country" (建国). Deng Xiaoping had anticipated that some would elect to stay abroad, but it was never anticipated by either the Chinese or American side that such considerable numbers would not return to China. As recently as 2013, the US National Science Foundation reported that 92 percent of Chinese students who had received PhD degrees in the United States still lived in the United States five years or more after graduation.[37] Chinese Ministry of Education figures further indicated that 45 percent of the Chinese 339,700 studying abroad in 2013 chose to remain abroad after graduation.[38] This "non-return" rate has diminished in recent years as many more—in fact, the majority—of Chinese graduates now return home. There have been several reasons for the increasing return rate. Increasingly competitive salaries with the West are one principal factor. Improved laboratories and research funding is another. In general, Chinese universities have markedly improved both their physical campuses and their research environments over the past decade. And a variety of commercial opportunities exist in China and in doing business with foreign countries. For all of these reasons, including family ties, Chinese students educated abroad are now returning home to work and live after completing their studies abroad.

Nor did American university administrators anticipate the huge financial infusion that Chinese students would provide through paying full tuition. In 2017–2018 academic year, 360,000 Chinese students studied on US campuses, and their paid tuition amounted to an estimated $13 billion.[39]

Although various (and some serious) problems have cropped up since about 2019 concerning Chinese students on American campuses—which I explore in greater depth in Chapter 7—overall, the enormous American investment in teaching and training Chinese students over the past four decades has been a net plus for the United States and therefore a successful element of engagement.

What Engagement Was Not

American engagement of China was essentially motivated by two main factors: advancing America's own national interests and transforming China in a more modern and liberal direction. The latter motivation definitely involved some affective (paternalistic) feelings on the part of Americans, as contributing to China's evolution in a more modern and liberal direction was seen as a reaffirmation of America itself. But it was also a rational and pretty pragmatic calculation on the part of different American actors. Contributing to China's modernization was thus both something done for China and in American self-interests.

What engaging China was *not* motivated by were sentiments of "friendship" or allyship. China has never been an ally of the United States, as alliances are—at bottom—reflections of commonly shared values. They also involve codified commitments of both parties to defend the other ally in case of attack (so-called "Article V" clauses, as is the case with NATO allies). American and Chinese strategic interests did indeed coincide over countering the Soviet Union, and regional actors Vietnam and North Korea in the early years—but the common security interests were not institutionalized as would be the case in an alliance. While individual Americans and Chinese certainly did form the personal bonds of friendship, and the Chinese government frequently liked to use the terms "friendship" and "old friend of China" to describe the overall and specific individual relationships, the American government always eschewed the use of these terms. As Michel Oksenberg aptly warned in 1980, following the normalization of relations,[40]

> We should not delude ourselves that we are building "friendly" relations with China, though on occasion it may be necessary to describe our relations in that way. Friendship implies a warmth and affection that China's leaders do not feel toward us as a nation. Self-interest, not sentiment, motivates them. Moreover, they will use our expressions of friendship against us, indicating that since we think of them as friends, we should treat them as such. Excessive professions of our friendship will imply to the Chinese a greater sense of American obligation and beneficence toward them than we are prepared to offer. Failure to deliver will then lead to Chinese accusations of betrayal and hypocrisy. Of course, within a national framework of self-interest, individual friendships can flourish.

Recognizing the validity of Oksenberg's warnings, it must also be said that he could not foresee the incalculable number of professional and personal relationships that have been forged over the decades of US–China engagement. Many of these are genuine and not expedient relationships. Thousands of Americans have lived in China, several million Chinese have studied in America, thousands have immigrated to the United States and joined American communities; intermarriages are common, business partnerships involve more than producing and exchanging goods and investment, and a variety of strands link the two societies together. I myself have a number of very good Chinese friends, a number of whom were my basketball teammates at Peking University. When I recently had dinner together with them in Beijing I asked myself: "Why can't US–China relations be so simple and straightforward as these friendships?" Therefore, despite the tactical and manipulative use of terms like "old friend of China" (老朋友), the term "friendship" also has real meaning in describing real relationships among the Chinese and American peoples.

Oksenberg's close friend and colleague Professor David M. Lampton has invested his entire career in engagement with China—as a professor in two different US universities, as director of two leading NGOs involved in direct engagement with China (the Committee on Scholarly Communication with

China and the National Committee on US–China Relations), as an adviser to the US government, and as a consultant to the private sector. In 2024, Lampton published his memoir recalling these experiences. In the conclusion he poses a series of rhetorical but important questions:

> One cannot dodge important questions: Was engagement a big mistake, a naïve period in which the United States strengthened a prospective enemy? Was constructive engagement misguided, rationalized by assumptions about the inevitability of democracy through economic and social interaction and the presumed palliative effects of modernization and globalization? Is engagement to be understood simply as a period in which short-term thinking, profit-hungry American businesses, and in their own way American universities, pursued perishable economic gains by building up what almost inevitably would become a strategic, economic, and technological competitor—a threat? Did we pay insufficient heed to the CCP and its goals, the country's vast reservoir of intelligent and increasingly well-educated people with a collective nationalist chip on its shoulders, and the PRC's need for legitimacy achieved not through political reform but by reclaiming the expansive territorial extent of the Qing Dynasty at its height?[41]

These are all excellent questions. Unfortunately, Lampton himself dodged and did not directly answer the very astute questions he posed. That would have been interesting and appropriate. Instead, he merely reflects,

> Because I have written elsewhere about the broad dimensions of gain during the forty-plus-year upswing starting in 1970, I will not rehearse that argument here other than to say that whether one considers the nutritional status of the Chinese people, life expectancy there, or their life opportunities, the gains have been enormous. Americans also benefitted mightily from China's entry into the global economic system, and the PRC's economic gains fueled by relatively high U.S. growth and helped keep inflation at bay for decades. While China benefited considerably in economic terms, the absolute gap in per capita GDP between the U.S. and PRC greatly widened in absolute terms in America's favor during the engagement period. There were, however, great inequities in the distribution of those gains in America. How America distributes its growth internally is its decision, not China's. That the United States squandered some gains in misguided wars and neglected human and physical infrastructure domestically for a long time is on Americans, not the Chinese.[42]

Since when was improving the nutritional status, life expectancy, and life opportunities of Chinese an *American* strategic priority and goal of engagement? And it is a highly contestable, if not dubious, assertion that "Americans have benefitted mightily from China's entry into the global economic system." China's entry into the global economic system has primarily benefited *China*. And what "relatively high U.S. growth" is he talking about? America's GDP growth has hovered around a modest 2.5 percent from 1990 to 2023[43]—while China's GDP growth over the same period averaged 9 percent, peaking at 14 percent several times.[44] And since when was narrowing the gap in relative GDP of the United States vs. the PRC a goal of engagement? Lampton claims that there were "great inequities in the distribution of those gains in America." What gains is he talking about? Tell that to the millions of American workers who lost their jobs because of outsourcing manufacturing to China, or to the tens of thousands of American farmers who had lost their farms before China became a major soybean importer.

Lampton himself references the fact that he has "written elsewhere" about the "gains of engagement." But if one checks the footnote reference, it is to his concluding chapter in the book *Engaging China: Fifty Years of Sino-American Relations* (which was a *festschrift* volume in his honor).[45] We considered this volume in Chapter 1, but Lampton's own chapter only briefly. Looking at it more carefully, he notes several specific "accomplishments" of engagement (or what he describes as "smaller aperture gains"). The first that he cites are improvements in China's food supply chain—which now has far fewer amounts of fruits and vegetables rotting before consumption, owing to "best practices" of storage, packaging, and handling taught to Chinese by the US National Academy of Sciences. "Small aperture" indeed. Then Lampton cites the improved flight safety record of Chinese airlines, which he credits to learning best practices from the US Federal Aviation Administration (a questionable assumption). He cites the sale of US cars and auto parts in China by General Motors as a plus attributable to engagement. Of course, GM shareholders might say so: GM sells one-third more vehicles in China than in the United States. But they are all manufactured in China! He then cites the example of Fuyao Glass Company, which employs two thousand American workers at its plant in Dayton, Ohio. I will grant that this employment is a good byproduct of two-way investment (as is GM's employment of Chinese workers at its plants in China), but Chinese investment in America is dwarfed by American investment in China (on average, prior to 2019, about $1.5 billion vs. $100 billion respectively). Two-way foreign direct investment has without doubt benefited Chinese workers far more than American workers. Then Lampton cites the benefits to China's public health system of working with US Department of Health and Human Services, National Institutes of Health, and Centers for Disease Control and Prevention. Again, this is an example of *Chinese* citizens being the beneficiaries of engagement (although, as the global pandemic of COVID-19 amply demonstrated, China did not practice "best practices" in sharing information with the World Health Organization).

These are the concrete examples Lampton provides of the benefits and accomplishments of engagement. If American engagement policy was primarily intended to improve the livelihoods of Chinese citizens, then I guess these are accomplishments. But they are all truly "small aperture" in comparison with the more truly strategic and grandiose goals of Engagement discussed earlier in this chapter: to modernize and marketize China's economy, to liberalize China's polity, to pluralize China's society (by introducing a range of freedoms), and to socialize China internationally (to adhere to the norms and practices of the global liberal order). Five decades later, it must be concluded that these American goals have all failed. China's economy today is a hybrid, where the state sector still accounts for almost half of GDP. Its political system is a one-party, one-person dictatorship. Its society now lives under the most stringent controls known since the draconian and uniform Mao era. And China is no advocate or practitioner of liberal practices in international organizations—to the contrary, Beijing aligns together with Putin's Russia, Iran, and other illiberal regimes in an attempt to undermine the liberal international order every single day. By these criteria, the goals of American engagement have not been met, and it can legitimately be argued that the Engagement strategy has indeed failed.

Having discussed the motivations for, and ideational elements of, the American engagement strategy in this chapter, we now turn—in the next two chapters—to more carefully consider its evolution over time and what I call the Engagement Coalition.

II

THE EVOLUTION OF ENGAGEMENT

Chapter 3
The Genesis of the Engagement Coalition

A key element of the Engagement strategy was to build as broad a base of support as possible inside the United States. No foreign policy (or major domestic policy for that matter) by the United States can be maintained without sustained broad-gauged support from the American public and their elected representatives. Various interest groups also advocate for their constituencies and special interests. The American government (executive branch and Congress) is also the object of intensive lobbying by foreign governments. This is the way democracies work.

In the case of US–China relations and American China policy, following the establishment of diplomatic relations in 1979, a wide coalition of powerful interest groups each came to hold a stake in the relationship. Each of the four strategies and seven tactics of engagement discussed in Chapter 2 represented different spheres of interaction and different sectors in American society. Individually, none of these interest groups would have been sufficient alone to maintain the relationship with China—but collectively they reinforced each other and added up to a comprehensive coalition. The formation of this coalition was to some extent intentional—as successive administrations and members of Congress sought to broaden and deepen the ties between the United States and China—but it was also, to a large extent, a byproduct of non-governmental actors taking their own initiative and building their own bridges to China. It was therefore both a top-down and bottom-up process.

Yet, the Engagement Coalition did not just spring upon the scene after 1979. To the contrary, the coalition and the engagement policies that were advocated had their origins much earlier. The coalition's nascent development before 1979 had much to do with its consolidation after 1979.

The Origins of the Engagement Coalition

First of all, it is important to understand that this was not the first time that domestic actors in the United States coalesced together to shape America's relations with China. I noted in the Preface and Chapter 1 that toward the end of the 19th century an "Open Door Constituency" (to borrow historian Michael Hunt's phrase) of traders, missionaries, diplomats, philanthropists, and medical workers came together to underpin and drive America's relations with China during the time of the imperial Qing dynasty.[1] This basic coalition broadened out following the revolution of 1911 and establishment of the Republic of China (ROC, also known as Nationalist China) to include American educators, scientists, doctors, more missionaries, military officers, politicians, members of Congress, scholars of China, business barons, diplomats, journalists, powerful media moguls (like Henry Luce), and presidents. All together, they constituted a powerful coalition that shaped popular American perceptions of China as well as forging close US relations with—and unending support for—Chiang Kai-shek's Nationalist government. This became known as the "China Lobby."

With the defeat of the Nationalists by Mao's Communists in 1949, the China Lobby did not die. Much to the contrary, it grew stronger and more influential as the Cold War unfolded and Washington clung to maintaining formal diplomatic relations and a mutual defense treaty with Chiang's regime, which had been defeated and driven off the mainland to the island of Taiwan. The China Lobby was primarily responsible for maintaining the meme of "Free China" on Taiwan ruled by the Chinese Nationalists (CHINATS) as distinct from the Chinese Communists (CHICOMS) who ruled the mainland.[2] During the early 1950s, as the debate over "Who Lost China?" gripped Washington, the China Lobby partnered with Senator Joseph McCarthy's witch hunt to ferret out supposed communist sympathizers in the US government and academia. As a result of the nationally televised inquisition, the careers of scores of distinguished diplomats in the Department of State, university professors, and some journalists were ruined. Groups such as the Committee of One Million, the American China Policy Association, and the Committee to Defend America by Aiding Anti-Communist China—all fanned the flames and hysteria of the time. Chiang Kai-shek's rump regime on Taiwan was the beneficiary—while America clung to the fiction that the ROC government on the island represented *all* of China in the United Nations and world affairs.

The China Lobby was rocked by the news of President Nixon's opening to (mainland) China in 1972, but it continued to fight a rearguard action to try and block US diplomatic recognition of the People's Republic of China (PRC)— until it happened in 1979. The China Lobby and their supporters in Congress were then instrumental in crafting the Taiwan Relations Act in the aftermath of the PRC recognition. While its clout diminished thereafter (relative to its previous influence), the group morphed into the "Taiwan Lobby" and continues to operate to this day. While nowhere near as strong and influential as it had been prior to 1979, the Taiwan Lobby has continued to maintain a presence in Washington and to be effective in advocating for Taiwan's interests.[3]

Following normalization in 1979, it took Beijing some time to figure out the necessity and art of lobbying in Washington, DC. The PRC never really took the role of Congress very seriously in those years, thinking that the US government was a mirror of their own, and all that was necessary when Beijing needed something was to contact the White House. Gradually, as the result of a series of events and disputes, Beijing gradually and grudgingly came to recognize that it needed to advocate for its own interests more broadly. By the late 1980s, and again following the rupture in relations as a result of the Tiananmen Square massacre on June 4, 1989, the PRC Embassy hired several law firms and lobbying groups to advocate for its interests with different US government departments and Congress. This was in part a reflection of the fact that PRC Embassy diplomats and officials had been very ineffective in directly cultivating relations with Congress—hence they fell back on simply paying lobbyists to do their bidding for them. Large "K Street" law firms like Akin Gump, Patton Boggs, Covington & Burling, Jones Day, and Hogan & Hartson were all hired as lobbyists by the Chinese Embassy and government—and all received seven-figure annual retainers.[4] While they take no money from Chinese entities, business advocacy groups such as the US–China Business Council (USCBC) and American Chamber of Commerce (AMCHAM) have also lobbied for policies that benefit Chinese commercial and diplomatic interests. The US–China Exchange Foundation, which is headquartered in Hong Kong but has ties to the United Front Work Department of the Chinese Communist Party (CCP), is also active in funding American media and university activities.

Thus, China lobbies (plural) are nothing new in American politics. They have a long history dating to the 19th century, they have sunk deep roots in different sectors of American society, and they have exerted an outsized influence on US government policies toward China. They have been very well funded and organized, and they have been susceptible to influence (and well-financed lobbying) by the Chinese themselves.

Early Advocates of Engagement

Readers may think that the Engagement Coalition only came together following President Nixon's historic visit to China in 1972 or following the normalization of diplomatic relations in 1979—but in fact, when one looks carefully, it is evident that the seeds of the coalition were sown much earlier.

Who Lost China vs. Lost Chance in China

In the autumn of 1949 and winter of 1950—just after Mao's Communist forces had defeated and driven Chiang Kai-shek's Nationalists from the mainland to the island of Taiwan and had proclaimed the new People's Republic of China on October 1, 1949—Washington was obsessed with handwringing, finger-pointing, and traitorous accusations about "Who Lost China?" In this visceral atmosphere, there were precious few in the capital city who contemplated the possibility of engaging and establishing formal diplomatic relations with the new PRC. It would certainly not be correct to say that there was a broad constituency in favor of such an action, but there were a handful who did advocate for it.

As the diplomatic historian Nancy Bernkopf Tucker's masterful study of this transitional period clearly demonstrates, there was one institution and a single individual who primarily advocated for recognizing, and interacting with, the newly established PRC and Chinese Communist regime.[5] The institution was the Department of State and the individual was Secretary of State Dean Acheson. Acheson was by far the lead advocate for such a course of action. He had been influenced by some State Department Foreign Service officers who had served in China, who recognized the support that the Chinese Communists had from the vast majority of Chinese people, and who generally viewed Chiang Kai-shek's regime with disdain. These diplomats would soon be caught up in the McCarthyite witch hunts searching for "communist sympathizers" in the State Department, and most were purged. But, for a brief period stretching from the summer of 1949 through the winter of 1950, these diplomats argued in favor of the United States formally recognizing the new communist regime—and their arguments won temporary favor with Secretary Acheson.

During this eight-month interregnum (roughly from July 1949 till February 1950), Acheson took several discrete steps to signal to Mao and the CCP leadership that the United States was interested in establishing direct lines of communication and *might* be interested in possibly recognizing the new regime.[6] Even if many of the "China hands" among Foreign Service officers did harbor sympathies for the Chinese Communists, Acheson did not. He was very pragmatic and hard-headed in the way that he approached the question of diplomatic recognition. In September 1949, just days before Mao stood atop Tiananmen Gate to proclaim the establishment of the PRC, Acheson gave a speech in New York in which he said:

> We maintain diplomatic relations with other countries primarily because we are all on the same planet and must do business with each other. We do not establish an embassy in a foreign country to show approval of its government. We do so to have a channel through which to conduct essential government relations and to protect legitimate United States interests.[7]

Whether or not there was a "lost chance in China"—to establish diplomatic contacts and even perhaps to have Mao visit Washington during this transitional time (as historian Barbara Tuchman and some others argued)[8]—any possibility of the United States recognizing and engaging with the new PRC regime and society disappeared on June 25, 1950, when the communist North Korean regime launched its lightning invasion of South Korea. The Cold War between the United States and the PRC commenced immediately on that day. This history is well-known and need not be reexamined here.[9]

What this illustrates is that most American diplomats are quite pragmatic and non-ideological. They are not intrinsically predisposed to hostile relations with adversaries—US diplomats are pragmatic and always looking for ways and avenues to manage differences with adversaries. This was true during the Soviet era and it was true with the PRC during the long Cold War and estrangement—as American diplomats opened up the "Warsaw channel" with the Chinese Communists (where both the United States and the PRC had embassies and met on-and-off for direct discussions between 1955 and 1970).[10] Once President Nixon undertook his bold rapprochement with the Beijing regime (which State Department diplomats knew nothing about), they were quick to hop on the bandwagon and support the new initiative. It is not the case that American diplomats are, by character, sympathetic to the PRC—but they are pragmatists and they do intrinsically *believe* in contact. It is their job to keep channels open, find ways to cooperate, never rupture ties, and always think about (maintaining the relationship) tomorrow. As former American Ambassador to Russia Michael McFaul notes in describing the "State Department culture" in his memoir, "Diplomats are trained to engage, not disengage."[11] McFaul's observation very much applies to China hands in the State Department. I have never met an American Foreign Service officer (and I have interacted with a considerable number) who is hostile toward the PRC. American diplomats have consistently been among the staunchest advocates of engagement with China—and this is why they come under fire from conservative members of Congress and in the media for being "soft on China."

Even if the State Department advocated on behalf of diplomatic recognition and engagement at the time (1949–1950), there was no broader coalition of actors or interests who advocated for such. The aforementioned pro-Nationalist China Lobby was dominant in American society, politics, and business. Once the Korean War broke out and the Cold War went into full swing, "Red China" had become a clear American adversary.

What If? Eisenhower, Kennedy, and Johnson Contemplations

Nonetheless, at three points during the 1950s and 1960s, advocates of engaging China emerged: first under President Eisenhower, second under President Kennedy, and the third time early in Lyndon Johnson's presidency.

By the time Dwight D. Eisenhower succeeded Harry Truman as president in 1953, the Cold War die had been cast and "Red China" was America's adversary and military enemy. At several points (1955, 1958, 1960), Eisenhower managed tense crises in the Taiwan Strait—and in each instance the president rebuffed advice from the Pentagon to possibly use nuclear weapons against the mainland. Although Eisenhower's eight years in office were tense times with the PRC, in 1956 Robert Bowie (Director of the Policy Planning Staff in the State Department) urged reexamination of US policy toward the PRC—advocating for granting it a seat in the United Nations, for relaxing controls on American journalists to travel to China, and for reconsideration of the trade embargo.[12] Bowie believed that the complete isolation of the PRC was not a sustainable policy. He was also, to some extent, testing the waters for Secretary of State John Foster Dulles's flirtation with a two-Chinas policy. Neither Bowie's suggestions nor Dulles's two-Chinas concept went anywhere, although the "Warsaw channel" ambassadorial talks did commence in 1955. These talks also failed to achieve anything substantive, as the two sides rarely got beyond scripted and well-worn "talking points" concerning Taiwan.

For Eisenhower as president, there was no "demand signal" for an opening to China coming from any quarter of American society. He was extremely cautious when it came to China.[13] Thus, in these years, there was no nascent Engagement Coalition waiting to spring forth—as was the case in Canada, Great Britain, France, and Japan. In each of these countries, a combination of the business community and some "friendship" groups were agitating for opening ties. These efforts were important in that when the governments in these countries finally did get around to seriously contemplating diplomatic recognition, a foundation had already been laid in the business world and among some leftist groups.

By the time John F. Kennedy was elected president and assumed office in 1961, tensions in the Taiwan Strait were running high (and had been a contentious point in the Nixon–Kennedy campaign debates the previous fall); the United States was beginning to become involved in the Vietnam War (on the assumption that the civil war there was really an attempt by Soviet Russia and "Communist China" to expand into Southeast Asia); and there was still no demand signal from American society calling for opening relations with China. Yet, Kennedy himself was not ipso facto predisposed against the idea of exploring certain options to loosen the tight Containment policy against the PRC. Kennedy was, in fact, quite curious about what was going on behind the "bamboo curtain,"[14] and he opined to his aides that there was something "irrational" about US policy. In fact, Kennedy evinced his discomfort in his October 1957 *Foreign Affairs* article "A Democrat Looks at Foreign Policy," in which he assailed existing China policy as "exaggeratedly military and probably too rigid," before concluding, "There have been—and still are—compelling reasons for the non-recognition of China, but we must be careful not to straightjacket our policy as a result of ignorance and fail to detect a change in the objective situation when it comes."[15]

Once in office, Kennedy ordered a thorough review of China policy. The President was pushing on an open door—as State Department officials George Ball, Averell Harriman, Roger Hilsman, James C. Thomson, and Allen Whiting were all contemplating the possibility of relaxing some strictures against the PRC.[16] Deputy Secretary of Defense James Forrestal was also apparently so inclined.[17] Kennedy met privately with Secretary State Dean Rusk in May 1961 to explore possible changes in China policy. During the private meeting, Rusk apparently offered up three options: move toward "dual recognition" of both the PRC and ROC (the two-Chinas policy); work to bring about reconciliation between Taipei and Beijing; or to sit tight and do nothing.[18] Kennedy selected the third option and refused to make any changes to policy, warning Rusk as he left the Oval Office, "And what's more Mr. Secretary, I don't want to read in the *Washington Post* or *New York Times* that the State Department is thinking about a change in our China policy!"[19] Generally speaking, Kennedy had his hands full with other foreign policy challenges and did not welcome it when the "China problem" intruded on his time. He is reported to have told his wife when China came up in conversation, "Jackie, time for the Bloody Marys!"

Kennedy's early years in office coincided with the famine that resulted from the Great Leap Forward (1958–1960, but the famine became evident in 1961–1962). The Canadian government had just relaxed its own grain embargo and had begun selling wheat to China. Rusk, Hilsman, and others counseled Kennedy to follow Canada's lead, and they also advocated for relaxing the ban on American journalists and citizens to travel to China, as well as for a partial relaxation of the trade embargo to allow for medicines and surgical instruments, and certain other low-technology items to be sold to the PRC.[20]

These ideas percolated in the minds of these men and in draft documents inside the State Department, but a consensus in favor of the initiatives never gelled. That did not deter Hilsman and Thomson from pressing further, while Whiting (as the lead State Department intelligence analyst on China and Asia) began to argue that the Sino-Soviet rift (emerging at the time) was real and could be potentially exploited strategically by the United States. Despite Kennedy's openness to new policy ideas, at this juncture he did not wish to take any definitive actions to alter the status quo in China policy. His close adviser Ted Sorensen recalls in his memoirs, "The only controversial foreign policy issue that he deliberately and explicitly postponed to his second term—when he would have larger popular and Congressional majorities—was US relations with

China, a power whose Communist takeover and involvement in the Korean War had made it an almost untouchable topic in American politics, but a topic that Kennedy knew had to be faced."[21]

Likely because some of his White House advisers (notably, confidants Theodore Sorenson and Arthur Schlesinger Jr., United Nations Ambassador Adlai Stevenson, and Under Secretary of State Chester Bowles) began to evince their unease over the rigid US policy, in the fall of 1963 the president then abandoned his caution and became more receptive to his advisers' entreaties. He tasked Hilsman (who had become Assistant Secretary of State for Far Eastern Affairs in May 1963, replacing W. Averell Harriman) to lead a drafting team of State Department officials to craft a public speech which could signal a "new approach to Communist China."[22] The speech was still being drafted when, on November 14, 1963, at what turned out to be his last press conference, in response to a journalist's question concerning the possibility of trade with China, Kennedy suddenly declared to the assembled journalists:

> We are not planning on trade with Red China in view of the policy that Red China pursues. But if the Red Chinese indicate a desire to live at peace with the United States, with other countries surrounding it, then quite obviously the United States would reappraise its policies. We are not wedded to a policy of hostility to Red China.[23]

This statement, in fact, amounted to a bombshell reversal of long-standing US policy (although it was not seen as such by the assembled media or by the foreign policy community). What Kennedy was doing was moving to a more flexible position and offering an explicit incentive to Beijing to alter its own virulent hostility toward the United States and its allies in Asia.

Eight days later President Kennedy was tragically assassinated in Dallas, Texas. Despite the ensuing trauma and sudden transition to the Lyndon Johnson presidency, Hilsman continued to complete the drafting of the speech. Secretary of State Rusk authorized him to deliver it to the Commonwealth Club in San Francisco on December 13, 1963. It was some speech—well worth rereading in full today, and it deserves our detailed attention here.[24] Clearly, enormous time, effort, care, and wordsmithing had gone into it. In retrospect, Hilsman (Photo 3.1) reflected that the speech was to combine "firmness, flexibility, and dispassion."[25]

In the speech, entitled "United States Policy Towards Communist China," Hilsman carefully balanced praise for the Republic of China on Taiwan, with denunciations of doctrinaire Chinese communist ideology and domestic polices (i.e., the Great Leap Forward) and aggression against its neighbors (unspecified), with distinctions comparing a more open Soviet Union (then still in

Photo 3.1 Roger Hilsman.
Photo credit: Public domain via Wikimedia Commons

the Khrushchev period of domestic liberalization and détente with the United States), with reflections on America's traditional relations with China, and some olive branches holding out the prospect of improved ties.

Hilsman opened his lengthy address with a series of important self-reflective observations:[26]

> For Americans, China presents a special problem in history. We first met Chinese civilization late in the decay of its imperial splendor. For more than a century we sent our traders, our missionaries, our educators, our doctors, and our good will. In the turmoil that followed the Chinese revolution of 1911 we felt a special kinship with China's culture and people. In World War II we became the staunchest of allies ... Americans—businessmen, missionaries, diplomats—have long felt a particularly close rapport with the Chinese.

Yet our involvement with China, while intense, was not wholly real: it was fed by illusions as well as good will ... We had little understanding of the ferment and weakness created by the collapse of the Confucian state. And we were little aware of the depth and fervor of Chinese nationalism in reaction to a sense of repeated humiliation at the hands of the West.

As a result, Americans were totally unprepared for the tragedy of the Chinese revolution: its capture by Marxism-Leninism and its transformation into a fiercely hostile force—hostile to the West and menacing to its neighbors. Our reaction was anger and disbelief, a sense of personal betrayal.

In the same reflective vein, toward the end of his speech, Hilsman admitted, "There has perhaps been more emotion about our China policy than about our policy toward any single country since World War II." With these words, Hilsman perfectly captured the shock and "sense of betrayal" that Americans felt over the "loss" of China when the Communists seized power, defeating the Nationalist regime that the United States had spent 38 years and untold billions of dollars supporting. Hilsman then went on to (hypocritically) proclaim a "deep friendship" with the "people on the mainland," while asserting that, "We have tried to be objective and to see to it that dislike of communism does not becloud our ability to see the facts." He blamed Beijing for refusing to exchange correspondents—which "could lower the wall of secrecy with which [China's leaders] surround themselves." He criticized the "closed and stagnant society on the mainland," and he labeled CCP leaders as "parochial" and "Marxist puritans," alleging that "there are few people on earth who are so sublimely confident as are the Chinese Communist leaders that they are always right and good ... These are men who comfortably clothe their own dictatorship in a cloak of doctrinal righteousness." Hilsman asserted, "Like the king in a fairy tale, they seem unaware that they have no clothes." He added,

We are confronted in Communist China with a regime which presently finds no ground of common interest with those whose ideals they do not share, which has used hatred as an engine of national policy. The United States is the central figure in their demonology and the target of a sustained fury of invective.

Despite his harsh attacks, which centered on the "inhumane" policies of the Great Leap Forward (in which we now know that approximately 40 million died of starvation), Hilsman then somewhat contradictorily declared, "There is some evidence of evolutionary forces at work in mainland China," after stating, "We have no reason to believe that there is a present likelihood that the Communist regime will be overthrown."

After excoriating the CCP leadership, Hilsman then turned to offer some olive branches to Beijing:

> Today, fourteen years have passed since the establishment of the Communist government in Peiping. It is time to take stock—dispassionately—of the greatest and most difficult problem we face in our efforts to assist in the development of a peaceful Far East. We pursue today towards Communist China a policy of the open door. We are determined to keep the door open to the possibility of change and not to slam it shut against any developments which might advance our national good, serve the free world, and benefit the people of China.

For good reason, Hilsman's speech attracted some national attention. The olive branches Hilsman laid out in San Francisco drew mixed reactions in the American media at first, but it then began to resonate more positively.[27] Senator George McGovern praised it. Some, including veteran diplomat and China hand Stanley Hornbeck, criticized it as a misrepresentation of US policy and another naïve attempt to pursue a two-Chinas policy.[28] The so-called China Lobby (Committee of One Million) was predictably critical, claiming that it was "soft on communism."[29] In retrospect, it was a turning point. As journalist John Pomfret observed in his monumental history of the US–China relationship, "Hilsman's speech had been a trial balloon, and it had floated."[30] Subsequently, it was no longer taboo to openly discuss an improved relationship with China. It would be a stretch, though, to conclude that with Hilsman's speech the Engagement Coalition had been born. It would take another decade to develop; the seeds of engagement had been planted and would begin to sprout during the second half of the decade.

Johnson Closes the Door

Had President Kennedy lived, it is quite likely that there would have been some forward movement toward an opening to China, but his successor Lyndon Johnson had no appetite for such. Johnson, of course, inherited the then-nascent Vietnam War from Kennedy—and he escalated America's involvement in it substantially. Johnson interpreted the war to be, in considerable part, a result of Communist China's aggression. In an important speech on April 7, 1965, at Johns Hopkins University in Baltimore, Johnson explicitly stated:

> Over this war—and all Asia—is another reality: the deepening shadow of Communist China. The rulers in Hanoi are urged on by Peking. This is a regime which has destroyed freedom in Tibet, which has attacked India, and has been

condemned by the United Nations for aggression in Korea. It is a nation which is helping the forces of violence in almost every continent. The contest in Vietnam is part of a wider pattern of aggressive purposes.[31]

Thus, Kennedy's exploratory feelers concerning China died early in the Johnson administration. Several of its advocates, including Hilsman, resigned their government positions. Nonetheless, outside of government there was some new momentum.

The Engagement Constituency Sinks Roots

President Johnson's radical escalation of the American involvement in the Vietnam War—which was premised on his belief that the war was all about containing Chinese expansionism in Southeast Asia—therefore closed the slightly open crack in the door that President Kennedy had left prior to his sudden and tragic assassination. While there was to be no further *official* contemplation by the US government under Johnson, nonetheless at the *unofficial* level, there was some forward movement.

Containment Without Isolation

Perhaps the most critical development was a series of hearings conducted by Senator J. William Fulbright and the Senate Foreign Relations Committee in March 1966.[32] These well-publicized public sessions followed on to a similar series on Vietnam that the committee undertook during January and February. Since those hearings inevitably raised questions concerning China's involvement, Senator Fulbright concluded that a separate set of hearings should specifically probe the complex issue of America's (non-)relations with China— which Fulbright envisioned as a means to stimulate a full national debate. Under bright television lights and cameras, over seven days and nine separate sessions, a parade of (mainly) leading academic China specialists offered their testimony to the committee: A. Doak Barnett, John King Fairbank, Benjamin Schwartz, John Lindbeck, Samuel Griffith, Morton H. Halperin, Alexander Eckstein, Harold C. Hinton, Donald Zagoria, George E. Taylor, David Rowe, Walter Judd, Hans Morgenthau, and Robert Scalapino.[33]

Perhaps the most noteworthy element to emerge from the hearings was A. Doak Barnett's distinction and call for "containment without isolation." Barnett, then a professor of government at Columbia University and a leading expert on China, paired his full endorsement of the continuation of the policy of "containment" toward China—which he defined as "both military and non-military measures to block threats posed by China to its neighbors," and deemed to

Photo 3.2 A. Doak Barnett.
Photo credit: Institute of Contemporary World Affairs

have been "fairly successful"—with his recommendation that the United States should no longer try to "isolate" China in world affairs.[34] Barnett put forward the view that a dual policy of "containment without isolation" would "aim on the one hand at checking military or subversive threats and pressures emanating from Peking, but at the same time would aim at maximum contacts with, and maximum involvement of, the Chinese Communists in the international community."[35] Barnett argued that by taking several specific steps, the United States could have a "moderating influence" on Beijing's behavior. Barnett identified three specific steps: "state a willingness for reciprocal diplomatic recognition; limit the present trade embargo to strategic items; and support a formula that would give United Nations seats to both Communist China and Nationalist China."[36] Barnett went further, advocating unequivocally, "Our aim, certainly, should be to work toward eventual establishment of diplomatic relations."[37]

Barnett's testimony was followed by that of John King Fairbank, the doyen of Chinese studies and professor at Harvard (Photo 3.3). Fairbank had been viciously attacked for his "communist sympathies" during the McCarthyite probes into "un-American activities" in early 1950s. Professionally damaged but undaunted, Fairbank had long been a quiet advocate for evaluating the PRC on its own terms and in the long sweep of Chinese history.[38] In his testimony before Senator Fulbright's Senate Foreign Relations Committee, Fairbank interestingly

Photo 3.3 John King Fairbank.

Photo credit: Public domain via Wikimedia Commons

finessed Barnett's suggestion for a shift in US policy toward "containment without isolation" by seeming to downplay the containment half of Barnett's equation: "Containment alone is a blind alley unless we add policies of constructive competition and of international contact." Fairbank unabashedly called for (his perceived) need to bring the PRC into the full panoply of international institutions, exchanges, and discourse. His was a radical proposal!

Professors Schwartz, Lindbeck, Eckstein, Zagoria, Hinton, Morgenthau, and Scalapino all subsequently endorsed Barnett's suggestion to cease the "isolation" of the PRC, although they disagreed concerning the continued efficacy of the policy of "containment." Unsurprisingly, Congressman Walter Judd and conservative scholars George Taylor and David Rowe opposed Barnett's initiative, while Professors Griffiths and Halperin were more circumspect. The Senate Foreign Relations Committee members probed and politely questioned their witnesses, but none of the committee members or the committee as a whole openly endorsed the "containment without isolation" proposal.

Senator Fulbright himself did subsequently publicly endorse Barnett's recommendations in some media interviews and in his own 1966 book *The Arrogance of Power.*[39] In calling the hearings, Committee Chairman Fulbright was one of the first prominent Americans to openly question the underlying premise of the Vietnam War as the Johnson administration defined it—namely, that North Vietnam was acting as a proxy for Communist China and that China was misunderstood by Americans. "China is not judged to be aggressive because of her actions; she is presumed to be aggressive because she is Communist," Fulbright observed in his memoirs.[40] In coming to this judgment, Fulbright drew on Fairbank's view that China was a "frustrated modernizer" rather than an aggressive power. Economic modernization, rather than exporting revolution, was seen by Fulbright, Barnett, and Fairbank as Beijing's primary goal (a *very* dubious and questionable assumption in 1966 as the Cultural Revolution raged inside of China and the CCP exported arms, materiel, and money to communist insurgent movements worldwide!). Based on this logic, these pro-engagers assumed and argued that a new American strategy which opened the door to China would facilitate China's broader accommodation with the West and thus help to facilitate China's economic modernization.[41]

Here we see the essence of Engagement School's arguments which would be made a decade later after Nixon had gone to China and the Carter administration was looking for persuasive arguments as it sought to normalize diplomatic relations with the PRC. It is no coincidence that Michel Oksenberg, the Carter administration's leading China specialist, used this very argument in trying to mobilize domestic support for normalization. He had been Barnett's PhD student and was his intellectual acolyte.[42] By the mid-late 1970s, there was more truth to this argument, as the radical Cultural Revolution had ended and the CCP leadership had set the country on the path of the "four modernizations." Perhaps Professors Barnett and Fairbank, probably America's two leading China experts at the time, were prescient and deeply understood China's intrinsic and long-standing "search for wealth and power,"[43] but it was a difficult argument to make while Mao's China was fomenting the chaotic Cultural Revolution domestically and exporting it abroad.

While the Fulbright hearings did not produce a change in American policy, they were a turning point—at least in terms of American *discourse* about how to deal with Communist China. No longer was it taboo to publicly discuss the possibility of establishing ties with the PRC. And remember that this was 1966—more than five full years *before* Henry Kissinger would take his secret visit to Beijing in July 1971, to be followed in February 1972 by President Nixon's groundbreaking visit. But it was becoming evident toward the late 1960s that at least some prominent Americans favored a shift in US policy. Nixon was also doing the math on how many nations in the United Nations General Assembly were increasingly supportive of giving the PRC China's seat and expelling the ROC from the body. The votes in favor had been increasing every year and the margins against the United States and other countries that continued to try to block the PRC's admission and expulsion of the ROC was shrinking. On October 25, 1971, with a roll-call vote of 76–35 (with 35 abstentions) the PRC was granted China's seat in the United Nations General Assembly and on the Security Council, while the Republic of China (Taiwan) was expelled from both bodies.

Following the Fulbright hearings, although the Vietnam War continued to rage with deployment of American forces reaching their zenith, the efforts to fashion a new policy toward the PRC began to move away from Washington, DC, and into the country at large. This was an important development. It was one thing to quietly contemplate such a momentous shift in US policy in the shiny corridors and offices of the State Department, or in open and public Congressional hearings—but it was quite another for the possibility to be discussed among the American public at large or among their representatives in Congress (Senator Fulbright himself had been an exception to the rule, openly raising the issue in a speech on the Senate floor on March 25, 1964).

The Emergence of the New China Lobby

Beginning during the mid-1960s, a nascent coalition of non-governmental groups and activist citizens began a grass roots campaign to raise consciousness among the American public about the PRC and to generate pressure on the US government to begin some sort of outreach and engagement to Beijing.

During 1964–1966, a few organizations began to engage their members on the question of China policy. The Quaker American Friends Service Committee (AFSC), the League of Women's Voters, the American Association of the United Nations, the American Chamber of Commerce, and some philanthropic foundations, all began to discuss the possibility of "exploring steps designed to more effectively open channels of communication with the people of mainland China."[44]

Several of the academics who had testified before the Fulbright Committee began to become publicly involved, perhaps most notably University of California, Berkeley political scientist Robert Scalapino (Photo 3.4).

Together with Cecil Thomas of the San Francisco branch of AFSC, Scalapino organized two public conferences (one in San Francisco and the other in Washington, DC). The first took place on the University of California campus on December 9, 1964, which attracted over 1,000 attendees.[45] Two northern California public television stations broadcast the conference live and the proceedings were widely reported in the press.[46] The second meeting, ambitiously entitled the National Conference on the United States and China, occurred over three days in Washington, DC (April 28–30, 1965), and was particularly

Photo 3.4 Robert A. Scalapino.
Photo credit: Public domain via Wikimedia Commons

animated (and chaotic), with 800 participants clamoring to express their views. The meeting was addressed by Senator George McGovern, two senior representatives of the State Department, a number of scholars from several elite east coast universities, and some businessmen.[47]

Momentum was building. Over one hundred similar gatherings were organized by the Quakers across the country during 1965–1966.[48] A national groundswell in favor of engagement with China was building.

The Three Committees

Scalapino was a very entrepreneurial academic who also believed deeply in public education. He worked together with Professors A. Doak Barnett (Columbia University), Lucian W. Pye (MIT), Alexander Eckstein (University of Michigan), Allen S. Whiting (University of Michigan), and others; together, they were instrumental in establishing the National Committee on US–China Relations (NCUSCR) on June 9, 1966. Scalapino was elected as its first chairman.[49] Fifty-eight years later (in 2024) the NCUSCR's own Statement of Purpose still reads:

The National Committee on United States–China Relations is a nonprofit educational organization that encourages understanding of China and the United States between citizens of both countries. Established in 1966 by a broad coalition of scholars and civic, religious, and business leaders, the Committee was founded in the belief that vigorous debate of China policy among Americans was essential and that balanced public education could clarify U.S. interests and strengthen our foreign policy. Similarly, the founders believed that over time dialogue with Chinese citizens would enhance mutual understanding, a basic requirement for stable and productive relations.

Over the decades, the NCUSCR's basic purposes have not changed, although its programs have developed in response to shifting needs and opportunities. The National Committee focuses its exchange, educational, and policy programs on international relations, economic development and management, governance and legal affairs, environmental and other global concerns, mass communication, and education administration—addressing these issues with respect to mainland China, Hong Kong, and Taiwan. The National Committee's programs draw strength from its members, who now number more than 700 Americans from all parts of the country, and nearly 60 corporations and professional firms. They represent many viewpoints but share the belief that increased public knowledge of China and US–China relations requires ongoing public education, face-to-face contact, and forthright exchange of ideas.[50]

From its inception in 1966 through 1972, the NCUSCR was focused exclusively on sponsoring public programs to discuss China; but following President Nixon's visit in 1972, the organization assumed a second function of organizing *exchanges* between the two societies. Over the decades, the NCUSCR has indeed played an instrumental, constructive, and commendable role in US–China relations. It was instrumental in the ice-breaking "ping-pong diplomacy" in 1972 (organizing the return visit of the Chinese ping-pong team to the United States) and it has undertaken a wide variety of exchanges and programs subsequently. It works very hard to be apolitical, non-partisan, and true to its founding principles—but over the past decade the NCUSCR has been increasingly out of step with both American (increasingly negative) views of China and with US government policy (see further discussion in Chapter 7, section "Non-Governmental Organizations"). The National Committee's mission and raison d'être, after all, is engagement with China.

The NCUSCR was one of three national organizations established around the same time, each of which had an eye on the future day when the United States and China would establish full relations. The other two were the National Council on US–China Trade (subsequently renamed the US–China Business Council) and the Committee on Scholarly Communication with Mainland China (later renamed Committee on Scholarly Communication with the People's Republic of China [CSCPRC] and then subsequently shortened to Committee on Scholarly Communication with China).

The CSCPRC was also established in 1966 under the joint sponsorship of the American Council of Learned Societies (ACLS), the National Academy of Sciences (NAS), and the Social Science Research Council (SSRC). There were two people involved before 1966 in creating the CSCPRC. The first was Harrison Brown, who was Foreign Secretary of the NAS. He had been involved with the Pugwash conferences on Science and World Affairs, a conclave comprised of scientists and policymakers that was established at the height of the Cold War and dedicated to arms control and abolition of nuclear weapons.[51] It was at Pugwash that Brown had met Zhou Peiyuan, a European-trained theoretical physicist and founding member of the Chinese Academy of Sciences. China had exploded its first atomic bomb on October 16, 1964, and American scientists realized that "there was more going on there than previously realized," according to Mary Brown Bullock, who later served as the longtime staff director of the CSCPRC.[52] Brown began discussions with the Department of State, as he did not want the NAS to start something that the State Department did not, at least implicitly, agree to. The second person involved in the pre–1966 brainstorming and planning was Professor John Lindbeck of Columbia University. Brown and Lindbeck together approached the ACLS and SSRC in 1964, and these discussions led to the creation of the CSCPRC in 1966 under tripartite sponsorship. From the beginning, the organization was physically based at the National Academy of Sciences in Washington, DC.

Established just as the anti-intellectual and xenophobic Cultural Revolution was breaking out in China, the CSCPRC had an inauspicious beginning— there were literally no Chinese universities or institutions of higher education and research with which to engage. Even if there were, the US government's own travel ban to China would likely have precluded any exchanges. Yet, those who established the CSCPRC did have the foresight to envision a day when such exchanges might be possible. The organization remained dormant until after President Nixon's visit to China in February 1972 and the issuing of joint Shanghai Communiqué, which included the statement:

> The two sides agreed that it is desirable to broaden the understanding between the two peoples. To this end, they discussed specific areas in such fields as science, technology, culture, sports and journalism, in which people-to-people contacts and exchanges would be mutually beneficial. Each side undertakes to facilitate the further development of such contacts and exchanges.[53]

It would be seven more years before diplomatic relations were officially established in 1979—thus facilitating a fuller menu of academic exchanges. But during the intervening period, the CSCPRC played a vital role in kick-starting exchanges between American and Chinese scientists and scholars. In 1972, the

CSCPRC initiated a multidisciplinary exchange program—that by 1978 had sponsored 30 American delegations that traveled to China, while hosting 37 Chinese delegations in the United States (together including approximately 700 individuals).[54] For its part, the NCUSCR sponsored 19 delegations to China and received 14 from China during the same period (1972–1978).[55]

These delegations were almost entirely in the sciences.[56] During the period of 1972–1979, the topics of Chinese delegations that visited the United States included the teaching of the medical sciences, hydro technology, high-energy physics, library science, physiology, insect hormones, biomedical engineering, seismology, laser research, agricultural mechanization, pharmacology, plant photosynthesis, molecular biology, petrochemicals, industrial automation, tumor immunology, astronomy, environmental science, meteorology, tunnel boring, marine sciences, nuclear and plasma physics, remote sensing, theoretical and applied mechanics, science policy, materials science, as well as renewable and new energy resources. American delegations to the PRC almost exactly paralleled these topics, but also included delegations on Chinese art and archaeology, Chinese history, early childhood education, linguistics, acupuncture, animal sciences, astronomy, cancer research, engineering education, plate tectonics and earthquake science, biochemistry, insect control, solid state physics, schistosomiasis, paleoanthropology, and rural small-scale industry. The selection of delegation topics says much about each sides' respective research interests (and what the other side would countenance).

It was no accident that scientific exchanges figured so prominently between the two sides during the 1970s. For China's part, the "four modernizations" had become a new focus of public policy after 1973, and China was cautiously opening its door to select West European countries. For America's part, engaging in a limited number of scientific exchanges was a way to maintain a minimum of momentum in the relationship, as it had bogged down following President Nixon's resignation during Gerald Ford's presidency (1974–1976). There was no real movement toward normalization. The stagnation in bilateral ties and loss of momentum continued after Jimmy Carter was elected and succeeded Ford as president in January 1977.

Carter came to office genuinely committed to finishing the normalization process—however there were three other foreign policy priorities that took precedence (the SALT II arms control agreement with the Soviet Union, renegotiating and ratifying the Panama Canal treaties, and the Camp David Middle East Peace Accords). Normalization with China, while a priority for the new administration, had to take fourth place in the queue. Thus, the operative question was *how* to push the relationship forward with Beijing during the interim period before the administration could really focus on finalizing the normalization process.

Carter and his National Security Advisor Zbigniew Brzezinski were both persuaded by Michel Oksenberg—the China specialist on the National Security Council staff—that science and technology was the perfect medium to keep the Chinese engaged given Beijing's own prioritization on modernization (especially after Deng Xiaoping returned to power in 1977 and gave an important speech to the National Science Conference in May 1978). The Chairman of the CSCPRC at the time was Frank Press, a renowned geophysicist whom Carter tapped to become his Science Adviser and head of the White House Office of Science and Technology Policy (OSTP). Press brought along with him to OSTP Anne Keatley, who had been the staff director of CSCPRC and was replaced by Mary Brown Bullock.[57] Together with Oksenberg and Ben Huberman (deputy director of OSTP), this group in the White House and at CSCPRC pushed ahead with an ambitious set of science and technology exchanges with China—which were important in their own right but also critically served to maintain needed momentum before full normalization of relations was consummated (this process is well described in a recent book by Pete Millwood).[58]

Another important impact of these scientific exchanges during the 1970s—as other scholars have noted—was to "humanize" the other side and erode the mutual narratives of the other as an adversary.[59] These modest scientific exchanges were supplemented by a growing trickle of tourists, businesspeople, and Chinese Americans visiting relatives during the decade. By 1977, an estimated 15,000 Americans had visited China while 1,000 Chinese had visited the United States.[60] In the United States, such exchanges also served to shift the perception of China from one of an ideological, communist, monolithic zealot to that of a modernizing developing country (albeit a socialist one). Similarly, as my own study of Chinese perceptions of America demonstrated, Chinese began to view the United States through more variegated lenses.[61]

The third American committee which played a role in beginning exchanges with China was the National Council on US–China Trade (NCUSCT), which was established March 1973—seven years after the NCUSCR and CSCPRC. If the National Committee established a bridgehead between professionals and those involved in the arts and sports, and the CSCPRC involved American scientists and academics, the NCUSCT similarly filled a need for a conduit in the commercial domain.

The Council's creation came about as the result of a confluence of stimuli.[62] The Nixon visit to China in 1972 seems to have been the original impetus, as an internal US government working group was formed just one month after the visit to explore the possibility of establishing some kind of governmental or non-governmental body to be a bilateral conduit for trade discussions. The possibility of creating an American counterpart to the China Council for the Promotion of International Trade (CCPIT) was one option considered. Nixon's visit in February 1972 was followed shortly thereafter in June by a Congressional visit led by House of Representatives members Gerald Ford and Hale Boggs. Their visit included meetings with Premier Zhou Enlai as well as CCPIT officials—both of whom were distinctly *un*enthusiastic about the possibility of trade with the United States. Upon their return to Washington, Ford and Boggs issued a report that raised the possibility of creating a "non-governmental" or "quasi-governmental" organization to facilitate trade with China.[63] Around the same time, the Nixon administration was approached by two businessmen (Boeing CEO Thornton Wilson and commercial lawyer Eugene Theroux) who pushed forward the idea of establishing a private non-governmental organization (NGO) to promote trade with China. The National Security Council under Henry Kissinger concluded that the US government should not be in the position of coordinating trade with China through an official body, but that the Department of Commerce should be supportive of such a private sector effort. With President Nixon's approval, as well as National Security Adviser Henry Kissinger and Secretary of Commerce Frederick Dent, Wilson and Theroux were given the green light to proceed.

Four months later, in April, a board of directors was created—representing a cross section of CEOs from major multinational corporations (Boeing, General Electric, J. C. Penny, Manufacturers Hanover Trust Bank, John Deere, PepsiCo, Cargill Grain). On May 31, 1973, the NCUSCT was formally established with a lavish event at the Mayflower Hotel in Washington, DC. The event attracted 500 companies. Christopher H. Phillips, then serving as Deputy US Ambassador to the United Nations, was elected as the first president of the NCUSCT. Although two-way trade that year registered only $800 million,[64] six years later—by the time of normalization in 1979—it had grown to $1.14 billion.[65]

From this time forward, the American business community became the most powerful lobby and constituency in the Engagement Coalition. Many would argue that "business was the ballast" in the relationship over decades. This is not to neglect or dismiss the important roles played by the other constituencies examined throughout the remainder of this chapter—but, clearly, the enormous sums of money involved in two-way trade in goods and services ($758 billion in 2022) and the political power of business in domestic American politics gave it an outsized influence in shaping US policy toward China (for better or for worse).

Thus, the "three committees" all played important roles is fostering the early engagement between different sectors of Americans and their Chinese counterparts during the 1970s following the Nixon opening, and they each continued to play critical roles as the principal institutional intermediaries on the American side following normalization (the CSCPRC discontinued operations in 1996).

The three committees were not the only organizations that served as interme-diaries between American society and the PRC. Two others merit mention. Both had "leftist" political orientations. The first was the Committee on Concerned Asia Scholars (CCAS)—an organization formed in 1968 by graduate students and some faculty from leading American universities (University of California, Berkeley; Stanford University; the University of Michigan; Columbia Univer-sity; and Harvard University), but it also included a considerable number of non-institutionally affiliated independent scholars.[66] Founding members of CCAS included a number of young scholars who would go on to have significant careers as academic China specialists—including Susan Shirk, Orville Schell, Norma Diamond, Joseph Esherick, Ed Friedman, Perry Link, Maurice Meisner, Paul Pickowitz, Elizabeth Perry, Carl Riskin, Mark Selden, John Dower, Bruce Cumings, and Marilyn Young.[67]

The principal purpose of CCAS was opposition to the Vietnam War. It did a considerable amount of organizing on-campus protests across the country. Although activism against the Vietnam War was the group's principal purpose, it also had a secondary interest in China. With respect to both China and the Vietnam War, CCAS was profoundly "anti-establishment"—criticizing the links between the US government and academia—which was clearly evident in the organization's founding Statement of Principles:

> We first came together in opposition to the brutal aggression of the United States in Vietnam and to the complicity or silence of our profession with regard to that policy. Those in the field of Asian studies bear responsibility for the con-sequences of their research and the political posture of their profession. We are concerned about the present unwillingness of specialists to speak out against the implications of an Asian policy committed to ensuring American domina-tion of much of Asia. We reject the legitimacy of this aim and attempt to change this policy. We recognize that the present structure of the profession has often perverted scholarship and alienated many people in the field.[68]

Prior to Nixon's trip to China in 1972, CCAS expressed interest in Mao's Cultural Revolution, but afterward it became more involved in advocating for US–China relations. To this end, it began to send small delegations to China beginning in March 1971. Some of these groups were received by Premier Zhou Enlai. After one trip, CCAS scholars published a paperback volume entitled *Inside the People's Republic!*—which included the transcript of one meeting with Premier Zhou as well as accounts of their travels (including to many Potemkin sites).[69] After having no opportunities to visit China for two decades, these visits were the first chances to peer behind the "bamboo curtain."[70]

The second group was the US–China People's Friendship Association (USCPFA).[71] It was founded in 1971 and its first president was William Hinton, a socialist farmer who had spent some years in China chronicling land reform and the plight of Chinese peasants after the revolution. His book *Fanshen* provided one of the first looks inside the PRC for American readers. Although many of those who involved themselves in the organization had leftist political leanings, this was by no means true of all. USCPFA quickly established branches across the country in many communities (chapters still exist nowadays in all 50 states) and it became the principal way that ordinary Americans could travel to China in those days. By 1980, it had 11,000 members.[72] As a "friendship" association, USCPFA received financial and logistic support from the Chinese Association of Friendship with Foreign Countries (one of the main "united front" organs of the CCP and PRC)—which covered in-country expenses for USCPFA delegations. By the mid-late 1970s, USCPFA were organizing two dozen "friendship tours" per year for curious and sympathetic Americans.[73] As such, USCPFA attracted the attention and monitoring by the FBI.

A third organization that was national in scope and was active in lobbying for possible US diplomatic recognition of the PRC and considering granting it membership in the United Nations was the United Nations Association of the United States (UNA–USA), previously known as the American Association of the United Nations (AAUN). Established soon after the creation of the United Nations itself at the San Francisco Conference in June 1945, the AAUN of course recognized the Republic of China as the government of China. But the Communist Chinese seizure of the mainland, the ROC's retreat to the island of Taiwan, and the establishment of the PRC in October 1949 put the AAUN in a bind. On the one hand, it was torn between following US government policy of continuing to recognize the ROC as the legitimate government of China and hence occupying China's seat in the United Nations and on the Security Council. On the other hand, the AAUN accepted the core principle of "universality" of including *all* governments that met the criteria of sovereignty as members of the United Nations.

Prima facie this suggested the two-Chinas solution—i.e., that both the ROC (representing only the island of Taiwan) and the PRC (representing mainland China) as the way out of the bind. The problem was, first, that *both* Chinese regimes maintained that they were the sole legitimate government of *all* of China and, second, that the island of Taiwan was an inalienable sovereign part of China (having reverted from Japanese colonial status to Chinese sovereignty at the end of World War II). Since the PRC did not have enough support from United Nations member states to seat it as a sovereign member and to expel the ROC during the 1950s and 1960s, the AAUN tried to straddle the divide and finesse the issue by arguing for "dual recognition," in effect a two-Chinas policy. Yet, how could an organization that was committed to the universal principles of representation *not* advocate for the seating of the PRC? In a statement from 1956 the AAUN said, "We can no longer hide our heads in the sand and refuse to recognize the problem of Communist China. Certainly, it is impossible to accept the delegates of a nation so long as it is in a state of war with the United Nations. But eventually peoples must be represented in the United Nations by governments in effective control, whether they are democratic or not."[74] The AAUN/UNA–USA continued to hold this two-China position (which, of course, neither the government in Beijing nor in Taipei endorsed) into the 1960s. But by the mid-1960s, the position was becoming increasingly untenable, and the association called on the Johnson administration to "state clearly the conditions under which it would be prepared to see the representatives of Peking take a seat in the United Nations."[75]

As the Vietnam War escalated and the groundswell of agitation across the country in favor of official diplomatic recognition of the PRC (even within a two-Chinas framework) began to grow, the association joined other groups in advocacy. In 1966 and 1967, the association produced two public reports discussing these possibilities of how to seat the PRC.[76] While exploratory, the UNA–USA was nonetheless a respected national organization and its leadership included notable Americans. Two of its leaders, Theodore Sorensen and Robert Roosa, were high-ranking officials in the Kennedy administration (Counselor to the President and Under Secretary of the Treasury, respectively).

Other American NGOs also were involved in advocating for US engagement with the PRC. One was the Fund for Peace—an NGO devoted to "preventing violent conflict and promoting sustainable security." It held an annual "convocation," the third of which was devoted to US relations with China, which took place on October 29, 1971, in advance of Nixon's forthcoming trip to China, and was co-chaired by former Chief Justice Earl Warren and Robert Roosa. It was an all-star gathering of prominent Americans, such as Averell Harriman. This meeting was perhaps the first to give the US foreign policy "establishment" imprimatur to the opening to China.

Periodic Congressional delegations (CODELS) also visited China during the decade of the 1970s, although the Chinese side limited their number owing to a lack of formal diplomatic relations. Some CODELS issued reports, most did not.[77]

Despite these newly opened channels of engagement by the United States with China, and the general curiosity and enthusiasm following the Nixon opening, there remained some skepticism concerning the potential for the development of society-to-society exchanges. Richard H. Solomon served as the China expert on the National Security Council staff from 1972 to 1976 during the presidencies of Nixon and Ford. On New Year's Day of 1978, exactly one year before the normalization of relations, Solomon published a significant article in *Foreign Affairs*. In it, he warned against precipitously moving too quickly to normalization without the requisite domestic support, arguing,

> There are no bilateral advantages for America in normalizing relations with the PRC. Peking is unable to finance a sizable expansion of trade with the United States even if it modifies the principle of "self-reliance." The PRC is not really interested in cultural contact with the United States, and scientific exchanges will be primarily to the advantage of the Chinese ... Since 1971 we have become more realistic about the limits of a bilateral relationship with the PRC. Scientific and cultural exchanges have grown slowly because of China's modest and controlled capacity for hosting foreigners, the political conditions Peking imposes on such contacts, and the limited areas for unfettered intellectual collaboration. The American academic community now complains about the restraints of "scholarly tourism" (that is, no real dialogue, much less cooperative research) and the limited willingness of the Chinese side to reciprocate contacts.[78]

Despite these cautionary warnings by Solomon, little did he know that the new Carter administration was already well progressed in their planning to proceed with secret negotiations with the Chinese leadership to consummate formal diplomatic normalization of relations by the end of the year.

While the full flowering of the Engagement Coalition would have to await formal diplomatic relations (because the two nations could literally not engage in the full range of normal ties between the two states absent formal relations), nonetheless, as we have seen in this chapter, the genesis of the Engagement Coalition was already entrenched and the seeds were planted which would bloom over the following decade. Thus, just as in the cases of Japan and Canada,[79] the NGOs that had been developed in the United States in anticipation of diplomatic relations were important in both helping to forge a domestic consensus in favor of official relations, as well as then being poised to spring into action once formal diplomatic relations were established.

The Nixon Breakthrough and Ford Interregnum

As I discussed at the beginning of Chapter 2, Henry Kissinger's and President Nixon's breakthrough outreach to China in 1971 and the historic visit in 1972 (see Photo 3.5) were motivated by several factors. Clearly, the main motivation was to forge a common strategic front against the Soviet Union. Two other interrelated motivations, as described in Nixon's *Foreign Affairs* article of 1967,

Photo 3.5 President Nixon arrives in China, February 21, 1972.
Photo credit: Public domain via Wikimedia Commons

were to "bring China into the family of nations," thus integrating China into the international community and thereby inducing change inside of China:

> Taking the long view, we simply cannot afford to leave China forever outside of the family of nations, there to nurture its fantasies, cherish its hates and threaten its neighbors. There is no place on this small planet for a billion of its potentially most able people to live in angry isolation ... The world cannot be safe until China changes. Thus, our aim—to the extent we can influence events—should be to *induce change*.[80]

Additionally (also as discussed in Chapter 2), Kissinger wanted to open a panoply of professional and people-to-people exchanges. Kissinger's National Security Council staff members Alfred Jenkins and John Holdridge prepared a memo which Kissinger presented to Chinese Premier Zhou Enlai's aide Xiong Xianghui, which included a 25-point proposal suggesting exchanges in sports, science, and journalism, among other fields. Xiong apparently welcomed the proposals but cautioned the Americans that these needed to be conducted on a "private" and "non-governmental" basis owing to the lack of diplomatic relations.[81] These were subsequently specifically mentioned in the Shanghai Communiqué of 1972 and were inserted at Kissinger's specific request to Winston Lord (the principal drafter of the communiqué on the American side).[82]

All of these motivations and goals of Kissinger and Nixon were welcomed and echoed on the Chinese side. Mao and Zhou Enlai wanted the American counterweight to the Soviet "Polar Bear," they wanted the PRC to join the United Nations and international institutional community, and they also sought change in China. What kind of change? Economic, scientific, and technological *modernization* (the "four modernizations" policy was first announced by Zhou Enlai in 1973). To this end, forging professional and societal exchanges with the United States was seen to be useful (but only *after* formal diplomatic relations were established).

Following Nixon's historic visit to China in 1972 and signing of the Shanghai Communiqué, all four of these processes commenced. However, they were slowed somewhat by Nixon's own problems with the Watergate scandal, which finally forced him from office on August 8, 1974.

His successor, President Gerald R. Ford, did his best to try and restore and maintain the momentum that had been disrupted by Watergate. His time in the presidency, though, was a relatively brief interregnum (August 1974–January 1977). The presidential election campaign against Jimmy Carter in 1976 was all-consuming for Ford, leaving little time for diplomacy. Ford had appointed Kissinger as Secretary of State, who did his best to keep contacts with the Chinese leadership.

However, the health of Chairman Mao and Premier Zhou Enlai were both failing during these years. Zhou had progressive intestinal cancer that weakened and hospitalized him for much of 1974–1975, before he died in January 1976. Mao too was suffering from a range of afflictions. In fact, the historic summit with Nixon almost never occurred. As Nixon's visit drew near in late 1971, Mao was experiencing increasingly declining health.[83] According to Mao's doctor Li Zhisui, Mao was experiencing the symptoms of congestive heart failure, a chronic lung infection, bronchitis and emphysema, edema, and other manifestations of what would later be diagnosed in 1974 as Lou Gehrig's disease (amyotrophic lateral sclerosis [ALS]). Just three weeks before Nixon's arrival, Dr. Li thought that Mao was perhaps at death's door following an apparent stroke on top of these other maladies. In January 1972, just a month before Nixon's arrival, Mao could barely stand when attending Marshal Chen Yi's funeral and, according to eyewitnesses, told Premier Zhou Enlai, "I don't think I can make it. Everything depends on you now ... You take care of everything after my death. Let's say this is my Will."[84] But Mao insisted that Dr. Li make him better in order to receive Nixon. This required round-the-clock intensive injections of antibiotics and steroids to control his lung infection and edema, oxygen to help his breathing, acupuncture to stimulate his reflexes, and other therapies to cope with the increasing dysfunctionality of his motor skills. The treatments had produced positive results, although Mao's edema still made him bloated and he had lost strength in his legs and arms.[85] He needed help from nurses to stand, move, sit, and use the bathroom. Sleeping pills helped him sleep. Just prior to Nixon's arrival, they gave Mao a shave and haircut—the first in more than five months—and propped him up (literally) in his overstuffed chair in the study adjacent to his bedroom. It all worked out. Mao was able to meet Nixon and change the global strategic order.

Despite rallying to meet Nixon, throughout this period Mao's health continued to deteriorate.[86] His degenerative ALS continued to progress—taking an increasing toll on the nervous system and motor skills. The muscles of Mao's throat and larynx were noticeably affected, which made it increasingly difficult for him to speak. He also suffered one or two more strokes, which resulted in partial paralysis of his left side. Muscular atrophy affected use of both his arms and legs. As he had great difficulty swallowing, Mao sometimes had to be fed intravenously and was given oxygen on a regular basis. His eyesight was also failing, and he could not easily read (even with a magnifying glass). "In July 1974 we learned that Mao was going to die," Dr. Li recalled, "he could not see a finger in front of his face and could only tell light from dark." He was having increasing difficulty talking, his tongue did not move, and he would often grunt in barely discernible words that seemingly only his nurse aide (and former lover) Zhang Yufeng and interpreter Nancy Tang (Tang Wensheng) could understand and render into intelligible Chinese.

Despite his deteriorating condition, Mao did continue to meet with the occasional visiting foreign leader, but these were rather perfunctory encounters. One of these visiting dignitaries was President Gerald Ford, whose small entourage visited Beijing on December 1–5, 1975.[87] By this time, Zhou Enlai was too ill to meet with Ford's party (which included Kissinger); instead, the President met with Deng Xiaoping, who had just been rehabilitated by Zhou to stand in for and succeed him. The meetings with Deng were focused primarily on countering the Soviet Union.[88]

The preparations for Ford's visit had not gone well, in fact they had gone badly. When Kissinger, Winston Lord, and a small advance team visited Beijing in October 1975 to prepare the logistics for the presidential visit, they were treated unusually coldly by the Chinese side. At the time, the Chinese side—with Deng Xiaoping back in power and empowered by Mao and Zhou to take charge of foreign affairs, including with the United States—were growing increasingly critical of Washington's détente policies with Moscow and what Beijing perceived to be a policy of "appeasement" and the "Munich mentality" (particularly with respect to an apparent acquiescence by Washington to the Soviet Union's sphere of influence over Eastern Europe). Beijing accused Washington of "standing on China's shoulders to resist the Polar Bear." Deng also perceived backsliding by the United States on making substantive progress toward the full normalization of diplomatic relations (as a result of the Water-gate scandal and Nixon's resignation). As such, prior to Ford's visit, the Chinese gave the American advance party an intentionally frigid reception. As Winston Lord recounts in his oral history, "This was the most unpleasant, frosty trip of all the trips I made to China from 1971 to 1976. The Chinese were very cold on substance, at meetings, and in their public toasts. They were very tough on détente and alleged that we were being naïve about the Russians … We were try-ing to prepare a communiqué for the Ford visit, as we had prepared the Shanghai Communiqué in 1971 for the Nixon visit. The Chinese resisted and rejected mentioning any real substantive progress in the communiqué … We were very unhappy when we left China because we saw this as a trip without any results and, perhaps, even without a friendly reception."[89]

Thus, the atmosphere leading up to the presidential visit was not good, and the American side was not entirely sure what to expect. As a sign of displeasure over the preparatory visit in October, the United States conveyed to the Chinese that instead of a perhaps weeklong visit to several Chinese cities, the visit would be limited to Beijing.

After arrival (see Photo 3.6), at the welcoming banquet in his honor at the Great Hall of the People, Ford said in his toast:

The moves that were taken in 1971 and 1972 by the leaders of China and the United States were of historic significance. I take this occasion to reaffirm my

Photo 3.6 Deng Xiaoping receives President Gerald Ford.

Photo credit: White House photograph, courtesy of Gerald R. Ford Presidential Library

commitment to the objectives and the principles that emerged from those first steps and specifically to the normalization of our relations ... The development of cultural and scientific exchanges, and trade, strengthens the ties between the Chinese and American peoples.[90]

Despite these words about the broader US–China relationship (and the elements that later comprised "engagement"), the subsequently declassified and publicly released transcripts of the closed-door discussions that President Ford and his party had with Deng and Mao focused entirely on the Soviet Union.

President Ford and his party had a two-hour meeting with Chairman Mao.[91] It had been uncertain that a meeting with Mao was even to take place, and the reasons became clear in their opening exchange:[92]

CHAIRMAN MAO: "So, how are you?"
PRESIDENT FORD: "Fine. I hope you are too."
CHAIRMAN MAO: "I am not well. I am sick."

Despite being a Marxist and thus atheist, Mao then told Ford that he was prepared to "go and meet God." Following this exchange, the remainder of the conversation dealt entirely with the Soviet Union and did not cover any other elements of "engagement." Although physically weakened, Mao's mental acuity was apparent to his American interlocutors, and the meeting ran a full two hours. As Winston Lord recently reflected to me, "This was my fifth and last meeting with him [Mao]. He declined physically over the years but remained mentally sharp. He thus exhibited extraordinary willpower. In rereading the transcripts of the meeting (in which I was the American notetaker), I am struck by how much detail he could summon, such as the policies of individual African countries."[93]

The Ford visit succeeded in temporarily restoring some momentum in the relationship, but it also revealed just how single-issue-oriented the relationship was at this juncture: joint efforts to counter the Soviet Union. All other dimensions of the relationship would have to await the presidency of Jimmy Carter.

Chapter 4

The Evolution of the Engagement
Coalition After Normalization

This chapter picks up the story of American engagement policy following President Nixon's dramatic breakthrough in 1971–1972 and the interregnum of President Gerald Ford's presidency 1974–1976—and carries it through the subsequent six presidencies and nine administrations. This is the period of "high engagement," a lengthy period of 36 years (1979–2016). The period of engagement officially ended with the Trump administration (2017–2021) and Biden administration (2021–2025).

Presidents Possess Agency

Of all the different actors and constituencies in the United States that affect US relations with China, probably the most important are presidents. The case can be made that the business community may be the most influential over time, but I would argue that presidents are the most impactful. While presidents come and go (and their administrations) establish the public position and the substantive policies of the US government toward China. They have considerable agency that other constituencies do not possess. Both because of their own individual worldviews (and how they perceive China), and because there has been a broad consensus across multiple domestic constituencies, six consecutive presidents (Carter through Obama) bought into the logic of engagement with China and carried out the Engagement strategy toward China. Therefore, these six presidents were not simply members of the Engagement Coalition—they were its *leaders*. This came to an abrupt halt with President Donald Trump, and President Biden's subsequent China policies had more in common with Trump's than with his predecessors (as we will see in Chapter 5).

We, therefore, begin by examining the statements of six presidents and eight administrations (Carter, Reagan, George H. W. Bush, Bill Clinton, George W. Bush, Barack Obama) concerning the purposes of engagement.[1] Readers should thus note that presidential statements concerning other aspects of US–China relations are not considered, as there are many useful primary and secondary sources that do so. The published records of each administration are filled with the lacunae of different policy issues. My intended purpose here is to focus very specifically on what each president (and some of their senior administration officials) said publicly concerning the purposes of engagement with China.

This is not at all to suggest that each did so consistently throughout their terms in office. In fact, with the exceptions of George H. W. Bush and Barack Obama, every single one of these presidents following Nixon did not immediately embrace the logic of engagement and the China policies that their predecessor had bequeathed to them—but they *all* eventually came around to accept this logic.

Gerald Ford was uncertain about how to proceed with the commitments that Nixon and Kissinger had made with China and that he inherited. Jimmy Carter was committed to realizing normalization, but on a very different set of terms from those of Nixon and Ford. Ronald Reagan came to office having campaigned against Carter's "sell-out" of Taiwan and promising to restore formal diplomatic relations with Taipei (Reagan preferred a "two-Chinas" policy, and he was prepared to sever the new relationship with Beijing in order to restore it with Taiwan). Once Reagan reconsidered and reneged on this campaign promise, and his administration managed to finesse the dilemma of arms sales to Taiwan in 1982, Reagan personally and his administration went "all in" on engagement with China.

George H. W. Bush took no convincing in order to embrace engagement from the outset, as he had served in Beijing as de facto ambassador and head of the US Liaison Office and had a strong commitment to engagement with China (undoubtedly the strongest among these presidents). The Tiananmen massacre of June 4, 1989, deeply tested that commitment—but Bush 41 never wavered in his core belief that engagement had to continue, no matter the shock of June 4.

Bill Clinton campaigned against Bush's post–June 4 "accommodation" of China (although he did not label it "appeasement"), famously criticizing Bush for "coddling dictators from Beijing to Baghdad." Clinton remained critical and aloof of China during his first term but came around to embrace engagement during his second term.

George W. Bush similarly campaigned against the Clinton/Gore administration's proclaimed "strategic partnership" with Beijing—arguing instead that China was a "strategic competitor." But nine months into his presidency, following 9/11, Bush too pivoted to embrace the logic and practices of engagement. His two terms were probably the smoothest and most productive that the two nations have had since the Reagan administration.

Barack Obama did not run against the Bush 43 China policy, and he accepted the broad rationale for engagement (especially the need to engage Beijing more deeply on issues of "global governance"), but he did want to make several key adjustments to China policy. If anything, Obama came into office committed to engagement—but progressively over eight years he grew more and more disenchanted with its results. By the end of his administration (2016 in particular), engagement was already unraveling—in theory and in practice.

The Carter Administration

What is most notable from reviewing the historical record and declassified memoranda of Carter's presidency is that there were *no* indications of seeking to engage China in transformational terms—i.e., to change China. In fact, the entirety of the empirical record reveals a president and his administration totally preoccupied with the mechanics of achieving normalization of relations. Hardly any documents—including Carter's own memoirs and daily White House diary,[2] those of Secretary of State Vance, National Security Advisor Zbigniew Brzezinski, National Security Council China specialist Michel Oksenberg, and the official Department of State's *Foreign Relations of the United States 1977–1980*, ever mention a future vision for US–China relations or the type of China that the United States would like to see emerge. There were no "vision statements." The closest that President Carter came were these statements at the time of normalization:

- Carter's statement when announcing normalization of relations: "Normalization—and the expanded commercial and cultural relations that it will bring—will contribute to the well-being of our nation."[3]
- Carter's New Year's message to Chinese Premier Hua Guofeng in 1979: "We pledge ... to enrich the lives of our peoples, both spiritually and materially, through trade, tourism, student and cultural exchanges, and cooperation in the sciences."[4]
- Carter's toast at the White House state dinner for Deng Xiaoping: "We've not entered this new relationship for any short-term gains. We have a long-term commitment to a world community of diverse and independent nations. We believe that a strong and secure China will play a cooperative part in developing the type of world community which we envision ... Despite our cultural, political, and economic differences, there is much for us to build on together."[5]

Publicly, Secretary of State Cyrus Vance also indicated no real vision for the relationship. He too was totally preoccupied with how to navigate the eight months of secret negotiations with Beijing and his running feud with National Security

Advisor Zbigniew Brzezinski.[6] The closest that Vance came was in a secret memo he prepared for Carter on the eve of Deng Xiaoping's visit:

> The factor which initially brought us together (1969–1972) was a common concern with the Soviet Union. But the importance of normalization transcends that. The relaxation of tensions between the United States and China can have a dramatic impact on the political and strategic landscape of Asia, and on the world … The series of agreements that we will either be signing or mentioning for the future—S&T, consular, cultural, trade, claims/assets, press representation—will contribute importantly to the public perception that normalization *does* make a difference … We want to broaden and thicken our relationship. For us, these agreements and the rapidly expanding relationships are important because they draw the Chinese further into involvement with us and the rest of the world. To the extent that the Chinese become part of the community of primarily non-Communist nations at this time in their development, so will our ties with China be more enduring when and if they are later tested by strategic and political strains.[7]

Here, we see in Vance's private words, illustration of the third strategy outlined in Chapter 2—to integrate China internationally—but it is quite interesting (and revealing) that this element of the engagement strategy is not evident in other public speeches or private memoranda of the Carter administration.

For his part, the closest that National Security Advisor Zbigniew Brzezinski came to articulating a "vision" for the US–China relationship was his banquet toast during his May 1978 trip to Beijing:

> Our commitment to friendship with China is based on shared concerns and is derived from a long-term strategic view. The United States does not view its relationship with China as a tactical expedient … We approach our relations with three fundamental beliefs: that friendship between the United States and the People's Republic of China is vital and beneficial to world peace; that a strong and secure China is in America's interest; that a powerful, confident, and globally engaged United States is in China's interest … The President of the United States desires friendly relations with a strong China.[8]

There is no mention in Brzezinski's statement of integrating China internationally, broadening scientific and cultural exchanges, trade, etc. If there is a vision for China here it lies precisely in the phrase (drafted by Oksenberg[9]) that the United States sought a "strong and secure" China. This is a phrase that the Carter administration subsequently used a number of times. One feels the irony rereading these statements today in light of China's comprehensive strength and power, even if Beijing does exhibit insecurity. In light of the American debate on whether "engagement failed" that I discussed in Chapter 1, and the premise of helping China to modernize as discussed in Chapter 2, one could reasonably ask: *Why* was it in America's strategic interests to support a "strong and secure" China? The answer at the time was that (a) China was a very poor and under-developed country; (b) China was under direct military threat from the USSR at the time; and (c) strengthening China helped America's strategic position vis-à-vis the Soviet Union. But in retrospect, critics of engagement would say that such an American policy was naïve to the extreme.

The one senior Carter administration official who evinced any desire or goal to change China domestically was Secretary of Treasury Michael Blumenthal, who told President Carter in an Oval Office meeting in March 1979,

> China is definitely ready to be influenced by the United States. They value their connections with us for economic reasons. It will be hard to influence their political system, for they remain inward-looking and maintain that China is the center of the universe. But if we can get to them economically, then we will be able to influence them politically.[10]

Other than these selective quotations, there was no real concept of transforming China in the historical record from the Carter administration. Even chief administration China specialist Michel Oksenberg—in a confidential and very telling memo from him to Brzezinski in October 1977 (see Photo 4.1)—noted,

> How we treat the Chinese—as superior, equal, patron, client, or whatever—has been an issue since Americans first came to Chinese shores in the late 1700s. If history teaches us anything, it is this: Efforts unilaterally to stipulate the terms of interaction between the Chinese and us, particularly with the intent of inducing them to behave like us, are bound to fail. We are engaged with the Chinese in the search for mutually satisfactory modes of interaction ... In conclusion, we must not approach Peking as supplicants. We must behave with self-dignity. At the same time, we must remain aware of the special strategic, his-toric, and diplomatic circumstances that surround our relationship with China and adjust ourselves accordingly.[11]

Here we see Oksenberg the Sinologist demonstrating his historical understand-ing of the relationship—something that was very necessary as the two countries approached each other following a hiatus of nearly three decades. What is particularly notable and interesting is that Oksenberg was trying to temper a resurgence of the "missionary impulse" from reasserting itself. Oksenberg understood the deep sense of aggrievement that the Chinese Communists har-bored toward the West and the United States. He was also a scholar of the

Photo 4.1 President Jimmy Carter with Michel Oksenberg in China, 1997.

Photo credit: Michel Oksenberg Papers, Box 16, Folder 29, Envelope 16, Hoover Institution Library & Archives

Chinese Communist political system and understood well how obstinate and incompatible its Leninist leaders and system would be to try and work with. At the same time, he was able to see beyond these impediments to understand how even the Chinese Communists could find some pragmatic behavior when it suited them. On this basis, Oksenberg knew that mutual business could be done.

Following normalization, the historical record indicates that the Carter administration logically pivoted from how to *achieve* normalization to how to *implement* it. This resulted in a dual focus. First, what exchanges should be carried out with the Chinese? Second, how far should US strategic technology export controls be relaxed for China?

In so doing, we see the essence of the tactics of engagement outlined in Chapter 2—namely engagement as *exchanges*—i.e., to exchange is to engage. From this perspective, it is the process of engaging the other side that matters. This is probably the way that the vast majority of those involved with managing relations with China (certainly US government officials) perceived engagement—to push forward the expansion of bilateral ties through an ever-widening net of exchanges. I do recognize that this is one major way—perhaps the main way—that the majority of those involved with China envisioned what they were doing. At least this was the case during the 1970s and the early 1980s. After 1984, however, as we will see, a more *transformative* motivation (to change China) came more to the fore.

The Reagan Administration

Ronald Reagan came to office as a dedicated anti-communist. Prior to being elected, President Reagan had an ideological predisposition against China as a communist country, yet his views were not that well-formulated or fully set in stone (as they were vis-à-vis the Soviet Union). He had never been to the mainland, but he had previously been to Taiwan in 1971 and 1978. He supported Taiwan as an example of "Free China" (although it was not yet a democracy), and thus he was not well-disposed to America's new diplomatic relationship with the People's Republic of China (PRC). When he ran against Gerald Ford for the Republican nomination in 1976, Reagan was openly on record as opposing diplomatic relations with China. Once normalization occurred under Jimmy Carter, Reagan was openly critical of "abandoning our ally" in Taiwan, and he campaigned in 1980 against Carter on a pledge that, if elected, he would reverse the decision and reestablish "official relations" with Taiwan.[12] Reagan berated Carter about "selling out our ally" during the presidential campaign debates.

Needless to say, Reagan's rhetoric greatly alarmed Beijing. Once elected, he invited Taiwan's representatives as official guests at his inauguration. That further infuriated Beijing. Prior to the election, during the late summer of 1980, Reagan dispatched his vice-presidential running mate George H. W. Bush, along with his foreign policy advisor Richard Allen and former CIA China hand James Lilley, to try and calm Beijing's nerves and to explain his thinking (Reagan basically favored a two-Chinas policy with two official embassies). When the small group returned from Beijing, they persuaded Reagan to make a public statement that finessed the issue and temporarily satisfied Beijing.[13]

This was hardly the end of Reagan's tensions with Beijing. His first Secretary of State, Alexander Haig, was a strong advocate of relations with China, viewing it (as he stated in his memoirs) as "strategically the most important nation on earth."[14] Reagan and Haig had many differences, which culminated in the latter's resignation in 1982, but one of the central tensions had to do with China.

Haig wanted a close strategic relationship with Beijing (as he had experienced and contributed to during the Nixon years)—so close that he advocated selling various weapons to the People's Liberation Army.

Their falling out also had to do with weapons sales to Taiwan. This hypersensitive issue had actually been left unresolved by the Carter administration in its normalization negotiations with Deng Xiaoping. Carter had told Deng during the final round of negotiations, and again in person at the White House in January 1979, that the United States continued to "reserve the right" to sell "carefully selected defensive articles and services" to Taiwan post-normalization, and this language became enshrined in the Taiwan Relations Act. But Beijing never accepted it and continued to press the new Reagan administration over the matter. Ultimately, this resulted in the two countries negotiating and concluding the third joint US–China Communiqué in August 1982. But the issue, as Haig recounts it, revealed much about Reagan's view of China:

> Taiwan was a very difficult question for Ronald Reagan. He is an anti-communist. For thirty years, Taiwan had symbolized the hope (it was not always regarded as an illusion) that the most populous and ancient civilization on earth would free itself of communism. The recognition of China shattered the illusion but left the hope intact. Reagan, like many others, had difficulty in grasping this truth ... Any suggestion of abandoning the Taiwanese, or subjecting them to insult, deeply offended his sense of the loyalty that old friends and long-time allies owed to one another.[15]

Reagan's reasoning, according to Henry Nau (a scholar of, and former official in, the Reagan administration), is that Taiwan was seen as "a kind of West Berlin in Asia, its significance going beyond a mere island."[16]

Haig was replaced as Secretary of State by George P. Shultz. Among other things, Shultz brought with him to office a view that the United States had been overly obsessed with its supposed strategic relationship with China. For Shultz, America had *real* allies in Asia (Australia, Japan, the Philippines, South Korea, and Thailand), while China was a temporary strategic partner at best. His views aligned much more with President Reagan's. Thus, we see in the final six years of the Reagan administration the emergence of an "Asia First China Policy"— rather than a "China First Asia Policy" as had been carried out under Nixon, Kissinger, Carter, Brzezinski, and Haig.[17] This tension in American policy— whether to prioritize relations with Beijing or with US allies in the region—has long been embedded in American Asian policy and has fluctuated from one administration to the next. Shultz described his views this way in his memoirs:

> We well understood the geostrategic importance of China ... recognizing this, we nevertheless sought to alter the thinking underlying our policy. My own attitude was a marked departure from the so-called "China card" policy: the idea

that the United States could maneuver back and forth, playing one big Communist power off against another. When the geostrategic importance of China
became the conceptual prism through which Sino-American relations were
viewed, it was almost inevitable that American policymakers became overly
solicitous of Chinese interests, concerns, and sensitivities ... On the basis of
my own experience, I knew it would be a mistake to place too much emphasis
on a relationship for its own sake.[18]

Shultz further recalled that, "Much of the history of Sino-American relations
since normalization of relations in 1979 could be described as a series of
Chinese-defined 'obstacles'—such as Taiwan, technology transfers, and trade—
that the United States had been tasked to overcome in order to improve the
overall relationship."

With the advantage of historical retrospect, Shultz's observations at the time
were very prescient—this is exactly what China has constantly done to the
United States over the subsequent four-plus decades. For much of this period,
Washington has been far too solicitous of Beijing—while Beijing has never
stopped making demands of Washington. Even in the wake of the June 4th
massacre, Deng Xiaoping had the gall to tell President Bush's emissaries Brent
Scowcroft and Lawrence Eagleburger that it was the United States that had been
responsible for the "turmoil" in Tiananmen Square and that it was the United
States that had to "untie the knot"![19]

Secretary Shultz's perspectives resonated with President Reagan's. He said in
his memoirs, "President Reagan's instincts and my own views on the People's
Republic of China were similar"[20]—while Reagan said of Shultz in his memoirs,
"We really see eye-to-eye."[21]

This is not the place to recount the evolution of Reagan's China policies
after Shultz replaced Haig, as this is well recounted in Shultz's own memoir
and other histories.[22] What can be said is that, following the August 1982 third
joint communiqué, bilateral tensions subsided substantially—which permitted
the Reagan administration to do what the Carter administration had started and
had envisioned: the full *institutionalization* of the bilateral relationship. During
the last six years of the Reagan administration, dozens of bilateral agreements
and "memoranda of understanding" (MOUs) were concluded between the two
governments, with countless more between American businesses, universities,
and other actors. It was, in fact, during this decade of the 1980s that the Engagement Coalition really emerged—and it is indeed ironic that it did so during the
presidency of such a staunch anti-communist as Reagan.

Reagan's own views about China also evolved considerably during
these years. In April 1984, Reagan made a state visit to China (see Photo 4.2),
reciprocating one by Chinese Premier Zhao Ziyang the previous January (I was

Photo 4.2   President Ronald Reagan meets Premier Zhao Ziyang, April 30, 1984.

Photo credit: Photo by Dennis Brack/Alamy Stock Photo

then an American exchange student at Beijing University and witnessed the entire visit, including meeting Reagan and Zhao at the state banquet, and working for ABC News during the visit).

This was Reagan's first visit to a communist country.[23] It obviously had an impact on him—aboard Air Force One on the way back to Alaska, when asked by a pool of reporters of his impressions of China, Reagan spoke extemporaneously at length about China's reforms, the "freedoms" he perceived to be sprouting, and his firsthand experiences, before then referring to the PRC as a "so-called communist country."[24] During the trip, Reagan also maintained his daily diary, in which he effused about all of the signs of "capitalism" and "free markets" that he saw, but also some of his personal experiences. In one speech Reagan also said, "[It is] my determination that China be treated as a friendly non-allied nation and that the United States [should be] fully prepared to cooperate in your modernization."[25] Of Chinese food, Reagan reflected on the first day, "We had our first go at a twelve-course Chinese dinner. We heeded Dick Nixon's advice and didn't ask what things were—we just swallowed them. There were a few items I managed to stir around on my plate and leave. We both did well with our chopsticks."[26]

One highlight of the visit was Reagan's speech at Fudan University in which the president spoke of his vision of the US–China relationship and engagement between the two societies, and he took a number of questions from Chinese students. As an American PhD student in China under the national exchange program, I was permitted to attend the event. It was a very heady atmosphere, and President Reagan spoke and took questions for nearly two hours. His comments were very broad-gauged and upbeat, and they were broadcast live on television (but without interpretation). It was one of the most positive and upbeat speeches about the US–China relationship given by an American president—befitting the sense of a new relationship in its early stages and filled with potential, but also the enthusiasm sweeping China at the time as Deng Xiaoping's reforms were beginning to spread. Living in China at the time (1983–1985), I personally experienced the growing positivity about the future. The mid-late 1980s were, in many ways, really the glory years of Sino-American relations, and Reagan's speech at Fudan captured it well. This period was very much focused on building ties between the two societies and peoples. Reagan concluded by saying, "I hope that when history looks back upon this new chapter in our relationship, these will be remembered as days when America and China accepted the challenge to strengthen the ties that bind us, to cooperate for greater prosperity among our people, and to strive for a more secure and just peace in the world."[27]

****

While on the subject of Reagan's 1984 visit to China, I must share a personal experience that I had. I have told this story to some people, and there were participants that remember and can verify it—but this is the first time I am telling the story in print. It is the story of how I (possibly) saved President Reagan's life.

The story unfolded on the eve of President Reagan's arrival in Beijing, about eight days beforehand. I was at a party at Beijing University with about 20 other foreign students crammed into a small dorm room in the foreign students' dormitory. I was seated between two female Czech students to my left and two men (one Palestinian and one Venezuelan) to my right. I was engaged in conversation with the Czechs (one of whom I still am in contact with), but I could overhear the conversation of the two young men.

The Palestinian, named Nazir, was a member of the militant Popular Front for the Liberation of Palestine (PFLP), and he had first come to China for paramilitary training (at a camp in Hunan Province he told me). After completing the training, he did not, or could not, return to Lebanon and he thus stayed on as a student at Peking University (Beida). Similarly, Wilfredo the Venezuelan had been a member of the Shining Path guerrilla movement in the Andes (mainly Peru but it also operated in Bolivia, Colombia, and Venezuela). He too had come to China for paramilitary guerrilla training and decided to stay on at Beida. I interacted with these guys on occasion, as we lived on the same floor in the

Shaoyuan foreign student's dormitory. Nazir was much more outgoing, while Wilfredo was much more reclusive (we nicknamed him "Beethoven").

At any rate, both had backgrounds with organizations that today would be labeled "terrorist," although in those years they were known as "national liberation movements." China was a major backer of such groups—sending arms, supplies, and money to them in Southeast Asia, Africa, the Middle East, and Latin America, and bringing some of their members to China for training. These groups were both explicitly "anti-imperialist" and anti-American (although I never felt any overt hostility from either one toward me), and it was not unusual that Chinese universities in those years had such individuals among the many "third world" students (at Beida we also had about 30 North Koreans).

As I was engaged in conversation with the Czechs, I could easily overhear the conversation between Nazir and Wilfredo (which was in Chinese, as that was their only shared language). At one point, Nazir said to Wilfredo, "*Ni zhidao, xia ge libai Meiguo Zongtong Ligen dao Beijing lai fangwen* [You know, next week American President Reagan is visiting Beijing]." Then there was a pause, before Nazir said, "*Hen rongyi sha ta!* [It would be easy to kill him!]." That certainly got my attention—but I did not turn to confront or query Nazir. I just kept listening, while trying to feign paying attention to the Czechs. Then Nazir told Wilfredo, "*Ligen zai Changcheng Fandian da zhongting jianghua. Cong yangtai hen rongyi sha ta* [Reagan is giving a speech in the atrium lobby at the Great Wall Hotel.[28] It would be very easy to kill him from the balcony]." Nazir then gestured as if firing a rifle.

Needless to say, I was very disturbed to overhear this conversation—but I did not confront or engage them. I left the party not long thereafter. But what I overheard disturbed and bothered me overnight. The next day I met my wife for dinner—she was a student at a different university (the Central Academy of Fine Arts)—and told her what I had overhead. The following day she telephoned me in my dorm and told me that she had just been shopping at the Great Wall Sheraton Hotel and had seen Nazir (she knew who he was) walking along the balconies overlooking the big atrium lobby where Reagan was due to speak!

This was all I needed to decide that I had to tell someone in the US Embassy. So, I hopped on my trusty Flying Pidgeon bicycle and hurriedly rode downtown to the embassy. The only diplomat I knew there was Leon Slawecki, the Cultural Affairs officer who was responsible for us on the official national exchange program. I told Leon what I had overheard, and that my wife had seen Nazir casing the hotel atrium. He told me to "stay right here," and he left the office, returning a five minutes later with two men dressed in dark suits with short hair (classic "G-Men"). They were part of the Secret Service security advance team that was already in Beijing prior to Reagan's arrival. "Tell these gentlemen what you just told me," Leon instructed. So, I told my story again. "Stay right here," the two G-Men told me. I sat patiently for another 10–15 minutes until they returned with a burly gentleman. "This is Mr. (Chas) Freeman, the Deputy Chief of Mission. Please tell him what you have told us." I dutifully told my story again. Mr. Freeman, who is a famous former US diplomat with long China experience (including serving as President Nixon's interpreter on his visit in 1972) and someone I have subsequently come to know, then told me, "Thank you for your patriotism and telling us. Go back to the university and do not tell a soul. We will take it from here."

About two days later, and two days before President Reagan arrived, the Beijing's Public Security Bureau (PSB) "swept" the entire Wudaokou university district in northwestern Beijing, where there were many technical colleges and some comprehensive universities like Beida, Renmin, and Tsinghua. The PSB physically and compulsorily loaded *all* students from developing "third world" countries on to buses that took them directly to the train station, where they were put on a train to Yantai, a seaside city in Shandong Province about 200 miles east of Beijing. The students were told this was a "mandatory holiday," and they stayed at Yantai for about two weeks—until well after President Reagan had departed. To this day, they do not have any idea of why they had this spontaneous mandatory "holiday." As for Nazir and Wilfredo, I suspect—but do not know for sure—that they were detained and interrogated prior to the Reagan visit. It was another month or two before I saw them at Beida, and I did not engage them (nor do I think they ever suspected that I had overheard their "plot").

I was at the President's speech at the Great Wall Sheraton Hotel on April 28, 1974.[29] My eyes gravitated to the balconies overlooking the atrium—which were filled with Secret Service and security personnel. Nazir and Wilfredo meanwhile were either under detention or far away in Yantai. Who knows how serious they were that initial evening, and where would they get a rifle in China? But when my wife saw Nazir casing the hotel balconies, where he could have had a clear shot down into the atrium, I realized that their conversation might not have been an idle one. How could I have lived with myself if I had done nothing, and the President of the United States had been assassinated in China?

This is a true story. Chas Freeman can vouch for it, and we have discussed it several times in recent years (he has also told me that the US Embassy and China's Ministry of Public Security had received reports of a possible Iranian assassination plot). I have since submitted a Freedom of Information Act request to declassify Secret Service files related to the incident.

****

The remainder of the Reagan administration witnessed continued broadening and strengthening of the bilateral relationship. As I have already noted, under the guidance of Secretary of State George Shultz, the US government was not particularly solicitous of China—just businesslike. Winston Lord served as US Ambassador to China throughout most of Shultz's term as Secretary of State, and later recalled to me,[30]

> Shultz had a hard-headed approach to China. I witnessed this first-hand when I was by his side throughout his long visit to China in 1987, which he called his best overseas visit ever as Secretary. He was politely firm generally and specifically on Taiwan, an issue he handled with consummate skill. And he was very assiduous about our alliances. He projected to the Chinese that we sought to flesh out and improve our relations, but without illusions or patronizing.

After the Taiwan arms sales issue was suitably addressed with the third joint communiqué in 1982, and President Reagan undertook his very positive state visit in 1984, the relationship was on solid footing. It was still relatively new though, as normalization of relations had only occurred in 1979—and, therefore, what was particularly needed was to put in place the institutional edifice of government-to-government and society-to-society relations. Institutionalizing these ties was the real essence of "normalization." The Carter administration had launched the process, but the Reagan administration completed it. In this vein, Ambassador Lord recalls that, "I saw as a core objective the need to inject positive elements in our relations to buttress the negative glue of balancing the Soviet Union—to erect ongoing foundations in case the Soviet factor disappeared (which it did shortly after my tenure)."[31] Ten years after formal relations were established on January 1, 1979, they were truly "normal." While the Reagan administration moved energetically to "normalize" bilateral relations, it continued to cooperate with China against Moscow. In the late 1980s, the United States and China continued to supply arms to the resistance in Afghanistan, operate listening posts along the Soviet border and shared intelligence, and sold $800 million of arms to China.

In reviewing the record of this decade, including *all* of President Reagan's public statements concerning China, I am struck by the straightforward businesslike prose the president used to describe how the United States approached the relationship with China. His other public speeches during the state visit in 1984 were quite effusive and positive about the potential future of the relationship. He was also typically forthright in speaking about the importance of freedom and human rights. Subsequently, he spoke more about the need to bring the two societies closer together. Indeed, that was one central element of engagement. For example, in 1986 Reagan did say in an interview,

> An objective of U.S. policy is to build an enduring relationship with the PRC, including a military one, which will support China's national development and maintain China as a force for peace and stability in the Asia-Pacific region and

the world. We believe that a more secure, modernizing, and friendly China, with an independent foreign policy and economic system more compatible with the West, can make significant contributions to peace and stability.[32]

This was probably Reagan's most fulsome articulation of American China policy and objectives during his entire presidency. Although there were "growing pains" for the new Sino-American relationship during the decade, the 1980s were very positive and heady years. China's image in the United States was very positive, bordering on euphoric, as the economic, social, and political reforms unfolded across China. American media regularly characterized the reforms as "capitalist." Nicholas Kristof, correspondent for *The New York Times*, coined the term "Market Leninism." Liberal political reform was indeed on the agenda of Deng Xiaoping, Hu Yaobang, and Zhao Ziyang, and Deng was twice honored by *Time* magazine as "Man of the Year" (1978 and 1985).

Yet, as author (and bureau chief of *The Los Angeles Times* in Beijing at the time) James Mann observed in his classic account of US–China relations from Nixon to Clinton,

> Reagan's remark about "so-called Communists" epitomized the delusions and the China euphoria that swept America during the 1980s ... America believed China was changing its political system more than it in fact was ... America's romantic view of China in the 1980s was sometimes belied by the realities that Reagan and other officials confronted during their visits to Beijing.[33]

Indeed, the 1980s were a very positive time in China and in US–China relations. I witnessed and personally experienced both (living in China in 1980, 1983, 1984, 1985, and 1987, and I visited in 1981 and 1989). Engagement became a reality during this time. If Americans were intoxicated with China and the potential for US–China interactions—the opposite was equally true. The decade was an extended period of 美国热 (America fever). It was a decade of mutual infatuation that has never been repeated in the relationship.

The George H. W. Bush Administration

President George H. W. Bush inherited a US–China relationship from Ronald Reagan in very sound shape. Indeed, Bush had played a key part in shaping it in his capacity as Vice President. Bush had fond memories and great affection for China stemming from his years as head of the American Liaison Office in Beijing (1974–1975).[34] Because of his time in Beijing, Bush fancied himself something of a China expert. Before President Reagan dispatched Bush to Beijing in 1980, in an effort to ameliorate PRC anxieties about Reagan's stated desire to restore official relations with Taiwan, Bush declined an offer for a briefing by the State Department's China experts—brusquely dismissing the offer, saying, "I know these people."[35]

Bush came to the presidency totally committed to the US–China relationship and to engagement with China. His diary-style memoir, written together with his National Security Advisor Brent Scowcroft,[36] indicates that he viewed the China relationship on three levels: building society-to-society ties, leveraging the strategic relationship against the Soviet Union, and on a personal level with Deng Xiaoping. Bush interacted with Deng somewhat during his years as Liaison Office chief, and thereafter continued to refer to him as his "old friend."

Bush believed strongly in the US–China relationship—so strongly that he took the unprecedented step for a new president of not making his first foreign trip to the United Kingdom and Europe. Instead, Bush went to Asia and made his third stop (after Tokyo and Seoul) in Beijing. His 48-hour stopover (February 25–27) in Beijing included high-level meetings with Deng (see Photo 4.3), Premier Zhao Ziyang, President Yang Shangkun, and other officials; he attended a Sunday church service, and he spoke effusively of the relationship to the Chinese public in a televised interview.[37]

Photo 4.3 President George H. W. Bush toasts with Senior Leader Deng Xiaoping at a banquet held at the Great Hall of the People in Beijing, China, on February 26, 1989.

Photo credit: Edward Nachtrieb/Alamy Stock Photo

But an ill-fated diplomatic dinner and incident cast a pall over the visit. This is a rather complicated story,[38] but it had to do with the US Embassy inviting Chinese dissident astrophysicist Fang Lizhi to a "Texas-style barbeque" at the Great Wall Sheraton Hotel (the same hotel as in my aforementioned Reagan story). En route to the dinner, Fang and his American escort Professor Perry Link were intercepted by Chinese security personnel and not allowed to attend. This incident caused a considerable kerfuffle. Other than this flap, the China visit went well (the Tokyo leg did not, as Bush became ill and fainted during an official welcoming dinner at the Prime Minister's residence), and Sino-American relations under the new president seemed to be off to a good start and on a good track ... until June 4, 1989.

With the June 4 massacre, all hell broke loose in the US–China relationship. The events over the preceding six weeks—the daily mammoth demonstrations in Tiananmen Square calling for democracy, press freedoms, and critiquing growing corruption and inflation—attracted global attention. During the night of June 3–4, heavily armed ground forces of the People's Liberation Army literally shot their way into Tiananmen Square (as it had been blockaded by Beijing's citizens and roadblocks), killing approximately 1,500 people and wounding several hundred others. These events need not be recounted and repeated here (but they need to be remembered).

Two dimensions are of importance here. The first was the profound positive impact that the dramatic demonstrations had on the American public—followed by the horrific shock and profound negative impact of the cold-blooded killings. Second, how did President Bush respond, and what did it mean for America's engagement with China?

The demonstrations themselves had been broadcast live on American television for six consecutive weeks. It was high drama and political theater. It was the very first time that China's citizens had ever confronted the communist government on such as scale.[39] If Vietnam was the first "living room war" for Americans, Tiananmen was the first "living room revolution," broadcast live and in technicolor on television daily for six weeks. The demonstrations increased in magnitude and intensity with every passing day, and they were entirely peaceful. At one point the students went on a hunger strike to protest the government's unwillingness to meet and directly discuss their demands. This just fueled the drama. American viewers heard Chinese students quoting American heroes such as Patrick Henry ("Give me liberty or give me death"), Benjamin Franklin, and Thomas Jefferson—and they literally saw the students from the Central Academy of Fine Arts (中央美术学院) fabricate and erect a replica of the iconic Statue of Liberty directly facing Mao's portrait on Tiananmen Gate (which was described by some journalists as "the great showdown of the 20th century").

Americans can be forgiven for believing that they were witnessing a political revolution inspired by the American example (for its part, the Chinese government also saw the demos as American-inspired—not by example, but rather, as alleged by Deng Xiaoping, through direct manipulation of the students). In some ways, the demonstrations were a logical outgrowth of the 1980s—a decade during which China emerged from the collective trauma of the xenophobic Cultural Revolution while "America fever" (美国热) swept urban society and particularly college campuses. It was a decade in which not only Americans were led to believe that China was abandoning communism and embracing capitalism—but, conversely, Chinese were inclined to believe that America was a model of modernity and democracy.

These twin perceptions coincided in Tiananmen. Importantly, for the purposes of this study, the images presented to the American public tapped into the long-standing American "missionary complex" to transform China into a liberal society, polity, and economy. Americans thought they were seeing a reaffirmation and vindication of their own system—and that China was, again, seeking to emulate the United States and throw off the vestiges of communism. Thus, when the Chinese military opened fire and forcibly ended the demonstrations, killing hundreds, American television viewers thought they were also witnessing the suppression of the American political model. Americans took it personally.

The impact of this massacre on US–China relations was profound, extremely negative, and long-lasting. This cannot be overstated, and it still haunts the relationship to this day. American public perceptions of China plummeted overnight—prior to the massacre 72 percent of the public held positive views of China, by July only 31 percent did (with 58 percent having negative views, according to Gallup).[40] For the United States, the killings had revealed the true draconian nature of the Chinese Communists. They were no longer seen as reformers—and certainly not political reformers—but as ruthless totalitarian Leninist despots. For the Chinese Communist leadership, the demonstrations were proof of what they had believed all along: the United States would *never* accept their rule as legitimate and had *always* sought to subvert or overthrow it.

With this new prevailing image in the United States, the very essence of the Engagement strategy was called into question. Although the United States "reengaged" with China after 1995, it was more circumscribed and more cautious. But a very central purpose of engagement—to make China more liberal politically—had been irreparably damaged. Interestingly and ironically, while this central purpose had been *implicit* in American strategy leading up to 1989, afterward it became much more *explicit*. While the presidents I have already surveyed in this chapter (Nixon, Ford, Carter, and Reagan) never really spoke about liberalizing China, the next four presidents (Bush 41, Clinton, Bush 43, and Obama) all did.

So, how did President Bush—"Mr. Engagement"—react to Tiananmen? In assessing exactly how Bush responded, we are helped by the fact that all of the classified records of that period in the Bush presidency have now been declassified and deposited at the George H. W. Bush Presidential Library at Texas A&M University in College Station, Texas. I was invited to lecture at the Scowcroft Institute for International Affairs at the university in May 2019 and took advantage by staying on a couple of extra days to go through Bush's presidential papers concerning China for 1989–1990. I had always wondered about the internal deliberations inside the US government, and with China's government, following Tiananmen. I took photographs of those documents that I deemed most pertinent to reconstructing how President Bush and other senior officials assessed the situation and decided to proceed in the weeks and months ahead, and these were subsequently posted online for public consumption on the Asia Society's website *ChinaFile*.[41] All of these documents were classified—many very highly (e.g., "Sensitive," "Eyes Only," Top Secret [Compartmentalized] Information).

Three overarching observations emerge from the documents. First, the documents clearly reveal the overwhelming *realpolitik* calculations and desire by President Bush personally to "preserve" the US–China relationship at all costs. These documents illustrate the President's higher regard for the importance of the relationship, over penalizing the Chinese authorities for their actions, and hence his obsession with getting the relationship "back on track." Also surprising to me was Bush's (inflated) self-regard for his own insights into China and his understanding of its history, owing to his time as Liaison Office representative in Beijing from 1974 to 1975, as well as his fawning language of his personal "friendship" with Deng Xiaoping. This was a turning point in the history of China and US–China relations, and Bush did not hesitate to choose the side of national interests over moral indignation or squeezing the Chinese Communist regime harder so that it might actually collapse or be overthrown. Oddly, there does not appear to have been any second-guessing of this approach in the administration over subsequent months as the communist regimes of Eastern Europe were being toppled by their citizens one after another during the second half of 1989. Bush and other senior US officials praised and encouraged the collapse of communism there, but not in China.

Second, also surprising and stunning to me was Deng Xiaoping's straightforward accusation (to Scowcroft at the meeting on July 2 in the Great Hall of the People) that it was the *American* side that had been a principal source of the "counterrevolutionary rebellion" (反革命暴乱) and it would be up to the American side to "untie the knot"! Deng made many other stark statements and accusations in this meeting. Scowcroft had gone to Beijing in the hopes of establishing a pathway through which the Chinese leadership could climb out of the traps they had laid and were in. Instead, Deng turned the tables on him, accusing the United States of fomenting the demonstrations and, thus making it responsible for healing the damaged relationship!

Third, the White House documents do not reveal any attempts to coordinate reactions and policies with allies or other governments. It was indeed surprising not to find a flurry of cables, phone calls, and presidential letters with other G-7 partners in the aftermath of Tiananmen and in advance of their summit in Paris on July 16–19 (although the summit did produce a statement on China[42]). For a president who placed such emphasis on consulting allies and other heads of state personally, this is a surprising (non-)finding.

Within 24 hours of the massacre, President Bush faced the press at the White House in a very charged political atmosphere. His instincts and thinking were clear:

> This is not the time for an emotional response, but for a reasoned, careful action that takes into account both our long-term interests ... And now is the time to look beyond the moment to the enduring aspects of this vital relationship for the United States ... I don't want to see a total break in the relationship, and I will not encourage a total break in the relationship.[43]

But then Bush goes on record as the first American president to publicly endorse democracy in China:

> It is important to act in a way that will encourage the further development and deepening of the ... process of democratization ... The process of democratization of Communist societies will not be a smooth one, and we must react to setbacks in a way which stimulates rather than stifles progress toward open and representative systems ... I believe the forces of democracy are so powerful ... I am convinced that the forces of democracy are going to overcome these unfortunate events in Tiananmen Square ... I happen to believe that the commercial contacts have led, in essence, to this quest for more freedom. I think as people have commercial incentives, whether it's in China or other totalitarian systems, the move to democracy becomes more inexorable.[44]

Four days later Bush himself described his thinking in his own diary:

> The tragic events of Tiananmen, events that began with some hope for peaceful resolution, seriously damaged our hard-won gains. I glumly began to fear that we might quickly find ourselves back at the point we had been in 1972. Tiananmen shattered much of the goodwill China had earned in the West. To many it appeared that reform was merely a sham, and that China was still the

dictatorship it had always been. I believed otherwise. The question for me was how to condemn what we saw as wrong and react appropriately, while also *remaining engaged* [emphasis added] with China, even if the relationship must now be "on hold."[45]

This recollection by Bush within a week of the massacre is very revealing, and it summarizes well what we have subsequently come to know. On June 20, 16 days after the massacre, Bush understatedly notes in his diary, "I'm sending signals to China that we want the relationship to stay intact, but it's hard when they are executing people."[46] Bush's attachment to "staying engaged" with China even went so far as his vetoing several key pieces of legislation and sanctions that Congress had passed in order to penalize Beijing over the Tiananmen killings.[47]

Subsequently, in an effort to maintain the relationship yet convey his deep concerns about Tiananmen, Bush dispatched National Security Advisor Brent Scowcroft and Deputy Secretary of State Lawrence Eagleburger on two trips to Beijing (the first was secret). On the first of these trips, in his meeting with Deng Xiaoping, Scowcroft informed Deng, "You and China could have no better friend than George Bush."[48] It was in this conversation when Deng pinned the blame for the "counterrevolutionary rebellion" in Beijing on the United States, informing Scowcroft of the Chinese proverb, "It is up to the person who ties the knot to untie the knot. Our hope is that the United States will seek to untie the knot."[49]

When these secret visits were discovered by the US media, a public and Congressional firestorm erupted, and Bush was put in the difficult position of defending his view of the US–China relationship and the need to remain "engaged." This put Bush at (extreme) odds with the Congress and American public opinion. Although his administration invoked a range of sanctions and suspensions on China, he also vetoed several Congressional bills mandating additional and tougher sanctions (including linking renewal of Most Favored Nation trading status to China's human rights). This is not the place to repeat this history, as it has been amply covered elsewhere.[50] What is interesting to note is how Bush defined the purposes of his China policy. On the second anniversary of the massacre, on June 4, 1991, he denounced the "the brutal and arbitrary use of deadly force" but then said, "Our goal is to remain *engaged* [emphasis added] over the long term with China in order to foster its return to a pattern of reform."[51] One week previous, in his Commencement address at his alma mater, Yale University, Bush said,

> We will continue to advance our interests and ideals—for free trade, for broader democratization, for respect for human rights throughout China ... The real point is to pursue a policy that has the best chance of changing Chinese

behavior ... The most compelling reason to renew MFN and *remain engaged* [emphasis added] in China is not economic, it's not strategic, it's moral ... It is wrong to isolate China if we hope to influence China.[52]

Thus, in these statements by President Bush, we see for the first time the (repeated) use of the term "engagement" as the *leitmotif* of US China policy—and for the first time any American president explicitly saying that the democratization of China is an explicit goal of the United States. Such language may have been implicit in previous president's China policies, but after 1989 it became explicit. Meanwhile, the *practice* of engagement—as distinct from the strategy for it—was radically reduced following Tiananmen. As Winston Lord, Ambassador to China under Reagan and Bush, noted at the time, "Based on both practical and moral grounds, thousands of individual decisions every week are wiping out or stretching out trade deals, investment, and scientific plans. In the cultural and academic areas—from ballet companies to art exhibits, from journalistic exchanges to student exchanges—a host of promising projects are dying or are placed in cold storage."[53]

The Clinton Administration

In his campaign for the presidency in 1992, Bill Clinton took direct aim at Bush's engagement policy by promising at the Democratic National Convention in 1992 "an America that we will not coddle tyrants from Baghdad to Beijing."[54] Clinton himself had never been to China, although he had been to Taiwan four times as Governor of Arkansas. Once he was elected president, China policy was seen as a hot potato that Clinton and his advisers (notably Chief of Staff Leon Panetta) wanted to stay well away from, as there was thought to be no political upside to trying to re-engage with the "butchers of Beijing." If anything, in its first term, the Clinton administration doubled down on a get-tough policy toward China. Anthony Lake, Clinton's National Security Advisor, set out the new administration's overall foreign policy in a speech entitled "From Containment to Enlargement," the central theme of which was that instead of "containing" communist countries (which, with the exceptions of China, Cuba, North Korea Vietnam, no longer existed following the collapse of the East European regimes in 1989 and the Soviet Union in 1991), the purpose of Clinton's foreign policy would now be to "enlarge the community of democracies." As such, Lake specifically singled out China (together with Iran and Iraq) as "backlash states" for bucking the global wave of democratization.[55] Moreover, Clinton himself went further by telling *The New York Times*, "One day [the PRC] will go the way of Communist regimes in Eastern Europe and the former Soviet Union, so [the US] must do what it can to encourage that process."[56] Such characterizations put a target on Beijing's back (and only confirmed America's subversive intent in the minds of China's gerontocratic rulers).

Although there was a general resistance to dealing with China (official exchanges remained suspended), by 1993 other G-7 countries had begun to relax their post-Tiananmen sanctions and had begun to selectively re-engage with Beijing. First, it was Japan and then European states. Nearly four years after the massacre, the United States appeared to be the outlier among Western governments. Nonetheless, there was not much pressure from within the executive branch departments, from Congress, or from American society to re-engage with China. Even the business community remained reticent, as China's economy was sharply contracting, foreign investment was soft, and a political pall still hung over the country. This began to change in the aftermath of Deng Xiaoping's "Southern Sojourn" (南巡) in February 1992, when he visited Guangdong Province and the Shenzhen Special Economic Zone and gave several "speeches" (more like utterances) encouraging a return to economic reform policies. Among other consequences, Wall Street began to re-engage and reinvest in China.[57]

The official relationship, however, remained in the deepfreeze until November 19, 1993, when President Clinton hosted Chinese president and leader Jiang Zemin at the inaugural Asia-Pacific Economic Cooperation (APEC) summit on Blake Island near Seattle. This was the first encounter between the US and Chinese heads of state following Tiananmen. Robert Suettinger, who served as a senior official with responsibility for China on Clinton's National Security Council staff, observed about the stakes for Jiang going into the meeting, "For Jiang, the meeting with Clinton was a critical appearance. Still untested and considered a Deng puppet without strong views of his own, Jiang had a complex and nearly impossible agenda for the scheduled one-hour meeting. He had to show himself as a tough and determined leader, but at the same time encourage the American leader to take a more balanced, long-term approach to China and to establish some personal rapport with him."[58]

Jiang Zemin apparently did not get the memo from the White House about the intended informal atmosphere and casual dress code—which was a harbinger of how the leaders interacted. Jiang showed up in a suit and tie while Clinton donned a leather bomber jacket, lumberjack shirt, blue jeans, and cowboy boots. Their one-on-one bilateral meeting (with aides and interpreters) did not go well. Jiang was very stiff and, uncharacteristically, stuck closely to his talking points.[59] Suettinger recalls that, "Jiang appeared nervous and seemed to address most of his remarks at the Chinese officials who accompanied him rather than at his American interlocutors." The discussions were apparently quite tense,[60] but nonetheless the Seattle get-together broke the ice, and the relationship began to thaw. A modicum of interactions between the two countries resumed. For the Americans, the principal issue of concern at the time was nuclear proliferation and China's practice of surreptitiously exporting materiel and expertise to Pakistan, Iran, and North Korea, along with M-11 medium-range ballistic missiles to Pakistan and assisting the Iranian defense industries broadly.[61]

The hangover from the Tiananmen massacre persisted, however, and China's human rights abuses now became formally linked to the administration's annual renewal of China's Most Favored Nation trading status. After a year of wrangling, on May 26, 1994 Clinton announced that he had decided to "delink" China's human rights abuses from annual Most Favored Nation status renewal. In doing so Clinton said, "I believe the question, therefore, is not whether we continue to support human rights in China ... I believe that we can do it by *engaging* [emphasis added] the Chinese ... We will have more intense and constant dialogue on human rights issues."[62] Then, in answering another journalist who asked the President, "Aren't you really bowing to Big Business and backing off of human rights?" Clinton responded, "I believe that the answer to what we should do is to *pursue a broader strategy of engagement* [emphasis added] ... and I think that it is far more likely to produce advances in human rights as well as to support our strategic and economic interests."[63]

Although, as we saw earlier in this chapter, President Bush 41 several times used "engage" as a verb—here we have, for the first time, a president using it as a noun and formally stating that the United States pursued a *strategy of engagement*. In a speech at the National Committee on US–China Relations in New York on May 17, 1996, Clinton's Secretary of State Warren Christopher reiterated, "Our focus must be on the long term, and we must seek to resolve our differences through *engagement*, not confrontation."[64] By Clinton's second term (1996–2000) the administration began to formally use the term "comprehensive engagement" to characterize its China policy.

The changeover of administrations in 1996 brought in a different group of senior officials. This included two prominent China scholars—Susan Shirk and Kenneth Lieberthal. Shirk took leave of absence from her professorial position at the University of California, San Diego, as did Lieberthal from the University of Michigan. Both were deeply experienced with Chinese affairs (as leading experts on Chinese domestic politics) and they brought a depth of firsthand on-the-ground research experience in China with them. Shirk became Deputy Assistant Secretary of State with responsibility for China, Taiwan, Hong Kong, and Mongolian affairs—while Lieberthal became Senior Director for Asia on the National Security Council staff.[65] Both were committed to re-engaging with China, and they both were given the go-ahead to do so by their bosses (Secretary of State Madeleine Albright and National Security Advisor Sandy Berger, respectively). The replacement of Tony Lake by Sandy Berger was also important, as Lake had prioritized human rights in China policy—while Berger was more open to a broader-gauged engagement policy.[66]

A similar dynamic occurred at the State Department, where new Secretary of State Albright adopted a more global and variegated China agenda in recognition of the fact that American national interests concerning China extended beyond the human rights agenda. This reorientation placed the "linkage" of human rights improvement to annual renewal of Most Favored Nation trading status front and center on the China agenda (which had been the case since the 1989 Tiananmen massacre). The American business community in particular was clamoring for such a "de-linkage," but other constituencies also found "their issues" held hostage to the Clinton administration's human rights policy. After considerable debate inside the administration, President Clinton was persuaded of the wisdom of de-linking annual Most Favored Nation status renewal to China's demonstrated "substantial progress" in improving human rights, and he issued an Executive Order in 1994 directing this.[67]

As the second Clinton administration opened, these senior officials moved with dispatch to leave the residual vestiges of Tiananmen (and the Taiwan Straits crises of 1995–1996) behind, and to open a new chapter in US engagement with China. The new initiative importantly included an exchange of state visits between President Clinton and President Jiang Zemin in 1996–1997, as well as granting China Permanent Normal Trade Relations (PNTR) and, in 1998, bringing to fruition the long-running negotiations over China's accession to the World Trade Organization (WTO). A brief description of these events follows, but—as per the focus of this entire chapter—I will concentrate on what was said about the US engagement strategy/policy (rather than the events themselves).

Jiang Zemin paid an official visit to Washington on October 29–31, 1997. He was the first Chinese president to do so in a decade (since Yang Shangkun in 1987), and the visit was filled with all the usual fanfare befitting a state visit: White House South Lawn honor guard and reception ceremony, formal black-tie formal dinner, staying in the official guest residence at Blair House, and lengthy discussions in the Oval Office. Before Jiang's arrival, Clinton informed the nation in his radio address,

> I am convinced the best way to promote our interests and our values is not to shut China out but to draw China in, to help it become a strong and stable partner in shaping security and prosperity for the future ... If we maintain *our steady engagement* [emphasis added] with China, building areas of agreement while dealing candidly and openly with our differences on issues like human rights and religious freedom, we can help China to choose the path of integration, cooperation ... but if we treat China as our enemy, we may create the very

outcome we're trying to guard against ... Our objective is not containment or conflict. It is cooperation.[68]

This was one of the most fulsome, yet succinct, descriptions of the purposes of engagement offered by an American president. Then again, just before Jiang's arrival, Clinton said in a speech at the Asia Society in New York, "The pragmatic policy of expanding our areas of cooperation with China while confronting our differences openly and respectfully, this is the best way to advance our fundamental interests and our values and to promote a more open and free China ... America must stay the course of engagement."[69]

In his welcoming speeches and banquet toasts during Jiang's visit, Clinton was typically loquacious on a range of issues in the US–China relationship, the role of the two nations in world affairs, and the positive potential for the relationship. His only really negative comment was to tell Jiang (spontaneously at a joint press conference) that, "The [Chinese] Government is on the wrong side of history," concerning the 1989 Tiananmen events.[70]

At the conclusion of Jiang's state visit, the two sides issued a joint statement—which added an important new phrase to the lexicon of engagement: "strategic partner." The operative sentence read, "The two Presidents are determined to build toward a constructive strategic partnership between China and the United States through increasing cooperation, to meet international challenges and promote peace and development in the world."[71] The exact phrasing has an interesting background. Prior to Jiang's visit to Washington, a team of White House officials, led by National Security Council Senior Director Sandra Kristof, traveled to Beijing to negotiate the wording of the joint statement. As is sometimes the case in diplomacy, and frequently in US–China diplomatic statements, protracted and heated haggling occurs over a few words and the sequence of them. Kristof was locked into such haggling late into the night with her counterpart, Assistant Foreign Minister and longtime America hand Yang Jiechi. As Kristof later recounted,

We went back and forth on a variety of words, and we ended up with *building toward a constructive strategic partnership*. The "building toward" was important to us, and it was the "strategic partnership" that was important to them ... And at the last minute, Yang and I went over to get a cup of coffee, and I said, "You know, we're down to this, why don't you give me 'building towards' and I'll give you 'constructive strategic partnership.' It says the same and is the answer to both of our needs." We reconfirmed that at the time that they were getting ready for the White House arrival ceremony, and that's how it came to be.[72]

Henceforth, the phrase "strategic partnership" became a key part of the Clinton administration's Engagement strategy. However, the American and international media regularly ignored the connotation of the future in "building towards"—instead reporting that the United States and China had *proclaimed* a "strategic partnership." No matter how many times American officials tried to caveat that the phrase was not intended to be a proclamation of present policy, but rather a hope for a desired future, such nuance was lost on the media and public. The phrase would come back to haunt the Clinton administration subsequently.

The following year, in 1998, Clinton made a reciprocal state visit to China (see Photo 4.4). A full nine days in duration (the longest trip Clinton made during his entire presidency and the longest trip that any American president has ever made to China, including Nixon in 1972), it was a made-for-television media extravaganza, as the President and his entourage visited Xian, Beijing, Shanghai, Guilin, and Hong Kong. From a public relations standpoint, the trip was a real success, it buoyed Clinton's sagging approval ratings at home (which had been tarnished by a series of scandals), and the trip breathed new life into America's engagement with China.[73]

Yet still unresolved was the issue of China's accession to the WTO and the need to make its Most Favored Nation status "permanent" (instead of having to be annually renewed by Congress). The Clinton administration's US Trade Representative, the astute and experienced commercial lawyer Charlene Barshefsky, had been locked into protracted negotiations with her Chinese counterparts for several years. The Clinton administration and the entire Engagement Coalition in the United States—most notably including the business community—saw the PRC's accession and PNTR as a critical step forward in locking China into the international trading system, but also to locking in key domestic reforms that would continue to propel further market reforms, the further opening of Chinese society to the world, and hopefully reigniting political reform in the country. What is important for readers of this book, and for our understanding of how the United States justified engagement with China, was the way that President Clinton sold PNTR to the American public—directly linking the economic arguments to advocacy for *political* reform in China.

Congressional approval for PNTR had to precede China's accession into the WTO, so President Clinton personally undertook a strong lobbying campaign of Congress and the American public. On June 3, 1999, on the tenth anniversary of the Tiananmen crackdown, Clinton began to make his case with a presidential statement;

> Trade remains a force for change social change in China—spreading the tools, contacts, and ideas that promote freedom. A decade ago, at Tiananmen, when Chinese citizens courageously demonstrated for democracy, they were met

Photo 4.4 President Bill Clinton and President Jiang Zemin at the state banquet honoring President Clinton's visit to China, Great Hall of the People, Beijing.

Photo credit: White House photo by Barbara Kinney, public domain via Wikimedia Commons

by violence from a regime fearful of change. We continue to speak and work strongly for human rights in China. A continued policy of principled, purposeful *engagement* reinforces these efforts to move China toward greater openness and broader freedom ... A policy of disengagement and confrontation would only strengthen those in China who oppose greater openness and freedom.[74]

As part of the Clinton administration's full-court-press to persuade Congress and the public that admitting China to the WTO was in American interests, the

President consistently made the argument that it would promote the political liberalization and possible democratization of China. In a major speech at Johns Hopkins University School of Advanced International Studies (my alma mater, and I was in the audience) on March 9, 2000, Clinton argued,[75]

> By joining the WTO, China is not simply agreeing to import more of our products; it is agreeing to import one of democracy's most cherished values: economic freedom. The more China liberalizes its economy, the more fully it will liberate the potential of its people—their initiative, their imagination, their remarkable spirit of enterprise. And when individuals have the power, not just to dream but to realize their dreams, they will demand a greater say.

Clinton was careful not to explicitly predict that economic liberalization would inexorably bring democratization, rather linking economic and personal freedoms. It was also in this speech that Clinton made his famous observation about trying to control the internet: "There's no question China has been trying to crack down on the Internet. Good luck! That's sort of like trying to nail Jello to the wall." In another speech to the Business Council, Clinton argued, "In the end, China will learn what people all over the world are now learning: You can't expect people to be innovative economically while being stifled politically."[76]

Thus, the Clinton administration reinforced the Engagement strategy (particularly during the second term) and followed in George H. W. Bush's footsteps of linking economic openness to political liberalization as well as integration into the international institutional order. Hence, WTO entry embodied all three elements of the Engagement strategy outlined in Chapter 2.

The George W. Bush Administration

As is often the case during American presidential election campaigns, the challenger often criticizes the incumbent administration's China policies. Such was the case with George W. Bush in his campaign against Al Gore. During the campaign, Bush criticized the Clinton-Gore view of China as a "strategic partner"—arguing, in distinct contrast, that China was a "strategic competitor" of the United States.[77]

This is the first time that *any* US president or would-be president referred to China publicly as a "strategic competitor." There were two reasons for it: first, that the term was a distinct rhetorical contrast with "strategic partner"; second, because it reflected the way in which the foreign policy team around Bush thought about China. This group—which principally contained Dick Cheney, Donald Rumsfeld, Condoleezza Rice, Colin Powell, Robert Zoellick,

Paul Wolfowitz, Richard Armitage, Stephen Hadley, and others—were known as "neo-cons" (neo-conservatives) and nicknamed themselves the "Vulcans" after the Greek God of Fire.[78]

While these individuals did not see the world, American foreign policy, or China in exactly the same way, there was considerable consensus among them concerning China and Asia policy. Some were more ideological and tended to view the PRC as a communist country, but all viewed China's growing material and military power as a likely long-term challenge to America's position in Asia and the world. They all subscribed to the "Asia First China Policy," first adopted by former Secretary of State George Shultz (see the section "The Reagan Administration")—the idea that the United States should prioritize its relationships with real allies and strategic partners in Asia.[79] As such, they did not believe that Washington should be overly solicitous of Beijing—as they argued that the second Clinton administration had been. Hence, as former Secretary of State and National Security Advisor Condoleezza Rice subsequently told me, "strategic competitor" was seen both a useful rhetorical device during the campaign, but it also reflected a deeper view that the PRC was in fact a strategic competitor and potential adversary.[80] This perspective had begun to percolate in Washington during the second Clinton term, when an informal group of China hawks known as the "Blue Team" emerged.

A slightly less hawkish interpretation among some of the Vulcans held that China should be viewed as a "major power"—which, while not a strategic partner, should nonetheless be worked with. This perspective was best exemplified in Condoleezza Rice's thinking. Rice, who was extremely close to Bush personally, was appointed as his National Security Advisor. She articulated this viewpoint in a major *Foreign Affairs* article published after the election but before the new Bush 43 administration took office. Rice had much of interest to say about China in this article:

> It is in America's interest to strengthen the hands of those who seek economic integration because this will probably lead to sustained and organized pressures for political liberalization. There are no guarantees, but in scores of cases from Chile to Spain to Taiwan, the link between democracy and economic liberalization has proven powerful over the long run. Trade and economic interaction are, in fact, good—not only for America's economic growth but for its political aims as well ... Even if there is an argument for economic interaction with Beijing, China is still a potential threat to stability in the Asia-Pacific region. Its military power is currently no match for that of the United States. But that condition is not necessarily permanent. What we do know is that China is a great power with unresolved vital interests, particularly concerning Taiwan and the South China Sea. China resents the role of

the United States in the Asia-Pacific region. This means that China is not a "status quo" power, but one that would like to alter Asia's balance of power in its own favor. That alone makes it a strategic competitor, not the "strategic partner" the Clinton administration once called it. Add to this China's record of cooperation with Iran and Pakistan in the proliferation of ballistic-missile technology, and the security problem is obvious. China will do what it can to enhance its position, whether by stealing nuclear secrets or by trying to intimidate Taiwan ... Human rights concerns should not move to the sidelines in the meantime. Rather, the American president should press the Chinese leadership for change ... U.S. policy toward China requires nuance and balance. It is important to promote China's internal transition through economic interaction while containing Chinese power and security ambitions. Cooperation should be pursued, but we should never be afraid to confront Beijing when our interests collide.[81]

We see in these excerpts a combination of classic Engagement theory aimed at inducing domestic economic marketization and international economic integration combined with political liberalization in China—but Rice coupled this with a more sober assessment of China's growing military power and its potential for revisionist (defined by her as "non-status quo") destabilizing behavior in Asia and the world.

The Bush 43 administration had barely settled into office when the Chinese came knocking on the door. A delegation led by Vice Premier Qian Qichen and Foreign Minister Yang Jiechi (China's senior America hand and an old friend of the Bush family) visited in March 2001. The Chinese wanted to take the pulse of the new administration and its views of the US relationship with China. It was no accident that the delegation did not fly straight to Washington—instead its first stop was in Houston, Texas, to visit the former President George H. W. Bush, reasoning, most probably, that the best way to shape the views and policies of George W. Bush was via his father. When the Chinese delegation got to Washington and had a meeting in the Oval Office with the new president and his aides, Bush told them, "Our relationship, of course, will be a complex relationship. There will be areas where we can find agreement, such as trade. There will be some areas where we will have disagreements ... It is in our nation's best interests that we have good relations with China."[82]

There was no indication here that the new administration sought to establish a more assertive or confrontational posture, as had been suggested during the campaign in 2000, in Rice's article, and through the appointment of many neoconservatives to top positions in the administration.

This modest beginning would be severely tested only ten days later, when an American EP-3 reconnaissance plane was intercepted and physically struck by a Chinese fighter pilot. The Chinese pilot's plane crashed into the South China Sea and he lost his life, but the American aircraft managed an emergency landing at a Chinese Air Force base on Hainan Island. Its 24 crew members were detained and interrogated, and a full-blown diplomatic crisis erupted. Public statements by President Bush were surprisingly measured (given the circumstances),[83] offering only the understatement: "This accident has the potential of undermining our hopes for a fruitful and productive relationship between our two countries."[84] The administration worked assiduously behind the scenes to get the crew and the plane released. This was accomplished through adroit diplomacy, and the crew was returned on April 11, 2001. President Bush welcomed the crew home with a public statement, but he refrained both from criticizing China over their detention or speaking about the negative implications of the event for US–China relations.[85] But behind the scenes, senior members of the administration bristled and the neo-cons argued that their suspicious views of China as a strategic competitor had been validated.

After the EP-3 incident, the administration sought to reestablish regular channels of communication with their counterparts in Beijing (which occurred mainly through State Department channels). In June, as he renewed PNTR for China, Bush did say, "The United States has a huge stake in the emergence of an economically open, politically stable, and secure China."[86] The summer of 2001 proceeded without incident, and a major deterioration in the relationship had been averted. Nonetheless, the neo-cons in the administration continued to harbor their suspicions of China. One had the sense that a storm was still brewing in the relationship.

An unanticipated and totally different kind of storm did erupt, however: a crisis of major proportions, but one that turned out to be extremely beneficial to the US–China relationship: 9/11 and the al-Qaeda terrorist attacks on the United States. In President Bush's own words, when he took his first foreign trip (to Shanghai) after the attacks,

> The President [referring to Chinese President Jiang Zemin] and the Government of China responded immediately to the attacks of September 11th. There was no hesitation: there was no doubt that they would stand with the United States and our people at this terrible time ... It is President Jiang and the Government of China standing side-by-side with the American people as we fight this evil force.[87]

Following 9/11, and because of China's cooperation with the United States, the following seven years of the Bush administration were extremely positive for the US–China relations. During his term in office, Bush visited China four times, and he welcomed President Jiang Zemin and his successor Hu Jintao on a combined six visits to the United States (see Photo 4.5).

It must be said that the Bush 43 administration witnessed the best extended stretch of ties since the Reagan administration. This extended to all aspects of the relationship—governmental and non-governmental. As President Bush himself reflected on the 30th anniversary of Nixon's relationship-opening visit to China, "We have had thirty years of growth in the US–China relationship. Our ties are mature, respectful, and important to both of our nations and to the world."[88] Six months later, when hosting President Jiang Zemin at his Texas ranch, Bush observed, "The United States seeks and is building a relationship with China that is candid, constructive, and cooperative."[89] Clearly, in retrospect, 9/11 proved to be a turning point for the better in US–China relations. Prior to those tragic incidents, and especially in the wake of the EP-3 surveillance plane crisis in May 2001, the Bush administration was poised for a much more hawkish and confrontational set of policies toward China.

Photo 4.5   President George W. Bush and President Hu Jintao, November 19, 2006.

Photo credit: White House photo by Eric Draper, public domain

But following 9/11, the two sides found common strategic cause and Beijing helped in some logistical ways to facilitate the US war against the Taliban and al-Qaeda in Afghanistan. The enemy of my enemy is my friend, as the old adage goes. This strategic convergence opened the door to seven years of positive relations and multifaceted cooperation.

The Engagement strategy, as outlined in Chapter 2, was fully embraced during the Bush 43 years: continued economic opening and marketization, strategic coordination, international integration, and political liberalization. Readers may wonder what I mean by the latter. I mean two things. First, during the Jiang Zemin and Hu Jintao periods in China—from 1995 to 2008, specifically—there was considerable political experimentation and liberalization occurring. This was *not* a period of political stasis in China, as stealthy yet substantive political reforms were undertaken. I detail these in my book *China's Leaders: From Mao to Now* (2023).[90]

Second, President Bush himself continually pushed for improved treatment of human rights in China, and he did so both privately and openly. He applied his "freedom agenda" to China as well as the Middle East and other countries. As he reflects in his memoirs, "I saw trade as a tool to promote the freedom agenda. I believed that, over time, that the freedom inherent in the market would lead people to demand liberty in the public square."[91] On another occasion, in 2003, when welcoming Premier Wen Jiabao to the White House, Bush said, "The growth of economic freedom in China provides reason for hope that social, political, and religious freedoms will grow there as well. In the long run, these freedoms are indivisible and essential to national greatness and national dignity."[92] Yet another time, in 2005, Bush argued, "As China reforms its economy, its leaders are finding that once the door to freedom is opened even a crack, it cannot be closed. As the people of China grow in prosperity, their demands for political freedom will grow as well."[93]

Bush did not come to these views only once he became president. As early as 1999, he asserted in his major foreign policy campaign speech at the Reagan Presidential Library, "Economic freedom creates habits of liberty. And habits of liberty create expectations of democracy. There are no guarantees, but there are good examples, from Chile to Taiwan. Trade freely with China, and time is on our side."[94] Condoleezza Rice, Bush's first National Security Advisor and subsequently Secretary of State, was similarly convinced: "[Yet] I firmly believe that political change will come to China ... The US can and must continue to advocate for a democratic China."[95]

Another noteworthy element of Bush's Engagement strategy came when his Deputy Secretary of State Robert Zoellick gave an important speech calling on China to become a "responsible [international] stakeholder."[96] Zoellick's speech drew on one of the central tenets of Engagement strategy since

Nixon—to integrate China into the international institutional order. That was not new; what was new is that Zoellick offered a partial "mission accomplished" proclamation—but coupled it with a fresh call for Beijing to do more. He argued, in essence, that the mission of making China a formal national member of a wide variety of international institutions had been *accomplished*. He did not use the term, but this is what international relations scholars refer to as "shallow" or "partial integration"—to be a formal member, but not a full upholder of the institution's norms and rules (which is known as "deep integration"). In his speech, Zoellick was calling out China for shallow and partial integration—paying the dues of membership but not really absorbing or behaving by the rules of the club. He was arguing that China adopted an *à la carte* approach to international institutional diplomacy and that it needed to become more deeply committed and embedded in the broad institutional architecture as well as the underlying liberal values and norms of the system.

Zoellick began his speech by proclaiming, "Our policy has succeeded remarkably well: the dragon emerged and joined the world." But he concluded his speech by saying, "We now need to encourage China to become a responsible stakeholder in the international system. As a responsible stakeholder, China would be more than just a member—it would work with us to sustain the international system that has enabled its success."

Chinese officials did not react well to the speech once they figured out what Zoellick was really arguing. I arrived in Beijing for a conference with senior scholars and officials (including Zheng Bijian, Hu Jintao's senior foreign affairs adviser) one day after his speech, and there was much confusion, followed by consternation. The Chinese interpreted the speech as condescending and as another American attempt to manipulate China and hold it down. As a Deputy Director of the International Department of the Chinese Communist Party assertively told me, "First you Americans tried to contain us during the Cold War. That failed. Then you tried to overthrow us in Tiananmen. That failed. Now you are trying to constrain us internationally. That will fail too!"[97]

While the Bush administration was trying to tie China deeper into international institutions, in an effort to get Beijing to adhere to liberal values of the postwar system,[98] it simultaneously tried to lock China in more fully to bilateral dialogues and institutional mechanisms. Over the previous decade, dating back to the second Clinton administration's attempt to re-engage with Beijing, a wide variety of government-to-government (ministry-to-ministry) dialogues had developed. By the end of the Bush 43 administration, they had totaled nearly 100 separate dialogue mechanisms. However, there was little coordination and a fair amount of redundancy among them. In an effort to centralize and better coordinate these bilateral mechanisms, President Bush tasked his Treasury

Secretary Hank Paulson in 2009 with establishing the Strategic & Economic Dialogue (SAED). It grew out of the separate Strategic Dialogue, which began in August 2005 between Deputy Secretary of State Robert Zoellick and China's Vice Foreign Minister Dai Bingguo (which convened six rounds biannually between 2005 and 2008 for the two sides to brief each other on global trends and hot spots), and a separate Economic Dialogue between officials in the two economic bureaucracies.

The SAED brought under one roof between 15 and 30 agency/ministry heads and a total of more than 150 officials from both sides.[99] It was an unprecedentedly large and sweeping undertaking (by any two governments in history). While the SAED did focus minds and added bureaucratic energy to the relationship, it was also unwieldy. In the view of President Bush's National Security Council aide and chief China advisor Dennis Wilder, "The fusing of the two dialogues into the SAED was a terrible idea. It lost the value of a small group interaction and simply became another talk shop."[100] But the real problem lay in the failure of both sides to follow up on the commitments they made in the joint statements that resulted from each meeting. These statements read more like aspirational "wish lists" than actionable policy documents. Both sides were to blame for the poor implementation. Nonetheless, the SAED was a new institutional innovation in the relationship and it exemplified institutional engagement (and readers should recall from Chapter 2 that institutional engagement was one of the eight key tactics of the Engagement strategy).

Without doubt, US–China relations thrived during the Bush 43 administration. President Bush's top China aide, Dennis Wilder, also credits the successful relationship in good part to Bush's personal relationships with China's leaders Jiang Zemin and Hu Jintao: "President Bush did things that no other president was able to do because of his strong relationships with Jiang and Hu," Wilder told me.[101] Chinese cooperation in the "war on terror" after 9/11 was surely also an important contributing factor. But so too were the economic and political reforms undertaken in China during the Jiang Zemin and Hu Jintao years. China was moving in the directions that engagement theory and strategy envisioned; not as distinctly as during the 1980s before Tiananmen, but engagement nonetheless seemed to be paying dividends.

The Obama Administration

The Obama administration inherited a very strong US–China relationship bequeathed to it by the Bush administration. As Obama and his foreign policy team essentially wanted to continue what they inherited—with a few adjustments—there was no need for Obama to campaign against his predecessor's China policy (as is so often the case). Obama and his administration thus inherited and largely embraced the Engagement paradigm, and there was considerable continuity at the outset of his presidency (this would change as the administration evolved, particularly in its second term). However, they made two initial adjustments to the Engagement policy.

First, they sought to enhance even further the idea that China could contribute more on a range of global challenges—especially global economic recovery, nuclear non-proliferation, and climate change. This was commensurate with Obama's and the Democratic Party's general emphasis on multilateralism and global governance. Obama and the Democrats saw the world through the prism of transnational challenges that threatened the planet and all of humankind—which therefore required multinational and multilateral collective responses. Obama's team believed that through intensive interaction with Beijing it could help to "shape China's choices" and policies in global governance.[102] As the world's two major powers, it logically followed that the United States and China needed to jointly partner in addressing a broad range of transnational challenges. So, the Obama administration embraced Robert Zoellick's and the Bush 43 administration's call for China to become a "responsible international stakeholder," a greater contributor to global governance, and a partner of the United States in doing so. While the Obama team could not use Zoellick's terminology (as all American administrations depart from their predecessor's lexicon), they nonetheless very much embraced the underlying logic of a global governance partnership with Beijing and sought to increase the quality of its contributions to regional and global problem-solving. Although the Obama administration did not go so far, there was talk at the time of a "G-2": the United States and China.[103]

The second Obama initiative that was somewhat distinct from the Bush 43's foreign policy was a greater emphasis on the Asia-Pacific region with a somewhat reduced emphasis on counterterrorism in the Middle East and Afghanistan. The Obama team thus launched what they called the "Pivot" policy—that is, to "pivot" away from the Middle East and toward the Asia-Pacific. Although the pivot had buy-in from senior officials at the National Security Council, Defense Department, and State Department, Assistant Secretary of State of East Asia/Pacific Affairs Kurt Campbell played a key role in conceptualizing the new policy,[104] while Secretary of State Hillary Clinton adopted it as her own signature initiative. Clinton launched it in a two-step rollout—first in an article in *Foreign Policy* magazine entitled "America's Pacific Century," which was coupled with a speech at the East–West Center in Honolulu.[105] Two years earlier, just after taking office, Clinton outlined her hopes for the US–China relationship in a speech to the Asia Society:

You know very well how important China is and how essential it is that we have a positive, cooperative relationship. It is vital to peace and prosperity, not only in the Asia-Pacific region, but worldwide. Our mutual economic *engagement* with China was evident during the economic growth of the past two decades ... Now, some believe that China on the rise is, by definition, an adversary. To the contrary, we believe that the United States and China can benefit from and contribute to each other's successes. It is in our interest to work harder to build on areas of common concern and shared opportunities.[106]

Clinton also prioritized democratic development, both in China and across the region. Clinton wrote in her memoirs, "A major goal of our strategy in Asia was to promote political reform as well as economic growth. We wanted to make the 21st century a time in which people across Asia become not only more prosperous but also more free ... It's not a secret that the epicenter of the anti-democratic forces in Asia is China."[107]

Secretary Clinton also made her very first foreign trip to China and Asia, just 30 days into her tenure. Over the next four years, she would visit China a total of seven times; her successor John Kerry made nine visits. Together, their 16 visits eclipsed the previous record of eleven combined visits set by George W. Bush's Secretaries of State Colin Powell and Condoleezza Rice.[108] President Obama himself visited China in his first year in office (see Photo 4.6) and met Chinese President Hu Jintao three times in 2009 alone.

While China was a key piece of the Obama administration's overall policy at the outset of their first term, it was embedded in a broader regional policy that emphasized American allies. The administration also acceded to the Association of Southeast Asian Nations' (ASEAN) Treaty of Amity and Cooperation (TAC), thus elevating Southeast Asia among US priorities. By the time it left office eight years later, the Obama administration's efforts to strengthen ties with Southeast Asia eclipsed all previous administrations.[109]

Thus, the Obama administration very much continued the Engagement strategy/policy of previous administrations. Reviewing *every* statement by President Obama concerning China throughout his term in office reveals the consistent theme of *cooperation*. His public terminology morphed somewhat during the eight years, but "cooperation," "partners," "comprehensive," "constructive," and "mutual interests" were regularly part of the President's vocabulary. In one speech to the SAED in 2009, he used all of these adjectives' multiple times.[110] He told President Hu Jintao in September 2009, "I am committed to pursuing a genuinely cooperative and comprehensive relationship with China ... given the growing number of common global and regional challenges that our countries face. I want to take cooperation on a range of global and regional and bilateral issues to a new level."[111] On his first state visit to China in November

Photo 4.6   President Obama and President Xi Jinping at state arrival welcome ceremony, November 12, 2014.

Photo credit: Official White House Photo by Chuck Kennedy, public domain

2009, Obama proclaimed, "Today, we have a positive, constructive, and comprehensive relationship that opens the door to partnership on the key global issues of our time."[112] At the same event, he used a new catch phrase, "The United States welcomes China's rise as a *strong, prosperous, and successful* member of the community of nations" [emphasis added].[113] By 2012, Obama used the same language in welcoming Vice President Xi Jinping at the White House: "We welcome China's peaceful rise and we believe that a *strong and prosperous China* is one that can help to bring *stability and prosperity* to the region and to the world."[114] A few months later he described the relationship as "practical, constructive, and comprehensive."[115] In 2014, Obama altered his phraseology somewhat to say, "The United States welcomes the rise of a prosperous, peaceful, and stable China that plays a responsible role in the world."[116]

Thus, the Obama team sought to prioritize engaging and working with Beijing on a range of global governance challenges. This was abundantly evident in the joint statement released at the conclusion of President Obama's state visit to China on November 15–18, 2009. The joint statement was one of the longest ever between the two governments (no fewer than 41 paragraphs), identifying numerous areas of potential cooperation: climate change, alternative energy development, public health, agriculture, space, science and technology, innovation, law enforcement, military-military, civil aviation, legal education, cultural exchanges, macroeconomic coordination, non-proliferation, North Korea, Iranian nuclear program, and other topics.[117] It was a diplomatic bureaucrat's dream document. Indeed, the senior official on the American side who was responsible for conceptualizing and drafting the statement—seasoned China hand Jeffrey Bader of the National Security Council staff—later referred to it as a "good compendium of our joint objectives."[118]

The joint statement that concluded the trip was detailed and left the optimistic impression that the two governments could work closely together to address global challenges. However, behind the scenes, the four-day trip had not gone all that well. The Chinese had treated America's new president very badly in protocol terms and some of his private discussions with Chinese leaders were reported to have been very testy. Obama's own memoirs characterized his meeting with the over-scripted and wooden Hu Jintao as the "usual sleepy affair," although he also claimed to have "put down a clear set of markers on US priorities."[119]

One unexpected outcome came when the President disembarked Air Force One in Shanghai. It was raining and he carried his own umbrella as he descended the stairs of the aircraft. This was covered live on Chinese television, causing considerable controversy among the Chinese public—as no Chinese leader would *ever* carry their own umbrella!

There were considerable behind-the-scenes struggles between Chinese and American officials over the President's itinerary. The Chinese side very carefully stage-managed every second of the visit, with the American side essentially backing down on almost all of its requests. This began with a "Town Hall" event that Obama was to hold with Chinese students in Shanghai. Originally, the American side had requested a presidential visit to a university campus and speech to students, as *every* visiting American president had done since Ronald Reagan. The Chinese refused. They were apparently very concerned about the public charisma of the new American president, who had already electrified large public audiences in Berlin, Prague, and Cairo. That was the last thing Chinese officials wanted. Finally, a compromise solution was struck whereby Obama would do a give-and-take session with a group of carefully selected students from a cross-section of Shanghai universities. The Americans requested an audience of 1,500, the Chinese insisted on 50.[120] The Americans wanted it broadcast live nationwide on Chinese Central Television (CCTV), but the Chinese insisted there would be no television broadcast—until they relented at the last second, with no public announcement, as the session was broadcast locally on Shanghai television (a somewhat censored version was subsequently streamed on the Xinhua.net website). Once the Obama entourage reached Beijing, the Chinese would allow no public events. There would be no customary address to the American business community or visit to a commercial joint venture. The Chinese government even refused a US Embassy list to invite local

Americans (of which I was one) to the state dinner in the Great Hall of the People. A private meeting with local US businesspeople and scholars, organized by the US Embassy and to which I had been invited, also had to be called off because of "scheduling difficulties." While I was not privy to the official events, I was living in Beijing at the time as a Fulbright Senior Scholar at the Chinese Academy of Social Sciences, and hence I could observe the visit.

The shabby and obstructionist Chinese treatment of Obama was intentional and not consistent with how previous American presidents had been treated. The US media coverage of the trip captured this negative dynamic.[121] In a subsequent discussion with me, US Ambassador Jon Huntsman recounted the many frustrations that the American side had encountered and endured.[122] Following the visit, Obama was said to have been irritated if not insulted by his treatment, and he subsequently became more skeptical of China during the remainder of his term on office.

By the time Obama met the new Chinese leader, Xi Jinping, at Sunnylands, California in 2013 for an "informal shirt-sleeves summit," in describing the relationship he dropped the previously used word "strong" in favor of "a peaceful, stable, and prosperous China is good for the world and for the United States."[123] This meeting also sparked a controversy about a new formulation: "Building a new model of major country relations" (新型大国关系). It was controversial because the Chinese side asserted in the post-summit press conference that Xi had advanced the new formulation and that the two leaders had agreed to it—when, in fact, the American side had not agreed to it—at least at the time. Three months later, however, when Xi and Obama met in St. Petersburg, Russia, for a G-20 summit and held a joint press conference, Obama told the media, "We had excellent meetings in Sunnylands earlier this year, and we've agreed to continue to build a new model of great power relations based on practical cooperation and constructively managing our differences."[124] Such formulations are extremely important in the Chinese system, as they constitute a *tifa* (提法)— a defining narrative that becomes the basis for policy and repetitive recitation by Chinese cadres and citizens.[125] The problem is that once foreigners agree to use them—especially verbatim—they are endorsing Chinese definitions of the concept and thus also get locked into the policy positions that flow from them.

The remaining seven years of Obama's presidency after the visit in 2009 witnessed a certain duality: on the public surface, his administration sought Chinese cooperation on global governance and regional challenges; under the surface, various issues became increasingly contentious and fraught. This began almost immediately after the visit to China in 2009 when the Chinese side personally rebuffed Obama at the Copenhagen Climate Change Summit (COP-15) by sending a junior official (He Yafei) to negotiate with the President and the conference collapsed with no US–China agreement. Tussles over many other bilateral, regional, and global issues accumulated and intensified over the remaining course of the administration—notably trade disputes, North Korea, Iran, cyber hacking and theft (of corporate and US government information), Chinese currency undervaluation, human rights and dissent (including the defections of dissident Chen Guangchen and Chongqing police chief Wang Lijun), Taiwan, the Dalai Lama, and the South China Sea.[126] It was in the White House Rose Garden on September 25, 2015, that Xi Jinping assured Obama publicly, "Relevant construction activities that China are undertaking in the South Nansha Islands do not target or impact any country and China does not intend to pursue militarization."[127]

By the end of the Obama administration, the US–China relationship had grown distinctly more strained and competitive in various realms. Sino-American competition had become the dominant factor in the international relations of Asia, producing pressures on regional countries to increasingly align with Beijing or Washington.[128] Trade disputes had become increasingly fraught, both because of the gargantuan US deficit as well as increasingly impediments faced by American businesses trying to operate in China. Chinese cyber hacking of the US government, corporations, think tanks, state and private sector actors was a rising and deeply troubling concern. China's own military modernization had made substantial progress in several areas, surprising many analysts and posing direct new challenges to US forces in the Indo-Pacific, to American allies in the region, and to Taiwan. Human rights in China, never good, had sharply deteriorated after 2009. Indeed, any signs of Chinese political reforms—which were evident under Hu Jintao's reign prior to that year—ground to a halt thereafter.[129]

The relationship was definitely in a downward trajectory as Obama's term drew to an end. Ever since Xi Jinping came to power in 2012, China had become increasingly repressive at home, assertive abroad, and more truculent as a potential partner. As James Mann observed in his book, "The Obama administration's initial policy of avoiding conflict with China led not to greater accommodation, but to more insistent Chinese demands and further testing of American resolve. When the Obama administration sought to be conciliatory, Chinese officials seemed to take that as confirmation of American weakness and China's growing power."[130] Year by year, Engagement was rapidly losing its efficacy in its spirit, in its intended purposes, and in practice.

Little did the world know that it was a harbinger for what was to come under President Trump.

III

THE ENGAGEMENT COALITION FRACTURES AND THE COUNTER-CHINA COALITION FORMS

Chapter 5
From Engagement to
Strategic Competition

"The U.S. and other liberal democracies were slow to let go of the hope that China, having been welcomed into the international system, would play by the rules. The Trump administration turned the assumptions that underpinned China policy on their head."
—Lt. General (Ret.) H. R. McMaster, National Security Advisor to President Trump, 2017–2018[1]

"We have to ensure that competition does not veer into conflict— and we also have to manage it responsibly."
—President Biden to President Xi Jinping at summit meeting, Woodside, California, November 15, 2023[2]

"When the facts change, I change my mind—what do you do, Sir?" This quotation, attributed to John Maynard Keynes in 1924, is germane to the American foreign policy establishment and the China Engagement strategy since the mid-2010s. By then, there was ample evidence that Xi Jinping's China had changed, and that consequently the basic assumptions and tenets of the four-decade-old US Engagement strategy required rethinking and revision as well. We saw in Chapter 1 that members of the American foreign affairs elite and the China policy community began an animated debate over the question "Did Engagement Fail?" in 2017 (kicked off by the Campbell–Ratner article). As the debate percolated, a transition of presidential administrations occurred from Obama to Trump.

This chapter examines how the Engagement strategy and Engagement Coalition fractured after 2017 during the Trump and Biden administrations, and how a new "Counter-China Coalition" has formed since then. I show how the Trump administration fundamentally broke away from both the premises and the practices of engagement that had been consistently pursued since the Nixon administration—by being the first to explicitly adopt a paradigm of "strateg competition" as the macro guide to China strategy and policies. Next, I describe how the Biden administration essentially and explicitly continued (albeit with less bombast) the paradigm shift initiated by Trump. And, finally, the chapter speculates about what China policies the second Trump administration (taking office in January 2025) may pursue.

Trump Turns the Tables

When Donald J. Trump took office on January 20, 2017, the US–China relationship was already under growing and serious stress during the final years of the Obama administration (as described in Chapter 4). The relationship was increasingly filled with mutual mistrust, suspicions, acrimony, alienation, and real policy differences. Like trees falling silently in a forest, the individual pillars of the Engagement Coalition were—one-by-one—becoming increasingly alienated and were progressively loosening their decades-long ties to China. The theoretical premises of Engagement—that China would become more politically and socially liberal, more economically market-oriented, and more normatively supportive of the international liberal order—were clearly not panning out. Quite to the contrary, China was becoming even more repressive and dictatorial politically, more economically and socially controlled, and more illiberal internationally. The proverbial Emperor (Engagement) increasingly was seen to have no clothes.

Trump's anti-China rhetoric during the campaign reflected and intuitively tapped into the growing disillusionment across multiple sectors of the American electorate. His China bashing played particularly well in America's heartland. Speaking to a frenzied campaign rally in Fort Wayne, Indiana, on May 2, 2016, Trump accused China of "raping" the United States: "We can't continue to allow China to rape our country, and that's what they're doing."[3] Trump used the term in reference to the yawning trade deficit, but his incendiary verbiage resonated with disgruntled Americans across the Upper Midwest, New England, the Atlantic Seaboard, and western states, who had experienced years of painful job losses, family financial pressures, and other social dislocations due largely to globalization and the outsourcing of manufacturing to China. This was not a figment of their imagination or a convenient scapegoat—it was real and personal—and Trump astutely tapped into their grievances with great political effectiveness. Countering China became a central plank in Trump's campaign for the presidency.

However, once he was elected and entered the White House in January 2017, Trump initially did a complete about-face and stunningly gave China everything it could have wanted. During his first year in office, Trump:

- withdrew from the Trans-Pacific Partnership (TPP);
- hosted Xi Jinping for a hastily scheduled leader-to-leader summit at Trump's Mar-a-Lago club in April;
- fawned flattery on Xi Jinping as a "great leader" and China as a "great nation";
- reiterated commitment to the "One-China" policy with respect to Taiwan (although he was the first president to violate it by accepting a congratulatory telephone call from Taiwan President Tsai Ing-wen);
- appointed a US ambassador (Iowa Governor Terry Branstad) with personal ties to Xi and an extremely pro-China background;
- refused to officially label China as a "currency manipulator" (which he had promised to do "on Day 1");
- did not level any trade tariffs on China (he had promised 45 percent tariffs);
- initiated a review of Treasury Department procedures to loosen regulations for Chinese investments in the United States;
- refrained from criticism of China's military buildup;
- did not say a word about human rights or repression in China;
- expressed a strong desire to work with Beijing on North Korea;
- questioned the value of American alliances in Asia and worldwide;
- promised that he would visit China on a state visit before the end of 2017.

With this stunning list of conciliatory gestures, Trump started off with an astoundingly soft and accommodating set of policies and initiatives toward Beijing. Xi Jinping and Chinese leaders in the Zhongnanhai probably could not believe their good fortune! Trump had reversed virtually all of his campaign rhetoric and promises in short order. If this is the way Donald Trump "makes deals" as a businessman[4]—by giving away the store at the outset of a negotiation—China's leaders could be forgiven for thinking that they were dealing with an inexperienced lightweight. During this first year in office, China's government was also able to quickly penetrate Trump's inner circle by cultivating his son-in-law Jared Kushner and daughter Ivanka Trump (Chinese Ambassador Cui Tiankai personally did so), as well as Secretary of Treasury Steven Mnuchin, Secretary of State Rex Tillerson, Secretary of Commerce Wilbur Ross, and National Economic Council Director Gary Cohn (all financiers/businessmen with close previous ties to China). Trump's personal friends and Wall Street tycoons, notably Stephen A. Schwartzman (Blackstone Group), John L. Thornton (Goldman Sachs), Hank Greenberg (American International Group), and others personally lobbied Trump to maintain close ties with China.[5]

These initial gestures culminated in a "state visit plus" by the President and First Lady to Beijing on November 8–10, 2017 (see Photo 5.1). Xi Jinping

Photo 5.1 President Xi Jinping and President Donald Trump review Honor Guard outside the east entrance of the Great Hall of the People in Beijing, November 9, 2017.

Photo credit: Imago/Alamy Stock Photo

and the Chinese government truly rolled out the red carpet, which included an unprecedented dinner in the Forbidden City.[6] The Chinese consciously played to Trump's narcissistic vanity, and it clearly worked. At the conclusion of the visit, the two sides issued a lengthy and very positive joint statement that covered a number of areas of bilateral cooperation.[7] It could have been taken right out of the playbooks of any of the presidential visits discussed in Chapter 4. It had all the classic ritual trappings of Engagement. All observers (including China's government) could be forgiven for believing that the Trump administration, like many before it, would abandon the campaign rhetoric critical of China in favor of continuing the tried-and-true policies and actions of Engagement.

However, following the presidential visit to Beijing, the Trump administration shifted course. It followed a dual track approach—the steps taken above to try and set a positive tone while simultaneously preparing for a major shift in China policy. That shift began in late March 2017, when senior officials held a "Principals Committee" meeting (an inter-agency meeting of Cabinet-level officials). This meeting was intended to be a "framing session" on China policy, according to Trump's second National Security Advisor H. R. McMaster.[8] To tee up the discussion, National Security Council staff aide Matt Pottinger coauthored a discussion paper with the State Department's Policy-Planning staff. According to General McMaster, "The paper and the Principals discussion focused on understanding the emotions, aspirations and interests that drive CCP [Chinese Communist Party] behavior; identifying vital U.S. interests at stake; assessing assumptions that underpinned previous policies; proposing U.S. policy objectives; and anticipating obstacles to progress."[9] General McMaster described how the meeting proceeded:

> At the start of the meeting, I read an excerpt from the Obama administration's China policy that reflected the forlorn hope, across multiple US administrations, that China, having been welcomed into the international community, would play by the rules and, as it prospered, liberalize its economy and, eventually, its form of governance. We had, over many years, succumbed to the cognitive traps of optimism bias and confirmation bias. The Pottinger paper was meant, in part, to jolt us back to reality. As I looked around the room, the magnitude of what we were about to do became clear: help the President effect the most significant shift in U.S. foreign policy since the end of the Cold War.[10]

This meeting occurred early in the administration and at the same time as more positive gestures were being offered, but it initiated what McMaster described as "the most significant shift in U.S. foreign policy since the end of the Cold War."

The next three years witnessed increased frictions and American pressure on China. Xi Jinping and China's leaders must not have known what hit them—and, as the Appendix describes, China's America specialists neither forewarned them nor foresaw the seismic shift coming in American policy. They should have, as the tremors had been evident for several years dating back throughout the Obama administration. Multiple constituencies in the Engagement Coalition had grown deeply disaffected with China—all they needed was leadership to fundamentally change the course of American policy. Donald Trump was that vessel.

Trump himself did not know much at all about China. He had never been there before he became President. All he knew—and cared about—was the yawning trade deficit (which had mushroomed to $347 billion by the time he took office). Other than this issue, which he naïvely viewed in zero-sum terms, he was very unknowledgeable about China. He had no real understanding of the hot-button Taiwan issue. He couldn't care less about human rights. He was dismissive of the PRC military's growing capabilities, and he questioned the US defense posture and alliances in the Asia-Pacific (and elsewhere). He did not really see China as a partner in global governance (despite the aforementioned joint statement in November 2017). China's repressive political system was inconsequential to him—indeed Trump *admired* Xi Jinping, frequently calling him a "strong leader."

But Trump was surrounded by White House officials and an administration made up of China hawks. Other than Kushner, daughter Ivanka (who herself had numerous investments and patents in China), Mnuchin, Ross, and Tillerson (all of whom had extensive previous business dealings with China), the Trump administration at senior and secondary levels consisted of hardliners when it came to China: Presidential Counselor Steve Bannon, Trade Advisor Peter Navarro, Secretary of State Mike Pompeo and his China advisor Miles Yu, Secretary of Defense James Mattis, US Trade Representative Robert Lighthizer, National Security Advisor General Michael Flynn, informal advisor Michael Pillsbury, and others were all in Trump's inner circle. They also composed something of a book club, devouring and discussing Pillsbury's *The Hundred Year Marathon* and Navarro's *Death by China*.[11] When General McMaster replaced Flynn as National Security Advisor, a more traditional "realist" mind and voice joined the inner circle.

Taken together, these men formed something of a team and they put together the blueprint for changing American China strategy. Navarro was a lesser-known economist from the University of California, Irvine (and *not* a China specialist) who joined the administration as Director of Trump's National Trade Council. Pillsbury (who was a Fellow at the conservative Hudson Institute) probably would also have been invited to join the administration, but that would have required him to qualify for security clearances (which he had had revoked twice in the past). Unlike Navarro, Pillsbury was a real China specialist, holding a PhD in Chinese politics from Columbia University, was reasonably fluent in Chinese, and had worked on Chinese military issues since the 1970s. He had managed to develop a presence in Washington China policy, defense, and intelligence circles (although he was ostracized and distrusted by most mainstream China specialists). So, he continued to lurk on the fringes of the Washington establishment, but because of his security clearance problem, Pillsbury was relegated to playing an outside advisory role. He did manage to get inside the Oval Office to brief Trump, Pence, and other senior officials on several occasions. He also allegedly undertook five trips to Beijing in the first year of the Trump administration, serving as something of a go-between.[12]

One other key figure who was not at all known at the time but who would come to play an absolutely central role in shaping and forging the Trump administration's China strategy and policies over the following four years was Matt Pottinger. Pottinger had been a young Reuters and *Wall Street Journal* correspondent in China for eight years (1998–2005), was fluent in the Chinese language, and was deeply knowledgeable about Chinese politics, economy, and society. As a journalist, he had been instrumental in uncovering the Chinese government's coverup of the SARS epidemic. He had also experienced first-hand the draconian hand of the Chinese security state—having been harassed, detained, and beaten up by Chinese security thugs. Because of the 9/11 terrorist attacks, Pottinger did something very unusual for a foreign correspondent: he quit his job and joined the US Marines. Very youthful in his appearance, energetic and outgoing, Pottinger did not fit the caricature of the Marine Corps—but he served and fought in three combat deployments in Iraq and Afghanistan from 2007 to 2010. While in Afghanistan, serving as an intelligence officer, his commanding officer was Lieutenant General Michael Flynn. When Flynn was catapulted into the job of being Trump's first National Security Advisor (where he did not last long), he remembered and recruited Pottinger to be one of his deputies for Asian and China affairs.

After Trump was elected, Pottinger served on the transition team, when he authored a 12-page strategy paper on China and Indo-Pacific policy that contained many of the ideas that would become the basis of the Trump administration's China and Asia policies.[13] First, he argued for the need to shore up US allies in the Asia-Pacific, who were growing nervous about the rise of China and were concerned about the depth of commitment of the United States to the region's security (as the Obama administration's "pivot to Asia" had been more bark than bite). Pottinger argued that, under Xi Jinping, China's strategic aim was nothing short of achieving hegemonic dominance over the region. Second, he argued for tougher economic policies on trade with China and punitive policies on industrial and intellectual property theft. Third, he outlined an administration whole-of-government offensive to combat China's influence operations and united front activities in American society.

Pottinger would go on to serve the entire Trump term (only resigning in protest over the Capitol insurrection on January 6, 2021)—surviving four National Security Council Advisors (Michael Flynn, H. R. McMaster, John Bolton, and Robert O'Brien). During his four years as Senior Director for Asia and then Deputy National Security Advisor, Pottinger was instrumental (almost single-handedly) in turning the "ship of state" away from an intrinsic and long-standing "cooperate with China" bureaucratic mission to a "compete with China" bureaucratic mission. As noted in Chapters 2 and 4, from the Carter through the Obama administrations, the entire executive-branch bureaucracy had been structurally and normatively oriented in ways to pursue cooperation with China. That was their raison d'être. As we saw in Chapter 4, the Carter administration's China specialist Michel Oksenberg had first conceptualized the idea of reorienting the bureaucracy away from its Cold War negative missions of countering China to a new post-normalization positive mission of cooperating and working with China. Over the intervening decades, countless formal agreements and institutionalized dialogues took shape—all aimed at advancing US–China cooperation. This bureaucratic institutionalization was deeply embedded in Washington and extremely difficult to change. Executive-branch departments and agencies had incentivized missions (and the resources from a supportive Congress) to get along with China and forge cooperation wherever possible. But Pottinger came to office not convinced of the logic or the need for such bureaucratic engagement—and he set about to change it. To do so was akin to changing the direction of an 80,000-ton ocean liner in mid-course: not at all easy. But he did it. I would venture to say that no single individual—including presidents themselves—have ever had such an impact on the federal bureaucracy as Matt Pottinger did. While he did encounter some resistance,[14] in the span of four years he managed to repurpose the entire executive-branch apparatus against China.[15] This was no small or simple feat. Turning bureaucracies of this magnitude, with their line-item budgets, around in such a short span of time was a Herculean undertaking.

There were two other individuals who were also key in the early stages of the Trump administration's China strategy. The first was Lieutenant General H. R. McMaster, who succeeded Lieutenant General Michael Flynn and served as National Security Advisor from 2017 to 2018. McMaster was a highly decorated US Army officer with command experience in Iraq and Afghanistan, but he is also a "defense intellectual" and successful author who holds a PhD in military history from the University of North Carolina. His Deputy National Security Advisor for strategy was Nadia Schadlow, a brainy scholar of defense studies and strategy, who had also served in government and at a major private foundation (Smith Richardson). McMaster tasked Schadlow with conceptualizing and drafting the Trump administration's first *National Security Strategy of the United States*, a document mandated by Congress of all new administrations. Other National Security Council staff members and parts of the executive branch had input to the *National Security Strategy*, but McMaster and Schadlow carefully oversaw and were largely responsible for drafting the document (Pottinger had major input on the China sections).[16]

The publication of the *National Security Strategy* was the first real indication that the Trump administration was thinking radically differently about China than its predecessors. The *National Security Strategy* argued that American foreign policy now occurred in an "era of great power competition" and it was the first ever to label China as a "revisionist power."[17] Other references to China included,

China and Russia challenge American power, influence, and interests, attempting to erode American security and prosperity. They are determined to make economies less free and less fair, to grow their militaries, and to control information and data to repress their societies and expand their influence.

China and Russia want to shape a world antithetical to U.S. values and interests. China seeks to displace the United States in the Indo-Pacific region, expand the reaches of its state-driven economic model, and reorder the region in its favor. Russia seeks to restore its great power status and establish spheres of influence near its borders.

For decades, U.S. policy was rooted in the belief that support for China's rise and for its integration into the post-war international order would liberalize China. Contrary to our hopes, China expanded its power at the expense of the sovereignty of others. China gathers and exploits data on an unrivaled scale and spreads features of its authoritarian system, including corruption and the use of surveillance. It is building the most capable and well-funded military in the world, after our own. Its nuclear arsenal is growing and diversifying. Part of China's military modernization and economic expansion is due to its access to the U.S. innovation economy, including America's world-class universities.

The *National Security Strategy* and the Pentagon's companion document the *National Defense Strategy of the United States* laid out a completely new vision of China as a revisionist and strategically competitive power that directly challenged American national interests. The *National Defense Strategy* said,

China is leveraging military modernization, influence operations, and predatory economics to coerce its neighboring countries to reorder the Indo-Pacific region to their advantage. As China continues economic and military ascendance, asserting power through an all-of-nation long-term strategy, it will continue to pursue a military modernization program that seeks Indo-Pacific regional hegemony in the near-term and displacement of the United States to achieve global preeminence in the future.[18]

Subsequently, in their last year in office, the Trump administration became the first-ever administration to publish a stand-alone official policy document specifically about China: *The United States Strategic Approach to the People's Republic of China*.[19] This extraordinary document is well worth reading in its entirety, but suffice to quote this:

Since the United States and the People's Republic of China (PRC) established diplomatic relations in 1979, United States policy toward the PRC was largely premised on a hope that deepening engagement would spur fundamental economic and political opening in the PRC and lead to its emergence as a constructive and responsible global stakeholder, with a more open society. More than 40 years later, it has become evident that this approach underestimated the will of the Chinese Communist Party (CCP) to constrain the scope of economic and political reform in China. Over the past two decades, reforms have slowed, stalled, or reversed. The PRC's rapid economic development and increased engagement with the world did not lead to convergence with the citizen-centric, free and open order as the United States had hoped. The CCP has chosen instead to exploit the free and open rules-based order and attempt to reshape the international system in its favor. Beijing openly acknowledges that it seeks to transform the international order to align with CCP interests and ideology. The CCP's expanding use of economic, political, and military power to compel acquiescence from nation states harms vital American interests and undermines the sovereignty and dignity of countries and individuals around the world ... Guided by a return to principled realism, the United States is responding to the CCP's direct challenges by acknowledging that we are in a strategic competition and protecting our interests appropriately.

The United States Strategic Approach was intended by the White House and its principal author (Pottinger) to be a modern-day equivalent of the George Kennan's "Long Telegram" and his famous anonymous *Foreign Affairs* July 1947 article, "The Sources of Soviet Conduct," that set the intellectual framing for the Cold War.[20]

Between these official documents, which bookended the four-year Trump administration, the intervening three years would witness escalating frictions, tit-for-tat sanctions, tariffs and counter-tariffs, and much fiery rhetoric from Trump personally and members of his administration. The ins-and-outs and ups-and-downs of the turbulent Trump years have been recounted in many places and do not require recapitulation here, while several books have been written about China policy during the Trump years.[21] During these intervening years, a series of high-profile speeches were given by senior cabinet officials in the Trump administration; when taken together, they fundamentally redefined the intellectual and policy bases of American China strategy and policies.

The first speech was from Vice President Mike Pence to the Hudson Institute on October 4, 2018.[22] Pottinger was the principal drafter of this speech. In it, Pence offered an all-around indictment of malign Chinese behavior at home and abroad. What was notable and new were two things. The first was his distinction between the Chinese Communist Party (CCP) and China—this was an important distinction and theme that would be continued throughout the Trump administration. That is, not to simply use "China" or "Chinese" as shorthand, but rather speak specifically of the CCP as the perpetrator of things America did not like (after the COVID pandemic broke out in 2019 and Trump inappropriately and provocatively began to speak of the "Chinese virus," there was a considerable domestic backlash over the racist connotations of the term, after which Trump stopped using it).[23]

The second new departure in the Pence speech concerned the CCP's "influence operations." This was a new concept and term that entered the lexicon of government, media, academia, and think tanks during 2018–2019. It was the result initially of Russian attempts to manipulate public opinion during the presidential election in 2016. But subsequently it began to come to light that organs of the CCP were attempting to penetrate and influence multiple stakeholders across the United States. To some extent, China's efforts to lobby Congress had been known for some time, as were clandestine attempts to make financial contributions to the Clinton/Gore campaign in 1996,[24] but in 2018–2019 a whole new and disturbing set of CCP influence activities were uncovered. Vice President Pence summed up the new phenomenon well:

> Beijing is employing a whole-of-government approach to advance its influence and benefit its interests. It's employing this power in more proactive and coercive ways to interfere in the domestic policies and politics of the United States ... The Chinese Communist Party is rewarding or coercing American businesses, movie studios, universities, think tanks, scholars, journalists, and local, state, and federal officials.
>
> Worst of all, China has initiated an unprecedented effort to influence American public opinion, the 2018 elections, and the environment leading into the 2020 presidential elections ... To that end, Beijing has mobilized covert actors, front groups, and propaganda outlets to shift Americans' perception of Chinese policies ... Senior Chinese officials have also tried to influence business leaders to condemn our trade actions, leveraging their desire to maintain their operations in China ... Beijing routinely demands that Hollywood portray China in a strictly positive light, and it punishes studios and producers that don't. Beijing's censors are quick to edit or outlaw movies that criticize China, even in minor ways ... Beyond business, the Chinese Communist Party is spending billions of dollars on propaganda outlets in the United States, as well as other countries ... But the media isn't the only place where the Chinese Communist Party seeks to foster a culture of censorship. The same is true of academia. Look no further than the Chinese Students and Scholars Associations, of which there are more than 150 branches across American campuses. China exerts academic pressure in other ways, too. Beijing provides generous funding to universities, think tanks, and scholars, with the understanding that they will avoid ideas that the Communist Party finds dangerous or offensive. China experts in particular know that their visas will be delayed or denied if their research contradicts Beijing's talking points ... The Chinese Communist Party is trying to undermine academic freedom and the freedom of speech in America today... When

it comes to Beijing's malign influence and interference in American politics and policy, we will continue to expose it, no matter the form it takes.[25]

This lengthy quotation excerpted from Pence's speech describes well the parameters of the CCP's influence activities/operations in the United States. When Pence's speech took place, the whole concept was new. Subsequently, however, over the next few years think tanks and research institutes, NGOs, intelligence agencies, and individual scholars in the United States and abroad began to dig into the issue.[26] We will examine this more carefully in the Chapter 7.

The second speech in the series of criticisms of China was by National Security Advisor Robert O'Brien in Phoenix, Arizona, on June 24, 2020; it was entitled "The Chinese Communist Party's Ideology and Global Ambitions."[27] As the title suggests, this speech took aim squarely at the CCP's adherence to Marxism–Leninism as a political ideology, and clearly framed US–China relations as a clash of ideologies reminiscent of the Cold War. Equating Xi Jinping specifically with Josef Stalin, O'Brien said, "As interpreted and practiced by Lenin, Stalin, and Mao, communism is a totalitarian ideology ... The Chinese Communist Party seeks total control over the people's lives. This means economic control, it means political control, it means physical control, and, perhaps most importantly, it means thought control." The speech then cataloged numerous examples of how the CCP is trying to control information outside of its borders all around the world, and he asserted that Xi Jinping's "Community of Common Destiny for Mankind" is a camouflaged blueprint for global domination. The speech concluded with a list of steps the United States (under Trump) was taking to push back against the CCP and PRC in seven areas.

The third salvo was a speech by FBI Director Christopher Wray on July 7, 2020, entitled "The Threat Posed by the Chinese Government and the Chinese Communist Party to the Economic and National Security of the United States."[28] As would be expected from an FBI Director, the speech focused on clandestine espionage threats and counter-intelligence. In his speech, Director Wrap claimed that he would provide "more detail on the Chinese threat than the FBI has ever presented in an open forum." Wray did indeed offer multiple examples. Some of these had previously been reported in the media, some were new. He also noted that the sheer volume of PRC intelligence activities had reached the point where the FBI was opening a new counter-intelligence investigation concerning China "every 10 hours." This dimension of malign Chinese activities affects commercial businesses, academia, state and local governments, national data bases (government and private), illicit technology theft, recruitment of informants and spies, and other illegal actions.

Next came Attorney General William Barr, who offered "Remarks on China Policy" on July 16, 2020, at the Gerald Ford Presidential Library.[29] Barr reiterated many of the same themes and accusations as Wray, particularly concerning commercial espionage. But he went further to chastise Hollywood and American corporations for self-censorship and capitulation under China's pressure: "Hollywood is far from alone in kowtowing to the PRC. America's big tech companies have also allowed themselves to become pawns of Chinese influence," asserted the Attorney General. He further claimed that, "The Chinese Communist Party also seeks to infiltrate, censor, or co-opt American academic and research institutions." Barr's speech seemed to be aimed as much at American institutions as at China.

The final broadside was Secretary of State Mike Pompeo's speech "Communist China and the Free World," delivered on July 23, 2020, at the Nixon Presidential Library in California.[30] Claiming to be the wrap-up to the series, the Secretary of State actually said little he had not said before in previous venues or what was not covered in the speeches by Pence, O'Brien, Wray, and Barr. It was more of a recantation and summation than an original contribution.

Pompeo again criticized past engagement policies, taking specific aim at the CCP, and framed the relationship very much in Cold War redux terms (as evident in the title of the speech). John Foster Dulles could have written it. Pompeo hurled multiple accusations and insults at China and the CCP—claiming, for example, that "China is not a normal law-abiding nation," that Xi Jinping is a "true believer in a bankrupt totalitarian ideology," and that CCP ideology is one that holds "a decades-long desire for global hegemony of Chinese Communism." Channeling former President Ronald Reagan's reference to Soviet arms control treaties, Pompeo claimed that in the case of China the American assumption should be "mistrust and verify." He also insinuated, not so subtly, that only regime and system change in China will suffice to make China what he described as a "normal country." In doing so, Pompeo called for forging a multinational and multilateral effort to meet "this challenge." "If the Free World doesn't change, Communist China will surely change us," Pompeo concluded.

Taken together, these speeches by senior Trump officials laid out the administration's whole-of-government indictments of China and the CCP. Of course, President Trump himself had an outsized impact on his administration's approach to China. He was—as in all policy areas—unpredictable, bombastic, provocative, and confrontational. I previously noted his racist use of the term "Chinese virus" to refer to COVID. Perhaps his biggest impact was in the economic and commercial domain—where he slapped an estimated total of $277.5 billion in tariffs on China,[31] starting a retaliatory and escalatory trade war. Trump apparently had no fear of rupturing the economic relationship between the two countries—perhaps the *central* element in four decades of US engagement policy. It was under his administration that a new term and pre-viously unthought-of concept of "de-coupling" of the two economies came into mainstream lexicon. At one point (on August 24, 2019), Trump even abruptly announced on Twitter that he "hereby ordered" all American companies to withdraw from China![32] He subsequently softened his directive by Tweeting, "U.S. companies should immediately start looking for an alternative to China, including bringing your companies HOME and making your products in the USA."[33]

After three years of *sturm und drang* in US–China relations (following the first year of bonhomie), the Trump administration exited and bequeathed to its successor Biden administration a fundamentally changed China policy.

The Biden Administration: The Through Train

If Beijing or anyone else expected a basic change in US China policy, much less a return to a full re-embrace of the Engagement paradigm when President Biden took office in January 2021, they were sadly mistaken and did not understand the fundamental shift that had occurred in the US government and society over the previous 4–6 years. The new administration exhibited considerable conti-nuity with the Trump administration, but without the bombast of Trump and with substantially more sophistication in conceptualization and execution of policy.

For nearly three years, the Biden administration also practiced a whole-of-government strategy to push back against and compete with China. In the last year and a half of the Biden administration, however, it returned to the old practices of Engagement—by reinitiating high-level exchanges and the "engage-ment as process" approach discussed in Chapter 2. This meant a return to the practice of the approach to "talk tough behind closed doors but talk." In between, though, the US–China relationship deteriorated even below that of the Trump years and reached rock bottom. It had *never* been so bad since the Nixon opening in 1972, even following the Tiananmen massacre. American public opinion plummeted to the point whereby fully 83 percent of the pub-lic held "unfavorable" views of China in 2023, according to the Pew Research Center, with 50 percent saying that China was the "greatest threat" to the United States.[34] Moreover, following the visit by former House of Represen-tatives' Speaker Nancy Pelosi to Taiwan in the summer of 2022, the Chinese side cut off virtually all direct communications with US officials and under-took unprecedented aggressive military drills around the island. Thereafter, for one year, the Biden administration's chief concern was to "reestablish channels of communication."

Off to a Rough Start

How did the Biden administration begin vis-à-vis China? If Beijing was anticipating or hoping for a "reset" to engagement and return of relations to a predominantly cooperative mode, that perspective was clearly not shared in Washington.

From the early statements by President Biden himself, as well as by Secretary of State Antony Blinken, National Security Advisor Jake Sullivan, Defense Secretary Lloyd Austin, Director of National Intelligence Avril Haines, and other senior administration officials, two things were abundantly clear.

The first was that the Biden administration was adopting an overall framework of "competition" with China. President Biden even used the term "extreme competition" in February 2021, while referring to China as "our most serious competitor" in his first major foreign policy speech. National Security Advisor Jake Sullivan used "intense competition" and "stiff competition," while Secretary of State Blinken described the US-China relationship as, "Competitive when it should be, collaborative where it can be, and adversarial where it must be." This phraseology indicated considerable continuity with the approach of the "strategic competition" approach of the Trump administration. Biden officials also emphasized the importance of a coordinated approach with multiple allies and partners to counter China's malign practices. The new administration's "Interim National Security Guidance," issued in March 2021 further stated, "Our enduring advantages will allow us to prevail in strategic competition with China or any other nation ... We will deter Chinese aggression and counter threats to our collective security, prosperity, and democratic way of life."[35]

Second, the new administration's statements highlighted the values-oriented approach the Biden team would take not only toward China, but also toward Russia and other authoritarian regimes as well. The Democratic Party in the United States has long had two main camps on foreign policy—the "values first" and the "realpolitik" camps. The Biden administration was dominated by the former school, particularly Blinken and Sullivan. Together, early on, they articulated a worldview that distinguished between supporting democracies and countering autocracies. The administration also included several high-ranking officials with responsibility for China affairs who came with strong backgrounds in human rights and democracy-promotion work in NGOs.

The values-centric focus was made clear, for example, in Secretary of State Blinken's telephone call with Yang Jiechi (then a Politburo member and China's foreign policy supremo) on February 5, 2021. President Biden himself also prioritized the Hong Kong, Tibet, and Xinjiang issues in his phone call with President Xi Jinping on February 10 (along with tough words on China's "coercive and unfair trading practices").

What about Beijing's early actions vis-à-vis the new Biden administration? The best indication of China's approach was captured in Yang Jiechi's speech to the Board of Directors of the National Committee on US–China Relations on February 2, 2021.[36] Instead of reassuring and acknowledging American concerns, Yang went out of his way to scold, lecture, and hector the United States. The speech was filled with stock propaganda phrases, which seemed aimed more at the CCP Propaganda Department in Beijing than at an elite American audience in New York. Beyond the turgid phraseology, Yang adopted a sanctimonious tone throughout his speech—casting all blame for the deterioration of relations in recent years on the Trump administration and not acknowledging a single thing that China has contributed to the precipitous downturn in ties. Yang went to great lengths to criticize the US government for its "misguided policies," "strategic misjudgments," "stumbling blocks," and other "erroneous" policies and actions—while simultaneously arguing that China only sought "cooperation." Toward the end, Yang did sketch out a brief menu for some pragmatic cooperative actions that should be explored by both sides. But this came only after a litany of tough language warning the United States to cease "interference in China's internal affairs" and to respect its "core interests"—specially mentioning Hong Kong, Tibet, and Xinjiang—and warning that "they constitute a redline that must not be crossed." Not surprisingly, warnings concerning Taiwan also figured prominently in Yang's address.

For his part, China's leader Xi Jinping used less strident language in his February phone call with President Biden, but still warned that, "The Taiwan question and issues relating to Hong Kong, Xinjiang, etc. are China's internal affairs and concern China's sovereignty and territorial integrity, and the U.S. side should respect China's core interests and act prudently."[37] Yang's speech and Xi's words—taken together with public statements by President Biden, National Security Advisor Sullivan, Secretary of State Blinken, and Secretary of Defense Austin—suggested that a significant clash-of-values was on the horizon.

That clash came just four weeks later in Anchorage, Alaska. The temperature outside was frigid (14 degrees Fahrenheit / -10 Celsius) when the most senior diplomats from the United States and China sat down at the Captain Cook Hotel on March 19 for their first face-to-face meeting. But the political temperature inside was scalding hot. On one side of the table sat Secretary of State Antony Blinken, National Security Advisor Jake Sullivan, and National Security Council Indo-Pacific Coordinator Kurt Campbell—on the other side was Yang Jiechi, Foreign Minister Wang Yi, and Chinese Ambassador to the United States Cui Tiankai. What normally begins with a perfunctory exchange of greetings and generalized statements about the importance of the relationship in front of journalists and television cameras (known as a "press spray") quickly descended into an acerbic war of words between the two sides.[38]

Secretary of State Blinken had publicly signaled in advance that the American side was going to detail its discontent over an expansive range of China's behavior (internal and external). Beijing knew in advance what was coming (whether it was wise to have signaled it so publicly in advance is debatable), so the Chinese side knew it was walking into an antagonistic and confrontational meeting. And they came prepared for verbal combat.

Blinken opened by saying, "We will discuss our deep concerns with actions by China, including in Xinjiang, Hong Kong, Taiwan, cyberattacks on the United States, and economic coercion towards our allies ... The United States' relationship with China will be competitive where it should be, collaborative where it can be, adversarial where it must be." To my knowledge, this was the first time in *any* administration that a senior American official had ever publicly used the term "adversary" to describe China.

Yang immediately shot back, "So let me say here that, in front of the Chinese side, the United States does not have the qualification to say that it wants to speak to China from a position of strength."[39] Yang then gave Blinken a blistering lecture. It included sharp accusations and critiques of US democracy, Washington's "Cold War mentality," America's own human rights problems (as epitomized by the Black Lives Matter movement), international invasions and use of force, "massacres of peoples in other countries," and "long-arm jurisdiction and suppression ... through the use of force or financial hegemony." Yang concluded with the terse claim, "I don't think that the overwhelming majority of countries in the world would recognize that the universal values advocated by the United States or that the opinion of the United States could represent international public opinion."[40]

State Councilor Wang Yi then chimed in:

China certainly in the past has not, and in the future will not, accept the unwarranted accusations from the U.S. side. In the past several years, China's legitimate rights and interests have come under outright suppression, plunging the China–U.S. relationship into a period of unprecedented difficulty. This has damaged the interests of our two peoples and taken its toll on world stability and development, and this situation must no longer continue. China urges the U.S. side to fully abandon the hegemonic practice of willfully interfering in China's internal affairs. This has been a longstanding issue, and it should be changed. It is time for it to change.

Blinken and Sullivan were put on their back feet by Yang's and Wang's calculated outbursts—they responded extemporaneously but defensively. All of this extraordinary back-and-forth diplomatic spat played out live on television worldwide. What the world saw and heard was the "new China"—a much more confident, combative, assertive, and acerbic diplomatic style than in the past (which subsequently became known as "wolf warrior diplomacy"). Yang and Wang won high praise at home in China for "standing up to the hegemon."

The new Biden administration thus got off to a hawkish beginning with China. It is important to understand what "competition" meant in the Biden administration's thinking. Competition had four main dimensions (domestic, bilateral, regional, and global) and a variety of functional ones (economic, technological, military, diplomatic, cultural, and political). This multi-spectrum simultaneous approach proceeds from the premise of rivalry. It was principally seen as a means to rebuild and strengthen the United States so that it can effectively compete against China well into the future. What made the Biden administration different from the Trump administration's approach was a clear recognition that effectively competing with China begins at home—with large-scale targeted investment into hard and soft infrastructure, education, research and development, technological innovation, and other dimensions of intrinsic national power.

In August 2021, Deputy Secretary of State Wendy Sherman traveled to Tianjin, China; this was the first face-to-face diplomatic encounter after the Anchorage meltdown. State Councilor and Foreign Minister Wang again scolded Sherman that China would not tolerate the United States claiming a "superior" position or approaching China from a "position of strength." Before Sherman's arrival, Wang further warned that China would provide her a "tutorial on how to conduct diplomacy as equals" (echoing Yang Jiechi's lecture in Alaska). Vice Foreign Minister (and now China's ambassador to the United States) Xie Feng was Sherman's official counterpart, and he also informed her that the United States was waging a "thinly veiled attempt to contain and suppress China" by "waging a whole-of-government and whole-of-society campaign to bring China down."

While Sherman went to China looking for ways to establish "guardrails" that would buffer the competition and disputes between the two sides, she was instead again met with an unyielding and sanctimonious stance from her interlocutors.[41] It was now clear that the Biden administration was dealing with an emboldened and confident, even arrogant, Beijing that had zero tolerance for criticism and would turn its defensiveness into offense by pushing back hard when Washington expressed concerns about China's behavior. In his address in Tiananmen Square commemorating the CCP's 100th anniversary in 2021, Xi Jinping captured this attitude when he bluntly proclaimed, "We'll never accept insufferably arrogant lecturing from those 'master teachers'! We will never allow any foreign force to bully, oppress, or subjugate us. Anyone who would attempt to do so will find themselves on a collision course with a great wall of steel forged by over 1.4 billion Chinese people."[42]

Going into 2022, tensions between Washington and Beijing were palpable and the relationship was fragile. US Ambassador to China Nicholas Burns said publicly that bilateral relations were at their "lowest moment" since Nixon's pathbreaking trip in 1972.[43]

Managed Competition

As 2022 unfolded, the Biden administration modified its public language somewhat by introducing two new concepts: "managed competition" and "responsible competition." In October, National Security Advisor Sullivan began a series of private meetings with his counterparts Yang Jiechi and Wang Yi in third countries, in an effort to reengage the Chinese in serious dialogue. In his meeting with Yang in Zurich, Switzerland on October 6, 2021, Sullivan used the term "responsible competition" in his discussions. But, immediately following, in its description of the meeting, Xinhua News Agency explicitly announced that, "China opposes defining the U.S.–China relationship in terms of 'competition.'"[44] "Managed competition" was a term suggested to the Biden administration through a variety of channels and by Asia Society President and former Australian Prime Minister Kevin Rudd.[45] Indeed, Sullivan had previewed his thinking in a *Foreign Affairs* article with Kurt Campbell just before assuming office.[46]

Then, six months later and fully a year and a half into the administration, the Biden foreign policy team finally offered the first systematic and public articulation of its China strategy. On May 13, 2022, Secretary of State Blinken gave a prominent address at George Washington University (as a faculty member and Director of the university's China Policy Program I was seated in the front row).[47] "Now, China is a global power with extraordinary reach, influence, and ambition ... The scale and scope of the challenge posed by the People's Republic of China will test American diplomacy like nothing we've seen before," Blinken told the audience. "China is the only country with both the intent to reshape the international order and, increasingly, the economic, diplomatic, military, and technological power to do it. Beijing's vision would move us away from the universal values that have sustained so much of the world's progress over the past 75 years," he claimed. Then Blinken offered a series of palliatives meant to soothe an insecure regime in Beijing: "We are not looking for conflict or a new Cold War"; "We don't seek to block China from its role as a major power"; "We do not seek to transform China's political system."

Then Blinken turned critical:

Rather than using its power to reinforce and revitalize the laws, the agreements, the principles, the institutions that enabled its success so that other
countries could benefit from them too, Beijing is undermining them. Under
President Xi Jinping, the ruling Chinese Communist Party has become more
repressive at home and more aggressive abroad. We see that in how Beijing
has perfected mass surveillance within China and exported that technology
to more than 80 countries; how it is advancing unlawful maritime claims in
the South China Sea, undermining peace and security, freedom of navigation,
and commerce; how it is circumventing or breaking trade rules, harming workers and companies in the United States but also around the world; and how it
purports to champion sovereignty and territorial integrity, while standing with
governments that brazenly violate them.

Finally, Secretary Blinken's speech offered a three-part policy shorthand, "The
Biden administration's strategy can be summed up in three words—'invest,
align, compete': We will *invest* in the foundations of our strength here at home—
our competitiveness, our innovation, our democracy. We will *align* our efforts
with our network of allies and partners, acting with common purpose and in
common cause. And harnessing these two key assets, we will *compete* with China
to defend our interests and build our vision for the future." It must be said that
these three pillars of the Biden administration's China strategy were more than
rhetoric.

With respect to the first pillar, with the CHIPS and Science Act of 2022,
the administration and Congress succeeded in some landmark legislation to
boost American productivity and innovation. The annual National Defense
Authorization Act and other legislation signed into law further strengthened the
domestic components of American China strategy.

Secondly, the administration meticulously and relentlessly sought to coordinate its China policies with Asian and European allies. It is fair to say that,
with both regions, there had never been closer consultation and collaboration
with US allies concerning China. While China definitely has an advantage in
the Global South (which the US has long neglected), it has lost considerable
ground and influence in Asia and Europe. The European Union, led by European Commission President Ursula von der Leyen, found a unified voice and
backbone as never before on China. Through the careful knitting together of
Indo-Pacific allies and partners by the Biden administration, including the new
initiatives of AUKUS (Australia, United Kingdom, United States), the Quad (US,
Japan, India, and Australia), and the US–Japan–South Korea troika, the United
States made great progress in pushing back against China across the region while

considerably strengthening a coalition of countries that share deep concerns about China. The US Department of State also established "China House"—a bureaucratic initiative to more closely monitor and counter China's actions from US embassies worldwide.

Third, while the "competition" leg of Blinken's three pillars was not clearly or well defined in his speech, it seems to have referred to taking a variety of counter-actions—unilaterally and multilaterally—against China in different domains. As such, the Biden administration sanctioned a number of Chinese officials and entities (unilaterally and in tandem with European and Asian allies); stepped up its counter-intelligence actions against China's influence and interference operations (see Chapter 6); more carefully vetted potential Chinese investments in the United States; maintained a wide range of tariffs on Chinese goods; continued to help strengthen Taiwan's defenses; carefully monitored and sanctioned PRC entities that aided Russian aggression against Ukraine; and sought to improve its public diplomacy efforts against China worldwide.

These initiatives by the Biden administration led China's leader Xi Jinping to claim in a speech on March 7, 2023, "Western countries led by the United States have implemented all-around containment, encirclement and suppression of China, which has brought unprecedented severe challenges to our country's development."[48] Clearly, the United States' efforts under the Biden administration had gotten under Xi's skin.

US–China relations were strained even further by the visit to Taiwan by House of Representatives Speaker Nancy Pelosi in August 2022. This was the highest-ranking American official or politician to visit the island since the normalization of US–China relations and passage of the Taiwan Relations Act in 1979—both of which stipulated that *no* senior American or Taiwan officials were permitted to visit each other's countries. Over the years, the American side had occasionally nibbled away at this stricture, sending the odd cabinet secretary, but never an official of Pelosi's rank (third in line to the presidency). Pelosi made her own decision to go to Taiwan, under the constitutional separation of powers, and the Biden administration did not stop her from going (it is unclear if it tried to do so). She went, and the PRC went ballistic—literally. It began firing ballistic missiles near—and over—the island, undertook large-scale naval exercises in the Taiwan Strait (and subsequently to the east and north of the island), and embarked on a very aggressive series of People Liberation Army Air Force (PLAAF) sorties into Taiwan's Air Defense Identification Zone (ADIZ) and airspace. For 75 years, China's ships and planes observed the "Central Strait Line" that runs down the middle of the Taiwan Strait. No longer. A "new normal" of PRC military presence in Taiwan's air and sea space has been established. In 2021, according to Taiwan military authorities, there were 972 incursions into its air space; in 2022, there were nearly 1,737 PLAAF sorties into Taiwan's across the Central Strait Line and into Taiwan's ADIZ, with a peak of 149 on one day.[49]

China also responded to the Pelosi visit by cutting off all military-to-military contacts with the United States and severely curtailing other official exchanges (which were quite minimal to begin with). It also stepped up its own aggressive and dangerous intercepts of American military aircraft flying in international airspace in the South China Sea and along China's coastline. The US Department of Defense reported no fewer than 282 "unsafe encounters" during 2023, and released a number of stunning and startling videos of these close encounters.[50] Some of these provocative and highly risky actions by PLAAF pilots came within 10–30 feet of US aircraft, including one incident when a Chinese fighter passed within 10 feet of a B-52 bomber over the South China Sea![51]

Then, to make matters worse and add further strains to a reeling relationship, in late January 2023, a Chinese military spy balloon overflew the United States, loitering over some intercontinental ballistic missile bases in Montana, before President Biden gave the order to shoot the balloon down off the East Coast of the United States. This sent the relationship into another tailspin, with Secretary of State Blinken abruptly canceling a trip to Beijing on the eve of departure (which was intended to agree a bilateral roadmap for restarting exchanges).

As a result of these cut-offs of communications and the very real and rising chance of a military mishap between American and Chinese military aircraft or ships, the Biden administration began an intensive campaign to "reopen channels of communication" with Beijing beginning in the spring of 2023. Classic "engagement diplomacy" ensued. During the summer of 2023, the Secretaries of Treasury (Janet Yellen) and Commerce (Gina Raimondo) both visited Beijing. Yellen had become the "good cop" of the Biden administration, giving several public speeches on the need *not* to decouple the two economies (while simultaneously "de-risking" in certain sectors that had national security concerns). Raimondo was more of the "bad cop"—arguing during her trip to China that the country was increasingly "uninvestable."[52] After her return, in a speech to a business group in Northern California, Raimondo starkly said, "China is the biggest threat we've ever had. China is not our friend."[53]

The modest return to "engagement diplomacy" was part of the diplomatic dance between Washington and Beijing in the run-up to the scheduled meeting between Biden and Xi Jinping near San Francisco in November 2023. "We have now been able to reconnect our two governments [following a lengthy hiatus]," US Ambassador to China Nicholas Burns observed.[54] It was America's turn to host the Asia-Pacific Economic Cooperation (APEC) forum, and as China's head-of-state Xi was slated to participate. This offered a "forced opportunity" for the two leaders to stage a summit and try and instill some new normalcy (at least the appearance thereof) into the strained relationship. The one-day-long tête-à-tête took place at a private villa south of San Francisco near Silicon Valley and the Stanford University campus (see Photo 5.2).

Although an enormous amount of preparatory work had been invested by both governments in advance of the presidential meeting, the announced results were underwhelming (given all of the sensitive and dangerous problems in the relationship).[55] The principal purpose of the meeting seemed simply to be meeting—to be meeting without rancor and acrimony, but rather with an air of diplomatic normalcy and positivity. It was all about the optics—to send visual signals to the Chinese public, the American public, and the world that the United States and China had returned to a semblance of stability and normalcy in their complex and often strained relationship. But there was no joint statement issued, as is normally the case after head-of-state summits. Instead, each side gave their own official readouts (which were not consistent with each other).

Substantively, the summit did produce a number of "deliverables." Perhaps the most important development was the reestablishment, following a lengthy hiatus, of defense and military-to-military dialogues and interactions. This included (according to the official Chinese readout) "high-level military-to-military communication, the China–US Defense Policy Coordination Talks, the China–US Military Maritime Consultative Agreement meetings, and to

Photo 5.2   President Joe Biden and President Xi Jinping meet at Filoli Estate, Woodside, California, November 15, 2023.

Photo credit: Xinhua/Alamy Stock Photo

conduct telephone conversations between theater commanders." Other "deliverables" included establishing a working group on artificial intelligence, a working group to promote tourism, cooperation in counter-narcotics and combating fentanyl trafficking, enhanced cooperation on climate change, an increase of airline flights between the two countries, and new commitments to expand people-to-people exchanges (students, youth, tourists, sports, business, sister city and other subnational exchanges). Ongoing bilateral dialogues were also renewed in the following areas (according to the White House readout): "commercial, economic, financial, Asia-Pacific, arms control and non-proliferation, maritime, export control enforcement, policy planning, agriculture, and disability issues."

The Chinese side was also very pleased that, apparently, President Biden reaffirmed the "five commitments", that he had previously made to Xi at their meeting in 2022 in Bali, Indonesia—namely, that (according to the Chinese readout),[56] "The United States does not seek a new Cold War, does not seek to change China's system, does not seek to revitalize its alliances against China, does not support Taiwan independence, and has no intention to have conflict with China." The White House readout did not indicate that Biden reiterated these five assurances, known in China as the "five noes"; this was a significant difference.

Instead, the official White House readout indicated that President Biden, "reaffirmed the United States' ironclad commitment to defending our Asia-Pacific allies"; "emphasized the United States' enduring commitment to freedom of navigation and overflight"; "underscored the universality of human rights ... and raised concerns regarding PRC human rights abuses, including in Xinjiang, Tibet, and Hong Kong" "emphasized the [U.S.] One China Policy has not changed and has been consistent across decades and administrations"; "raised continued concerns about the PRC's unfair trade policies, non-market economic practices, and punitive actions against U.S. firms, which harm American workers and families"; and "emphasized that the United States and China are in competition."[57]

The discrepancies between the two governments' official readouts—while not surprising—did raise questions about what was actually said concerning a number of the most sensitive issues in the US–China relationship. Nonetheless, the big takeaway from the meeting was that engagement as process (as defined in Chapter 2) was returning to the relationship. After three years of intense competition and downward spiraling relations, senior Biden officials (and Biden himself) were all reaching back into their well-worn playbook of bureaucratic engagement.

Coming out of the San Francisco summit, Biden officials did their best to "spin" the results. US Ambassador to China Nicholas Burns told a public audience at the Brookings Institution in Washington,

We are systemic rivals ... Our job is to wage the competition [with China], but responsibly. We're competing with China—but we're also engaging with China ... We have to compete, but drive down the prospect of conflict. Complexity defines the relationship. We're focused on competition—in security, technology, trade, human rights—but also have to work together where we can. We have to think about the "balance of interests."[58]

Ambassador Burns concluded by cautiously observing, "I don't feel optimistic about the future of US–China relations. I'm hopeful, but realistic." For his part, National Security Advisor Jake Sullivan said in January 2024,

We realize that efforts, implied or explicit, to shape or change the PRC over several decades did not succeed. We expect that the PRC will be a major player on the world stage for the foreseeable future. That means that even as we compete, we have to find ways to live alongside one another. Competition with the PRC does not have to lead to conflict, confrontation, or a new Cold War. The United States can take steps to advance its interests and values and those of its allies and partners on the one hand, while responsibly managing competition on the other. Being able to do both of those things is at the heart of our approach.[59]

The remainder of the Biden administration witnessed a change of *tactics*, but not necessarily substance vis-à-vis China. The result of this partial bureaucratic "re-institutionalization" of the relationship (partial because it was only at the ministerial level) was a new and welcome stabilization of the previously fractious and dysfunctional relationship, and it did represent a modest return to part of the previous administrations' strategy of Engagement. As I discussed in Chapter 2, this represented one of the four elements of the Engagement strategy—engagement as (bureaucratic) *process*. That is, to speak—and complain—directly to Chinese government counterparts about some aspects of China's behavior, while looking for areas where the two nation's interests coincide, and they could potentially work together. It is important, though, not to mistake engagement as process as engagement of substance. That is, to speak directly and critically by no means implies agreement of perspectives and policies.[60] If anything, Chinese officials now just tend to ignore American entreaties. While important to do so, the actual agenda of discordant issues discussed at the California meeting remained lengthy and troublesome for the United States: the Russian invasion of Ukraine and China's diplomatic, economic, and political support for the Putin regime and Russian arms industry; militarization of occupied islands in the South China Sea and coercion against the Philippines, an American ally: military pressure against Taiwan; exports of chemical precursors that produce fentanyl; human rights abuses; Chinese cyber hacking and espionage; and a wide range of trade, technology, and investment disputes.[61]

The Surge in Anti-Americanism

Even people-to-people exchanges—which Xi told Biden at their San Francisco summit was a priority for the Chinese side—did not progress. In fact, they *regressed*. By the end of 2024, less than 1,000 American students were studying in Chinese universities. Many forms of American cultural activities in China—including those sponsored by the US Embassy and Consulates on topics such as mental health treatments, women's entrepreneurship, film screenings, university fairs, scholarly speakers, and other cultural exchanges—have been blocked by Chinese authorities. This prompted US Ambassador Nicholas Burns to take the rare step of publicly denouncing these actions.[62] Burns told *The Wall Street Journal*, "I've been concerned for my two-plus years here about the very aggressive Chinese government efforts to denigrate America, to tell a distorted story about American society, American history, American policy. It happens every day on all the networks available to the government here, and there's a high degree of anti-Americanism online ... We've had innumerable conversations with the government of China about this and nothing has changed, but nothing gets fixed."[63]

The steady stream of anti-American polemics is, of course, nothing new. It stretches back consistently over 75 years of CCP rule. I have published a whole book and several articles about it.[64] It has never stopped—it just escalates and deescalates in quantity, volume, and invective—and it has gotten much more severe during the Xi era.[65]

Perhaps the most fulsome diatribe was published in 2023 by the official state Xinhua News Agency. Entitled "US Hegemony and Its Perils," Xinhua accused the United States of practicing five types of hegemony (political, military, economic, technological, and cultural).[66] The official report included the following:

> Since becoming the world's most powerful country after the two world wars and the Cold War, the United States has acted more boldly to interfere in the internal affairs of other countries, pursue, maintain and abuse hegemony, advance subversion and infiltration, and willfully wage wars, bringing harm to the international community. The United States has developed a hegemonic playbook to stage "color revolutions," instigate regional disputes, and even directly launch wars under the guise of promoting democracy, freedom

and human rights. Clinging to the Cold War mentality, the United States has ramped up bloc politics and stoked conflict and confrontation. It has overstretched the concept of national security, abused export controls and forced unilateral sanctions upon others. It has taken a selective approach to international law and rules, utilizing or discarding them as it sees fit, and has sought to impose rules that serve its own interests in the name of upholding a "rules-based international order."

The hegemonic, domineering, and bullying practices of using strength to intimidate the weak, taking from others by force and subterfuge, and playing zero-sum games are exerting grave harm. The historical trends of peace, development, cooperation, and mutual benefit are unstoppable. The United States has been overriding truth with its power and trampling justice to serve self-interest. These unilateral, egoistic and regressive hegemonic practices have drawn growing, intense criticism and opposition from the international community.

China opposes all forms of hegemonism and power politics and rejects interference in other countries' internal affairs. The United States must conduct serious soul-searching. It must critically examine what it has done, let go of its arrogance and prejudice, and quit its hegemonic, domineering and bullying practices.[67]

As the Biden administration drew to a close and the November 2024 presidential election between Donald Trump and Kamala Harris was on the horizon, there was much speculation about what the victor's China policies might be.[68] This book is going to press in December 2024, just after Donald Trump's decisive electoral victory.

The Prospects for a Second Trump Administration's China Policies

In anticipating what the second Trump administration might pursue in its strategy and policies toward China, it is instructive to look back in time. The single most notable aspect of China policies during the first Trump administration and through the Biden administration was their *consistency* and *continuation*. The differences between the two administrations were minor and more a matter of degree than fundamental substance. There was thus a "through train" in virtually all areas of China policy—diplomatic and political, military and security, economic and commercial, political ideology, cyber and espionage, technology, education, human rights, and other domains; in each sphere there existed essential continuity from the first Trump administration through the Biden administration.

There were a few differences, though. President Trump and his senior administration officials during the first term were much more accusatory and bombastic in their rhetoric than President Biden and his senior officials were. Trump and his administration offered many public condemnations of China—whereas Biden himself and his officials offered far fewer. The Biden administration, by contrast, did far more substantively to strengthen alliances abroad and build coalitions against China than the Trump team ever did, while at home Biden worked together with Congress to pass important legislation intended to strengthen the American technological, educational, and research foundation to effectively compete with China.

Thus, the first thing I would anticipate in Trump 2.0 is *further continuity* with the past eight years of China policies. Four years ago, many America watchers and officials in Beijing anticipated that President Biden would break with Trump's radical shift on China and return to the old policies of "engagement" (see Appendix). They were proven dead wrong then (and it revealed a fundamental intelligence failure by China's America specialists), and they will be proven incorrect again if they think that US policy is going to revert to the pre-2017 cooperative policies of engagement with China.

In anticipating the future, Trump personally is the biggest wildcard because of his demonstrated unpredictability (and narcissism). Although he and his administration were, after their first year in office, highly critical of CCP and government policies, as well as of Xi Jinping himself, Trump 2.0 could abruptly pivot and reach out to Xi in the same way he previously did toward North Korea's Kim Jung-un. For example, in a campaign speech in Grand Rapids, Michigan, on July 21, 2024, Trump used fawning language and made clear his respect for Xi—describing him as "brilliant," "smart," and "a fierce person because he controls 1.4 billion people with an iron fist." If Trump tried a gambit to orchestrate some kind of rapprochement directly with Xi Jinping, he would be putting himself deeply at odds with the entire Republican Party, his own administration, many in Congress, most Democrats and American citizens—all of whom view China as America's No. 1 competitor and adversary.

One area to watch with Trump is the degree of coordination with American allies and partners in their China policies. As noted, this was a distinguishing hallmark and real achievement of the Biden administration (perhaps the best coordination in history)—but given Trump's demonstrated antipathy for alliances, it is quite possible that this coordination could fracture. That would leave America to face China increasingly alone, and that would be a very negative development. It is *exactly* what Beijing constantly hopes for and works toward. "Divide and rule" and the ancient Chinese stratagem of *yi yi zhi yi* (以夷制夷, to use the barbarians to control the barbarians) is a time-tested tactic of China.

Concerning America's support for the defense of Taiwan, Trump has indicated that he views Taiwan in the same financially transactional way he views NATO allies: "Taiwan should pay us for defense; you know, we're no different from an insurance company," Trump told Bloomberg in an interview on July 17, 2024. It is difficult to know if Taiwan could "buy" renewed commitments for its defense from Trump and his administration.

A Trump administration trade policy would likely be a doubling down on the aggressive one he adopted the first time around. He has already threatened slapping 60 percent across-the-board tariffs on China. The PRC, the world, and America's own economy should prepare for considerable stresses from an even tougher tariff policy. It should also be anticipated that Beijing will retaliate with its own stiff tariffs, its own export controls, and its own sanctions, as well as putting pressure on American businesses operating in China. This could result in an all-out trade war. Thus, further and deepened US-China frictions can be anticipated.

It is also highly likely that the second Trump administration will double-down on the Biden administration's stiffened technology export controls on China and continue to restrict Chinese investments in the United States via the Treasury Department's Committee on Foreign Investment in the United States (CFIUS) mechanism. The technology decoupling that is already underway (both the result of Xi Jinping's own technology autonomy efforts as well as American actions) is likely to accelerate.

Another important factor to consider is personnel. Several of president-elect Trump's high-level appointees are demonstrated China "hawks" with lengthy track records of criticizing China and the CCP. This includes designated appointments of (pending confirmation in some cases) Secretary of State Marco Rubio, National Security Advisor Mike Waltz, CIA Director John Ratcliffe, and others. Rubio has invested a significant part of his Senate career to mastering the details of China policy in different domains, and he may be *the* single most knowledgeable Member of Congress about China. He has been outspoken and unafraid to take the Xi Jinping regime to task for a variety of its malign actions. He has also authored or coauthored a variety of legislative bills concerning China's human rights abuses, Xinjiang, and Hong Kong. Rubio is also under sanction by the Chinese government and forbidden to enter China, which is going to make it very difficult for Rubio to interact with Chinese officials (it will be interesting to see how—and if—this is finessed by the PRC). For his part, Trump's National Security Advisor designate Congressman Mike Waltz also has a demonstrated record of very hawkish statements and policy positions concerning China and the CCP. Waltz, a former US Army Green Beret, was elected to Congress in 2018 (representing his Florida district) and he has served on the House of Representatives Armed Services and Intelligence committees. While not as deeply knowledgeable about China as Rubio, Waltz has also done his homework. His public statements have been stark. In 2021 he wrote on X (formerly Twitter) that, "We are in a Cold War with the Chinese Communist Party. I, for one, will fight to the end to ensure the United States and the free world do not one day bow to the Chinese Communist Party." Trump has also appointed former State Department diplomat Alex Wong as Waltz's Deputy National Security Advisor. Wong possesses some experience on China, having previously served as Deputy Assistant Secretary of State for East Asian and Pacific Affairs and as Deputy Special Representative for North Korea in the first Trump administration. He too has a history of highly hawkish statements and perspectives on China. Wong has argued that the CCP predicates its own legitimacy on diminishing and countering US interests.[69] Trump's CIA Director Designate John Ratcliffe also has a long record of highly critical, hawkish, and even alarmist statements concerning China. Ratcliffe also previously served in the first Trump administration as Director of National Intelligence. In that capacity he wrote in *The Wall Street Journal* on December 3, 2020: "If I could communicate one thing to the American people from this unique vantage point, it is that the People's Republic of China poses the greatest threat to America today, and the greatest threat to democracy and freedom worldwide since World War II. The intelligence is clear: Beijing intends to dominate the U.S. and the rest of the planet economically, militarily, and technologically."[70] Trump has also named Peter Navarro as Senior Economic Advisor in the White House. Navarro, who recently served four months in a federal prison for contempt of Congress related to the January 6, 2021, US Capitol insurrection, was one of the main architects of Trump's first-term commercial policies aimed at China (together with Robert Lighthizer, who is also expected to receive a senior position in the second Trump administration). At the time of this writing, other senior appointments to the second Trump administration remain unclear, but it can likely be anticipated that others will also hold hawkish views of China.

Regardless of the personnel who populate the Trump administration 2.0, there is already considerable momentum—and, more importantly, allocated financial resources—across the executive branch bureaucracy and in Congress to continue a wide variety of policies intended to counter China. The "Counter-China Coalition" is now deeply entrenched. Engagement is d-e-a-d. The only remaining question is how the second Trump administration—like the Biden administration—manages the comprehensively competitive and friction-ridden relationship with China, short of going to war.

Chapter 6
Inside the Beltway: The US Government

"The United States recognizes the long-term strategic competition between our two systems. Through a whole-of-government approach and guided by a return to principled realism ... the United States Government will continue to protect American interests and advance American influence."

—*The United States Strategic Approach to the People's Republic of China*, May 26, 2020[1]

"Western countries led by the United States have implemented all-around containment, encirclement and suppression of China, which have brought unprecedented severe challenges to our country's development."

—Xi Jinping, March 6, 2023[2]

Just as engagement with China occurred in various sectors and parts of the United States, so too is the disengagement process occurring to differing degrees in a range of institutions and localities. This chapter examines how the US federal government in Washington, DC, has reoriented its policy and institutional approach to China during the Trump and Biden administrations—from full-spectrum engagement to whole-of-government comprehensive competition. It focuses primarily on the national security and other bureaucracies in the executive branch, as well as how a new "Counter-China Coalition" has emerged in Congress.

The Executive Branch

When normalization of full diplomatic relations occurred on January 1, 1979, the US executive branch bureaucracies sprang into action to forge collaborative relationships with their institutional counterparts, thus attempting to turn negative bureaucratic missions aimed at countering the other into positive cooperative ones. Indeed, in the very first year after normalization, no fewer than

35 intergovernmental agreements were concluded. This process was described at the time by Michel Oksenberg (President Carter's chief China advisor and himself a leading scholar of Chinese bureaucracy) as "marrying bureaucracies." As discussed in Chapter 6, this was not an accidental or ad hoc process—it was very deliberate. On the one hand, forging bureaucratic partnerships and interactions is the normal substance of government-to-government relations, so it was only natural that the American and Chinese governments would try to forge such ties. But there were two other primary motivations. First, it was thought at the time that the Sino-American relationship was far too dependent on common shared strategic opposition to the Soviet Union—thus it needed a broader and deeper foundation as it developed following normalization. Second, the Carter and Reagan administrations sought such interactions to contribute to the "transformative" efforts by the United States to change China and to help China modernize.

The reason that this history is relevant to the present is because under the current competitive conditions in US–China relations, the two bureaucracies are now involved in the exact reverse process. They are either engaged in "institutional decoupling," thus breaking off any collaborative relationship, or they are reshaping their positive cooperative missions backward into more negative missions to once again counter the other.

One way this is occurring is by simply not renewing previous agreements and memoranda of understanding (MOUs). A large number have simply lapsed. Many that remain in force have gone dormant. Another method, undertaken by the Trump administration, was to entirely break off the large-scale Strategic and Economic Dialogue (SAED) process of the George W. Bush and Barack Obama administrations, the Joint Commission on Commerce and Trade (JCCT), and a number of other bilateral dialogues. During the Obama administration, there existed just under 100 bilateral dialogues; under Trump they shrunk to less than ten, and only a few were continued by the Biden administration. This was unilateral on the American part, as the Chinese side did not seek to do so. China loves dialogues (so much so that it causes many foreign interlocutors to complain of "dialogue fatigue"). The ostensible reason the Trump administration terminated the dialogues was that they were viewed as a "trap" to tie the US government up in endless discussions that produced little resolution of issues of concern to the American side, and the implementation of the agreed communiqués was normally marginal, while China continued on with its troublesome practices and building its national strength.

Accordingly, many US government departments and agencies have begun programs to scrutinize, curtail, or block exchange programs with their Chinese counterparts. Congress is also playing an active role in this process through passing multiple acts of legislation mandating such scrutiny and reporting requirements. The Department of Education, the National Institutes of Health, National Science Foundation, and other federal funding agencies have stepped up reporting requirements of American universities involved in collaborative research with China or those that receive grants or gifts from China. The Federal Communications Commission is now more closely policing the operations of Chinese radio and television organs inside the United States, with several Chinese state media organs now being required to register as "foreign missions" under the Foreign Agents Registration Act (FARA). The Department of Defense has curtailed a wide range of interactions it previously undertook with the People's Liberation Army (PLA); the PLA has also unilaterally suspended a variety of exchanges. NASA has been forbidden by law from collaborating with its counterpart, the Chinese National Space Administration. Quiet but cooperative work in securing nuclear stockpiles between Sandia National Laboratories and its Chinese counterpart has also slowed down (if not stopped). The Treasury Department's Committee on Foreign Investment in the United States (CFIUS) has ramped up its scrutiny of Chinese investments, blocking many deals. The Department of Commerce has considerably tightened export controls on China and its Bureau of Industry and Security has developed an "Entities List" of Chinese companies, research institutions, universities, government agencies, and individuals that are considered dangerous to US national security. As the COVID-19 pandemic revealed, the previous active collaboration between the two countries' Centers for Disease Control (CDC) has become dysfunctional. Even meteorological and weather data are no longer regularly shared. For their part, many Chinese bureaucracies have similarly pulled back from their previous interactions with their American counterparts.

Congress

The executive branch is not the only governmental actor that shapes American policy and relations with China. Congress has had a long—but episodic—impact as well. Yet, Congress has never been more proactively engaged in shaping China policy than since 2017 (the 117th and 118th Congresses)—so argues my George Washington University colleague and scholar Robert Sutter in his recent book *Congress and China Policy*.[3] Sutter's seminal study is the bible on the subject. Let us first review some of Sutter's principal observations concerning Congressional roles in China policy prior to recent years, before examining in more detail its recent proactivity.

Historical Patterns

Overall, Sutter concludes that, "Although at various times a number of members of Congress were enthusiastic boosters of administration initiatives toward China, an overall pattern of Congress serving as an obstacle to presidential efforts to engage more deeply with China at the expense of other American interests and values occurred repeatedly."[4] Sutter notes that during the Nixon, Ford, Reagan, and George W. Bush administrations there existed general "interbranch comity," but that during the Carter, George H. W. Bush, Clinton, and Obama administrations Congress stood in substantial opposition to these administrations' China policies. This opposition was expressed via leading individual members in both houses, through committee hearings and publications, through resolutions, through blocking of administration legislative initiatives, and through occasional overriding of presidential vetoes. Examples included Congressional resistance to the implementation of the Carter administration's normalization of relations in 1979, and notably the Taiwan Relations Act; the Congressional outrage and opposition to the George H. W. Bush administration's soft reactions to the Tiananmen massacre; the Clinton administration's efforts to reengage China following the Taiwan Straits crises in 1995–1996, and the 493–1 Congressional resolution that the Clinton administration should grant a visa to Taiwan President Lee Teng-hui (which triggered the Taiwan Strait crisis of 1995); and the Obama administration's efforts to engage China on a range of issues at a time when China was becoming more assertive and belligerent abroad. Sutter also notes that when different administrations tended to prioritize diplomacy with and be an ardent suitor of Beijing, and to relatively downplay relations with American allies, Congress was resistant to this "China First" diplomacy. But when administrations followed "Asia First" diplomatic priorities of Reagan's Secretary of State George Shultz (see Chapter 4), Congress was much more supportive.

In brief, Congress has demonstrated long-standing skepticism of China—but never more so than since 2018, Sutter finds. During the Reagan and George W. Bush administrations, Congress tended to follow the administration's lead on China policy (and was thus supportive of engagement). In other periods and administrations, Congress either was not fully supportive or stood in opposition to the administration's engagement with China.

Of course, Congress has been susceptible to perpetual lobbying from various interest groups: human rights advocates, religious groups, labor unions, farmers, think tanks, ethnic groups (including Chinese American organizations, such as the Committee of 100), the Taiwan lobby, Tibetan and Uighur activists, and the American business community. Yet, generally speaking, these various and sundry groups have advocated for their own special interests and rarely came together in a coalition on Capitol Hill. As one study of the role of interest groups' impact on China policy observed, "Groups with seemingly divergent interests and opposing ideologies can still form an alliance in pursuit of a shared goal—but once these coalitions have achieved their objective, the marriage can be dissolved quickly."[5] Although Permanent Normal Trade Relations (PNTR) did finally pass the Congress, and was signed into law, and China was admitted to the World Trade Organization (WTO) in 2001, it was a *battle royale* prior to passage, and the coalition that prevailed was very diverse and quickly splintered thereafter. In fact, the PNTR/WTO coalition may well have been the last pro-engagement coalition to have existed on Capitol Hill.[6]

The Emergence of the "Counter-China Coalition"

As Robert Sutter's study principally argues, the period since 2017 has been unprecedented in the activism, scope, tenacity, and broad-based Congressional opposition to China. He observes that, "Congressional actions of the past five years (2017–2022) have been the most important and enduring Congressional role in the history of US policy towards China."[7] Separately, Sutter told me, "I found from early 2018 onwards bipartisan majorities in Congress reflected very serious alarm about China's multifaceted challenges—threats—to the US well-being. This sense of danger posed by China was unprecedented in the history of Congressional treatment of China."[8]

What kind of challenges, specifically? Sutter notes three. First, "China's rapid development of military power." Second, "China's longstanding efforts using state-directed development policies to plunder foreign intellectual property rights and undermine international competitors." Third, "China's challenge to global governance: China seeks to legitimate its predatory economic practices and territorial expansionism; [to] counter programs promoting accountable governance, human rights, and democracy; [to] undermine US alliances seen [as] impeding China's rise; and [to] support forceful foreign advances of Vladimir Putin's Russia and other authoritarian and often corrupt world leaders."[9]

Another recent and careful study of Congress and China policy from the Carnegie Endowment for International Peace perceptively describes the differences among Congressional members this way:

> Some members take a view of China reminiscent of President Ronald Reagan's view of the Soviet Union in his first term, when he called it the "evil empire" and greatly increased defense spending. For these members, there

are grave, existential stakes for America in the unfolding competition. They see America as locked in an intense ideological rivalry with China, which they say aims to supplant the United States as the world's superpower. They warn that unless America acts now, and forcefully, to counter China's rise, the country will find itself hemmed in by China's military, economic, and technological power in just a few years. Other members focus more heavily on the economic aspects of the competition. These economic hawks assess that the country's economic relationship is badly in need of reform. They agree with the "neo-Reaganites" that the problem is serious, but [they] focus on the need for measures to strengthen America's domestic competitiveness in order to better compete with China. They hope that a healthier economic relationship will reduce other sources of tension and help stabilize US–China relations over the long term.[10]

What is remarkable and particularly noteworthy about the recent surge in Congressional activism on China is the broad cross-section of interests, issues, and actors involved in what I call the "Counter-China Coalition." This coalition is truly bipartisan and comprises multiple constituencies—hence giving it strength and staying power. It has become cliché—but true—to note that Congress cannot seem to agree on anything—except China.[11] The coalition is not episodic or temporary. It has deep roots, deep pockets, depth of political passion, and longevity. Unlike previous China-related coalitions in Congress which, as noted earlier, tended to be episodic and quick to splinter, this time it is different. As long as China acts in a manner that is seen to be aggressive, autocratic and illiberal, and challenges both American diplomatic and security interests in the Asia-Pacific and beyond, as well as threatening the specific interests of various domestic interest groups inside the United States, the Counter-China Coalition will thrive and be an important constraint on executive branch efforts to reengage with China.

This is how foreign policy is made—and should be made—in American democracy. The executive branch has its own agency and prerogatives, but Congress represents voters and domestic interests and is the vehicle through which these interest groups impact policy. In other words, Congress has much more than simply the "power of the purse"—it is a separate autonomous branch of government, and it reflects the electorate's majority will. It is critical to recognize that considerable majorities of the American people have turned against China in recent years. In April 2023, fully 83 percent of surveyed Americans held a "negative" and "unfavorable" view of China, with 38 percent perceiving China as an "enemy," 52 percent a "competitor," and only 6 percent as a "partner."[12] The new Counter-China Coalition is also bipartisan in nature, among both Republicans and Democrats (89 percent of Republicans and 81 percent of Democrats held negative views of China in 2023).[13] This hardening of anti-China perspectives is also reflected across generations. A poll jointly conducted by *The Economist* and YouGov in 2023 indicated that roughly 25 percent of younger Americans aged 18–44 viewed China as an "enemy," compared with 52 percent of those aged 45+.[14] The same survey found that only 22 percent of those in the younger cohort viewed China as "friendly," while only a paltry 4 percent of those in the 45+ cohort did.

Forms of Congressional Activism on China

Congress has sought to demonstrate its newfound activism and exert its influence on China in various ways—via Congressional hearings; issuing reports; drafting and passing legislation; Congressional delegations (CODELs) at home and abroad; special committees and commissions; through issuing non-binding "Sense of the Congress" resolutions; issuing legislative directives and restrictions; through funding executive branch requested budgets; through funding denials; and through members' public statements.

Hearings
Holding public hearings (as well as closed-door classified ones) is one of the most important functions of Congress. They serve to educate and inform both members and the public, they bring evidence into the public domain, and they exemplify the "check and balance" function vis-à-vis the executive and judicial branches. A study by Evan Medeiros in 2023 found that between 2019 and 2022 the Congressional committees held between 10–15 China-specific hearings each year.[15] The most active committees in holding China-related hearings have been the House Armed Services Committee; House Permanent Select Committee on Intelligence; House Foreign Affairs Committee and Subcommittee on East Asia & Pacific; Senate Select Committee on Intelligence; Senate Foreign Relations Committee and its Subcommittees on East Asia & Pacific and International Cybersecurity Policy; Senate Armed Services Committee; the House and Senate Homeland Affairs Committees, and others. As a representative sample, consider the following committee hearings topics (2017–2022): the House Foreign Affairs Committee;[16] House Intelligence Committee;[17] Senate Foreign Relations Committee;[18] Senate Armed Services Committee;[19] and Senate Intelligence Committee.[20]

Legislation
Drafting, considering, and passing bills into law is a fundamental Congressional function. By the 116th and 117th Congresses (2019–2021 and 2021–2023,

respectively) Congress considered more bills concerning China than other regions and countries in the world: approximately 375 per session.[21] Altogether, the number of bills about China introduced in Congress increased *sixfold* between 2013 and 2021 (between the 113th and 116th Congresses).[22] At one point in the 118th Congress (October 2023), there were approximately 450 pending draft bills and more than 100 pending resolutions dealing with China.[23] Not all draft bills become law, of course, but the sheer totality of this legislation is testimony to the dramatically increased attention paid to China in Congress. A Carnegie Endowment study indicates that the vast majority (40 percent) of all Congressional bills on China are related to security and defense.[24]

Some of the most noteworthy pieces of China-related (or related to Taiwan and Hong Kong) passed legislation includes the CHIPS and Science Act (2023), the Innovation and Competition Act (2021), the Endless Frontier Act (2023), the China Trade Relations Act (2023), the Taiwan Travel Act (2018), the Taiwan Policy Act (2022), the Hong Kong Human Rights and Democracy Act (2019), Hong Kong Autonomy Act (2020), and Uyghur Forced Labor Prevention Act (2021). Many other individual draft bills wind up being incorporated in omnibus legislation (most notably, the annual National Defense Authorization Act and Consolidated Appropriations Act).

Congressional delegations

Another traditional Congressional activity is fact-finding CODELs abroad. One recent interesting study by the Center for Strategic & International Studies shows that CODELs to the People's Republic of China (PRC) began to steadily nosedive in 2014 (from a high of 20 in that year) before plummeting to zero in 2019, and they have remained flat and virtually nonexistent since. Senator Chuck Schumer (D-NY) did lead a bipartisan CODEL to China in 2023, but that was the exception to the rule. By stark contrast, CODELs to Taiwan began to skyrocket in 2020, reaching 40 in 2023.[25]

The Two China Commissions

Congress has two standing "commissions" which monitor China and aspects of US–China relations, hold public and closed-door hearings, produce annual reports, and recommend actions to be taken by Congress and the executive branch: the US–China Economic Security Review Commission (USCESRC) and the Congressional-Executive Commission on China (CECC). Unlike Congressional committees, neither commission has subpoena powers, nor can they write legislation. Both are truly advisory in their functions (including advising on legislation), and both are also investigatory bodies. Both were created and constituted under public law in 2000. The former is composed of 12 Congressionally appointed "commissioners" while the latter is made up of nine Senators, nine members of the House of Representatives, and five senior administration officials appointed by the President. Both commissions have professional staff of 10–20 individuals. The USCESRC focuses primarily on China's external capacities and activities, while the CECC is primarily focused on China's domestic behavior related to repression and human rights (although it has recently begun to investigate the PRC's "transnational repression"). Taken together, the two commissions' purviews and work are very complementary.

According to its mandate, the CECC is charged with "monitoring China's compliance with international human rights standards, to encourage the development of the rule of law in the PRC, and to establish and maintain a list of victims of human rights abuses in China. The Commission's professional staff is made up of US experts on China specializing in religious freedom, labor affairs, Tibet and ethnic minorities, the Internet and free flow of broadcast and print information, and law and legal reform, including commercial law reform."[26] The CECC's annual reports contain very detailed and useful assessments of (the lack of) freedom of expression, freedom of religion, civil society, criminal justice, access to justice, ethnic minority rights, governance, the status of women, worker rights, population control, human trafficking, public health, environment and climate, business and human rights, Tibet, Xinjiang, Hong Kong, and Macau.[27] The CECC also maintains a thorough database on political prisoners in China.[28] Since 2021, the Commission has also focused its attention on the erosion of Hong Kong's autonomy since the implementation of the National Security Law.

The US–China Economic & Security Review Commission has a "legislative mandate to monitor, investigate, and submit to Congress an annual report on the national security implications of the bilateral trade and economic relationship between the United States and the People's Republic of China, and to provide recommendations, where appropriate, to Congress for legislative and administrative action."[29] It too holds a series of hearings with expert witnesses throughout the year and issues highly informative annual reports.[30] Each annual report also contains very specific recommendations for both executive branch actions and Congressional legislation and exercise of its oversight functions. The Report to Congress of 2023 included informative sections on bilateral US–China economic and trade relations, China's global and regional diplomacy, China's overseas espionage activities, China's global legal reach, China's global influence and interference activities (overseas united front and external propaganda work), China's domestic workforce, China's domestic economy, the PLA's relations with foreign militaries, China's defense innovation and civil-military fusion program, and China's relations with Europe, Taiwan, and Hong Kong.[31] The report of 2022 included sections on Chinese Communist Party (CCP) decision-making, China's cyber capabilities, China's energy strategy,

China's trade practices, China's activities and influence in South and Central Asia, China's role in global supply chains, as well as on Taiwan and Hong Kong.[32]

The Select Committee on the Strategic Competition Between the United States and CCP

Another important Congressional development was the creation in January 2023 of the House of Representatives Select Committee on Strategic Competition Between the United States and the CCP.[33] The committee was initially chaired by well-credentialed 39-year-old Representative Mike Gallagher (R-Wisconsin), a third-term Congressman, a decorated Marine who served two tours in Iraq, a recipient of an MA in Security Studies and PhD in International Relations from Georgetown University, and a Princeton University undergraduate. While Gallagher had never been to China, he began to develop an interest in it as a strategic challenge when serving together in Iraq with fellow Marine Matt Pottinger (see discussion of the Trump administration in Chapter 5). Kevin McCarthy (D-California), former Speaker of the House of Representatives, was impressed with Gallagher and appointed him to chair the committee when he directed that it be established. The ranking member of the committee is Raja Krishnamoorthi (D-Illinois), and it contains thirteen Republican and eleven Democratic members.[34] From its inception, the committee went out of its way to be bipartisan and to project an image of such. The committee also has a considerable staff and budget. The media-savvy staff has produced dozens of videos for social media, drawing public attention to China's alleged malign behavior.[35] Apparently for family reasons, Gallagher suddenly announced in March 2024 that he was resigning his seat in the House of Representatives and would not be running for reelection; he was succeeded as committee chair by John Moolenaar (R-Michigan).

The Select Committee holds public hearings and internal briefings, undertakes investigations (including field trips by members), issues reports, and advises Congress on legislation (although the committee is not empowered to produce legislation like other committees, its individual members can introduce bills).[36] Committee Chairman Gallagher set the tone for the committee's work at its initial hearing (televised in prime time): "Just because Congress is divided, we cannot afford to waste the next two years lingering in legislative limbo or pandering for the press. We must act with a sense of urgency. Our policy over the next ten years will set the stage for the next hundred."[37] Embellishing with dramatic prose, Gallagher continued, "This is an existential struggle over what life will look like in the 21st century—and the most fundamental freedoms are at stake." Channeling Ronald Reagan's comparison of totalitarianism to a crocodile Gallagher continued, "We're merely feeding the crocodile that will eventually eat us. We must not be intimidated."[38]

It is unusual, but no accident, that the committee chose to name itself as the Select Committee on Strategic Competition Between the United States and the CCP—rather than with the PRC. This distinction between the CCP and the PRC, and between the CCP and the "Chinese people," are distinctions that first began under the Trump administration. They are important and good distinctions. They much more precisely designate the exact institution with which the United States has so many difficulties, and thus does not pillory the PRC as a state or nation, or more broadly with the Chinese people. As Ambassador to China Nicholas Burns publicly stated in December 2023, "We are systemic rivals, but the people of China are not our enemy."[39]

The topics of the Select Committee's ten hearings in 2023 provide a good indication of its foci and orientation: "CCP Transnational Repression: The Party Effort to Silence and Coerce Critics Overseas"; "Discourse Power: The CCP's Strategy to Shape the Global Information Space"; "Systemic Risk: The Chinese Communist Party's Threat to US Financial Stability"; "Commanding Heights: Ensuring US Leadership in the Critical and Emerging Technologies of the 21st Century"; "Risky Business: Growing Peril for American Companies in China"; "Leveling the Playing Field: How to Counter the Chinese Communist Party's Economic Aggression"; "The Chinese Communist Party's Ongoing Uyghur Genocide"; "The Chinese Communist Party's Threat to America." The Select Committee has undertaken a number of investigations,[40] and has released a number of reports,[41] the most significant of which issued to date was *Reset, Prevent, Build: A Strategy to Win America's Economic Competition with the Chinese Communist Party.*[42] Among its 130 policy recommendations, this report suggested that China's Most Favored Nation trading status be returned to an annual renewal basis or perhaps revoked altogether.

One unusual aspect of the committee's work has been to take field trips around the United States, as well as CODELs abroad (to the United Kingdom, Australia, South Pacific, and Taiwan). Inside of the United States, the committee has held investigatory hearings and roundtables in the Midwest (Detroit, Iowa, and Wisconsin), on Wall Street and in New York City, in Los Angeles and Hollywood, in San Francisco and Silicon Valley.

The committee has adopted a "name and shame" approach to many of its investigations. This included issuing a joint letter to the Presidents of the US–China Business Council and National Committee on US–China Relations castigating the two organizations for co-hosting a $40,000 per head "welcome dinner" in honor of President Xi Jinping in San Francisco on November 15, 2023.[43] The letter stated, "USCBC's and NCUSCR's decision to profit from selling access to the senior-most CCP official responsible for the Uyghur genocide raises serious questions about whether these organizations are playing responsible roles in the bilateral relationship." The letter then demanded both organizations to "provide a complete list of individuals, companies, financial institutions, and other entities that have purchased tickets to the CCP dinner and provide a separate list of individuals and companies that have paid the $40,000 fee to sit at the table with Xi." It is unclear if the USCBC and NCUSCR ever complied with the Select Committee's requests.[44] Afterward, Gallagher chided those corporate executives in attendance who paid the fees: "It may buy you a meal with Xi, but it can't buy you a conscience."[45] Gallagher himself criticized the Biden administration's China policy as "zombie engagement" and has slammed US businesses that deal with China as accepting "golden blindfolds."[46]

The Select Committee has gained a lot of attention and has considerable momentum (at the time of writing). Its overall impact, however, remains to be seen. So does its existence. The committee is not a permanent Congressional committee and serves at the pleasure of the Speaker of the House of Representatives. It has been renewed for the 119th Congress (2025–).

The US–China Working Group

The final Congressional entity of note is the US–China Working Group, a bipartisan caucus of House members. Created in 2005, the bipartisan Working Group is co-chaired by Representatives Rick Larsen (D-Washington) and Darin LaHood (R-Illinois), includes 27 members,[47] and sees its mission as: "The U.S.–China Working Group seeks to build diplomatic relations with China and educate Members of Congress through meetings and briefings with business, academic and political leaders from the U.S. and China. The USCWG provides accurate information to Member of Congress and offers a forum for open and frank discussion with Chinese leaders."[48]

While the Working Group has a distinct history of pro-engagement with China, it too has begun to alter its tone as the US–China relationship has soured and China has come under growing criticism in Congress in recent years. In 2023, Representative Larsen released a "White Paper" for "enhancing US competitiveness with China."[49] It is a very sensible document which recognizes that times have changed and even a self-described "pragmatic engager" also needs to change his views under new circumstances. In it, Larsen interestingly distinguishes three different cohorts among his Congressional colleagues on China: "*Punishers*, who seek to harm China for lost jobs, stolen intellectual property, and other offenses; *Decouplers*, who wish to sever the bilateral relationship partially or entirely; and *Salvagers*, who view engagement with China as necessary to achieving US policy goals."[50] Larsen's paper offers a four-part strategy for effective competition with China: "recognizing existing areas of conflict and competition; expanding the playbook to include both offensive and defensive measures to compete with China; identifying areas where cooperation is in both nations' interests; and getting our own house in order." The 22-page document offers a considerable number of very specific and very sensible policy recommendations in six categories (national security; development and diplomacy; jobs, business, investment, and trade; technology; education; domestic renewal).

These examples of the new activism in Congress (and considerable hostility) concerning China both reflect the profoundly changed mood in the country as well as its own increasing role in shaping American policies toward China. We now turn to the other remaining US government actors that shape American policies—the national security community.

The National Security Community

The US national security community was really the first constituency to sound the alarm to identify China as a potential adversary and threat to the United States. While other constituencies—businesses, NGOs, academics, states and localities, Congress, and the executive branch of different administrations—all continued to buy into the logic and substance of engagement with China, beginning in the late-1990s and early-2000s the national security community began to exhibit unease with engagement and with China's growing power.

The "national security community" is, of course, not monolithic. For the purposes of this chapter, we will focus only on three components: the US military, the intelligence community (IC) and counterintelligence (CI) community.

The Military

The American military's view of China is, of course, reactive and responsive to China's own military modernization. This is not the place to delineate and describe the considerable progress made by the PLA and all of its services (ground, air, naval, cyber, missile) over the past two decades. When I published my book *Modernizing China's Military: Progress, Problems & Prospects* in 2002, the broad consensus among PLA watchers was that the PLA was far from being a modern military with regional or global power projection capabilities. It was thought to completely lack the capabilities to cross the 90-mile Taiwan Strait to successfully invade the island, which was ridiculed at the time as having to be a "million-man swim." China had no real surfacedecades to today. In the interim, navy to speak of and its range was restricted inside of the 1,000 nautical mile "first island chain"; its two nuclear-powered submarines never left port and its diesel subs were noisy and easy to detect and sink; its air force was composed of vintage Soviet MiGs made in the 1950s–1970s; its intermediate and intercontinental missile forces were relatively small and all the rockets were liquid-fueled and thus slow to launch; its logistics were fragmented and poorly coordinated; its force structure was bloated, its training regimen was unfit for multiple weather conditions, and it had not experienced actual combat since the 1979 border war with Vietnam (in which the PLA was humiliated by more competent Vietnamese forces). In short, the PLA in 2000 was largely a joke.

Fast-forward two decades to today. In the interim, from 1992 to 2020, China's defense spending increased 790 percent in real terms.[51] At the time of writing, the PLA has the following impressive capacities: the world's largest surface navy (370+ ships, including 140 major surface combatants) that has deployed as far away as the Mediterranean, Baltic Sea, throughout the Indian Ocean littoral, and well eastward into the Pacific Ocean; it has three deployed aircraft carriers, as well as a dozen deployed nuclear-powered attack submarines (SSBN and SSN); a wide range of amphibious warfare ships capable of landing troops on Taiwan; its ground forces have been streamlined and now undertake training exercises in all-weather conditions; its air force is now composed of entirely fourth- and fifth- generation fighters, as well as intercontinental bombers, both of which can be refueled in-flight; its strategic rocket forces now include nearly 3,000 deployed missiles of various ranges (ICBMs = 350, IRBMs = 500, MRBMs = 1,000, SRBMs = 1,000, GLCM = 300[52]) and is fielding a nuclear ICBM force that could total 1,000 by 2030 and 1,500 by 2035 (many of which will be deployed in three new fields of missile silos in western China[53]); it has highly sophisticated cyber forces; its logistics have been substantially upgraded and centralized; it has a large number of satellites and considerable anti-satellite capabilities, and a growing space force; it is fielding hypersonic weapons; and a self-sufficient defense industrial base.

The PLA has come a very long way in a relatively short period of time. Except for a couple of categories (such as deployed nuclear weapons) in which Russia is still superior to Chinese forces and capabilities, the Chinese military is now second only in the world to the United States (and in some areas possesses equal or better capabilities). These PLA capabilities are best and most accurately described in the Pentagon's annual report to Congress *Military and Security Developments Involving the People's Republic of China*.[54] There also exist a number of informative non-governmental assessments.[55]

China's rapid and full-scope military progress has alarmed the Pentagon. In his testimony before the House Armed Services Committee in 2020, former Deputy Secretary of Defense Michèle Flournoy alarmingly informed the committee,

America's military advantage is rapidly eroding vis-à-vis China in light of their modernization efforts. In fact, if we just stay the current course, a rising China will likely achieve overmatch in a number of key capability areas, undermining or at least calling into question our ability to deter effectively, to defend our interests, to protect our allies and partners, and ultimately to prevail at acceptable levels of cost and risk.[56]

Flournoy is no "hair on fire" defense hawk—she is a well-respected defense intellectual and experienced policymaker at the highest levels of the Pentagon.

Accordingly, Secretary of Defense Lloyd Austin identified the PLA as the US military's "pacing challenge." The *National Defense Strategy* released by the Department of Defense in 2022 clearly states,

> The most comprehensive and serious challenge to U.S. national security is the PRC's coercive and increasingly aggressive endeavor to refashion the Indo-Pacific region and the international system to suit its interests and authoritarian preferences. The PRC seeks to undermine U.S. alliances and security partnerships in the Indo-Pacific region.[57]

The Biden administration's Assistant Secretary of Defense for Indo-Pacific Affairs, Ely Ratner, told the House Armed Services Committee in March 2022,

> We continue to update our concepts, capabilities, and force posture to defend the homeland, deter aggression, and prepare to prevail in conflict. We are prioritizing capabilities relevant to the China challenge, to enable a joint force that is lethal and able to strike adversary forces and systems at range; resilient and able to gain information advantage and maintain command and control through adversary disruptions; survivable and agile in the face of adversary attacks that seek to reduce combat power and mobilization speed; and able to provide the logistics and sustainment needed for operations in a highly contested environment.[58]

Admiral John Aquilino, then Commander of the Indo-Pacific Command, told the same House hearing, "INDOPACOM's mission is to prevent conflict through the execution of integrated deterrence, and should deterrence fail, we must be prepared to fight and win."[59]

China has also become the main driver of the US defense budget: "This is a strategy-driven budget—and one driven by the seriousness of our strategic competition with the People's Republic of China," Secretary Austin told the Senate Armed Services Committee in March 2023.[60] The *National Defense Strategy* of 2022 further states,

> The 2022 NDS advances a strategy focused on the PRC ... and it seeks to prevent the PRC's dominance of key regions while protecting the US homeland

and reinforcing a stable and open international system. A key objective of the NDS is to dissuade the PRC from considering aggression as a viable means of advancing goals that threaten vital US national interests.[61]

The *National Defense Strategy* then elaborates a variety of means of "integrated deterrence" to be used against adversaries: deterrence by "denial, by resilience ('the ability to withstand, fight through, and recovery quickly from disruption'), and by direct and collective cost imposition."[62] It then contains a specific section on how these and other forms of deterrence and "escalation management" would be applied in a conflict with China.[63]

Dispersion of forces across the vast Indo-Pacific AOR (area of operation), mobility and flexibility, extended logistics lines, multi-spectrum warfare, and partnership with other allied forces in the region are all central to the strategy of the Department of Defense and Indo-Pacific Command (INDOPACOM) to fight the PRC (if necessary). Accordingly, different US military services and branches are all developing their own deterrence and warfighting doctrine and training for potential combat with the PLA. The US Army and Marine Corps are training in tropical and mountainous environments,[64] while the US Navy is surging ships and submarines into the western Pacific and eastern Indian Ocean. The US defense industry has been instructed to considerably increase its production of long-range stand-off precision guided munitions. At the same time, the Pentagon has instructed US defense industries to limit the use of parts manufactured in China, so as to avoid serious supply-chain vulnerabilities in both peacetime and wartime.[65]

In addition to real-time and real-life training to potentially fight Chinese forces, the Pentagon, INDOPACOM, and an endless number of US defense contractors regularly undertake wargames and "tabletop exercises" to simulate actual wartime combat against PLA forces. Many of these have to do with helping to defend Taiwan, but they also include exercises in the South China Sea, around the Malacca Straits, the Andaman Sea, the East China Sea, the Yellow Sea, and the western Pacific Ocean. Unfortunately, a considerable number of such simulated wargames conclude that Chinese forces would be extremely difficult to fight effectively over a period of time and could well prevail against US forces (especially in Taiwan contingencies).[66] "The Chinese just ran circles around us—they knew exactly what we were going to do before we did it," commented General John Hyten, former Vice-Chairman of the Joint Chiefs of Staff.[67]

Almost all of these wargames describe horrific costs and consequences for the United States—with thousands of likely military deaths and casualties, dozens of sunk naval assets, hundreds of downed aircraft, rapidly depleted stocks of munitions, difficult and endangered reinforcements and resupplies, likely strikes against US military assets on Guam, in Hawaii, and in other US-allied Asian countries (Japan, South Korea, the Philippines, Australia, Singapore, and Thailand) and possible strikes against the American homeland. If China did escalate a conflict by striking these other sovereign states, a limited Taiwan conflict would quickly morph into a pan-regional war of China vs. many other nations.

And all of these devastating consequences say nothing about destruction on the island of Taiwan as well as on the Chinese mainland. Meanwhile, as the Americans have been engaged in abstract wargaming, under Xi Jinping's twin policies of "self-reliance" and "daring to struggle," China has tangibly been stockpiling (since 2021) strategic commodities: food, fuel, energy, metals, industrial inputs, munitions, cash, and other assets, while "sanction-proofing" its economy.[68] Storage capacity for both crude oil and natural gas have been increasing year-on-year since 2020, China's wheat and maize stocks are now 51 percent and 67 percent of world supplies (up from 5 to 10 percent respectively since 2018), while stocks of soybeans (China's largest agricultural import) have doubled since 2018.[69] The Ukraine War has taught China many lessons, as Beijing envisions itself potentially being in Moscow's position.[70]

The Intelligence Community

China has also become the No. 1 priority for both the IC, which collects information about China outside of the United States, as well as the counterintelligence (CI) community, which is tasked with combating PRC intelligence activities inside of the United States. Altogether, the IC consists of 18 separate agencies, all of which have China-related missions.[71] Nine of these are associated with the Department of Defense, seven with other cabinet departments, and two are "independent" agencies (Central Intelligence Agency [CIA] and Office of the Director of National Intelligence [ODNI]). An increasing percentage of the IC budget ($100 billion per year) is now allocated to China (although it is not known how much).

The Director of National Intelligence (DNI) and the Office of Director (ODNI) sit at the top of the sprawling IC. During the Biden administration, the DNI was Avril Haines. Each year the DNI delivers an annual "threat assessment" on behalf of the IC to the Senate Select Committee on Intelligence. In her oral testimony to the Select Committee in 2023 (that accompanied an official written submission), Director Haines devoted a considerable portion of her testimony to China, which included the following statements:[72]

> The People's Republic of China—which is increasingly challenging the United States economically, technologically, politically, and militarily around the world—remains our unparalleled priority. The Chinese Communist Party, or

CCP, under President Xi Jinping will continue efforts to achieve Xi's vision of making China the preeminent power in East Asia and a major power on the world stage. To fulfill Xi's vision, however, the CCP is increasingly convinced that it can only do so at the expense of U.S. power and influence, and by using coordinated, whole-of-government tools to demonstrate strength and compel neighbors to acquiesce to its preferences, including its land, sea, and air claims in the region and its assertions of sovereignty over Taiwan. In brief, the CCP represents both the leading and most consequential threat to U.S. national security and leadership globally and its intelligence-specific ambitions and capabilities make it for us our most serious and consequential intelligence rival.

Director Haines's in-person testimony touched on a variety of elements covered in the much lengthier Annual Threat Assessment document from 2023.[73] The China section of the Threat Assessment accounted for 6 out of 37 total pages, which further elaborated the IC's integrated assessment of China. This included the following key judgments with respect to the United States:

> Beijing sees increasingly competitive US–China relations as part of an epochal geopolitical shift and views Washington's diplomatic, economic, military, and technological measures against Beijing as part of a broader US effort to prevent China's rise and undermine CCP rule ... Beijing is accelerating the development of key capabilities that it believes the People's Liberation Army (PLA) needs to confront the United States in a large-scale, sustained conflict ... Beijing is reorienting its strategic posture for strategic rivalry with the United States because its leaders have concluded that its current capabilities are insufficient.
>
> China will remain the top threat to US technological competitiveness, as Beijing targets key sectors and proprietary commercial and military technology from US and allied companies and institutions ... China probably currently presents the broadest, most active, and persistent cyber espionage threat to US Government and private sector networks. If Beijing feared that a major conflict with the United States were imminent, it almost certainly would consider undertaking aggressive cyber operations against US homeland critical infrastructure and military assets worldwide. Beijing uses a sophisticated array of covert, overt, licit, and illicit means to try to soften US criticism, shape US power centers' views of China, and influence policymakers at all levels of government. PRC leaders probably believe that a US bipartisan consensus against China is impeding their efforts to directly influence US national-level policy regarding China. Beijing has adjusted by redoubling its efforts to build influence at the state and local level to shift US policy in China's favor because of Beijing's belief that local officials are more pliable than their federal

counterparts. PRC actors have become more aggressive with their influence campaigns, probably motivated by their view that anti-China sentiment in the United States is threatening their international image, access to markets, and technological expertise. Beijing's growing efforts to actively exploit US societal divisions using its online personas move it closer to Moscow's playbook for influence operations.

The IC is charged with four principal types of activities, all of which apply to China: collection, analysis, covert action, and counterintelligence. Collection and covert action occur by various means—technological and human—inside of China as well as in other countries outside of China. China is now a *global* intelligence target for the IC as Chinese actors and activities around the world are an increasing priority. In 2022, the Department of State created a new Office of China Coordination (informally called "China House"), which is an effort to have a centralized collection effort concerning China from US embassies and consulates worldwide, and to assign "China-literate" Foreign Service Officers to US embassies and consulates in many countries.[74] The CIA is similarly assigning an increasing portion of China officers to its stations around the world. Third countries are also good places to recruit Chinese informants, who can be activated when they return to China. Under the Biden administration, the CIA has apparently doubled its spending on China.[75]

The principal priority, however, remains collection inside of China itself. Because of the various difficulties of collecting intelligence in and on China, the PRC is known as a "hard target" (perhaps the hardest of hard targets). Human intelligence collection inside of China is highly risky and has become much more so under Xi Jinping's rule. "It is high-risk, and it is true that things get compromised," admitted David Marlowe, the CIA's Deputy Director for Operations, in a rare public appearance in May 2023.[76]

As has been reported in American media, the CIA's human spy network in China was significantly compromised and disrupted by China's counterintelligence agency (the Ministry of State Security [MSS]) during 2010–2012. The MSS apparently penetrated and compromised the clandestine communications means that the CIA station in China used to communicate with their agents, resulting in the arrest and execution of "at least twenty informants," according to knowledgeable US government sources.[77] An unknown number of Chinese informants were caught and imprisoned, and some were executed. At least one individual was reportedly shot in the courtyard of a government building in front of his coworkers (as a deterrent to them). It is also thought that a Chinese mole inside the CIA had supplied the names and workplaces of some agents. That mole was Jerry Chun Shing Lee. Lee was a naturalized American citizen who was born in Hong Kong, grew up in Hawaii, served 4 years in the US

Army, and then spent 13 years as a CIA case officer from 1994–2007.[78] When the FBI arrested Lee in 2012, he had in his possession handwritten names of CIA assets in China, operational notes from clandestine meetings, and covert facility locations.[79] Lee plea-bargained with prosecutors (after supplying the US government with key information about Chinese intelligence activities) and was only convicted on a single charge of conspiracy to commit espionage before being sentenced to prison for 19 years. Lee is hardly the only known case of China's penetration of the CIA, going all the way back to Larry Wu-tai Chin, who worked for the CIA's translation service (Foreign Broadcast Information Service) for 37 years before being caught in 1985.[80] In between there have been a number of other arrests and convictions of members of the IC and US military who had committed espionage and passed US secrets to China (Jerry Lee was only one of three in 2019 alone[81]).

The consequences for US intelligence of the more recent takedown of the CIA's network in China were "horrendous, horrendous, horrendous," said a former senior US official with knowledge of China's crackdown.[82] For his part, when asked about it at the Aspen Security Forum in 2023, CIA Director William Burns publicly stated the following:[83]

Questioner (Mary Louise Kelley): "I'm going to push you on this, because about a decade ago China rolled up a lot of CIA operations in China. A dozen or more CIA sources were arrested, or worse, executed. Have you rebuilt?"

Director Burns: "Yeah. We've made progress and we're working very hard over recent years to ensure that we have strong human intelligence capability to complement what we can acquire through other methods."

It was indeed more than a little surprising that Director Burns was willing to discuss the case publicly, but even more so what he said about rebuilding the network—which drew quick attention in Beijing, where the MSS has redoubled its already intensive counterintelligence efforts. Since Xi Jinping came to power in 2012, he has launched a broad and intensive nationwide effort to unmask, expose, and ferret out "foreign spies." The MSS itself is directing the "whole of society mobilization" in which "the participation of the masses should be normalized."[84] Under China's new counterintelligence initiative, warnings against foreign spies are aired on television and posted on social media; university faculty are made to take courses on protecting state secrets; primary and secondary school students are even taught about foreign spies; neighborhood monitors (a relic from the Maoist past) have been remobilized to keep a careful eye on the comings-and-goings of foreigners (visiting a Chinese home can again be dangerous for foreigners as well as the Chinese hosts); Chinese women are warned not to date foreign men; while foreign businesspeople, students, and teachers are now under increased surveillance and occasional questioning or detention. A national hotline and website have been established to report possible spying, and cash rewards of up to RMB 500,000 ($70,000) are being offered by the MSS for public tips on foreign spies,[85] while some local governments (like Chongqing) have established their own counter-espionage regulations and enforcement capabilities.[86]

China is indeed a dangerous and risky place for foreigners today. The expansive Amendments (made in 2023) to the Counter-Espionage Law (from 2014) have made it even more so (see discussion in Chapter 7). The amended law has sent shivers down the spines of foreign businesses, diplomats, NGO employees, and academics. Partially as a consequence, in June 2023, the US State Department elevated China to a Level 3 Travel Advisory to Mainland China: "Reconsider travel to Mainland China due to the arbitrary enforcement of local laws, including in relation to exit bans, and the risk of wrongful detentions."[87] A raft of new data protection laws that severely restrict cross-border corporate data flows, as well as recent raids on US companies Bain & Company, Mintz Group, Capvision, and other consulting firms that do corporate research have added to the risks.[88]

By law US intelligence agencies are forbidden from collecting intelligence inside of the United States—although, in the wake of 9/11, the IC (mainly the National Security Agency [NSA]) was permitted to obtain search warrants under the Foreign Intelligence Surveillance Act (FISA) and FISA Court to wiretap (communications intercepts) or otherwise monitor certain individuals in the United States homeland. While the NSA is not permitted to "target" American citizens for collection abroad, it does regularly intercept email communications and text messages from targeted Chinese—who may be communicating with Americans (all US professionals who exchange emails with Chinese interlocutors should be aware of this).

The IC's analysis of collected intelligence occurs inside the United States or in official US institutions abroad. The CIA is the main institution for all-source analysis, although it is also undertaken by the ODNI, Defense Intelligence Agency, Bureau of Intelligence and Research of the State Department, the NSA, and National Reconnaissance Office, Department of Homeland Security's Office of Intelligence and Analysis, Department of the Treasury Office of Intelligence and Analysis, and other agencies.

In 2021, CIA Director William Burns established a new "China Mission Center" inside the agency.[89] In launching it Burns said, "[It] will further strengthen our collective work on the most important geopolitical threat we face in the 21st century, and increasingly adversarial Chinese government."[90] The new China Mission Center has considerably increased the personnel, resources, technologies, and analytical techniques devoted to China at CIA (other IC agencies has similarly increased their resources for and focus on China). Director Burns has also publicly stated, "The CIA has committed substantially more resources toward China-related intelligence collection, operations, and analysis around the world—more than doubling the percentage of our overall budget focused on China over just the last two years."[91] Burns also convened a weekly meeting on China in his seventh-floor office at CIA headquarters in Langley, Virginia.[92]

Counterintelligence

Under United States Public Law Title 50, Chapter 44, Section 3003, "The term 'counterintelligence' means information gathered, and activities conducted, to protect against espionage, other intelligence activities, sabotage, or assassinations conducted by or on behalf of foreign governments or elements thereof, foreign organizations, or foreign persons, or international terrorist activities."[93] In Chapter 7, I will discuss separately China's "influence" operations and activities inside the United States. Such influence operations and activities often occur at the borderline of counterintelligence. While illicit, malign, and often covert, they are not always illegal and are thus to be distinguished from *espionage*. Both espionage (which comes in a variety of forms) and influence operations/activities are undertaken by CCP organs, PRC government organs and intelligence agencies, and the PLA. China's intelligence apparatus is bureaucratically sprawling, quite sophisticated, and increasingly active and aggressive abroad.[94] According to James Olson, former chief of counterintelligence at the CIA, "The Chinese are mounting a massive espionage, cyber, and covert action assault on the United States ... If the American people fully understood the audacity and effectiveness of this campaign, they would be outraged and would demand action. Our top priority in US counterintelligence today—and into the future—must be to stop or to drastically curtail China's spying."[95]

Although the FBI is on the frontline of tracking and countering Chinese espionage and intelligence activates inside the United States, oversight and coordination of CI efforts now falls to the National Counterintelligence and Security Center (NCSC), which is part of the ODNI. Since 2021, NCSC has included the National Insider Threat Task Force, which operates under the joint leadership of the Attorney General and DNI and it is charged with "deterring, detecting, and mitigating insider threats, including the safeguarding of classified information from exploitation, compromise, or other unauthorized disclosure."[96] This mission includes ferreting out human spies (in collaboration with individual agency's CI services) as well as various technological penetration of classified material. The ODNI also includes a Foreign Malign Influence Center,[97] which was established in September 2022.[98]

The US government's counterintelligence efforts against Chinese intelligence operations inside of the United States are substantial. Various CI officials, most notably FBI Director Christopher Wray, have identified China as America's No. 1 counterintelligence adversary. "When we tally up what we see in our investigations—over 2,000 of which are focused on the Chinese government trying to steal our information or technology—there is just no country that presents a broader threat to our ideas, our innovation, and our economic security than China," Director Wray said in a speech at the Reagan Presidential Library in 2022, adding that every one of the Bureau's 56 field offices has active China cases and the FBI opens a new counterintelligence case against China about twice a day.[99] In the speech Wray further observed, "China may be the first government to combine authoritarian ambitions with cutting-edge technical capability. It's like the surveillance nightmare of East Germany combined with the tech of Silicon Valley." Elsewhere, Wray has also succinctly asserted, "The greatest long-term threat to our nation's information and intellectual property, and to our economic vitality, is the counterintelligence and economic espionage threat from China."[100] China's espionage efforts are far-flung and sometimes brazen, according to Director Wray: "They're going after everything. What makes the PRC intelligence apparatus so pernicious is the way it uses every means at its disposal against us all at once—blending cyber, human intelligence, corporate transactions, and investments to achieve its strategic goals."[101]

The range of American targets of Chinese espionage and covert intelligence programs includes cyber hacks of virtually *all* US government agencies and senior officials' email accounts. For example, in 2023, Secretary of State Blinken, Secretary of Commerce Raimondo, and US Ambassador to China Nicholas Burns all had their personal email accounts hacked. In 2013–2014, Chinese operatives managed to successfully penetrate the Office of Personnel Management. This astounding penetration resulted in *21 million* US government personnel files with highly personal information collected in the course of security clearance investigations being stolen (which could be used for blackmail or targeting individuals for espionage).[102] In 2017, Chinese cyber hackers penetrated the credit-rating bureau Equifax, which held sensitive personal data on approximately 150 million American homeowners and bank account holders;[103] in 2015, the giant medical insurer Anthem Blue Cross/Blue Shield was hacked and 80 million personal medical records were stolen; Marriott Hotels lost 500 million guests' records (including credit card numbers) in 2014; and countless American companies have had their proprietary information and trade secrets stolen by Chinese hackers (worth an estimated $225–$600 *billion* per year, according to the FBI).[104] Chinese cyber espionage targets many types of technologies and industries,[105] but priority targets have been military-related technologies and weapons systems, as well as the ten priority areas of its *Made in China 2025* strategy (information technology, numerical control tools, aerospace equipment, shipbuilding, railway equipment, energy saving devices, medical devices, new materials, agricultural machinery, power equipment).[106] FBI Director Christopher Wray summed up the scope and impact of China's espionage to his "Five Eyes" (US, UK, Canada, Australia, New Zealand) counterparts:

> The People's Republic of China represents the defining threat of this generation, this era. There is no country that presents a broader, more comprehensive threat to our ideas, our innovation, our economic security, and ultimately our national security. We have seen efforts by the Chinese government—directly or indirectly—trying to steal intellectual property, trade secrets, personal data—all across the country. We're talking everything from Fortune 100 companies to smaller start-ups. We're talking about agriculture, biotech, healthcare, robotics, aviation, academic research. We probably have somewhere on the order of 2000 active investigations that are just related to the Chinese government's efforts to steal information.[107]

The race to develop cutting-edge capabilities in the all-important field of artificial intelligence (AI) is also a Chinese espionage priority (as well as an FBI and corporate priority to counter it). Not only is AI an espionage target, but it is also increasingly a means of espionage itself.[108] Chinese capability in acquiring AI and other technologies is not simply a matter of stealing it—it is often for sale in Silicon Valley! Chinese actors can simply—and legally—just *buy* cutting-edge capabilities.[109] Another method used is to buy start-up tech companies that have filed for bankruptcy.

China's cyberwarriors also target critical American communications and transportation infrastructure nodes. In his Congressional testimony in 2024, FBI Director Christopher Wray said, "China's hackers are positioning on American infrastructure in preparation to wreak havoc and cause real-world harm to American citizens and communities, if or when China decides the time has come to strike. Chinese government hackers are busily targeting water treatment plants, the electrical grid, transportation systems, and other critical infrastructure inside the United States."[110] Wray also revealed that Chinese cyberattacks on US infrastructure had reached "unprecedented levels,"[111] and the US government had disrupted a large-scale Chinese penetration of civilian cyber networks known as Volt Typhoon.[112] PLA hackers had penetrated the computer systems of about two dozen infrastructure facilities during 2023—including a water treatment facility in Hawaii, a major West Coast port, at least one oil and gas pipeline, and the Texas power grid.[113] In late 2024 it was revealed that an even more audacious Chinese hacking effort—labeled Salt Typhoon (by Microsoft)—had successfully managed to penetrate *all* of America's leading (and many smaller) telecommunications networks, including Verizon, AT&T, and T-Mobile! This unprecedented hack allowed the intruders (believed to be China's MSS) to actually listen in on phone conversations and read personal text messages on these national networks (but not encrypted carriers like WhatsApp or Signal). This brazen and broad intrusion permitted the Chinese hackers to monitor the conversations of national security officials and politicians (including, at the time, the inner circle of presidential candidate Donald Trump). Senator Mark Warner (D-Virginia), Chairman of the Senate Intelligence Committee, said he was stunned by the breadth and depth of the full-scope breach of America's telecommunications networks. "This is far and away the most serious telecom hack in our history—it makes Colonial Pipeline and Solar Winds look like small potatoes," Senator Warner told *The New York Times* on November 23, 2024.

The Executive Director of the Department of Homeland Security's Cybersecurity and Infrastructure Security Agency attributed these Chinese efforts "in part to preposition themselves to be able to disrupt or destroy that critical infrastructure in the event of a conflict ... or to cause societal chaos inside the United States."[114] This suspicion was echoed by NSA Director General Timothy Haugh in 2024.[115] Similar attempted hacks of logistics facilities in Hawaii and the West Coast of the continental United States strongly suggest such active attacks would accompany a US–China conflict over Taiwan or elsewhere in the Asia-Pacific region. The ODNI's 2023 Annual Threat Assessment (mentioned earlier in this chapter) warned that China "almost certainly is capable of launching cyberattacks that would disrupt US critical infrastructure, including oil and gas pipelines and rail systems."[116] In retaliation for the multi-year effort to place malware in America's electrical grids, defense systems, and other critical infrastructure, the Department of the Treasury slapped sanctions on several Chinese entities affiliated with the MSS in March 2024.[117] The most likely scenario for disrupting such critical domestic infrastructure would be in a time of conflict over Taiwan, say US officials.

China's cyber espionage against the United States is undertaken by Chinese military, state and public security organs, university and research institute affiliated groups, and individuals. In 2013, it was revealed that PLA Unit 61398, based in a 12-story office block on the outskirts of Shanghai, had sought to penetrate a wide range of American infrastructure and corporate entities.[118] The FBI has posted "Wanted" posters online of Chinese individuals either indicted or sought for illegal cyber hacking against American targets.[119] The FBI also has a dedicated and informative public webpage concerning Chinese espionage threats which includes a "wanted list" of Chinese fugitives "wanted for a variety of crimes against US interests on behalf of China."

The FBI and America's other intelligence services (notably the NSA) are doing all they can to combat Chinese cyber hacking, but the sheer volume of the challenge is difficult to cope with. FBI Director Wray shockingly told a Congressional Committee in 2024, "If you took every single one of the FBI cyber agents, intelligence analysts and focused them exclusively on the China threat, China's hackers would still outnumber FBI cyber personnel by at least 50 to 1."[120]

Another counterintelligence challenge for the FBI concerns academics in American universities who are lured to China with lucrative contracts through the Thousand Talents program. Actually, there are dozens, perhaps 100, of such talent recruitment programs; Thousand Talents is hardly the only one.[121] A large number of academics with full-time faculty appointments in American universities have accepted such "dual" appointments with Chinese universities—usually *without* the permission of their American employer. In recent years, these talent recruitment appointments have been exposed and cracked down on by US universities, as well as by the US Justice Department. Perhaps the most noteworthy case involved Chemistry Department Chair Charles Lieber of Harvard University, who was arrested, tried, fined, and briefly imprisoned after being found guilty of fraudulently disguising income and evading taxes. The Justice Department found that, "Specifically, the terms of Lieber's three-year Thousand Talents contract with Wuhan University of Technology (WUT) entitled Lieber to a salary of up to $50,000 per month, living expenses of up to $150,000 and approximately $1.5 million to conduct joint research at WUT."[122] While Lieber was not accused of transferring sensitive information or violating US export controls, the counterintelligence threat is that some scientists and engineers are in a position to do so. There has also definitely been some overzealousness by the FBI and counterintelligence authorities in pursuing and prosecuting academic of Chinese descent.[123]

Finally, one other counterintelligence dimension involves what has become known as "transnational repression"—the attempt by the Chinese government and private sector actors to track, intimidate, and silence Chinese diaspora critics and dissidents overseas. A number of cases and incidents have been uncovered and prosecuted in recent years,[124] as Xi Jinping's government has stepped up its surveillance and harassment of overseas critics.[125] One particularly brazen example involved the arrest of 44 Chinese nationals (including 40 Ministry of Public Security officers) who were operating a "police station" in New York City.[126] In one recent case, an ethnic Chinese man was convicted in a Brooklyn federal court of monitoring and providing detailed information to agents of China's Ministry of State Security concerning Chinese nationals living in the New York area involved in activities related to Hong Kong, Taiwan, Tibet, and Uighurs.[127] The man, Wang Shaojun, was convicted of acting as an agent of a foreign government and faces up to 25 years in prison. In the summer of 2023, a group of three men were convicted in a similar case for stalking dissidents in New Jersey.[128] The responsibility to counter such actions in the United States falls to the FBI,[129] although local law enforcement agencies are also involved.

This chapter has focused on the US national government and its departments and agencies. In the next chapter we move "outside the (Washington, DC) Beltway" to explore several sectors of American society and how they have experienced the disengagement and decoupling process of recent years with China.

Chapter 7
Outside the Beltway: Non-Governmental Actors

"The Chinese government is engaged in a broad, diverse campaign of theft and malign influence, and it can execute that campaign with authoritarian efficiency. They're calculating. They're persistent. They're patient. And they're not subject to the righteous constraints of an open, democratic society or the rule of law. They will use an all-tools and all-sectors approach—and that demands our own all-tools and all-sectors approach in response."

—Christopher Wray, Director of the Federal Bureau of Investigation[1]

"In a complicated great power relationship, you don't want the two peoples pulled apart."

—Nicholas Burns, US Ambassador to China[2]

In this chapter, we turn from the governmental to non-governmental sector in the United States and from Washington, DC, to the rest of the country. It is this non-governmental sphere which so thoroughly embraced the opportunity to engage both *with* China and, in many cases, *in* China. As discussed in Chapter 2, the expansive private sector was a huge part of—and in many ways constituted the real essence of—engagement: people-to-people exchanges; university partnerships and student exchanges; US states and localities; think tanks; philanthropic foundations; journalists and media; doctors and scientists; scholarly researchers in a range of fields; and the business community. There was hardly any sector of American society that did *not* engage with China. Many of these American actors began to operate and work together with their Chinese counterparts *in* China—while Chinese in these sectors also came to the United States to interact with their American counterparts.

This two-way interchange was, by and large, extremely positive for both sides. This was how "China won America." But things have dramatically changed, and China has now "lost America." "Engagement as exchanges" with China (the fourth element of the Engagement strategy described in Chapter 2) is no longer seen as beneficial to many American institutions, citizens in the United States, and the different sectors that constituted the Engagement Coalition.

There have been multiple reasons for the fracturing of this coalition. One principal factor has been the sheer asymmetrical nature of these exchanges. No matter the sector—higher education, business, tourism, media, localities, etc.—there was never any *numerical* reciprocity, as Chinese actors swamped and overwhelmed American actors. The disproportionate asymmetrical nature of exchanges with Chinese counterparts left many Americans feeling that they were being taken advantage of. Exchanges had become very one-sided over time, and China was benefiting far more than America and Americans. A second important factor is that a variety of actors encountered substantial—and unacceptable—obstacles and obstructionism from their counterparts in China. Simply pursuing their professional missions became exceedingly difficult. A third, more recent, factor has been China's multifaceted "influence operations" and espionage inside of the United States. More generally, two broader factors have contributed to the fact that China has "lost America": domestic changes in America and in China."

America Changes

The first lies within America itself, most notably the various elements of Donald Trump's nativist Make America Great Again (MAGA) movement.[3] Several strands of MAGA thinking have targeted China. First, and perhaps most importantly, is the anti-globalization sentiment in the United States. Globalization is viewed by the MAGA movement as directly responsible for the hollowing out of American industries—particularly across the Midwestern states as a result of the outsourcing of American manufacturing to China. But instead of blaming American companies for this outsourcing or for failing to upgrade factories and wages to stay globally competitive, the MAGA movement and the (post-)industrial working class blamed China. The United States suffered a "China shock" in the decade after the country's entry into the World Trade Organization (WTO) in 2001, hemorrhaging an estimated 560,000 manufacturing jobs.[4] During his first presidential campaign, Trump tapped directly into this resentment—arguing that China was "raping" America; at one point as President, he threatened to "order" all American companies with production facilities in China to "reshore" and bring their manufacturing home to America. The bestselling book *Hillbilly Elegy* by J. D. Vance, Trump's Vice-President elect, captured well the devastated lives in Appalachia, the Midwest, and across rural America.

Another part of the MAGA anti-globalization argument targeted "liberal elites" who promoted an open global trade agenda and institutions such as the WTO. At its heart, the MAGA movement is profoundly anti-elitist and anti-liberal, and they blame "liberal East Coast elites" for the entire process of engaging with China—based on faulty and fuzzyheaded liberal assumptions about either "shaping China" or "integrating China" into a global liberal order (which MAGA supporters also despise and oppose). Although the MAGA movement is concentrated in the heartland of the country between the two coasts and represents mainstream working-class America's distrust of college-educated elites, it is also responsive to Trump's isolationist worldview of "America First." As nativists, they do not like challengers to American power and primacy from any rival, notably China.

Another contributing factor was the fact that COVID-19 originated in China and caused many across the heartland of America to blame China for it and consequently for the devastating losses of one million American lives. This also led to the racist remarks of President Trump concerning the "Chinese virus," and to physical and verbal assaults on Asian Americans. COVID-19's disruption of supply chains that brought goods to the United States from China, including pharmaceuticals and masks, was another related source of resentment toward China among average Americans. It made Americans suddenly realize just how dependent on China the United States had become as a result of "engagement." Americans like to think of their country as powerful and autonomous from others—the COVID-19 crisis drove home this dependency in direct ways. It made many Americans deeply uncomfortable.

Anti-China fearmongering is also spread to MAGA supporters through social media. Former Trump adviser Steve Bannon's "War Room" podcast, Charlie Kirk's "Turning Point USA," "The Clay Travis and Buck Sexton Show," "The Michael Savage Show," and previously the "Rush Limbaugh Show" (Limbaugh died in 2021) are all popular among the MAGA right and all peddle a steady stream of anti-China invective.[5] FOX News has also broadcast a regular diet of anti-China narratives to its viewers.

In addition, the Christian right is a core component of the MAGA movement. For this substantial constituency, the Chinese Communist Party (CCP) is seen as (a) communist, thus (b) atheist, and (c) repressive of religious and other freedoms. In fact, however, the Chinese government and constitution (Article 13) permits five religions to be practiced (Buddhism, Catholicism, Daoism, Islam, and Protestantism), and all are actively practiced in China today. While 19.9 million mainland Chinese identify as practicing Christians,[6] the Christian right in the United States believe otherwise. Bob Fu (Fu Xiqiu), a Christian pastor in Midland, Texas, has been very active in the Republican Party and in bringing American Christians' attention to the plight of their brethren in China, and the NGO that he founded (China Aid) has done much good work to support Chinese Christians.[7]

Thus, China represents a perfect storm that fuses together core beliefs and deep grievances for the MAGA movement and many average Americans across the heartland. These MAGA sentiments aligned with two other groups in America.

First, there was a growing sense among a cross-section of foreign policy specialists that Engagement had "failed" to transform China into a more liberal political system or a more liberal international actor (see Chapter 1), as the Engagement strategy had envisioned and intended. Second, both the more traditional conservative wing of the Republican Party and the Tea Party "freedom caucus" in Congress increasingly viewed China as a communist regime, which had an ideology and a system antithetical to American politics and values. This perspective, of course, echoes the Cold War. China is now increasingly seen by many in this cohort as an incarnate of the Soviet Union—but one on steroids. Worse yet, across the domestic political spectrum there is increasing awareness and recognition of China's new power: economic, military, and technological. Rather than confining itself as an actor in Asia, suddenly China has been showing up on all continents and in far-flung oceans.[8] In July 2024, its bombers (together with Russian bombers) even entered Alaska's Air Defense Identification Zone for the first time,[9] and it may just be a matter of time before Chinese and Russian naval vessels exercise off the coast of California, Oregon, or Washington state (*that* will shake up Americans!).

Moreover, in the wake of the Global Financial Crisis (2008–2009), China began to act much more assertively, even aggressively, in regional and global affairs. An earlier version of the angry nationalist "wolf warrior diplomacy" suddenly emerged, with Chinese diplomatic spokespersons becoming very acerbic, caustic, and verbally aggressive. The year 2010 thus became known as China's "Year of Assertiveness."[10]

China's newfound power and prowess stunned all observers, as it seemingly emerged very suddenly (although it has been growing steadily for years). Americans had grown accustomed to thinking about China as a large Asian developing country struggling to modernize itself, but one that lagged very far behind the United States and the West. Thus, some Americans began to wonder: What have we done to contribute to this emerging Frankenstein? And *why*? What kind of fuzzyheaded liberal naïveté had led the United States to directly fuel China's modernization and rapid rise?

As Beijing began to be more and more truculent and difficult for Washington to partner with in the very international institutions where the United States had assumed China would become a "responsible stakeholder," it became increasingly clear to careful observers (scholar Elizabeth Economy was one of the first) that the multi-decade effort to institutionally integrate China into the international institutional order (one of the four core strategies of Engagement discussed in Chapter 2), for it to contribute constructively as a good global citizen, and to be "socialized" into liberal norms of these international institutions of global governance, had been a fool's errand. Beijing proved itself to be Hobbesian and Darwinian instead of Kantian (those who view society and world affairs as anarchical, predatory, and survival-of-the-fittest—instead of intrinsically cooperative and collective). China was showing itself to be an extremely self-interested global actor that held and promoted very illiberal values and policies, aligning itself with other illiberal rogue states such as Vladimir Putin's Russia, the Ayatollah's Iran, and the Kim dynasty's North Korea.[11] During the 2010s, Beijing also began to establish a series of alternative regional organizations, which intentionally excluded the United States and Western countries: the Shanghai Cooperation Organization, China–Arab Cooperation Forum, Forum on China–Africa Cooperation, China and Central and Eastern European Countries Forum, Forum of China and Community of Latin American and Caribbean States, and the BRICS (Brazil, Russia, India, China, South Africa).[12]

All of this contributed in America to the odd combination of *alarm* about the newly emerging strong and illiberal China coupled with *disappointment* that China was not turning out the way that the engagement theorists had expected. Further, as we will explore in this chapter, beginning around 2015, China was discovered to be undertaking various illicit and covert actions to "influence" average Americans, American elites, American officials, American media, American educational and research institutions, American elections, American states and localities, and American business.[13] Actually, such attempted influence dates back decades and is institutionally embedded in the CCP's "united front" and intelligence systems—but it was not until the mid-2010s that the US government woke up to the degree and range of CCP penetration of American institutions and society.

By the time the 2024 Republican presidential election primaries rolled around, China again became a regular target. In a throwback to Cold War rhetoric of the 1950s and 1960s, candidate Republican Nikki Haley regularly referred to "Communist China" rather than just "China" on the campaign trail, while her early rivals Florida Governor Ron DeSantis, former Vice President Mike Pence, and entrepreneur Vivek Ramaswamy were all sharply critical of China. Haley's critique of "Communist China" was quite specific (channeling Senator Marco Rubio's China positions during the 2016 primaries) and she minced no words. In her announcement kicking off her presidential campaign in February 2024, Haley issued a forceful condemnation of China, characterizing it as the "strongest and most disciplined enemy" ever faced by the United States. "China's dictators want to cover the world in communist tyranny. We are the only ones who can stop them," Haley said.[14] Such a perspective resonated with many Americans of both political parties. "Yes, I view China as an enemy—which has practically been preparing for war with us for years," Haley told CNN in primetime in September 2023.[15] Haley's campaign website read, "Communist China is an existential threat. It's destroyed our jobs and stolen our secrets to build a massive military. Freedom is the only way to leave Chinese Communism on the ash heap of history."[16] "Chinese communism must be condemned and never congratulated," she said in a speech to the American Enterprise Institute.[17] Candidate Haley further elaborated on her China policy in a 2023 *Wall Street Journal* op-ed:[18]

> The Communist Party is preparing China for war. Xi Jinping has said it. America has to stop wasting time ... China has spent decades preparing to fight. America is now in a dangerous situation against a powerful enemy. The hour is late, but it isn't too late to wake up and take charge of our future. If we rally now, the Chinese Communist Party will end up on the ash heap of history, like the Soviet Communist Party before it.

While Haley was not successful in gaining the Republican Party's nomination (which she lost to Donald Trump), her critique of China was widely shared and captures a prevalent bipartisan sentiment in the country.

To understand America's recent disaffection and disillusionment with its relationship with China thus requires an understanding of what has transpired in American political culture over the past decade, notably the beliefs of the MAGA movement. Donald Trump is their vessel, as he has tapped into the spectrum of revisionist beliefs held by MAGA members, for whom China represents evil and an existential threat to the American way of life.

Therefore, across the country and across the political spectrum, there has been a sea change in the way that many Americans perceive China. By 2023, fully 83 percent of Americans polled by Pew held an "unfavorable" and "negative" perception of China.[19] This has not been a temporary shift in perceptions—it represents a secular downward trend over the past eight years (as Figure 0.1 indicates). Other survey companies report similar results. Gallup found that 85 percent of Americans held negative views of China in 2023.[20] This included 94 percent of Republicans, 82 percent of Democrats, and 83 percent of independents.[21] The Chicago Council on Global Affairs found in 2023, for the first time ever, that a record level of Americans (58 percent) view "China's development as a world power as a critical threat to the vital interest of the United States."[22]

China Changes

The second broad cause of disengagement lies in China. Beginning with Xi Jinping's ascension to power in 2012 and the regime's paranoia about Western (especially American) political and cultural subversion, the CCP and government agencies began a systematic crackdown on, and rollback of, the non-governmental American presence *inside* of China. As a result, a draconian dragnet has descended over China, and normal operating life has been made extremely difficult (and in many cases impossible) for American and other foreign non-governmental actors.

Concomitantly, malign Chinese activities inside of the United States have also increased (see Chapter 6). These included a range of activities: covert espionage; the dissemination of disinformation (both via legally operating Chinese media organs and surreptitious propaganda fronts, as well as via US media); "united front" operations aimed at co-opting the American Chinese diaspora community; direct interference in US elections; and a wide range of so-called influence operations carried out through a variety of means in American society, academia and think tanks, Congress, state and local governments, and the business community.[23] This chapter examines a number of these activities of People's Republic of China (PRC) and the "disengagement" impacts they have had on these sectors in the United States.

There has thus been a mutual "securitization" of the relationship, with both sides "mirror-imaging" and viewing the others' presence and activities inside its borders increasingly through the lens of—and threatening to—its national security. Even where national security is not considered to be endangered, both sides have made it increasingly difficult to carry out normal professional activities, such as scholarly research, journalistic reporting, ordinary business, societal exchanges, and philanthropic activities. This has resulted in a de facto decoupling and disengagement of the two societies.

At the same time, it is very important to note that the pressure put on these American actors in China and Chinese actors in America has not been *total*, but it has been widespread and significant. That is, exchanges and activities in each of these aforementioned spheres continue, but at various degrees of curtailment. Many have been terminated or suspended, but by no means all. It is thus a mixed picture, with some exchanges and activities continuing, but many others being impacted, curtailed, or halted.

In Chapter 5, we saw how the Trump and Biden administrations pushed back against what they perceived to be malign actions by China—in America, in Asia, and in the world. By this line of analysis, it has been Xi Jinping's China that has exercised agency first and has been the independent variable, while the United

States has *reacted* to Chinese actions and has been the dependent variable. There is, I believe, considerable truth in this causal analysis. Under Xi Jinping, the CCP and China's government organs have considerably ramped up their repression inside of China and have brought considerable pressure to bear on American (and other foreign) actors inside the country; they have definitely expanded its subversive actions inside the United States;[24] have substantially increased military pressure on Taiwan; China has increased its coercive policies and actions against a wide range of American allies in Asia, Europe, and elsewhere around the world; and Beijing has been an uncooperative revisionist actor in global governance institutions. By this line of analysis, it is America that is reacting to China.

However, the opposite argument is also plausible. That is, from the perspective of the CCP and government, it has been the United States that has been trying to subvert its political system, retard its economy, pressure it militarily, ringfence the country with American-led alliances in Asia, deploy military forces all around its periphery, intervene in Taiwan, and constrain China's growing presence around the world. From Beijing's perspective, it is America that is the aggressor. In the words of Xi Jinping in 2023, "Western countries led by the United States have implemented all-around containment, encirclement and suppression of China, which has brought unprecedented severe challenges to our country's development" (以美国为首的西方国家对我实施了全方位的遏制,围堵,打压).[25]

Xi has a point. Although it cannot be said that the United States is seeking to "contain" China externally and it is not clear what he means by "suppression" (although he likely refers to US efforts to restrict China's technological development), it is evident that the United States has been seeking to "encircle" China through its diplomatic and security partnerships with China's neighbors. Chinese commentators, including Xi, have long misused the term "containment" (遏制) to describe contemporary American policy toward China. During the 1950s and 1960s, the United States certainly did carry out a containment policy against the PRC as a subset of its containment policy of the USSR (see Chapter 3). There was a total trade embargo, zero academic exchanges, no tourism, no journalism, no government interactions, no nothing. *That* was containment. With President Nixon's opening in 1972, the United States abandoned containment as a strategy in favor of engagement with China, and there is no country in the world that subsequently did more to assist China's development and bring it into the international community than the United States. It is thus both factually incorrect and disingenuous for Chinese commentators to describe American policy as "containment." Xi should have just left it at "encirclement," but he would have been much more accurate to use the terms "political subversion" (政治颠覆) or "peaceful evolution" 和平演变). As I described in

Chapter 2 (and it is the central argument of this book), it has long been the American desire, intention, strategy, and policy to evolve China in more liberal political, economic, and social directions. So, Xi would not have been incorrect had he used these terms.

While unusually explicit, Xi's statement in 2023 is entirely consistent with his perspective of an embattled China which needs to "struggle" (奋斗) against the United States and the West in order to survive. Throughout his 12 years in power, Xi has repeatedly and continually expressed this viewpoint, urging his countrymen to "fight" and "struggle" against American "hegemony," and urging the People's Liberation Army to "prepare to fight and win wars," as documented so well in China scholar Bates Gill's book *Daring to Struggle: China's Global Ambitions Under Xi Jinping*.[26] In Xi's view, it is China that is reacting to America. Like his "best and bosom friend" Vladimir Putin, Xi sees China as engaged in an epic existential struggle with the United States and with the American-led liberal international order. In China scholar Susan Shirk's view, this has led Xi's CCP and government to "overreach" and undermine its previous four decades of reformist development while diminishing China's global position and reputation.[27]

In both Gill's and Shirk's views (both of their books are well worth reading), it is Xi Jinping who has overreacted, has exercised agency, has abandoned Deng Xiaoping's directive to "bide time and hide brightness" (韬光养晦), and who is primarily to blame for the deterioration of the US–China relationship in recent years. However, Shirk (and some other American scholars, whose views we will examine in Chapter 8) also argues that it is the United States that has *also* overreacted: "China's overreach has triggered an American overreaction that is almost self-defeating. Based on an exaggerated view of China's threat to the United States and lack of confidence in our own strengths, we have reverted to extreme measures against China that undercut our strengths and reinforce the hawkish elements in China," Professor Shirk asserts.[28]

Whether one accepts the American perspective that Xi's China has been the catalyst in launching new initiatives meant to constrain and subvert the United States—or whether one accepts the Chinese perspective that it is the United States that seeks to do the same to China—either way, it has produced an action–reaction dynamic in the US–China relationship. Both sides have increasingly "securitized" the relationship domestically. This is particularly the case in Xi's China, where national security has become the paramount policy priority. Since issuing his "Comprehensive Security Outlook" (总体安全观) in 2022, Xi has identified no fewer than 22 different types of "national security,"[29] and he used the term (国家安全) no fewer than 91 times in his speech to the 20th Party Congress in 2022. In an internal speech to Ministry of Public Security personnel entitled "Strictly Guard Against and Crackdown on Infiltration,

Subversion, Disturbances, and Destruction Activities by Internal and External Hostile Forces," Xi's Minister of Public Security Zhao Kezhi instructed his cadre, "We must intensively implement the 'Comprehensive National Security Outlook,' and strictly guard against internal and external hostile forces intent on subverting and overthrowing the state by activities that cause chaos."[30]

There has always been a distinct difference in the way that Americans and Chinese think about "national security." For Americans, at least prior to the Oklahoma City bombing of 1995 and al-Qaeda terrorist attacks in New York and Washington on 9/11 in 2001, national security was thought of primarily as *external* to the United States and involving the US military (this has evolved, of course, as domestic terrorism, militias, and cyber threats have permeated inside of the country's borders). For the PRC, though, national security has always included both internal and external dimensions. Unlike the United States, China does not have the luxury of friendly neighbors and secure borders—and it has long had to deal with successionist ethnic groups (Uighurs and Tibetans), and an unfinished civil war with Taiwan, as well as with political dissent and some domestic opposition to the communist regime. Ever since the 1950s, when John Foster Dulles announced his policy of "peaceful evolution," the CCP has perceived the United States to be an active threat to its *political* security. American and Western liberal ideas have also long been seen as a threat to communist China's *cultural* security. It is precisely for these reasons that American NGOs and American educators in China have come to be seen as such a threat by the Xi regime.

Since coming to power, Xi Jinping has unleashed a sustained reign of repression and comprehensive controls on China not seen since the Maoist era (the post–Tiananmen massacre crackdown in 1989–1991 was intense but largely limited to Beijing and relatively short-lived). Xi has also reembraced Marxist ideology, while practicing Leninist dictatorship. No sector of society has escaped the reach of Xi's regime.[31] Combating so-called foreign hostile forces (外国敌对势力) has been a centerpiece of Xi's campaign. The Central Political and Legal Affairs Commission (which is the highest-level party/government organ overseeing all internal security) has convened special work conferences devoted to combating these foreign hostile forces.[32] On April 16, 2023, Minister of State Security Chen Yixin convened a special plenary conference of security organs in Beijing to discuss Xi Jinping's instructions on enhancing national security.[33] In his speech to the conclave, Minister Chen invoked Xi's own instructions for "building a new national security pattern and system." Chen quoted Xi as stating,

The current international situation is complex and severe, the international struggle is becoming increasingly intense, and system confrontation has become a significant feature of the game of great powers ... China's national security involves a full range of issues at home and abroad. In order to build a new security pattern, it is necessary to integrate the two major domestic and international situations. Internally, we should take the maintenance of political security as the foundation, crack down on infiltration, sabotage, subversion, and successionist activities by hostile forces.[34]

The Ministries of Public and State Security have had their budgets and their briefs expanded to ferret out any and all dissent and potential "subversion." The Ministry of State Security (MSS) even took the unusual step of establishing a public WeChat account and, on August 1, 2023, with an initial posting entitled "Counter-Espionage Requires Mobilization of the Entire Society," launching a national effort to ferret out foreign spies.[35] According to one assessment, the MSS WeChat channel "pumps out a stream of rousing content, from slickly produced videos to chest-thumping screeds that denounce foreign hostile forces trying to contain China."[36] The MSS also offers rewards of up to RMB 500,000 (approximately $70,000) to Chinese citizens who report suspected spies, and the ministry has established a telephone hotline and internet platform for reporting spies (www.12339.gov.cn).[37] Since 2023, the MSS has nabbed several Chinese nationals who were accused of spying for the CIA. Two individuals, surnamed Zeng and Hao, were allegedly recruited while studying abroad in Italy and Japan respectively, and conveyed information to the CIA after returning to China (Zeng worked for a "military-industrial group" while Hao worked in a ministerial-level government agency).[38]

Under the new surveillance system, intellectuals and professors have been subjected to regular monitoring and the closest state scrutiny in many years, while teachers at all levels must strictly toe the Party line. The use of Western textbooks (in the original or in translation) has been officially banned by the Ministry of Education (although some teachers still surreptitiously use them, mainly in translation). Course syllabi now have to be vetted and approved by university Party committees, cameras and microphones have been installed in classrooms to monitor lectures, students sometimes report on professors who stray from the Party line, and some faculty have been relieved of their positions and punished for saying or publishing heretical things. Hundreds of defense lawyers (who try to defend accused citizens) have been detained and many charged with "subverting state power." Popular bloggers and individuals who transmit unacceptable social media posts are also subject to interrogation and punishment under China's Cybersecurity Law (2016), which prohibits "fabricating or disseminating false information or rumors and disturbing public order"—all under the mandate of what Xi has termed the "struggle for public opinion" (he has also designated the internet as an "ideological battlefield").[39]

Anyone who shares a "rumor" or other designated illicit social media posting faces up to three years in prison. Chinese private media has sometimes pushed the envelope of investigative journalism in the past, but now it (together with all official state media) has also been brought to heel by Xi. In February 2016, Xi made a highly publicized and carefully choreographed visit to the headquarters of Xinhua News Agency, CCTV, and *People's Daily* in Beijing,[40] where he demanded "absolute loyalty" of the media to the CCP. Xi did not mince his words: "All the work by the Party's media must reflect the Party's will, safeguard the Party's authority, and safeguard the Party's unity. They must love the Party, protect the Party, and closely align themselves with the Party leadership in thought, politics and action."[41]

In addition to the Cybersecurity Law, the government adopted several other sweeping draconian laws between 2014 and 2016—all aimed at severely restricting any kind of autonomous behavior in the public sphere: the National Security Law, Counter-Espionage Law, NGO Law, Charity Law, and Counterterrorism Law. Among the many restrictions contained in these laws was a common thread to severely constrict and closely monitor any foreign connections. This grew out of the CCP's paranoia arising from the "color revolutions" in Eastern Europe, Eurasia, and the alleged subversive roles played by foreign NGOs (particularly those linked to the United States).[42] The Hong Kong National Security Law (2019) mirrored these others. Another spine-chilling policy was the Central Committee General Office Document No. 9 (2013), the *Communiqué on the Current State of the Ideological Sphere*.[43] Document No. 9 makes very clear the subjects that are considered heretical and threatening to China's national security: Western constitutional democracy, Western "universal values," civil society, neoliberalism, freedom of the press, practicing "historical nihilism" and undermining the history of the CCP, and questioning or criticizing "socialism with Chinese characteristics."[44]

The regime's broadside against so-called foreign hostile forces started during Xi's second term (2017–2022),[45] and has intensified further in his third term (2022–).[46] It is this contextual backdrop in Xi Jinping's China that explains much of what American entities have been experiencing in China in recent years.

Non-Governmental Organizations

American non-governmental organizations (NGOs) have a long, proud, and generally positive history of operating in China. Churches and missionaries operated throughout China from the 18th through the 20th centuries. As historian Mary Brown Bullock's writings have so well documented and demonstrated, American philanthropies, educational, and medical NGOs sunk deep roots in Republican China (1912–1949).[47]

Following the normalization of relations in 1979, and particularly during the 1990s–2000s, American philanthropies, foundations, universities, educational exchange organizations, and an eclectic range of private sector NGOs again began operating in the country. This must be seen as the *return* of American philanthropy to China following a 30-year hiatus. Some of these—such as the China Medical Board, Yale–China, Oberlin in China, and the Rockefeller Foundation—simply resumed their pre–1949 activities, but most were new to China. The centuries-long "missionary impulse" of Americans to export their religious and liberal values, professional skills, and "best practices" in efforts to shape China's modernization returned with a vengeance.[48]

During Xi Jinping's tenure, however, American NGOs have come under far greater constraints and scrutiny, with many deciding to terminate their operations. This pressure has been evident in many ways. Perhaps the most significant has been legal. In 2016, China's National People's Congress promulgated the "Law of the People's Republic of China on Administration of Activities of Overseas Nongovernmental Organizations in the Mainland of China."[49] The new law specified the parameters of permitted NGO activities: "Foreign NGOs are permitted to work in economics, education, science, culture, health, sports, environmental protection, poverty, and disaster relief but must not endanger China's national unity, security, or ethnic unity; and must not harm China's national interests, societal public interest, or engage in or fund for-profit, political, or religious activities."[50]

The negative impact of this draconian law on foreign and American NGOs and foundations was immediate. Registered international NGOs (INGOs) dramatically plummeted from over 7,000 to less than 400 in just the 2 years immediately following implementation of the law.[51] China's own Ministry of Public Security (with which all INGOs must register) listed 685 legally registered INGOs in 2023, of which 150 were American.[52] According to the authoritative *China Development Brief* (itself an NGO that had operated in Beijing but was forced to relocate to Hong Kong), those that remain, run an eclectic gamut—including the Almond Board of California, the American Heart Association, Blessing Hands, Give Me Hope Foundation, Caterpillar Foundation, The Conference Board, Conservation International, Cotton USA, American Petroleum Institute, China Medical Board, US Dairy Export Council, US Soybean Export Council, US Chamber of Commerce, Conservation International, International Crane Association, Environmental Defense Fund, International Fund for Animal Welfare, Nature Conservancy, Orbis International, Project HOPE, the Paulson Institute, Special Olympics, International Association of Amusement Parks and Attractions, Rocky Mountain Institute, Nature Conservancy, National

Geographic Society, Rockefeller Brothers Fund, the Ford Foundation, Bill and Melinda Gates Foundation, World Resources Institute, Winrock International, US–China Educational Trust, and a number of others.[53]

Those American NGOs that remain operating in China are all in the fields of export promotion, public health and medicine, poverty alleviation, environmental protection, wildlife protection, sports, and tertiary education. With the exception of the Ford Foundation,[54] those whose work was related to legal, social, and political reform have all been squeezed out and have withdrawn from the country (some initially decamped to Hong Kong but they have subsequently left there too, following the Hong Kong government's promulgation of its own National Security Law in 2020, which has specifically taken aim at foreign NGOs). The American Bar Association and a number of major American law firms have also downsized or closed up shop in China.[55] As Mary Brown Bullock observes, the multi-decade American effort to promote reform in these three spheres has come to a screeching halt.[56]

Thus, American NGOs—which had been a key part of the Engagement Coalition and had established a strong position and positive reputation in China—have come under substantial pressures from Chinese governmental authorities in recent years. Most have pulled out of the country. Those that remain are in a very limited range of humanitarian assistance, environmental work, and trade promotion. Those that were involved with governance and politics have been forced out. The Carter Center, International Republican Institute (IRI), and National Democratic Institute (NDI)—which were involved in promoting and monitoring local elections—have been ordered to cease operations (and in the cases of IRI and NDI, their directors and board members have been individually sanctioned and are no longer permitted to travel to China). This negative trend can be expected to continue as long as the CCP and government remain politically insecure and take a suspicious (hostile) view of Western democracies.

Meanwhile, Chinese partner organizations (*all* foreign NGOs *must* have an officially registered Chinese partner/sponsor) have also come under increased scrutiny. As China opened to the world since the 1980s and the government became more tolerant of non-state actors, *Chinese* NGOs also began to proliferate (especially since 2000). China scholar (and my George Washington University colleague) Bruce Dickson cites the Ministry of Civil Affairs own data: in 2018, China had a total of 783,764 NGOs, including 360,399 "social organizations" (社会团体), 416,733 private non-commercial enterprises, and 6,632 foundations, with an additional 1.5 million unregistered.[57] The entire sphere of civil society has come under much closer scrutiny and controls by Xi's regime, and there has been a significant crackdown on and contraction of Chinese NGOs.[58] Since Xi Jinping came to power, the Chinese party-state has gone to great lengths to monitor, co-opt, and control such "social organizations."[59] They are all now compelled by law to register with both the Ministry of Civil Affairs and Ministry of Public Security, their administrative personnel and participants are scrutinized, their finances are audited, and their activities and operations are closely monitored.

This tightened control is the direct result of the regime's paranoia about Western penetration of such groups and their potential (even without Western penetration) to serve as platforms for activities not under the control of the party-state. This is no accident, as the CCP has closely studied—and learned the lessons from—the roles played by civil society actors in pressuring and overthrowing other authoritarian regimes.[60] Similarly, the CCP and PRC government organs have carefully studied how other authoritarian countries (notably Russia and Iran) have dealt with international NGOs (known as "authoritarian learning"),[61] and, in turn, China has increasingly begun to export "best" (read: worst) practices for controlling INGOs to other countries across the Global South.

Educational Exchanges

The topic of educational and scholarly exchanges with China can be divided into two parts: exchanges in China and exchanges in the United States. A further distinction also needs to be made between *educational* and *scholarly* exchanges. The former spans exchanges at multiple levels of education—secondary, university-level, and executive education—where students are taught in the classroom. The latter distinction, for the purposes of this book, involves research by American scholars in China.

There are (or were) a number of American high schools that have exchange programs in and with China. Many did not survive the COVID-19 era suspensions. One that has endured is my own former boarding school, the Verde Valley School in Sedona, Arizona—which has a program that brings about 30 Chinese high school students from its partner school in Shanghai for a semester in residence (one can only imagine the visual shock these students must experience between urban Shanghai and the picturesque red rock Oak Creek Canyon in northern Arizona). Prior to COVID-19, there were an estimated 80,000 Chinese students per year studying in American high schools (as many Chinese parents assumed—probably correctly—that this would give their kids a leg-up on admission to American universities). But I am not aware of American secondary school students going *to China* for study—for short-term group visits or summer language study yes, but not semester or year-long study in China. Of course, there are a number of expatriate international and American schools in China (our son attended the Western Academy of Beijing for eighth grade, while I was on a Fulbright fellowship at the Chinese Academy of Social Sciences in 2009–2010).

Programs that send American university-level students to China were far more substantial. I say "were" because the number of American students studying in China precipitously plummeted from 15,000 per year pre–COVID-19 to 211 in 2022, only 350 in 2022, and approximately 700 in 2023 (see Figure 7.1) according to the State Department and US Ambassador to China Nicholas Burns.[62] This sharply contrasts with still over 350,000 Chinese students currently studying in American universities.

There are a number of reasons for this precipitous decline—some generic, some specific to China. According to the International Institute for Education, there has been a general decline of American students studying abroad since 2017, and there was a precipitous drop-off because of COVID-19 in 2020 (by 2022, it had begun to rebound).[63] General tensions in US–China relations and the negative press coverage about China in American media has also been a contributing factor. The State Department's "Level 3 Travel Advisory" is a further deterrent (especially for parents), as the Advisory tells Americans

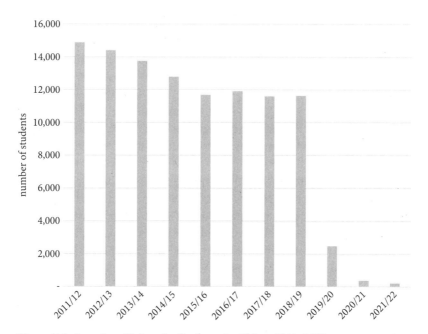

Figure 7.1 American University Students in China, 2011–2022.

Source: Institute of International Education, Open Doors Report IIE ID374169, "US College and University Students Studying in China, 2011/12–2021/22," https://opendoorsdata.org.

to "reconsider travel because of arbitrary enforcement of local laws, including in relation to exit bans, and the risk of wrongful detentions."[64] A number of students note that the increased surveillance environment, monitoring of foreigners, internet restrictions, and dull propagandistic classroom content have all deterred many from wanting to go to China. Random and infrequent acts of violence against Americans is also concerning (four faculty members from Cornell College in Iowa were stabbed in a park in Jilin in northeast China in June 2024). Social life for foreign students has also deteriorated under Xi Jinping's xenophobic crackdown—China is no longer a fun place to study (as it once was).[65] Bars and clubs have been shuttered in many cities, and there is a sense of constant surveillance. For those who simply wish to learn Chinese, Taiwan has become an increasingly attractive alternative. Cost is another factor, as airplane tickets are exorbitantly expensive, tuition and rooming costs are not cheap, and there is often more financial support to study elsewhere in Asia or Europe.

Another increasing deterrent is the extreme difficulty of earning a security clearance with the US government if an American has lived in China for any significant period of time (months or years). US government agencies, particularly intelligence agencies, have a de facto bias against granting security clearances to such individuals—given the potential that they could have been recruited by Chinese intelligence agencies while studying in China. This is not an abstract fear. One well-known case involved a student (Glenn Duffie Shriver) who was recruited by the Ministry of State Security while studying Chinese in Shanghai. The MSS paid Shriver $70,000 to register for the Foreign Service exam (which he did but failed), and then paid him to try and join the CIA. Shriver met over 40 times with MSS handlers and was found out by the FBI, which has a video about the case on its website.[66] The Justice Department prosecuted Shriver, who was sentenced to 48 months in prison for conspiring to provide national security information to Chinese intelligence agents.[67]

Another cause has to do with the sharp curtailment in bilateral university-to-university student exchange programs by the Chinese side. In 2021, China's Ministry of Education abruptly curtailed 84 of the 286 university exchange programs Chinese universities had worldwide, 19 of which were with American universities.[68] Notwithstanding these terminations, four American universities maintain "campuses" and joint programs in China: NYU–Shanghai;[69] Duke–Kunshan;[70] the Stanford University Center at Beijing University;[71] and Johns Hopkins–Nanjing University.[72] These are all in-residence programs where significant numbers of American students stay for at least one term or semester, often earning dual institutional degrees. Two other unique programs are the Schwartzman College at Tsinghua University[73] and the Yenching Academy at Beijing University[74]—each of which trains a highly select group of foreign (not just American) students in year-long modules. Some intensive language programs also continue (the most notable of which is the Inter-University Program at Tsinghua University[75]). Some universities that have short-term exchange programs that send students to China for a semester have resumed post–COVID-19; one is my university (George Washington University), which sends about a dozen students to Fudan University in Shanghai for a semester or academic year as part of the "Global BA" program. Stanford University maintains a "Center" on the campus of Beijing University (a beautifully designed courtyard building) and it sent a group of 20 undergraduates to study there during the spring quarter of 2024. But these in-country programs are the exception to the norm. The University of Chicago and Cornell have both terminated their in-China programs on Renmin University campus in Beijing. Others, such as the University of Iowa and Ohio State University, suspended their in-China programs during COVID-19 and are uncertain if they will resume.

Given these factors, the opportunity costs for wanting to study in mainland China have risen. This *will* have a deleterious impact on American's future ability to understand China, with real potential implications for the next generation of China hands.[76] The US government's overly zealous—virtually default—denial of security clearances for Americans who have studied or conducted research in China seems particularly counterproductive. Rigorous background checks combined with polygraph exams should be enough to ferret out any traitorous spies. The US government—notably the State Department, intelligence agencies, FBI counterintelligence, and other law enforcement organs—are shooting themselves in the foot and handicapping America's ability to draw on the language skills and substantive expertise to understand and analyze the country's primary rival and (potential) adversary.

Scholarly Exchanges

The COVID-19 lockdowns in China also negatively affected opportunities for scholarly research and professional interactions for American scholars. Some of these interactions involved collaborative research (mainly in the sciences but also some in the social sciences). Without being able to travel back and forth or be in residence *in China*, much previous collaboration was brought to a halt. The Trump administration's abrupt termination of the Fulbright Program in mainland China and Hong Kong did not help.

Notwithstanding these logistical impediments, Xi's regime also instituted a variety of new regulations which posed further obstacles. Any Chinese university or research institute that seeks to hold an international conference has to apply *six* months in advance to a variety of central government organs (including the Ministry of Public Security) for permission. This includes submitting a full name list of foreign participants *and* transcripts of their intended speeches or paper presentations (this makes international conferences virtually impossible). Research fieldwork opportunities (the ability to physically visit or live in rural areas) have been almost completely terminated, and urban research is similarly constrained. The ability to conduct social surveys (which had always been constricted) are now next to impossible to carry out. Archives that had previously been open for research (notably the No. 1 Qing Archives in Beijing and the No. 2 Republican Archives in Nanjing) were abruptly closed to foreign researchers (and to many Chinese scholars too), while all central and many provincial archives on post–1949 PRC are similarly closed off. Interview opportunities with local and central-level officials require multiple levels of official permission and are rarely granted. Even public city and university libraries now restrict access to foreigners. Taken together, these restrictions have brought US scholarly research opportunities in China to a virtual halt. Despite these growing systemic and institutional restrictions, some American and Chinese scholars do continue to share data and carry out collaborative research with each other. This is particularly true in the natural and medical sciences, but also in some social sciences (notably economics and business) and in some areas of Chinese history.

While COVID-19 restrictions on travel to China are gradually being lifted at the time of writing, and a handful of conferences have begun to take place again (but some have also been abruptly canceled), it is still too early to say whether the Chinese authorities will permit a resumption of normal scholarly research in China.[77] This is very doubtful. Early indications are that the research environment remains very fraught, with strict "national security" laws and regulations affecting many areas of scholarship and research.[78] Some American scholars report being interrogated about their academic publications by Chinese Embassy and Consulate personnel when applying for a visa, while there have been some instances of scholars with visas in hand being refused entry into the country and forced to return to the United States on the next flight out.

The situation became even more serious on April 26, 2023, when Xi Jinping's regime suddenly unveiled an updated and expanded version of the Counter-Espionage Law (the initial version was issued in 2014). The new law dramatically expands the range of foreign activities in China that the authorities can investigate and prosecute. The foreign business community is directly affected, but so are foreign scholars. The new law includes instructions to Chinese security personnel for "search and seizure" of baggage, electronic devices (computers and cell phones), and other personal belongings, as well as physical raids on residences and offices. The extremely broad and elastic definitions of "national security" can apply to any kind of information normally collected by researchers.

The new draconian environment under Xi certainly also has significant implications for the election of research topics by foreign scholars and students. There is so much that is now *not researchable* inside of China—either through in situ fieldwork, in archives, in libraries, in personal interviews, and via electronic sources. China has significantly closed-up under Xi, reversing the opening-up of previous decades. The PRC government clearly does not want foreign scholars snooping around and conducting research. Xi Jinping's own broadside against what he terms "historical nihilism" (历史虚无主义) is a further restriction, as foreign research projects (if they are to be approved by the authorities, and *all* foreign research projects *must* be approved by the Chinese educational and public security authorities, which use very strict benchmarks of evaluation) must now conform to the new ideological dogmatism of "Xi Jinping Thought in the New Era." This affects a very wide range of fields, but certainly research on the history of the CCP (党史) and national history (国史).

The years when American and foreign scholars could roam the country by train and other means, live in villages, observe factory workers, interview officials, and other research modalities is over. The result is that, ironically, the field of contemporary China studies may be coming full circle and returning to a research environment not unlike the 1950s–1960s: peering into China from the outside.[79] This may require dusting off research tools used in the 1950s through 1970s.

This new research environment also has real implications for how American professors should advise their graduate students in selecting their PhD research topics and devising their research plans. Doing field research on many subjects inside of China now definitely carries a distinct risk to one's physical security and the real possibility of arrest and detention. The research environment in China has fundamentally changed and much for the worse.[80] It is thus incumbent on all researchers (regardless of field) to familiarize themselves with this new and risky environment, and not take such risks.

The Impact on American Universities

Universities have been a key sector in American engagement with China. The engagement in higher education dates back to the 1870s, when the first group of Chinese students came to America to study. This trend accelerated and deepened during the Republic of China era (1912–1949), but it was during this time that American universities began to sink deep roots inside of China itself.[81] The United States was *the* most important external actor in developing and shaping Chinese higher and professional education during these decades. These exchanges were terminated after 1949 by the new CCP regime. But, beginning in the 1980s, the ties were reactivated and became a core element of engagement. It has been a generally positive and mutually beneficial dimension of US–China relations. Yet, like so many other sectors and areas of Sino-American exchanges, educational exchanges have encountered substantial problems in recent years.

There is little doubt that American universities became important stakeholders and beneficiaries in "engagement" with China.[82] Benefits directly accruing to US universities and colleges included, first and foremost, several tens of millions of Chinese students who came to study and who paid (after the initial tranche in the 1980s) substantial tuition fees (Chinese students are estimated to contribute $15 billion per year to the American economy in tuition payments and expenditures).[83] A second substantial benefit was the high percentage who remained in the United States after graduation, many becoming American citizens and Green Card holders, thus contributing directly to American innovation, society, and the economy. A third benefit was the research collaboration that occurred between Chinese and American scholars across many fields, while Chinese graduate students filled the ranks of teaching assistants, mainly in STEM fields. Considerable numbers of Chinese graduates have entered academia themselves, diversifying and enriching the Academy. Fourth, US colleges and universities are the beneficiaries of contracts with Chinese businesses for a range of services. Disclosures made available by the US Department of Education indicated approximately 2,900 contracts with public universities valued at $2.32 billion between 2012 and 2024.[84] Fifth, while often very reticent to speak in class, Chinese students offered valuable perspectives to the American classroom and their classmates (if there was a problem, it was that Chinese students tend to live in a social bubble with other Chinese students and do not integrate well on campuses and in American society generally). The reluctance to speak in class has become worse in recent years, as "peer-monitoring" of mainland Chinese and Hong Kong students by each other has become a real problem.

Thus, heretofore, the teaching and training of Chinese students in American universities over the past several decades has accrued multiple direct benefits to the United States and indirectly to the advancement of research and knowledge in a variety of fields (thus being a contribution to humankind). Those students who have returned to China after completion of their studies have also directly contributed to the modernization and professionalization of their home country. Recalling the four purposes of the Engagement strategy outlined in Chapter 2, this was one of its principal purposes. Also, as discussed in Chapter 2, a corollary intended purpose (or hope) was that these returned students (known as "sea turtles" or 海归) would become agents of political liberalization and change. This has not occurred. Even if they had *wanted* to be such agents of change, the domestic dangers of trying to do so were a strong deterrent.

These benefits have existed for several decades; however, beginning in the 2010s, several concerning phenomena began to occur on American campuses, which have caused legitimate concern and have had the net effect of many universities and colleges pulling back on their engagement with China. Anyone interested in a full-scope examination of the China challenges confronting American universities, and sensible ways of coping with these challenges, should consult two studies: *A Preliminary Study of PRC Political Influence and Interference Activities in American Higher Education*, authored by Anastasya Lloyd-Damnjanovic and published by the Woodrow Wilson Center; and *University Engagement with China: An MIT Approach*, written by the Massachusetts Institute of Technology (MIT) China Strategy Group.[85] The challenges confronting US universities have included the following.

Confucius Institutes

Launched in 2004 under the Hanban (an organ of the Ministry of Education), China's Confucius Institute (CI) programs began to rapidly proliferate worldwide. By 2019, there were 110 CIs on American campuses (plus 501 Confucius Classrooms at the secondary school level). Their stated and intended purpose was to teach "Chinese language and culture." While the vast majority did concentrate on language instruction, controversies began to arise over teaching of the "cultural" dimension and the censorship imposed by CI instructors on classroom discussion of politically sensitive topics. However, accusations that the CI textbooks were teaching American students Communist propaganda were untrue; I personally reviewed all six levels of Hanban/CI textbooks and found *no* overt political content. Moreover, at most US institutions which had one, there was a firewall between the CI and the university's Chinese studies curriculum, and CI teachers were not members of faculty. There was, however, a problem, and it became a *real* problem: the public programming that many CIs undertook—which frequently were about "China-friendly" topics, hosted visiting Chinese scholars and officials, and they *never* permitted events that were critical of China or covered topics deemed sensitive by Chinese authorities (and most CIs had a CCP member in residence).

Criticism and scrutiny of CIs began to increase sharply after 2014, and they were criticized by Members of Congress (notably, Florida Senator Marco Rubio) as "trojan horses" peddling Chinese Communist propaganda, infiltrating US universities, and infringing on freedom of thought and education. The money received by recipient US institutions (on average between $50,000–$200,000 per year) was viewed by Members of Congress as suspect and more evidence of Chinese Communist infiltration of American campuses. A Senate investigation of CIs concluded that approximately $158 million was distributed by the Hanban to CIs in the United States between 2006 and 2018.[86] That is not pocket change for cash-strapped US colleges and universities.

As the controversy brewed, several state legislatures (e.g., Texas, Florida, and Pennsylvania) ordered CIs in their states to be terminated. Executive branch and Congressional investigations followed.[87] By 2019, Congress added a provision to the National Defense Authorization Act that any university or college that had a CI would not be eligible for simultaneous funding from the Department of Defense (DOD). This was a "showstopper" for the vast majority of universities that had CIs (including my own at George Washington University), even though DOD created a workaround waiver in certain instances.[88] Thus, during 2020–2022, the vast majority of CIs across the United States were quickly terminated. The calculation for university administrators was straightforward: maintain a CI and receive no funding from DOD and have your institutional reputation sullied with the US government and Congress—or close it down and stay in their good graces. Even on campuses where faculty and administrators exercised strict oversight of their CI (as we did at George Washington University), the downside risks vis-à-vis the US government were too high.

CSSAs, Communist Party Cells, and Ties to the PRC Embassy/Consulates

If CIs were generally benign and the dangers were overblown (in my view, although many disagree), a very real problem concerns ties between the PRC Embassy in Washington and Consulates in New York, Chicago, Los Angeles, San Francisco (and formerly Houston) with the Chinese Students and Scholars Association (CSSA) branches on most American campuses.[89] CSSAs began to be established as early as the 1980s, and as of 2019 CSSAs existed on 150 American college campuses.[90] CSSAs maintain *direct* ties to, maintain private communications with, and receive funding from, PRC diplomatic missions. CSSAs do not operate on a financial shoestring: PRC embassy and consulate funding varies (and is not disclosed), but in one shocking case it was revealed that the "Southwest CSSA"—which was established in 2003 and oversees campuses in California, Arizona, New Mexico, and Hawaii—filed for tax-exempt status as a public charity with the Internal Revenue Service (IRS) in 2016, and the tax forms required in the application reported $107,304 in "gifts and contributions" but no money was reported from fundraising or membership dues, nor was its list of "donors" disclosed.[91]

While CSSAs undertake a variety of on-campus activities for Chinese students (and other students interested in China) that are benign, such as organizing Chinese Lunar New Year celebrations, and they serve to assist newly arrived students from China—they also monitor and report to the embassy/consulates about on-campus activities (organized by other student groups or university programs) related to Taiwan, Tibet, Xinjiang, human rights in China, and similar topics. They also occasionally mobilize PRC students for public activities (to protest the Dalai Lama or to welcome visiting Chinese dignitaries), and often organize "study sessions" for Chinese students on "patriotic" topics and important CCP and government documents (such as Xi Jinping's speeches to the 19th and 20th Party Congresses).

Thus, CSSAs are the "eyes and ears" of the Chinese government and a CCP tool on American campuses. While there is considerable variation among CSSAs across the country, I strongly believe that they should all be terminated *immediately*. At a minimum, they should all be mandated to register under the Foreign Agent Registration Act (FARA).

In addition, many Chinese students and visiting scholars in the United States are members of the CCP, and there are many CCP cells that have been established on a number of US campuses.[92] This is not a new or recent issue—it dates back to a CCP directive from 1990 to establish Party cells on campuses in more than 20 countries.[93] This directive was updated in 2019, according to a *Financial Times* investigation: "In 2019, the Chinese Communist Party's Central Committee released a new rule requiring members studying abroad to 'contact' Party cells at home at least once every six months. A year later, the Communist Youth League began asking its 74 million members aged between 14 and 28 to 'regularly report personal situations' while studying abroad."[94] These Party members enforce "peer-monitoring" on campus, which has become a big problem worldwide.[95] I have personally witnessed this in my own classes at George Washington University. These Party cells also distribute information from China to Chinese students. One survey conducted by the *Financial Times* journalists indicated,

> In interviews, Chinese student party members in New York, Boston, California and Washington told the FT they followed the requests from Party cells in China as they were keen to maintain their membership, which they saw as an asset for their career development ... The students said they regularly received political study materials, ranging from President Xi Jinping's latest speeches to Party history, from Party cells back home. They also said they occasionally participated in online webinars on how to 'tell a good China story' to their American peers.[96]

I believe that these improper activities should also be investigated and curtailed.

Financial Donations

Another problematic dimension of Chinese ties to American universities involves funding from PRC sources.[97] Thanks to growing wealth accumulation in China, prosperous Chinese are beginning to develop the practice of philanthropy and to exercise giving both at home and abroad. This is potentially a good thing for American universities, but it also comes with distinct and serious risks. Of course, all institutions of higher education cultivate lifetime giving from both graduates and their families. Given the numbers of Chinese students matriculating from American universities and the wealth of many of their families back in China, as well as their own potential career earnings, Chinese donations have become a growing priority for university development officers. Such philanthropy is not always motivated purely by love for one's alma mater; there are often strings attached. Some Chinese graduates from US universities also seem to believe that they can ensure, or at least enhance, their own children's chances of acceptance into top colleges through charitable gifts.

The amounts of foreign charitable giving to US universities are large in total—so large that there are few accurate estimates. Section 117 of the Higher Education Act of 1965 requires all institutions of higher education to report any *single* foreign gift of more than $250,000 with the US Department of Education (DOE), and with IRS via Form 990. Until public and Congressional attention began to be drawn to the question of Chinese donations in 2019, American universities were often very lax in meeting their legally-mandated reporting obligations (in 2020, the DOE even admitted that as much as $6.5 *billion* in foreign donations had gone unreported by US universities).[98] The DOE data show that nearly one-quarter of the *reported* filings from 2014 to 2019 ($1.2 billion) came from sources in mainland China and Hong Kong.[99] Hong Kong has been a convenient source of such donations. Several US universities (e.g., MIT, Brown, University of Pennsylvania, and the University of California) have established separate "foundations" with offices in Hong Kong that give tax breaks to Hong Kong residents who contribute to these foundations ($26 million between 2014 and 2019). Because of their foreign domicile, these foundations are not required to inform the IRS of their donors. Despite the importance of Hong Kong as a pass-through for Chinese donors, gifts are also made directly.

Since 2019, when the media and Congress began to shine a spotlight on Chinese donations and DOE's incomplete (to put it mildly) enforcement, the Department, the IRS, and universities themselves, have all become more stringent and responsible in carrying out their legal obligations. Because of the large amounts involved and their lax reporting in the past, the DOE opened individual investigations into Harvard, Yale, and Stanford.[100] Figure 7.2 depicts the major recipient US universities.

Given the government's extensive role in China's economy, acceptance of all Chinese gifts and grants requires strict due diligence that should go above and beyond the standard practices currently employed by universities for other charitable giving.

This is also an issue with some Hong Kong–based or US-based foundations that are linked directly or indirectly to the Chinese government or to enterprises and families that have prospered with the help of the Beijing government. The most notable case is the China–United States Exchange Foundation

University	Total Donations	Chinese Donations	% Chinese
Harvard	$567.1	$196.6	34.7%
Yale	$369.2	$189.2	51.2%
Stanford	$311.5	$122.1	39.2%
Penn	$200.3	$95.0	47.4%
MIT	$564.0	$76.7	13.6%
Columbia	$188.0	$62.3	33.1%
NYU	$159.6	$56.7	35.5%
Chicago	$146.2	$46.6	31.9%
USC	$101.3	$43.6	43.0%
Cornell	$162.8	$42.8	26.3%
Caltech	$84.2	$37.6	44.7%
Princeton	$102.9	$37.4	36.4%
UC Berkeley	$124.9	$32.3	25.8%

Figure 7.2   Chinese Donations to Top American Universities.

Source: Hannah Reale, "China's Donations to US Universities," *The Wire China*, September 13, 2020, https://www.thewirechina.com/ wp-content/uploads/2020/09/Chinas-Donations-to-U.S.-Universities. pdf (Chinese donations to US universities, 2014–2019; donations include Hong Kong; data from US Department of Education).

(CUSEF).[101] CUSEF was established in 2008 on the initiative of former Hong Kong Chief Executive and shipping magnate Tung Chee Hwa (C. H. Tung) who is now Chairman Emeritus of the foundation. Tung has also served as Vice Chairman of the Chinese People's Political Consultative Conference (CPPCC), the CCP's highest-level united front organization, and he was a delegate to both the CCP's 19th and 20th Party Congresses in 2017 and 2022 respectively. CUSEF undertakes a range of programs aimed at Americans that can accurately be described as influence-seeking activities. As such, and to its credit, CUSEF has registered in the United States under the Foreign Agents Registration Act (FARA). Its lobbying activities include sponsoring all-expenses-paid tours of China for delegations composed of what the foundation's website refers to as "thought leaders," including journalists and editors, think-tank specialists, and city and state officials. CUSEF has not often collaborated with American universities and think tanks, but it did offer funding to the University of Texas at Austin for its China Public Policy Center. However, after receiving criticism from Senator Ted Cruz (R-Texas) and others, the university declined the grant. CUSEF grants have, however, gone to leading US think tanks—such as the Brookings Institution, the Carnegie Endowment for International Peace, and the Asia Society. There is no evidence, however, of CUSEF having influenced the published products of these organizations.

There have not yet been many offers by Chinese donors—private, corporate, or government—to fund faculty positions or centers for Chinese studies on US campuses. But there have been some. One instance that I know of came in 2014, when my university (George Washington) was approached by Fudan University in Shanghai with a proposal for a $500,000 *annual* grant to establish a Center for Chinese Studies in partnership with Fudan on the campus in the heart of Washington, DC. The Chinese side had three main conditions for the grant: (1) that a series of Chinese officials and other visitors would be given public platforms for frequent speeches; (2) that faculty from the Chinese partner university could teach China courses on the US university campus; and (3) that new Chinese studies courses would be added to the university curriculum. Although administrators and development officers were more than tempted, George Washington University turned down the lucrative offer (on the advice and united opposition of its Chinese studies faculty). In another instance in 2017, the Johns Hopkins University School of Advanced International Studies (SAIS) announced that it had received a substantial gift from CUSEF for an endowed junior faculty position, as well as program funding for a Pacific Community Initiative (SAIS administrators stated that there were no political or other strings attached to these grants). Georgetown University has also received CUSEF funding for its Initiative on US-China Dialogue on Global Issues, which also includes some faculty funding.

China is not the only authoritarian government that has given or facilitated gifts to American academic institutions or think tanks, but it is one of the wealthiest. There is little *direct* evidence that PRC-originated gifts have compromised the intellectual independence of the recipient institution, but it remains a danger. The trend toward large gifts from Chinese sources, many with some kind of government linkage, underscores the need for vigilance in enforcing a stricter code of due diligence and transparency on the part of university administrations and faculties.

Censorship and Self-Censorship

Another category of troubling Chinese influence on American campuses involves the vexing issue of self-censorship among scholars in Chinese studies. While they sometimes push the boundaries, intellectuals and professionals in China all intrinsically know how to self-censor and conform to the CCP's prescribed and proscribed criteria. This is described well in a much-quoted essay by Perry Link, who discussed censorship within China as the "anaconda in the chandelier" syndrome.[102] The majority of foreign scholars who study China have also learned long ago what topics and viewpoints to avoid while in China. But once outside of China and back in their home countries, these scholars have often been critical of the Chinese authorities and policies. Only in rare instances *prior* to the Xi Jinping era were foreign scholars and writers penalized or banned from China for things that they published abroad. This has changed in recent years, as the PRC government has considerably stepped-up monitoring of what foreign scholars and writers publish and say abroad. As a result, visas are more frequently denied, and a growing number of scholars now live under partial or complete bans. I know this personally, as I was put on an "invitation ban" list from 2015 to 2023 as a result of a single article that I published in *The Wall Street Journal*.[103] I describe this incident more fully in the Preface of this book. Other American scholars have endured similar banishment by the Chinese government. I am aware of a number of other American China specialists and former US government officials who are on a visa ban list (under no circumstances will they be given a visa, professional or tourist). State Department officials have informally told me that they are aware of 25–30 such Americans.

This newly politicized environment in China has cast a long shadow over American academia.[104] One informal survey evinced considerable reticence to return to China.[105] Some American scholars, led by Center for Strategic & International Studies's Scott Kennedy, have tried to draw attention to the negative impact that the paucity of scholarly exchanges with China potentially has had, and they have published a report calling for the "recoupling" of the US and Chinese scholarly communities.[106]

Pressure on Universities

Another related dimension has to do with Chinese government pressure on American universities. The Chinese government has demonstrated a penchant for using institutional collaborations as points of leverage when US universities have hosted the Dalai Lama or held other events deemed politically sensitive or offensive to the Chinese government. In such instances, existing collaborative exchange programs have been suspended or put on hold, planned visits of university administrators have been canceled, programs between university institutes and centers have been suspended, and Chinese students wishing to study at these US institutions have been counseled to go elsewhere. Such punitive actions resulting from campus visits by the Dalai Lama have been taken against Emory University, the University of Maryland, the University of California, San Diego, and others. At the University of Maryland, which hosted the Dalai Lama in 2013, there was temporary fallout, but then, following a graduation incident in 2017, the Chinese government again halted cooperation with Maryland, seriously damaging one of the most extensive university exchange programs with China. On four occasions of which I am personally aware, senior administrative officers at my university (George Washington) have been contacted by the Chinese Embassy to request that planned events on campus be canceled (two events concerning Taiwan, one concerning Xinjiang, and one concerning Tibet). In each case, my university refused, and the events took place as planned (although students twice reported that the events were being filmed by unknown individuals).

In the Classroom

Another growing problem concerns Chinese students who record or film classroom lectures and post it on the internet or social media. It is not that widespread of a problem (at the time of writing), but I personally had an experience with it in 2023, when a student in my Chinese Foreign Policy course posted a video clip on WeChat that he had surreptitiously taken on his cellphone of one of my lectures together with criticism of my lecture content (this was brought to my attention by another student and the offending student was reprimanded by GWU). The real problem, though, is that some Chinese students monitor *each other*—for saying things in class that transgress official Chinese policies. Chinese students have long been reticent to participate fully in class, but such peer monitoring has become more pronounced in recent years.

Such cases establish a worrying precedent of Chinese intrusion into American academic life. But, as with most American institutions and sectors of society, universities must wrestle with how to *continue* with their China relationships—while, at the same time, trying to put in place safeguards against malfeasance and establishing better reciprocity in the relationship. Cutting off educational relationships with China is a non-starter. The question is: *How* to properly manage them?

American universities' relationships with China are complex and involve all of the issues discussed in this section: managing branch campuses and joint university partnerships in China, Chinese students and organizations on US campuses, American students on Chinese campuses, American scholars attempting to conduct research in China, facilitating Chinese scholars' research in America while protecting national security, properly vetting (and reporting) donations from China, dealing with censorship and self-censorship, maintaining academic integrity and ethics, and other dimensions.

What to Do?

As a consequence of these issues gaining much greater prominence in recent years, a considerable number of individual American universities as well as organizations such as the Association of Universities (AAU), Association of Public and Land Grant Universities (APLU), American Council on Education

(ACE), American Association of State Colleges and Universities (AASCU), and the National Association of Independent Colleges and Universities (NAICU), have all undertaken efforts to better understand these challenges, to exchange information, and to put in place new standards and procedures (coordinated when possible) to cope with these challenges. After much deliberation and consultation, the AAU has published a very thoughtful and useful set of recommendations for American colleges and universities.[107] The Massachusetts Institute of Technology has undertaken a systematic study of the subject, also with well-reasoned recommendations.[108]

At the heart of these studies' recommendations are the interrelated core issues of keeping American universities open to students and researchers from other societies, and maintaining full freedom of academic inquiry in teaching, study, and research—which is fundamental to the mission of the liberal university— while simultaneously establishing safeguards to protect these freedoms against encroachments from China and other authoritarian states. Striking this balance is not easy, but it is imperative to the continued success of American higher education.

It would be profoundly self-defeating to close the doors (even partially) to students from China, India, or elsewhere. In recent years, the US government has been intentionally restricting visas and preventing about 3,000–5,000 Chinese students from enrolling in graduate studies in STEM (science, technology, engineering, mathematics) fields;[109] this is ultimately counterproductive. Concomitantly, it is not just a matter of continuing to attract students and researchers from abroad—but it is also a matter of *retaining* a large portion of them to stay to live and work in the United States after completion of their studies. In 2017, 90 percent of the STEM students from China who had earned their PhDs in the United States between 2000 and 2015 were still in the United States.[110]

Such retention in the case of Chinese graduates and those who had earned Green Cards and obtained citizenship long ago became much more fraught in the wake of the Justice Department's 2018–2022 "China Initiative."[111] This controversial program came under fire for racial profiling and witch-hunt-like prosecutions. As a result, the Justice Department revised and rebranded the program—but damage had been done. Perhaps the best-known case of overzealous investigations and prosecutions involved distinguished MIT mechanical engineering professor Chen Gang.[112] Professor Chen's case was illustrative of the stigma that Asian and Asian American researchers had begun to feel. A study commissioned by the Asian American Scholar Forum (which represents 7,000 scientists, researchers, and scholars) surveyed 1,304 scientists of Chinese descent employed by American universities and found that 72 percent did not feel professionally or physically safe in the United States, and many were considering returning to China.[113] Resignations from their US university appointments and departures to take up appointments in China began to rise sharply in 2020, when more than 1,400 US-trained Chinese scientists left the United States for China (a 22 percent increase from the previous year).[114]

Despite this negative trend, there have been real problems with US-based faculty who participate in China's Thousand Talents program (simultaneously holding remunerated faculty positions in American and Chinese universities), double-dipping by receiving grants from China's government and corporate sector (thus circumventing US law and university regulations), illicit technology transfer, intellectual property theft, and (in some cases) espionage.

These myriad challenges to American higher education related to China have come seemingly suddenly to US universities in recent years—but they have also had a very salutary and positive effect. University administrators were "asleep at the switch" before; now, many administrators are awake and aware of the downsides and lurking dangers of US academic relationships with China. Universities' compliance with DOE and IRS reporting requirements has been improved, while liaison with the FBI has improved where warranted.[115] Many universities have now instituted new annual reporting requirements for faculty concerning conflicts of interest. On the other hand, such external and internal oversight can go too far and have the unintended result of impinging on legitimate collaborative research (in non-sensitive fields) between American and Chinese scholars and scientists. Both educational exchanges and scholarly collaboration *are legitimate* and should not be choked off.

The main challenge going forward will be to spread "best practices" from the handful of universities that have "woken up" and put in place a set of new guidelines and policies to the large majority of colleges and universities which are still not up-to-speed. The MIT blueprint and the Hoover Institution study's recommendations should serve as sensible points of departure.[116]

The Business Community

$758.4 *billion*: this stunning figure is much of what one needs to know about the US–China commercial relationship. This was the figure for total trade in goods and services between the two countries in 2022.[117] The next most important figure to know is $367.4 billion (also 2022).[118] That is the total deficit that the United States ran in goods trade with China ($562.9 billion in imports minus $195.5 billion in exports). Two other relevant figures are $126.1 billion (total stock of US foreign direct investment in China) and $28.7 billion (total stock of PRC FDI in America).[119]

From these figures, three things are clearly evident. First is the sheer *magnitude* of US–China trade (China does more trade on aggregate with the European Union and with the Association of Southeast Asian Nations, but they are collectivities of multiple states, while the US trades more with Canada and Mexico than with China). The stakes are huge. The US–China Business Council claims that "one million Americans make a living out of exporting to China,"[120] although US Secretary of Commerce Gina Raimondo says that "China is now our third largest export market and those exports support 750,000 American jobs."[121] Second is the deep *asymmetry* of the gargantuan deficit that the United States runs with China ($367.4 billion), which is not sustainable (at least politically). Third, the *differences* in total stock of FDI reveals just *how long* the United States has been investing in China and just *how much* it has invested in China's modernization, while the relative dearth of Chinese FDI in the United States shows that it is a latecomer and relatively uninfluential (many other countries invest far more in the US than the PRC does).

Clearly, the US–China commercial relationship is of enormous importance to the United States. The United States has traded with China since 1784, when the clipper ship *Empress of China* sailed from Boston to Guangzhou. The sheer size of China's population and consumer market has tantalized Western business since the 19th century, when John D. Rockefeller's Standard Oil Company sold its first kerosene lamps in China in 1863 and salivated over the prospects of "oil for the [millions of] lamps in China."[122] Fast-forward 150 years, and the rationale for American business being in China is now more multifaceted beyond consumer sales. As Craig Allen, President of the US–China Business Council, described it to me,

China is 17 percent of the world's population, and it is responsible for about 30 percent of global growth. China is the largest market for nearly everything and we need to be there if we are to be globally competitive. We need China's economies of scale. We need Chinese talent. China is the only place that has the scale to perform a number of critical industrial steps. China is totally integrated into Asia and the world, and we would be noncompetitive if we were not there. We are not in China because we are greedy or craven. We are there because we must be. If we are not there, American competitiveness will be severely impacted. If we are not in China, the Europeans, Japanese, and Koreans will eat our lunch, and America will seriously lose our competitive position on a global basis. If we are not there, inflation would be much higher, especially for low-income Americans.[123]

Trade, investment, and the economic/commercial dimension of the US–China relationship seemed hardly important when the two countries embarked on their relationship back in 1972. Two-way trade in that year totaled only $95.9 million. Ambassador John Negroponte recalls some State Department officials wondering at the time, "What are we going to buy from these people?"[124] Given the laggard state of China's economy then, such skepticism can be forgiven—but, clearly, no one foresaw the extraordinary and explosive growth in the commercial relationship over the subsequent half century. Nor did anyone anticipate the historically unprecedented modernization of China's economy, and the significant contributions that the United States has made to China's development. The United States has been instrumental in the PRC's economic and technological development (to say nothing of American contributions to the Chinese higher educational system, medical system, legal system, scientific research, civil society, and many professional sectors). However, I have never once heard or read a Chinese official or scholar crediting—much less thanking—the United States for the instrumental role that it has played in China's modernization. To be certain, it is the Chinese people *themselves* who are due the vast majority of the credit for their nation's remarkable economic progress—but foreign nations (led by the United States, Europe, Japan, and South Korea) have all been important additive factors, while Russia has been a very significant source of assistance to China's military modernization.

It is not necessary here to retell the lengthy saga—and ups and downs—of the American business experience in China. This has been done ably by Randall Stross,[125] Jim Mann,[126] Charles W. Freeman III,[127] Craig Allen,[128] Jim McGregor,[129] and others. Nor is it necessary to retell the broadly positive and important role that the US business community played over five decades in the broad process of American "engagement" with China. Indeed, it is fair to say (and many have said it) that the business community has been *the* main ballast in the relationship—which has served as a steadying influence when the relationship experienced shocks and strains in other dimensions of relations.

It is thus also fair to say that it has been the American business community which has been the most important advocate for better US–China relations. Fair or foul weather, the business community has never wavered in its unvarnished support for US engagement with China. Whether this is a good or bad thing, it is a fact. Personally, I have serious questions and deep doubts about the role that American business has played in recent years (post–2017) in the broader context of the relationship. That is, as the relationship has broadly deteriorated and many other sectors of American society have come to openly question the direction of—and their relations with—China under Xi Jinping, the business community has remained the single greatest continuing advocate for US relations with China. *Never* do they *ever* publicly criticize China. This has not only been the case during Xi Jinping's tenure—the tendency toward self-censorship dates back decades. Some would call this craven self-interest (to make money) and putting profits over conscience. Others put a more positive gloss on it. Craig Allen, the President of the US–China Business Council claims that, "We have confidence that the success of US business in China will benefit both countries, both peoples, and contribute to overall geopolitical stability ... [Yet] at the end of the day, the United States and China are going to collaborate in the service of humanity, or we fail to collaborate—to the detriment of humanity."[130] Such inflated rhetoric is delusory. Despite encountering difficulties in recent years, the business community continues to be *the primary* advocate of US engagement with China. No other constituency comes close.

Yet, just like every other sector in the United States and every other constituency in the Engagement Coalition, the business community's relations with China have hit rocky waters in recent years and significant strains have emerged in the commercial relationship. American corporations, companies, and commercial entities have all experienced considerable new obstacles (recognizing that there have *always* been obstacles) in doing normal business in China. Thus, the US commercial footprint in China is shrinking, frustrations and fears of doing business in China have grown, profits are relatively reducing, some companies are relocating their manufacturing facilities and supply chains to other countries, many are not putting *new* investments into China, and there now exists a distinct nervousness and uncertainty never previously present in the C-Suites and corporate boardrooms of American companies.

This section of the chapter tries to unpack the complexities (and contradictions) facing American businesses in China today. It does so in three subsections: macro evaluations of the business climate in China; impediments to doing business in China; and the degree of pullback and "decoupling" by US businesses from China.

The Climate for US Business in China

There are several annual surveys of American businesses in China that provide good longitudinal data and qualitative perspectives about the conditions on the ground generally affecting corporate experiences, decision-making, and profitability. Among these, the American Chambers of Commerce in Beijing and Shanghai (AMCHAM) and the US–China Business Council (USCBC) are the most consistent over time, detailed in their survey methodologies, and valuable in their findings.

Overall, these surveys have noted significant and secular declines in business confidence in recent years. In its survey from September 2023 of 325 member companies, Shanghai AMCHAM found that just 52 percent were "optimistic" about their five-year business outlooks—an all-time low since the surveys began in 1999. The decline has also been rapid, falling from the confidence rate of 78 percent as recently as 2021. Some 68 percent of respondents claimed profitability in 2022, the lowest in 15 years, but less than half saw their revenues grow during the year.[131]

AMCHAM China (Beijing) found in its survey from 2024 of 343 member companies that their confidence level was divided over China's investment environment between "improving" (28 percent), "deteriorating" (35 percent), and "staying the same" (37 percent), while 39 percent of companies reported feeling "less welcome" in the country.[132] Market access (lack of), regulatory enforcement, public procurement, and licensing practices were the main areas of "unfair treatment" reported by the companies surveyed. Overall, the top five business challenges identified were (highest to lowest) rising tensions in US–China relations; inconsistent regulatory interpretation and unclear laws and enforcement; rising labor costs; concerns about data security; and increasing competition from privately-owned Chinese companies.[133] Only 49 percent claimed that their China operations were profitable.

The USCBC's member survey from 2023 yielded findings similar to AMCHAM.[134] The top ten identified challenges were (in order) (1) Geopolitics and US–China relations; (2) data, personal information, and cybersecurity rules; (3) export controls, sanctions, and investment screening; (4) competition with Chinese companies (private and state-owned); (5) licenses and approvals; (6) uneven enforcement of laws and regulations; (7) international travel; (8) transparency (lack of); (9) intellectual property protection; (10) China's industrial policy.[135] The USCBC survey has long been known for its relatively more optimistic character (as compared with AMCHAM Beijing), but the survey of 2023 was distinctly and unprecedently gloomy. Of the 117 companies surveyed, 43 percent indicated that the business environment was "deteriorating," while 39 percent said it was "not improving," and only 19 percent found it to be "improving" (over 2022).[136] The five-year outlook for their businesses in China registered 49 percent positive, 23 percent neutral, and 28 percent negative. Thirty-five percent reported declining profitability in 2023, with 21 percent unchanged, and 44 percent enjoying increased profitability.

Despite considerable nervousness and a high sense of unpredictability, 58 percent of companies reported no prospective change in their "resource commitments" into China, 18 percent said they will decrease, and 25 percent said they will increase investments. Significantly, 79 percent reported no plans to move any or all of their operations out of China, while 23 percent did plan to move to other countries or "home-shore" to the United States.[137]

Clearly, many name-brand American firms continue to do well and to *expand* in China. Starbucks currently operates 6,000 stores across the country and has announced its intention to open an additional 3,000 by 2025 (this ambitious goal amounts to opening a new store every nine hours until reaching 9,000).[138] China accounted for a significant percentage of US multinationals' global earnings in 2022: Apple (19 percent), Corning Materials (33 percent), Texas Instruments (55 percent), Wynn Resorts (70 percent).[139] Walmart's revenue in China increased 225 percent between 2015 and 2022, Nike's by 190 percent, and Nvidia's by 650 percent.[140] On the other hand, IT firms Amazon, Google, Yahoo, and LinkedIn are all unwilling to operate in mainland China.

Indeed, many companies are reducing their exposure in China and they are preparing for uncertain contingencies. In 2023, foreign direct investment (FDI) fell to its lowest level in 30 years. Apple and Google have already shifted some production of their smartphones to India and Vietnam respectively.[141] In the case of Apple, it is not only a question of the increased difficulties of doing business in China, it also has to do with declining sales of Apple products to Chinese consumers who seem to have soured on Apple's brand. For the decade between 2012 and 2022, China was the second-largest market for iPhones after the United States, accounting for 20 percent of the company's worldwide sales.[142] In the first quarter of 2024, iPhone sales in-country declined by 25 percent.[143] Part of Apple's recent problems in the Chinese market have to do with increased domestic competition, particularly from Huawei and Xiaomi. Increased domestic competition has also directly impacted Elon Musk's Tesla production and sales in China, which also fell by 19 percent during the first quarter of 2024, as electric vehicles (EVs)produced by Chinese firms BYD and SAIC have gained substantial market share—which Musk publicly criticized (which did not endear him to the PRC government). Musk and Tesla, which bet big on China and their Shanghai production plant, are finding themselves increasingly sidelined in the Chinese marketplace and cold-shouldered by Chinese officials.[144]

While relatively few firms are pulling out of China altogether, most are limiting their China exposure.[145] This is referred to as the "China Plus" strategy: stay in China (because of huge sunk costs and continued, albeit declining, profitability) but diversify to other countries. This trend seems to be intensifying. Southeast Asia, South Asia, central Europe, Mexico, and Latin America are the prime beneficiaries. Most companies have drawn up contingency plans for relocating production and supply chains on relatively short notice, if necessary. A declining number remain profitable (earnings of General Motors in China have fallen by almost 70 percent since 2014[146]). Thus, there is an apparent disconnect in the USCBC survey between the long list of corporate concerns and their declining profitability, yet nearly 79 percent say they remain committed to staying in China. Still, the 23 percent which are relocating operations is a significant empirical indicator of the deteriorating business climate, and it will be important to watch this factor carefully going forward.

Other surveys provide a wider aperture to include a mixture of American and European firms with operations in China. Such, for example, was a survey from November 2023 of 35 China-based CEOs by The Conference Board (a New York-based business think tank and NGO), which revealed that CEO "confidence level" dropped precipitously during the year—from 72 percent confidence level in early 2023 to only 54 percent by the end of the year (a score below 50 reflects more negativity than positivity).[147] Consequently, the survey found, 40 percent of CEOs anticipated a decrease in their capital investments in 2024. Not only are CEOs not planning to expand their investments, but Chinese government data also reveal that international firms *withdrew* more than $160 billion in total investment from China during 2022–2023.[148] Total FDI into China has radically plummeted since 2021. According to Chinese government data, *total* FDI (from all countries) in 2023 was only $33 billion, the lowest since 1993 in the aftermath of the Tiananmen massacre.[149] FDI declined by 80 percent year-on-year from 2022 to 2023 and—for the first time ever—FDI registered a decline during the fourth quarter of 2023.[150] This is stunning in both speed and scope, and reminds one of the dialogue between two characters in Ernest Hemingway's 1926 novel *The Sun Also Rises*, when Bill asks his friend, "How did you go bankrupt?" to hear Mike's response, "Two ways—gradually and then suddenly." The rapidity of the decline in FDI is stunning enough, but even more so when one considers the *decades* of high-volume FDI inflows—which, since 2005, have ranged between $100–$350 billion annually,[151] and have *averaged* about $138 billion per year from 2012 to 2022.[152]

The environment for American and foreign businesses in China is getting worse—much worse.[153] AMCHAM Shanghai's annual member survey from 2023 noted, "2023 was supposed to be the year investor confidence and optimism bounced back. That has simply not materialized. Instead, business sentiment has continued to deteriorate."[154] As Jim McGregor—an extremely experienced and savvy American who has lived and worked in China for more than three decades as a journalist, businessman, business consultant, and author of *One Billion Customers: Lessons from the Frontlines of Doing Business in China*—observed to Tom Friedman of *The New York Times*, "The US business community loved China—there were always tensions, but there used to be a sense of opportunity and partnership. For China to turn the business community sour on China took hard work, but China did it."[155]

Impediments for American Business in China

The bloom has clearly worn off the rose when it comes to foreign investor confidence about China. There are many reasons for this. Some reasons are more general and pertain to the many negative macroeconomic indicators afflicting China's economy. Among other warning signs, these include:

- Difficulty in meeting the 5 percent GDP growth target in 2023 (it grew by 5.2 percent). Looking ahead, it will be difficult to sustain even this level (while the PRC government predicts growth "around 5 percent" in 2024, the World Bank predicts growth of only 4.5 percent and IMF 3.9 percent over the next five years).
- Loss of consumer confidence and consumption spending. In 2022, consumer spending (so-called final consumption) accounted for 53.2 percent of GDP, and the Chinese government has been relying on this element (along with an expanded service sector and innovation) as the three pillars to power China's economy through the "middle income trap." After rising from 2010 to 2019, a secular decline began thereafter.[156]
- The Debt-to-GDP ratio is now around 300 percent. That is "red light flashing" territory, with major property developer giants like Evergrande and Country Garden having defaulted on their debts ($300 billion and $186 billion in liabilities in 2021 and 2023, respectively). The weak real estate demand is sharply exacerbating the problem (the Rhodium Group estimates that China has 23 to 26 million unsold apartments). The IMF estimates that China's local governments are $9 trillion in debt for infrastructure financing alone.
- Exports fell for the *first* time in 2023 (-4.6 percent), imports were off -5.5 percent, while inbound FDI is way down as noted earlier (only $22 billion for that year). Meanwhile, capital outflows are surging ($11.8 billion in the third quarter of 2023 alone, according to the PRC's State Assets and Foreign Exchange Administration) as Chinese try hard to move their assets overseas and find safe havens for investment.
- A declining birth rate (China's population actually declined in 2022 for the first time since the Great Leap Forward famine in 1960).
- The high youth unemployment rate is the fifth highest in the world (21.3 percent, although some estimates are as high as 50 percent). China's youth ages 16–24 face very gloomy job prospects, have a very hard time finding marriage partners, and have very difficult prospects of buying an apartment.
- Pensioners are really feeling squeezed, and the savings rate—once the highest in the world—is slipping.

- The commercial sector is filled with "zombie companies" (those that require government subsidies to survive) as Xi Jinping's pro-state growth policies continue to discriminate against the private sector generally and the tech sector specifically.

While these are all very concerning indicators that signal a dramatically weakening economy, bear in mind that in 2023 it was still a $17.89-trillion economy in nominal terms with very deep pockets and reserves ($3.1 trillion).

There are also some reasons for the increased pessimism that pertain to a variety of concerning steps recently taken against foreign businesses and American businesses specifically. Long-standing problems include: intellectual property right (IPR) theft, bureaucratic red tape and regulatory obstacles to investment and in-country distribution, a capricious legal environment, an uneven playing field tilted in favor of domestic Chinese companies that enjoy industrial policy subsidies and other protection from foreign competition, and outright blocks on certain foreign companies. These are not new problems, and they have bedeviled US businesses for decades.

Yet, a new set of recent and troubling actions by Chinese government authorities have added to these ongoing concerns:

New restrictions on cross-border data flows. [157] These new regulations make it unclear if branch offices and facilities of foreign firms in China can legally transmit data to their home companies abroad. How are firms to efficiently operate with this concern? Even without it, the propensity of China's security services to monitor foreign email communications makes normal operating procedures worrisome, while there have been multiple instances of cross-border ZOOM meetings being monitored—and interrupted—by China's cyber police.[158]

Security service raids on the offices of US companies. In 2023 alone the consulting firms Bain & Co., Capvision, and the Mintz Group were all raided by local PRC government security services.[159] Among other jobs, these firms conduct "due diligence" on Chinese firms that are potential joint venture partners or are preparing to list on the Hong Kong or foreign stock exchanges.

Exit bans placed on foreigners "under investigation" by the authorities and *increased detentions of foreigners.*[160] The Dui Hua Foundation (a very credible independent American NGO based in San Francisco) keeps close track of detained Americans in China, and in December 2024 it estimated that there were more than 200 Americans imprisoned in Chinese jails and at least 30 others who were subject to exit bans. This has become a real problem not only for those detained or banned from leaving the country, but the risks have become a serious deterrent to expatriates thinking about working in—or even traveling to—China. Accordingly, the US State Department has issued a Level 3 Travel

Advisory for China (the ban was downgraded to Level 2 in November 2024 following a US–China prisoner swap which brought three Americans, who had been convicted of crimes in Chinese courts, home:[161]

Summary: Reconsider travel to Mainland China due to the arbitrary enforcement of local laws, including in relation to exit bans, and the risk of wrongful detentions. Exercise increased caution when traveling to the Hong Kong SAR due to the arbitrary enforcement of local laws. Reconsider travel to the Macau SAR due to a limited ability to provide emergency consular services. Exercise increased caution when traveling to the Macau SAR due to the arbitrary enforcement of local laws.

Increased censorship pressures. Self-censorship is nothing new for American or foreign companies in China, as they have long learned (unfortunately) that any public criticisms of Chinese government policies or actions that "hurt the feelings of the Chinese people" will immediately, directly, and negatively impact their operations in China. The USCBC member company survey from 2023 found that 45 percent of companies felt increasing pressure to make (or not make) statements about politically sensitive issues. Foreign businesses simply cannot operate in China if they do not self-censor, issue no criticisms, and remain silent. That (ethically bankrupt) complicity is the cost of doing business there. Recent instances include Marriott Hotels, the owners of the NBA's Houston Rockets and Golden State Warriors, Intel, Disney, Starbucks, Calvin Klein, and Coach—who have *all* had to make public apologies after either statements by their executives or their websites' depictions of Taiwan and/or Hong Kong were found to be offensive by Chinese authorities.[162] Big Hollywood studios have long been known to censor movie scripts so as not to offend Beijing, lest they lose the rare opportunity to distribute films inside China (only six American films are permitted for domestic distribution every year).[163] Many apparel companies (notably, Nike) have found themselves caught between a rock and a hard place to comply with the Uyghur Forced Labor Prevention Act of 2020.

Not only do corporate executives commit self-censorship, but some go out of their way to fawn praise on China's government and leaders. It is one thing—and bad enough—to self-censor in order to do business in China—but it is even worse to say flattering things about the Chinese government and its leaders in order to stay in their good graces. This practice might be called "pandering to the panda."

Take, for example, the Greenbergs—Hank and Evan—the father-son magnates of the US insurance industry (AIG and Chubb).[164] The Greenbergs have been unabashed advocates of US–China engagement and US business with China for decades, and the Greenberg's C.V. Starr Foundation has donated millions to organizations that promote such engagement. Another example is Stephen Schwartzman, the Wall Street financier, CEO of The Blackstone Group (which manages over $1 trillion in assets), who founded the Schwartzman College at Tsinghua University with a $117 million gift (loosely modeled on the Rhodes Scholars at Oxford, Schwartzman Scholars spend one academic year at the college).[165] Yet another example is John Thornton, a former senior executive at Goldman Sachs, Chairman of the Board of Trustees of both the Asia Society and the Brookings Institution (after whom the Brookings China Center is named), and currently Executive Chairman of Barrick Gold. In 2003, Thornton decamped to Beijing, where he taught at the Tsinghua University Business School for a number of years, while serving as an adviser to the Chinese government—which bestowed the Friendship Award of the PRC on him in 2008 (the highest honor accorded to foreign nationals).[166] Thornton shares this dubious distinction with Vladimir Putin, Raúl Castro, Nursultan Nazarbayev, and several others. Another example is Steve Wynn, the casino mogul, Republican Party megadonor, and owner of Wynn Resorts (70 percent of its global revenue comes from the Macao hotels/casinos). Wynn became so publicly sycophantic of China and Xi Jinping that the US Justice Department sued him in 2022 for his failure to register under FARA.[167]

All of these individuals have gone out of their way to praise and pander to the Chinese government, its leaders, and their policies. In return, they have had very high-level access to China's leaders and have made a considerable amount of money. These individuals are hardly unique. One could add to the list many other Wall Street tycoons. The moral to the story is, if you want to get along with China and get things done in China, do not criticize China—if you want to be really successful, go out of your way to publicly praise China (one can only assume that they lavish praise in closed-door meeting with Chinese officials).

Human resource barriers. Add to these new and recent impediments the rising costs of salaries for in-country hires coupled with the increased difficulty of attracting and retaining expatriates to live and work in China (and Hong Kong). Maintaining and paying staff in China directly impacts firms' cost of operations and profit margins. It has been increasingly difficult for foreign multinationals to find the qualified expatriates to send to China—and when they can find them, the combined costs of airfares, salaries, office and apartment rents, international schools, cooks/cars/drivers and office staff, all add up. The difficulties began in the decade of the 2000s, when the air pollution in Beijing and other cities became seriously life-threatening. Then came COVID-19—when many expats stayed in-country (because their jobs were there) and tried to endure the draconian lockdowns, but many also left.[168]

Legal deterrents. The recently revised Anti-Espionage and State Secrets Laws have serious implications for American and foreign businesses. The former was first promulgated in 2014, and the latter was originally issued in 1988 and last updated in 2010. In July 2023, a considerably revised version of the Anti-Espionage Law was adopted, while an updated version of the State Secrets Law adopted on May 1, 2024. It is important to note that these two laws are just the latest in a series of 15 security-related laws passed in recent years. Collectively, they have become a huge concern, and deterrent, to foreign businesses in China.

The revised Anti-Espionage Law caused considerable consternation in the business and diplomatic communities, and it attracted widespread critical media coverage around the world.[169] The updated law expands the definition of espionage to cover "all documents, data, materials, and articles concerning national security and interests as included for protection." This expanded definition is important because it could be applied to market research, business intelligence, and "due diligence" firms. One interpretation of the law's broad, ambiguous, and elastic definitions of "national security" described these potential applications:

Corporations doing business with the US government might be deemed to be conducting intelligence activities. Market research and business intelligence might now be considered espionage if documents, data, materials, and items related to national security are involved. Hiring a former government official might constitute coercion. Hiring anyone with knowledge of issues related to national security or relevant technologies might subject a corporation to investigation and sanction. Foreign firms involved in technology collaborations with Chinese enterprises may violate the law if their collaboration relates to national security. Corporate users of data centers and cloud services in China might be investigated if that data relates to national security.[170]

Lester Ross, a longtime lawyer and expert in Chinese law who has resided in Beijing for three decades, observed about the new law:

Enforcement of the law is to be led by state security organs with support from police and relevant agencies handling state secrets and military matters. However, the enumeration of acts that constitute espionage in the revised law actually lacks specificity regarding the activities' relationship to national security. This potentially makes the provision of any information or data that has not been published in officially licensed media subject to a possible allegation of espionage. Indeed, even web scraping or accessing material previously in the public domain but subsequently withdrawn might potentially constitute espionage as information removed from the public domain may subsequently be deemed to constitute a national secret. Furthermore, under Article 10 of the revised law, any foreign organization, entity or individual, and anyone who aids them in the gathering of information that is deemed to relate to national security, is potentially vulnerable to investigation for espionage. Considering that national security in other documents has been defined to comprise at least 16 separate categories of activity deemed related to national security [it] is very broad.[171]

In 2024, China's government updated its State Secrets Law to include a new and broad category of "work secrets" (工作保密).[172] This term could literally include any information related to technology, manufacturing designs, or other normal workplace data.

Taken together, these two newly revised laws—plus the 13 others concerning "national security" (国家安全), have sent chills throughout the foreign business community, law firms, and embassies in China, as well as the home domiciles of multinationals.

As if these concerns of American businesses operating in China are not enough—then there is Taiwan. A mainland military attack on Taiwan, combined with all of the horrific potential consequences, would have devastating effects on American and foreign businesses operating in both mainland China and Taiwan, as well as global economic and technological disruptions. In probably the most informed assessment available, The Rhodium Group (a very high-quality research firm based in New York City) *conservatively* estimates the direct global economic impact of an attempted blockade of the island alone would amount to at least $9 trillion in lost commerce, to say nothing of "the ripple effects from trade and supply chain disruptions."[173] As the world's 16th largest trading economy, and one that is 100 percent reliant on trade by sea and air, a blockade would be devastating for Taiwan. Taiwan is also home to TSMC, the world's most cutting-edge silicon chip fabrication company. Here, the Rhodium study concludes,

A rough, conservative estimate of dependence on Taiwanese chips suggests that companies in these industries could be forced to forego [*sic*] as much as $1.6 trillion in revenue annually in the event of a blockade. Beyond the immediate effect on corporate revenues from lost semiconductor production, the global economy would face significant second-order impacts that would likely add trillions more in economic impact. Many industries depend on the availability of goods and equipment containing Taiwanese chips. These include e-commerce, logistics, ride-hailing, entertainment, and other industries that collectively employ tens of millions of people. Spare parts and components for critical public infrastructure, such as telecommunications and medical devices, could become scarce. Ultimately, the full social and economic impacts of a chip shortage of that scale are incalculable, but they would likely be catastrophic.[174]

In the event of a Taiwan conflict, most American firms would be compelled to comply with US government directives. In September 2022, the chief executives of America's three largest banks—JP Morgan Chase, Bank of America, and Citigroup—testified before Congress, and all committed to comply with any US government demand to pull out of China if Taiwan were attacked.[175] These banks' exposure in China is substantial: together with Morgan Stanley, the four banks had a combined exposure of $48 billion in China in 2022 (although down 16 percent from 2021).[176]

To De-risk or Decouple?

Given all of these risks and challenges facing American businesses operating in and with China, it is appropriate to consider the question whether the United States should not—to some extent—"decouple" its interdependent economy from China's. The Trump administration offered a guarded "yes," but the emphatic response from the Biden administration was a succinct "no." Secretary of the Treasury Janet Yellen in particular went out of her way to deliver this message explicitly on several occasions.[177] As she told the US–China Business Council's Golden Jubilee Gala dinner in December 2023, "I and other US officials have repeatedly stated that the United States does not seek to decouple from China. This would be damaging to both our economies and would have negative global repercussions."[178] Secretary Yellen was the "good cop" in the Biden administration's China policy, while other cabinet secretaries (the Secretaries of State, Defense, Justice, and Commerce) were the proverbial "bad cops" in forthrightly criticizing China's behavior in different domains. Even still, in her speeches, Secretary Yellen made crystal clear that the US would prioritize "national security" over commerce when necessary.

On the other hand, the United States *is* pulling back in its commercial relationship with China. It has become fashionable to refer to this as "de-risking" rather than decoupling. The term "de-risking" was coined by European Commission President Ursula von der Leyen in an important speech in March 2023 (probably the single most important speech *ever* given about China by any European Union official).[179] De-risking involves a number of proactive and defensive measures intended to insulate and protect one's economy and technological base from malign and predatory Chinese policies and actions.

In a major speech about the US–China commercial and economic relationship at MIT in November 2022, Secretary of Commerce Gina Raimondo described how she saw the overall macro situation:[180]

> Over the past decade, China's leaders have made clear that they do not plan to pursue political and economic reform and are instead pursuing an alternative vision for their country's future. They are committed to *increasing* the role of the state in society and the economy, constraining the free flow of capital and information, and decoupling economically in a number of areas, including many technology sectors of the future. They have firewalled their data economy from the rest of the world. And they are accelerating their efforts to fuse their economic and technology policies with their military ambitions. China today poses a set of growing challenges to our national security. It is deploying its military in ways that undermine the security of our allies and partners and the free flow of global trade. It dominates the manufacturing of many critical elements and goods and has exploited other economies' dependence on its market for political coercion. It also seeks to dominate certain advanced technology sectors, while using many of those technologies to advance its military modernization and undermine fundamental human rights at home and abroad.

Then, Secretary Raimondo laid out concrete specific steps that the Biden administration was taking to "de-risk":

> Together with the private sector, we are going to bolster our system of export controls, enhance our investment screening regimes, strengthen our supply chain resiliency, and develop innovative solutions to counter China's economic coercion and human rights abuses. We have released a set of rules that impose systematic and technology-specific Export controls to limit China's ability to purchase and manufacture certain very advanced computing chips that are used to train large-scale artificial intelligence models, and which power the country's advanced military and surveillance systems, as well as the manufacturing equipment used to make these cutting-edge chips. We are also modernizing our review of inbound investment ... to direct a focus on certain critical new risk factors when evaluating potential inbound investment, such as technological leadership, supply chain dependency, and foreign company access to our personal data. I also want to underscore the priority that we are placing on ensuring that our companies are not complicit in China's gross human rights abuses.

In the summer of 2023, Secretary Raimondo traveled to Beijing and Shanghai. While her public statements during the trip were measured but clear about the need for a "level playing field" and the Chinese government to remove barriers to trade and investment, she did make headlines by proclaiming, prior to her departure, "Increasingly I hear from American business that China is [now] *uninvestable* because it has become too risky."[181] Indeed, instead of investing into China, foreign firms have *withdrawn* $160 billion in total earnings from China during six successive quarters from April 2022 through September 2023.[182] In October 2023, foreign investors pulled an additional $8.8 billion from Chinese stocks and bonds.[183] Even Silicon Valley venture capitalists have gotten cold feet about investing in China's tech industry.[184]

Xi Jinping had a golden opportunity to reassure Corporate America at a gala dinner organized by the US–China Business Council and National Committee on US–China Relations in conjunction with Xi's visit to San Francisco for the Asia-Pacific Economic Cooperation (APEC) forum. On the sidelines of APEC Xi held a bilateral head-of-state meeting with President Biden in November 2023 (see Photo 5-2). The co-sponsors of this gala dinner had the audacity to charge $40,000 for the "privilege" to sit at the head table with President Xi ($2,000 a head bought a seat at the auxiliary tables). Xi could not have asked for a more receptive audience—all of the titans of Corporate America paid the fees to be in attendance and gave him a standing ovation as he entered the hotel ballroom. But Xi squandered the opportunity. Instead of *reassuring* US businesses about China's commercial openness, or telling them how the PRC would take concrete steps to level the playing field, Xi offered only well-worn propaganda platitudes.[185] There was not a single sentence in his speech concerning the business environment in China—a curious omission given the audience. The CEOs in attendance received very critical press coverage, and a Congressional committee demanded a name list of those in attendance. "Talk about not knowing what time it is," observed the business-friendly *Wall Street Journal*.[186] "Xi offered no hints of concessions to business or even interest in more investment in the Chinese economy. The speech was propaganda at its finest," said a senior business executive who attended the dinner.[187]

Despite the dour and sour mood among American investors and businesses, a full or even substantial decoupling of the two countries' economies is neither feasible nor desirable.[188] "De-risking and diversifying, not decoupling" is the way that President Biden's National Security Advisor Jake Sullivan described the situation in his April 2023 speech at the Brookings Institution.[189] The integration and interdependence of the two economies is extremely deep and beneficial to both overall. But the trendline is definitely downward, the political risks and commercial barriers in China are increasingly high, and businesses and institutional pension funds are reducing their footprints and investments in China.[190] Capital only goes where there are incentives to be, and China has become much less attractive.

American States

Subnational diplomacy between "sister" localities—states/provinces/cities—in the United States and China have been a part of US–China relations and the engagement policy since the 1980s. While they have never received much media or scholarly attention—until recent years when they have come under increasing scrutiny by the US government and Congress—these subnational relationships have been at the heart of the engagement process between American and Chinese societies. To construct such ties was an intentional part of the Carter and Reagan administrations' early engagement strategies, while subsequent administrations quietly approved while American localities took their own initiatives to forge links with Chinese counterparts (although frequently it was the Chinese side which was the proactive party, with US local and state governments responding, often unwittingly, to Chinese entreaties).

Most American states and governor's offices have international commerce promotion offices that work with China to promote two-way trade and investment, while most states have tourism promotion bureaus, and some states have international educational exchange offices. There is nothing wrong or intrinsically nefarious about such subnational connections. President Dwight D. Eisenhower launched the sister-cities program back in 1956. However, in recent years it has been discovered that some of these ties have gone beyond commerce, education, and tourism, to also facilitate PRC and CCP political influence and interference in US domestic affairs. As *The Wall Street Journal* observed in April 2024, "From Florida to Indiana and Montana, an expanding array of local proposals, bills, laws and regulations aim to block Chinese individuals and companies from acquiring land, winning contracts, working on research, setting up factories and otherwise participating in the US economy. State officials, overriding traditional local interests such as drawing investment and creating jobs, say they are acting where Congress hasn't to address grassroots American distrust of the Chinese Communist Party. The states have generally been moving faster on China legislation than Congress."[191]

In one particularly brazen and widely reported case, in September 2024, a former member of New York Governors Andrew Cuomo and Kathy Hochul's staff (Linda Sun) was indicted on ten criminal charges including violating FARA.[192] Working in liaison with the Chinese Consulate General in New York, Ms. Sun had repeatedly blocked meetings between the governors and Taiwan representatives, blocked any critical comments about China in the governors' speeches, and facilitated meetings with PRC representatives—all in return for payments in cash and kind.[193] A similar instance emerged just a month later when it was revealed that a key fundraising aide to New York City Mayor Eric Adams (Winnie Greco) also had close ties to PRC Consulate officials as well as in China.

Like Linda Sun, Greco blocked the Mayor's potential interactions with individuals from Taiwan and promoted pro-China narratives in his speeches. She also arranged trips to China for Adams, an unknown number before he became Mayor and at least six times after taking office in 2021. As of this writing, Ms. Greco had not been charged with any crimes, but she is under investigation and she abruptly resigned as Adams's Director of Asian Affairs in October 2024.

The concerns about China have mushroomed very quickly across the country since 2022. While an extreme and empirically inaccurate statement, Virginia Republican Governor Glenn Youngkin typifies the growing paranoid view sweeping across state governments, "China has a very clearly stated objective: and that is to dominate the world and do that at America's expense."[194]

China's United Front Outreach to America's Grassroots

For China's part, such "people-to-people diplomacy" (人民外交) and "cultural diplomacy" (文化外交) have been a long-standing feature of the CCP's "united front" policies internationally, dating back to the 1950s.[195] On September 21, 1949, Chairman Mao famously proclaimed, "We have friends all over the world!" (In fact, the new PRC had precious *few* international friends at the time).[196]

Various CCP united front organs have subsequently been charged with building such ties abroad—notably the Chinese People's Association for Friendship with Foreign Countries (中国人民对外友好协会 or 对外友协); Chinese Peoples Institute of Foreign Affairs (中国人外交学会); and the International [Liaison] Department of the CCP (中共对外联络部), which specifically cultivates ties with foreign political parties and subnational politicians.[197] The CCP United Front Department (中共统战部) also uses "cut-outs"—such as CUSEF based in Hong Kong. The United Front Department's Overseas Chinese Affairs Office (侨务事务办) works directly through a variety of Chinese American and Chinese diaspora organizations, the most important of which are the Committee of 100 and the National Association for China's Peaceful Reunification (中国和平统一促进会).[198] A number of prominent Chinese Americans active in these organizations have been appointed as "overseas delegates" to the CCP's annual Chinese People's Political Consultative Congress (中国人民政治协商会议)—the preeminent united front body in the PRC. Another very active united front affiliated organ in the United States is the China General Chamber of Commerce (美国中国总商会 or CGCC). Established in 2005 to promote investment, trade, and business ties, the CGCC has worked hard to build connections with local American politicians (this is not intrinsically illicit as doing business locally often requires the support of local governments, politicians, and commercial associations). The CGCC has over 1,500 member companies (both Chinese and American), with headquarters in New York City and regional offices in Chicago, Houston, Los Angeles, San Francisco, and Washington, DC.[199]

Inside the United States, all of these PRC entities work with counterpart organizations such as the US–China People's Friendship Association and the National Committee on US–China Relations. With respect to working with state and local politicians, the Chinese People's Association for Friendship with Foreign Countries (CFPACC) is by far the most important. In 2011, it partnered with the National Governor's Association to establish a "China–U.S. Governor's Forum," and Hilary Rodham Clinton (who was then Secretary of State) signed a Memorandum of Understanding establishing it. But in 2020, the US Department of State nullified the agreement that established the program on the basis that "CFPACC's actions have undermined the Governor's Forum's original well-intentioned purpose." The China–US Governor's Forum is not the only state-level organization that CFPACC has created. In 2016, it launched the China–US Sub-National Legislatures Cooperation Forum. This body met every year from 2016 to 2019 (alternating between Honolulu, Wuhan, Las Vegas, and Shijiazhuang) before moving to a virtual format during COVID-19 (it is unclear if it continues to meet, although the Governor's Forum has been terminated by the American side).[200]

The CCP and PRC have thus long sought to cultivate foreign individuals, institutions, and local officials to hold positive views of China, to visit China, and report back to their home countries about the "real China." Sometimes these efforts were focused on socialist-leaning citizens (so-called fellow travelers), sometimes on media journalists, sometimes on "opinion shapers" in academia and think tanks, sometimes on social media aimed at foreign publics, sometimes on prominent local citizens, often on the Chinese ethnic diaspora, and sometimes on local politicians.[201] *American Interests and Chinese Influence* (the important report by Hoover Institution and Asia Society from 2019) was the *first* to uncover and systematically catalog a wide range of such efforts inside the United States (full disclosure: I was a member of the working group that researched and wrote the report),[202] and since then many other publications by think tanks and Congress have appeared and provide detailed information of the CCP's efforts to penetrate, influence, and interfere in American public opinion and politics.[203] In 2023, several prominent Senators introduced the "Countering Corrupt Influence Act (CCP Influence Act)" to legislate against such activities.[204]

Such "influence activities" include news manipulation and placing disinformation in American media and social media.[205] This is hardly unique to the United States and is a global phenomenon known in Chinese as 外宣

(foreign propaganda).[206] In the United States, it has also involved attempts to influence the presidential elections in 2020 and 2024.[207]

The recent and critical attention paid to these malign activities inside the United States has cast a pall over the wide range of sister state/city relationships, which had grown steadily over the decades and had rarely been questioned. Thus, like all of the other dimensions of US–China engagement, this sphere of direct society-to-society contact has also encountered difficulties in recent years.

This section seeks to unpack these subnational relationships and explain the reasons behind the recent downturn. Before doing so, though, it is extremely important to reiterate that subnational diplomacy between countries— including between United States and others—has long been seen as an impor- tant component of normal international relations. It is the essence of society-to- society and cultural diplomacy. Building such transnational ties at the grassroots level provides real ballast to American foreign policy and has long been viewed by the national government in Washington as both a natural and impor- tant component of America's engagement with the world. In fact, the Biden administration established a Subnational Diplomacy Unit in the Department of State with a Special Representative for City and State Diplomacy, headed by Nina Hachigian, former ambassador to Association of Southeast Asian Nations (ASEAN).[208]

Ties That No Longer Bind

The earliest partnerships (also known as "twinnings" or "pairings") were estab- lished in 1979 between San Francisco/Shanghai, Tianjin/Philadelphia, Nan- jing/St. Louis, and the state of Ohio with Hubei Province. Since then, now 36 American states and 31 Chinese provinces have established ties (in some cases more than one), and over 200 sister-city relationships that have been established. Altogether, President Xi Jinping and China's State Council claimed a total of 284 sister state/province/city pairings in 2023.[209] In some cases, even city districts and counties have established formal ties—e.g., Beijing's Haidian District and Berkeley, CA; Beijing's Chaoyang District and Brooklyn, NY; Beijing's Xicheng District and Pasadena, CA; Beijing's Shunyi District and Loudon County, VA; Suzhou and Queen Anne's County, MD; etc.[210]

Over four decades, these pairings all grew, but unevenly. Every American state had some part in the engagement with China, but some more than others. Bilat- eral ties and exchanges exist at a variety of levels, but commerce has led the way for all. Readers interested in the details are encouraged to consult a brilliant

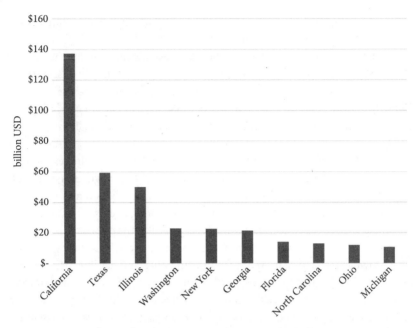

Figure 7.3 Top 10 US States Total Trade Volume with China 2023.

Source: US International Trade Administration, 2024, "TradeStats Express, State Trade by Partner (countries and regions)," https://www.trade.gov/data-visualization/tradestats-express-state-trade-partner-countries-and-regions.

interactive map created by The Rhodium Group, which shows all investments state-by-state, province-by-province, even county-by-county and industry-by-industry. On this map you can click on your state and county and see what Chinese investments there are (if any).

Not surprisingly, the state of California has led the way. Figure 7.3 and Figure 7.4 reflect the total trade figures as well as exports/imports for the top ten US states trading with China in 2023. Two-way investment has also been important for the state, with Chinese total FDI stock into California from 1990 to 2020 of $36.79 billion and US FDI into China during the same period of $55.07 billion.[211] Yet, there has been a secular decline in bilateral FDI since 2016.

Tourism and people-to-people exchanges have also been a source of revenue for California; in 2019, there were 1.5 million visitor trips that generated $4 billion in visitor spending.[212] Many California Governors—from Jerry Brown to Gavin Newsom—have paid official visits to China. After California, Texas, New York, Washington, Michigan, Ohio, Florida, Virginia, and Illinois have had the strongest commercial partnerships with China (see Figure 7.5).

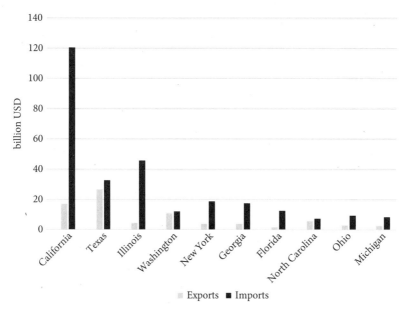

Figure 7.4 Top 10 US States Imports/Exports with China 2023.

Source: US International Trade Administration, 2024, "TradeStats Express: State Trade by Partner (countries and regions)," https://www.trade.gov/data-visualization/tradestats-express-state-trade-partner-countries-and-regions.

As with all of the other sectors we have examined in this chapter and in Chapter 6, *disengagement* began in 2017. This is clearly evident when examining the commercial (trade and investment) data, tourist numbers, higher education exchanges, and official visits. For example, during the three-year period between 2014 and 2016, American Governors paid at least 23 visits to China, only 12 did in 2017–2019, zero in 2019–2022, and only 1–2 per year in 2023–2024.[213] The souring and deterioration of subnational ties can be seen and measured in many other ways.

One indicator is the deluge of anti-China legislation being considered in state-houses, some of which have been adopted into law. Two researchers tracked the surge in such state-level legislation and found 81 proposed or adopted bills between 2017 and 2022, compared with only three between 2012 and 2016.[214] Another source cites "more than 100 pieces of proposed or adopted anti-China legislation between 2020 and 2022, a fourfold increase from the 2017–2019 period,"[215] while another study noted 27 states had pending China legislation in 2023.[216] Florida led the way with Governor Ron DeSantis (he was also a presidential candidate at the time) introducing a raft of laws and executive orders to constrict the Florida–China relationship. These included "legislation meant to

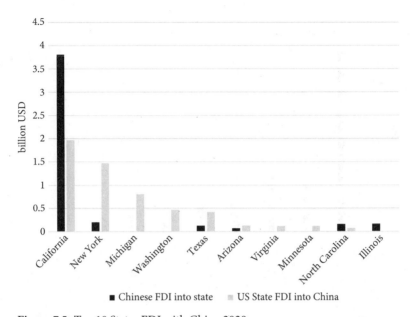

Figure 7.5 Top 10 States FDI with China 2020.

Source: US–China Investment Project, 2024, "FDI Data," https://www.us-china-investment.org/fdi-data.

hold China accountable for the COVID pandemic, require businesses and universities to divulge their ties to China, pressure the state pension fund to divest from China, and—most dramatically—prohibit real estate purchases by Chinese nationals."[217]

Florida was not the only state to consider or adopt such legislation. Texas briefly considered racist and xenophobic laws to ban its university system from admitting Chinese students, while more than ten states have sought to restrict ties between their universities and colleges with Chinese counterparts.[218] Michigan and Virginia have banned Chinese companies that build electric vehicle batteries (although in the case of Virginia it was a Ford plant that used Chinese technology).[219] Indiana banned the state's pension funds from investing in China. More than half of all states do not permit the use of TikTok on government issued cellphones, while Montana became the first state to outlaw the downloading of TikTok altogether.[220]

The land ownership issue has become especially heated.[221] A number of states are considering legislation that would ban Chinese nationals or Green Card holders from purchasing land over a certain size,[222] with four separate pieces of federal legislation pending in Congress.[223] In fact, the Chinese-owned share of *all* agricultural land in the United States only accounts for less than 1 percent

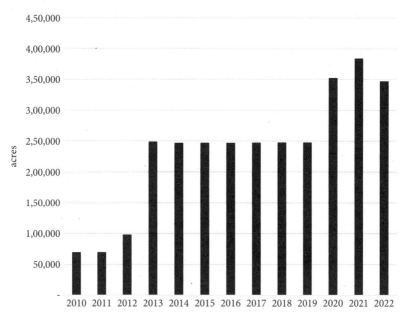

Figure 7.6 Chinese Ownership of US Farmland, 2010–2021.

Source: USDA Farm Service Agency, annual, Foreign Holdings of US Agricultural Land, https://www.fsa.usda.gov/programs-and-services/economic-and-policy-analysis/afida/annual-reports/index.

(16th among all foreign owners according to the US Department of Agriculture [USDA]), a total of 350,000 acres in 2020.[224] Figure 7.6 shows the levels of Chinese agricultural ownership over time.

According to USDA data, Chinese land ownership shrunk slightly from 384,000 to 347,000 acres between 2021 and 2022.[225] By contrast, Canadians own nearly 13 million acres of American farmland, an area nearly as large as the state of West Virginia (China's holdings are about the size of Los Angeles). One case that did raise eyebrows was Chinese billionaire (and San Francisco resident) Chen Tianqiao's ownership of 200,000 acres of prime Oregon forest land (which is not considered agricultural land).[226] Another somewhat sensational case concerned Chinese purchase of a corn milling plant that could process 25 million bushels of corn into animal feed and other derivative products per year, but was situated only 12 miles from the strategic Grand Forks Air Force Base in North Dakota.[227] The $70 million Chinese offer by the Fufeng Group would have given a major boost to the local economy, but it was blocked after local, state, and national officials, as well as the US Air Force, raised objections. There is a legitimate concern about such landholding near military and national security facilities, and the Committee on Foreign Investment in the

United States (CFIUS) has terminated several such purchases (in California, Florida, North Dakota, Oregon, and Texas) since 2020. Following the Fufeng case, several other states moved to block prospective Chinese land purchases and commercial investments. By July 2024, a total of 227 military sites were designated as subject to CFIUS review if foreigners were involved in attempted nearby land purchases.[228]

Beyond Chinese investments and land purchases, broader concerns have arisen in recent years about the PRC and CCP politically influencing state and local officials. Perhaps the most egregious case involved the state of Utah, where an Associated Press investigation uncovered a multiyear effort by Chinese operatives to penetrate the Mormon Church (Church of Jesus Christ of Latter-Day Saints) and Utah Legislature.[229] But the Utah case is far from unique. Many states have been targeted by the PRC to strengthen subnational ties.

China's approach to American states is not random or slipshod. The PRC Embassy in Washington, DC, and regional consulates in Chicago, New York, Los Angeles, San Francisco (and previously Houston) all regularly track the statements and actions of state and local politicians in their jurisdictions. Additionally, Tsinghua University's Center for Globalization Studies partnered with the Minzhi International Research Institute (a Beijing think tank with ties to one of China's eight so-called democratic parties under the united front of CPPCC) in 2019 to evaluate and rank the governors of all 50 American states in terms of their attitudes toward China—either "friendly," "tough," or "ambiguous." The survey studied various public statements of the 50 governors, and found that "among the 50 governors, 17 are 'friendly' to China, 14 have 'ambiguous' attitudes toward China, 6 are 'tough' on China, and 14 have made no clear or public statement on China."[230]

Those considered "friendly" to China included the governors of Alabama (Kay Ivey), Arizona (Doug Ducey), Colorado (Jared Polis), Delaware (John Carney), Idaho (Brad Little), Indiana (Eric Holcomb), Maine (Janet Mills), Massachusetts (Charlie Baker), Montana (Steve Bullock), New Hampshire (Chris Sununu), North Carolina (Roy Cooper), North Dakota (Doug Burgum), Oregon (Kate Brown), Tennessee (Bill Lee), Utah (Gary Herbert), Vermont (Phil Scott), and West Virginia (Jim Justice). Those considered "tough" on China included the governors of Florida (Ron DeSantis), Georgia (Brian Kemp), Missouri (Mike Parson), New York (Andrew Cuomo), South Carolina (Henry McMaster), and Wyoming (Mike Gordon). The "ambiguous" governors included Arkansas (Asa Hutchinson), California (Gavin Newsom), Hawaii (David Ige), Iowa (Kim Reynolds), Kentucky (Matt Bevin), Louisiana (John Bel Edwards), Maryland (Larry Hogan), Michigan (Gretchen Whitmer), Nebraska (Pete Rickets), Ohio (Mike DeWine), Pennsylvania (Tom Wolf), South Dakota (Kristi Noem), Texas (Greg Abbott), and Washington (Jay Inslee). One can certainly question the location of these individuals on the Chinese spectrum, but it is interesting that such estimates are done (much less published).[231]

Beginning in 2018, the federal government in Washington began to take closer notice of the PRC's and CCP's linkages at the subnational level across the United States. The original impetus for this was Vice President Mike Pence's speech to the Hudson Institute on the Trump administration's China policy (discussed in Chapter 5).[232] Subsequently, Secretary of State Mike Pompeo gave a high-profile speech to the National Governor's Association Winter Meeting in February 2020.[233] This speech was preceded by similar speeches by the FBI Director and Attorney General and, taken together, described a variety of efforts by the PRC and CCP to penetrate and manipulate American states and localities. For its part, the Biden administration continued such warnings. In January 2022, FBI Director Christopher Wray gave another high-profile speech at the Ronald Reagan Presidential Library in California entitled "Countering Threats Posed by the Chinese Government Inside the U.S."[234] In its annual Homeland Threat Assessment in 2024, the Department of Homeland Security has warned of a variety of threats from China—espionage, potential sabotage of critical infrastructure, disinformation, economic manipulation, drugs (fentanyl), cyberattacks, transnational repression, and other forms of "malign influence."[235]

The National Counterintelligence and Security Center has also issued a special report on "Protecting Government and Business Leaders at the U.S. State and Local Level from the People's Republic of China (PRC) Influence Operations."[236] Among other findings, the report notes,

The PRC understands U.S. state and local leaders enjoy a degree of independence from Washington and may seek to use them as proxies to advocate for national U.S. policies Beijing desires, including improved U.S. economic cooperation with China, and reduced U.S. criticism of China's policies towards Taiwan, Tibetans, Uyghurs, pro-democracy activists, and others ... Leaders at the U.S. state and local levels risk being manipulated to support hidden PRC agendas. PRC influence operations can be deceptive and coercive, with seemingly benign business opportunities or people-to-people exchanges sometimes masking PRC political agendas. Financial incentives may be used to hook U.S. state and local leaders, given their focus on local economic issues ... By their nature, these efforts can have a corrosive effect on targeted societies. They can also threaten the integrity of the U.S. policy making process and interfere in how U.S. civil, economic, and political life functions.

Individual U.S. localities may be unaware that their partnerships with cities and provinces in China are centrally coordinated and managed ... The PRC may view the U.S. business community as an especially important vector to influence local, state, and national leaders, given that companies are key constituents of, and often contributors to, politicians at all levels. The PRC may use market access, investments, or economic dependency as leverage, and overtly press U.S. business leaders, particularly those with commercial interests in China, to lobby Washington for policies Beijing favors.

The report concludes with a series of "best practice" recommendations for US states and localities to better guard against such potential malign PRC and CCP practices. Another careful study of the subject by Kyle Jaros, a University of Notre Dame scholar, also offers some very sensible recommendations and "best practices," which include,[237]

- keeping state-level officials fully informed about the evolving risks and opportunities involved in working with PRC partners;
- helping states develop common norms and red lines for engagement with Chinese counterparts;
- countering efforts by the PRC to instrumentalize subnational economic, educational, and exchange linkages for the purposes of covert political influence, espionage, or national security advantage;
- providing financial support to enable state governments and major city governments to develop in-house institutional capacity for monitoring exchanges with foreign countries generally and China relations specifically;
- conducting public outreach and education to help US businesses, universities, and ordinary citizens understand the structure and nature of the Chinese party-state and its links with the business world and nongovernmental organizational sector;
- enhancing state-to-state communication and coordination around approaches to China relations to share best practices and develop common baselines (platforms such as the National Governor's Association, National Conference of State Legislatures, and the US Conference of Mayors should play leading roles in this regard);
- strengthening mechanism at the federal level for intergovernmental communication and coordination around China relations.

These are all extremely sensible recommendations, with which I fully concur. I would only add that they cannot be ad hoc and left to individual states to absorb and implement. Such efforts must be led by the *federal* government, must be adequately resourced, coordinated, and sustained. The Department of Homeland Security would be the natural national institution to lead such an effort. I would like to suggest that an NGO—specifically the National Committee on US–China Relations (NCUSCR)—be involved in such an effort, but unfortunately, the

NCUSCR is far too deeply immersed in the idea of *expanding*—not mitigating—engagement with China. Since its inception (see Chapter 3), NCUSCR's raison d'être has been *engagement* with China. They are thus (in my view) not an objective organization, at least for purposes such as this—which involves *disengagement* from China (this judgment does not apply to many of their other public outreach activities or "Track II" exchanges with Chinese counterparts).

* * * *

This (perhaps overly lengthy) chapter has explored a variety of actors and sectors "outside the Beltway" of Washington, DC, across the vast United States of America. We have looked specifically at changes in the American body politic, changes in China that have affected US non-governmental actors, at educational and scholarly exchanges, at the US business community, and at American states and localities. I believe that this selection captures the most important sectors in American society which interact with China. Inevitably, however, many other actors have not been addressed or have been neglected. One could, for example, examine various occupational sectors in American society—farmers, industrial workers, unions, journalists, educators, suburbanites, men and women, LGBTQ, different ethnic groups, etc.—but that will have to be left to others to undertake (and it should be done). I have tried my best in this chapter to describe the four important sectors I selected and to show how each has been impacted by, and have contributed to, the deterioration of the US–China relationship and the relative disengagement of these American constituencies.

While this chapter has looked "outside the (Washington) Beltway" and Chapter 6 looked "inside the Beltway," Chapter 8 focuses specifically on the policy expert community. It examines the (still ongoing) debates among experts in think tanks, universities, NGOs, journalism, and some in Congress, concerning what US strategy and policy toward China should be.

IV

SEARCHING FOR A
NEW CHINA STRATEGY

Chapter 8
The Great American China Policy Debate

"Although Washington remains bitterly divided on most issues, there is a growing consensus that the era of engagement with China has come to an unceremonious close. The debate now is over what comes next?"

—Kurt Campbell, Deputy US Secretary of State, and Jake Sullivan, National Security Advisor[1]

"I think, ultimately, they [China] want to overtake the United States as the dominant country globally. And we don't want that to happen. We don't want to live in a world where the Chinese are the dominant country."

—Nicholas Burns, US Ambassador to China[2]

In Chapter 1, we examined the American debate (2016–2021) over whether the US strategy of engagement with China had failed or not. We examined the major proponents and opponents, their arguments and counterarguments. As with most debates, there was no precise winner or loser, no precise conclusion, and no precise endpoint to the debate. There were those who claimed that Engagement had failed to realize its original objectives (which was the subject of Chapter 2)—not the least of those who advocated this position were officials in the Trump and Biden administrations. Then there were those who pushed back, offering several counterarguments: (a) it was the Trump administration (not China) that unilaterally torpedoed Engagement; (b) it was never an intended goal of engagement to "change China"; or (c) Engagement had just not yet fully worked and more time was needed. This was a fairly time-bound debate (beginning in 2016, reaching a crescendo in 2018, continuing into 2019, before dissipating in 2020–2021).

Since that time, another distinct debate has ensued—over the content of what future US strategy toward the People's Republic of China (PRC) should be. This debate grew out of the previous one, it still continues in 2024 (at the time of writing), but it has ranged more broadly than the simpler question whether the engagement strategy had failed or not. The current debate is more about the broad parameters of what US strategy and policy should be in the "post-engagement" era. This chapter unpacks this diverse debate.

Watching the Watchers

Studying and understanding specialists' perceptions and images are useful in understanding policy debates in a country and often inside of governments—thereby unearthing the ideational origins and bases of foreign policies. Therefore, if one wishes to know what US strategy and policies toward China may be in the near- to medium-term future, one would do well to delve deeply into the debates currently taking place among China specialist and foreign policy experts in the United States (which is what this chapter does).

Like Gilbert Rozman's studies of China's Soviet experts,[3] David Engerman's study of American Sovietologists,[4] and more recently David McCourt's study of America's China and Russia experts,[5] I have long been a "watcher of watchers." My doctoral dissertation 35 years ago was on China's America Watchers,[6] and I have long been interested in foreign policy experts' debates in other countries.

Mediums and Modalities

The community of experts in the United States who analyze China and debate China policy is hardly monolithic. In order to understand the differences of viewpoints, one should contextualize the individual, as specialists' articulated perceptions often say as much about the perceiver as the perceived. That is, the training and socialization of the specialist, as well as their native political culture and professional environment, all contribute indirectly to shaping one's worldview, belief system, and specific perceptions. Insights drawn from sociology and social psychology have helped political scientists study foreign policy elites in the United States and other countries since the behavioral revolution of the 1960s.

In the United States, there are distinct professional "cultures" in universities across America, in Washington think tanks, in NGOs, in federally funded research and development centers (FFRDCs),[7] in for-profit consultancies and government contractors (so-called Beltway Bandits),[8] in US military war colleges,[9] and in elite invited-membership organizations, such as the Council on Foreign Relations or the Aspen Strategy Group.

All of these institutional types have their own distinct professional cultures. Some are rather secretive—literally because they work with classified information (as well as unclassified). This is the case of FFRDCs and consultancies/contractors. FFRDCs do, however, maintain a serious research culture that straddles the boundary between academic and intelligence research, and they produce serious empirical work products for their "customers" in the US government. Unfortunately, Washington think tanks have long since abandoned their former "book culture" and now are all oriented around analyzing current and recent events while chasing the proverbial media and social media cycles, where writing op-eds, short studies, and X (formerly Twitter) postings are now the name of the game. There is very little "deep research" still occurring in Washington think tanks (in my view), and their professional staffs have become glorified media pundits (each think tank maintains regularly updated internal records of "media appearances" by their staff—which is euphemistically known as "impact"). Nor is holding a PhD still a required bona fide for appointment as a senior fellow in the top Washington think tanks (today the top China specialist at the Brookings Institution only has a BA degree, and one at the Center for Strategic & International Studies (CSIS) only holds an MA).

On the other hand, in contrast to Washington think tanks, NGOs (such as the Asia Society or National Bureau of Asian Research) and membership organizations (such as the Council on Foreign Relations) do produce in-depth analytical and policy studies and occasional books (these organizations have absorbed the in-depth research previously done by think tanks). So do the partially federally funded US Institute of Peace and Woodrow Wilson Center. For their part, university-based academics largely do real scholarly research—but their professional culture is highly theoretical, and their publications are aimed primarily at each other (not government consumers or the public). University academics, by and large, operate in an isolated intellectual bubble. Although this is largely the case, a subset in social science departments and professional schools of international affairs do actively participate in foreign policy debates.

While there is interaction among these communities, it is not as much as one might assume; they are each fairly self-contained worlds. Although foreign policy experts do certainly rotate in-and-out of government (the proverbial "revolving door") there is actually not that much interaction *between* these different institutional sectors. *Within* them, yes—experts sometimes move from one think tank to another, scholars from one university to another, and consultants from one firm to another—but my impression is that there is not that much movement *between* these worlds. Think-tankers are hardly ever recruited by universities, although think tanks recruit from universities. If one does not hold a PhD, there is no opportunity to gain a tenured or tenure-track university appointment (adjunct teaching appointments or fixed-term appointments as "professors of practice" are possible in some university policy schools). Those working in FFRDCs, with the notable exception of the RAND Corporation, have virtually no public profile and are essentially intelligence analysts who work in the private sector (fulfilling contract research for the intelligence community or other US government departments).

Policy debates in the public square are, of course, intrinsic to American democracy. They constitute valued elements of the democratic process—not only because they are intrinsically *representative* and *pluralistic*, but also because it is *assumed* that out of the often-contentious cacophony of policy debates comes consensus and informed policy. While partisanship certainly plays a role in policy debates—dividing debaters among party lines, hawks vs. doves, or other cleavages—and an egocentric desire to promote oneself does sometimes play a role, there nonetheless exists the assumption that debaters' motives are ethical and driven primarily by pure analytical opinion drawn from empirical facts (even if ideology plays a role). At least this is the Weberian "ideal type." However, the recent work of Columbia University political scientist Elizabeth Saunders reveals that motivations which shape the argumentative orientations among foreign policy debaters are multiple, not so pure, and sometimes unethical.[10] Such policy debates also intrinsically take place among elites and for elites—primarily those in the aforementioned institutions inside the Washington Beltway. To some extent, as "elite cue theory" holds, the public in democracies (voters) do look to elites for cues as to how they should think about foreign policy and national security issues,[11] but generally speaking, elite discourse is almost entirely insular and circular.

Where do these elites make their views known and debate with each other? The mediums through which these foreign (and China) policy elites debate with each other primarily include the op-ed pages of major newspapers (*The New York Times, Wall Street Journal,* and *The Washington Post*), sometimes books, the occasional online social media posting, and foreign policy journals such as *Foreign Affairs* (other than the respected journal *International Security*, it is rare to find policy-relevant articles in academic journals). Public events (captured on YouTube) are another venue, but the debate is primarily carried out through publications. Whether or not these publications ever really have impact on actual policy is, in fact, questionable. Nine times out of ten, these published pieces just go into a kind of amorphous "discourse cloud." Ironically, one place where such debates and publications do have an impact is *outside* the United States. Research institutes, scholars, and journalists in Europe and Asia intensively and carefully follow US China policy debates—often seeing in them more coherence than in fact exists.

This context is important background to understanding the differing professional worlds in which participants and contributors to American debates on China occur. The Great American China Policy Debate that I examine in this chapter has largely been waged in the public domain by individuals in Washington think tanks, by some university-based scholars, and by NGOs.

Categorizing the American Debate on China

Different observers will no doubt distinguish different schools of thought and lines of argument amid the voluminous forest of analytical writings. Indeed, the challenge is to find distinct clusterings and not focus only on individual trees within the forest.

Prior to joining the Biden administration as Coordinator for Indo-Pacific Affairs on the National Security Council (and later Deputy Secretary of State), Kurt Campbell—himself a significant contributor to the debates—divided the "Washington Establishment" into five camps.[12] "The first school of thought—and the most prestigious—was the Engagement School," Campbell argued. The second school, in which Campbell included himself, was the "allies first model." The third was "the small school and ideologically extreme school that China is the enemy and that we have to get ready and gear up." Campbell's fourth school "wanted to pursue the old approach of focusing on one regional issue at a time, hoping to win China's cooperation without sparking broader confrontation."[13] Campbell's fifth group, as described to *The New York Times* correspondent David Sanger, was the "globalist school"—those who did not view China through the prism of great power competition, but rather who "focus on the existential transnational issues like climate change and pandemic prevention."[14]

Professor McCourt's recent study, which I noted at the outset of this chapter, offers a different schema. It was based both on publications by American China and Russia specialists as well as on approximately 150 original individual interviews. Like others involved in "watcher watching," McCourt divides American China and Russia specialists into distinguishable categories. Within the China watchers, he distinguishes four distinct schools of thought: Strategic Competitors, Engagers, New Cold Warriors, and Competitive Coexisters. These are interesting and empirically grounded clusterings of distinct lines of argument. I do not dispute these distinctions; I understand the basis of his categorizations and agree in essence with them. They parallel my own reading of the evidence, but mine are slightly different.

I distinguish five schools of thought: The Stealthy Rival School, the Comprehensive Competition School, the Strategic Empathy School, the Re-Engagement School, and the Managed Competition School. While these are distinct lines of overall argument and schools of thought, they are not all mutually exclusive—either in the content of the arguments or in those who make them. For example, there is some overlap between the Stealthy Rival, Comprehensive Competition, and Managed Competition Schools; there is also some overlap between the Strategic Empathy and Re-Engagement Schools, and between the Re-Engagement and Managed Competition Schools. These distinctions are not "ideal types" (in the Weberian sense) or caricatured stereo-types; they represent what I see as distinct lines of analysis, argument, and evidence.

The Stealthy Rival School

This first cohort of contributors to the Great American China Policy Debate is, in fact, relatively small, and they have argued their ideas primarily through books rather than articles. This cohort is of the general view that the Chinese Communist Party (CCP) and PRC government possess a coherent, multifaceted, long-term conspiratorial strategy and plan to systematically build up China's comprehensive power, deceive America domestically, and stealthily maneuver worldwide to disrupt, outflank, and undermine the global position of the United States. This conspiratorial Chinese strategy is, however, not secret (this school argues). It is "hiding in plain sight," if only one reads Chinese publications in the original language. Analysts who make this claim base their analyses on publications of Chinese authors: most openly published, but some internal so-called *neibu* (内部) publications. The core viewpoint of this school is made explicitly clear in the subtitles of the most noteworthy examples of this cohort's works: Michael Pillsbury's *The Hundred Year Marathon: China's Secret Strategy to Replace America as the Global Superpower*; Bill Gertz's *Deceiving the Sky: Inside Communist China's Drive for Global Supremacy*; Rush Doshi's *The Long Game: China's Grand Strategy to Displace American Order*; Robert Spalding's *War Without Rules: China's Playbook for Global Domination*; and Ian Easton's *The Final Struggle: Inside China's Global Strategy*.[15]

In terms of their backgrounds, this school is an eclectic group. Three of these representative authors hold PhDs (Pillsbury from Columbia University, Doshi from Harvard, Spalding from the University of Missouri). Three have served in the US government (Pillsbury at the Defense and State Departments, Spalding in the Defense Department and National Security Council, Doshi at the National Security Council). Four have worked in think tanks (Doshi at Brookings, Pillsbury at the Heritage Foundation and Hudson Institute, Spalding at the Hudson Institute, Easton at the Project 2049 Institute). Two currently hold academic appointments (Doshi at Georgetown University and Easton at the US Naval War College). Four have high degrees of proficiency or fluency in the Chinese language (Pillsbury, Spalding, Doshi, Easton), and one has served in the US Embassy in China (Brigadier General Spalding as Defense Attaché). In terms of institutional affiliations, academic training, and professional background, the outlier in this group is Bill Gertz, who has spent his entire career as a journalist (at *The Washington Times*) and book author.

While an eclectic group, they all share in common analyses of China's drive for global supremacy and desire to displace the United States as the global superpower, and they all argue that this desire springs from a deep-seated, sophisticated, and integrated plan which seeks to take advantage of America's weaknesses in different domains (dysfunctional democracy, open society, laissez-faire economy, aging technologies, under-resourced diplomacy, strategic overreach, intelligence gaps, and military vulnerabilities).

While these studies all share this general line of analysis and argument, it is also important to recognize that the Stealthy Rival School is different from the large number of more generic "China threat" books. Today, an Amazon book search under "China Threat" generates 20 such volumes.[16] The Stealthy Rival School certainly sees China as a threat, but their analyses are less focused on the military dimension and potential for war (especially over Taiwan), and they are more focused on China's motivations, strategies, and tactics for displacing the United States *short of war* (adopting the classic Sun Tzu maxim to defeat your enemy without engaging in direct combat). The Stealthy Rival School also shares some things in common with the next school of thought I will examine—the Comprehensive Competition School—yet their core arguments are somewhat different. Both schools share the view that the United States and China are locked into an indefinite competition for global primacy and that this competition plays out across multiple domains. However, the Stealthy Rival School looks at both the motivations and the manifestations of the competition whereas the Comprehensive Competition School tends to look only at the arenas of the competition.

Let us look more carefully at these motivations and manifestations in the Stealthy Rival School, beginning with Michael Pillsbury's book *The Hundred Year Marathon* (the title alludes to the century from which the Chinese Communists came to power in 1949 to the anticipated centenary of the PRC in 2049, when China will be strong enough to have replaced the United States as the world's leading power).

At the core of this school's analysis is that China (its leaders, strategists, and officials) are not reactive, but proactive. They do not operate in the short-term, but for the long term ... the very long term. China's elites operate according to a Grand Strategy and grand plans. This grand strategy—as best explicated in Pillsbury's book—derives from two main sources: first, ancient imperial Chinese history and stratagems and strategists (like Cao Cao, Zhu Geliang, Gou Jian, Sun Tzu, and others); second, lessons to be learned from the "century of shame and humiliation," 1842–1949 (百年国耻). Chinese leaders, officials, and strategists may operate tactically and in response to specific situations, but their moves are very deliberate and in accord with a set of core principles and ancient stratagems. Nothing in Chinese behavior occurs spontaneously or in an ad hoc fashion. Self-discipline is highly valued and ever-present.

Chinese strategists also think cyclically and not linearly, and they believe history evolves through distinct repetitive epochs (时代). Moreover, stasis is an abnormal and temporary state in societies on earth and between heaven and earth—*fluidity and flux* are thought to be the normal "state of nature." This is not to say that stability is not prized in Chinese society—it is. But stability, stasis, and equilibrium are seen as temporary in the Chinese mindset—unless stability is *imposed* from above by the state. Given that all things are in flux all the time, Chinese strategists draw on traditional concepts, particularly of *shi* (势)— i.e., the means for navigating dynamic fluidity. The concept of *shi* is central in Pillsbury's understanding of Chinese calculations. Such navigation involves constantly appraising the relative "balance of forces" (力量平衡) between China and other countries. Under such fluid and dynamic conditions, the victorious party will be the one that is most maneuverable and flexible. This requires constantly adapting tactics (while not losing sight of the short-, medium-, and long-term goals).

The ultimate goal is to maintain full *control* over both those inside of China's borders and—to the extent possible—in the world beyond China. The means of external control derive from those used domestically—namely to "condition" others to *conform* to China's and the ruling Party's desires. Conformity is a conditioned state. Control can only be brought about under conditions of preponderant *state strength*. Conformity is brought about through a combination of unrelenting indoctrination, surveillance, coercion, and knowing that if self-induced conformity breaks down, aberrant behavior will be punished. This school sees modern-day China as obsessed with regaining its "wealth and power" (富强) and predominant strength lost as the Qing dynasty unraveled (1644–1911). Internal disorder and weakness only invites manipulation and aggression by others (内乱外患). Chinese are actually very Darwinian: in an anarchical and dangerous world, only the strong survive. They are also quintessentially Realist: only power, preferably preponderant power, matters. Even if not preponderant, the skillful use of asymmetrical strategies and tactics can offset others' greater power assets. This is what "China's Great Rejuvenation" (中国大福星)—the national mission from the late-Qing to Xi Jinping—is all about.

Pillsbury also reveals the history of Sino-American relations that the Chinese Communists tell themselves and teach everyone in China. This is a history of American aggression, subversion, and attempts subjugate China:

In short, Chinese leaders believe the United States has been trying to dominate China for more than 150 years, and China's plan is to dominate us instead.

Chinese leaders view the global environment as fundamentally zero-sum, and they plan to show the same lack of mercy toward America that they believe the long line of China-hating American imperialists—dating back to John Tyler—have showed toward them. China's view of America would be less troubling if Chinese leaders weren't prepared to act on their misconceptions. While China doesn't at first glance seem to be preparing to take on the United States, the hard truth is that China's leaders see America as an enemy in a global struggle they plan on winning.[17]

There are various ways to take advantage of the vulnerabilities of China's adversaries, the Stealthy Rival School argues. Pillsbury, as well as the other members of the Stealthy Rival School, also argue that the Chinese are adept and adroit at exploiting American largesse and naïveté. Taking advantage of an adversary's ignorance and self-delusions has a long history in Chinese statecraft. Westerners and Americans may have preyed on China during the 19th and 20th centuries, but they also are seen as deluded enough as to try to help China modernize. While successive Chinese regimes (Qing, Republican, Communist) all primarily viewed the West as predatory, they all also recognized that Westerners offered things that China needed. Says Pillsbury,

China's Marathon strategy depends heavily on goodwill from other countries, especially the United States. That goodwill translates into massive foreign investment, the acceptance of Chinese exports, indulgences when the government or state-affiliated organizations are caught stealing technology or violating WTO rules and looking the other way on human rights abuses. Western countries offer such concessions primarily because their leaders are convinced that, overall, China is moving in the "right" direction toward freer markets, productive international cooperation, and political liberalization.[18]

Taking from the United States and others what would make China stronger is, in fact, a long-standing strategy dating to the Qing dynasty's Self-Strengthening Movement (自强运动) of 1861–1895. Why *not* make this tactical adjustment—when the broad strategic goal is to become stronger precisely in order to *resist* the West? If the foreigners are foolish enough to help us build up our capacities to resist them, why not let them? The Chinese Communists also know well that it was Lenin who observed that "the capitalists will sell us the rope with which we will hang them." Of course, the trick for China has been to *selectively* absorb what would strengthen it, while at the same time filtering out the harmful effects of the West: to "protect Chinese essence while using Western methods for application" (中学为体, 西学为用). Deng Xiaoping was clear about the risk when he observed, "If you open the window for fresh air, you have to expect some flies and mosquitos to blow in."

Another adopted historical tactic is to use asymmetrical tactics against stronger powers. These include mobilizing a "united front" (统战) of others to reinforce your weaknesses, exploit the adversary's vulnerabilities, and outflank the opponent (also known as "using barbarians to control barbarians" or 以夷制夷), using subversion inside the opponent's society and state, and developing asymmetrical weapons (such as "assassin's mace") to exploit the adversary's weaknesses.

Pillsbury also emphasizes the role that intentional *deception* plays in ancient, modern, and contemporary Chinese strategy and tactics. "The Chinese value highly the importance of deception stratagems."[19] Deception is a tried-and-true tactic dating to Sun Tzu's third century BCE *The Art of War* (孙子兵法) and the ancient *36 Stratagems*.[20] A key part of deception is the use of *disinformation* to confuse the adversary. A prominent example in recent times was China's propaganda campaign of "China's peaceful rise" (中国和平崛起).

Having rung the alarm bell as to what he perceives to be China's true intentions (to displace the United States as the primary global power) and elaborating the tactics it is using to do so, Pillsbury then discusses what the 2049 China-dominated world will look like:

> In sum, if the China Dream becomes a reality in 2049, the Sinocentric world will nurture autocracies; many websites will be filled with rewritten history defaming the West and praising China; and pollution will contaminate the air in more countries as developing nations adopt the Chinese model in a race to the bottom in food safety and environmental standards. As environmental degradation expands, species could disappear, ocean levels will rise, and cancer will spread. Some international organizations will not be able to step in as effectively as they can today because they will be marginalized. Chinese state-owned monopolies and Chinese-controlled economic alliances will dominate the global marketplace, and one of the world's mightiest military alliances may be controlled by Beijing, which will be able to easily outspend the United States on military research, troop levels, and weapons systems.[21]

Pillsbury paints a pretty bleak picture of a China-dominated world at mid-century. Time will, of course, tell as to whether his prophesies are correct. But his deep knowledge and explication of Chinese strategies and tactics are well-informed and to be taken seriously.

Rush Doshi's magnum opus *The Long Game: China's Grand Strategy to Displace American Order* is another example of the Stealthy Rival School. While Doshi's 419-page tome is a very impressive study and he shares in common with others in this school the idea that China is steadily and stealthily maneuvering to become *the* global power by mid-century, his focus and evidence is much more contemporary when compared with Pillsbury.[22] The Chinese actions he examines all come from the 1990s through 2010s—essentially, the Jiang Zemin, Hu Jintao, and Xi Jinping periods of rule. To his credit as a China scholar, Doshi dug through a large corpus of writings from these two decades (including the *Selected Works* of Jiang, Hu, and Xi, as well as their senior advisers). Doshi's book was originally his doctoral dissertation at Harvard, and in many ways, it still reads like it. His study cites an enormous corpus of Chinese writings, and this is truly a great strength of the volume: the evidentiary basis is extremely sound and thus gives his arguments strong credibility.

In brief, Doshi argues that the PRC under Jiang Zemin, Hu Jintao, and Xi Jinping has pursued a tripartite set of strategies in pursuit of its goal to displace America and achieve primacy. Doshi lays out in chapter-length assessments how the three strategies become manifest across three dimensions—political (by which he means diplomatic), economic, and military.

The first strategy is what he calls the strategy of *blunting*: "to blunt American power" under the broad strategic guidelines of "hiding capabilities and biding time."[23] This latter phrase is the English rendering of Deng Xiaoping's famous *taoguang, yanghui* (韬光养晦) dictum from 1989. Then Doshi shifts the analysis to the next phase of displacement: *building*. That is, how China is going about methodically constructing an alternative regional system (in Asia) and world order. Here too he walks the reader through the political (diplomatic), economic, and military dimensions of this effort. So, the first step in China's grand strategy, as Doshi sees it, is to blunt and neutralize the United States—and then, during the 21st century, to stand up an alternative order and to solicit buy-in from other nations (principally in the Global South).

Having set in place these building blocks—during the 2010s under Xi Jinping in his view—Beijing then shifted to a third discernible stage: *expansion*. That is, to consolidate all the elements of "building" the alternative order. During this phase, under Xi, China has really gone on the offensive to interfere directly in a wide variety of nations through political "influence" operations, through economic coercion, and through erecting a variety of new regional organizations around the world (Brazil, Russia, India, China, South Africa [BRICS]; Shanghai Cooperation Organization [SCO] ; Forum on China-Africa Cooperation [FOCAC]; China Arab Cooperation Forum [CACF]; China Eastern Europe Cooperation [CEEC]; Asia Infrastructure Investment Bank [AIIB]; Community of Latin American and Caribbean States [CELAC]; and others). These institutional efforts at new order-building all illustrate (with the possible exception of the Asia Infrastructure Investment Bank) the conformity to Chinese norms and practices, many deeply illiberal.

Doshi concludes his study with a chapter on how the United States should go about blunting China's efforts. He argues that the United States needs to be sophisticated in its response and measured in its application of valuable resources. He argues for an "asymmetric" American strategy to match China's own asymmetrical strategies and tactics. Rather than "matching China dollar-for-dollar, ship-for-ship, and loan-for-loan," he writes, Washington should adopt a "cost effective" approach that "denies China hegemony in its home region and worldwide."[24] He then lays out a quite thorough and sophisticated menu of steps that the United States could take in the economic, military, and diplomatic spheres to *blunt* China's own initiatives and undermine its position worldwide—while doubling down on core American strengths and comparative advantages. It is indeed interesting to read Doshi's set of recommendations (on pages 317–329 of the book) in light of what the Biden administration undertook during its first three years in office. Doshi served during these three years as a leading China hand on Biden's National Security Council staff, having been brought on board by his mentor Kurt Campbell.

For some, Doshi and Pillsbury have really "cracked the code" of China's aspirations, strategies, and modalities for undermining the United States and attempting to establish itself as the predominant power by mid-century. Personally, I think there is much to be learned from their analyses.

The other two principal examples of the Stealthy Rival School are Brigadier General (US Air Force, retired) Robert Spalding's book *War Without Rules: China's Playbook for Global Domination*, and Ian Easton's study *The Final Struggle: Inside China's Global Strategy*. Neither of these books (nor their authors) are political fringe crackpot, chest-thumping, ideological manifestos. Both men read and speak Chinese and know about China. Spalding, a former Air Force B-2 stealth bomber pilot who flew missions as part of the 509th Bomb Wing at Whiteman Air Force Base in Missouri, went on to serve as the US Defense Attaché in Beijing before becoming chief China strategist for the Chairman of the Joint Chiefs of Staff and then Director of Strategic Planning on the National Security Council staff in the White House. Easton is younger but has had a career immersed in China and Taiwan issues. Before recently joining the faculty as an associate professor at the US Naval War College in 2023, he was on the staff as CNA Corporation and the Project 2049 Institute, both based in Arlington, Virginia. He previously studied Chinese at Fudan University in Shanghai and National Taiwan University before receiving his MA in China Studies from National Cheng-chi University in Taipei.[25]

Spalding's book follows one he published in 2019 entitled *Stealth War: How China Took Over While America Slept*. They should really be read in tandem, especially as *Stealth War* deals principally with the domestic American dimensions of China's quest for dominance, while *War Without Rules* deals with the international dimensions. Both books—the author maintains—are a "call to arms" for America to "wake up" and grasp the severity and complexity of its multidimensional struggle with China. In *Stealth War*, General Spalding opens with an interesting admission:

> Some cynics will accuse me of being alarmist or sensationalist. These peo-ple are afflicted with the same blind spot I once had. I have examined why I was so oblivious to CCP aggression and why the rest of the world still has a similar blind spot. I now attribute it to hubris—our cocksure confidence in ourselves and our system. Our belief that America's socioeconomic model, its war machine, and its political model are the best in the world—has helped to fuel a profound confidence that we can overcome any challenge. That con-fidence has proven shortsighted. The blind spot remains in place—and has increased in size ... Blinded by our own greed and the dream of globaliza-tion, we've been convinced that free trade automatically unlocks the shackles of authoritarianism and paves the way to democracy ... And we've been duped.[26]

Contrary to its title, which suggests military warfare, *Stealth War* is a fairly cur-sory cruise across both military and non-military aspects of what Spalding sees as Beijing's multifaceted strategy to undermine and neutralize the United States in multiple domains. He begins by referencing the book *Unrestricted Warfare*, authored in 1999 by two senior colonels of the People's Liberation Army (PLA), which was the first Chinese book (it was published in Beijing and translated into English) to describe how in time of war with the United States, China should be prepared to disrupt and damage the US power grid, Wall Street finan-cial services, physical infrastructure (dams, ports, interstate waterways), and oil pipelines and storage facilities. When the book was translated, it had a stun-ning impact on the Pentagon, which heretofore had only thought of possibly fighting the Chinese military with weapons in the Taiwan theater. As a result of *Unrestricted Warfare*, US national security planners had to consider—really for the first time—"asymmetrical" attacks on the American homeland. I myself happened to be a consultant to the Pentagon at the time and recall well sev-eral classified and unclassified sessions to discuss the provocative book. It was taken very seriously inside of the US defense and intelligence establishment but was dismissed by some non-governmental China specialists as an exercise in "science fiction." More than 20 years later, such dangers have become manifest with Chinese cyber penetrations of all this critical infrastructure, and they are openly discussed by the Director of National Intelligence, the Director of the FBI, the Secretary of the Department of Homeland Security, and other agencies (as described in Chapters 6 and 7).

Spalding's book spends a lot of time discussing China's cyber threats, but also other technological challenges. He also rings the bell on Beijing's Belt & Road Initiative (BRI)—which he argues is a multifaceted geostrategic, energy, and military threat to America's worldwide interests. *Stealth War* may be intended as a "wake-up call"—but it is not a detailed, analytically rigorous, or sophisticated study. His second book, *War Without Rules*, is a continuation of the first, but on a global basis. That is, he uses excerpts from *Unrestricted Warfare* and constructs his own chapters around the various strategies and tactics described by the two PLA colonels—to argue how China is systematically deploying *nonmilitary* means to undermine the United States in various spheres. The book is actually more of a simple stream-of-consciousness narrative than a serious analytical exercise. It is also rather polemical. In the conclusion he argues that to frame China through a lens of "engagement," "management," "challenge," or "competitor"—all miss the mark. China, Spalding claims, is *already at war* with the United States—a war employing non-military means. The United States, he argues, needs to "wake up" and see what China is doing. All in all, General Spalding's two books are, I think, overly simplistic and overreactive, even if he does draw attention to how Beijing may be maneuvering on a global chessboard to outflank and undermine the United States (in this regard echoing Doshi and others).

This is also the subject of Ian Easton's *The Final Struggle*. Where Spalding's two books are rather simplistic, not thoroughly researched or documented, Easton's is the opposite. It is accessibly and knowledgeably written, and his 731 footnotes to a wide range of secondary English and primary Chinese language sources are an indication of the thoroughness of his research. Because of its esoteric co-publishers, Easton's book has received little, if any, attention to date.

Like Pillsbury and Doshi, Easton focuses largely on China's strategy for global dominance. This, he argues, is buried in Xi Jinping's writings as well as a series of books published by the PLA National Defense University. Easton claims that these materials reveal a systematic plan to control the global commons—in natural resources, energy supplies, global finance, food, sea lanes, information technologies, supply chains, etc. He further claims that China's Military–Civilian Fusion (军民结合) program is actually a blueprint for global technology dominance as well as providing the PLA with cutting-edge weaponry. He argues that China's vast data collection efforts via Tik Tok, Alipay, WeChat, and other platforms will ultimately dictate consumer's choices worldwide. Like Spalding, Easton argues that the US government and society are asleep at the switch and do not even realize the CCP's stealthy schemes to penetrate—and ultimately control—American and foreign societies. It all seems overstated, as is the case with Spalding's book, but Beijing's various nefarious methods do deserve closer scrutiny and countermeasures by democratic governments worldwide.

The final example of the Stealthy Rival paradigm is the book by former journalist Bill Gertz of *The Washington Times*. Gertz has a long and well-established reputation inside the Washington Beltway for his muckraking, often derisive, and sometimes defamatory articles. That is, he has made a career out of attacking those officials and China experts whom he considers to be soft on China. I know, as I was one (among many) who Gertz publicly attacked in his articles. In fact, I believe it was Gertz who originally coined the term "panda hugger" to describe such individuals. He definitely was among those to coin the term "Blue Team"—a designation for a group of China hawks (the term was drawn from wargame jargon for opposing red vs. blue armies, with the "blue team" defending the United States against "red team" aggressors).[27] While he and other Blue-Teamers consider themselves to be the guardians of the republic against those who they think are appeasing and selling out American national interests to China, their diatribes echo the excesses of the McCarthy era.

China, and American engagement with it, have long been the staple of Gertz's accusatory publications. Of relevance to the Stealthy Rival School in the recent Great American China Policy Debate is his book *Deceiving the Sky: Inside Communist China's Drive for Global Supremacy*. Like the other authors in this genre I have discussed, Gertz devotes individual chapters of his 230-page exposé to China's different means that he says add up to a comprehensive and concerted effort to undermine the United States and establish global hegemony: asymmetric warfare; anti-satellite weapons and space warfare; cyberattacks; traditional and non-traditional espionage and intelligence collection; international propaganda; economic coercion; conventional, nuclear, and hypersonic weapons; island reclamation, maritime expansion and "string of pearls" port-building; the export of high-tech surveillance systems; infiltration of 5G broadband networks worldwide; intellectual property theft; corporate expansion and takeovers of foreign firms; and so on. Gertz writes in a fairly detailed way about each of these Chinese methods and activities. He does not make them up and he is not fabricating the evidence, and perhaps these malign dots can be connected, but Gertz's narrative nonetheless has a highly conspiratorial character to it. One gets the sense that, in his view, China is on the verge of taking over the world. Like other contributors to the Stealthy Rival School, Gertz does draw needed attention to a wide range of malign interactional activities that the PRC and PLA are undertaking. This does provide a service, as it increases awareness and hopefully stimulates defensive countermeasures by various governments, even if it does evince a kind of breathless and seemingly overly conspiratorial narrative.

The Comprehensive Competition School

Of the five schools discussed in this chapter, the Comprehensive Competition School is the largest and most complex to parse and summarize. That is because competition is all-pervasive and permeates most areas of the US–China relationship.

The term "competition" has certainly become the leitmotif among American foreign policy specialists for characterizing the American relationship with China.[28] As we saw in Chapter 6, Congressional committees have held multiple hearings on the US strategic competition with China,[29] and indeed an entire Congressional committee has been established (the House Select Committee on Strategic Competition Between the United States and the Chinese Communist Party). Think-tank websites, social media, and newspaper editorial pages frequently carry discourse on US–China competition, policy journals are replete with such articles (a search of the leading journal *Foreign Affairs* from January 2018 through May 2024 reveals no fewer than 989 articles published concerning "US–China competition"!). Whole books have been published on the subject,[30] while prestigious think tanks and research organizations such as the Atlantic Council, American Enterprise Institute, Council on Foreign Relations, Aspen Strategy Group, and Asia Society churn out reports on how to effectively compete with China.[31] The RAND Corporation even prepared and published a lengthy report for the US government entitled *A Guide to Extreme Competition with China*, while another RAND study cataloged in considerable detail China's global influence in various areas (media, soft power, military, security, espionage economic, diplomatic, cultural, historical, informational, with a variety of regional and country case studies) and recommends specific actions the United States could adopt to counter Chinese influence.[32]

Meanwhile, US government officials and documents increasingly use the terminology of competition to describe the relationship and American policy. President George W. Bush was actually the first to officially describe China as a "strategic competitor" during the presidential campaign in 2000, directly contradicting the second Clinton administration's depiction of China as a "strategic partner," but then the Bush administration largely dropped the term after entering office. Although the term continued to float around among scholars and policy analysts, it then largely went into a 16-year hibernation until "strategic competition" became the official centerpiece used by the Trump administration in a variety of official documents and speeches (see Chapter 5). The Biden administration also adopted "competition" as its central intellectual descriptor and policy organizing construct, albeit with different adjectival modifiers. President Biden himself spoke of "extreme competition" in February 2021, but later in the year he used "healthy competition" when speaking with President Xi Jinping. On various public occasions, Biden's National Security Advisor Jake Sullivan used "intense competition" and "stiff competition," but also "responsible competition." For his part, Secretary of State Antony Blinken described the relationship as "competitive when it should be, collaborative where it can be, and adversarial where it must be," while former Deputy Secretary of State Wendy Sherman used "healthy competition" and "responsible competition." Blinken, Sullivan, and Sherman all used "competition" in their face-to-face meetings with Chinese interlocutors. The Biden administration's Indo-Pacific Strategy described its policy this way: "We will [also] seek to manage competition with the PRC responsibly."[33]

I was one of the first to characterize the United States and China as "competitors" in an article published in 2000, during the heyday of engagement.[34] Today, I think of and describe the relationship between the United States and China as one of *indefinite comprehensive competitive rivalry*. It is now primarily a *competitive* relationship in which each side seeks to strengthen itself vis-à-vis the other and takes actions and counteractions against the other. It is *comprehensive* in that the competition stretches across virtually all functional issue areas and all geographic regions of the world (even into outer space). It has become a classic great power *rivalry* whereby each increasingly contests the other's presence and influence worldwide, and it exhibits the classic reactive and escalatory elements of a "security dilemma." It is not time-bound and can be expected to last *indefinitely* into the future. So, readers should count me as a member of the Comprehensive Competition School.

The United States and China compete directly and indirectly over many things. As China scholar Harry Harding has astutely noted, they also bring to the competition parallel perceptions:

> Each country believes that its position is virtuous while insisting the other's is not. Both believe that they are exceptional, although in different ways: Americans think their country is the exceptional embodiment of universal values; Chinese think their long history and unique culture shows that they can be an exception to those Western values whose universality they reject. Both countries think they are destined for international leadership and insist that their leadership will be accepted because their intentions are benign.[35]

Parsing the current complex menu of US–China competition is a daunting task—because of the sheer enormity and complexity of the data set. Rather than delving into the thousands of publications on US–China competition, let me briefly consider some different dimensions of comprehensive competition, with illustrative examples of American perspectives of different aspects.

Ideological Competition

The respective ideologies (democracy vs. socialism) and the two differing political systems have long been a significant variable and sphere of contention and competition between the two powers. This was at the very center of the Cold War and Sino-American difficulties during the 1950s and 1960s. It receded following the pragmatic Nixon–Mao rapprochement in the 1970s and the "reform and opening" decade of the 1980s. It returned somewhat following the Tiananmen massacre in 1989, but it was again sublimated during the 1990s and the first decade of the 21st century. But with the Xi Jinping era in the 2010s–2020s, ideology has very much returned as an important driver of Chinese calculations, while the United States also became more ideological under Trump and Biden. Since Xi Jinping came to power in 2012, with his regime dramatically intensifying repression, the nature of China's political system has again risen to the surface as one of the primary problems in the bilateral relationship from the American perspective. America's ideological differences with the PRC are not limited to the CCP's domestic repression—they also very much have to do with contrasting and competing images of world order.[36]

It was the first Trump administration (2017–2021) that refocused attention on the ideological dimension, as various senior officials explicitly reframed the Sino-American competition as fundamentally ideological. Former Secretary of State Mike Pompeo's speech at the Nixon Library in July 2020 and National Security Advisor Robert O'Brien's speech in June 2020 were both ideological calls to arms,[37] while Trump's Deputy National Security Advisor (and top China adviser) Matt Pottinger observed after leaving office, "The ideological dimension of the competition is inescapable, even central."[38]

Conservative Washington scholars/think-tankers Hal Brands (Johns Hopkins SAIS) and Zack Cooper (American Enterprise Institute) similarly point to the centrality of ideology in US–China competition:

> The Washington–Beijing rivalry is driven by competing ideals and systems of government as much as by competing interests ... [Yet] purging ideology from American statecraft would be both ahistorical and unstrategic. The United States won the Cold War precisely because it put values near the center of that competition. Likewise, if Washington hopes to understand Beijing today, to mobilize its democratic friends for a long struggle, and to exploit its asymmetric advantages, it must take ideology seriously ... Leaving values and morality to the side would eliminate one of the United States' greatest advantages and make it harder to rally coalitions at home and abroad. It would play into Beijing's hands by making the rivalry a struggle over military dominance rather than a contest over what philosophical principles should structure domestic

governance and international order. Purging ideology from American strategy, as the realists recommend, is neither possible nor desirable.[39]

The return of ideology as an important driving variable is not likely to recede unless the CCP regime again reverts to a "softer" and more tolerant form of authoritarian rule that again appears to be moving in a convergent political trajectory with liberal systems (as was the case from 1980 to 1989 under Deng Xiaoping, Hu Yaobang, and Zhao Ziyang, or from 1996 to 2008 under Jiang Zemin and Hu Jintao). A return to such a politically reformist path will have to await the post-Xi era. From my perspective, the differing political systems are really *the core problem* in US–China relations. Competition certainly exists in other realms, as explored below, but incompatible political systems lie at the heart of the differences between the two sides. As the American political system has itself displayed multiple signs of dysfunctionality (most notably during the Trump years), Chinese officials have watched with glee and stepped up their criticisms of the American political system and various social maladies. "The East is rising and the West is declining" (东上,西下), Xi Jinping proudly proclaimed in 2014. Xi has also given several speeches predicting that socialism will inevitably triumph over capitalism, and he has relentlessly reinserted the study of Marxism–Leninism into the national educational curriculum. In one speech in 2014, Xi reportedly claimed, "The battle for mind control happens on a smokeless battlefield. It happens inside the domain of ideology. Whoever controls this battlefield can win hearts. They will have the initiative throughout the competition and combat ... When it comes to combat in the ideological domain, we don't have any room for compromise or retreat. We must achieve total victory."[40]

It is extremely important for Americans to recognize that Xi and the CCP very much view China's relationship with the United States through an ideological lens (as is made clear in Chapter 7 and the Appendix). For America's part, as described in Chapters 5 and 6, there are many who view the main challenges coming from China as ideological and political in nature. Other than former Secretary of State Mike Pompeo, probably the leading exponents of the "ideological struggle" school of China policy are Matt Pottinger and Mike Gallagher. Their *Foreign Affairs* article from 2024 entitled "No Substitute for Victory: America's Competition with China Must Be Won, Not Managed" included this thinly veiled statement bordering on a full call for regime change (which many readers interpreted it as being):

What would winning look like? China's communist rulers would give up trying to prevail in a hot or cold conflict with the United States and its friends. And the Chinese people—from ruling elites to everyday citizens—would find inspiration to explore new models of development and governance that don't rely on repression at home and compulsive hostility abroad.[41]

This statement drew a sharp rebuke by Deputy Secretary of State Kurt Campbell, who, when asked about this final sentence from Pottinger and Gallagher at a public session at the Stimson Center in Washington on June 13, 2024, responded that pursuing a policy of regime change would be "reckless and likely unproductive ... I do not believe it is in our interest at the current juncture to add to our [policy] list 'Let's try to topple the other leading power on the global stage,' despite our differences."[42]

Meanwhile, President Biden and his administration also cast US policy in somewhat ideological terms, notably Biden's own making of the contest between democracies and autocracies a centerpiece of his administration's foreign policy. When asked by CBS "60 Minutes" to describe the nature of US–China competition, Biden's Ambassador to China Nicholas Burns replied, "It's a competition of ideas, a battle of ideas: our idea, America's big idea, of a democratic society and human freedom—versus China's idea that a communist state is stronger than a democracy. We don't believe that. So, there is a battle here of whose ideas should lead the world? And we believe those are American ideas."[43]

Economic and Technological Competition

The elements in this realm are so many and so complicated that no short summary can do them justice. Readers are referred back to Chapter 7, where I discussed the many difficulties on America's trade and investment relationship with China.

The skewed playing field that China presents to American and foreign businesses is hardly a new problem, but it has gotten much worse in recent years. So-called overcapacity and the dumping of Chinese goods on the American and European markets—previously solar panels and more recently electric vehicles—has become pervasive, and the WTO seems incapable of handling the glut. But bilateral trade and investment, with its gargantuan surplus in China's favor, is by no means the only competitive challenge. China's industrial policies and subsidies, notably in the dozen high-technology sectors prioritized in Beijing's *Made in China 2025* initiative, continues to undermine American competitiveness in multiple sectors of production and commerce.

China's economic coercion against other countries—several of them American allies like Australia, Japan, South Korea, and the Philippines—has become a newer and very serious problem.[44] The US government has been working through the G-7 to establish a collective means to support countries subjected to Beijing's economic punishment and push back against such coercive measures.

Similarly, maintaining effective US government economic sanctions on Chinese corporate entities and individuals that violate American laws and policies is another competitive element. As of mid–2024, over 1,000 Chinese nationals and entities were on the US government's Specially Designated Nationals and Blocked Persons (SDN) list, the non–SDN Chinese Military Industrial Complex list, and the Entity List.[45]

As the United States and others learned during the COVID-19 pandemic, the world has become far too dependent on supply chains running through China. Unraveling and decoupling some of these linkages is difficult, but nonetheless it is proceeding apace. Establishing "supply chain resilience," "de-risking," "reshoring," or "friend-shoring" production have become the new watchwords for many companies and countries. As I noted in Chapter 7, raids on American firms in China by its state security authorities constitute another new problem which negatively affects the competitive calculations of US companies either already operating in China or thinking about entering the country.

These are all competitive business challenges. If they are not bad enough, the real new battleground of competition with China lies in the realm of *technology*. China has become a "near-peer competitor" of the United States,[46] and the two countries are now locked into a full-scale, intensive, and high-stakes competitive race to win the race of technological innovation and new emerging technologies—in the fields of artificial intelligence (AI), robotics, quantum computing, nanotechnology, biotechnology, military hypersonic weapons, 5G and 6G broadband, fintech, e-commerce, and—perhaps above all—semiconductor production.[47] The Biden administration and US Congress took important strides to strengthen America's technological competitiveness through the American Innovation and Competitiveness Act in 2021 and the CHIPS and Science Act in 2022.

One aspect of this tech competition is keeping cutting-edge American foundational and applied technologies out of the hands of China. To this end, the Trump and Biden administrations both significantly strengthened Department of Commerce export controls. The Commerce Department's Bureau of Industry and Security has increased the use of its Entity List to restrict trade in dual-use technologies with China.[48] These actions have made progress in stemming the flow of key technologies to China. In the reverse direction, the Biden administration took new steps to block Chinese investment into commercial technology ventures in the United States. President Biden's Executive Order from March 2022 strengthened both the regulatory powers of Committee on Foreign Investment in the United States (CFIUS)—a branch of the US Treasury Department—and the purview of technology investments subject to

CFIUS review and controls.[49] Other executive orders have placed limits on China's firms seeking to invest in AI and supercomputing,[50] as well as restricting high-end microchip exports.[51] The Biden administration has worked to carefully delimit these restrictions in what National Security Advisor Jake Sullivan describes as a policy of "a high fence and small yard."[52]

Strategic Competition

The other principal area of comprehensive competition is in the strategic-military domain. This includes three main areas: strategic competition for position and influence in Asia, strategic competition in the world, and military competition (including Taiwan).

The Asian region (whether described as the Asia-Pacific or Indo-Pacific) has always been the geostrategic epicenter of US–China interactions.[53] American and Chinese presence and activities in the region have not always been viewed as explicitly competitive (excepting Taiwan), but this is now predominantly the case. In terms of security, China has never been happy about the five American alliances, the US military presence throughout the region, or intelligence-gathering near China. While Beijing may have previously tolerated these realities, it has long resented them. Chinese civilian and military leaders have grown more and more opposed and outspoken in recent years. Beijing constantly monitors the alliances for signs of strain and fissures, eager to exploit any and all. Such has particularly been the case with respect to the alliances with Thailand and the Philippines. US security assistance to Taiwan has always been a particularly neuralgic Chinese concern, but in recent years Beijing has also increasingly expressed its discontent with US military relationships in Southeast Asia—notably with Singapore, Malaysia, Brunei, the Philippines, Thailand, and Vietnam. It is also extremely critical of the growing US security relationship with India, and Beijing views the development of the Quad (the US, Japan, Australia, and India) with deep suspicion. As an indication of its frustration, at the National People's Congress in March 2023, Xi Jinping unprecedentedly and unequivocally bluntly stated, "Western countries led by the United States have implemented all-around containment, encirclement, and suppression of China, which has brought unprecedented severe challenges to our country's development."[54]

For its part, China's military capabilities have steadily improved, and its operations have broadened throughout the region. The PLA Navy is now the largest one in the *world*, while its growing inventory of missiles has provided the capacity to reach Guam and attack American targets at long range. Its strategic rocket forces have embarked on a sustained buildup of its land-based intercontinental ballistic missiles (ICBMs). China's island building and deployment of military assets in the South China Sea are becoming a real game changer in regional security. Some analysts, notably Elbridge Colby in his book *Strategy of Denial*, make the case for a much more robust American military presence throughout the Indo-Pacific to counter China.[55] For his part, Biden's Secretary of Defense Lloyd Austin described China's military modernization as the "pacing threat" for the entire US military. Clearly, the Pentagon and Indo-Pacific Command (INDOPACOM) now view China as the single most significant comprehensive threat to stability and security in the Indo-Pacific region (while North Korea remains a secondary but always significant threat) and are planning and training accordingly for multiple contingencies and multi-spectrum conflict with China's military and cyberwarriors.

Taiwan remains, by far, the most dangerous flashpoint in US–China security competition. Contradicting the Taiwan Relations Act, President Biden publicly claimed four times that the United States would come to the defense of Taiwan if China attacks it. Easier said than done, however. Many knowledgeable observers argue that urgent and multidimensional steps need to be taken to fortify Taiwan's defenses, strengthen the US military's deterrence against PRC aggression, and urgently prepare for possible actual combat.[56] As such, the Pentagon and INDOPACOM have been intensively working on a variety of means to maintain an effective deterrent—and, if necessary, to prevail in a conflict against the PLA.

Throughout Southeast Asia, China has increased its presence and influence—diplomatically, commercially, and culturally—and Beijing sees itself in clear competition with the United States in the region.[57] The Belt and Road Initiative is a significant tool in Beijing's toolbox, as many Southeast and South Asian countries are in dire need of roads, rails, ports, electric grids, hospitals, schools, water treatment, internet connectivity, and a variety of governance enhancements. But Beijing has also dramatically stepped up its economic aid, cultural presence, public diplomacy, united front activities, and diplomatic presence throughout the Association of Southeast Asian Nations region and Indian Ocean littoral states. Beijing has also combined influence activities with the threat of economic penalties against Australia and New Zealand—thus alienating both countries—while ramping up its presence in the South Pacific islands. Similar tactics have been used against South Korea. Meanwhile, the most tension-prone of China's regional relationships—with Japan—remains fragile.

For America's part, the Obama administration prioritized the region with its "pivot" or "rebalance" policy, the first Trump's administration followed with its "Free and Open Indo-Pacific" initiative, and the Biden administration focused even greater attention and resources on the region. Under all three administrations, Washington has sought to constrain and restrict China's regional position and influence.

Overall, while it must be said that China's position and influence has increased relative to that of the United States in Southeast Asia, the two powers are definitely locked into intensified regional competition. In 2020, I published a whole book specifically on this subject;[58] in 2023, I led an Asia Society project that produced an important report offering specific recommendations for US policy.[59] The competition remains fluid, however. There are already apparent signs that Beijing may be overplaying its hand toward a number of countries. In my view, Washington has underplayed its own hand, as the United States has many intrinsic strengths and considerable respect across the region. Without a doubt, Sino-American competition across Asia is intensifying and will be a long-term phenomenon. However, Washington really needs to up its game to compete more effectively.

As China has "gone global,"[60] so too has its competition with the United States. Once geographically limited to Asia and Africa, China is now a true international actor. As it has expanded its presence, interests, and influence on all continents, it has bumped up against long-standing American presence and relationships in many parts of the world. This is particularly the case in Europe,[61] Latin America (both Central and South America), and increasingly throughout the Middle East and Africa.[62] Some regions and countries have yet to fully grasp the new great power rivalry, some are in denial, while others are beginning to wrestle with the consequences and their policy options.

Simply by virtue of China's newfound presence in these regions, the United States views and defines China as a geostrategic competitor. Hegemons do not like peer competitors, especially those that enter the hegemon's traditional regional spheres of influence.[63] The competitors are thus usually viewed in zero-sum fashion. This need not necessarily be the case, as the two powers' interests overlap in places and they could undertake helpful actions in parallel, such as development assistance, debt relief, Millennium Development Challenge goals, disaster relief, pandemics, counterterrorism, and other areas. Unfortunately, such collaborative thinking is currently lacking in both capitals. Once a "competition mindset" is set in place, it tends to take on an inexorable and reinforcing zero-sum dynamic of its own. Everything is perceived through the prism of contested influence. This is, for example, the way that Washington has often viewed the BRICS, the AIIB, the New Development Bank (NDB), and the string of China's regional cooperation forums: the SCO, the CASCF, the CEEC grouping, the FOCAC, the China–CELAC, and the Pacific Islands Forum.[64] Beijing sees these institutions as examples of the "new type" of cooperative diplomacy and security—as distinct from the US model of bilateral and multilateral alliances—which it seeks to promote in world affairs.[65] In contrast, from Washington's perspective, these organizations are proof positive of China expanding its spheres of influence.

US–China competition also extends to multilateral international institutions and global governance.[66] Washington thus increasingly views Beijing as a global "revisionist" power that seeks to undermine and overturn the post–World War II so-called Liberal International Order.[67] Following the first Trump administration's intentional efforts to erode that order, the Biden administration set it as a top priority to rejoin institutions and reconstruct the normative order. For its part, China's role in global governance has certainly been a work-in-progress, but it has been a generally positive evolution. Over time, China has progressively become an institutional member of international society and gradually assimilated many of the norms and rules of international institutions. Yet it has also long evinced both ambivalence and discomfort with the liberal order it has joined (despite benefiting substantially from it). While China has become more constructively involved and invested in global governance, it is now trying to proactively shape the global governance agenda in an illiberal direction since Xi Jinping came to power. This puts it at increasing variance with the United States and other liberal democratic states.

The Comprehensive Competition School is thus voluminous. Most contributions focus on individual dimensions of the competition—technology, economics, defense, soft power, and so on. Multiple reports from think tanks have dissected the different dimensions of the comprehensive competition. This includes reports by the Aspen Strategy Group,[68] Atlantic Council,[69] Brookings Institution,[70] Council on Foreign Relations,[71] and the Task Force on US China Policy of the Asia Society Center on US–China Relations and University of California, San Diego (of which I am a member).[72] Former Obama administration official and China expert Evan Medeiros also edited a significant book that systematically examined different dimensions of the US–China competition.[73]

In all of the multiple dimensions I have discussed, the United States and China are certainly locked into comprehensive competition. The biggest risk today may be, as Evan Medeiros has aptly described it, "not that China's rise will fade away (and Washington will have overreacted). Instead, it is the possibility that the United States will fail to build and sustain support for long-term competition across all dimensions of power."[74]

The Strategic Empathy School

The Strategic Empathy School is composed of a relatively small group of former US military officers, intelligence officials, a few academics, and some think-tankers. Some have training and expertise in Chinese studies and language, some do not. Those university-based academics who do not come from the security studies field, those who do have such background hold significant university appointments.

"Strategic empathy" is a recently coined term, although it has earlier origins during the Cold War and earlier Sino-American antagonism. Historian Zachary Shore is generally credited with originating the term and concept of strategic empathy.[75] Shore defines the term as "the skill of understanding what drives and constrains one's adversary."[76] In other words, strategic empathy involves "getting inside the head" of one's potential and real adversaries. The *Merriam-Webster Dictionary* defines empathy as "the action of understanding, being aware of, being sensitive to, and vicariously experiencing the feelings, thoughts, and experience of another," while the *Oxford English Dictionary* defines it as "the ability to imagine and understand the thoughts, perspective, and emotions of another person."

While strategic empathy may be a recently used term, it is hardly a new concept. As a concept, this is the essence of intelligence collection and analysis. This is what the CIA does 24/7: to try to gain insights into the personalities and thinking of leaders and elites in foreign countries. During the Cold War, considerable resources and effort were expended not just by the CIA, but also by academic specialists on the Soviet Union and China (some on contract with the US intelligence community). One of my doctoral supervisors at the University of Michigan, Allen S. Whiting, was a particular trailblazer in such analysis.[77] Other notable scholars who have tried to "read the minds" of Soviet and Chinese leaders and "crack the operational code" of those regimes included Nathan Leites, Lucian Pye, Richard Pipes, Adam Ulam, John W. Lewis, Richard Solomon, William Zimmerman, Merle Fainsod, Vladimir Zubok, Stephen Kotkin, Joseph Torigian, and others. "Peering into the Politburo" is nothing new. All such scholars have seen the need to understand the historical context—as well as the Leninist organizational *apparat*—within which these communist leaders operated as essential to both anticipating their likely moves as well as developing countermeasures to blunt them.

Actually, I find the term "strategic empathy" to not be entirely accurate—because (in my view) empathy implies *sympathy* or *compassion* for a rival or adversary. Understanding the history, strategic calculus, strategic culture, and individual proclivities of adversarial leaders is certainly necessary—but one does not have to sympathize with, or feel compassionate for, them. Understand yes, sympathize no. Both Soviet/Russian and Chinese leaders share a schizophrenic and simultaneous sense of greatness and a sense of grievance born out of past Western aggression, deprivations, and humiliations. I tell my students that these two overriding beliefs—the contradictory senses of *grandeur* and *grievance*—drive Chinese Communist calculations. One must certainly understand and be alert to this "schizophrenia" on the part of the Russians and the Chinese—precisely in order to *anticipate* how certain actions by the United States or the West (or Japan) may appear to provoke ancient anxieties and neuroses. But such anticipation should not be reason to *not* undertake a given action against China or Russia. The United States and the West must act in its own interests when they must. One way to preempt or circumscribe possible negative Chinese or Russian reactions is to provide *advance warnings*—which may alleviate *over*reactions and may serve to help serve to "soften the blow" without compromising one's own interests.

This said, the value and virtue in the concept of strategic empathy is *not* to "mirror-image." History is replete with such mirror-imaging—the transposition of one's own self-identities, belief systems, worldviews, and expectations on to the Other. General H. R. McMaster (President Trump's second National Security Advisor and a Senior Fellow at the Hoover Institution) describes this as "strategic narcissism."[78] It can often lead to misinterpretation, miscalculation, and mistakes. Yet, as with strategic empathy, it does not mean that one should *not* undertake a certain policy action just because it is premised on values or perceptions one draws from their *own* national experience or national interests. If it is in your national interests to do something, then it is justified. But *first* a government should ask themselves two key questions: (1) Are we simply mirror-imaging and therefore mis-defining the situation? (2) Have we "put ourselves in the other's shoes" and do we fully understand how the other party sees and defines a situation? If this "due diligence" is honestly addressed, then policymakers should be able to make their decisions based on their national interests and the circumstances at the time.

As applied to China and China policy, General McMaster argues that at the outset of the Trump administration, when he served as National Security Advisor and accompanied President Trump on the 2017 "state visit plus" trip to Beijing, he felt the need to "infuse our approach to China with a strong dose of strategic empathy. The first step was to appreciate the influence of historical memory on Chinese communist leaders ... The selective use of history—both the history they invoked and the history they averted—revealed the emotions and worldview that drive Chinese Communist Party goals."[79] Initially, at least, McMaster only seemed to grasp one half of China's historical legacy: the legacy of grandeur and greatness. About the lavish treatment the presidential party received during the visit in 2017, McMaster reflected,

> The 2017 visit to the Forbidden City was meant to depict China's increasingly active foreign policy as a return to a natural order. The Forbidden City was the destination for foreigners to bow before the emperor's authority, pay tribute, and to supplicate for privileges, that the emperor might bestow upon them. Xi wanted his visitors to recognize as inevitable that Chinese power would once

again underpin an international system in which Chinese leaders granted privileges in exchange for recognition of China's superiority. As we walked through the Forbidden City it was easy to view Chairman Xi as supremely confident. He wanted to be seen as the unchallenged ruler of an increasingly powerful and apparently harmonious country.[80]

But then, having walked past the Forbidden City's "three great halls"—the Hall of Supreme Harmony, Hall of Central Harmony, and Hall of Preserving Harmony—the Trump tour party reached the imperial apartments at the north end of the Forbidden City, when the tour guide pointed out where the "last emperor" Pu Yi had lived before abdicating the throne in 1924 "in the midst of China's century of shame and humiliation."[81] The dual messaging of the Forbidden City tour was not lost on McMaster.

The irony of McMaster's brief foray into Chinese history was that it infused and reinforced his own sense of how the Trump administration needed to jettison the past policy of "engagement" that had been axiomatically accepted by multiple previous administrations and to replace it with an altogether new paradigm. General McMaster recalls in his memoir, "Our National Security Council staff's assessment of China policy in 2017 began with an emphasis on strategic empathy. We needed to ground our approach to China in a better understanding of the motivations, emotions, cultural biases, and aspirations that drive and constrain the CCP's actions."[82] What McMaster and his National Security Council Senior Director for East Asia Matt Pottinger did was to assess the CCP's core motivations that constitute its worldview:

> The recognition that the CCP was obsessed with control and determined to achieve national rejuvenation at the expense of US interests and the liberal international order led to the adoption of new assumptions. First, China would not liberalize its economy nor its form of government. Second, China would not play by international rules and would instead try to undermine and eventually replace them with new ones more sympathetic to its interests. Third, China would continue to combine its form of economic aggression, including unfair trade practices, with a sustained campaign of industrial espionage to dominate key sectors of the global economy and lead in the development and application of disruptive technologies. Fourth, China's aggressive posture was designed to gain control of strategic locations and infrastructure to establish exclusionary areas of primacy. Finally, absent more effective competition from the United States and like-minded nations, China would become more aggressive in promoting its statist economy and authoritarian political model as an alternative to free-market economics and democratic governance.[83]

What they could also have emphasized was the CCP's deep paranoia about external subversion, so-called color revolutions, fear of autonomous civil society, as well as the deep sense of grievance and revanchism that flows from its "century of shame and humiliation" narrative. But, overall, this assessment by McMaster and Pottinger was an accurate assessment, and it fed directly into the *National Security Strategy of the United States* (2017), which I discussed in Chapters 1 and 5.[84] McMaster concluded that, "The Obama administration was not the first to base its China policy on the belief that engagement would foster cooperation, but Pottinger and I believed that it should be the last. We set out to build bipartisan support for the most significant shift in US policy since the end of World War II ... We could no longer adhere to the narcissistic view that defined China in aspirational terms: what the West hoped China might become."[85]

While McMaster, Pottinger, and other members of the Trump foreign policy and national security team may have identified the CCP's worldview correctly, their corollary policy prescriptions were anything but indulgent of the CCP's many insecurities, neuroses, and paranoia. Rather, Trump's team viewed these as potential *weaknesses* to be exploited, not to be accommodated. What followed, as described in detail in Chapter 5, were three years of unrelenting criticism and pressure on Beijing.

However, other members of the Strategic Empathy School do not at all agree with the assessment by the Trump's team. Instead, while these others also note the CCP's many neuralgias and insecurities—they instead argue for American policies that do not feed or provoke these insecurities. They also argue that China is driven by its own oft-stated desire for development, a need to ensure its security, and the drive for reclaimed national grandeur. Let us examine several examples.

In 2024, renowned China scholar David M. Lampton teamed up with former senior US intelligence official and Stanford University professor Thomas Fingar for an important article in *The Washington Quarterly*.[86] The authors attempt to explain the deterioration of Sino-American relations from Beijing's perspective. They argue that the PRC's (which they intentionally seem to refer to instead of the CCP) behavior and policies toward the United States is driven by a number of factors. First, they argued that China is defensive and simply pushing back against provocative American actions: "In short, US policy and action is a central driver of China's behavior. Beijing responds to American initiatives in ways deeply resonant with its own history and the repertoire of foreign policy tools that its history provides."[87] Second, they attribute PRC behavior to a deeply embedded sense of vulnerability: "Current PRC behavior is better understood as the product of perceived weakness and fragility."[88] They then go on to repeat the hearty perennial that China since the Qing dynasty has pursued consistent and coherent goals:

> China's primary national goals ... have remained remarkably constant. These goals are prosperity and security (wealth and power). To achieve them, China must have domestic tranquility, a modern economy, and a strong military ... This package posits a hostile and threatening external environment and emphasizes achievement of relative economic autarky, tighter domestic social control, ideological conformity, a leader-in-charge approach to governance, and deep suspicion of foreigners ... This policy cluster highlights and seeks to reduce the country's vulnerability to Western influence and subversion.[89]

Fingar and Lampton go on to emphasize the fear-of-subversion factor and dangers of domestic instability, and to catalog how a series of actions by the Obama, Trump, and Biden administrations have all fueled China's insecurities and have produced defensive policy actions which they term Beijing's "protection package." They also view China's international actions as reactive to the United States: "Deep suspicion of imputed US intentions predisposes Beijing to do what it can to impede Washington from achieving its objectives all around the world. In doing so, thwarting the United States may sometimes be more important than advancing Chinese interests. A basic axiom of Chinese foreign policy is that as US–China friction increases, Washington seeks to destabilize China's periphery, running the gamut from close-in surveillance of the mainland to Tibet, Taiwan, and Xinjiang, and cultivating security ties with China's most problematic neighbors (Japan, Vietnam, and India, among others)."[90]

Based on this empathetic reading of China's calculus, Fingar and Lampton offer the policy suggestion to "eschew gratuitous behaviors that push PRC hot buttons and trigger predictable reactions, which make meaningful dialogue difficult."[91] Their article is a useful reminder for American and Western readers of how the US–China relationship looks from Beijing—but I would argue again that understanding Beijing's logic and calculus does not mean that the US should indulge it. American China policy, and foreign policy in general, must be made 100 percent in America's own national interests—not just out of fear of provoking another's insecurities and possible reactions.

Another example of the Strategic Empathy School was a multi-authored (by Michael D. Swaine, Ezra F. Vogel, Paul Heer, J. Stapleton Roy, Rachel Esplin Odell, Mike Mochizuki, Avery Goldstein, and Alice Miller) rebuttal to an article by Princeton professor Aaron Friedberg published in the influential journal *Foreign Affairs*.[92] Authored by widely respected China scholars, one leading Japan scholar, and a former US Ambassador to China, this article was scathingly critical of Friedberg's original article.[93] If readers seek a "one-stop-shop" summary critique of the Comprehensive Competition School, this is it. Space here does not permit a full recitation of the authors' arguments, and readers would do well to read it in its entirety. It is systematic, scathing, and even caustic in tone in countering Friedberg's original article. To be fair, much of this critique is a comprehensive criticism of the Comprehensive Competition School—i.e., of those who advocate policies that bring pressure to bear on Beijing. Like their op-ed "China Is Not an Enemy," published in 2019 in *The Washington Post*, [94] which includes three of the individuals (Swaine, Roy, and Vogel) who coauthored the article in *Foreign Affairs*, they are particularly upset by *American* policy that seeks to confront China. In this regard, the latter article is not entirely an example of strategic empathy for Beijing as it is a condemnation of Washington's calculus and policies.

Nonetheless, they embrace strategic empathy perspectives when they state,

> Hawkish positions on China often proceed from flawed presumptions. Friedberg claims that the bulk of Beijing's policy disagreements with the West arise from its authoritarian political system. He ignores the fact that many of China's international concerns have grown out of longstanding nationalist beliefs and cultural attitudes that long predate communist rule. These include the resentment produced by over a century of predatory Western behavior in East Asia, a profound and at times bristling pride in China's rise, and deep-seated fears that a more freewheeling domestic political process could jeopardize the stability that has facilitated greater prosperity. Such nationalistic attitudes and concerns would prevail even in a democratic China; there is no reason to believe that China's system of governance is what makes Beijing eager to protect what it regards as its territory and reestablish itself as a major power in Asia and the world.[95]

This is classic strategic empathy—i.e., the Beijing regime's policy calculus and modus operandi are to be explained by the country's unique culture, history, and geography. The authors do not, however, go so far as to explicitly state that the United States should indulge and accommodate China's self-perceptions, but they do so implicitly.

For his part, Friedberg was invited to reply to the rebuttal to his original article. Friedberg met the sharpness of the article by Swaine and his colleagues with his own daggers. He countered that the critique "is replete with intemperate, derogatory, and dismissive language intended to discredit and marginalize rather than engage with an opponent's views ... I believe that the authors misunderstand the threat China now poses and understate its severity. The threat is a product of China's growing material power coupled with the distinctive character of its domestic regime." He continued,

As their capabilities and confidence have grown, China's rulers have started to push back against both the material strength and the physical presence of the United States and its democratic allies, as well as the subversive appeal of their liberal democratic ideals. Beijing seeks to undermine the credibility of US security guarantees and to divide democracies from one another while continuing to penetrate and exploit their societies, economies, and information spheres.[96]

This sharp exchange is a prime illustration of the deep differences, and occasional venom, that is sometimes on display in the Great American China Policy Debate and the China watching community.

There are several other examples of the Strategic Empathy School. One is the strategic-affairs scholar Charles Glaser, formerly my colleague at George Washington University, now relocated to MIT. Glaser is one of a number of strategic specialists who have "parachuted" into the study of the Chinese military and strategy in recent years (there is nothing wrong with that, as those without lengthy academic training on China often have important insights). Glaser's logic and argument falls squarely into the Strategic Empathy School even though he is by no means a China specialist, has no training in China studies, cannot read or speak the Chinese language, and is not schooled in the lacunae of Chinese strategic thought. Rather he comes at China-related issues as a cold and proud "Realist" who, he claims, is looking out for America's best interests. Glaser's analyses are careful, but he draws alarming and controversial conclusions from them. In a pair of jarring articles, one in *International Security* and the other in *Foreign Affairs*, Glaser called for an essential US abandonment of Taiwan as well as American alliances in East Asia. In each article he argues for "accommodating" Beijing, so as not to provoke it. Glaser argues that,

> First, [territorial] accommodation can satisfy or partially satisfy an adversary that wants to change the status quo, thereby reducing the costs the adversary is willing to pay to further change the status quo, which in turn reduces the probability of war. Second, accommodation can enhance an adversary's security by shrinking the military threat the state poses or by signaling the state's benign motives, or both—which in turns increases the state's own security. Third, accommodation can reduce military competition between the state and its adversary, which under a range of conditions can improve both states' security.[97]

Glaser's "accommodation" is, in my view, outright appeasement.

Glaser explicitly calls for "ending the US commitment to Taiwan," which together with other "accommodating" moves by Washington concerning the East and South China Seas, would be part of a US–China "grand bargain" that he argues would yield the positive effects of lessening tensions, removing "security dilemma" dynamics, and pacifying Beijing.[98] He stunningly states, "Ending the U.S. commitment to defend Taiwan could greatly moderate the intensifying military competition between the United States and China, which is adding to strains in their relationship."[99] Glaser admits in passing that the commitment of the United States to Taiwan involves values, but he brushes this aside in favor of the cold calculus of national interests—and he does not view America's long-standing support for Taiwan to be in the US national interest. Glaser seems most concerned by the escalating competitive and confrontational dynamic between Washington and Beijing, and he is trying to alleviate the growing tension through removing what he sees as the main provocation to Beijing. Perhaps I am misreading him, and his article is long and convoluted, but when it was published, he was a definite outlier in US China policy circles (to say nothing of Taiwan) and he came under sharp attack. He still is an outlier, as not a single analyst has embraced his call to remove the US defense commitment to Taiwan.

In 2021, Glaser published another shocking article—this time doubling down on Taiwan by stating unequivocally, "Taiwan is not a vital US interest."[100] In yet another article, Glaser reiterates his view starkly: "Taiwan is the linchpin of China's security concerns; therefore, ending the US commitment to Taiwan might transform the US–China military competition ... [if] the United States believes China is motivated largely by security, then it should give weight to policies that are less threatening to China."[101]

Even worse, Glaser called for a "reevaluation" of American alliance commitments in East Asia. Using the same logic that he applies to Taiwan, Glaser seems to see these alliances as provocative to Beijing and premised on antiquated assumptions about maintaining American "primacy" in East Asia. This is the same argument made, in many publications, by Australian scholar and strategist Hugh White, although White goes further by arguing that the future of his native Australia, indeed all of Asia—and perhaps the world—clearly lies with China and it is thus best to get on the proverbial China train sooner rather than later.[102] This view is also shared by former Singaporean official and author Kishore Mahbubani.[103] Like White and Mahbubani (and Xi Jinping himself), Glaser views the United States as a "declining power." As such, he states,

> [F]or the declining power, the best option may be to cut back on its commitments. In East Asia, that would mean giving Beijing greater leeway in the South China Sea, letting go of Taiwan, and accepting the United States is no longer the dominant power it once was in the region.[104]

Such extremist views go well beyond Strategic Empathy or even "accommodation"—they represent clearcut appeasement. Needless to say, such defeatist views are anathema to American strategic planners in Washington and Honolulu at INDOPACOM.

Another significant voice in the Strategic Empathy School is Michael Swaine of the Quincy Institute for Responsible Statecraft. Before joining Quincy, Swaine had a long and distinguished career at the RAND Corporation and Carnegie Endowment for International Peace and he has served as a consultant to various parts of the Department of Defense. Over the years, he has published prolifically about China's military and defense strategy, and about US–China relations. It is difficult to summarize such a long and distinguished record of publications, but I think it is fair to say that his writings in recent years are notable for two overriding sets of analysis and argument. Like Glaser's, Swaine's first argument is that the American alliances in Asia and the US military footprint and defense doctrine in the Indo-Pacific are highly provocative to China and thus are destabilizing and do not advance US national security interests.[105] Second, in Swaine's view, it is the United States that—under the Trump and Biden administrations—has primarily caused the significant deterioration of the US–China relations, and that the US government needs to return to a policy of engagement and cooperation with Beijing.[106] In this telling, Washington has been the provocateur and Beijing is simply acting defensively and rationally. Classic strategic empathy. Yet, Swaine also recognizes the real dangers and risky dynamics present in the US–China–Taiwan military domain, and— to his great credit—has led a Track 2 dialogue with PLA interlocutors on crisis management.[107]

Another example of the Strategic Empathy School is Johns Hopkins University (formerly Cornell University) Professor Jessica Chen Weiss. In a widely read essay that she published in *Foreign Affairs* in 2022, Weiss took on the contemporary wisdom in Washington and the Biden administration (in which she had just served as a Council of Foreign Relations fellow on the State Department's Policy Planning Staff) concerning competing with China. The article was not viewed positively by some of her former colleagues in the State Department and US government, as it was seen as violating long-standing norms of not publicly contradicting administration policy.[108] Her expressed views did not necessarily derive from, but predated, her brief government service and experiences. I remember speaking with Jessica before she went to work in the State Department, and she was quite critical of the administration's policies of competing with China, so I counseled her that she may wish to keep those views to herself while serving on the Secretary of State's Policy Planning staff. Her year in government service did not change her mind—instead only seemingly reinforcing her previous convictions. Her lengthy article was published within days of her leaving government service.

In her article Weiss echoes the oft-stated arguments of those in the Re-Engagement School who find fault with the more confrontational turn in American policy since 2017. Weiss counsels that, "rather than looking back nostalgically at its past preeminence, Washington must commit, with actions as well as words, to a positive-sum vision of a reformed international system that includes China and meets the existential need to tackle shared challenges." She continues, "Even in the absence of a crisis, a reactive posture has begun to drive a range of U.S. policies. Washington frequently falls into the trap of trying to counter Chinese efforts around the world without appreciating what local governments and populations want."[109] To be fair, Weiss did not explicitly align her views with those of Beijing, but her critique of Washington's strategy and policies of intensively competing with China certainly echo Beijing's standard line. In another *Foreign Affairs* article entitled "The Case Against the China Consensus," published in September 2024, Weiss doubled down on her original article and arguments.

With her two articles, Weiss became a contrarian voice in Washington and something of a poster child for those who argue that the US government's competition policies are misguided. While noting the need to call out malign Chinese practices, Weiss's main argument seems to be that the US needs to pursue a more positive vision and agenda for its relationship with China. That is fine in the abstract—but *where exactly* does such cooperative potential exist, given that China's behavior contradicts and challenges American interests across almost all issue areas? She also argued, in a separate interview about her first article, that Washington needs to provide "reassurances" to Beijing, and not only threats.[110] This is classic strategic empathy: don't provoke Beijing's many sensitivities, don't antagonize it unnecessarily, and offer gestures of reassurance in the hope of inducing cooperation. In both the article and the interview defending it, Weiss tried to thread the needle between the need to criticize malign Chinese behavior and the need to not demonize the country. Weiss's arguments are nuanced, and I do not wish to oversimplify them. Her main argument, though, is that the "competition paradigm" tends to be inherently zero-sum—and that does not necessarily lead to a stable and productive relationship with China (the leitmotif of the Re-Engagement School).

Another noteworthy example of the Strategic Empathy School is Paul Heer. Trained as a diplomatic historian at George Washington University with a doctoral dissertation on George Kennan's Asia policy,[111] Heer was a longtime analyst in the CIA's Office of China Analysis—working his way up from a junior analyst to capping his career as the National Intelligence Officer for East Asia from 2007–2015. Although he was not trained in Chinese studies and has no Chinese language abilities, Heer nonetheless became an astute analyst of China's domestic and foreign policies. After retiring from the CIA and decades in Washington, he moved to Chicago and became a freelance writer and think-tank affiliate. After decades of not being able to publish in the public domain, Heer exploded post-retirement by publishing dozens of articles in recent years. He has also been working on a book manuscript that explicitly argues for strategic empathy in understanding China and crafting American policy toward the country.

Actually, Heer is difficult to pigeonhole. That is, some of his writings echo the Re-Engagement School, some mirror elements of the Comprehensive Competition School, some agree with the Managed Competition School. Many are critical of assertive US policies, statements, and actions toward China,[112] and he often argues that American commentators on China frequently "overstate and oversimplify" China's capabilities and aspirations.[113] At bottom, though, Heer argues that however appropriate Washington's criticism may sometimes be or however necessary US government or military actions to counter China's own assertiveness may be, there is still a need for American analysts and policymakers to understand the dynamics in China and among its leadership which cause them to take the actions that they take. Classic strategic empathy, as defined by Zachary Shore.[114] In one of his articles Heer explicitly states, "Washington could benefit from a better understanding of the Chinese mindset through the exercise of some 'strategic empathy'—but such an approach is often equated with 'sympathy' and is thus preemptively rejected."[115] Yes, if empathy equals sympathy, then I believe that it *should* be rejected. Heer adds in the same article that,

> Indeed, the CCP's persistent fear that engagement might change China should be sufficient reason to sustain it. This is why mere condemnation of the CCP regime, however justifiable, will have limited utility and success in either liberalizing China or yielding other strategic benefits for the United States. Washington can and should continue to censure Beijing when it engages in horrendous activities and exceeds or violates international norms in its behavior. The United States should also continue bolstering its capabilities and strategies to vigorously resist, deter, and counter Beijing's offensive actions and agenda. But this must be accompanied by pragmatic and persistent efforts to engage with CCP leaders in pursuit of the full range of material US interests and American security and prosperity. This should also include concerted efforts to better and more accurately understand the Chinese mindset.[116]

Actually, this article by Heer is filled with criticisms of Chinese behavior, much more so than in his other publications. One reason may be the negative criticism he received to another article published one week earlier, entitled "Engagement with China Has Not Failed—It Just Hasn't Succeeded Yet."[117] Heer begins the follow-up article by observing, "Among other responses to that article were some vehement attacks on my judgment, integrity, and loyalty to the United States. I was accused in particular of rarely if ever acknowledging the horrific nature of the CCP, and I was advised that my credibility depended on my willingness to publicly condemn it." Thus, in the subsequent article (published on July 25, 2022) Heer went out of his way to criticize and condemn a range of PRC behaviors, labeling it as a "repugnant regime."[118]

Other times Heer seems too indulgent of the Chinese regime and its actions. In one article, entitled "What Is Really Driving Chinese Aggression?" he excuses a wide range of belligerent behavior—toward Taiwan, Hong Kong, territorial disputes in the South China Sea, East China Sea, Xinjiang, and "wolf warrior" public diplomacy—all as "defensive and reactive" to external stimuli.[119] Like some other observers (most notably Michael Swaine and Charles Glaser), Heer argues that Washington should abandon any pretentions to maintaining its "primacy" in East Asia.[120]

In this article, Heer also reiterates his long-standing view that China is *not* trying to exclude the United States from the region. "China *is* pursuing hegemony in East Asia," he says, "but *not* an exclusive hostile hegemony." "It is not trying to exclude the United States from the region or deny American access there." Here, Heer is clearly pushing back against those who believe exactly the opposite. He also adopts the Strategic Empathy argument that "[p]olicies and strategies aimed at upholding US primacy in East Asia are likely to be counterproductive because such an approach ... would reinforce Beijing's belief that the United States seeks to contain China by keeping it subordinate within its own region. This would increase the chances of Beijing feeling compelled to adopt a more confrontational and aggressive posture."

Paul Heer has published a lot,[121] with many insights and analyses, but in one article he sums up his bottom line: "The biggest obstacle to American understanding of China appears to be Washington's seeming determination to misunderstand China—rather than grant any credibility and legitimacy to its strategic outlook and goals."[122] To all strategic empathizers, China must be seen as it sees itself.

The Re-Engagement School

As might be surmised, this school consists of those who were previously supporters of, and stakeholders in, the original Engagement Coalition. Most of the members of this school have spent their entire professional careers *practicing* engagement. In fact, virtually *all* contributors to the five schools of thought examined in this section of the book were previously card-carrying members of the original Engagement Coalition. The only difference with the Re-Engagement School is that—unlike all the others—they have not substantially changed their views in reaction to changed circumstances brought on by Xi Jinping. To the contrary, they believe and argue that moving away from Engagement is a huge strategic mistake on the part of the United States. And, therefore, only returning to Engagement with China will rectify the mistake.

Remember from Chapter 2 that the beauty of the Engagement strategy was that it offered something for multiple constituencies across the country, and thus various interest groups had buy-in and became stakeholders in the relationship. Fundamentally, every constituency bought into the premise that direct contact between Americans and their Chinese counterparts was a good thing, the deeper the better, that engagement with the United States would contribute to the modernization and liberalization of China over time, the PRC's integration into the (US-led) international order, and that there were both direct and indirect benefits to be gained from such interactions and integration. Different constituencies in the United States would benefit directly, while China's broader engagement with the world and the post–World War II international order was also seen as beneficial to American global interests. Many European, Asian, and other nations also accepted this strategic policy logic—as they pursued their own versions of engagement with China.

Despite periodic disruptions in the bilateral relationship (most notably the Tiananmen massacre), engagement with China was rarely questioned. While some Democrats felt that engagement was too indulgent of the abuse of human rights and repression inflicted by the Chinese communist regime, and some Republicans questioned the long-term wisdom of strengthening China's capacities through trade and technology transfer, these naysayers were at the margins of US policy discourse on China—while a strong bipartisan center continually bought into the logic of Engagement. It became axiomatic. For decades, the US foreign policy establishment produced report after report on the need for continued bilateral cooperation and integration of China internationally. This was further evidenced by continually expanding executive-branch bureaucratic interactions with their Chinese government counterparts, deepening state and local ties, a vast proliferation of academic and civil society interactions, ever-broadening trade and commercial relations, considerable tourism, immigration, and inter-societal exchanges.

Thus, the US government's Engagement (with a capital "E") produced engagement (with a lowercase "e") of multiple non-governmental constituencies, breeding many supporters across America. But some were more deeply committed than others. These were the individuals responsible for *managing* the engagement and relationship—US diplomats, key NGOs, some leading academics who had close ties to government and philanthropic funders of engagement activities, and the business community. Put another way, there was a difference between the *orchestrators* of Engagement and the beneficiaries of engagement.

It is thus perhaps quite natural that it is precisely these people—the orchestrators of Engagement—who have been the quickest to praise the record of Engagement (often defensively, I would observe) *and* to call for a return to it as the best approach to current and future China policy.

The first example of the Re-Engagers are the two main NGOs (and their presidents) which have been at the center of engagement for half a century: the National Committee on US–China Relations (NCUSCR) led by Stephen Orlins and the US–China Business Council lead (USCBC) by Craig Allen. This is no surprise, as the very raison d'être of the NCUSCR and USCBC is engagement with China! In Chapter 3, we traced the origins of these two advocacy organizations back to the 1960s. Both are *advocacy* organizations—they both advocate for engagement with China—as such, the 501 (c) (3) tax exempt status of both organizations should be examined by the Internal Revenue Service (IRS) for violating IRS "political and legislative lobbying" statutes. While this has been the bread and butter of the NCUSCR since its inception, it has also had an additional mission of educating Americans about China, but its main job has been to facilitate the physical exchanges of Americans going to China and Chinese coming to America. As such, its mission has concentrated most directly on one of the four pillars of Engagement as described in Chapter 2: engagement as *process*— sending people back-and-forth between the two countries. The people who were sent on the delegations that were exchanged were largely in support of the other three pillars of Engagement outlined in Chapter 2: to modernize and marketize the Chinese economy, to liberalize the Chinese political system and society, and to integrate China into the international liberal order.

Orlins has served as president of the NCUSCR since 2005, two decades of service (far longer than any of his predecessors). Prior to that, he had been a businessman and lawyer in China and Asia, as well as serving as a legal advisor to the Department of State (1976–1979) and was thus involved in laying the legal framework for the normalization of diplomatic relations in 1979. It is his *job* to promote cooperative relations between the United States and China—and he does this unabashedly and without reservation (too much so for some). While publicly criticizing China is not normally part of Orlins's track record or toolkit, the NCUSCR and Orlins do engage with Chinese counterparts on some of the most troublesome issues in the US–China relationship. This is exactly what the defenders of Engagement argue is perhaps *the* single most important aspect of engagement—to literally engage in straightforward conversations with Chinese counterparts about differences as well as commonalities in the relationship. To build bridges, bridge differences, and (where possible) to forge cooperation is, they argue, the *essence* of engagement. Again, this is the engagement as process component of the four elements of the Engagement strategy outlined in Chapter 2.

Orlins's speeches and articles are too many to parse here—but suffice to say they all share one common theme in common: the need for engagement and re-engagement.[123] While he bemoans the atrophy in relations in recent years and constantly calls for the need to repair the strained ties, in one article in the *South China Morning Post* (2021) Orlins offered a sweeping indictment of the Trump administration for triggering the nosedive in relations.[124] This is not unlike other dyed-in-the-wool engagers who primarily blame the American side with cratering the relationship—rather than the United States as *responding* to malign Chinese behavior.

Orlins's counterpart as president of the USCBC is former Ambassador Craig Allen, who served in the position from 2018–2024. Formerly a career Foreign Commercial Officer with the US Department of Commerce and trade negotiator with the US–China Joint Commission on Commerce and Trade, Allen served twice in the US Embassy in Beijing, once in the American Institute in Taiwan, and in the US Embassies in Japan, South Africa, and Brunei (where he was the Ambassador). He is a deeply experienced diplomat and US–China trade expert. While he often was directly engaged in hardball negotiations with his Chinese counterparts over trade disputes, once he was appointed as president of the USCBC, Allen became an unabashed advocate for US business with and in China. As he proudly proclaimed at his inaugural USCBC gala dinner in 2018, "We need *more* trade with and *more* investment from China!"[125] Since then, Allen has continued to advocate expanding US businesses in China, and he expresses discontent with US government policies under the Trump and Biden administrations that seek to limit it. He also advocates for US businesses in China when he meets with his Chinese counterparts. In both public and private, Allen claims that it is his job and responsibility to be an advocate for American workers through advocating for expanded exports to China. As he told the USCBC 50th anniversary celebration gala dinner in December 2023, "We support American companies doing business in China—to benefit American citizens from across this great land: farmers, truckers, ranchers, fishermen, actors, longshoremen, university professors, waiters, hospitality workers, and on and on. More than a million of our fellow citizens are employed due to trade with China."[126]

Without engagement with China, there can be no trade and investment. It is thus no surprise that Ambassador Allen and the USCBC are unabashed advocates for intensified engagement with China. USCBC Board Chairman Evan Greenberg is even more of an outspoken advocate for trade and business with China.[127] Decoupling of the two economies is not in their interests, and they are outspoken critics of those who wish to decouple, de-risk, and otherwise constrain US–China trade and investment. Evan Greenberg's father, the indefatigable Maurice R. Greenberg, joined together with 22 former senior US government officials and diplomats (including former ambassadors to China Gary Locke and Stapleton Roy), business titans, and NGO luminaries (including Steve Orlins and Craig Allen) in taking out a paid full-page advertisement (costing approximately $194,000[128]) in *The Wall Street Journal* on April 3, 2023, addressed to Presidents Joseph Biden and Xi Jinping, calling for "the leadership of both the United States and China to work together diligently to repair and stabilize the state of affairs between our two countries ... to alleviate the heightened temperature and better manage our many differences."[129]

Former Treasury Secretary and longtime engagement advocate Henry Paulson is also an outspoken critic of the "post-engagement" China policies of the Trump and Biden administrations, and he relentlessly advocates for re-engagement with China.[130] Paulson does allow that "some level of decoupling is inevitable," but his North Star remains "recoupling" the two economies.

Other former high-level US government officials are also in favor of maintaining some degree of "engagement as process" with Chinese government interlocutors. Former National Security Advisor Stephen Hadley argues that such direct engagement has—in itself—a stabilizing effect on a strained relationship and that such direct exchanges of contrasting views are the only way to make them clearly understood by the other side and possibly to narrow differences.[131] Former US Trade Representative Charlene Barshefsky, who in 2024 was appointed as Chair of the Board of Directors of the NCUSCR, shares a similar view.[132] This view of "engagement as process" (via face-to-face contact) is increasingly common—and is, in fact, the basis of the Managed Competition School (see the section "The Managed Competition School").

Not surprisingly (because this is what they do on a daily basis), former senior State Department officials are also among the foremost advocates of re-engagement. Career diplomat and former ambassador to China J. Stapleton Roy has been one such advocate. Ambassador Roy was born and raised in China and spent most of his distinguished diplomatic career involved with US–China relations. He is one of the most knowledgeable and sensible advisers on US policy and relations with China, and he is also carefully listened to by Chinese government officials in Beijing. Ambassador Roy was also among the five signatories of the "China Is Not an Enemy" op-ed in *The Washington Post* described above and in Chapter 2, which blamed the breakdown of relations in recent years primarily on the US government and argued for a return to the *processes*, if not the premises, of engagement. Ambassador Roy has been one of the clearest thinking strategists on US China policy in the current ongoing debate. He does not simplistically advocate for a return to engagement for engagement's sake—he believes that there is no realistic alternative, and that it is in American national interests to maintain regular dialogue with the Chinese leadership and governmental authorities no matter what the differences are. Ambassador Roy is particularly hard-headed in pushing the US government to think in longer terms and to more clearly define exactly what type of relationship the United States wishes to have with Beijing.[133] What are the end goals? What are the real priorities? What resources and tools should the US adopt in pursuit of those goals and priorities? What exactly does "competition" as a policy strategy really mean? Is it inherently zero-sum or can it be positive sum? At the end of the day, Ambassador Roy has argued that engagement is not a choice but a necessity for the United States—engagement defined as the process of interaction. However, he bristles at—and rejects outright—the suggestion that the US policy of engagement was *ever* intended to liberalize or democratize China.

Susan A. Thornton is another senior career Foreign Service Officer who has been outspoken in her advocacy of the need to maintain engagement with China. She too was sharply critical of Trump administration China policy— and she paid personally for her disagreements, as Secretary of State Pompeo blocked her nomination to become Assistant Secretary of State for East Asia & Pacific Affairs. Following the blockage, Thornton resigned after nearly 30 years in the Foreign Service. Understandably embittered, she unleashed on the Trump administration's China policies,

> The current "get tough" approach bears more resemblance to the antics of an overly cocky teenager than major power diplomacy. Administration officials refuse to meet Chinese counterparts, humiliate Chinese leaders with "tweet storms" and trash-talk Chinese initiatives and companies on the global stage. The FBI director names China a "whole-of-society threat," and a high-ranking political appointee State Department official asserts that the United States is involved in a "clash of civilizations" with China "because Chinese are not Caucasians." U.S. military encroachments and surveillance missions close to Chinese territory spur a daily high-stakes game of cat and mouse, and US officials assert publicly that Washington and Beijing are already in a "cyber war." U.S. district attorneys travel the country to warn about talking shop to ethnic Chinese co-workers. Rafts of anti-China legislation spew from the printers of congressional staffers. And there are many other, more risky gambits being unspooled behind the black curtain. Even during the most hair-trigger days of the Cold War, the Soviet Union was not treated to such mindless and peripatetic hostility from the U.S. government.[134]

Since leaving government service Thornton retired to her farm in Maine but has remained particularly outspoken in favor of re-engaging with China. As she put it in one interview, "The notion that we're not going to cooperate with China—it's the second largest economy in the world—is just a fantasy. The sooner we dispense with that fantasy and get on with it, the better off we'll be."[135] With this reputation, not surprisingly she is popular in China and is invited there frequently.

Other advocates of re-engagement are senior and respected academics who have also spent their lives practicing and advocating for engagement with China. The most notable such individual is Professor David M. Lampton, whose views on engagement we have already sampled in Chapter 2 and in the Strategic Empathy School. Lampton is not only an intellectual advocate of engagement—but he has spent much of his career outside of universities leading two of the key organizations involved in engagement: the Committee on Scholarly Communication with the People's Republic of China and the National Committee on US–China Relations. He personifies engagement. He has also been an adviser to many philanthropic foundations (including serving as Chairman of the Board of Trustees of the Asia Foundation). During his decades on the faculty of Ohio State and Johns Hopkins Universities, he has been one of the nation's leading specialists and public intellectuals on China and US–China relations.[136] Since the late Michel Oksenberg and Ezra Vogel, there is probably no academic who has been more deeply involved in the practice of US engagement with China.

In one interview in 2024, Lampton summed up his thinking about engagement: "Engagement was not a strategy. Engagement was not a plan. Both of our societies, for about 40 years, saw their interests as broadly compatible and complementary. So, I argue that engagement was propelled by powerful interests at all levels of both societies for a long time and those engaged in the interaction thought they not only were doing well, but also good."[137] While Lampton realizes that the US–China relationship today is deeply and systemically strained, and he argued in 2015 that it was at a "tipping point,"[138] he nonetheless calls for re-engagement. But re-engagement on what basis? "The United States must avoid setting its strategic goals in a way that implies it is trying to keep China externally weak, divided and isolated, and that regime change is the US goal written in invisible ink," Lampton wrote in an article published in 2024.[139] This viewpoint is also illustrative of the Strategic Empathy School.

Other scholars are quite concerned that the United States needs to recalibrate its China policy, be much less confrontational, and look for mutual areas of common concern on which to work together. One example is the book *Engaging China: Rebuilding Sino-American Relations* by Portland State University professor emeritus Mel Gurtov,[140] who offers a detailed "menu" for re-engagement (built mainly around cooperation on transnational issues).[141]

Thus, those who argue in favor of a return to engagement (re-engagement) with China do so almost entirely from the definition of "engagement as process" as outlined in Chapter 2. They *do not* accept the three other definitions of the original purposes of engagement—to modernize the Chinese economy, to liberalize the Chinese political system and society, and to socialize China in the international liberal order. Some, like Gurtov and even the Biden administration, do implicitly seem to accept the third definition of integrating China into the international (liberal) order in pursuit of addressing common transnational challenges—e.g., climate change, public health pandemics, renewable energy, counter-narcotics, global macroeconomic stability, cybersecurity, artificial intelligence, etc. This is a good segue to the Managed Competition School.

The Managed Competition School

The Managed Competition School is something of a hybrid between the Comprehensive Competition and Re-Engagement Schools. It recognizes that systemic and strategic competition is *the* defining characteristic of US–China relations, and it accepts that taking proactive steps to compete with China in various realms is necessary. At the same time, this school is concerned and very conscious of the fact that unconstrained competition carries real risks—including the risk of deadly conflict—and therefore they believe that it is incumbent on both sides to try to reduce the risks by working together to adopt specific measures to "buffer" the competition, to build "guardrails" and various management mechanisms to bound the competition.

This is precisely what the Biden administration meant when it regularly invoked its standard language to "manage competition responsibly."

National Security Advisor Jake Sullivan described it this way:

> We expect that the PRC will be a major player on the world stage for the foreseeable future. That means that even as we compete, we have to find ways to live alongside one another. Competition with the PRC does not have to lead to conflict, confrontation, or a new Cold War. The United States can take steps to advance its interests and values and those of its allies and partners on the one hand, while responsibly managing competition on the other. Being able to do both of those things is at the heart of our approach. And, in fact, the United States has decades of experience talking to and even working with our competitors when our interests call for it ... Detailed, dogged diplomacy is necessary to manage the friction that is endemic to a strategic competition between two major powers ... We aim to continue the pace of intensive interaction with the

PRC that has helped both sides manage areas of difference and unlock cooperation on areas where our interests align. We're not planning to recreate the
now outdated structures and mechanisms from an earlier period in the bilateral
relationship. And we're definitely not interested in dialogue just for dialogue's
sake. But we do see value in launching and shepherding a select number of
working-level consultations in discrete, carefully chosen areas to advance our
interests and achieve results. In the period ahead, we hope we can work with the
PRC to deepen crisis communication mechanisms to reduce the risk of conflict.
We're ready to coordinate on climate, health security, global macroeconomic
stability, and new challenges like the risks posed by artificial intelligence. We'll
also talk to Beijing about challenging regional and global issues, from the Red
Sea to the Korean Peninsula. And we'll work to advance progress on a range of
bilateral issues too, including people-to-people ties.[142]

Without using the term "managed competition," Sullivan and Campbell actually laid out the essentials of the approach (before the Biden administration took
office) in their article published in 2019 in *Foreign Affairs*, "Competition Without Catastrophe: How America Can Both Challenge and Coexist with China."[143]
In this article, they argued,

> Rather than relying on assumptions about China's trajectory, American strat-
> egy should be durable whatever the future brings for the Chinese system. It
> should seek to achieve not a definitive end state akin to the Cold War's ultimate
> conclusion but a steady state of clear-eyed coexistence on terms favorable to
> U.S. interests and values. Such coexistence would involve elements of competi-
> tion and cooperation, with the United States' competitive efforts geared toward
> securing those favorable terms. This might mean considerable friction in the
> near term as U.S. policy moves beyond engagement—whereas in the past, the
> avoidance of friction, in the service of positive ties, was an objective unto itself.
> Going forward, China policy must be about more than the kind of relationship
> the United States wants to have; it must also be about the kinds of interests the
> United States wants to secure. The steady state Washington should pursue is
> rightly about both: a set of conditions necessary for preventing a dangerous
> escalatory spiral, even as competition continues.

More recently, American Ambassador to China Nicholas Burns describes the
duality in US–China relations this way:

> The two countries have a highly competitive relationship across a number
> of areas. That includes the security realm in the Indo-Pacific, technology—
> which in many ways is the heart of the competition now between the two

countries—economics, trade, and human rights. We have to assume this is going to continue. We've been talking to the Chinese about the need to acknowledge this competition and try to manage it effectively. It takes up a lot of time in this relationship.[144]

On another occasion, at the Council on Foreign Relations in New York, Ambassador Burns said, "Competition is the driving thrust of the relationship, but engagement and cooperation is very important for our national interests as well. I hope that we can keep those two contradictory thoughts in mind, maybe two halves of an equation."[145] In another speech at the Brookings Institution in Washington, Burns stated, "We are systemic rivals ... Our job is to wage the competition, but responsibly. We're competing with China, but we're also engaging with China."[146]

The concept of managed US–China competition has its antecedents in the détente phase of the Soviet–American Cold War. The détente processes were not mutually exclusive to the geostrategic competition but were supplementary and complementary.

In an article published in the journal *Asia Policy* in 2017, and then again subsequently in an op-ed in *The Wall Street Journal* (2020), I think I might have been the first to use the term "managed competition" to describe US policy toward China, and I still count myself as a member of the Managed Competition School (as well as the Comprehensive Competition School). In these articles, I argued that the détente of the Soviet–American Cold War offers many poignant lessons for today's Sino-American rivalry, and therefore it is worthwhile to reopen that toolbox and dust off some of the tools.[147] Soviet–American détente was a protracted and multilayered set of reinforcing processes. Some involved multiple countries, such as the Conference on Security and Cooperation in Europe (CSCE) and the Helsinki Accords, which could possibly be adapted in the case of China. Unofficial Track 2 exchanges of experts and the creation of socalled epistemic communities played important roles in the Cold War. These examples from the Soviet–American experience need to be fully reexamined to explore potentially reusable mechanisms. Several other notable individuals with considerable direct experience with Soviet–American and US–Russia relations who have also seen the parallels to the détente phase of the Soviet–American relationship include Stanford scholar and former US ambassador to Russia Michael McFaul and former Secretary of State and Hoover Institution Director Condoleezza Rice.[148]

While some see these parallels, others think they are badly misplaced. In a widely read (including in Beijing, where I was the week after it was published) article from April 2024 in *Foreign Affairs* entitled "No Substitute for Victory: America's Competition with China Must Be Won, Not Managed," Matt Pottinger and Mike Gallagher sharply attacking the détente analogy as well as the entire concept of managed competition:

No country should relish waging another Cold War. Yet a Cold War is already being waged against the United States by China's leaders. Rather than denying the existence of this struggle, Washington should own it and win it. Luke-warm statements that pretend as if there is no Cold War perversely court a hot war; they signal complacency to the American people and conciliation to Chinese leaders. Like the original Cold War, the new Cold War will not be won through half measures and timid rhetoric. Victory requires only admitting that a totalitarian regime that commits genocide, fuels conflict and threatens war will never be a reliable partner. Like the discredited détente policies that Washington adopted in the 1970s to deal with the Soviet Union, the current approach will yield little cooperation from Chinese leaders while fortifying their conviction that they can destabilize the world with impunity ... The Biden administration offers up managing competition as a goal, but that is not a goal; it is a method, and a counterproductive one at that. Washington is allowing the aim of its China policy to become *process* [emphasis added]; meetings that should be instruments through which the United States advances its interests become core objectives in and of themselves.[149]

While the Cold War with the Soviet Union had differing characteristics from the possible Cold War 2.0 with China, the two also exhibit many similarities. The United States and Soviet Union not only had their "tripwires" and "red lines," but they also established a wide variety of conflict avoidance, confidence-building, and crisis-management mechanisms. Not surprisingly, many of these lie in the security/military domain: things like "hotlines" and communications frequencies between military authorities at multiple levels in the chain of command; pre-notification of military exercises and large-scale movement of troops or weapons; arms-control agreements; "rules of the road" for accidental air and sea encounters; crisis escalation controls (including mutual commitments to "no first use" of nuclear weapons); forbidding cyberattacks on civilian infrastructure; bans on anti-satellite weapons and the placing of kinetic systems in outer space; and convening of a variety of meaningful military-to-military dialogues and civilian dialogues (governmental and Track 1.5 and 2) on geostrategic perspectives and policies. There is time and opportunity to try to put in place a variety of confidence-building mechanisms and risk-mitigation measures, create channels of communication and crisis-management mechanisms between military and civilian authorities, and plan non-escalatory reactions to anticipated or possible moves by the other side. Such actions are very much needed in an attempt to buffer, bound, and stabilize the escalating competition today and into the future.

Others who belong to the Managed Competition School include leading Washington think-tankers Scott Kennedy (CSIS) and Ryan Haas (Brookings Institution).[150] Haas's book *Stronger: Adapting America's China Strategy in an Age of Competitive Interdependence* offers a variety of useful suggestions for competing while mitigating risks of conflict in the relationship.[151] In particular, he discusses the need for mutual "risk reduction" and "reciprocal restraint" between Washington and Beijing. Like some who belong to the Re-Engagement School, Haas also argues in favor of intensified engagement with Beijing on global governance issues.[152]

Another prominent example of the Managed Competition School is former Australian Prime Minister (and now Ambassador to the United States) Kevin Rudd. The centerpiece of his important book *The Avoidable War* (2022) and a companion article in *Foreign Affairs* is that, if not managed effectively, the US–China relationship could very easily result in calamitous war.[153] These two publications describe in some considerable detail the various differences that are driving the two sides toward intensified "strategic competition"—but he also maps out a number of steps for effective "managed strategic competition" and avoiding a catastrophic conflict. In addition to his ample political and diplomatic experience, Rudd is also a trained Sinologist and perceptive China watcher (fluent in Chinese and a recent recipient of a PhD from Oxford with a dissertation on Xi Jinping). When it comes to China, Rudd knows of what he speaks. It is highly likely that he conveyed his prescription for managed competition to the White House and State Department during the Biden administration. Among the numerous suggestions for "managing strategic competition," Rudd—like several others—thinks that the best potential for effective management and finding potential collaboration lies in the realm of global governance and reforming the international institutional order.[154] This makes good sense, as no global transnational issue can be effectively addressed without the participation of the United States and PRC.

In short, the essence of the Managed Competition School is for the United States to assertively "compete" with China through a variety of domestic and international means—but, at the same time, to "manage" the competition by engaging in direct dialogue with Beijing on all matters. This is the classic "engagement as process" approach. Prior to mid-2022, however, the Biden administration was all competition and no management. The relationship between the two governments had broken down and become virtually dysfunctional as they were barely talking with each other. Military-to-military exchanges had been terminated altogether (by the Chinese side). The relationship had hit its lowest point in the half century since the Nixon–Mao opening.

In 2023, though, the administration made a concerted effort to rebuild "channels of communication" between the two sides. As Kurt Campbell, the administration's top Asia hand, put it, "We believe, at this juncture, the critical effort in front of us is ensuring that there is a higher degree of effective, systemic communication between the leadership of our two countries."[155] A roadmap to restart reciprocal exchanges was agreed when Biden and Xi Jinping met in Bali, Indonesia, in November 2021. The White House readout in the meeting indicated that Biden "reiterated that this competition should not veer into conflict and underscored that the United States and China must manage the competition responsibly and maintain open lines of communication."[156]

Unfortunately, the schedule of planned exchanges was soon short-circuited by the "spy balloon incident" of January/February 2022—when a Chinese reconnaissance balloon floated 60,000 feet over the continental United States, hovering for days over ICBM sites in Montana. It turns out that this was far from the first time that Chinese spy balloons had transited American airspace. China's military balloon reconnaissance program has been going on for a number of years, based on Hainan Island. After the Montana incident occurred, American intelligence revealed that there had been several previous flyovers near sensitive military facilities on the Hawaiian island of Kauai (where anti-missile lasers are tested), near Pearl Harbor itself, near the massive US military base on the island of Guam, as well as over Florida and Texas.[157] After US Air Force fighters shot the balloon down off the East Coast of the United States on February 4, 2022, another six-month hiatus in face-to-face meetings ensued. By mid-2023, they hesitantly restarted. China hawk Representative Mike Gallagher labeled the renewed contact as "zombie engagement."[158]

The carefully orchestrated series of exchanges at the ministerial/cabinet secretary level culminated in another leaders' summit near San Francisco in November 2023. As described in Chapter 5, this summit meeting did serve to stabilize the relationship. After that, a pattern of episodic exchanges began again—but such meetings were few and far between. Still, the two sides at least began talking again. The US administration was, however, wary of falling into China's "dialogue trap"—where dialogues become over-institutionalized and over-scripted. David Sanger, diplomatic correspondent of *The New York Times*, observed that "the risk was that those meetings could become talk for talk's sake, the sort of empty diplomacy that the Biden team had described as a failure of past administrations."[159] National Security Advisor Jake Sullivan explained to Sanger his view of the difference between "engagement" and "diplomacy": "Engagement is premised on the theory that deeper interdependence with

China, and working groups with China to resolve issues, would produce changes in Chinese behavior." Diplomacy, on the other hand, according to Sullivan, is about "managing conflict."[160] This is an interesting definition of engagement which combines the "engagement as process" approach with attempts to induce change in Chinese behavior, all of which are part of the definition I provided in Chapter 2. But it is difficult to see how engagement as process differs from normal diplomacy. For example, this is the way that the State Department described the meeting (in May 2024) between Deputy Secretary of State Kurt Campbell and Executive Vice Foreign Minister Ma Zhaoxu:

> Deputy Secretary of State Kurt M. Campbell hosted People's Republic of China (PRC) Executive Vice Foreign Minister Ma Zhaoxu for an official visit in Washington on May 30, 2024. The candid and constructive discussion was part of ongoing efforts to maintain open lines of communication between the United States and PRC and responsibly manage competition in the relationship ... The Deputy Secretary emphasized that although the United States and PRC are in competition, both countries need to prevent miscalculation that could veer into conflict or confrontation. Both sides reaffirmed the importance of maintaining open channels of communication at all times and committed to continue diplomacy and consultations in the United States and the PRC in the period ahead.[161]

From Defensive to Proactive Managed Competition

The kind of managed competition practiced by the Biden administration is what I call "defensive managed competition." It is *reactive* and intended to keep a lid on the inevitable frictions arising from comprehensive competition. An alternative would be more *proactive* managed competition, where the two sides together seek to establish a series of frameworks and agreements similar to the late détente phase in Soviet–American relations. During that phase, Moscow and Washington moved beyond arms control to negotiate and establish frameworks for European and Eurasian security (the Conference on Security Cooperation in Europe) and human rights (the Helsinki Agreements). As Philip Zelikow and Condoleezza Rice illustrate in their firsthand account of the period,[162] the ability to break through and go beyond the narrow Soviet–American arms-control agenda depended on two key factors: creative leadership and bold new thinking. It was not until Mikhail Gorbachev became the Soviet leader and decided that his country and regime were not likely to endure without sweeping fundamental reforms domestically (*perestroika* and *glasnost*) and internationally, that necessitated such "new thinking." At first, the Americans were equally caught in the arms-control mental trap, but Secretary of State James Baker persuaded President George H. W. Bush that truly new thinking was required if the frozen frontiers in Europe were to be reconceptualized and redrawn (the CSCE process), and human rights in the Soviet Union and East European communist states could also be qualitatively improved through a new collaborative framework (the Helsinki Process).

Such bold "new thinking" is definitely needed today in the US–China relationship. Both sides need to think boldly beyond a narrow and reactive managed competition framework—and reach for a broader bilateral scaffold, particularly in two areas: human rights in China and the security architecture in Northeast and Southeast Asia. This would require truly new thinking on the part of both leaderships. Concerning the human rights dimension, one should not be at all optimistic that Xi Jinping would be willing to permit anything like the Helsinki Process to be constructed with China today. If China had a reformist leader along the lines of previous Chinese leaders Zhao Ziyang, Hu Yaobang, Jiang Zemin, or Hu Jintao, there *might* be such an opportunity to explore a Helsinki-like process—but *not* with the draconian dictator Xi Jinping. We will have to wait for the post-Xi era and hope that a more reformist leader—similar to these previous ones—who would come to power. Concerning the Asian security architecture, there may be scope for bridging the differences between the Chinese schema for non-alliance-based security organizations and the long-standing American preference for alliances. After all, in the Soviet–American case, CSCE *supplemented* the American alliance system, and it was not necessary to alter or dissolve NATO (as pre-Gorbachev Soviet leaders had long insisted). Finding a mutually acceptable architecture for Asian security, which would include *parallel* but overlapping structures, is conceivable—perhaps even under Xi Jinping—but some truly creative thinking and some protracted difficult negotiations (which necessarily would include other Asian states) would be required.

Thus, while "defensive managed competition" is certainly useful as a device for "bounding" comprehensive competition and keeping the peace, a more elastic type of "proactive managed competition" is worth considering and pursuing.

* * * *

The Great American China Policy Debate will surely continue. Such animated discourse is in American democratic DNA. Through the cacophony of dueling perspectives and sometimes heated rhetoric, policy ideas are floated, considered, criticized and counter-criticized—and sometimes consensus is built and specific policy proposals are adopted. In some ways, though, it is not so much the outcome that matters as much as the *process* of debate. It may be cumbersome and messy, but it is the essence of democracy and often produces good policy. As Winston Churchill is credited with observing, "The Americans can always be trusted to do the right thing, once all other possibilities have been exhausted."

In Chapter 9, I turn from examining others' policy prescriptions and offer my own.

Chapter 9
Conclusion: Toward a New China Strategy

"For any administration, China is in its own category—too big to ignore, too repressive to embrace, too difficult to influence, and very, very proud."
— Madeleine Albright, former US Secretary of State[1]

"Engagement was effectively dead by 2016. In today's era of great power competition, 'managed competition' and 'competitive coexistence' have replaced 'engagement,' R.I.P."
— Joseph S. Nye, Harvard University[2]

"We deal with China as we find it, not as we desire it. Conversely, China has to deal with America as it is, not as Beijing may wish it to be."
— David M. Lampton, Johns Hopkins University[3]

This book has covered a number of dimensions of America's relations with—and policies toward—China, and it has tackled a fairly lengthy period of time—75 years from 1949 to 2024 (with some discussion in Chapter 1 that goes all the way back to the 1780s through the 19th and early 20th centuries). It has concentrated on exploring three principal puzzles: First, how to explain the repetitive fluctuation in the relationship from amity to enmity to amity to enmity over time? Second, what was the American "Engagement" strategy all about, and what did it intend to accomplish? Third, after five decades, why and how has that Engagement strategy come asunder and fractured, and what has it been replaced by?

With respect to the first puzzle—the reasons for the repetitive fluctuation in the relationship, oscillating repeatedly between amity to enmity over many decades (if not centuries)—one principal explanation, indeed the core argument of the book, is that the main driver of the fluctuation has to do with *American expectations* of China and America's centuries-long "missionary complex" to try to shape China and move it in more "modern" and liberal directions. That is, the *externalization* of American expectations on to the Other (in this case, China) has been the main independent variable, while the main dependent variable has been either China's compliance *or* nonconformity with these expectations. When China was generally complying with and conforming to American expectations of liberal development (in all spheres), and not resisting it, the relationship has been generally cooperative and stable. Basically speaking, when China was seen by the United States to be incrementally moving in a seemingly liberal direction—economically, socially, intellectually, politically, and internationally—and did not resist American paternalism, Americans instinctively believed that the relationship was moving in the "right" direction. However, when China's own nationalism and self-interests led it to resist American paternalistic expectations, practices, and presence, then frictions quickly arose and the relationship became strained, acrimonious, and unstable. This is the *macro dynamic* in the Sino-American relationship over time as I see it, and the bottom-line takeaway of this study.

This takeaway not only goes far toward accounting for the fluctuations in the relationship from the Carter administration (1976–1980) to the present (2024), but this pattern has actually been repeated numerous times since the 1780s (250 years!). To be sure, it is not the *only* variable which has caused fluctuation in the relationship—as both crises and troublesome episodes have periodically jarred it, while the two powers' national interests sometimes diverged or collided. Oftentimes China sublimated its discomfort with American policies and efforts to change China so as to accommodate its own broader interests of modernization and security. It is also true and important to recognize that, until very recent years, China has always been the weaker party and thus it *needed* the United States for its modernization and security. It was an asymmetrical relationship. However, with China's increased strength and America's relatively declining power, Beijing has been much more inclined toward, and capable of, "pushing back" to protect its perceived interests. Thus, shifting power dynamics impinge upon the perceptual dimension of the relationship.

Whether or not one accepts this argument, there is no denying the repetitive oscillating cycles of amity/enmity and cooperation/friction over time. Historians of US–China relations have referred to this as the "love–hate cycle."[4] The intellectual puzzle is *why*? What causes the fluctuation? To reiterate, this study argues that the principal reason has been America's attempts to mold and shape China, on the one hand, and China's responses (either accepting or resistant) on the other.

This raises the further question of whether the recent deterioration of relations and period of increased and intense acrimony (from 2017 to 2024) is simply another periodic downswing in the long relationship—that will pass, as the two countries will eventually re-engage, rediscover each other, and rebuild a more amicable relationship? After all, this has occurred many times in the past—as the pendulum swung from confrontation back to more cooperative interactions. *Or is this time really different?* Is the competition now so broad, deep, and systemic, and the power dynamic no longer so asymmetrical in America's favor, that this current mutual hostility is really the "new normal"? Despite the historically oscillating pattern that would lead one to expect a return to a more cooperatively normal relationship, this time the *structural* dynamics in the relationship have really changed as China has become America's "peer competitor."

Add to this the important fact that Xi Jinping has been a very different type of Chinese leader—no longer willing to "hide brightness and bide time" (韬光养晦) and sublimate China's deep suspicions of the United States to the interests of maintaining America's contributions to China's modernization and security. As a result of these factors, China has a newfound confidence and hubris.

It has been Xi Jinping's policies and the behavior of his regime which have so thoroughly challenged American national interests, policy priorities, moral sensibilities, and attempts to shape China which have produced American responses and counteractions. Chapters 5, 6, and 7 have chronicled both the actions of Xi's regime and America's counteractions. Xi and his regime have definitely exercised agency in the relationship. Seen in this way, it is *America* that has been reacting to China's behavior. But, at the same time, Xi's China has been reacting to what it sees as subversive and highly confrontational "anti-China" policies emanating from the United States. Thus, there *is* an action–reaction–re-reaction dynamic at work here. Both sides have exercised agency.

This study has also taken a deep dive into the history and elements of America's decades-long "Engagement" strategy toward China. Chapter 3 revealed that the logic of engagement actually had its origins as far back as Eisenhower, Kennedy, and the very early Johnson administration. It far predated President Nixon's stunning opening to China in 1971–1972. Indeed, there was a groundswell of popular and elite support for altering America's Containment policies toward the People's Republic of China (PRC) which Nixon was alert to and which may have contributed to his calculations that there would be domestic support for his ice-breaking initiative. In Chapter 4, I then traced how six successive American presidents and their administrations (Carter through Obama) understood and practiced the strategy and policies of Engagement. Critical understanding of how and why this strategy prevailed over such a long period of time requires that we understand "Engagement" to be both a *governmental strategy* (which I normally have capitalized as "Engagement") and *interaction* between the two societies. The Engagement strategy spawned an extremely diverse range of domestic American actors that literally engaged (with a small "e") with their counterparts in China. As described in Chapter 2, this broad range of domestic American actors forged a de facto Engagement Coalition—both in Washington and nationwide, across numerous political constituencies, interest groups, and institutions. The beauty of engagement was that it had something in it for everyone—as all of these diverse actors became stakeholders in the strategy and the relationship. That is how foreign policy is supposed to work in a democracy.

This book also shows in some considerable detail—in Chapters 5, 6, and 7—exactly how all of these constituencies each came to believe that their interests were no longer benefitting as much (if at all) from their engagement with China—and indeed that China was actually *harming* their interests. One by one, these domestic American actors all began to "peel away" from the Engagement Coalition: executive branch departments of the federal government in Washington, Congress, all the 50 American states, the national security community, NGOs, universities, foreign policy and China experts, and (to a lesser extent) the business community.

As the Engagement Coalition fractured, I argue, it has been replaced by the Counter-China Coalition. To be sure, this new coalition remains somewhat inchoate and is still taking shape. It was easier to find commonalities to engage with China previously than it is nowadays to find them to disengage from and oppose China. There are also real costs to disengagement— literal costs (financial) and costs imposed by the two governments (in the form of sanctions, travel bans, and disruption of institutional exchanges). *Both* the United States and the PRC governments engage in these punitive measures. The relationship has become mutually "(over-)securitized." As the new Counter-China Coalition has taken shape, its constituent elements all share in common an alienation from China, frustrations with how various Chinese authorities and institutions have tried to block their activities inside of China, and how various Chinese actors themselves have penetrated *into* the United States (thus violating American laws and transgressing a range of American interests).

In this evolving environment, where one coalition has fractured and the other is still forming, something of a policy vacuum has existed in terms of the future direction of American strategy, policies, and relations with China. What happens when policy vacuums exist in American democracy? Americans enter into intense debates with one another. That is what Chapters 1 and 8 are all about respectively: the "Did Engagement Fail?" debate of 2016–2019 (Chapter 1) and its successor, the Great American China Policy Debate of 2020–2024 (Chapter 8). I delved deeply into these twin debates. As with most debates, clear winners and losers are usually illusive. Rather, there is a kind of competitive cacophony where different voices assert their positions and try to win adherents. Sometimes, a general consensus emerges in such national-level debates. Such is the case with the "Did Engagement Fail?" debate, with a broad and fairly clear consensus emerging that the answer was "yes" (it did fail to achieve at least one of its main aims, to politically liberalize China). Yes, there were naysayers who disagreed that Engagement had failed, but they were a distinct minority. These previous advocates for engagement have simply morphed into a new school of re-engagement. However, as Chapter 8 details, this cohort is but one of *five* schools of thought that are currently competing to prevail in the ongoing debate over how to cast a new American China strategy.

Contextual Factors Affecting American China Policy

Of course, American strategy and policies toward China do not occur in a vacuum disassociated from broader contextual factors that affect and constrain American choices of strategy and policies. This section identifies a number of these factors.

The Relative Decline of American Power and Diffusion of Global Power

Ever since the so-called unipolar moment[5] in the aftermath of the collapse of the Soviet Union and end of the Cold War, the era of American predominance and primacy has steadily dissipated. America's share of the global economy was 40 percent in 1960, it shrunk to 34 percent in 1985 and 30 percent in 2000, and it is 24 percent today. Other measures of power reveal similar *relative* declines in America's once predominant role. This is by no means to suggest that the United States is no longer a superpower and the comprehensively strongest power on the planet—but it is empirically the case that it is no longer "predominant," and the United States no longer enjoys "primacy." Recognizing this reality, as Harvard Professor Joseph S. Nye has argued in recent years, the United States still possesses tremendous intrinsic attributes and resilience. To paraphrase Mark Twain, reports of its decline have been exaggerated. In 2020, during COVID-19 and the first Trump administration, the United States seemed to many around the world to be in inexorable eclipse. It had indeed squandered significant soft power and its economy had eroded. But by 2024, both have been rebuilt. Meanwhile, China's economy has entered a secular decline. No one is any longer predicting that China aggregate GDP will overtake that of the United States by 2030. Indeed, there is now discussion of "peak China" (China having past its peak of growth).[6] Its soft power and international reputation have similarly tanked.

Nonetheless, the world is a dynamic and fluid place, and the United States needs to continually adapt and adjust. In this new environment, I see the world as currently "trifurcating," with three important trends of note occurring in international relations.

First, in the wake of the rise of China and Russia's aggressive war against Ukraine, the "West" has rediscovered itself. Transatlantic consultation and cooperation have not been stronger or more solid in years. NATO has had new life and purpose breathed into it (including the addition of Finland and Sweden). I have been studying US–European approaches to China for decades, and it is apparent to me that convergence and coordination on China policy has perhaps never been closer and stronger than during the Biden administration. This said, such transatlantic comity can never be assumed and always needs to be cultivated. Supportive of transatlantic strength has been the solidarity of the five American allies in Asia. Although the alliance with Thailand remains wobbly, the other four (with Australia, Japan, the Philippines, and South Korea) have all been significantly strengthened during the Biden administration.

The second and deeply concerning trend is what I call the new "Axis of Illiberalism"—composed of Russia, China, Iran, and North Korea.[7] These four authoritarian/totalitarian despotic states support each other in many political, diplomatic, economic, technological, and military ways—thus offsetting their own intrinsic weaknesses and vulnerabilities. All four are under an array of sanctions by the West and isolation in the international community, and together they present real challenges to Western democracies. They are all deeply aggrieved states which share in common deep antipathy for the United States, toward liberalism and democracies, and toward the postwar Liberal International Order; they are all pervasive violators of human rights and basic freedoms of their citizens. Russia and China are engaged in territorial aggression (in Ukraine and the South China Sea, respectively), while Iran contributes to instability across the Middle East. North Korea is a constant existential threat to South Korea, as well as to Japan, and more recently the Kim regime has taken the unprecedented provocative step of sending its military forces to fight on the Russian side against Ukraine. Unlike the expansive Western coalition I have just described, these four illiberal repressive states have few followers, adherents, and *no allies*. This said, only North Korea can be described as truly isolated. China obviously has extensive diplomatic and economic ties around the world, Putin's Russia has managed to evade the Western sanctions regime with the assistance of China and India, and Iran maintains some ties in the Middle East and with Europe. The fact that these four states find common cause and bond together with each other actually speaks volumes about their relative isolation.

Within this four-way axis, the China–Russia relationship is by far the most consequential for the United States and the West. This relationship is currently at its closest and highest level *ever* (even exceeding the heyday of the Sino-Soviet alliance and partnership of the 1950s). Much has been published about the relationship in general and the Putin–Xi relationship in particular,[8] so there is no need to probe that further here. Suffice to say that, in my view, the Beijing–Moscow "Comprehensive Strategic Partnership of Coordination" is much more than a tactical expedient. It reflects similar political systems, a common Marxist–Leninist heritage, a common strategic outlook (anchored on opposing the United States and global liberal norms), some common bilateral complementarities, well-institutionalized ties between the two governments, two militaries, two security services, two scientific and technological establishments, two military-industrial complexes, and common border provinces in the Russian Far East and Chinese northeast (东北).

As was the case during the 1950s, when the United States adopted the "wedge strategy" to try and split the Sino-Soviet alliance (which eventually fractured on its own and not as the result of American pressure), it would behoove American interests if the current Sino-Russian partnership fractured. But, as during the earlier period, there is not a great deal that the United States can do to induce a split today. This is not to say that there are not possible fissures to exploit, however. Much depends, in my view, on the Russian leadership. As I see it, Putin is the key variable. As long as Vladimir Putin rules Russia and pursues his anti-Western policies and seeks to restore Russian hegemony over much of the former Soviet Union, he will find common cause and support from Beijing. The one area of potential friction is in Central Asia, which Putin covets in his hegemonic quest but where China has established a deep presence. If Putin were to be replaced as Russian leader, his replacement may revert to a more Western orientation (another strong strand in Russian traditional geopolitical thinking). Under such circumstances, China would find itself more isolated. Xi Jinping is less of a variable, as Chinese interests in Eurasia are more constant and the Chinese are not as intrinsically hostile to the West as Putin is. Thus, if the United States and the West seek to undermine the China–Russia entente the best way to pursue it is to bring all possible pressure to topple the Putin regime and allow a post-Putin Russia to embark on a new and more variegated foreign policy that is not hostile to the West. Similarly, a less pro-Russian and anti-American Chinese regime could also change the dynamic. But that will have to await the post-Xi era.

The third trend is the diffusion of power and the rising importance of the Global South (countries south of the Equator)—the highly diverse and broad set of countries (140 of the 191 member states of the United Nations). The United States may still be a superpower—but it is one in a highly diversified world, one where China has sunk deep roots and enjoys a significant following with this broad swath of countries. To my mind, one the greatest failures of American foreign policy in general and China policy in particular has been the failure to craft a broad Global South strategy and a specifically crafted Global South component to its China strategy. One notable voice who has called for the same is my respected Hoover Institution colleague Elizabeth Economy.[9]

These three global trends constitute important context within which the United States must pursue its broad foreign policy and national security interests, but also its China strategy specifically.

The Multinational and Multilateral Necessities of a Successful China Strategy

America could never really "go it alone" in its China policies, and it certainly cannot today or in the future. A successful China strategy can never be unilateral or even strictly bilateral. By necessity, it must be multinational (among nations) and multilateral (among international institutions). This is even more the case as US primacy has dissipated and the United States now exists in a more diverse international environment.

Under conditions of this diminished and diversified power structure, American allies and non-allied partnerships serve as critical multipliers for the United States. Fortunately, the United States has many such multipliers. A total of *56 nations* are *formal* allies—defined as defense treaties with clauses of mutual defense (so-called Article IV clauses): 32 members of NATO, 19 members of the Rio Treaty and Organization of American States, and 5 Asia-Pacific nations (Australia, Japan, the Philippines, South Korea, and Thailand).[10] In addition, the United States today has 18 designated "Major Non-NATO Allies." Further, the US Departments of State and Defense both have extensive sets of formal "strategic partnerships" around the world.

While not all of these countries view China in exactly the same way, there is considerable overlap with the US government's perceptions and policies. Indeed, a large majority of these states have also encountered real difficulties with Xi Jinping's China—notably those in NATO and the European Union as well as four of five Asia-Pacific allies (Thailand being the outlier). To the extent that Washington can embed its China policy multinationally with these like-minded states, so much the better (the Biden administration did an excellent job of this). Keeping these allies and partners on side should *never* be taken for granted by Washington—they require constant reaffirmation and rejuvenation. Ally management is what former Secretary of State George Shultz referred to as "diplomatic gardening" (i.e., constant cultivation).

A related contextual reality is the evolving international institutional order—the United Nations and the broad range of regional *multilateral* organizations around the world. These international bodies are an extremely important component of international affairs and are themselves evolving (and in real need of revision and upgrading). The United Nations alone has 17 agencies. Regional organizations such as the Association of Southeast Asian Nations (ASEAN), the Organization of American States (OAS), the African Union (AU), the Gulf Cooperation Council (GCC), and the European Union (EU) are all highly relevant; to the extent that the United States can find synergies in its China policies with member states of these organizations, so much the better. Of course, China is also competing for influence in each of these organizations *and* it has established its own set of separate regional groupings—such as the Forum on China–Africa Cooperation, the China–Arab Cooperation Forum, the Shanghai Cooperation Organization, the China–Latin American and Caribbean States Cooperation Forum, and the BRICS.[11] All of these organizations interact with both the United States and China and all play outsized roles in their own regions. American China policy must ipso facto be embedded in these regions.

Complex Bilateral Interdependence

Another hugely important conditioning factor in the US–China relationship is the deep and complex interdependence between the two economies and societies. Social and economic decoupling is an empirical impossibility, even if there are real pressures from each government to do so to some extent. The book *Stronger: Adapting America's China Strategy in an Age of Competitive Interdependence* (published in 2021 by Ryan Hass, China specialist at Brookings Institution) illustrates a variety of the complex linkages that exist between the two societies.[12] Yet, the interdependencies are asymmetrical. For example, there are *millions* of former PRC nationals who have immigrated to the United States and virtually no Americans who have emigrated to China (yes, American expats work there, but only a handful have become PRC citizens). Many of the millions of these immigrant Chinese maintain deep ties to their original homeland and regularly return to do business and visit relatives, while at the same time having become important contributors to the fabric of American society.

The commercial and economic interdependencies are also profound. In 2023, the two nations did $575 billion in goods trade. Excluding the ten collective nation-states of the ASEAN, which now ranks as China's leading trading partner, and the 27 member states of the European Union (which ranks second), the United States is China's largest trading partner. For its part, the US–China

Business Council estimates that exports of goods and services to China support one million American jobs.

Nearly 160,000 Chinese students still enroll in US universities every year, two-way tourism is picking up again, collaborative research in the sciences goes on, and other people-to-people exchanges exist. Nonetheless, as described particularly in Chapters 6 and 7, the institutional linkages between the national-level and state governments, between NGOs, media, and other sectors of the two societies have either been broken off or have atrophied badly (likely never to be restarted). Thus "institutional decoupling" is real, even if economic and social decoupling is not.

Rapid Technological Innovation

The US–China relationship is also conditioned by the ongoing burst in new technological innovations sweeping the planet—changing the nature of communications, of production and commerce, of warfare, of governance, of almost everything in the daily lives of developed countries (developing countries have been largely left out). At the forefront of this new technological revolution are innovations in artificial intelligence. Also of cutting-edge importance is quantum computing, advanced robotics, bio- and nanotechnology, new materials, virtual reality, augmented reality, clean technologies, blockchain, and the Internet of Things. China's *Made in China 2025* program (中国制造 2025) identified these and other new innovations as national priorities back in 2015. Today and into the future, the United States and China are both key contributors to, competitors in, and directly affected by these technological trends.

Domestic Realities

Last, but certainly not least, in terms of contextual factors that will condition the making and implementation of American strategies and policies toward China are the "structural" domestic realities in both the United States and China.[13] While both societies are dynamic and always changing to some extent, there are factors that are quite constant and not likely to change.

In the case of China, the assumed continuities include the sheer size of the country, population, national economy (second largest in the world at $17.9 trillion GDP), and hence its ability to navigate downturns in economic growth or economic shocks; the deeply institutionalized Leninist political system, the Sinified Marxist political philosophy underlying it, and the significant public support for the Chinese Communist Party (CCP); the assumed likelihood (but with less certainty) of Xi Jinping's rule enduring through 2030; the claim to Taiwan as an inherent and intrinsic sovereign part of China; and the regime's continued emphasis on domestic security, which perceives the United States as a genuine subversive threat.

In the case of the United States, the assumed continuities include secure borders and friendly neighbors; the world's largest economy ($28.6 trillion); the rule of law; the institutions and processes of democracy despite continuing deep divisions and periodic paralysis between the Democratic and Republican parties; a strong belief in, and continued funding for, the world's strongest military; world-class scientific and technological innovation; and energy independence.

Despite these continuities, and inherent "strengths" of both systems, nothing is preordained. Shocks to these systems can—and do—happen. One should *never* assume complete continuity in domestic politics and the iron laws of economics guarantees respective cyclical fluctuations. In both countries presidential leadership is a key factor, particularly in the case of Xi Jinping, who has had an outsized impact on all aspects of his country—but with whom there exists considerable discontent in China. American presidents are more circumscribed by the democratic system and various interest groups which contribute to shaping China policies.

A Strategy for "Assertive Competition" Toward China

After this lengthy book providing others' perspectives and policies on American China policy, in this section I wish to provide my own views and suggestions. To my mind, for the United States, China is a geostrategic challenge, a military adversary, an economic and technological competitor, and an ideological rival. As such, the United States needs a comprehensive and systematic strategy for competing effectively with China across all of these spheres.[14] Such a strategy contains both broad principles and more narrow components.

Broad Principles

Indefinite comprehensive competitive rivalry: The United States and China have entered a lengthy and indefinite period characterized by this four-part term (which I elaborated in Chapter 8). I hasten to add that "competition" is not a codeword for confrontation or containment. Competition means just that—to compete proactively and assertively with China on all fronts. Competing is what rivals do, and China is America's rival. To be effective, competing includes both offensive and defensive elements. The United States must simultaneously strengthen itself (making itself more competitive) while pressuring and limiting—not helping—China's pursuit of strength and global influence. In international relations theory this is sometimes referred to, respectively, as "defensive realism" and "offensive realism." Some may well legitimately ask: What is it that the United States and China actually are competing over? Relative domestic strength and global influence is precisely what the two rivals are competing over. That means increasing all elements of American comprehensive national power vis-à-vis China, while offering a persuasive vision for world order that influences other nations. As Hoover Institution Senior Fellow Elizabeth Economy succinctly noted in a 2024 CSIS study, "It is a competition for the values and structure of the international system itself and leadership of that system."

Also, simply using the term "strategic competition" is insufficient—because to many American experts "strategic" primarily signifies the military/security domain. Today's *competition* between the United States and China is *comprehensive* in scope, and affecting multiple realms: military/security, political systems, ideology and values, diplomacy, economic/commercial, media, culture and soft power, governance practices, public diplomacy and "influence operations," espionage, technology, innovation, the Indo-Pacific region, and global competition in all of these functional areas and in international institutions. In each area, China is a competitor of the United States—pursuing contradictory (and often diametrically opposed) policies and practices—and it must be dealt with as such. This is an increasingly intensified dynamic, although not yet a zero-sum one in all domains. In every one of these areas, the United States and China find themselves in disagreement and competing for advantages and influence vis-à-vis the other. It is also a *rivalry* in classic great power terms—both symmetrically between the world's two leading powers and asymmetrically in terms of rising vs. established powers (the so-called Thucydides' Trap). And the competition is temporally *indefinite* in character—it is likely to last decades into the future.

Practicing comprehensive competition against another power is complicated. As Johns Hopkins University scholar Hal Brands astutely argues in his superb book *The Twilight Struggle: What the Cold War Teaches Us About Great Power Rivalry Today*,[15]

> In essence, long-term competition is an ongoing open-ended contest for influence between great powers ... Long-term competition is interactive: it requires outplaying an antagonist that is trying to outplay you. It means ... molding the larger international environment to limit the adversary's options ...
>
> Long-term competition occurs in a world of finite resources, as no one has the advantage in every dimension of rivalry, countries must tolerate weakness

somewhere if they are to enjoy strength anywhere. The essence of long-term competition, then, is strategic choice: countries must choose where to focus and where to economize; they must deftly apply limited means while forcing a competitor to squander its own. Above all, long-term competition rewards countries that pit their strengths against a competitor's vulnerabilities and translate moments of opportunity into lasting advantage.

Long-term competition is comprehensive. The military balance invariably casts its shadow over any competition, but power is multidimensional, so struggles over power are multidimensional too. Long-term competition thus requires integrating multiple forms of influence into an integrated whole.

Long-term competition ... plays out over years, decades, generations. It rewards the incremental strengthening of position rather than the quest for quick, decisive triumph ... Commitment is imperative.

Long-term competition is a test of systems as much as statecraft. It is the measure of whose political, social, and economic model can best generate and employ power ... And because long-term competition is a contest of systems, shrewd players will ruthlessly exploit a rival's internal weaknesses.

These is sage advice from Professor Brands. His whole book should be required reading for all American strategists as they formulate competitive strategies toward China today and into the future.

Assertive competition: The United States should embrace comprehensive competition with China and do so *assertively*. Passivity is a recipe for failure, and multitasking is required. As in sports, a winning strategy requires playing defense proactively and controlling the pace of play on offense. The United States should constantly push forward American interests and priorities, while pushing back against malign Chinese behavior that challenges US interests and values on a *global* basis. The United States should not shy away from competing assertively or think it is some kind of negative approach simply because it is not of the Kantian paradigm of cooperation which underpinned decades of Engagement. China is not a friend or partner of the United States; it is America's competitor, rival, and possible adversary. We are again living in a Realist age of great power rivalry. The United States needs to throw off the mental and policy shackles that lead it to instinctively think solely in terms of engagement, diplomacy, and cooperation—and rather adopt a much more tough-minded and competitive mindset. Doing so requires a much higher tolerance for friction in the relationship. Sometimes competition requires confrontation. This said, a fractious and friction-plagued relationship is potentially dangerous— thus establishing "floors," "guardrails," "buffers," and other "confidence-building mechanisms" to constrain the competition is also important.

Compete constantly, cooperate selectively: The United States has many more differences with China than interests in common. As such, a strategy of "competing first and cooperating second" is realistic and prudent. Recognizing that this is now a primarily competitive relationship, we must also recognize that there remain some limited areas of important potential *cooperation* between the United States and China—primarily in the arena of "global governance." This includes working together with China on global economic stability, counterterrorism, artificial intelligence, climate change, pandemics, sea-lane security, nuclear nonproliferation, regional security and peacekeeping, counternarcotics production and smuggling, managing migration, and other transnational problems. These are all significant and important issues, on which the United States and China (together with others in the international community) should always try to collaborate. Bilateral and multilateral bureaucratic efforts should be made to forge cooperation where possible in these areas. Such cooperation does not necessarily have to be collaborative. That is, parallel actions by each government can, de facto, be cooperative through their complementarity.

If there is one "good news" story in Chinese diplomacy during Xi Jinping's tenure, it is that China has really "stepped up" and increased its contributions in global governance—but the bad news is that the PRC remains an aggrieved, dissatisfied, and "revisionist" state. Together with Putin's Russia, Xi's China is pushing back against the norms and practices of the Liberal International Order, while still working within the system when it benefits Beijing's interests. While the China–Russia illiberal partnership is a serious challenge to the United States and the West, there nonetheless remains overlap between the American and Chinese governments in these aforementioned issues. In pursuing limited and targeted cooperation, the United States should not appear to be the eager suitor. Beijing recognizes how its national interests are affected in some (but not all) of these aforementioned areas, and it has to arrive at its own pragmatic decisions to work with the United States on a case-by-case basis. One challenge for Washington will be to avoid Beijing's frequent tactic of "linkage": we will help you (the United States) here if you help us (the PRC) there. Case-by-case *compartmentalization* should be the preferred policy approach.

Revisit the Cold War toolbox: While the US–China competitive rivalry is not exactly the same as the Cold War with the Soviet Union was, it is worthwhile to revisit the previous policy toolbox and dust off playbooks and tactics used by the United States back then. While some instruments from the Cold War may be reusable, equating China with the Soviet Union is not entirely applicable. While they have several similarities, there are also fundamental differences. As Kurt Campbell and Jake Sullivan observed, "China today is a peer competitor that is more formidable economically, more sophisticated diplomatically, and more flexible ideologically than the Soviet Union ever was."[16] I would add to this list that China is thoroughly institutionally integrated into the international system, Chinese citizens are thoroughly integrated into American society, and there are huge numbers of Chinese students in US universities—*none* of which were the case with the former Soviet Union. Recognizing these differences, China's economy—while a hybrid mixture of the state, collective, and private sectors—is still in essence a planned economy cloned from the Soviet *Gosplan* model, while China's political system remains *entirely* Leninist in structure and norms, and it is run by a *Communist* Party whose governing ideology remains Marxism–Leninism. In many real ways, the organization and behavior of the Chinese Communist party-state remains a Soviet organizational byproduct. I have always told my students, "To understand China, you need to understand the Soviet Union first."

Moreover, some Chinese tactics today—such as its "united front" and disinformation operations, its espionage, its development of asymmetric weapons, global military deployments, cultivation of client states and proxies, and two-against-one "strategic triangle" maneuvering—were all staples of the USSR, and American tactics for combating them vis-à-vis China in this era could benefit from drawing on earlier experiences and practices. The United States also has prior experience competing with China during the Cold War, which is instructive.[17]

While these negative elements of Soviet/Chinese behavior are still very relevant, so too were the *cooperative* dimensions of the Cold War. In the final section of Chapter 8, I discussed the need for "proactive managed competition" (as distinct from "defensive managed competition"). The idea here is to look for—and reach beyond—the types of mechanisms aimed at decreasing the risks of conflict—arms control agreements, military confidence-building measures, Track II dialogues, crisis management mechanisms, hotlines, and so on—in order to explore negotiated human-rights frameworks and regional security architectures. This is what the United States and Soviet Union successfully did during the Gorbachev–Bush 43 years, and the US–China relationship today could well do with some similar bold and creative thinking in the human rights and security realms.

No matter how competitive and fraught the US–China relationship is, we can never stop engaging in *dialogue* with Chinese interlocutors at several levels, bilaterally and multilaterally. The dialogues may not always be substantive or fulfilling for the American side (often they are not), as the Chinese tend to reflexively and rigidly adhere to their talking points, often use formulaic slogans (口号), are sometimes rude and caustic ("wolf warrior" approach), and eschew flexibility or real give-and-take. But cutting off all dialogue is counterproductive. That said, constant reevaluation and retooling the formats of such dialogues is always a good idea.

More Specific Observations and Policy Recommendations

Moving from broad guidelines to more targeted ones, what follows are my eight recommendations for how the United States can effectively and assertively compete with China. Readers should first note that these are all recommendations solely related to *competing* with China—they do not include the usual litany of issues on the US–China agenda—e.g., Taiwan, People's Liberation Army, commercial market access, human rights, climate change, and so on. There exist innumerable reports that parse this litany of these specific US–China policy issues which readers can consult.

1. Develop a comprehensive China competition strategy: To pursue comprehensive competition requires a comprehensive strategy. The individual elements need to interrelate and be parts of a broad holistic strategy. Ad hoc and uncoordinated efforts will be far less successful than those that follow a design and set of thought-through purposes. Whole-of-government and whole-of-society approaches are to be encouraged. Pushback in itself is *not* a strategy, although it is a principal *tactic* of competition.

A comprehensive competitive China strategy requires *integrating* the strategic, diplomatic, military, intelligence, technological, economic, public diplomacy, educational, cultural, soft power, and other elements of national power into an integrated strategy coordinated by the National Security Council at the White House. This in turn requires that a separate China Directorate be created in the National Security Council, staffed with perhaps 20 experts (some seconded from other departments, and some political appointees), with a single individual "China Czar" responsible for coordinating across the federal bureaucracy and possessing some authority vis-à-vis the 50 American states and commercial companies. The China Directorate should lead an inter-agency process that determines effective counteractions to be taken by different US government departments and agencies domestically and around the world vis-à-vis China. The China Directorate should also closely liaise with Congress and have a small team responsible for such.

To effectively compete with China globally, the US government needs to develop systematic and comprehensive knowledge about China's activities worldwide. The United States has been a global power since World War II and should remain so. If China were to come to dominate *any* region of the world, it would intrinsically *not* be in American interests. US intelligence agencies and *every* US Embassy in the world should prioritize tracking China's activities (in this regard, the Biden administration's creation of "China House" in the Department of State and the CIA's China Mission Center were good beginnings), and this information needs to be pooled by the National

Intelligence Council, filtered, and fed into the National Security Council's China Directorate.

2. Rebuild at home: America's long-term competition with China will only be successful if we invest in the core elements of competitiveness in the United States: strengthen education at all levels, invest in science and technology, prioritize innovation, rebuild infrastructure, radically reduce the national debt, retrain the workforce for the post-industrial world, and fix the broken immigration system. The Biden administration and Congress made a good start in these regards, but it needs to be sustained and invested in on a continuing basis. The United States also needs to remain firmly committed to and practice its own liberal democratic political values.[18] The United States will not be a role model for other countries and peoples, and effectively compete with the appeal of China's authoritarian model, if the American political system is dysfunctional, if it cannot conquer the existing racism and sexism in society, narrow the income gap, rebuild infrastructure, and correct other maladies that compromise the American Example. America's soft power has always been one of the greatest strengths of the United States, but admiration of America has declined worldwide in recent years; without admiration, and the respect that comes with it, the United States will find it more difficult to leverage its other elements of power vis-à-vis China.

In the realm of technological competition with China, the US needs to heighten vigilance and invest in cutting-edge research. Chinese cyber hacking, espionage, and intellectual property theft have reached epidemic proportions. The United States needs to strengthen its defenses in many ways—including increasing awareness among universities of the threats. Export controls should continually be strengthened vis-à-vis China (including via third countries). The first Trump administration and the Biden administrations both made important efforts in these domains, with the support of Congress, and they need to be continued into the second Trump administration.

Full decoupling of the US and Chinese economies is neither desirable nor feasible, but in the areas of advanced technology and protecting America's comparative advantages as well as national security, *some* decoupling from China *is* advisable. It just makes prudent sense. We also need to invest considerable sums into basic scientific research in order to maintain all American comparative advantages in innovation.

3. Be confident and exhibit it: In the competition for global position and influence, the United States should capitalize on its relative comparative strengths and take advantage of Beijing's relative weaknesses. Unlike the former Soviet Union, China today is truly a global *actor* although not necessarily a *power*. As my book *China Goes Global: The Partial Power* (2013) argued, the PRC can still be accurately described as a "partial power."[19] Its power and influence are uneven. The PRC still has virtually *no* global conventional military power projection capacity, has very poor soft power appeal and is viewed with increasing suspicion all around the world (as evidenced in multiple Pew polls), is seen to be a mercantilist, coercive, and exploitative economic actor, has *no allies*, and is not diplomatically very influential on a global level. China's many relative weaknesses are de facto American assets and to be exploited to the benefit of the United States in the competition.

Thus, we should not *overestimate* China. It is a big and increasingly strong country, but it is also filled with multiple systemic weaknesses: its aging population and gender imbalance; rigid single-party-state political system; state-dominated fiscal system and non-convertible currency; rigid educational system; high income inequality (.47 Gini Coefficient); repression of civil society, dissent, and religion; draconian controls over Tibet and Xinjiang; controlled media; high level of corruption and kleptocracy; capital out-flight; industrial overcapacity; ballooned corporate and local government debt (approximately 300 percent of GDP); slowing GDP growth; deflation; the Middle Income Trap; housing market bubbles and overbuilding (ghost cities); environmental degradation; and a dictatorial leader with no succession plan. In the competition with the United States, these are all vulnerabilities for China. China is not a 10-foot-tall Giant—we should not overestimate it, and we should be cognizant of—and where possible exploit—its multiple weaknesses.

Externally, the United States has a much longer history of relations with most countries in the world than does the PRC.[20] Security assistance is one of America's real comparative advantages. America's 56 formal allies and 18 Major Non-NATO Allies are particular assets and advantages for the United States. China has *no* allies or close security partnerships (other than with Russia). No other nation comes close to America's global security footprint, and this goes far beyond weapons sales to include a wide variety of security assistance and force enhancement programs. American multinational corporations also have a much better international reputation for corporate social responsibility, transparency, and lack of corruption than their Chinese counterparts. Similarly, many American government and private sector aid programs compare favorably with Chinese ones (China does have a good track record, mainly in Africa, in the areas of public health, primary and secondary education, agriculture, and infrastructure). Concerning soft power and cultural exchanges more broadly, the United States again possesses many strengths vis-à-vis China.

The United States possesses many admirable attributes—but none more important than its *openness*. This was recently driven home to me when Professor Joseph Nye and I visited the US Embassy in Beijing in April 2024. As we approached the embassy gate, there was an enormous queue—five rows deep—stretching all around the block. There were probably 1,000 Chinese wait-ing, all with appointments, to apply for visas. I pointed out, "Joe, now *that* is soft power!" The father of the concept of soft power readily concurred. There are no visa lines hundreds deep at any Chinese Embassy anywhere in the world, and nobody wishes to emigrate to China and become a Chinese citizen.

At the same time, the United States needs to recognize that its global image has been significantly tarnished in recent years by the first Trump administration's actions, the January 6 insurrection at the US Capitol, the political gridlock and democratic dysfunction in Washington, mass shootings, racial incidents and police brutality, decaying infrastructure, and other domestic maladies. While these are sources of shame and causes for humility, the fact that the US media, government, legal system, and public all wrestle with these weaknesses openly and in a democratic fashion is a *strength* of the United States in its soft power competition with China and other autocratic states.

4. Coordinate closely with allies and a wide range of partner countries: The United States can never afford to "go it alone" in implementing its China strat-egy and policies. The United States must work in tandem and effectively with Asian, European, and other countries vis-à-vis China. Targeted policies and tai-lored actions should be developed to counter and offset China's presence and malign activities worldwide, while systematically advancing American national interests. Many countries around the world have anxieties about China, they are growing in number, and this can be used to American advantage. The US approach should be to dilute and frustrate China's attempts to create client states, create regional spheres of interest, lock up resources, and expand its military footprint.

Global competition also requires *prioritization*, as the United States does not possess the capacity or the resources to do everything everywhere all at once. Washington should prioritize several regions: Central and South America, South and Southeast Asia, Central and Southern Europe, and the Middle East. Africa and Central Asia are second- or third-tier priorities. Even concentrating on these regions will require considerable diplomatic, financial, and military resources. The aforementioned new National Security Council's China Direc-torate should develop plans tailored to each region, and private sector think tanks can play a useful role in these regionally tailored efforts.[21] Presenting polit-ical, diplomatic, security, and economic alternatives to nations in these regions can sometimes be stand-alone American efforts, whereas sometimes—such as building infrastructure—the US can partner with Japanese, European, or other allies and countries to provide alternatives. No nation wants to be beholden to China (as is increasingly evident along the "Belt and Road"), and *all* seek multiple external partners. As such, in competing with China worldwide, it would be a profound *mistake* to explicitly ask or push countries into a false binary "choice" between the United States and China. Most countries seek to have positive relations with *both* Washington and Beijing. Therefore, the United States needs to "help them hedge" (as my colleague and retired US diplomat David Shear argues) while providing clear alternative options to their reliance on Beijing.

5. Dramatically increase efforts in US public diplomacy and strategic communications: Among other arenas, the US–China global competition is being waged in—and to a significant extent will be determined by—the *public information domain*. The inadequacy of our public diplomacy and strategic communications has been my single greatest complaint and criticism of the US government's China policies over several successive administrations. It absolutely *must* be corrected. We urgently need a sophisticated multifaceted worldwide strategic communications program aimed at countering China's narratives and advancing our own. This involves both governmental organs and non-governmental media, as well as cultural exchange programs. And it needs to be bureaucratically anchored in, centralized, and coordinated from the National Security Council in the White House.

Serious consideration should also be given to resurrecting the US Information Agency (USIA). Throughout the Cold War, USIA (founded in 1953) was a crucial and successful public diplomacy instrument. It penetrated the Soviet "information iron curtain" with accurate news via radio broadcasts and other means, while simultaneously pursuing its primary mission of "telling America's story to the world." After the Soviet–American contest "went global" and the two superpowers began competing for influence in the "Third World," USIA became a vital tool in advancing policies and narratives. By 1961, the agency employed 11,000 personnel, had 202 offices worldwide in 85 nations, operated 101 radio stations, provided information and programs to an additional 4,000 (non-American) radio stations, operated a network of libraries accessible to the foreign publics, sponsored a range of arts and culture exhibitions, and published a variety of magazines and some academic journals (including the highly regarded *Problems of Communism*).[22] Having "won" the Cold War USIA was abolished in 1999. This was a huge mistake that should be reversed; USIA should be reestablished, perhaps rebranded, and given the new mission of countering propaganda from China, Russia, Iran, and radical Islam, while rediscovering its old mission of educating the world about the United States, its values, and its foreign policy.

We live in an unprecedented, instantaneous information age. To be successful in the competition with China, the United States *must* effectively influence the international narratives *about China*—its domestic and international behaviors—as well as the narratives about the United States. Perceptions matter, a lot. The United States must win the "battle of narratives" with China for global hearts and minds.[23] The United States has a great number of intrinsic strengths and several comparative advantages over the PRC—but to date it has been *failing* and *losing* the public diplomacy and strategic communications competition with Beijing, which runs a very well-resourced and fairly sophisticated international propaganda offensive.[24] In some regions—notably Southeast Asia, Latin America, and Africa—China is already dominating regional media. In these regions, China has become a main source of news content via feeds from Xinhua and other PRC state media sources, while the United States is covered infrequently and its media feeds are too expensive for many foreign outlets to subscribe to (whereas China's are either free or inexpensive). Moreover, the reporting *about* China is overwhelmingly positive in the Global South, while reporting on the United States tends to be negative.

The battle of narratives also very much extends to China itself. As former Secretary of Defense and CIA Director Robert Gates told the 2024 Aspen Security Forum,

> [Vis-à-vis China], we have neglected the kind of strategic communications programs we had all through the Cold War directed at the East Europeans and the Russians, about what was really going on in their countries. All we did was to tell the truth. Part of our strategy should be getting under the skin of these guys [the CCP] and getting the word to their people about what is going on in their country.[25]

Transparency is a key tool to combat China's malign influence at home and abroad ("the best disinfectant is sunlight"). In this context, a spotlight should be shone on these Chinese activities—whether it is "debt-trap diplomacy" on Belt and Road projects; coercive economic diplomacy; the political and economic squeezing of Hong Kong and increased pressures on Taiwan; economic support for Russia, North Korea, and Iran; ethnic and religious repression in Xinjiang, Tibet, and other restrictions of human rights; the surreptitious ownership of foreign media; exporting censorship; co-opting foreign politicians; manipulating Chinese diaspora communities; and other malign activities. *Exposing* these Chinese activities is absolutely critical in America's competition with China. In many ways, the Chinese government's *own* negative behavior is one of America's greatest assets in its contest with China, and it must be taken advantage of (but if foreign publics are unaware of malign Chinese behavior and interference in other societies, or if China's own propaganda efforts are effective in repressing such information, it is to Beijing's benefit).

The Department of State's Global Engagement Center (GEC) has begun to focus on this issue and has begun to mount an effort to counter Chinese propaganda worldwide,[26] but the State Department's GEC and Bureau of Public Diplomacy are woefully under-resourced and lack strategic thinking concerning China. Greater coordination and resources are required in the US government, and urgently.[27] The Active Measures Working Group of the Cold-War era—an inter-agency body that coordinated and undertook efforts to combat Soviet disinformation and propaganda—may be a model worth reexamining.[28] Public diplomacy officers in the field really need to step up their games and proactively promote the value and contributions of the United States in their countries/regions while raising concerns about Chinese practices with foreign publics.

6. Maintain official dialogues and unofficial people-to-people exchanges with China: It never hurts, and often helps, to listen and talk. No matter how strained relations get, it is important to maintain open lines of communication with the Chinese government in Beijing and variety of subnational and non-governmental actors across China.

Such communication, however, should be a *vehicle* to addressing substantive issues—it should not be seen as an end in itself. The United States should also avoid the "trap" of institutionalizing such dialogues. Small is beautiful. Flexible issue-specific intergovernmental working groups are the most effective mechanisms. Further, in dealing with the government in Beijing, Washington should avoid any temptations for a "Grand Bargain" or Chinese pressures for a new (fourth) joint communiqué. These may have been feasible back in the Nixon–Kissinger era, but those days are long past.

Non-governmental and people-to-people exchanges remain an important part of the US–China relationship, although they have considerably attenuated in recent years. There are real reasons for this attenuation (outlined in Chapters 6 and 7), and they cannot be easily rebuilt given the draconian controls and surveillance in Xi Jinping's China. Only when China truly opens up again and respects international practices of professional interactions can the United States have "normal" non-governmental exchanges with PRC counterparts. This very much applies to *scholarly exchanges*, where the severe constrictions placed on American and foreign scholars in China are currently prohibitive and not conducive to normal academic exchange (whereas in the United States there are few restrictions placed on PRC scholars). In the domain of all non-governmental exchanges, the overriding principle should be to have—to the greatest extent possible—both *quantitative and qualitative **reciprocity***. Professional exchanges are unsupportable and unsustainable if they are not essentially reciprocal, equal, and fair. Long gone should be the days when the United States indulged the asymmetrical nature of private sector exchanges.

The reciprocity principle should also apply to media personnel. This too is true both quantitatively and qualitatively. There should be a rough equivalent number of journalists accredited in each country (I suggest 50). For many years, there has been a severe asymmetry in the numbers of accredited journalists, in China's favor. For example, prior to the tit-for-tat expulsions in 2020, there were 160 Chinese journalists accredited in the United States but only 98 Americans accredited in China (and half of these were not doing journalistic work per se, as they were in country on journalist visas but worked for Dow Jones or Bloomberg providing financial services to Chinese clients).[29] Being an American or foreign correspondent in China has always been an unusually tough job, as there has been regular harassment and impediments to their work, but under Xi Jinping's regime these barriers have been heightened, according to the annual reports of the Foreign Correspondents Club of China.[30] Since the 1960s, the PRC has also used its media organs overseas as non-official covers for its intelligence officers, including inside the United States, and counterintelligence vigilance needs to applied here as well.

7. Bring the American business community onside: In my view, the US business community is a significant vulnerability—not an asset—in an effective American strategy to compete with China. Of course, some business must be done with China—and there is *a lot* of it (over $600 billion annually)—but the American government, American corporations, and the American people need to realistically ask themselves: Is this business really in the US *national* interest? A simple look at the yawning and sustained deficit in traded goods and services that the US has run for decades with China ($279.4 billion in 2023) may suggest not.

But the issue is far deeper than the trade deficit—trade should be about much more than corporate profits and exchanging goods and services. The American corporate sector needs to understand that some—much—of what it does in China is *strengthening an existing rival and a potential adversary.* That is what US business has been doing in many domains for decades. In my view, one should not trade with a potential adversary (except in the most low-end manufactured goods and perhaps agricultural products).

Yes, trade benefits some of the American workforce, and approximately one million US workers are tied to trade with China (according to the US–China Business Council). It certainly benefits American farmers, as China is America's leading agricultural export market. It benefits the US automotive industry as Chinese consumers buy American vehicles (all of which are made *in* China by

Chinese workers). Chinese love to watch the NBA (but the NBA repeatedly capitulates to Chinese government pressures). But in many other domains (many technologies, higher education, energy, semiconductors, aircraft, new materials) trading with, and investing in, China only serves to strengthen America's competitor and rival.

It may be time to consider resurrecting and applying the "Trading with the Enemy Act" in certain instances. Leaving it to the consciences of corporate executives is not going to work, as US corporate leaders have long demonstrated that they cannot see beyond their profit margins to recognize the broader common national good and national security interests of *not* strengthening a rival by doing business with China. Leaving it to the Commerce Department to police sensitive technology exports to China, while important, is also insufficient. Both the White House and Congress have their own responsibilities in bringing American business to their senses. Some serious "tough talk" needs to take place between the executive branch and Corporate America. CEOs and those who promote business with China need to be hauled before Congress and the American people to explain themselves in public hearings. "Naming and shaming" is an effective deterrent. I fully recognize that my perspectives on this dimension of US–China relations will be controversial and certainly not welcome among the business community—but this is the way I feel. Do others share this perspective?

8. Strengthen American capacities to understand China: The United States will be significantly handicapped in its competition with China if it does not possess strong governmental and non-governmental analytical capacity and resources. The US intelligence community is already prioritizing China, as described in Chapter 6, but it will be a constant challenge to find the resources—financial, human, and technological—to maintain analytic capacities that constantly adapt to changes in China, in collection means, and in analytical methods.

To a real extent, US government capabilities will only be as good as the personnel in government service. That places a significant responsibility on the shoulders of American universities and colleges to continually train a strong cadre of knowledgeable China hands. China studies in the United States is the best in the world—bar none—but it requires constant improvement and dedicated funding. The National Defense Education Act of 1958, which was spurred by the Soviet launch of Sputnik, played a key role in developing Soviet and Slavic Studies in the United States—which, in turn, played a key role in prosecuting the Cold War against the former Soviet Union.[31] To some extent, China studies were a corollary beneficiary of this funding stream. In the case of China, though, private sector American philanthropic foundations (Ford, Rockefeller, and Luce) played instrumental roles in building the China studies field. I have written about this elsewhere.[32] Today and into the future, the United States needs—indeed *requires*— a similar well-resourced national investment into contemporary China studies.

Not every government employee who works on China can be previously trained in Chinese studies. This means that the US government needs a robust program for in-service *executive education*. That is, to take tailored short courses (1–3-weeks-long) taught by either existing US government personnel or outside experts. To some extent, the Foreign Service Institute in Arlington, Virginia, and the National Intelligence University in Bethesda, Maryland, meet this need. But tailored courses should be taught directly in government agencies. I have taught a number of such short courses over the years, and they have been very well received. One reason is that the "students" (US government personnel) tend to work on very finite subjects concerning China and thus do not have much, if any, understanding of the "Big Picture" of how the Chinese system (CCP, government, military) is organized and functions or how their niche subject matter fits into China's larger government directed programs.

Here is an unusal suggestion: why not establish a college (not university) dedicated solely to the study of China (China College)? Such a college would naturally be established in or near Washington, DC. It would be a 100 percent *private* institution, but it would receive a combination of Congressional, federal, state (from Maryland, Virginia, or the District of Columbia), and private funding. Its organization, faculty, and curriculum would be organized according to the principal elements that we need to know about China: history, politics, economy, society, culture (the humanities), military and security, and the Chinese language. Students would *not* necessarily go to China as part of their studies (although perhaps to Taiwan), thus making their eligibility for government security clearances much easier. This would require that the Chinese language program be vigorous. Faculty could be either hired full-time or as part-time adjuncts (drawing from US government agencies in some cases). They would all be bona fide China specialists. As most US universities do not permit their faculty to hold simultaneous joint appointments with other universities and colleges, faculty employed by other institutions in the United States could be tapped for occasional lectures in their areas of expertise. Graduates of such an envisioned China College would be hired by various US government agencies as well as in the private sector. It would only be open to US citizens and Green Card holders.

The Most Realistic US Policy Goal: A Relationship of "Competitive Coexistence"

Given the multiple complexities, inherent dangers, and the comprehensively competitive nature of the US–China relationship, there is no realistic prospect or false nirvana of returning to an amicable and cooperative bilateral relationship. And, as this book has argued, the US strategy of "Engagement" is dead. D-E-A-D. May it rest in peace (R.I.P.). One can debate, as we saw in Chapters 1 and 2, whether Engagement failed to achieve its intended purposes or not (personally I think it did), but, regardless, the strategy and policies associated with Engagement (capital "E") are finished even if the modalities of engagement (small "e") continue in some sectors. The suspicions and frictions in the relationship now run too deep and are so comprehensive that the original premises of Engagement are outdated—*unless* the CCP and PRC return to a more reformist and "liberal" mode of governance characteristic of the pre-Xi era. Unless and until that were to occur, the Humpty Dumpty of Engagement cannot be resurrected and put back together again.

I want to be very clear here: I am *not* advocating for regime change—that would be highly irresponsible, reckless, costly, and impossible to achieve. But as was evident during *specific segments* of the eras of Deng Xiaoping (1978–1989), Jiang Zemin (1996–2002), and Hu Jintao (2002–2008), the CCP and PRC have in the past moved in more open and quasi-liberal directions—economically, politically, intellectually, and socially.[33] Seen in this light, it is the era of Xi Jinping that has been the *aberration* in Chinese politics over the past 45 years. As this book has principally argued, when China has moved in more free, open, tolerant, and liberal directions domestically, and has not challenged or threatened American security interests regionally or globally, *then* the United States has been more able to cooperate and work constructively with China. It has been the American desire for—and expectations of—China to liberalize that has been the main independent variable in the relationship, while China's responses to—or compliance with—these expectations has been the main dependent variable. The desire to "change China" is deeply rooted in American DNA, it has not changed in 250 years, and it is not going to change. Thus, the independent variable is constant. But the dependent variable has been anything but fixed. China has often sought to accept American patronage and paternalism, but at other times China's own deep and proud nationalism has resented and resisted American intentions and physical presence. That has been *the* "rub" in US–China relations—American paternalism vs. Chinese nationalism—and it is what has accounted for the frequent oscillations in the relationship over time.

This being the case, "competitive coexistence" is the best that can be hoped for, and worked toward, as a mutual bilateral policy goal of both Beijing and Washington. Competitive coexistence is a kind of equilibrium and is comparable to the détente phase of the Cold War. It keeps the peace and keeps the strategic competition "cold" (non-kinetic). It allows for certain types of bilateral exchanges, multilateral interactions, and limited cooperation. It is not a zero-sum contest but can rather be thought of an indefinite soccer match with ebb-and-flow between the two contestants but where there is no ultimate winner. Yet, such a contest is not a Hobbesian anarchical free-for-all. There have to be mutually accepted *norms*, if not rules, of conduct by both parties. The Cold War, in its détente phase, established such norms and rules (especially under the Conference on Security Cooperation in Europe and the Helsinki Final Act). Establishing such norms, expectations, and rules of conduct was a long and very complicated negotiated process between Moscow and the West. It did not stop the USSR or USA from intensely competing with, and even threatening, each other. But it did successfully establish such stabilizing mechanisms, which kept the peace and maintained order in the European theater and the world.

I thus believe that such a model of ***competitive coexistence***—under conditions of comprehensive competition—between the United States and China is probably the most realistic and achievable policy framework for today's rivals.

Appendix
China Interprets American Engagement and Post-Engagement

"If China had a democratic government, someone there right now would surely be demanding to know: how did we lose America?"
—Thomas Friedman, *The New York Times*[1]

This Appendix turns the tables around by examining China's perceptions of American China policy. Specifically, its addresses three questions:

- How have Chinese analysts and scholars interpreted the American strategy of Engagement? What do they say were the intended purposes of Engagement and how do they see its evolution over time?
- What reasons do Chinese analysts and scholars attribute for the abrupt and fundamental change in US strategy from Engagement to Strategic Competition since 2017?
- Has there been a "Who Lost America?" debate in China? If not, why? Do Chinese analysts view China as having *any* responsibility for the deterioration of US–China relations and the fundamental change in US strategy and policies?

I address these three questions through a few interviews with some of China's America specialists during a visit to Beijing in the spring of 2024, but mainly by tapping into an extensive data set of journal articles (and some books) published in Chinese over the past 15 years (but with a particular focus on the period after 2017) published in the online China National Knowledge Infrastructure (CNKI) periodical index.[2] The articles all come from the main periodicals concerned with the United States and international relations: 美国研究 (*American Studies*) published by the Institute of American Studies of the Chinese Academy of Social Sciences; 现代国际关系 (*Contemporary International Relations*) published by the China Institutes of Contemporary International Relations; 国际问题研究 (*International Studies Research*) published by the China Institute of International Studies; 外交评论 (*Foreign Affairs Review*) and 外交学院学报 (*Foreign Affairs College Study Journal*) published by China Foreign Affairs University; 国际展望 (*International Outlook*) published by the Shanghai Institute of International Studies; 国际战略研究简报 (*International*

Strategic Research) published by the China Institute of International Strategic Studies; 世界经济与政治 (*World Politics and Economics*) published by the Institute of World Economics and Politics of the Chinese Academy of Social Sciences; 当代世界 (*Contemporary World*) published by the International Department of the Chinese Communist Party (CCP); 和平与发展 (*Peace and Development*) published by the China Association for International Friendly Contact, and a few others. The following analysis taps into this Chinese language literature (much of it heretofore unexplored), and I am most grateful to several of my student research assistants (see Acknowledgments) for generating the articles from CNKI, summarizing them, and helping with translations. Readers should bear in mind that it is *not* an examination of what Chinese analysts and scholars say about the ups and downs of US–China relations over time; rather, it is very focused on the aforementioned three sets of questions. The evidentiary basis also only includes official statements made by the government of the People's Republic of China (PRC) when they pertain directly to these three sets of questions.

The American Engagement Strategy and Its Evolution

China's America specialists have generally interpreted the US engagement policy (接触政策) as having been a centerpiece of American China strategy since the 1980s—but not a consistent element. When I asked Da Wei (one of China's leading America specialists, formerly director of the America section of the China Institutes of Contemporary International Relations [CICIR] and now Professor and Director of the Institute of Strategic Studies at Tsinghua University) how he understood the US engagement policy and its evolution, he distinguished between three broad periods and purposes: first, 1972–1989, when the primary purpose was "strategic and to jointly counter the USSR"; second, from the 1990s to 2016, when the United States sought to "shape China's moving towards economic marketization and political liberalization"; and, third, since 2017, when "competition and containment" have become prominent.[3] When I asked Professor Da why he thought that the US Engagement strategy had fractured, he attributed it to two factors: the "narrowing of the power gap" between the two countries, and to the fact that "China had not developed in the direction the US had expected."

When I visited Beijing in April 2024, I had the opportunity for a roundtable discussion organized by Professor Da at his Tsinghua University institute. It was specifically designed (after I gave an opening presentation) to address my research questions of how China's America experts understood the American Engagement strategy.[4] One participant, a professor at Renmin University, opined that "the US Engagement strategy was intended to change China from a planned economy to a market economy, and into a democratic political system like the United States." Another America hand from CICIR observed that,

"Regime change in China was an element of the Engagement strategy originally, then to keep China from rising was added. Then it became more comprehensively competitive. During the Cold War, the US Engagement strategy was more about security and diplomacy—but in the post–Cold War period it became more about economics and politics. Now we need to change strategic competition to strategic reassurance." Another scholar from the CASS Institute of American Studies astutely observed, "Looking back, the Engagement policy did not fail, it was quite successful. Just because a couple divorces after 45 years does not mean that the marriage was a failure from the start." "We feel that the Biden administration has intensified competition, and there is no more engagement," said another scholar from the People's Liberation Army (PLA) National Defense University. The Renmin University professor added, "Chinese scholars use the term 'competition' (竞争) frequently to describe US–China relations, even if the government doesn't."

In their publications, a variety of analysts distinguish between two principal features of engagement. The first was literally to maintain interactions between the US and Chinese governments and societies. This is a more literal definition of engagement—to "exchange" (交往). The second consistent definition, though, emphasizes America's attempts to foment "peaceful evolution" (和平演变) in China's political system—to evolve it from a socialist political system into a non-socialist system. There is a long history of CCP and PRC accusations and criticisms of alleged American attempts of peaceful evolution, dating back to Chairman Mao's own October 1959 speech (in response to John Foster Dulles's use of term in 1955).[5] These two features are in fact viewed as *twin elements*—the contact between the two societies, particularly inside of China, is the vehicle through which peaceful evolution is promoted. This has been a consistent view of the CCP, so argues former Central Party School theorist and professor Cai Xia,[6] and virtually all CCP and government officials. Given all of the evidence presented in this book, they are thus not incorrect when they argue that it *has* been a consistent American strategy and policy over many decades to shape, evolve, liberalize, and change China's political system and society.

Many authors argue that the 1980s was the heyday of US engagement with China, as the two governments and societies began to establish a presence in each other's society and educational institutions. Chinese authors also recognize that the "1989 chaos" (八九年动乱) or "political turmoil" (政治暴乱) sharply curtailed these exchanges and that official US policy recoiled thereafter.[7]

Subsequently, most attribute the term "engagement" (接触) to the Clinton administration. Several America hands argue that the second Clinton administration's engagement policy was a necessary adjustment to the failed "pressure tactics" of the first Clinton term, as they argue it was forced to abandon the linkage of renewing Most Favored Nation trading status to China's human rights record.[8] In this view, engagement was a capitulation to reality. In Clinton's first term, this CICIR author argued, "The US failure to promote China's peaceful transition from socialism to democracy, and ultimately achieving the strategic goals of liberalizing and Westernizing China, required an adjustment of tactics. While there was no change in the goals of liberalizing and Westernizing China, new emphasis was placed on political and economic dialogues, and military exchanges between the two countries developed steadily."[9] Seasoned America watcher Chu Shulong, then at CICIR, also argued that the shift in Clinton's China policy from pressure to engagement was an expedient necessity.[10] Chen Jiamin of China Foreign Affairs University (CFAU) concurred: "US containment pressures did not result in China's political system developing in the direction desired, the US had to change its approach and adopt a broader strategy of engagement."[11] Another CFAU professor argued that the United States had no choice but to shift course and policy, as US sanctions against China had failed, the United States needed China's business, and punitive trade measures were ineffective in promoting human rights and American values.[12] This author, Zhang Yiting, argued that the Clinton administration concluded that it was better to "enmesh" (纠缠) China in a series of exchange mechanisms than to pressure it.[13] Another scholar from Beijing University warned that the shift in tactics should not obscure Washington's principal aim—to advance peaceful evolution and undermine the CCP.[14] The tactics may have changed, but the goals had not. Niu Jun, a noted historian from the Institute of American Studies at the Chinese Academy of Social Sciences, also agreed that US policy had *always* been to "facilitate a broad peaceful evolution in China from communism to democracy, thereby supporting forces that advance economic and political freedoms."[15]

Yang Jiemian, then President of the Shanghai Institute of International Studies, observed that the shift in Clinton's engagement policy from the first to the second term was the result of five broader considerations: the adoption of a "piecemeal problem solving approach"; China's growing comprehensive power; its rapid economic growth and potential market; the failure of pressure tactics; and the growing convergence of interests among a variety of domestic American actors that sought exchanges with China (Yang specifically mentioned academia, media, and local communities).[16] Others noted that while the Clinton administration was becoming more conciliatory toward China, it was simultaneously strengthening American ties with Asian countries all around China—thus pursuing a dual "engagement + containment" (接触与遏制) strategy.[17] Actually, this theme is quite commonplace among China's America watchers. CFAU scholar Li Shouyuan also distinguished between three factions (三个派系) in American China policymaking: the engagement faction, which seeks to strengthen cooperation with China; the containment faction, which adheres to the "China threat theory" (中国威胁论); and a centrist faction which "maintains contact with China while secretly containing it."[18] Li further argued that all three factions adhere to the "Cold War mentality" (冷战思潮) of pursuing hegemonic dominance over China while seeking to subvert the CCP political system through "peaceful evolution."[19]

Yet others, such as Liu Jianfei of the Central Party School, further warned that the United States would never abandon its efforts to "change China" (变中国): "America still fantasizes that China can abandon its current system and gradually become a member of the democratic alliance ... Anti-communism is the common position of both the engagement and containment camps," wrote Liu in 2002.[20]

In an article published in 1996, China's leading America specialist, Wang Jisi, then Director of the Institute of American Studies at the Chinese Academy of Social Sciences (subsequently at Beijing University and the Central Party School), defined America's engagement policy (for which he used the term 交往, "to have contact with") as being motivated by three main characteristics: "to collaborate with China in numerous sectors that align with US interests; to influence and change China domestically; and to constrain China's global actions within the existing international framework."[21] By contrast to engagement, Wang Jisi also identified a "China threat" school in American policy, which he argued was based on four perceptions: the perception of socialist totalitarianism as a direct threat and challenge to democracy; the belief that China's rise will disrupt and redefine the prevailing international order; economic concerns stemming from China's vast exports of low-cost goods; and cultural clashes where Confucian thought is seen as challenging Western Christian ideology.[22] Zhu Feng, another prominent America specialist (then a professor at Beijing University, subsequently at Nanjing University), argues that the "China threat theory" is rooted in political ideology, specifically "the American democratic ideology that believes autocratic communist regimes are inherently aggressive."[23]

Almost all of China's America specialists argued that the George W. Bush administration came to office in 2001 prepared to adopt a hardline and confrontational policy toward China,[24] but that the 9/11 terrorist attacks in New York and Washington forced it to adopt a moderated policy of engagement—because the Bush 43 administration needed China's cooperation in the war against the Taliban and al-Qaeda in Afghanistan.[25] Despite this tactical alteration in policy, authors such as Professor Wu Xinbo of Fudan University, also one of China's leading and most astute Americanists, wrote that the Bush administration's practiced a dual policy of "deterrence plus hedging": deterring China from using military force against Taiwan while strategically hedging against China by strengthening US ties to countries all around the PRC.[26]

Toward the end of the Bush administration, Deputy Secretary of State Robert Zoellick added a new wrinkle to the US policy of engaging China (see Chapter 4) by calling for China to become a "responsible international stakeholder" (负责任的国际利益相关者). As I learned firsthand when visiting Beijing just after Zoellick's speech in September 2005, Chinese officials were at first confused by the concept—but then interpreted it as condescending criticism. Of course, we *are* responsible stakeholders in the international system, many argued. Who are you Americans to say we need to become "responsible"?

This was a refrain I repeatedly heard during my visit. But one interlocutor at the CCP's International Department saw something more sinister in Zoellick's call—he saw it as a trap to constrain China and thus benefit American power and primacy. As the department's deputy director assertively told me, "First you Americans tried to contain us during the Cold War. That failed. Then you tried to overthrow us in Tiananmen. That failed. Now you are trying to constrain us internationally. That will fail too!" (as he pounded the table for emphasis).[27]

The Obama administration took office on the heels of the Global Financial Crisis (GFC) of 2008–2009 (全球金融危机), which virtually all of China's America specialists agreed was a watershed event and turning point in the relationship—because it signaled, according to most, the real decline of the United States. As I noted in my book *Beautiful Imperialist: China Perceives America, 1972–1990*, China's America watchers have long predicted—and have long hoped for—America's decline (美国衰落). They have been repeatedly proven wrong. But with the GFC, this time many argued that America's day as the world's preeminent power had finally come.

As a result, many argued, the United States now needed China more than ever—thus necessitating a renewed engagement policy; they argued that Washington now had to treat China as a real equal.[28] One article identified two competing schools of thought in China's internal debate about American decline: those who saw the United States as in inexorable decline, and those who argued that America still possessed considerable residual strengths.[29] Some, such as Major General Zhu Chenghu of the PLA National Defense University, argued that while the GFC had dealt a "heavy blow" to the economic strength of the United States, America still possessed considerable other elements of "comprehensive power" (综合国力). General Zhu noted in particular America's continental geographic size, its total GDP, its capacity for technological innovation, its unparalleled military power, its global system of alliances, the supremacy of the US dollar, its soft power, its vast natural resources (including food), and its leading position in international institutions.[30] Similarly, Chu Shulong of CICIR argued that America's hard and soft power remained unparalleled.[31] Two Tsinghua University scholars noted America's declining manufacturing base, rising income inequality, exorbitant national debt, and the social and cultural crises besetting American society.[32] Others, such as CICIR's leading America hand (and current CICIR president) Yuan Peng, saw a more ominous future as a result of the GFC. Yuan noted that because the economic gap between the United States and China had narrowed as a consequence of the crisis, tensions between the two leading powers would actually intensify.[33] This reasoning is consistent with power transition theory, as Beijing University scholar Zhu Feng noted.[34] In a similar vein, Tsinghua University's Yan Xuetong, a prominent "realist" international relations theorist, foreshadowed Graham Allison's "Thucydides Trap" argument by observing in 2010 that the "structural contradictions" (机构性矛盾) between the two powers were going to intensify and become more acute.[35] Others noted how the GFC had badly damaged American credibility and soft power in the world.[36] Other analysts predicted that Washington would now have to show real "respect and restraint" (尊重加克制) toward China.[37]

I was living in Beijing during 2009–2010, as a Senior Fulbright Scholar at the Institute of World Economics and Politics of the Chinese Academy of Social Sciences, and I encountered all of these perspectives. There was a distinct sense of hubris in attitude and assertiveness in policy emanating from Beijing (2010 would euphemistically become known among China specialists as China's "year of assertiveness").

Then, as the Obama administration unveiled its "pivot" or "rebalance" policy to the Asia-Pacific, Chinese analysts began to wrestle with the implications. Tao Wenzhao, a senior America specialist at the CASS America Institute wrote that the new policy had a dual purpose: to check the rise of China and to inject new stimulus into the flagging American economy through new investment in the military-industrial complex.[38] Others, such as Liu Jianfei of the Central Party School, argued that the strategic shift to Asia potentially posed a new threat to China's security.[39] Some, such as Xia Liping of the Shanghai Institute of International Studies, were more soberminded. Xia argued that a combination of domestic economic constraints, limitations on US military deployments, and the vast geography of the Asia-Pacific region, would all serve to make Obama's Asia Pivot more rhetoric than reality.[40] Xia was proven correct.[41]

By the end of the Obama administration, many Chinese analysts were increasingly of the view that American power had inexorably declined. Chinese strategists sensed a global and regional power vacuum, an indecisive president, and a lame duck administration.[42]

One very interesting article by Li Haidong, a professor at CFAU, published just at the end of the Obama administration, parsed the debates over China policy that were occurring in 2016 in the United States. It is one of just a few articles published at the time which picked up on the discontent with engagement among some American foreign policy and China specialists. Professor Li had just completed a year in Washington, DC, as a visiting Fulbright scholar at Johns Hopkins SAIS, and he made good use of his time there, interviewing a wide range of foreign policy and China experts (which he describes as 知华派, literally the "faction knowledgeable about China").

In his article, Li identified five separate contending lines of argument and schools of thought. The first school draws on the "traditional premises" of classic Engagement strategy: "mutual accommodation" (互相容纳) and cooperation (合作) in order to establish an "equilibrium" (平衡) in international order. US–China international cooperation is seen as more important that China's internal character. This school further advocates that the United States should abandon the notion of sustaining its "primacy," acknowledging the reality that American power is in decline. Proponents of this school also argue for an "inclusive" regional security framework in the Asia-Pacific where the United States and China exercise mutual accommodation and restraint. Li specifically cites David

M. Lampton and Michael Swaine as the most noteworthy examples, whom he describes as "moderate and pragmatic," but acknowledges that this faction has "faced resistance in recent years."[43]

Li's second school is admittedly similar to the first in that they advocate for a China policy of "selective engagement, cooperation, and strategic restraint." One difference with the first school is that the second views the international system as increasingly "diffused, multipolar, and not having a center of gravity," as argued in Charles Kupchan's book *No One's World: The West, the Rest, and the Coming Global Turn*. Under such quasi-anarchic conditions, where there is no hegemon or concert of powers to ensure world order, dangers abound. Thus, the second school argues, according to Li, that the United States and China need to "meet each other halfway" (an explicit reference to Lyle Goldstein's book *Meeting China Halfway: How to Defuse the Emerging US–China Rivalry*) and find areas of "practical engagement and cooperation" (实施接触与合作). Indicative of this school was James Steinberg and Michael O'Hanlon's book *Strategic Reassurance and Resolve: US–China Relations in the 21st Century*.

Professor Li's third school is epitomized by Chas W. Freeman Jr., a former high-level US diplomat who argues that America's power is declining comprehensively; the United States has endured repeated international failures because of an excessively militarized approach which shortchanges pragmatic diplomacy, led by the "military-intelligence clique" (国防情报团); an ideological predisposition to look for enemies (which Freeman described as "enemy deprivation syndrome"); and a refusal to adapt to the reality of China's rise and to grant it a legitimate role as a "rule maker."[44] Li says that Freeman's views have also "encountered resistance" in US policymaking circles.

Li's fourth school is an eclectic group that includes Michael Pillsbury, Robert Rubin, Hank Paulson, and John Ikenberry. What these four have in common, according to Li, is that China is divided between "hawkish forces" (鹰派) and "reformists" (改革派), and that US policy should be aimed at countering the former and empowering the latter.

Li's fifth school are advocates of "containing China" (遏制华). They argue that US–China relations are inherently competitive with minimal areas of mutual interest and cooperation, that American global primacy must be maintained at all costs, that China's domestic political regime is a fundamental problem, and—on these bases—containment of China and slowing its rise is the wisest American strategic policy.[45] Li says that this school prominently includes Robert Blackwill, Ashley Tellis, John Mearsheimer, and Aaron Friedberg.

After delineating his five schools of US China policy, Li Haidong offered a number of astute observations about the "increasingly pessimistic character" (悲观色彩渐浓) in American strategic thinking about China occurring toward the end of the Obama administration. He noted that a number of American China specialists who used to favor the traditional engagement policy had become increasingly disillusioned and had adopted a more pessimistic tone in their assessments of China and China policy. The reasons he attributes for the shift included the following:

> An increasing number of elites in the US tend to believe that the US has not succeeded in driving China's internal liberalization or fully integrating China into the US-led international system. The growing pessimism in US policy toward China is due to the disappointment with China's lack of liberalization despite its rise. The belief that China's middle-class growth would lead to democratic reforms has been challenged, and the US sees China as ideologically anti-Western and a security threat. Calls for a tougher approach toward China have increased as the basis for the engagement and integration policies erodes ... The US believes that its leadership position in the Asia-Pacific and even globally has been substantially threatened by China. The US aims to prevent the emergence of hostile hegemonic powers in the Asia-Pacific region, including China, which is seen as challenging its leadership position in international affairs ... The contradictions between China and the US and China regarding the type of international order to be established are becoming increasingly acute: the US advocates a unipolar order led by itself with alliances, while China rejects this and emphasizes multipolarity and respect for sovereignty
> ... Economic and trade relations have always been considered the ballast for stabilizing China–US relations ... but many American elites now view the trade relationship unfavorably. They believe that China's rise has led to US job losses, particularly in manufacturing. American business groups accuse China of unfair trade practices and cyber theft. Economic issues are increasingly linked to security concerns, complicating US–China trade relations ...
> The American domestic assessment of whether there will ultimately be a war between China and the United States is also undergoing changes. US–China competition is intensifying in geopolitics, economics, and culture. A war between the two countries is seen as unlikely but not impossible. US policy elites are becoming less optimistic about cooperation and engagement with China. There is growing concern that conflicts and crises in US–China relations may increase. The US views China as a strong opponent to its global leadership and liberal international order.[46]

This is a remarkable and extremely perceptive set of insights into the changing American thinking about China and China policy at the time. I commend Li Haidong. His is the *only* such analysis that I have been able to find in scouring numerous Chinese journals and articles, which recognized that a fundamental shift was occurring in American thinking about China. Unlike most analyses which are ephemeral and simply "take the temperature" of the US–China relationship at any given time, Li dug more deeply into the debates taking place among American policy experts, divided them into groups (his divisions and those he included in each category are questionable, however), but his real contribution was to accurately capture the growing consensus that the long-standing strategy of Engagement was eroding.

The fact that other America watchers *completely missed* this subterranean seismic shift occurring inside the Beltway in 2014–2016 is a sad commentary on China's supposed America specialists, and it constitutes a significant *intelligence failure* on their part at the time (although most contributors to these journals were academics and not intelligence analysts per se, CICIR personnel excepted[47]). As we will see in the next section, this simmering discontent erupted and informed the Trump administration's dramatic shift in China policy in 2018. China's supposed America specialists did not see it coming (except perhaps Li Haidong).

Analyzing the Trump Administration's Break with Engagement

Like much of the world, China's America watchers were flummoxed by, and hard-pressed to explain, Donald Trump's election in 2016. In this section, I will examine their analyses of two elements. First, what were the factors that led to Trump's electoral victory? Second, what was their understanding of the Trump administration's China policy, particularly its abandonment of the Engagement paradigm that had held sway across all previous administrations? Relatedly, once the Trump administration replaced Engagement with a new doctrine of "strategic competition," how did Chinese analysts understand it—and why hadn't they seen it coming?

Despite their failure to anticipate either Trump's electoral victory or the looming shift in America's China policy under Trump, China's America watchers actually demonstrated, following the election, a pretty good understanding of the forces that gave rise to Trump's MAGA movement and his electoral victory.

For example, Diao Daming of the Institute of American Studies at the Chinese Academy of Social Sciences published an insightful article just five weeks after the election which listed a number of factors that contributed to Trump's victory:

> The election was influenced by the discontent of American voters, particularly among lower-class whites, and it was fueled by longstanding discontent and fear of Americans, especially concerning the economy, employment, social issues, ethnic relations, international status, and security. Globalization contributed to economic hollowing-out and demographic diversity due to immigration, intensifying grievances. The slow economic recovery after the 2008 financial crisis left people dissatisfied. Employment growth in low-end services and a shrinking middle class caused frustrations. The prospect of becoming a nation without an ethnic majority also sparked an identity crisis among white Americans. Economic challenges, extremism, and gun control issues further escalated tensions between white working-class individuals and minorities, driving animosity ... Trump

effectively channeled the grievances of the white working-class population, promoting "America First" and blaming immigration and trade for the country's problems. The "anti-establishment" sentiment also influenced the political outcome of the election, reflecting widespread distrust of and aversion toward political elites. Trump embraced the "anti-establishment faction" (反建制派), appealing to those dissatisfied with Washington elites and seeking change. His unconventional approach resonated with voters looking for a candidate outside traditional politics, despite his controversial rhetoric ...

The 2016 election also saw widespread use of social media, transforming political campaigns. Social media became a crucial source of information for young voters, it created echo chambers and allowed anti-establishment candidates like Bernie Sanders to mobilize support ... Overall, the 2016 election set in motion a lengthy process of party reconfiguration and potential political change. The election's impact on society and the potential for new movements should not be underestimated. The dual core voter structure of Baby Boomers and Millennials influences political dynamics. The internet and social media facilitate mobilization, empowering grassroots sentiments to challenge political elites ... The 2016 election resembled a social movement driven by anti-establishment sentiment among blue-collar white voters mobilized through social media. Trump's "America First" ideology appealed to them, while Clinton's campaign struggled to address their concerns.[48]

Wang Xi of the History Department at Beijing University agreed that Trump was able to capitalize on the "anxieties and fears" of Rust Belt working-class voters, and his "core message of white nationalism and populism inspired them."[49] Despite Trump's victory, several Chinese analysts noted the increased political polarization of the American public, based on mutually extreme ideological views (liberalism vs. populism).[50] This polarization manifested itself in "frequent government shutdowns, political gridlock, and the inability to formulate and implement significant social policies," according to Zhou Qi of the Institute of American Studies of the Chinese Academy of Social Sciences.[51] One analyst predicted that Trump's victory brought with it inherent tensions with the traditional Republican establishment faction (建制派), which foreshadowed struggles in Congress between the traditionalists and newly elected populists.[52] Zhang Yi, also of CASS/IAS, pointed to the "three big divides" (三大分裂) in America: the economic divisions, racial divisions, and cultural divisions.[53] Yet other analysts at the CASS Institute of World Economic and Politics noted the rising appeal of conspiracy theories circulating on obscure social media sites like QAnon.[54] Some America watchers noted how the distrust of establishment elites became manifest in attacks by Trump's adviser Steve Bannon and others on the "deep state" (深层国家), and in "deconstructing the administrative state" (解构行政国).[55]

Once the Trump administration entered office, China's America watchers were at first cautious and circumspect, not really knowing what to expect from the new president and his team. While alarmed that Trump took a congratulatory phone call from Taiwan's President Tsai Ing-wen, breaking with previous precedent of not interacting with Taiwan's head of state, they were relieved when he soon thereafter reiterated his administration's commitment to the One China Policy.[56] They did correctly anticipate a tougher set of economic and commercial policies from Trump, based on his rhetoric on the campaign trail. Da Wei, then the head of the America Institute at CICIR, also warned that the neoconservatives who populated the new administration could launch a much more hardline policy toward China, that the Chinese government should prepare for potential tensions in 2017, but that Beijing could also take advantage of Trump's anticipated isolationist policies and play a greater role in global governance.[57] One CASS America Institute analyst thought that there was perhaps a silver lining for China in Trump's isolationist approach to foreign policy, as it may represent a turn from "remaking others" (including China) to "remaking itself."[58] Another analyst, Jiang Fangfei, thought that the Trump administration would abandon the "hedging" and "soft balancing" policies against China pursued by the Obama administration in favor of a more confrontational approach that would pursue elements of containment.[59] He was one of the few who anticipated the seismic shift to come in American China policy.

The uncertainty and speculation about what Trump may or may not do changed abruptly to considerable concern once the Trump administration released its *National Security Strategy* in December 2017. As discussed in Chapter 5, this document signaled the official abandonment of the Engagement strategy in favor of a new policy of strategic competition. CASS researcher Ni Feng observed that it "marks a new era of comprehensive and strategic competition between the United States and China."[60] Wu Xinbo of Fudan University concurred that the emphasis of *National Security Strategy* on "great power competition" signaled that the United States would pursue unilateralism, abandoning multilateralism and withdrawing from international institutions. Wu said that China should brace itself for "extreme rhetoric and confrontational actions."[61] He too was right. While such analyses did foreshadow the monumental changes that were to come, they did not actually anticipate them. That is, such analyses *reacted* to events that occurred, rather than *predicting* the scope of the policy changes that the Trump administration would enact. Nor did they, with two exceptions, analyze the disenchantment with the Engagement strategy that had surfaced. In addition to the previously discussed Li Haidong article, the only other exception I could find was an article from August 2018 by Fudan University scholar Wei Zongyou, who astutely noted that,

During the Obama administration, skepticism about the engagement policy toward China grew within the US. Some believed that China had benefitted greatly from engagement while becoming increasingly dissatisfied with the US-led international order. China's assertive foreign policy and attempts to challenge existing rules and US hegemony raised concerns. Furthermore, China's political system did not undergo the anticipated liberalization.[62]

Following the publication of the *National Security Strategy*, China's America watchers continued to react to the steady stream of confrontational rhetoric and actions taken by the Trump administration. Analyses focused on Trump's trade war and tariffs, economic decoupling, the "new technology Cold War," blaming China for the COVID-19 pandemic, and the extreme rhetoric of Trump administration officials.[63] One article identified those in the Trump administration responsible for the new "adversarial policy" (敌手政策) which treated China as an "enemy" (敌人), specially naming Secretary of State Pompeo, National Security Advisor Robert O'Brien, Deputy National Security Advisor Matt Pottinger, and external advisers Michael Pillsbury, Steve Bannon, and Frank Gaffney.[64] Other analysts lamented the Trump administration's termination of government-to-government exchanges and the strict limitations placed on Chinese diplomats and visiting scholars in the United States.[65]

While China's America watchers wrote quite a lot about the changes in the Trump administration's China policies, *none*—not a single one—explored the *reasons* for the qualitative shift in US policy, and *none*—not a single one—attributed the changes in US policy to *anything* that *China* had done to cause the United States to react and change its policies. In the unanimous view of China's America specialists, the changes in the Trump administration's policy had to do *entirely* with internal American factors associated with the neoconservatism and populism of the Trump administration—and *nothing* that China said or did to cause the reaction from Washington. It was the United States that was 100 percent entirely to blame for the deterioration of the Sino-American relationship, in their view. China had zero agency or responsibility. Moreover, there were no analyses of how the Engagement Coalition fractured, how the Engagement policy lost its efficacy, and why it all unraveled so quickly.

Even China's top diplomat, former ambassador to the United States, and seasoned America hand Yang Jiechi squarely placed the blame for the deteriorated relationship on America and the Trump administration. In a speech to the Board of Directors of the National Committee on US–China Relations in New York in 2021, Yang asserted,

> For the past few years, the Trump administration adopted misguided policies against China, plunging the relationship into its most difficult period since the establishment of diplomatic ties. Some in the United States, sticking to Cold War thinking, perceive China as a threat. Their rhetoric and actions have interfered in China's internal affairs, undermined China's interests, and disrupted exchanges and mutually beneficial cooperation between the two sides. There have been attempts to seek "decoupling" and a so-called "new Cold War." Such moves, going against the trend of the times,

have seriously damaged China–US relations as well as the fundamental interests of the two people.[66]

Evaluating the Biden Administration

Soon after President Biden and his administration assumed office, China's leading America specialist Wang Jisi took the measure of the new administration:

> Under Biden, official US rhetoric on China has become less belligerent but still reflects an antagonistic mood. China has "an overall goal to become the leading country in the world, the wealthiest country in the world, and the most powerful country in the world," Biden said at his first press conference in March. "That's not going to happen on my watch, because the United States is going to continue to grow and expand."[67]

Another America hand, Zhao Kejin of Tsinghua University, predicted that, "The Biden administration will not change the consensus on US strategic competition with China. Since 2017, the United States has recognized China as a strategic competitor, and both the US Congress and society have formed a consensus on this matter."[68] Others noted that the technology sphere will become the new realm of competition between the two countries, and they correctly predicted a tightening of American export controls, restrictions on inbound Chinese investments, and other regulatory barriers aimed at "suppressing" (压制) China's high technology development.[69] Still others anticipated—and then analyzed—the renewed US emphasis strengthening relations with Asian nations all around China's periphery.[70]

As China's America specialists wrestled with the potential implications of Biden's election in 2020, some anticipated—at least hoped—that it would auger a return to America's Engagement policy and a new era of Sino-American cooperation. Still reeling from the jarring experience of the Trump administration's extremely hawkish policies and actions, these America hands assumed that the "establishment faction" (建制派), led by the US business community and "old engagement faction" (老接触派), would reassert themselves and thought at least the relationship would be somewhat steadied. Some argued that since Biden himself had spent his career supporting engagement with China, including extensive time spent with Xi Jinping personally, it could be anticipated that he would revert to a more traditional policy of engagement with China.[71]

These wishful thinkers were, however, countered by more seasoned America hands who cautioned that there was likely to be much more continuity with, than change from, the Trump administration. One assessment by Da Wei, formerly one of the chief America hands at the Ministry of State Security's CICIR, who had relocated to the University of International Relations (国际关系学院, the Ministry of State Security's training school), warned that there would be no "back to the future" (回到未来)—i.e., a return to engagement applied to the future.[72] Their reasoning was that Biden's defeat of Elizabeth Warren and Bernie Sanders for the Democratic Party's nomination signaled the eclipse of the "neoliberal wing" (新自由主义派) of the party. For China policy this meant, they argued, that the free-traders and globalization liberal elites were now being replaced by more conservative Democrats who viewed China as a competitor instead of a partner. This assessment was echoed by Zhang Zhaoxi, a researcher in CICIR's America Institute, in an article assessing the personnel who assumed the senior foreign policy positions in the new Biden administration—a group he designated as "liberal hawks" (自由鹰派). This group—which included Jake Sullivan, Antony Blinken, Ely Ratner, Kurt Campbell, Rush Doshi, and Mira Rapp-Hooper—believed in, and were putting together, a strategy of "comprehensive competition" (综合竞争) toward China.[73] In his article Zhang observed that,

> The Liberal Hawks emphasize ideological confrontation, stressing the delineation of international camps based on liberal democratic systems and values, and they seek to maintain and consolidate American hegemony through global political and economic systems and rules. They also consider overseas intervention a crucial means to protect their strategic interests ... Compared to the emotional and extremist approach of the Trump administration, the Liberal Hawks have refined the logic of strategic competition with China. They believe the fundamental flaw in the engagement policy with China was the assumption that engagement would fundamentally change China's political system and foreign policy. In their view, the starting point of US policy toward China is to maintain America's dominant position and system leadership ... The Liberal Hawks have clarified the meaning of strategic competitors, asserting that China is the only competitor capable of continuously combining economic, diplomatic, military, and technological strength to challenge the United States.[74]

Fudan University's Wu Xinbo, one of China's most astute observers and scholars of US–China relations, agreed that,

> The goal of US China policy is to meet the challenge from a stronger and more active (积极的) China and to maintain US hegemony and dominant influence. The Biden administration has repeatedly emphasized that the US should deal with China from a position of strength and has repeatedly reminded China not to misjudge the US as being in decline.
>
> The Biden administration's suppression of China is all-encompassing. In the areas of values, the US has continued to pressure China on issues such as Xinjiang, Hong Kong, and human rights. In the areas of trade and technology, the Biden administration has retained the tariffs unleashed by Trump, renewed a large number of sanctions against China, and has forced a number of Chinese companies to delist from the US stock market. In the geopolitical arena, the US has enlisted the European Union, Japan, India,

Southeast Asia, and Australia to cooperate on China. On the military front, the US has continued to pressure China in the South China Sea and Taiwan and it has increased the presence of US troops in the region.[75]

I would observe that Wu Xinbo and these other America hands had an *absolutely accurate* assessment of the Biden administration's China policies. What they did *not* accurately do is to assess any blame on China for its transgressions. That is, Professor Wu lists a variety of actions taken by the United States in separate policy realms, but in *none* does he explain for Chinese readers what exactly it is that the United States specifically objects to in each area. What is it *exactly* about Xinjiang, Hong Kong, Tibet, and human rights that the United States objects to? *Why* does the United States apply tariffs and sanctions on Chinese commercial entities and individuals? *What exactly* do the European Union, Japan, India, Southeast Asia, and Australia agree on concerning China and *why*? What is it exactly that the United States and others are concerned about China's actions in the South China Sea and vis-à-vis Taiwan? Are these objections justified? Wu and *all* other Chinese analysts *never ever* ask or address these questions in their articles. Their analyses are entirely *one-sided*. China can never do any wrong, China is always the aggrieved and injured party, China has nothing to apologize or adjust for, and it is always the United States which is wrong and responsible for any and all tensions in China's bilateral relations.

If Wu and other America hands never admit that China's own behavior, policies, rhetoric, and actions may have contributed to the deterioration of the US–China relationship, what do they counsel China should do in the face of such American actions? Normally, these authors are highly reluctant to offer any of their own policy suggestions in print. This article by Wu Xinbo, however, was an exception to the rule. Wu offered four specific suggestions:

1. China should increase contact and dialogues with the US. While the Biden administration emphasizes competition as its main focus, China should advocate expanded cooperation. Both governments need to define the lowest boundaries of their core interests in order to prevent the relationship from spiraling out of control.
2. China should struggle resolutely to condemn US interference in China's internal affairs, and defend China's sovereign interests in Taiwan, Hong Kong, Xinjiang, and Tibet.
3. China should mobilize third parties, strengthen the China–Russia comprehensive strategic partnership, improve relations with the European Union, strengthen the strategic partnership with ASEAN, and increase its presence in the Middle East, Africa, and Latin America.
4. China should enhance shaping of the public opinion atmosphere.[76]

For their part, Chinese government officials have consistently refused to use the "C word" (competition) to describe the Biden administration's China policy or the US–China relationship. As President Xi Jinping himself said in his speech when visiting San Francisco for a summit meeting with President Biden in November 2023,

> The Number 1 question for us is: are we adversaries or are we partners? This is the fundamental and overarching issue. The logic is quite simple. If one sees the other side as a primary competitor, the most consequential geopolitical challenge and a pacing threat, it will only lead to misinformed policymaking, misguided actions, and unwanted results.[77]

China's Ministry of Foreign Affairs former Spokeswoman Mao Ning has specifically pushed back on the characterization of the relationship as competitive: "China does not shy away or flinch from competition. It is beneath a responsible country to use competition as a pretext to smear other countries and restrain their legitimate right to development."[78] Mao Ning's colleague Wang Wenbin similarly said, "The US should stop treating China as an imaginary enemy and correct the wrong behavior of engaging in major power confrontation under the guise of competition."[79] Of all Chinese officials, State Councilor and Foreign Minister Wang Yi has been the most outspoken in criticizing the American use of "competition" to frame the US–China relationship, saying in a speech to the Asia Society in New York in 2022, "Undeniably, China and the US have competition in areas like economy and trade, and China does not fear such competition. However, we do not agree that China–US relations should be simply defined by competition, because this is not the entirety or the mainstream of the relationship. We need healthy competition that brings out the best in each other, not vicious competition that aims at each other's demise."[80]

A "Who Lost America?" Debate in China

The third issue that this Appendix examines is the question whether there has been a "Who Lost America?" debate in China. That is, as just noted, do China's America specialists and foreign policy experts ever evince *any* self-criticisms of China and Chinese behavior for having contributed to the significant changes in US strategy and policy toward China since 2017, and the corresponding deterioration of the Sino-American relationship? Did China exercise any agency and bear any responsibility for these sharp changes? Is there any awareness of China's causes and contributions to these changes in US policy and hence the relationship?

In most countries, at least democratic countries where debates are open and participants in debates often identify and accept self-blame, this would be natural. As we saw clearly in Chapters 1 and 8, the Americans have heatedly debated China policy and there has been a significant cohort that places at least *some* blame on the United States for abandonment of Engagement, the sharp shift to strategic and comprehensive competition, and the deterioration of the overall relationship. Even in closed authoritarian systems like China's, there is a long history of internal foreign policy debates, and there is an extensive American literature (which we examined in Chapter 8) that has explored foreign policy debates in the former Soviet Union and China. Such debates are, to be sure, usually quite oblique, and it thus requires careful "content analysis" of open-source policy journals, books, and interviews (if possible) to ferret out the lines of division and debates.

This is precisely why I have included this Appendix in this book. I wanted to undertake a careful and detailed examination of the relevant Chinese language literature concerning the US Engagement strategy and the post-Engagement—in order to establish two things: first, the Chinese understanding of the Engagement strategy, and second, the Chinese understanding of the post-2017 shift in US strategy to the strategic competition paradigm. In the latter case in particular, we have the empirical evidence of how Chinese analysts understand the shift from Engagement to post-Engagement. While there was evidence of a range of views concerning the causes of the shift, *every single one* attributed it 100 percent to the United States! China, in the views of this extensive data set of articles published by America watchers, held *no responsibility*—none—for the change in American policy and therefore in the deterioration of the relationship.

This is quite shocking—but it is not really surprising. In my five decades of studying and analyzing US–China relations and China's foreign relations generally, *not a single time* have I ever found China's government, or international relations scholars, admit fault on China's behalf when China and another country have disputes. Nor has China *ever* officially apologized to another country for any action it has taken. For that matter, to my knowledge, the CCP and China's government have only *twice* admitted that serious domestic policy mistakes had been made—in the cases of the Great Leap Forward economic policy and resulting famine (that resulted in the deaths of 30–45 million) of 1958–1961, and of the Cultural Revolution of 1966–1976 (which is officially termed "an extreme leftist error" or 最走派错误).

Once again, in the subject of this Appendix and book, we see China's analysts accepting zero blame for their own government's and ruling Party's actions. It is always the other side's fault. China's leading and most experienced America specialist, Professor Wang Jisi of Peking University, explains it most clearly:

Some US watchers in China, myself included, find the country we have studied for years increasingly unrecognizable and unpredictable. We should do our own self-reflection to examine what went wrong. Political polarization, power struggles, scandals, a lack of confidence in national establishments, tweets doubling as policy announcements, the frequent replacement of top officials in charge of foreign affairs, vacancies in important government positions—similar problems existed before, but their intensity and scope have been particularly stunning since the 2016 US presidential election. The way the Trump administration is wielding US power and influence is bewildering to Chinese political analysts ... It has become harder and harder for foreign-policy makers in China to discern what rules the Americans want themselves and others to abide by, what kind of world order they hope to maintain, and where Washington is on major international issues.[81]

In a subsequent, extremely candid and quite remarkable, article in *Foreign Affairs*, Wang Jisi explained China's perceptions to his American audience. It is such an important article that it merits these extensive excerpts:

In the United States, China's rise is a source of neuralgia and anxiety. Unsurprisingly, in China, the country's growing status is a source of confidence and pride. Against this backdrop, many Chinese analysts highlight the political dysfunction, socioeconomic inequality, ethnic and racial divisions, and economic stagnation that plague the United States and other Western democracies. They also point out that many developing countries and former socialist countries that emulated Western models after the Cold War are not in good shape, and they note how Afghanistan and Iraq, the two places where the United States has intervened most forcefully, continue to suffer from poverty, instability, and political violence. For all these reasons, many Chinese, especially the younger generation, feel fully justified in meeting U.S. pressure with confidence and even a sense of defiant triumphalism.

Underneath the recent hardening of Chinese views on the United States lies a deeper, older source of antagonism. In Chinese eyes, the most significant threat to China's sovereignty and national security has long been U.S. interference in its internal affairs aimed at changing the country's political system and undermining the CCP. Americans often fail to appreciate just how important this history is to their Chinese counterparts and just how much it informs Beijing's views of Washington ...

The CCP believes that all these perceived U.S. attempts to foment dissent and destabilize China are part of an integrated American strategy to Westernize (*xihua*) and split up (*fenhua*) China and prevent the country from becoming a great power. Beijing believes that Washington was the driving force behind the "color revolutions" that took place in the first decade of this century in former Soviet states and that the U.S. government has ginned up protest movements against authoritarian regimes around the world, including the Arab revolts of 2010–11. The CCP believes that those alleged U.S. interventions will supply a blueprint for Washington to undermine and eventually topple the party. The central government and Chinese official media acknowledge no distinctions among the U.S. government's executive branch, the U.S. Congress, American media, and American-based non-governmental organizations. The CCP views all American institutions and individuals that criticize or take action against

Beijing as players in a well-planned, well-organized campaign of subversion, and the Party brands any Chinese citizen or group that has in one way or another been backed by the United States or American organizations as a "stooge" or "political tool" of Washington ...

Just as American views on China have hardened in recent years, so have many Chinese officials come to take a dimmer view of the United States. The conventional wisdom in Beijing holds that the United States is the greatest external challenge to China's national security, sovereignty, and internal stability. Most Chinese observers now believe that the United States is driven by fear and envy to contain China in every possible way. And although American policy elites are clearly aware of how that view has taken hold in China, many of them miss the fact that from Beijing's perspective, it is the United States—and not China—that has fostered this newly adversarial environment, especially by carrying out what the CCP views as a decades-long campaign of meddling in China's internal affairs with the goal of weakening the party's grip on power. Better understanding these diverging views of recent history would help the two countries find a way to manage the competition between them and avoid a devastating conflict that no one wants.[82]

While it is indeed important that Wang Jisi published such an article that illuminates for an elite American audience in English just how the United States and its actions are apparently universally viewed by officials, experts, and even ordinary Chinese (老百姓), there is still *no admission* in the article that China has done *anything* which is a legitimate cause of concern for the United States (and others). There is no mention of China's non-democratic one-party neo-totalitarian political system under the rule of a single strongman dictator; its extensive human rights abuses; its closed internet and control of information; its genocidal incarceration and inhumane treatment of Uighurs; its racist "assimilation" programs of ethnic Tibetans; its dramatic military buildup; its overt criticisms and attempts to undermine American alliances in Asia and Europe; it multifaceted economic and military coercion against Taiwan; the periodic bullying of its neighbors India, Vietnam, and the Philippines; its building and military fortification of islands in the South China Sea; and so on.

All that Wang Jisi can admit which may justify American concerns is his meek statement: "It is not difficult to understand why U.S. officials see China as a competitor ... Americans increasingly feel that in the contest with China, the momentum is with Beijing."[83]

So, if China accepts no responsibility for its own malign actions and policies that threaten not only American interests and values but also international law, then what does the Chinese side think is the way forward to a more stable and productive relationship with the United States? Here again, Wang Jisi's observations are telling:

In China, elites and ordinary people alike generally view politics as a struggle for power and material interests. The most common Chinese understanding about US strategy toward China is that unless and until China's national power exceeds that of the United States, there will be no way to modify Washington's arrogant, aggressive approach.[84]

China's America watchers and officials seemingly have no capacity for self-reflection and self-criticism.

This is not at all encouraging for the future of US–China relations. It takes two to tango. If the United States and China are ever going to pull themselves out of the current trough in relations, it is going to take *both sides* to admit some fault and responsibility for their own actions that have contributed to the extreme deterioration of the relationship. The American side definitely must itself undertake some serious self-reflection, and it has already engaged in an animated domestic debate as we have witnessed in Chapters 1 and 8. Americans and democratic societies have a capacity for such introspection and debate— indeed, it is a principal strength of the United States as a democracy. China, as a Leninist autocracy, has no such capacity. Therein lies a fundamental systemic source of friction and instability in the relationship.

Acknowledgments

Books may be written alone, but they cannot be written without the significant support of others.

In this case, I owe special and considerable thanks to the two institutions which provided prestigious fellowships and where I wrote this book in residence.

During September 2023 through January 2024, I had the honor of being selected as a Distinguished Fellow at the Kissinger Institute for US–China Relations of the Woodrow Wilson International Center for Scholars in Washington, DC. I am particularly indebted to Rob Litwak, Senior Vice President at the Wilson Center, and Robert Daly, Director of the Kissinger Institute, for their warm hospitality and stimulating collegiality. Ever since my own stint on the staff of the Wilson Center in 1986–1987, Rob has been a close personal friend and much respected professional colleague. Since he became Director of the Kissinger Institute in 2013, Robert has done much to bring the best scholarship and sensible policy discourse about China to Washington, DC, and into the public square. I also benefited much from discussions with Wilson Center Fellows in my cohort, particularly Huang Yasheng, Steve Jackson, and Klaus Larres. Steve also deserves special thanks for his yeoman's assistance with preparing the graphics in the book. The Wilson Center librarians were also super kind and extremely helpful in tracking down a number of sources for me. Director of Fellowships Kim Conner and her exemplary team made me feel most welcome back to my "old home" (this was my third time in residence at the Wilson Center and I cannot say enough positive things about this unique institution and "living memorial" to the 28th President of the United States).

Subsequently, from February through June 2024, I had the additional privilege and pleasure of being a Distinguished Visiting Fellow at the Hoover Institution at Stanford University, named in honor of the 31st President of the United States. I am truly deeply indebted to the Honorable Condoleezza Rice, the 66th Secretary of State and the Director of the Hoover Institution, as she kindly invited me to spend part of my sabbatical at Hoover. I enormously admire Condi, who I have known on-and-off since we were both PhD students during the 1980s (she at Stanford, me at Michigan). What Condi has accomplished in her life and career is probably without parallel in the history of the United States, and she is an exemplary American in so many ways. Larry Diamond, Hoover William L. Clayton Senior Fellow and Stanford professor, was also instrumental in inviting and welcoming me. I also greatly admire Larry as a scholar, as a brave advocate for civic and democratic freedoms worldwide, and as a good friend.

While at Hoover, I also greatly benefited from discussions with Senior Fellows Elizabeth Economy, Jim Ellis, Niall Ferguson, Sumit Ganguly, Stephen Kotkin, H. R. McMaster, Amy Zegart, and Philip Zelikow; with Distinguished Visiting Fellows Joseph Nye and Rose Gottemoeller; with National Security Affairs Fellows David Arulanantham and Nicholas Shenkin; with Distinguished Research Fellow Glenn Tiffert; and with Fellow Erin Baggott Carter.

Also at Stanford, I gained a lot from discussions with Michael McFaul, Director of the Freeman Spogli Institute for International Studies and distinguished Professor. I admire Mike greatly as a scholar, as a steadfast advocate of democracy, and for what he has contributed to the United States in his official capacities on the National Security Council and as Ambassador to Russia during the Obama administration (which was not at all easy), and I am pleased to count him as a personal friend (we first met on a trip together to Kazakhstan in 1990). Professors Andrew Walder and Jean Oi, whose close friendship and support date back to our days together as graduate students at the University of Michigan in the early 1980s, made my wife and me feel welcome in Palo Alto. Professors Kathryn Stoner, Scott Sagan, and diplomat-in-residence Laura Stone took time to talk with me. These are all extremely accomplished professionals and scholars, and they all made me feel very welcome in a totally new environment. The intellectual milieu at Hoover and Stanford is extraordinarily rich, and I tried to take full advantage by participating in numerous seminars and conferences.

Sabbaticals are one of the very best things about being a professor. They come every seven years. If used well, they should infuse one with several kinds of new capital: intellectual, cultural, personal, professional, and geographic. My stay at Stanford and Hoover ticked all of these boxes and definitely proved to be one of the very best sabbaticals I have ever had (and I have had some good ones). This book simply would not have been written without spending the valuable and productive time at the Hoover Institution and the Woodrow Wilson Center, two centers of national and international renown. They are both credits to our nation and their presidential namesakes, and I am proud to have been associated with each.

For granting me the sabbatical, I am most grateful to George Washington University's Elliott School of International Affairs and the Department of Political Science. Elliott School Dean Alyssa Ayres, Political Science Department chair Eric Lawrence, and university Provost Christopher Bracey are due special thanks for supporting my sabbatical application. I am now in my 28th year as a faculty member at George Washington University—which has been enormously rewarding, especially my faculty colleagues and the more than 3,000 students I have taught. I am grateful for the university's support of my various professional activities. I am also deeply indebted to Christopher J. Fussner, Elliott School alumnus and a former undergraduate classmate of mine, for his nearly 40 years of unstinting financial and personal support for the China Policy Program at George Washington University (which I established in 1998 and have directed ever since).

For this book, I am also in the debt of five of my former Elliott School graduate students who served as research assistants: Madeleine Craig-Scheckman, Ben Wasserstrom, Sheldon Xie, Luya Zhang, and David Zhong (David was also my intern research assistant at the Wilson Center). Maddie also helped to dig up a huge amount of information and produce the graphics on American states' interactions with China. Each of these research assistants dug deeply into a variety of American and Chinese materials, which considerably strengthened the evidentiary basis of the book.

I am also truly indebted to colleagues who read parts of the manuscript concerning US government administrations in which they served as senior China policymakers: Winston Lord (Nixon, Ford, Reagan, and Clinton), Doug Paal (Bush 41), Ken Lieberthal (Clinton), Dennis Wilder (Bush 43), Evan Medeiros (Obama), and H. R. McMaster (Trump). Each helped to correct and refine my judgments, and I am truly grateful to each for their time and careful reading of previous drafts of relevant sections.

Other colleagues who have epitomized collegiality by commenting on specific parts of the manuscript include Craig Allen, Richard Bush, Rick Inderfurth, Loch Johnson, Winston Lord, Henry Nau, Nicholas Shenkin, Robert Sutter, Andrew Walder, and Amy Zegart. Each helped to fine-tune certain sections and saved me from errors in their areas of expertise. Of course, all remaining errors and omissions are my own fault (and there are no doubt some).

I also am grateful to Oxford University Press (OUP) for a thoroughly professional production and publication process. This is my tenth book published with OUP, dating back to 1994. I have had the distinct pleasure of having David McBride as my editor for the past five volumes. Dave has become one of the most noteworthy commissioning editors of books on international relations and in the China field, and I am honored to be included in the distinguished list of important authors and books that he has built. I am also grateful to two anonymous OUP reviewers who offered constructive critiques and for recognizing the novelty of my approach and argument. Once the book entered the production process, Lacey Harvey and Devasree Vasudevan expertly guided it through all of the complexities before the author had the pleasure of holding a bound copy. I am also most grateful to Elizaveta Friesem for her expert copyediting. I am deeply grateful to Dave, Lacey, and the entire OUP team for all of their professionalism and expert work.

Last, but not least, I have had the support, love, and companionship of my spouse of 42 years: Ingrid Larsen. Ingrid has had to endure far too many discussions and descriptions of various book chapters from me, and she has been a wonderful and constructive "sounding board." Our two wonderful sons, Chris and Xander, are also a daily source of pride and support. Our new grandson James came into the world during the year when I was writing this book, offering a wonderful diversion and welcome addition to my life. While perhaps cliché, I also benefited from the daily companionship of "man's best friend," our beloved golden retriever, Cooper. While the book was mainly written in Washington, DC, and Palo Alto, California, the finishing touches were completed where I have done much of my book writing during my career—at our family cabin near Traverse City, Michigan—and my home in Arlington, Virginia.

I owe all of those above a deep debt of thanks.

Notes

Preface

1. David Shambaugh, *China's Communist Party: Atrophy and Adaptation* (Berkeley, CA: University of California Press, 2013).
2. David Shambaugh, *Modernizing China's Military: Progress, Problems, and Prospects* (Berkeley, CA: University of California Press, 2002).
3. David Shambaugh, *Beautiful Imperialist: China Perceives America, 1972–1990* (Princeton, NJ: Princeton University Press, 1991).
4. David Shambaugh, *China Goes Global: The Partial Power* (New York, NY: Oxford University Press, 2013).
5. David Shambaugh, *China's Future* (Cambridge, UK: Polity Press, 2016).
6. David Shambaugh, *China's Leaders: From Mao to Now* (Cambridge, UK: Polity Press, 2021).
7. David Shambaugh, *Where Great Powers Meet: America & China in Southeast Asia* (New York, NY: Oxford University Press, 2021).
8. Jeannette Shambaugh Elliott and David Shambaugh, *The Odyssey of China's Imperial Art Treasures* (Seattle, WA: University of Washington Press, 2005).
9. Pew Research Center, "Views of China and Xi Jinping," https://www.pewresearch.org/global/2024/07/09/views-of-china-and-xi-jinping.
10. The White House, *National Security Strategy of the United States of America*, https://trumpwhitehouse.archives.gov/wp-content/uploads/2017/12/NSS-Final-12-18-2017-0905.pdf; The White House, *United States Strategic Approach to the People's Republic of China*, https://trumpwhitehouse.archives.gov/wp-content/uploads/2020/05/U.S.-Strategic-Approach-to-The-Peoples-Republic-of-China-Report-5.24v1.pdf.
11. See Antony J. Blinken, Secretary of State, speech at George Washington University, May 26, 2022, "The Administration's Approach to the People's Republic of China," https://www.state.gov/the-administrations-approach-to-the-peoples-republic-of-china.
12. See "China Should Worry Less About Old Enemies, More About Ex-Friends," *The Economist*, December 15, 2018.
13. My dissertation was subsequently revised and published as Shambaugh, *Beautiful Imperialist*, op. cit.
14. I do not know of any other foreigner who has been a residential visiting scholar in so many CASS institutes.
15. David Shambaugh (ed.), *Tangled Titans: The United States and China* (Lanham, MD: Rowman & Littlefield, 2013). I recount my sense of unease at the time in the Preface of this volume.
16. David Shambaugh, "The Coming Chinese Crack-Up," *Wall Street Journal*, May 6, 2015.
17. See Shambaugh, *China's Communist Party*, op. cit.

Chapter 1

1. Philip Zelikow and Condoleezza Rice, *To Build a Better World* (New York, NY: Twelve, 2019), pp. 426–427.
2. See Susan Shirk, *Overreach: How China Derailed Its Peaceful Rise* (New York, NY: Oxford University Press, 2023); Bates Gill, *Daring to Struggle: China's Global Ambitions Under Xi Jinping* (New York, NY: Oxford University Press, 2022).
3. I personally witnessed this while living in China at the time. See David Shambaugh, "The Year China Showed Its Claws," *Financial Times*, February 16, 2010.
4. See Evan Osnos, *Wildland: The Making of America's Fury* (New York, NY: Farrar, Straus, Giroux, 2021).

5. For an excellent analysis of the rise of populism and illiberalism in the United States, see Alan S. Kahan, *Freedom from Fear: An Incomplete History of Liberalism* (Princeton, NJ: Princeton University Press, 2023), chapter 11.

6. Among the studies that advance this argument are Gordon H. Chang, *Fateful Ties: A History of America's Preoccupation with China* (Cambridge, MA: Harvard University Press, 2015); Jonathan Spence, *To Change China: Western Advisors in China* (New York, NY: Penguin, 2002); John Pomfret, *The Beautiful Country and the Middle Kingdom: America and China, 1776 to the Present* (New York, NY: Henry Holt & Co., 2016); James C. Thomson, *While China Faced West: American Reformers in Nationalist China* (Cambridge, MA: Harvard University Press, 1969); John Curtis Perry, *Facing West: Americans and the Opening of the Pacific* (New York, NY: Praeger, 1994); Akira Iriye, *Across the Pacific: An Inner History of American–East Asian Relations* (New York, NY: Harcourt, Brace & World, 1967); Peter Buck, *American Science and Modern China* (Cambridge, MA: Cambridge University Press, 2010); David L. Andersen, *Imperialism and Idealism: American Diplomats in China, 1861–1898* (Bloomington, IN: Indiana University Press, 1986); James C. Thomson, *Sentimental Imperialists: The American Experience in East Asia* (New York, NY: Harper & Row, 1981).

7. Richard Madsen, *China and the American Dream: A Moral Inquiry* (Berkeley, CA: University of California Press, 1995).

8. See Tyler Dennett, *Americans in Eastern Asia* (London: Forgotten Books, 2015; originally published in 1922), pp. 372–378.

9. Michael H. Hunt, *The Making of a Special Relationship: The United States and China to 1914* (New York, NY: Columbia University Press, 1983), p. 172.

10. Anson Burlingame, "Speech in New York, June 23, 1868," https://china.usc.edu/anson-burlingame-speech-new-york-june-23-1868.

11. See Xu Guoqi, "Anson Burlingame: China's First Messenger to the World," in Xu Guoqi (ed.), *Chinese and Americans: A Shared History* (Cambridge, MA: Harvard University Press, 2014).

12. Pomfret, *The Beautiful Country and the Middle Kingdom*, op. cit., p. 65.

13. Andersen, *Imperialism and Idealism*, op. cit., pp. 47–48.

14. Ibid., p. 46.

15. Ibid., p. 51.

16. Ibid., p. 53, p. 55.

17. Frederick Low (1869–1874), Benjamin Avery (1874–1875), George Seward (1876–1880), James B. Angell (1880–1881), John R. Young (1882–1885), and Charles Denby (1885–1898).

18. Office of the Historian, United States Department of State, "Secretary of State John Hay and the Open Door in China, 1899–1900," https://history.state.gov/milestones/1899-1913/hay-and-china.

19. Hunt, *The Making of a Special Relationship*, op. cit.

20. The White House, *National Security Strategy of the United States of America*, December 2017, https://trumpwhitehouse.archives.gov/wp-content/uploads/2017/12/NSS-Final-12-18-2017-0905.pdf.

21. National Archives, *The United States Strategic Approach to the People's Republic of China*, May 26, 2022, https://trumpwhitehouse.archives.gov/wp-content/uploads/2020/05/U.S.-Strategic-Approach-to-The-Peoples-Republic-of-China-Report-5.24v1.pdf.

22. Kurt M. Campbell and Ely Ratner, "The China Reckoning: How Beijing Defied American Expectations," *Foreign Affairs* (March/April 2018), pp. 60–70.

23. Ibid., p. 61.

24. Kurt M. Campbell and Ely Ratner, "Rejoinder by Campbell and Ratner," in "Did America Get China Wrong? The Engagement Debate," *Foreign Affairs* (July/August 2018).

25. John J. Mearsheimer, *The Tragedy of Great Power Politics* (New York, NY: W. W. Norton, 2001).

26. Aaron L. Friedberg, *A Contest for Supremacy: America, China, and the Contest for Supremacy in Asia* (New York, NY: W. W. Norton, 2012).

27. Quoted from Masahiro Okoshi, "U.S. Engagement with China a 'Strategic Blunder': Mearsheimer," *Nikkei Asia*, February 21, 2022.

28. Aaron L. Friedberg, *Getting China Wrong* (Cambridge, MA: Polity Press, 2022).

29. Ibid., p. 163.

30. Robert D. Blackwill and Ashley J. Tellis, *Revising U.S. Grand Strategy Towards China* (New York, NY: Council on Foreign Relations Special Report No. 72, March 2015); Robert D.

Blackwill, *Implementing Grand Strategy Towards China* (New York, NY: Council on Foreign Relations Report No. 85, January 2020).

31. Robert Zoellick, "Whither China: From Membership to Responsibility?" Remarks to the National Committee on US–China Relations, September 21, 2005.

32. Graham Allison, *Destined for War: Can America and China Escape the Thucydides' Trap?* (New York, NY: Mariner Books, 2017).

33. Joseph S. Nye, "What Killed US–China Engagement?" *Taipei Times*, January 6, 2024.

34. Ibid.

35. "Fireside Chat with Condoleezza Rice and Robert M. Gates," Aspen Security Forum, July 19, 2024, https://www.youtube.com/watch?v=mlD9cvaPDy4&list=PL7fuyfNu8jfPTKp6PJ2y JugSfxXEDyEqM&index=29.

36. Orville Schell, "The Death of Engagement," *The Wire China*, June 7, 2020.

37. Ibid.

38. See David Shambaugh, "Q&A: David Shambaugh on Why U.S. Engagement with China Is Already Dead in Spirit," *The Wire China*, November 7, 2021.

39. Harry Harding, "Has U.S. China Policy Failed?" *The Washington Quarterly*, Vol. 38, No. 3 (Fall 2015). All subsequent quotations from Harding's article are ibid., various pages.

40. Wang Jisi et al., "Did America Get China Wrong? The Engagement Debate," *Foreign Affairs* (June 14, 2018).

41. J. Stapleton Roy, "Engagement Works," ibid.

42. Thomas W. Christensen and Patricia Kim, "Don't Abandon Ship," ibid.

43. Joseph S. Nye, "Time Will Tell," ibid.

44. Juan Zhang, "Ambassador Winston Lord: Reflection, Review, and Hope for US–China Relations," US–China Perception Monitor, November 30, 2023.

45. Ibid.

46. M. Taylor Fravel, J. Stapleton Roy, Michael D. Swaine, Susan A. Thornton, and Ezra Vogel, "Opinion: China Is Not an Enemy," *The Washington Post*, July 3, 2019. The sequential listing of the authors' names was alphabetical, per *The Washington Post* custom.

47. "Open Letter: China Is Not an Enemy," *National Committee on US–China Relations*, https://www.ncuscr.org/open-letter-china-is-not-the-enemy.

48. See "Stay the Course on China: An Open Letter to President Trump," *The Journal of Political Risk*, https://www.jpolrisk.com/stay-the-course-on-china-an-open-letter-to-president-trump.

49. Alastair Iain Johnston, "The Failures of the 'Failure of Engagement' with China," *The Washington Quarterly*, Vol. 42, No. 2 (June 2019).

50. Ibid., p. 99.

51. George W. Bush, "A Distinctly American Internationalism," speech at the Ronald Reagan Presidential Library, November 19, 1999.

52. Stephen Orlins, "As US–China Strategic Rivalry Heats Up, Don't Forget the Successes of Engagement," *South China Morning Post*, June 9, 2018.

53. Ibid.

54. Andy Rothman, "The Benefits of Engagement," *The Wire China*, March 28, 2021.

55. Jonathan D. Pollack and Jeffrey A. Bader, "Looking Before We Leap: Weighing the Risks of US–China Disengagement," Brookings Policy Brief, July 2019.

56. Anne F. Thurston (ed.), *Engaging China: Fifty Years of Sino-American Relations* (New York, NY: Columbia University Press, 2021).

57. Thomas Fingar, "The Logic and Efficacy of Engagement: Objectives, Assumptions, and Impacts," ibid., p. 41, p. 43.

58. Ibid., p. 49.

59. See his memoir David M. Lampton, *Living U.S.–China Relations: From Cold War to Cold War* (Lanham, MD; Rowman & Littlefield, 2024).

60. David M. Lampton, "Engagement with China: A Eulogy with Reflections on a Gathering Storm," in Anne F. Thurston (ed.), *Engaging China: Fifty Years of Sino-American Relations* (New York, NY: Columbia University Press, 2021), p. 394.

61. Although there are many examples and variations of the "competition paradigm," it is perhaps best exemplified in Evan Medeiros (ed.), *Cold Rivals: The New Era of US–China Strategic Competition* (Washington, DC: Georgetown University Press, 2023).

62. See, for example, Paul Heer, "Engagement with China Has Not Failed: It Just Hasn't Succeeded Yet," *The National Interest*, June 14, 2022.

63. James Mann, *The China Fantasy: How Our Leaders Explain Away Chinese Repression* (New York, NY: Viking Press, 2007).

Chapter 2

1. Joseph S. Nye, "What Killed US–China Engagement?" *Taipei Times*, January 6, 2024.
2. Orville Schell, "The Death of Engagement," *The Wire China*, June 7, 2020.
3. Ai Weiwei, "No, Capitalism and the Internet Will Not Free China's People," *The New York Times*, October 23, 2022.
4. See Nancy Bernkopf Tucker, *Patterns in the Dust: Chinese–American Relations and the Recognition Controversy, 1949–1950* (New York, NY: Columbia University Press, 1983).
5. Richard Nixon, "Asia After Viet Nam," *Foreign Affairs* (October 1967).
6. Joint Communique Between the United States and China, February 27, 1972, https://digitalarchive.wilsoncenter.org/document/joint-communique-between-united-states-and-china.
7. Author's communication with Winston Lord, September 28, 2023.
8. See James C. Thomson, *While China Faced West: American Reformers in Nationalist China, 1928–1937* (Cambridge, MA: Harvard University Press, 1969); Peter Buck, *American Science and Modern China, 1876–1936* (Cambridge, UK: Cambridge University Press, 1980); Mary Brown Bullock, *An American Transplant: The Rockefeller Foundation and Peking Union Medical College* (Berkeley, CA: University of California Press, 1980); Mary Brown Bullock, *The Oil Prince's Legacy: Rockefeller Philanthropy in China* (Stanford, CA: Stanford University Press, 2017); Bridie Andrews, *The Making of Modern Chinese Medicine, 1850–1960* (Honolulu, HI: University of Hawaii Press, 2014); William C. Kirby, *Empires of Ideas: Creating the Modern University from Germany to America in China* (Cambridge, MA: Harvard University Press, 2022). American perceptions of China during this period are well captured in T. Christopher Jesperson, *American Images of China, 1931–1949* (Stanford, CA: Stanford University Press, 1996).
9. Michel Oksenberg, "China Policy for the 1980s," *Foreign Affairs* (Winter 1980/1981).
10. I offer definitions and distinctions between these terms in my book Shambaugh, *China's Future* (Cambridge, UK: Polity Press, 2016).
11. Francis Fukuyama, "The End of History?" *The National Interest*, No. 16 (Summer 1989).
12. Press Conference by the President, June 5, 1989, https://www.chinafile.com/library/reports/us-china-diplomacy-after-tiananmen-documents-george-hw-bush-presidential-library.
13. William J. Clinton, "Remarks to the Asia Society and the United States–China Education Foundation Board," *Public Papers of the Presidents of the United States (1997)*, p. 1428.
14. "Remarks in Kyoto," November 16, 2005, *Public Papers of the Presidents of the United States (2005)*, p. 1726.
15. For specific discussion, see Shambaugh, *China's Future*, op. cit., and David Shambaugh, *China's Leaders: From Mao to Now* (Cambridge, UK: Polity Press, 2021).
16. John Foster Dulles, "Challenge and Response in United States Policy," *Foreign Affairs*, Vol. 36, No. 1 (October 1957); "Briefing on the World Situation," Hearings Before the Committee on Foreign Affairs, House of Representatives, Eighty-Sixth Congress, January 28–29, 1959.
17. Schell, The Death of Engagement," op. cit.
18. Nixon, "Asia After Viet Nam," op. cit.
19. See Alastair Iain Johnston, *Social States: China in International Institutions, 1980–2000* (Princeton, NJ: Princeton University Press, 2008).
20. See Elizabeth Economy and Michel C. Oksenberg (eds.), *China Joins the World: Progress and Prospects* (New York, NY: Council on Foreign Relations, 1998).
21. See David Shambaugh, "China and the Liberal International Order," in Nicholas Burns, Leah Boutinis, and Jonathon Price (eds.), *The World Turned Upside Down: Maintaining American Leadership in a Dangerous Age* (Washington, DC: The Aspen Institute, 2017), https://www.aspeninstitute.org/wp-content/uploads/2017/11/FINAL-ASG-World-Upside-Down-FINAL.REV_.pdf.
22. See Robert Zoellick, "Responsible Stakeholder," *National Committee on US–China Relations*, https://www.ncuscr.org/fact/robert-zoellicks-responsible-stakeholder-speech.
23. Michel Oksenberg, "A Decade of Sino-American Relations," *Foreign Affairs* (Fall 1982).

24. I had the privilege of serving as Oksenberg's assistant on the National Security Council staff in 1977–1978, and I distinctly recall him arguing this in personal conversations, in meetings, and in memoranda.
25. Oksenberg, "A Decade of Sino-American Relations," op. cit.
26. Oksenberg, "China Policy for the 1980s," op. cit.
27. For an excellent tracing of bilateral bureaucratic relations, see Bonnie S. Glaser, "The Diplomatic Relationship: Substance and Process," in David Shambaugh (ed.), *Tangled Titans: The United States and China* (Lanham, MD: Rowman & Littlefield, 2013).
28. Oksenberg, "China Policy for the 1980s," op. cit.
29. State Council of the People's Republic of China, "China, US Have Established 284 'Sister' Pairs," April 30, 2022, https://english.www.gov.cn/news/internationalexchanges/202204/30/content_WS626c754fc6d02e533532a1c1.html.
30. See Professor Dickson's excellent and nuanced discussion in his book Bruce J. Dickson, *The Party and the People: Chinese Politics in the 21st Century* (Princeton, NJ: Princeton University Press, 2021).
31. Quoted in Charles W. Freeman III, "The Commercial and Economic Relationship," in David Shambaugh (ed.), *Tangled Titans: The United States and China* (Lanham, MD: Rowman & Littlefield, 2013).
32. Source: US Department of Commerce, "Trade with China," https://www.bis.doc.gov/index.php/country-papers/3268-2022-statistical-analysis-of-u-s-trade-with-china/file.
33. See David Shambaugh and Gudrun Wacker (eds.), *American and European Relations with China: Advancing Common Agendas* (Berlin: Stiftung Wissenschaft und Politik, 2008).
34. "From Reform and Opening to Opening Without Reform: Lessons from the Ford Foundation's Law Program in China," https://www.fordfoundation.org/work/learning/learning-reflections/from-reform-and-opening-to-opening-without-reform-lessons-from-the-ford-foundation-s-law-program-in-china.
35. Ibid.
36. For a superb overview of these programs and the history of US–China legal exchanges, see Jamie P. Horsley, "Revitalizing Law and Governance Collaboration with China," The Brookings Institution, November 2020.
37. Figure cited in Luke Kelly, "How China Is Winning Back More Graduates from Foreign Universities Than Ever Before," *Forbes*, January 25, 2018.
38. Zhongguo Jiaoyu Bu (中国教育部), "2016年度我国出国留学人员情况统计," March 3, 2017, http://www.moe.gov.cn/jyb_xwfb/xw_fbh/moe_2069/xwfbh_2017n/xwfb_170301/170301_sjtj/201703/t20170301_297676.html.
39. BBC, "How Reliant Are US Colleges on Chinese Students?" June 12, 2019.
40. Oksenberg, "China Policy for the 1980s," op. cit.
41. David M. Lampton, *Living U.S.–China Relations: From Cold War to Cold War* (Lanham, MD: Rowman & Littlefield, 2024), p. 380.
42. Ibid., p. 382.
43. See "Annual Growth of the Real Gross Domestic Product of the United States from 1990 to 2023," *Statista*, https://www.statista.com/statistics/188165/annual-gdp-growth-of-the-united-states-since-1990.
44. See "GDP Growth (Annual %)—China," https://data.worldbank.org/indicator/NY.GDP.MKTP.KD.ZG?locations=CN.
45. Anne F. Thurston (ed.), *Engaging China: Fifty Years of Sino-American Engagement* (New York: Columbia University Press, 2021)

Chapter 3

1. See Michael Hunt, *The Making of a Special Relationship: The United States and China to 1914* (New York: Columbia University Press, 1983).
2. The classic account is Ross Y. Koen, *The China Lobby in American Politics* (New York, NY: Harper and Row, 1974). Also see Wayne Morse, "The Influence of the China Lobby," in Benson Lee Grayson (ed.), *The American Image of China* (New York, NY: Frederick Ungar Publishing Company, 1979).
3. See James Mann, "Congress and Taiwan: Understanding the Bond" and Richard C. Bush, "Taiwan Policy Making Since Tiananmen: Navigating Through Shifting Waters," in Ramon

H. Myers, Michel C. Oksenberg, and David Shambaugh (eds.), *Making China Policy: Lessons from the Bush and Clinton Administrations* (Lanham, MD: Rowman & Littlefield, 2001).

4. These firms must register under the Foreign Agent Registration Act (FARA) and declare their activities and funding sources.

5. Nancy Bernkopf Tucker, *Patterns in the Dust: Chinese–American Relations and the Recognition Controversy 1949–1950* (New York, NY: Columbia University Press, 1983), especially chapter 10.

6. See discussion in Tucker, ibid., pp. 188–193.

7. Quoted in ibid., p. 191.

8. See Barbara W. Tuchman, "If Mao Had Come to Washington: An Essay in Alternatives," *Foreign Affairs* (October 1972), https://www.foreignaffairs.com/articles/asia/1972-10-01/if-mao-had-come-washington-essay-alternatives.

9. Of the enormous literature on the topic, I particularly commend Thomas W. Christensen, *Useful Adversaries: Grand Strategy, Domestic Mobilization, and Sino-American Conflict, 1947–1958* (Princeton, NJ: Princeton University Press, 1996).

10. See Office of the Historian, US Department of State, "US–China Ambassadorial Talks, 1955–1970," https://history.state.gov/milestones/1953-1960/china-talks

11. Michael McFaul, *From Cold War to Hot Peace: An American Ambassador in Putin's Russia* (Boston, MA: Houghton, Mifflin, Harcourt, 2018), p. 320.

12. See discussion in Nancy Bernkopf Tucker, *The China Threat: Memories, Myths, and Realities in the 1950s* (New York, NY: Columbia University Press, 2012).

13. This is very well traced in ibid., especially pp. 182–185.

14. John Pomfret, *The Beautiful Country and the Middle Kingdom: America and China, 1776 to the Present* (New York, NY: Henry Holt & Co., 2016), p. 426.

15. Quoted in Foster Rhea Dulles, *American Foreign Policy Towards Communist China, 1949–1969* (New York, NY: Thomas Y. Crowell Co., 1972), p. 189. See John F. Kennedy, "A Democrat Looks at Foreign Policy," *Foreign Affairs*, October 1, 1957, https://www.foreignaffairs.com/articles/united-states/1957-10-01/democrat-looks-foreign-policy.

16. At the time, in 1961, Rusk served as Secretary of State, Hilsman was Assistant Secretary of the Bureau of Intelligence and Research (INR), Rice was a staff member of the Secretary's Policy Planning staff, Thomson was assigned to the Office of Far Eastern Affairs, and Whiting was Chief of the Far Eastern Division of INR.

17. Roger Hilsman, *To Move a Nation: The Politics of Foreign Policy of John F. Kennedy* (Garden City, NY: Doubleday & Co., 1967), p. 348.

18. This is recounted in Charles J. Pellegrin, "'There Are Bigger Issues at Stake': The Administration of John F. Kennedy and United States–Republic of China Relations, 1961–63," in John Delane Williams et al., *John F. Kennedy History, Memory, and Legacy: An Interdisciplinary Inquiry* (Grand Forks, ND: University of North Dakota Press, 2010).

19. Ibid., p. 102, citing Rusk's memoirs Dean Rusk, *As I Saw It* (New York, NY: W. W. Norton, 1990), pp. 282–284.

20. This derives from conversations I had with Allen Whiting in 1997 and 2001.

21. Ted Sorensen, *Counselor: Life at the Edge of History* (New York, NY: Harper, 2008), p. 352.

22. In his memoirs, Hilsman specifically credits the following State Department officials with helping to draft it: James C. Thomson Jr., Lindsey Grant, Allen S. Whiting, Joseph W. Neubert, Abram Manell, and Robert W. Barnett. See Hilsman, *To Move a Nation*, op. cit., p. 351.

23. President John F. Kennedy, News Conference No. 64, November 14, 1963, *John F. Kennedy Presidential Library*, https://www.jfklibrary.org/archives/other-resources/john-f-kennedy-press-conferences/news-conference-64.

24. The speech is available in the *Department of State Bulletin*, Vol. 50 (1964), pp. 11–17.

25. Hilsman, *To Move a Nation*, op. cit., p. 351. This chapter (chapter 24) in Hilsman's memoirs goes into considerable detail about the speech.

26. All quotations in this section are from *Department of State Bulletin*, op. cit.

27. Hilsman credits Allen Whiting's background press briefings with generating positive coverage. Hilsman, *To Move a Nation*, op. cit., p. 355.

28. Stanley K. Hornbeck, "Policy Regarding China: What Did Mr. Hilsman Disclose at San Francisco?" *World Affairs*, Vol. 126, No. 4 (Winter 1963–1964), pp. 238–243.

29. Hilsman, *To Move a Nation*, op. cit., pp. 355–356.

30. Pomfret, *The Beautiful Country and the Middle Kingdom*, op. cit., p. 431.

31. Lyndon B. Johnson, "Peace Without Conquest," address at Johns Hopkins University, April 7, 1965.
32. For a summary of the hearings, see "Developments in China Studied," *CQ Almanac 1966*, pp. 424–429, http://library.cqpress.com/cqalmanac/cqal66-1301704.
33. The oral and written testimony of the hearings were published as *U.S. Policy with Respect to Mainland China* (Washington, DC: U.S. Government Printing Office, 1966). Excerpts were published in Akira Iriye (ed.), *U.S. Policy Toward China* (Boston, MA: Little, Brown & Co., 1968).
34. See E. W. Kenworthy, "China Expert Asks US to Ease Policy," *The New York Times*, March 9, 1966.
35. Iriye, *U.S. Policy Toward China*, op. cit., p. 127.
36. Kenworthy, "China Expert Asks US to Ease Policy," op. cit., p. 7.
37. Ibid., p. 129.
38. Fairbank set out his views in detail at the time in his book John King Fairbank, *China: The People's Middle Kingdom and the U.S.A.* (Cambridge, MA: Belknap Press of Harvard University Press, 1967).
39. J. William Fulbright, *The Arrogance of Power* (New York, NY: Vintage Books, 1966),
40. I am indebted to Mao Lin for drawing this to my attention. See Mao Lin, *Bringing China Back into the World: The Historical Origin of America's Engagement Policy and Its Implications for Contemporary US–China Relations* (Washington, DC: Woodrow Wilson Center China Fellows Occasional Paper, 2023), p. 109.
41. Ibid.
42. See Michel Oksenberg and Steven Goldstein, "The Chinese Political Spectrum," *Problems of Communism*, Vol. 23, No. 2 (March/April 1974).
43. See Benjamin I. Schwartz, *In Search of Wealth and Power: Yen Fu and the West* (Cambridge, MA: Harvard University Press, 1964); Orville Schell and John Delury, *Wealth and Power: China's Long March to the 21st Century* (New York, NY: Random House, 2014).
44. Norton Wheeler, *The Role of American NGOs in China's Modernization: Invited Influence* (London: Routledge, 2013), pp. 28–29.
45. Kazushi Minami, *People's Diplomacy: How Americans and Chinese Transformed US–China Relations During the Cold War* (Ithaca, NY: Cornell University Press, 2024), p. 23.
46. Richard Madsen, *China and the American Dream: A Moral Inquiry* (Berkeley, CA: University of California Press, 1995), p. 33.
47. Ibid., p. 36.
48. Minami, *People's Diplomacy*, op. cit.
49. Madsen, *China and the American Dream*, op. cit., also provides an account of the establishment of the NCUSCR, which draws on an unpublished manuscript in NCUSCR archives by Robert Mang, "Origins of the National Committee on US–China Relations."
50. National Committee on U.S.–China Relations, "Who We Are," https://www.ncuscr.org/about.
51. See Pugwash Conference on Science and World Affairs, https://pugwash.org/about-pugwash.
52. Information on the establishment of the CSCPRC is based on an email from Mary Brown Bullock, former staff director of the CSCPRC, November 6, 2023.
53. Office of the Historian, U.S. Department of State, "Joint Statement Following Discussion with Leaders of the People's Republic of China," February 27, 1972, https://history.state.gov/historicaldocuments/frus1969-76v17/d203.
54. Cited in Pete Millwood, *Improbable Diplomats: How Ping-Pong Players, Musicians, and Scientists Remade US–China Relations* (Cambridge, MA: Cambridge University Press, 2023), p. 17.
55. Ibid., pp. 17–18. Also see Kathlin Smith, "The Role of Scientists in Normalizing U.S.–China Relations," *Annals of the New York Academy of Sciences*, Vol. 866, No. 1 (December 1998), pp. 114–136.
56. A complete listing is available in Appendix H of David M. Lampton with Joyce A. Medancy and Kristen M. Williams, *A Relationship Restored: Trends in U.S.–China Educational Exchanges, 1978–1984* (Washington, DC: National Academy Press, 1986), pp. 239–241. For a good overview of the science and education exchanges during this period, see Minami, *People's Diplomacy*, op. cit., chapters 3 and 4.
57. For her recollections of her time as staff director of CSCPRC, see Mary Brown Bullock, *China on My Mind* (Atlanta, GA: Xlibris, 2023).

58. Millwood, *Improbable Diplomats*, op. cit., especially chapter 6. Millwood's study is by far the best on the development of the "three committees" and the important roles that they played during the pre-normalization period.

59. Harry Harding, *A Fragile Relationship: The United States and China Since 1972* (Washington, DC: Brookings Institution Press, 1992), pp. 54–60; Madsen, *China and the American Dream*, op. cit.; and Millwood, *Improbable Diplomats*, op. cit., p. 23.

60. Harding, ibid., p. 56.

61. See David Shambaugh, *Beautiful Imperialist: China Perceives America, 1972–1990* (Princeton, NJ: Princeton University Press, 1991).

62. The origins and establishment of the NCUSCT are well described by Millwood in *Improbable Diplomats*, op. cit., pp. 156–161. Also see Min Song, *Economic Normalization: Sino-American Trade Relations from 1969–1980*, PhD diss., University of Georgia, 2009.

63. Eugene Theroux, "The Founding of the Council," *China Business Review*, Vol. 20, No. 4 (1993), p. 2.

64. In 1973, China's *total* foreign trade amounted to less than J. C. Penney's annual revenue! Ibid.

65. Harding, *A Fragile Relationship*, op. cit., Table A-2, p. 364.

66. See Committee of Concerned Asian Scholars, https://en.wikipedia.org/wiki/Committee_of_Concerned_Asian_Scholars.

67. CCAS founding members are all listed in ibid.

68. Ibid.

69. First\hand accounts and memorabilia of the participants can be found at University of California-San Diego, "CCAS Trips to China in the Eserly 1970s," https://exhibits.ucsd.edu/starlight/ccas.

70. Committee on Concerned Asian Scholars, *Inside the People's Republic!* (New York, NY: Bantam Books, 1972).

71. See US–China People's Friendship Association, https://www.uscpfa.org/about-uscpfa; https://en.wikipedia.org/wiki/US-China_Peoples_Friendship_Association; Paul B. Trescott, *From Frenzy to Friendship: A History of the US–China People's Friendship Association* (Carbondale, IL: US–China People's Friendship Association).

72. "About USCPFA," https://www.uscpfa.org/about-uscpfa.

73. Minami, *People's Diplomacy*, op. cit., p. 123.

74. Quoted in James Wurst, *The UN Association–USA: A Little Known History of Advocacy and Action* (Boulder, CO: Lynne Reinner Publishers, 2016), p. 40

75. Ibid., p. 249. I am grateful to Ed Elmendorf, my cousin and former President of the UNA–USA, for drawing this history to my attention.

76. United Nations Association of the USA, *China, the United Nations, and United States Policy* (New York, NY: United Nations Association of the United States, 1966–1967). Robert V. Roosa was responsible for compiling the reports.

77. See, for example, "China Report: Report of a Special Congressional Delegation," U.S. Government Printing Office, July 1973.

78. Richard H. Solomon, "Thinking Through the China Problem," *Foreign Affairs* (January 1, 1978).

79. See Yoshihide Soeya, *Japan's Economic Diplomacy with China, 1945–1978* (Oxford: Clarendon Press, 1999); Ryosei Kokubun, Yoshihide Soeya, Akio Takahara, and Shin Kawashima, *Japan–China Relations in the Modern Era* (London: Routledge, 2017); Paul Evans, *Engaging China: Myth, Aspiration, and Strategy in Canadian Policy from Trudeau to Harper* (Toronto: University of Toronto Press, 2014).

80. Richard Nixon, "Asia After Viet Nam," *Foreign Affairs* (October 1967).

81. Minami, *People's Diplomacy*, op. cit., p. 39. The original memorandum can be found in *FRUS, 1969–1976*, volume E-13, document 43.

82. Author's personal communication with Winston Lord, September 28, 2023.

83. The following description derives from Li Zhisui, *The Private Life of Chairman Mao* (London: Chatto & Windus, 1994), chapters 80 and 81.

84. This description comes from Zhou and Mao's interpreter Ji Chaozhu (who may well have been the eyewitness). See Ji Chaozhu, *The Man on Mao's Right* (New York, NY: Random House, 2008), p. 250.

85. Ji Chaozhu confirms Dr. Li's account of Mao's condition, ibid., p. 254.

86. The description of Mao's health is drawn largely from Li Zhisui, *The Private Life of Chairman Mao*, op. cit., chapters 82 and 84, as well as from Roderick MacFarquhar and Michael Schoenhals, *Mao's Last Revolution* (Cambridge, MA: Harvard University Press, 2008), pp. 413–414.

87. "President Arrives in China for Talks," *The New York Times*, December 1, 1975.

88. Transcripts of these discussions are available at Gerald R. Ford Presidential Library and Museum, https://www.fordlibrarymuseum.gov/library/document/0331/1553946.pdf.

89. Association of Diplomatic Studies and Training (ADST) Foreign Affairs Oral History Project, "Ambassador Winston Lord," p. 384, https://www.adst.org/OH%20TOCs/Lord,%20Winston.pdf.

90. The White House, "The President's Toast at the Welcoming Banquet in Peking," December 1, 1975: http://www.fordlibrarymuseum.gov/library/document.

91. See Gerald R. Ford Presidential Library and Museum, "Memorandum of Conversation" (in Beijing), December 4, 1975.

92. See Gerald R. Ford Presidential Library and Museum, https://www.fordlibrarymuseum.gov/library/document/0331/1553946.pdf.

93. Author's personal communication with Winston Lord, March 24, 2024.

Chapter 4

1. Presidents Nixon and Ford are not considered here, as they were in Chapter 3.

2. Jimmy Carter, *White House Diary* (New York, NY: Farrar, Straus, and Giroux, 2010).

3. President Jimmy Carter, "Address to the Nation: Diplomatic Relations Between the United States and the People's Republic of China," December 15, 1978, *Public Papers of the Presidents of the United States (1978)*, pp. 2264–2266.

4. President Jimmy Carter, "Premier Hua Guofeng of the People's Republic of China: New Year's Message from the President," January 1, 1979, *Public Papers of the Presidents of the United States (1979)*, p. 1.

5. President Jimmy Carter, "Visit of Vice-Premier Deng of China: Toast at the State Dinner," January 29, 1979, *Public Papers of the Presidents of the United States (1979)*, pp. 192–195.

6. Cyrus Vance, *Hard Choices: Critical Years in America's Foreign Policy* (New York, NY: Simon & Schuster, 1983).

7. "Memorandum from Secretary of State Vance to President Carter," January 26, 1979, *Foreign Relations of the United States, 1977–1981*, p. 728, p. 731.

8. Zbigniew Brzezinski, *Power and Principle: Memoirs of the National Security Advisor, 1977–1981* (New York, NY: Farrar, Strauss, and Giroux, 1983), p. 217.

9. I know this firsthand, as I served as Oksenberg's assistant at the National Security Council during 1977–1978 and was involved in the preparation of materials for Brzezinski's visit in May 1978.

10. "Memorandum of Conversation: Summary of the President's Meeting with Secretary Blumenthal," March 1979, *FRUS*, op. cit., p. 827.

11. "Why We Treat the Chinese Differently: Memorandum from Michel Oksenberg of the National Security Council Staff to the President's Assistant for National Security Affairs (Brzezinski)," October 7, 1977, *FRUS*, p. 255.

12. James Mann, *About Face: A History of America's Curious Relationship with China, from Nixon to Clinton* (New York, NY: Vintage Books, 1998), p. 116.

13. Ibid., p. 118.

14. Alexander M. Haig, *Caveat: Realism, Reagan, and Foreign Policy* (New York, NY: MacMillan, 1984), p. 30.

15. Ibid., p. 198.

16. Email exchange with Henry Nau, January 8, 2024.

17. While Shultz was the leader of the "Asia First" faction, his views were supported by William Clark, Gaston Sigur, James Lilley, Paul Wolfowitz, and Richard Armitage. See discussion in Mann, *About Face*, op. cit., p. 132.

18. George P. Shultz, *Turmoil and Triumph: My Years as Secretary of State* (New York, NY: Charles Scribner, 1993), pp. 381–382.

19. See "Memorandum of Conversation: Meeting with Deng Xiaoping of the People's Republic of China" (Sensitive, Secret, Eyes Only), July 2, 1989, https://www.documentcloud.org/documents/6184537-U-S-Government-Documents-Following-Tiananmen.js, pp. 18–32, quotation on p. 22.
20. Shultz, *Turmoil and Triumph*, op. cit., p. 381.
21. Ronald Reagan, *The Reagan Diaries* (New York, NY: Harper Collins, 2007), p. 211.
22. Shultz, *Turmoil and Triumph* op. cit., chapter 22; Mann, *About Face*, op. cit., chapters 6 and 7.
23. See Christopher Wren, "China Undergoing a New Revolution: Nation Reagan Will See Bears Little Likeliness to Spartan State Visited by Nixon," *The New York Times*, April 23, 1984.
24. Mann, *About Face*, op. cit., p. 147; "Question-and-Answer Session with Reporters on the Trip to China," May 1, 1984, *Public Papers of the Presidents of the United States (1984)*, pp. 610–613. Also see Lou Cannon, "Reagan Ends Trip with Dream of Friendship," *The Washington Post*, May 1, 1984. According to Reagan biographer Henry Nau, "The potential change in China's domestic system away from communism was Reagan's north star." Email exchange with Author, January 8, 2024.
25. "Remarks to Chinese Community Leaders in Beijing, China," April 27, 1984, *Public Papers of the Presidents of the United States (1984)*, pp. 579–584.
26. Reagan, *The Reagan Diaries*, op. cit., p. 234.
27. Ronald Reagan, "Remarks at Fudan University in Shanghai, China," April 30, 1984, *Public Papers of the Presidents of the United States (1984)*, pp. 603–607.
28. How Nazir knew about the planned speech at the Great Wall Sheraton is unclear, although American students, the business community, and other specially invited American guests had already been invited by the US Embassy to the event.
29. For the text of President Reagan's speech, see "Remarks at a Reception for Members of the American Community in Beijing, China," April 28, 1984, *Public Papers of the Presidents of the United States (1984)*, pp. 589–591.
30. Author's correspondence with Winston Lord, November 18, 2023.
31. Ibid.
32. "Written Responses to Questions Submitted by Japanese News Organizations at the Tokyo Economic Summit," May 2, 1986, *Public Papers of the Presidents of the United States (1986)*, pp. 544–547.
33. Mann, *About Face*, op. cit. p. 147.
34. Bush's account of these years can be found in his memoir Jeffrey A. Engel (ed.) and George H. W. Bush, *The China Diary of George H. W. Bush: The Making of a Global President* (Princeton, NJ: Princeton University Press, 2008). Bush's memoir reveals that he spent most of his time in Beijing playing tennis, going for bicycle rides, attending diplomatic cocktail receptions, and being frustrated by his almost complete inability to get any official (or unofficial) appointments with Chinese officials. The latter can be explained by the combination of lack of formal diplomatic relations together with the factional infighting in the leadership toward the end of Mao's life.
35. Harry Harding, *A Fragile Relationship: The United States and China Since 1972* (Washington, DC: Brookings Institution Press, 1992), p. 229.
36. Ibid., and George Bush and Brent Scowcroft, *A World Transformed* (New York, NY: Alfred Knopf, 1998).
37. "Interview with Chinese Television Journalists in Beijing," February 26, 1989, *Public Papers of the Presidents of the United States (1989)*, p. 142.
38. Ambassador Winston Lord recounts the incident in his oral history "A Dissident for Dinner: George H. W. Bush's Ill-Fated Banquet in China," Association for Diplomatic Studies and Training (ADST), September 24, 2015, https://adst.org/2015/09/a-dissident-for-dinner-george-h-w-bushs-ill-fated-banquet-in-china.
39. On April 15, 1976, there had been another spontaneous uprising in Tiananmen Square, eulogizing the deceased and beloved Premier Zhou Enlai and protesting the failure of the government to formally mourn him. The demonstrations were put down within 48 hours. In December 1986, there had also been student demonstrations on campuses in Hefei, Nanjing, and Shanghai, but these were stopped peacefully by the authorities.
40. Harding, *A Fragile Relationship*, op. cit., Table A-1, p. 363.
41. See https://www.chinafile.com/conversation/other-tiananmen-papers.
42. See http://www.g8.utoronto.ca/summit/1989paris/china.html.

43. "The President's News Conference," June 5, 1989, *Public Papers of the Presidents of the United States (1989)*, pp. 13–19.
44. Ibid.
45. Bush and Scowcroft, *A World Transformed*, op. cit., pp. 97–98.
46. Ibid., p. 102.
47. The legislation and Bush's vetoes are discussed in Kerry Dumbaugh, "Interest Groups: Growing Influence," in Ramon H. Myers, Michel C. Oksenberg, and David Shambaugh (eds.), *Making China Policy: Lessons from the Bush and Clinton Administrations* (Lanham, MD: Rowman & Littlefield, 2001).
48. "Memorandum of Conversation: Meeting with Deng Xiaoping of the People's Republic of China" (Sensitive, Secret, Eyes Only), July 2, 1989; https://www.chinafile.com/conversation/other-tiananmen-papers.
49. Ibid.
50. See, for example, Robert Suettinger, *Beyond Tiananmen: The Politics of US–China Relations, 1989–2000* (Washington, DC: Brookings Institution Press, 2003); David M. Lampton, *Same Bed, Different Dreams: Managing US–China Relations, 1989–2000* (Berkeley, CA: University of California Press, 2001); Harding, *A Fragile Relationship*, op. cit.; Robert S. Ross, "The Bush Administration: The Origins of Engagement," in Myers, Oksenberg, and Shambaugh, *Making China Policy*, op. cit.
51. George H. W. Bush, "Statement on China," June 4, 1991, *Public Papers of the Presidents of the United States (1991)*, p. 605.
52. George H. W. Bush, "Remarks at the Yale University Commencement Ceremony in New Haven, Connecticut," May 27, 1991, *Public Papers of the Presidents of the United States (1991)*, pp. 565–568.
53. Winston Lord, "China and America: Beyond the Big Chill," *Foreign Affairs* (Fall 1989).
54. See William J. Clinton, "Address Accepting the Presidential Nomination at the Democratic National Convention in New York," July 16, 1992, https://www.presidency.ucsb.edu/documents/address-accepting-the-presidential-nomination-the-democratic-national-convention-new-york.
55. Anthony Lake, "From Containment to Enlargement," address at the Nitze School of Advanced International Studies, Johns Hopkins University, September 21, 1993. The text is available in *Department of State Dispatch*, 4, no. 39 (September 27, 1993), and from the Clinton Presidential Library, https://clinton.presidentiallibraries.us/items/show/9013.
56. Quoted in Orville Schell, "The Death of Engagement," *The Wire China*, June 7, 2020.
57. I am grateful to Ken Lieberthal for pointing this out.
58. Suettinger, *Beyond Tiananmen*, op. cit., pp. 181–182.
59. Thomas Friedman, "The Pacific Summit: Leaders at Summit Seek Strong Pacific Community," *The New York Times*, November 21, 1993.
60. "Remarks and an Exchange with Reporters Following Discussions with President Jiang Zemin of China in Seattle," November 19, 1993, *Public Papers of the Presidents of the United States (1993)*, pp. 2022–2025.
61. See Evan S. Medeiros, *Reluctant Restraint: The Evolution of China's Nonproliferation Policies and Practices, 1980–2004* (Stanford, CA: Stanford University Press, 2007). Medeiros's study is, by far, the most thorough examination of the subject.
62. "The President's News Conference," May 26, 1994, *Public Papers of the Presidents of the United States (1994)*, p. 991.
63. Ibid., p. 992.
64. Quoted in Lampton, *Same Bed, Different Dreams*, op. cit., p. 54.
65. Lieberthal succeeded Sandra Kristof as Senior Director in July 1998.
66. I am indebted to Ken Lieberthal for pointing this out.
67. See David M. Lampton, "America's China Policy in the Age of the Finance Minister," *The China Quarterly*, No. 139 (September 1994); Chi-hung Wei, "Engaging a State That Resists Sanctions Pressure: US Policy Towards China, 1992–1994," *Millennium: Journal of International Studies*, Vol. 43, No. 2 (2014).
68. "The President's Radio Address," June 14, 1997, *Public Papers of the Presidents of the United States (1997)*, p. 735.

69. William J. Clinton, "Remarks to the Asia Society and the United States–China Education Foundation Board," October 24, 1997, *Public Papers of the Presidents of the United States (1997)*, p. 1428.

70. "The President's News Conference with President Jiang Zemin of China," October 29, 1997, *Public Papers of the Presidents of the United States (1997)*, p. 1449.

71. "China–U.S. Joint Statement," October 29, 1997, http://us.china-embassy.gov.cn/eng/zmgx/zywj/lhsm3/200310/t20031023_4917631.htm.

72. Verbatim interview by Robert Suettinger with Sandra Kristof, in Suettinger, *Beyond Tiananmen*, op. cit., p. 318.

73. A good account of the trip is provided in Suettinger, ibid., pp. 344–351.

74. "Statement on the Decision to Extend Normal Trade Relations Status with China," June 3, 1999, *Public Papers of the Presidents of the United States (1999)*, p. 874.

75. See   https://archive.nytimes.com/www.nytimes.com/library/world/asia/030900clinton-china-text.html; https://www.youtube.com/watch?v=LrV6BSBtFV0.

76. William J. Clinton, "Remarks to the Business Council," February 24, 2000, *Public Papers of the Presidents of the United States (2000)*, p. 299.

77. Thomas W. Lippman, "Bush Makes Clinton China Policy an Issue," *The Washington Post*, August 20, 1999. Bush's first use of the term "strategic competitor" was in a speech at the Reagan Presidential Library, November 19, 1999: "Text of Remarks Prepared for Delivery by Texas Gov. George W. Bush at Ronald Reagan Presidential Library, Simi Valley, Calif. on November 19, 1999," https://www.washingtonpost.com/archive/business/technology/1999/11/19/text-of-remarks-prepared-for-delivery-by-texas-gov-george-w-bush-at-ronald-reagan-presidential-library-simi-valley-calif-on-november-19-1999/1e893802-88ce-40de-bcf7-a4e1b6393ad2.

78. See James Mann, *The Rise of the Vulcans: The History of Bush's War Cabinet* (New York, NY: Penguin, 2004). Others in what might be called the "outer ring" of Bush's foreign policy advisors were Aaron Friedberg, Jim Kelly, Doug Feith, John Bolton, Michael Green, Steven Yates, and Peter Rodman. Dennis Wilder subsequently joined the National Security Council as Senior Director for Asia, on secondment from CIA.

79. Indeed, many of this group had served under and worked with Shultz during the Reagan administration.

80. Author's discussion with Condoleezza Rice, Stanford, California, December 2, 2022.

81. Condoleezza Rice, "Campaign 2000: Promoting the National Interest," *Foreign Affairs* (January 1, 2001).

82. "Remarks Prior to Discussions with Vice Premier Qian Qichen of China and an Exchange with Reporters," March 22, 2001, *Public Papers of the Presidents of the United States (2001)*, pp. 285–286.

83. See, for example, https://www.c-span.org/video/?163504-1/us-surveillance-plane-crash; https://www.cbsnews.com/news/bush-to-china-it-is-time.

84. "Remarks Calling on China to Return the United States Military Crew and Surveillance Aircraft," April 3, 2001, *Public Papers of the Presidents of the United States (2001)*, p. 364.

85. "Remarks on Plans for Release of United States Navy Aircraft Crewmembers in China," April 11, 2001, *Public Papers of the Presidents of the United States (2001)*, p. 384.

86. "Statement on Renewal of Normal Trade Relations Status for China," June 1, 2001, *Public Papers of the Presidents of the United States (2001)*, p. 605.

87. "The President's News Conference with President Jiang Zemin of China in Shanghai, China," October 19, 2001, *Public Papers of the Presidents of the United States (2001)*, p. 1262.

88. "The President's News Conference with President Jiang Zemin of China in Beijing," February 21, 2002, *Public Papers of the Presidents of the United States (2002)*, p. 264.

89. "The President's News Conference with President Jiang Zemin of China in Crawford, Texas," October 25, 2002, *Public Papers of the Presidents of the United States (2002)*, p. 1898.

90. David Shambaugh, *China's Leaders: From Mao to Now* (Cambridge, MA: Polity Press, 2023).

91. George W. Bush, *Decision Points* (New York, NY: Crown Publishers, 2010), p. 427.

92. "Remarks at a Welcoming Ceremony for Premier Wen Jiabao of China," December 9, 2003, *Public Papers of the Presidents of the United States (2003)*, p. 1700.

93. "Remarks in Kyoto," November 16, 2005, *Public Papers of the Presidents of the United States (2005)*, p. 1726.

94. "Text of Remarks Prepared for Delivery by Texas Gov. George W. Bush at Ronald Reagan Presidential Library, Simi Valley, Calif. on November 19, 1999," op. cit.

95. Condoleezza Rice, *No Higher Honor: A Memoir of My Years in Washington* (New York, NY: Crown Publishers, 2011), p. 645.

96. Robert Zoellick, "Whiter China? From Membership to Responsibility," Remarks to the National Committee on US–China Relations, September 25, 2005.

97. Interview at CCP International Department, October 2, 2005, Beijing.

98. On China's integration into the international institutional and global governance order, see Ann Kent, *Beyond Compliance: China, International Organizations, and Global Security* (Stanford, CA: Stanford University Press, 2000); Michel Oksenberg and Elizabeth Economy (eds.), *China Joins the World: Progress and Prospects* (New York, NY: Council on Foreign Relations, 1998); Alastair Iain Johnston, *Social States: China in International Institutions, 1980–2000* (Princeton, NJ: Princeton University Press, 2008); David Shambaugh, *China Goes Global: The Partial Power* (New York, NY: Oxford University Press, 2014), chapter 4; David Shambaugh, "China and the Liberal International Order," in Nicholas Burns, Leah Bitounis, and Jonathon Price (eds.), *The World Turned Upside Down: Maintaining American Leadership in a Dangerous Age* (Washington, DC: The Aspen Institute, 2017); Harry Harding, "China's Views of International Norms and Institutions," in Gudrun Wacker and David Shambaugh (eds.), *American and European Relations with China: Advancing Common Agendas* (Berlin: SWP, 2008), https://www.swp-berlin.org/publications/products/research_papers/2008_RP03_shambaugh_wkr_ks.pdf; Katherine Morton, "China's Global Governance Interactions," in David Shambaugh (ed.), *China & the World* (New York, NY: Oxford University Press, 2020).

99. Bonnie Glaser, "The Diplomatic Relationship: Substance and Process," in David Shambaugh (ed.), *Tangled Titans: The United States and China* (Lanham, MD: Rowman & Littlefield, 2013), p. 158.

100. Email exchange with Dennis Wilder, December 28, 2023.

101. Ibid.

102. Email exchange with Evan Medeiros (who served on Obama's National Security Council staff at the time), January 5, 2024.

103. The G-2 concept was first put forward in 2005 by C. Fred Bergsten in his book *The United States and the World Economy*, and then again in his "A Partnership of Equals: How Washington Should Respond to China's Economic Challenge," *Foreign Affairs* (July/August 2008). For a contrarian view of the US–China G-2 concept, see Elizabeth Economy and Adam Segal, "The G-2 Mirage," *Foreign Affairs* (May/June 2009). For Bergsten's rejoinder to Economy and Segal, see "Two's Company," *Foreign Affairs* (September/October 2009).

104. See Kurt M. Campbell, *The Pivot: The Future of American Statecraft in Asia* (New York, NY: Twelve Books, 2016).

105. Hillary Clinton, "America's Pacific Century," *Foreign Policy*, October 11, 2011.

106. Hillary Clinton, "U.S.–Asia Relations: Indespensible to Our Future," February 13, 2009, https://2009-2017.state.gov/secretary/20092013clinton/rm/2009a/02/117333.htm.

107. Hillary Rodham Clinton, *Hard Choices* (New York, NY: Simon & Schuster, 2014), p. 60, p. 63.

108. Trips tabulated in Alexandra Sharp, "U.S. Engagement with China in 3 Charts," *Foreign Policy*, December 1, 2023.

109. See David Shambaugh, *Where Great Powers Meet: America & China in Southeast Asia* (New York: Oxford University Press, 2021).

110. "Remarks at the United States–China Strategic and Economic Dialogue," July 27, 2009, *Public Papers of the Presidents of the United States (2009)*, pp. 1177–1180.

111. "Remarks Prior to a Meeting with President Hui Jintao of China in New York City," September 22, 2009, *Public Papers of the Presidents of the United States (2009)*, pp. 1435–1436.

112. "Remarks at a Town Hall Meeting and a Question-and-Answer Session in Shanghai, November 16, 2009, *Public Papers of the Presidents of the United States (2009)*, p. 1687.

113. Ibid., p. 1689.

114. "Remarks Prior to a Meeting with Vice-President Xi Jinping of China," February 14, 2012, *Public Papers of the Presidents of the United States (2012)*, p. 150.

115. "Remarks Prior to a Meeting with President Hu Jintao in Los Cabos, Mexico," June 19, 2012, *Public Papers of the Presidents of the United States (2012)*, p. 816.

116. "Remarks at the Asia-Pacific Economic Cooperation CEO Summit in Beijing," November 10, 2014, *Public Papers of the Presidents of the United States (2014)*, p. 1424; "Remarks Prior to a Meeting with President Xi Jinping in Beijing, China," November 1, 2014, *Public Papers of the Presidents of the United States (2014)*, p. 1439. The phrase "plays a responsible role in the world" was used only in the second of these two quotations by Obama.

117. The White House, "U.S.–China Joint Statement," November 17, 2009, https://obamawhitehouse.archives.gov/realitycheck/the-press-office/us-china-joint-statement.

118. Jeffrey A. Bader, *Obama and China's Rise: An Insider's Account of America's Asia Strategy* (Washington, DC: Brookings Institution Press, 2012), p. 55.

119. Barack Obama, *A Promised Land* (New York, NY: Crown Books, 2020), p. 481.

120. Ibid., p. 57.

121. See, for example, Jonathan Wiseman, Andrew Browne, and Jason Dean, "Obama Hits a Wall on His Visit to China," *Wall Street Journal*, November 19, 2009; Helene Cooper, "China Holds Firm on Major Issues in Obama Visit," *New York Times*, November 17, 2009.

122. Author's private discussion with Ambassador Jon Huntsman, US Embassy, Beijing, November 28, 2009.

123. "Remarks Prior to a meeting with President Xi Jinping of China in Rancho Mirage, California," June 7, 2013, *Public Papers of the Presidents of the United States (2013)*, p. 551.

124. "Remarks Prior to a Meeting with President Xi Jinping of China in St. Petersburg," September 6, 2013, *Public Papers of Presidents of the United States (2013)*, p. 1007.

125. See Michael Schoenhals, *Doing Things with Words in Chinese Politics* (Berkeley, CA: University of California Center for Chinese Studies, 1992).

126. See Bader, *Obama and China's Rise*, op. cit.; Rodham Clinton, *Hard Choices*, op. cit.

127. "Remarks by President Obama and President Xi of the People's Republic of China in Joint Press Conference," September 25, 2015, https://obamawhitehouse.archives.gov/the-press-office/2015/09/25/remarks-president-obama-and-president-xi-peoples-republic-china-joint.

128. See David Shambaugh, "President Obama's Asia Scorecard," *The Wilson Quarterly* (Winter 2016).

129. See the discussion in my books, David Shambaugh, *China's Future* (Cambridge, UK: Polity Press, 2016) and David Shambaugh, *China's Leaders: From Mao to Now* (Cambridge, UK: Polity Press, 2023); also see Susan Shirk, *Overreach: How China Derailed Its Peaceful Rise* (New York, NY: Oxford University Press, 2022).

130. James Mann, *The Obamians: The Struggle Inside the White House to Redefine American Power* (New York, NY: Viking Press, 2012), pp. 177–178.

Chapter 5

1. H. R. McMaster, "Why Trump Went Hard on China, and Biden Will Follow," *Politico*, April 15, 2021.

2. The White House, "Remarks by President Biden and Xi Jinping of the People's Republic of China Before Bilateral Meeting," Filoli Historic House & Garden, Woodside, California, November 15, 2023.

3. Jeremy Diamond, "Trump: We Cannot Allow China to Continue to Rape Our Country," CNN, May 2, 2016.

4. See Donald J. Trump, *The Art of the Deal* (New York, NY: Random House, 2015).

5. See Bob Davis and Lingling Wei, *Superpower Showdown: How the Battle Between Trump and Xi Threatens a New Cold War* (New York, NY: Harper Business, 2020), pp. 165–171; John Pomfret, "The Thornton Touch," *The Wire China*, March 6, 2022.

6. The "state visit plus" to Beijing is covered in detail from the firsthand perspective of Trump's National Security Advisor H. R. McMaster in his book *Battlegrounds: The Fight to Defend the Free World* (New York, NY: Harper, 2020), pp. 91–99.

7. National Archives, "President Donald J. Trump's State Visit to China," https://trumpwhitehouse.archives.gov/briefings-statements/president-donald-j-trumps-state-visit-china.

8. McMaster, "Why Trump Went Hard on China, and Biden Will Follow," op. cit.

9. Ibid.

10. Ibid.

11. Michael Pillsbury, *The Hundred Year Marathon: China's Secret Strategy to Replace America* (New York, NY: St. Martin's Griffin, 2016); Peter Navarro and Greg Autry, *Death by China: A Global Call to Action* (Upper Saddle River, NJ: Pearson FT Press, 2011).

12. Josh Rogin, *Chaos Under Heaven: Trump, Xi, and the Battle for the 21st Century* (New York, NY: Houghton, Mifflin, Harcourt, 2021), p. 39.

13. This revised document was declassified and made publicly available at the end of the Trump administration. See National Security Council, "US Strategic Framework for the Indo-Pacific," https://trumpwhitehouse.archives.gov/wp-content/uploads/2021/01/IPS-Final-Declass.pdf.

14. Author's discussion with H. R. McMaster, June 19, 2024, Stanford, California.

15. See Bob Davis, "Matthew Pottinger on Flipping the U.S.–China Paradigm on Its Head," *The Wire China*, June 26, 2022.

16. Author's discussion with H. R. McMaster, June 19, 2024, Stanford, California.

17. The White House, *The National Security Strategy of the United States*, December 2017, https://trumpwhitehouse.archives.gov/wp-content/uploads/2017/12/NSS-Final-12-18-2017-0905.pdf, p. 25.

18. Department of Defense, *National Defense Strategy of the United States*, https://dod.defense.gov/Portals/1/Documents/pubs/2018-National-Defense-Strategy-Summary.pdf.

19. The White House, *The United States Strategic Approach to the People's Republic of China*, May 26, 2022, https://trumpwhitehouse.archives.gov/wp-content/uploads/2020/05/U.S.-Strategic-Approach-to-The-Peoples-Republic-of-China-Report-5.24v1.pdf.

20. This is reported by *The Washington Post*'s columnist Josh Rogin, who claims in his book that Pottinger told him this was the intention. See Rogin, *Chaos Under Heaven*, op. cit., p. 197.

21. In addition to media coverage, see Davis and Wei, *Superpower Showdown*, op. cit.; Rogin, *Chaos Under Heaven*, op. cit.; Newt Gingrich, *Trump and China: Facing America's Greatest Threat* (New York, NY: Center Street Publishers, 2019).

22. See "Vice-President Mike Pence's Remarks on the Administration's Policy Towards China," https://www.hudson.org/events/1610-vice-president-mike-pence-s-remarks-on-the-administration-s-policy-towards-china102018.

23. Truth be told, I and several other China specialists had a phone call with National Security Council official Matt Pottinger in which we urged him to stop the President from using this racist language, and within a day he did stop (at Pottinger's suggestion).

24. Bob Woodward, "Findings Link Clinton Allies to Chinese Intelligence," *The Washington Post*, February 10, 1998, https://www.washingtonpost.com/wp-srv/politics/special/campfin/stories/cf021098.htm.

25. "Vice President Mike Pence's Remarks on the Administration's Policy Towards China," op. cit.

26. The most significant American effort was the Working Group on Chinese Influence Activities in the United States, led by Orville Schell and Larry Diamond and a joint project undertaken by the Asia Society and Hoover Institution. See Larry Diamond and Orville Schell (eds.), *China's Influence & American Interests Promoting Constructive Vigilance* (Stanford, CA: Hoover Institution Press, 2019).

27. See Robert C. O'Brien, "The Chinese Communist Party's Ideology and Global Ambitions," June 24, 2020, https://trumpwhitehouse.archives.gov/briefings-statements/chinese-communist-partys-ideology-global-ambitions.

28. See Christopher Wray, "The Threat Posed by the Chinese Government and the Chinese Communist Party to the Economic and National Security of the United States," July 7, 2020, https://www.fbi.gov/news/speeches/the-threat-posed-by-the-chinese-government-and-the-chinese-communist-party-to-the-economic-and-national-security-of-the-united-states.

29. See Attorney General William P. Barr Delivers Remarks on China Policy at the Gerald R. Ford Presidential Museum, July 16, 2020, https://www.justice.gov/opa/speech/attorney-general-william-p-barr-delivers-remarks-china-policy-gerald-r-ford-presidential.

30. See Michael R. Pompeo, "Communist China and the Free World's Future," https://2017-2021.state.gov/communist-china-and-the-free-worlds-future-2.

31. See Table 1 in Tom Lee and Jacqueline Varas, "The Total Cost of US Tariffs," American Action Forum, May 10, 2022.

32. Jeanne Wahlen, Abha Bhattarai, and Reed Albergotti, "Trump 'Hereby' Orders US Business Out of China. Can He Do That?" *The Washington Post*, August 24, 2019.

33. Kevin Breuninger, "Trump Says He's Ordering American Companies to Immediately Start Looking for an Alternative to China," CNBC, August 24, 2019.

34. Pew Research Center, "Americans Are Critical of China's Global Role—As Well as Its Relationship with Russia," April 12, 2023, https://www.cnbc.com/2023/07/27/pew-research-50percent-of-americans-view-china-as-top-threat-to-the-us.html.

35. The White House, *Interim National Security Guidance*, March 2021, https://www.whitehouse.gov/wp-content/uploads/2021/03/NSC-1v2.pdf, p. 20. The Biden administration's full *National Security Strategy*, released in October 2022, included a much fuller explication of the various challenges the PRC posed to US national security interests: The White House, *The Biden-Harris Administration's National Security Strategy*, https://www.whitehouse.gov/wp-content/uploads/2022/10/Biden-Harris-Administrations-National-Security-Strategy-10.2022.pdf. Also see The White House, *Indo-Pacific Strategy of the United States*, February 2022, https://www.whitehouse.gov/wp-content/uploads/2022/02/U.S.-Indo-Pacific-Strategy.pdf.

36. "NCUSCR Conversation with Politburo Member Yang Jiechi," February 1, 2021, https://www.ncuscr.org/yang-jiechi-event-transcript.

37. The White House, "Readout of President Joseph R. Biden Jr. Call with President Xi Jinping of China," February 1, 2021, https://www.whitehouse.gov/briefing-room/statements-releases/2021/02/10/readout-of-president-joseph-r-biden-jr-call-with-president-xi-jinping-of-china.

38. Some of the discussion in this section is drawn from David Shambaugh, "A Hot Exchange in Cold Alaska," *China–US Focus*, March 25, 2021.

39. "How It Happened: Transcript of the US–China Opening Remarks in Alaska," *Nikkei Asia*, March 19, 2021.

40. Transcript can be found at https://hk.usconsulate.gov/n-2021031801.

41. Some of the discussion in this section is drawn from David Shambaugh, "China Stands Up to America," *China–US Focus*, August 4, 2021.

42. "Full Text of Xi Jinping's Speech on the 100th Anniversary of the CCP," https://asia.nikkei.com/Politics/Full-text-of-Xi-Jinping-s-speech-on-the-CCP-s-100th-anniversary#:~:text=As%20a%20nation%2C%20we%20have,%2C%20oppress%2C%20or%20subjugate%20us.

43. See Iain Marlo and Anna Montiero, "China Ties at 'Lowest Moment' Since 1972, US Ambassador Says," *Bloomberg*, June 9, 2022.

44. Some of the discussion in this section is drawn from David Shambaugh, "Still Wide Apart," *China–US Focus*, October 6, 2021.

45. I am told that Rudd personally lobbied National Security Council Advisor Jake Sullivan and Indo-Pacific Coordinator Kurt Campbell, as well as Secretary of State Antony Blinken (all of whom he knew) to adopt the concept of "managed competition," which he also fully explicated in an article "Short of War: How to Keep the US–Chinese Competition from Ending in Calamity," *Foreign Affairs* (March/April 2021), and in his book Kevin Rudd, *The Avoidable War: The Dangers of a Catastrophic Conflict Between the US and Xi Jinping's China* (New York, NY: Public Affairs, 2022). I also used this term in my article "As the US and China Wage a New Cold War, They Should Learn from the Last One," *Wall Street Journal*, July 31, 2020.

46. Kurt Campbell and Jake Sullivan, "Competition Without Catastrophe: How America Can Both Challenge and Coexist with China," *Foreign Affairs* (September/October 2019).

47. Antony J. Blinken, "The Administration's Approach to the People's Republic of China," speech at George Washington University, May 26, 2022, https://www.state.gov/the-administrations-approach-to-the-peoples-republic-of-china; also see David Shambaugh, "About Time: The Biden Administration Rolls Out Its China Policy," *China–US Focus*, May 30, 2022.

48. Keith Bradsher, "China's Leader, with Rare Bluntness, Blames US Containment for Troubles," *The New York Times*, March 7, 2023.

49. Amy Chang Chien and Chris Buckley, "China Sends Record Number of Military Planes Near Taiwan," *The New York Times*, September 18, 2023; John Feng, "China Doubles Military Flights Around Taiwan," *Newsweek*, January 2, 2023.

50. "Department of Defense Releases Declassified Images, Videos of Coercive and Risky PLA Operational Behavior," US Department of Defense, October 17, 2023, https://www.defense.gov/News/Releases/Release/Article/3559903/department-of-defense-releases-declassified-images-videos-of-coercive-and-risky. This website shows multiple live film images of these encounters.

51. Defense Visual Information Distribution Service, "Unprofessional Intercept of US B-52 over South China Sea," https://www.dvidshub.net/video/901664/unprofessional-intercept-us-b-52-over-south-china-sea.

52. See Ana Swanson and Keith Bradsher, "The US and China Are Talking Again: Where It Will Lead Is Unclear," *The New York Times*, August 31, 2023.
53. "China Rips US for Seeing It as 'Enemy' After Raimondo Remarks," Bloomberg, December 4, 2023.
54. Council on Foreign Relations, "C.V. Starr & Co., Annual Lecture on China: A Conversation with Ambassador Nicholas Burns," December 12, 2023, https://www.youtube.com/watch?v=bAcC5BVxfRE.
55. Some of the discussion in this section is derived from David Shambaugh, "Are Sino-American Relations Back on Track?" *China–US Focus*, November 18, 2023.
56. Ministry of Foreign Affairs of the People's Republic of China, "President Xi Jinping Meets the US President Joe Biden," November 16, 2023, https://www.fmprc.gov.cn/mfa_eng/zxxx_662805/202311/t20231116_11181442.html; An Gang, "A Future-Oriented San Francisco Vision," *Beijing Review*, November 23, 2023.
57. The White House, "Readout of President Joe Biden's Meeting with President Xi Jinping of the People's Republic of China," November 15, 2023.
58. The Brookings Institution, "A Conversation with US Ambassador to China Nicholas R. Burns on US–China Relations," December 15, 2023.
59. The White House, "Remarks and Q&A by National Security Advisor Jake Sullivan on the Future of US–China Relations," January 30, 2024.
60. This point is made in David Pierson and Olivia Wang, "China and U.S. Are Back at the Table, but the Conversation Has Limits," *The New York Times*, February 3, 2024; and in Nathaniel Sher and Andrew Weaver, "Engagement Lite: The Logic of Biden's Engagement with China," *The Diplomat*, February 3, 2024.
61. See Michael R. Gordon and Brian Spegele, "Blinken Presses Xi on Russia Help," *Wall Street Journal*, April 27–28, 2024.
62. Jonathan Cheng, "In Rare Rebuke, US Ambassador Accuses China of Undermining Diplomacy," *Wall Street Journal*, June 25, 2024.
63. Ibid.
64. See David Shambaugh, *Beautiful Imperialist: China Perceives America, 1972–1990* (Princeton, NJ: Princeton University Press, 1991); David Shambaugh, "China's America Watchers," *Problems of Communism*, Vol. 37, Nos. 3/4 (May/August 1988); David Shambaugh, "Anti-Americanism in China," *The Annals* of the American Academy of Political and Social Science, Vol. 497 (May 1988); David Shambaugh, "Chinese Images of America During the People's Republic of China," in David Shambaugh (ed.), *Mutual Images and U.S.–China Relations* (Occasional Paper No. 32 of the Asia Program of the Woodrow Wilson International Center for Scholars, 1988).
65. Chris Buckley, "Behind Public Assurances, Xi Jinping Has Spread Grim Views on US," *The New York Times*, November 13, 2023; Wang Wen, "Why China' People No Longer Look Up to America," *The New York Times*, August 9, 2022.
66. Xinhua News Agency, *US Hegemony and Its Perils*, February 2023, https://english.news.cn/20230220/d3a4291d44f2499ea20710ae272ece72/c.html.
67. Ibid.
68. See David Shambaugh, "Speculating About Trump vs. Harris China Policies," *China–US Focus*, July 31, 2024, https://www.chinausfocus.com/foreign-policy/speculating-about-trump-vs-harris-china-policies.
69. See Alex Wong, "Competition with China: Debating the Endgame," Ronald Reagan Presidential Foundation and Institute, October 16, 2023.
70. John Ratcliffe, "China Is National Security Threat No. 1," *Wall Street Journal*, December 3, 2020.

Chapter 6

1. Trump Administration White House, *The United States Strategic Approach to the People's Republic of China*, May 26, 2020, https://trumpwhitehouse.archives.gov/wp-content/uploads/2020/05/U.S.-Strategic-Approach-to-The-Peoples-Republic-of-China-Report-5.24v1.pdf.
2. Original source: http://www.news.cn/politics/leaders/2023-03/06/c_1129417096.htm; https://news.rthk.hk/rthk/en/component/k2/1690845-20230307.htm. See also Keith Bradsher, "China's Leader, with Rare Bluntness, Blames U.S. Containment for Troubles," *The New York Times*, March 7, 2023.

3. Robert G. Sutter, *Congress and China Policy* (Lanham, MD: Lexington Books, 2023). See also Sutter's study *Congress Ensures Continuity in US Policy Toward China and Taiwan* (Washington, DC: East-West Center Occasional Paper No. 2, 2024).

4. Ibid., p. 1.

5. Kerry Dumbaugh, "Interest Groups: Growing Influence," in Ramon H. Myers, Michel C. Oksenberg, and David Shambaugh (eds.), *Making China Policy: Lessons from the Bush and Clinton Administrations* (Lanham, MD: Rowman & Littlefield, 2001), p. 117.

6. In a previous book, Professor Sutter explored the MFN/PNTR debate during the Bush and Clinton administrations in considerable detail. See Robert G. Sutter, *U.S. Policy Toward China: An Introduction to the Role of Interest Groups* (Lanham, MD: Rowman & Littlefield, 1998), chapters 3–4.

7. Sutter, *Congress and China Policy*, op. cit., p. 216.

8. Personal communication with Professor Sutter, January 8, 2024.

9. Sutter, *Congress and China Policy*, pp. 215–216.

10. Christopher S. Chivvis and Hannah Miller, *The Role of Congress in U.S.–China Relations* (Washington, DC: Carnegie Endowment for International Peace, November 2023), p. 2.

11. See Christopher Carothers and Taiyi Sun, "Bipartisanship on China in a Polarized America," *International Relations*, published online September 26, 2023, https://doi.org/10.1177/0047117823120148.

12. Pew Research Center, "Americans Are Critical of China's Global Role, as Well as Its Relationship with Russia: Most See Little Ability for the US and China to Cooperate," April 12, 2023.

13. Ibid. Also see David Shambaugh, "The New Bipartisan Consensus on China Policy," *China–US Focus*, September 21, 2018.

14. "Ageism: How Young Americans See China," *The Economist*, March 25, 2023, p. 23.

15. Evan S. Medeiros, *The New Domestic Politics of U.S.–China Relations* (New York, NY: Asia Society Policy Institute's Center for China Analysis, December 2023), p. 16, Figure 2.

16. "China's Pursuit of Emerging and Exponential Technologies"; "The Military and Security Challenges in the Indo-Pacific Region"; "Strategic Competition with China"; "Climate Change in the Era of Strategic Competition"; "DOD's Role in Competing with China"; "National Security Challenges and US Military Activities in the Indo-Pacific Region"; "Checking China's Maritime Push"; "China's Technological Rise: Challenges to US Innovation and Security"; "The Tragic Case of Liu Xiaobo"; "Strengthening US–Taiwan Ties"; "US Economic Strategy Amid China's Belt & Road"; "US Policy Toward Tibet: Access, Religious Freedom, and Human Rights"; "China in Africa: The New Colonialism?"; "Reenforcing the US–Taiwan Relationship"; "Chinese Investment and Influence in Europe"; "Russian and Chinese Nuclear Arsenals"; "China's Predatory Trade and Investment Strategy"; "China's Growing Influence in Asia and the United States"; "China's Expanding Influence in Europe and Eurasia"; "Chinese and Russian Influence in the Middle East"; "Dollar Diplomacy or Debt Trap? Examining China's Role in the Western Hemisphere"; "Authoritarianism with Chinese Characteristics: Political, Religious, and Human Rights Challenges in China"; "China's Maritime Ambitions"; "The End of One Country, Two Systems? Implications of Beijing's National Security Law in Hong Kong"; "Taiwan and the United States: Enduring Bonds in the Face of Adversity"; "Scenarios in a Cross-Strait Conflict"; "US–European Cooperation on China and the Broader Indo-Pacific"; "Changing Dynamics in the South China Sea."

17. "China's Worldwide Military Expansion"; "China's Threat to American Government and Private Sector Research and Innovation Leadership"; "China's Digital Authoritarianism: Surveillance, Influence, and Political Control"; "US–China Relations and Its Impact on National Security and Intelligence in a Post-COVID World."

18. "America's Leadership in the Asia-Pacific" (five separate hearings); "A Multilateral and Strategic Response to International Predatory Economic Practices"; "The China Challenge" (three separate hearings); "A New Approach for an Era of US–China Competition"; "The Hong Kong Emergency: Securing Freedom, Autonomy, and Human Rights"; "Advancing Effective US Competition with China: Objectives, Priorities, and Next Steps"; "Advancing US Engagement and Countering China in the Indo-Pacific and Beyond"; "Advancing Effective US Policy for Strategic Competition with China in the 21st Century"; "Atrocities in Xinjiang: Where Do We Go from Here?"; "Strength Through Partnership: Building the US–Taiwan Relationship"; "The Future of US Policy on Taiwan"; "China's Role in Latin America and the Caribbean"; "China's Role in the Middle East."

19. "The United States' Strategic Competition with China."

20. "Beijing's Long Arm: Threats to US National Security"; "Countering the People's Republic of China's Economic and Technological Plan for Dominance"; "The Comprehensive Threat to America Posed by the Chinese Communist Party."
21. Chivvis and Miller, *The Role of Congress in U.S.–China Relations*, op. cit., p. 4. Russia slightly outpaced China in the 117th Congress, largely because of sanctions on Moscow related to Ukraine conflict.
22. Ibid., p. 3.
23. I am grateful to Susan Lawrence of the Congressional Research Service for this information. Private communication, October 11, 2023. For a full record of all China-related bills and resolutions under consideration in Congress, see Congress.gov, https://www.congress.gov/search?q=%7B%22source%22%3A%22legislation%22%2C%22search%22%3A%22china%22%7D.
24. Chivvis and Miller, *The Role of Congress in U.S.–China Relations*, op. cit., p. 7. Note that this figure does *not* include the annual National Defense Authorization Act (NDAA), which includes a very wide range of items and funding related to China.
25. See Trustee China Hand Blog Post, Scott Kennedy, "Codels: Fortifying Congress's Role on China Policy," CSIS, October 13, 2023, https://www.csis.org/blogs/trustee-china-hand/codels-fortifying-congresss-role-china-policy.
26. See https://www.cecc.gov; https://www.cecc.gov/about/frequently-asked-questions.
27. https://www.cecc.gov/publications/annual-reports/2022-annual-report.
28. https://www.cecc.gov/resources/political-prisoner-database.
29. https://www.uscc.gov/about-us.
30. https://www.uscc.gov/annual-reports.
31. https://www.uscc.gov/sites/default/files/2023-11/2023_Annual_Report_to_Congress.pdf.
32. https://www.uscc.gov/annual-report/2022-annual-report-congress.
33. https://selectcommitteeontheccp.house.gov.
34. Eliot Chen, "Who's Who on the China Select Committee," *The Wire China*, February 12, 2023.
35. See https://selectcommitteeontheccp.house.gov/media/videos.
36. See Charles Hutzler, "The Committee That Ended the Age of Engagement?" *ChinaFile*, June 10, 2024, https://www.chinafile.com/reporting-opinion/features/committee-ended-age-of-engagement.
37. Cate Cadell, "At House Hearing on Chinese Communist Party, Bipartisan Show of Concern: New Committee's First Hearing Elicits Condemnation in Beijing," *The Washington Post*, March 1, 2023.
38. Quoted in Mark Magnier, "US House Panel Targeting Chinese Influence Makes Its Mark, to Mixed Reviews," *South China Morning Post*, December 27, 2023.
39. The Brookings Institution, "A Conversation with US Ambassador to China Nicholas R. Burns on US–China Relations," December 15, 2023.
40. https://selectcommitteeontheccp.house.gov/media/investigations.
41. https://selectcommitteeontheccp.house.gov/documents/reports.
42. https://selectcommitteeontheccp.house.gov/media/policy-recommendations/reset-prevent-build-strategy-win-americas-economic-competition-chinese. See also Cate Cadell, "House Committee Calls for Reset on China–US Economic Relations," *The Washington Post*, December 12, 2023.
43. https://selectcommitteeontheccp.house.gov/media/letters/letter-american-business-executives-dinner-xi-jinping.
44. Ibid. Note that $40,000 bought a seat at the head table with Xi, all others had to pay $2,000 to attend the dinner.
45. Quoted in Brent Crane, "Chairman Mike," *The Wire China*, January 7, 2024.
46. Phelim Kine, "'Certain Things Require a Machete': House China Committee Chair Defends Approach to Beijing," *Politico*, December 31, 2023.
47. See Rick Larsen (D-WA), "US-China Working Group," https://larsen.house.gov/uscwg.
48. Ibid.
49. See Rick Larsen, *US-China White Paper: A Four-Point Strategy to Enhance US Competitveness and Leadership*, https://larsen.house.gov/uploadedfiles/2023_china_white_paper.pdf.
50. Ibid.
51. SIPRI, "SIPRI Military Expenditure Database," https://www.sipri.org/databases/milex.

52. US Department of Defense, *Military and Security Developments Involving the People's Republic of China 2023: Annual Report to Congress*, p. 67, https://media.defense.gov/2023/Oct/19/2003323409/-1/-1/1/2023-military-and-security-developmentsinvolving-the-peoples-republic-of-china.pdf.

53. Chris Buckley, "Fear and Ambition Propel Xi's Nuclear Acceleration," *The New York Times*, February 4, 2024.

54. Ibid.

55. See, for example, Bates Gill, *Daring to Struggle: China's Global Ambitions Under Xi Jinping* (New York, NY: Oxford University Press, 2022), chapter 5; Phillip C. Saunders, Arthur S. Ding, Andrew Scobell, Andrew N. D. Yang, and Joel Wuthnow (eds.), *Chairman Xi Remakes the PLA: Assessing Chinese Military Reforms* (Washington, DC: National Defense University Press, 2019); M. Taylor Fravel, *Active Defense: China's Military Strategy Since 1949* (Princeton, NJ: Princeton University Press, 2019).

56. Statement of Michèle A. Flournoy, January 15, 2020, in Committee on Armed Forces, House of Representatives, *Department of Defense's Role in Competing with China* (US Government Printing Office, 2020), p. 4.

57. U.S. Department of Defense, 2022 *National Defense Strategy of the United States*, https://apps.dtic.mil/sti/trecms/pdf/AD1183514.pdf, p. 4.

58. Statement of Hon. Ely S. Ratner, Assistant Secretary of Defense for Indo-Pacific Security Affairs, US Department of Defense, to Committee on Armed Forces, House of US Representatives, March 9, 2022 (US Government Printing Office, 2023), p. 5.

59. Ibid., p. 7.

60. C. Todd Lopez, "Competition with China Drives FY 2024 Budget Request," *DOD News*, https://www.defense.gov/News/News-Stories/Article/Article/3343663/competition-with-china-drives-fy-2024-budget-request.

61. Department of Defense, *2022 National Defense Strategy of the United States*: https://media.defense.gov/2022/Oct/27/2003103845/-1/-1/1/2022-national-defense-strategynpr-mdr.pdf.

62. Ibid., pp. 8–9.

63. Ibid., p. 10.

64. See Damien Cave, "US Military Returns to the Jungle, Training for a Very Different Threat," *The New York Times*, December 15, 2023; Michael R. Gordon, "The Marines Transformed to Take on China," *Wall Street Journal*, December 29, 2023.

65. Doug Cameron, "Pentagon Pushes Defense Companies to Limit Use of Chinese Supplies," *Wall Street Journal*, September 18, 2022.

66. See Matthew Tetreau, "Where the Wargames Weren't: Assessing 10 Years of US–Chinese Military Assessments," *War on the Rocks*, September 22, 2023; Center for New American Security (CNAS), *Dangerous Straits: Wargaming a Future Conflict over Taiwan*, June 2022; Center for Strategic and International Studies (CSIS), *The First Battle of the Next War: Wargaming a Chinese Invasion of Taiwan*, January 2023; Michael Hirsh, "The Pentagon Is Freaking Out About a Potential War with China (Because America Might Lose)," *Politico*, June 9, 2023.

67. Hirsh, ibid.; Tara Copp, "'It Failed Miserably': After Wargaming Loss, Joint Chiefs Are Overhauling How the US Military Will Fight," *Defense One*, July 26, 2021.

68. See John Pomfret and Matt Pottinger, "Xi Jinping Says He Is Preparing China for War: The World Should Take Him Seriously," *Foreign Affairs* (March 29, 2023); "China Wants to Insulate Itself Against Western Sanctions," *The Economist*, February 26, 2022; Zongyuan Zoe Liu, "China Is Hardening Itself for Economic War," *Foreign Policy*, June 26, 2022.

69. "An Ill Wind: Why Is Xi Jinping Building Secret Commodity Stockpiles?" *The Economist*, July 27, 2024.

70. See Evan Feigenbaum and Adam Szubin, "What China Has Learned from the Ukraine War," *Foreign Affairs* (February 14, 2023).

71. Office of the Director of National Intelligence, "Who We Are," https://www.dni.gov/index.php/what-we-do/members-of-the-ic.

72. Office of the Director of National Intelligence, "DNI Haines Opening Statement to the Senate Select Committee on Intelligence on the 2023 Annual Threat Assessment of the US Intelligence Community," March 8, 2023, https://www.dni.gov/index.php/newsroom/congressional-testimonies/congressional-testimonies-2023/3685-dni-haines-opening-statement-on-the-2023-annual-threat-assessment-of-the-u-s-intelligence-community.

73. Office of the Director of National Intelligence, *Annual Threat Assessment of the U.S. Intelligence Community*, https://www.dni.gov/files/ODNI/documents/assessments/ATA-2023-Unclassified-Report.pdf.

74. Department of State, "Secretary Blinken Launches the Office of China Coordination," December 16, 2022, https://www.state.gov/secretary-blinken-launches-the-office-of-china-coordination; Nahal Toosi and Phelim Kine, "Biden Launches 'China House' to Counter China's Growing Global Clout," *Politico*, December 16, 2022.

75. Cited in Edward Wong, Julian E. Barnes, Muyi Xiao, and Chris Buckley, "Chinese Spy Agency Rising to Challenge the CIA," *The New York Times*, December 27, 2023.

76. Quoted in Warren P. Strobel, "American Spies Confront a New, Formidable China," *Wall Street Journal*, December 26, 2023.

77. Dan De Luce, "China Has Become a Tough Target for US Spies," NBC News, March 8, 2023.

78. Amy B. Zegart, *Spies, Lies, and Algorithms* (Princeton, NJ: Princeton University Press, 2022), pp. 166–167; Department of Justice, "Former CIA Officer Sentenced for Conspiracy to Commit Espionage," US Department of Justice, https://www.justice.gov/opa/pr/former-cia-officer-sentenced-conspiracy-commit-espionage; Zack Montague, "Ex-CIA Officer Sentenced to 19 Years in Chinese Espionage Conspiracy," *The New York Times*, November 22, 2019.

79. Zegart, ibid.

80. See   https://www.cia.gov/readingroom/docs/CIA-RDP90-00965R000504650019-5.pdf; https://en.wikipedia.org/wiki/Larry_Wu-tai_Chin.

81. Department of Justice, "Former CIA Officer Sentenced," op. cit.

82. Quoted in Warren P. Strobel, "American Spies Confront a New, Formidable China," op. cit.

83. "Fireside Chat with William Burns," Aspen Security Forum, July 20, 2023.

84. Quoted from a MSS WeChat posting as reported by Vivian Wang, "China to Its People: Spies Are Everywhere, Help Us Catch Them," *The New York Times*, September 2, 2023; see also Wong et al., "Chinese Spy Agency Rising to Challenge the CIA," op. cit.

85. Wang Xiangwei, "Why China's Top Spy Agency Is Stepping Out of the Shadows," *South China Morning Post*, February 5, 2024.

86. Yukio Tajima, "China Mobilizes Public Against 'Spying,' from Maps to Finance," *Nikkei Asia*, January 20, 2024; Joe Leahy, "China's Feared Spy Agency Steps Out of Shadows," *Financial Times*, January 22, 2024.

87. US Department of State, "China Travel Advisory," https://travel.state.gov/content/travel/en/traveladvisories/traveladvisories/china-travel-advisory.html.

88. Helen Davidson, "China Targets Foreign Consulting Companies in Foreign Spying Raids," *The Guardian*, May 9, 2023.

89. See Shane Harris, "CIA Creates New Mission Center to Counter China," *The Washington Post*, October 7, 2021.

90. De Luce, "China Has Become a Tough Target for US Spies," op. cit.

91. William J. Burns, "Spycraft and Statecraft," *Foreign Affairs* (March/April 2024); Warren P. Stroebel, "US Struggles to Spy on China, Its Leading Espionage Priority," *The Wall Street Journal*, December 26, 2023.

92. Ibid.

93. See Legal Information Institute, "50 U.S. Code 3003 Definitions," https://www.law.cornell.edu/uscode/text/50/3003#3.

94. See Peter Mattis and Matthew Brazil, *Chinese Communist Espionage: An Intelligence Primer* (Annapolis, MD: Naval Institute Press, 2019); Nicholas Eftimiades, *Chinese Espionage Operations and Tactics* (N.P.: Vitruvian Press, 2020); Alex Joske, *Spies and Lies: How China's Greatest Covert Operations Fooled the World* (Sydney: Hardie Grant, 2022); Dennis F. Poindexter, *The Chinese Information War: Espionage, Cyberwar, Communications Control and Related Threats to the United States*, 2nd ed. (N.P.: MacFarland Publishing, 2018).

95. James M. Olson, *To Catch a Spy: The Art of Counterintelligence* (Washington, DC: Georgetown University Press, 2021), p. 1.

96. See https://www.dni.gov/index.php/ncsc-how-we-work/ncsc-nittf.

97. See https://www.dni.gov/index.php/fmic-who-we-are.

98. For a useful survey of US government efforts to counter various types of PRC influence see, Kenton Thibaut, *Effective US Government Strategies to Address China's Information Influence* (Washington, DC: Atlantic Council and DFRLab, 2024), https://www.atlanticcouncil.org/wp-

content/uploads/2024/07/Chinas-Weaponization-of-the-Global-Information-Environment.
pdf.

99. Christopher Wray, "China's Quest for Economic, Political Domination Threatens American Security," February 1, 2022, https://www.fbi.gov/news/stories/director-wray-addresses-threats-posed-to-the-us-by-china-020122. Text of speech is "Countering Threats Posed by the Chinese Government Inside the US," January 31, 2022, https://www.fbi.gov/news/speeches/countering-threats-posed-by-the-chinese-government-inside-the-us-wray-013122.

100. See https://www.fbi.gov/investigate/counterintelligence/the-china-threat.

101. Quoted in Julian Barnes and Edward Wong, "In Risky Hunt for Secrets, US and China Expand Global Spy Operations," *The New York Times*, September 17, 2023.

102. Christopher Wray, "The Threat Posed by the Chinese Government and Chinese Communist Party to the Economic and National Security of the United States," address to the Hudson Institute, July 7, 2020, https://www.fbi.gov/news/speeches/the-threat-posed-by-the-chinese-government-and-the-chinese-communist-party-to-the-economic-and-national-security-of-the-united-states.

103. Calder Walton, "China Has Been Waging a Decades Long, All-Out Spy War," *Foreign Policy*, March 28, 2023.

104. See Federal Bureau of Investigation, *China: The Risk to Corporate America*, https://www.fbi.gov/file-repository/china-exec-summary-risk-to-corporate-america-2019.pdf.

105. See William C. Hannas, James C. Mulvenon, and Anna Puglisi, *Chinese Industrial Espionage: Technology Acquisition and Military Modernization* (London: Routledge, 2013); William C. Hannas and Didi Kirsten Tatlow, *Beyond Espionage: China's Quest for Foreign Technology* (London: Routledge, 2020).

106. See Institute for Security and Development Policy, *Backgrounder: Made in China 2025* (2018), https://isdp.eu/content/uploads/2018/06/Made-in-China-Backgrounder.pdf; MERICS, *Made in China 2025* (2016), https://merics.org/en/report/made-china-2025.

107. Scott Pelley, "China Stealing Technology Secrets—From AI to Computing and Biology, 'Five Eyes' Intelligence Leaders Warn," 60 Minutes, October 22, 2023.

108. See Robert McMillan, Dustin Volz, and Aruna Viswanatha, "China Is Stealing AI Secrets to Tubocharge Spying, US Says," *Wall Street Journal*, December 25, 2023.

109. I am indebted to Amy Zegart for pointing this out to me.

110. Didi Tang, Eric Tucker, and Frank Bajak, "US Says It Blocked a China Cyber Threat, but Warns Hackers Could Still Disrupt Lives of Americans," Associated Press, January 31, 2024.

111. Joe Parkinson and Drew Hinshaw, "FBI Director Says China Cyberattacks on US Infrastructure Now at Unprecedented Scale," *Wall Street Journal*, February 18, 2024.

112. Cate Cadell and Joseph Menn, "FBI Says It Shut Down Sources of Chinese Infrastructure Hacks," *The Washington Post*, January 31, 2024.

113. Ellen Nakashima and Joseph Menn, "China's Cyber Army Is Invading Critical US Services," *The Washington Post*, December 11, 2023; Lily Hay Newman, "The NSA Seems Pretty Stressed About the Threat of Chinese Hackers in US Critical Infrastructure," *Wired*, November 10, 2023.

114. Quoted in Nakashima and Menn, "China's Cyber Army Is Invading Critical US Services," op. cit.

115. Niharika Mandhana and Gordon Fairclough, "China's Chaos Threat Worries NSA Chief," *Wall Street Journal*, June 4, 2024.

116. Nakashima and Menn, "China's Cyber Army Is Invading Critical US Services," op. cit.

117. David Sanger and Mark Landler, "U.S. and Britain Say China Hacked into Infrastructure and Voter Rolls," *The New York Times*, March 26, 2024.

118. David Sanger, David Barboza, and Nicole Perlroth, "Chinese Army Unit Is Seen as Tied to Hacking Against the U.S.," *The New York Times*, February 18, 2013.

119. See https://www.fbi.gov/wanted/cyber/apt-41-group; https://www.fbi.gov/wanted/cyber/apt-10-group; https://www.fbi.gov/wanted/cyber/fujie-wang; https://www.fbi.gov/wanted/cyber/chinese-pla-members-54th-research-institute; https://www.fbi.gov/wanted/cyber/sun-kailiang; https://www.fbi.gov/wanted/cyber/gu-chunhui.

120. Cadell and Menn, "FBI Says It's Shut Down Sources of Recent Chinese Infrastructure Hacks," op. cit.

121. Estimate provided in Author's interview with FBI agent, April 10, 2024. On China's talent recruitment programs, see David Zweig, *The War for Chinese Talent in America: The Politics of*

Technology and Knowledge in Sino-US Relations (New York, NY: Columbia University Press, 2024).

122. United States Attorney's Office, District of Massachusetts, "Former Harvard University Professor Sentenced for Lying About His Affiliation with Wuhan University of Technology; China's Thousand Talents Program; and Filing False Tax Returns," April 26, 2023, https://www.justice.gov/usao-ma/pr/former-harvard-university-professor-sentenced-lying-about-his-affiliation-wuhan.

123. See Zweig, *The War for Chinese Talent in America*, op. cit.

124. See https://www.state.gov/promoting-accountability-for-transnational-repression-committed-by-peoples-republic-of-china-prc-officials/; https://www.justice.gov/opa/pr/five-men-indicted-crimes-related-transnational-repression-scheme-silence-critics-people-s; https://www.justice.gov/opa/pr/two-arrested-and-13-charged-three-separate-cases-alleged-participation-malign-schemes-united; https://www.justice.gov/opa/pr/us-citizen-and-four-chinese-intelligence-officers-charged-spying-prominent-dissidents-human; https://www.justice.gov/opa/pr/five-individuals-charged-variously-stalking-harassing-and-spying-us-residents-behalf-prc-0; https://www.justice.gov/usao-edny/pr/nine-individuals-charged-superseding-indictment-conspiring-act-illegal-agents-people-s; https://www.justice.gov/opa/pr/us-citizen-and-four-chinese-intelligence-officers-charged-spying-prominent-dissidents-human; https://www.justice.gov/opa/pr/man-charged-transnational-repression-campaign-while-acting-illegal-agent-chinese-government.

125. See Didi Kirsten Tatlow, "Xi Jinping Ramps Up China's Surveillance, Harassment Deep in America," *Newsweek*, December 3, 2022.

126. See Office of Public Affairs, U.S. Department of Justice, "40 Officers of China's National Police Charged in Transnatioal Repression Schemes Targeting U.S. Residents," April 17, 2023, https://www.justice.gov/opa/pr/40-officers-china-s-national-police-charged-transnational-repression-schemes-targeting-us.

127. Maia Coleman, "Queens Man Is Convicted of Spying on Dissidents for China," *The New York Times*, August 6, 2024.

128. Karen Zraick, "Three Are Convicted of Harassing Family on Behalf of China's Government," *The New York Times*, June 209, 2023.

129. See Federal Bureau of Investigation, "Transnational Repression," https://www.fbi.gov/investigate/counterintelligence/transnational-repression.

Chapter 7

1. Christopher Wray, "The Threat Posed by the Chinese Government and Chinese Communist Party to the Economic and National Security of the United States," Address to the Hudson Institute, July 7, 2020, https://www.fbi.gov/news/speeches/the-threat-posed-by-the-chinese-government-and-the-chinese-communist-party-to-the-economic-and-national-security-of-the-united-states.

2. Council on Foreign Relations, "C.V. Starr & Co. Annual Lecture on China: A Conversation with Ambassador Nicholas Burns," December 12, 2023, https://www.youtube.com/watch?v=bAcC5BVxfRE.

3. On the MAGA movement generally, see the excellent book Isaac Arnsdorf, *Finish What We Started: The MAGA Movement's Ground War to End Democracy* (Boston, MA: Little, Brown, 2024).

4. Cited in Noah Barkin and Gregor Sebastian, "Tipping Point? Germany and China in an Era of Zero-Sum Competition," The Rodium Group, February 15, 2024.

5. Stuart A. Thompson, "Steve Bannon's Podcast Is Top Misinformation Spreader," *The New York Times*, February 9, 2023.

6. See Isabelle Ong, "Have China's Christians Peaked? Pew Researches the Data Debate," *Christianity Today*, August 30, 2023.

7. See ChinaAid, *Religious Freedom for All of China*, https://chinaaid.org/about.

8. See David Shambaugh, *China Goes Global: The Partial Power* (New York: Oxford University Press, 2013).

9. See Paul Sonne, "Russia and China Carry Out First Joint Bomber Patrol Near Alaska," *The New York Times*, July 25, 2024.

10. See, for example, Michael D. Swaine, "Perceptions of an Assertive China," *China Leadership Monitor*, No. 32 (2010), http://media.hoover.org/sites/default/files/documents/CLM32MS. pdf; Alastair Iain Johnston, "How New and Assertive Is China's New Assertiveness?" *International Security*, Vol. 37. No. 4 (Spring 2013).

11. See Anne Applebaum, *Autocracy, Inc.: The Dictators Who Want to Run the World* (New York, NY: Random House, 2024).

12. See Srikanth Kondapalli, "Regional Multilateralism with Chinese Characteristics," in David Shambaugh (ed.), *China & the World* (New York, NY: Oxford University Press, 2020).

13. The most definitive study of these "influence activities" in the United States remains Larry Diamond and Orville Schell (eds.), *China's Influence and American Interests: Promoting Constructive Vigilance* (Stanford, CA: Hoover Institution Press, 2019).

14. Quoted from Will Steakin, "Nikki Haley Is Running for President as a China Hawk—But Her Record Suggests Otherwise," https://abcnews.go.com/US/nikki-haley-running-china-hawk-record-suggests-picture/story?id=104726771#:~:text=In%20her%20February%202024%20announcement,faced%20by%20the%20United%20States.

15. Ebony Davis, "Nikki Haley Says She Views China as an Enemy in Pointed Rebuke," September 10, 2023, https://www.cnn.com/2023/09/10/politics/nikki-haley-china-cnntv/index.html.

16. https://nikkihaley.com/2023/09/27/nikki-haley-my-plan-to-unleash-americas-secret-weapon-economic-freedom.

17. https://ny1.com/nyc/all-boroughs/politics/2023/06/27/attacking-both-biden-and-trump-nikki-haley-lays-out-strategy-for-china.

18. Nikki Haley, "Nikki Haley: My Plan to Confront the Chinese Threat," *Wall Street Journal*, June 26, 2023.

19. See Pew Research Center, "Views of China," July 27, 2023, https://www.pewresearch.org/global/2023/07/27/views-of-china.

20. See Megan Brenan, "Record Low: 15% of Americans View China Favorably," Gallup, March 7, 2023, https://news.gallup.com/poll/471551/record-low-americans-view-china-favorably. aspx.

21. Ibid.

22. See Chicago Council on Global Affairs, "Americans Feel More Threat from China Now Than in the Past Three Decades," https://globalaffairs.org/research/public-opinion-survey/americans-feel-more-threat-china-now-past-three-decades.

23. For the most systematic study of such "influence operations" is Diamond and Schell, *China's Influence and American Interests*, op. cit. This volume includes a detailed bureaucratic organizational chart of China's sprawling apparatus that operates overseas (Appendix 1).

24. I say "expanded" because many malign Chinese activities have been carried out inside the United States for years, but they have not been recognized until recently.

25. Original source: http://www.news.cn/politics/leaders/2023-03/06/c_1129417096.htm; https://news.rthk.hk/rthk/en/component/k2/1690845-20230307.htm. See also Keith Bradsher, "China's Leader, with Rare Bluntness, Blames U.S. Containment for Troubles," *The New York Times*, March 7, 2023.

26. Bates Gill, *Daring to Struggle: China's Global Ambitions Under Xi Jinping* (New York, NY: Oxford University Press, 2023).

27. Susan Shirk, *Overreach: How China Derailed Its Peaceful Rise* (New York, NY: Oxford University Press, 2023).

28. Ibid., p. 316.

29. For excellent analysis of this topic see Katya Drinhausen and Helena LeGarda, "'Comprehensive National Security' Unleashed: How Xi's Approach Shapes China's Policies at Home and Abroad," MERICS, September 15, 2022; Jude Blanchette, "The Edge of an Abyss: Xi Jinping's Overall National Security Outlook," *China Leadership Monitor*, No. 73 (September 2022); Sheena Greitens, "National Security After China's 20th Party Congress," *China Leadership Monitor*, No. 77 (August 2023).

30. "Gongan Buzhang: Yanmi fangfan daji jing nei wai didui shili shentou dainfu daoluan pohuai huodong" [Minister of Public Security: Strictly Guard Against and Crackdown on Infiltration, Subversion, Disturbances, and Destructive Activities by Internal and External Hostile Forces], November 3, 2020, https://new.qq.com/rain/a/20201103A09GDY00 (Author's translation).

31. See Vivian Wang, "Eyes and Ears: Rising Arsenal Across China. Xi Tightens His Grip to Fend Off Any Unrest," *The New York Times*, May 27, 2024.

32. See, for example, "Zhongyang Zhengfa Wei yaoqiu renqing xingshi: jing nei wai didui shili congwei tingzhi pohuai huodong" [The Central Political and Legal Affairs Commission Requires a Clear Understanding of the Situation: Hostile Forces at Home and Abroad Have Never Ceased Their Destructive Activities], *Sohu Wang*, January 11, 2021, https://www.sohu.com/a/44475052_137462 (Author's translation).

33. "Chen Yixin: Shenru xuexi guanche dang de ershida jingshen jiakuai goujian xin anquan geju" [Chen Yixin: Deeply Study and Implement the Spirit of the Party's 20th Congress and Accelerate the Establishment of a New Security Pattern], Zhongguo Zhengfu Wang, April 16, 2023, https://gov.cn/lianbo/2023-04/16/content_5752098.htm (Author's translation).

34. Ibid.

35. "Spooked," *The Economist*, September 23, 2023.

36. See Chun Han Wong, "China Casts CIA as Villain in New Anti-Spying Push," *Wall Street Journal*, August 24, 2023.

37. "Guojia Anquan Bu kaitong hulianwang jubao shouli pingtai" [The Ministry of State Security Launches an Internet Reporting Platform], *Zhongguo Zhengfu Wang*, April 15, 2018, https://www.gov.cn/xinwen/2018-04/15/content_5282639.htm (Author's translation).

38. See Wong, "China Casts CIA as Villain in New Anti-Spying Push," op. cit.

39. See U.S. Library of Congress, *Government Responses to Disinformation on Social Media Platforms: China*, July 24, 2020, https://www.loc.gov/law/help/social-media-disinformation/china.php.

40. See Edward Wong, "CCP News Alert: Chinese Media Must Serve the Party," *The New York Times*, February 16, 2016; "Xi Jinping Asks for 'Absolute Loyalty' from State Media," *The Guardian*, February 19, 2016.

41. Ibid.

42. "Zhongqingju (Zhongyang Qingbao Ju) yong 5 shouduan zai chaoguo 50 guo cehua 'Yanse Geming'" [The CIA Uses Five Methods to Plot 'Color Revolutions' in More Than 50 Countries], Xinwen Wang, May 4, 2023, http://www.news.cn/world/2023-05/04/c_1129587958.htm (Author's translation).

43. See "Document No. 9: A Chinafile Translation," *ChinaFile*, https://www.chinafile.com/document-9-chinafile-translation.

44. "Document No. 9," ibid.

45. See "Gong An Bu: Yanmi fangfan daji jing nei wai didui shili shentou dianfu daoluan pohuai huodong" [Ministry of Public Security: Strictly Guard Against and Crack Down on Infiltration, Subversion, Disturbance, and Destruction Activities by Hostile Force Both Within and Outside the Country], *Tengxun Xinwen*, November 3, 2020, https://new.qq.com/rain/a/20201103A09GDY00 (Author's translation).

46. See "Chen Wenqing zhuchi zhaokai Zhongyang Zhengfa Weiyuanhui Quanti Huiyi qiandiaoyi youli jucuo guanche luoshi dang de ershida jingshen jianjue weihu guojia anquan he shehui wending" [Chen Wenqing Presides over the Full Meeting of the Central Political and Legal Affairs Commission, Emphasizing the Implementation of the Spirit of the 20th Party Congress with Strong Measures to Resolutely Safeguard National Security and Social Stability], *Renmin Wang*, November 29, 2022, http://politics.people.com.cn/n1/2022/1129/c1001-32577106.html (Author's translation).

47. Mary Brown Bullock, "Strategic Adaptation: American Foundations, Religious Organizations, and NGOs in China," in Anne F. Thurston (ed.), *Engaging China: Fifty Years of Sino-American Relations* (New York, NY: Columbia University Press, 2021); Mary Brown Bullock, *An American Transplant: The Rockefeller Foundation and Peking Union Medical College* (Berkeley, CA: University of California Press, 1980); Mary Brown Bullock, *The Oil Prince's Legacy: Rockefeller Philanthropy in China* (Stanford, CA: Stanford University Press, 2011).

48. For earlier Western efforts, see Jonathan Spence, *To Change China: Western Advisors in China* (New York, NY: Penguin, 2002).

49. See Chinafile, "The China NGO Project: Laws and Regulations," https://www.chinafile.com/ngo/laws-regulations/law-of-peoples-republic-of-china-administration-of-activities-of-overseas.

50. Articles 3 and 5; ibid.

51. See D. D. Wu, "More Than 7000 Foreign NGOs in China: Only 91 Registered So Far," *The Diplomat*, June 2, 2017, https://thediplomat.com/2017/06/more-than-7000-foreign-ngos-in-china-only-72-registered-so-far; Edward Wong, "Clampdown in China Restricts 7000 Foreign

Organizations," *The New York Times*, April 28, 2016. The 400 figure is given in Bruce Dickson, *The Party and the People: Chinese Politics in the 21st Century* (Princeton, NJ: Princeton University Press, 2021), p. 108. Another source lists 591 registered foreign NGOs by 2021: see Mark Sidel, "Securitizing Overseas Nonprofit Work in China: Five Years of the Overseas NGO Law Framework and Its New Application to Academic Institutions," *USALI Perspectives*, Vol. 2, No. 6 (November 11, 2021).

52. See "Registration of Overseas NGOs," https://ngo.mps.gov.cn/ngo/portal/toInfogs.do?p_type=1. I am indebted to Vicky Tu for this reference.

53. China Development Brief, "NGO Directory," https://chinadevelopmentbrief.org/ngo-directory.

54. See The Ford Foundation, "China Overview," https://www.fordfoundation.org/our-work-around-the-world/china.

55. See Eliot Chen, "Foreign Law Firms Feel the Chill in China," *The Wire China*, December 17, 2023.

56. Brown Bullock, "Strategic Adaptation," op. cit., p. 221.

57. Dickson, *The Party and the People*, op. cit., p. 266, note 8, citing Ministry of Civil Affairs, http://www.mca.gov.cn/article/sj/tjjb/sjsj/2018/20180608021510.html.

58. See "Minzheng Bu Shehui Zuzhi Guanli Ju fuze tongzhi jiu 2023 nian daji zhengzhi feifa shehui zuzhi zhuanxiang xingdong youguan wenti da jizhe wen" [The Responsible Comrade of the Ministry of Civil Affairs Bureau of Social Organization Administration Answers Journalists' Questions Regarding the Special Action to Crack Down on and Rectify Illegal Social Organizations in 2023], *Zhongguo Zhengfu Wang*, August 18, 2023, https://www.gov.cn/zhengce/202308/content_6899050.htm (Author's translation).

59. See "Kaichuang weihu guojia anquan de zhanxin jumian: Xin Shidai Zhongguo weihu guojia anquan shuping" [Creating a New Situation of National Security Maintenance: A Review of China's National Security in the New Era], *Zhongguo Zhengfu Wang*, September 21, 2022, https://www.gov.cn/xinwen/2022-09/21/content_5710913.htm.

60. See David Shambaugh, *China's Communist Party: Atrophy & Adaptation* (Berkeley, CA and Washington, DC: University of California Press, 2013); David Shambaugh, "Learning from Abroad to Reinvent Itself: External Influences on Internal CCP Reforms," in Cheng Li (ed.), *China's Political Trajectory* (Brookings Institution Press, 2008); Stephen Kotkin, *Uncivil Society: 1989 and the Implosion of the Communist Establishment* (N.P.: Modern Library, 2010).

61. See Elizabeth Plantan, "Transnational Civil Society and Authoritarian Politics in China and Russia," Woodrow Wilson Center China Fellowship 2022–2023 Occasional Paper; and Applebaum, *Autocracy, Inc.*, op. cit.

62. See Janis Mackey Frayer and Jennifer Jett, "How the US–China Clash Is Being Felt on Campus," NBC News, June 2, 2023; Paul Basken, "American Students Still All but Absent from China," *Times Higher Education*, December 21, 2023, https://www.statista.com/statistics/374169/china-number-of-students-from-the-us/; William Yang, "Bilateral Tensions Cause the Number of American Students in China to Plummet," VOA News, December 19, 2023.

63. See International Institute of Education, "U.S. Study Abroad," https://opendoorsdata.org/annual-release/u-s-study-abroad.

64. See U.S. Department of State, "China Travel Advisory," https://travel.state.gov/content/travel/en/traveladvisories/traveladvisories/china-travel-advisory.html#:~:text=Mainland%20China%20-%20Level%203A%20Reconsider,the%20risk%20of%20wrongful%20detentions.

65. See, for example, Keith Richburg, "American Students Have Soured on China. That's Bad for the U.S.," *Washington Post*, May 22, 2024.

66. FBI, "Game of Pawns," https://www.fbi.gov/video-repository/newss-game-of-pawns/view.

67. Department of Justice, "Michigan Man Sentenced to 48 Months for Conspiring to Spy for the People's Republic of China," January 21, 2011, https://www.justice.gov/opa/pr/michigan-man-sentenced-48-months-attempting-spy-people-s-republic-china.

68. The full list of terminations, including the 19 American exchange programs, is listed in "Zhuyi! 84 ge gaoxiao shuoshidian tingzhi banxue" [Attention! 84 University Programs Have Ceased Operations], *Shouji Xinlang Wang*, September 9, 2021, https://finance.sina.cn/insurance/bxzx/2021-09-09/detail-iktzqtyt4922972.d.html (Author's translation).

69. See https://shanghai.nyu.edu.

70. See https://www.dukekunshan.edu.cn.

71. See https://scpku.fsi.stanford.edu.

72. See https://sais.jhu.edu/hopkins-nanjing-center.

73. See https://www.schwarzmanscholars.org.

74. See https://yenchingacademy.pku.edu.cn.

75. See https://iupchinesecenter.org.

76. See Rory Truex, "Where Have All the American China Experts Gone?" *The Washington Post*, January 3, 2024.

77. This discussion is drawn from my article Shambaugh, "The Evolution of American Contemporary China Studies: Coming Full Circle?" *Journal of Contemporary China*, Vol. 33, No. 146 (March 2024).

78. See Karin Fischer, "Slamming the Door on Scholarship," *Chronicle of Higher Education*, February 21, 2023.

79. See Shambaugh, "The Evolution of American Contemporary China Studies," op. cit.

80. See Emily Baum and Yingyi Ma, *China Studies in an Uncertain Age* (New York, NY: American Council of Learned Societies, 2023); and Shambaugh, ibid.

81. See Peter Buck, *American Science and Modern China* (Cambridge, MA: Cambridge University Press, 2010); Brown Bullock, *An American Transplant*, op. cit.; Phillip West, *Yenching University and Sino-Western Relations* (Cambridge, MA: Harvard University Press, 1976); Thomson, *While China Faced West: American Reformers in Nationalist China* (Cambridge, MA: Harvard University Press, 1969), op. cit.

82. See, for example, Institute of International Education, *US–China Educational Exchange: Perspectives on a Growing Partnership* (New York, NY: Institute of International Education, 2008).

83. Gitnux, "Chinese Students in the US Statistics and Trends," https://gitnux.org/chinese-students-in-us-statistics/#:~:text=Table%20of%20Contents&text=In%202020%2C%20around%20380%2C000%20Chinese,USC%20hosting%20the%20most%20students.

84. James T. Areddy, "Research for Sale: How Chinese Money Flows to American Universities," *Wall Street Journal*, April 15, 2024.

85. Anastasya Lloyd-Damnjanovic, *A Preliminary Study of PRC Political Influence and Interference Activities in American Higher Education* (Washington, DC: Woodrow Wilson Center Kissinger Institute on China and the United States, 2018); The MIT China Strategy Group, *University Engagement with China: An MIT Approach* (Cambridge, MA: MIT, November 2022).

86. Cited in Elizabeth Redden, "Who Controls Confucius Institutes?" *Inside Higher Education*, February 27, 2019.

87. See, for example, United States Government Accountability Office (GAO), *China: Observations on Confucius Institutes in the United States and U.S. Universities in China*, Testimony Before the Permanent Subcommittee on Investigations, Committee on Homeland Security and Governmental Affairs, February 28, 2019.

88. See National Academy of Sciences, *Confucius Institutes at U.S. Institutions of Higher Education, Consensus Study Report: Waiver Criteria for the Department of Defense* (Washington, DC: National Academies Press, 2023).

89. For an excellent overview of CSSAs, see Bethany Allen-Ebrahimian, "China's Long Arm Reaches into American Campuses," *Foreign Policy*, March 7, 2018.

90. Statistic given in Bethany Allen-Ebrahimian, "Chinese Government Gave Money to Georgetown Chinese Student Group," *Foreign Policy*, February 14, 2014.

91. This case is detailed in Allen-Ebrahimian, "China's Long Arm Reaches into American Campuses," op. cit.

92. See Bethany Allen-Ebrahimian, "The Chinese Communist Party Is Setting Up Cells at Universities Across America," *Foreign Policy*, April 18, 2018.

93. As noted in Lloyd-Damnjanovic, *A Preliminary Study of PRC Political Influence and Interference Activities in American Higher Education*, op. cit., citing Zhang Yu, "CPC Members Encounter Obstacles While Trying to Establish Party Branches Overseas," *Global Times*, November 28, 2018.

94. Sun Yu, "China Exerts New Control Over Its Young Expats in the US: Students and Workers Who Have Joined the Communist Party Say They Have Been Asked to Spread Propaganda," *Financial Times*, July 1, 2024.

95. See Peter Foster, Sun Yu, Andrew Jack, and Chan Ho-him, "China Accused of 'Transnational Repression' of Students," *Financial Times*, May 13, 2024.

96. Sun Yu, "China Exerts New Control Over Its Young Expats in the US," op. cit.
97. Part of this section is drawn from the chapter I co-authored on universities in Diamond and Schell, *China's Influence and American Interests*, op. cit.
98. See US Department of Education, Office of the General Counsel, *Institutional Compliance with Section 117 of the Higher Education Act of 1965*, March 2020, https://www2.ed.gov/policy/highered/leg/institutional-compliance-section-117.pdf.
99. As cited in Hannah Reale, "China's Donations to U.S. Universities," *The Wire China*, September 13, 2020.
100. See respectively United States Department of Education Office of General Council, "Notice of 20 U.S.C. Investigation and Record Request/Harvard University," https://www2.ed.gov/policy/highered/leg/harvard-20200211.pdf; U.S. Department of Education Office of General Counsel, *Institutional Compliance with Section 117 of the Higher Education Act of 1965*, https://www2.ed.gov/policy/highered/leg/yale-20200211.pdf;https:www2.ed.gov/policy/highered/leg/stanford-20200810.pdf.
101. CUSEF's official website: https://www.cusef.org.hk. For a detailed exposé of CUSEF, its united front ties, and its use of American consultants for various activities, see John Dotson, "The China-U.S. Exchange Foundation and United Front 'Lobbying Laundering' in American Politics," *Jamestown Foundation China Brief*, Vol. 20, No. 16 (2020).
102. Perry Link, "China: The Anaconda in the Chandelier," *New York Review of Books*, April 11, 2002.
103. David Shambaugh, "The Coming Chinese Crackup," *Wall Street Journal*, March 6, 2015.
104. See Shambaugh, "The Evolution of American Contemporary China Studies," op. cit.; "Slamming the Door on Scholarship," *Chronicle of Higher Education*, op. cit.
105. ChinaFile, "Will I Return to China?" https://www.chinafile.com/conversation/will-i-return-china; Sheena Chestnut Greitens and Rory Truex, "Repressive Experiences Among China Scholars: New Evidence from Survey Data," *The China Quarterly*, No. 242 (June 2020).
106. See Scott Kennedy (ed.), *U.S.–China Scholarly Recoupling: Advancing Mutual Understanding in an Era of Intense Rivalry* (Washington, DC: CSIS, 2024).
107. American Association of Universities, "Engagement with China: Recommendations for American Colleges and Universities," (n.d.): https://www.aau.edu/sites/default/files/AAU-Files/Constituent%20Meetings/CFR%20Meetings/Reporton HigherEdEngagementwithChina(NCUSCR%202019)(002).pdf.
108. The MIT China Strategy Group, *University Engagement with China*, op. cit.
109. Ibid.
110. Ibid.
111. See U.S. Department of Justice, "Information About the Department of Justice's China Initiative and a Compilation of China-Related Prosecutions Since 2018," https://www.justice.gov/archives/nsd/information-about-department-justice-s-china-initiative-and-compilation-china-related.
112. Ellen Barry and Katie Benner, "U.S. Drops Its Case Against M.I.T. Scientist Accused of Hiding China Links," *The New York Times*, January 20, 2022.
113. See Asian American Scholar Forum, "New Report Showcases Climate of Fear Among Asian-Origin Scientists and Researchers," September 23, 2022, https://www.aasforum.org/2022/09/23/new-report-showcases-climate-of-fear-among-asian-origin-scientists-and-researchers.
114. Figure cited in Sha Hua and Karen Hao, "US-China Tensions Fuel Outflow of Chinese Scientists from US Universities," *Wall Street Journal*, September 22, 2022.
115. The FBI has been proactive in educating educators about the risks and potential dangers related to China. See FBI, *China: The Risk to Academia*: https://www.fbi.gov/file-repository/china-risk-to-academia-2019.pdf/view#:~:text=The%20FBI%20produced% 20several%20resources,protect%20themselves%20from%20counterintelligence%20threats.
116. The MIT China Study Group, *University Engagement with China*, op. cit.; Diamond and Schell, *China's Influence and American Interests*, op. cit., chapter 4; in particular, pp. 65–70.
117. Office of the US Trade Representative: The People's Republic of China (2022), https://ustr.gov/countries-regions/china-mongolia-taiwan/peoples-republic-china.
118. Ibid.
119. Ibid.

120. "Q&A: Craig Allen on U.S. Business Confidence in China," *The Wire China*, March 27, 2022. Also see US-China Business Council, "How Trade with China Benefits the United States," https://www.uschina.org/how-trade-china-benefits-united-states.

121. "Remarks by U.S. Secretary of Commerce Gina Raimondo on U.S. Competitiveness and the China Challenge," delivered at MIT, November 30, 2022, https://www.commerce.gov/news/speeches/2022/11/remarks-us-secretary-commerce-gina-raimondo-us-competitiveness-and-china.

122. See Alice Tisdale Hobart, *Oil for the Lamps of China* (N.P.: Eastbridge Books, 1933); and Brown Bullock, *The Oil Prince's Legacy*, op. cit.

123. Author's email exchange with Craig Allen, March 30, 2024.

124. Cited in Freeman III, "The Commercial and Economic Relationship," in David Shambaugh (ed.), *Tangled Titans: The United States and China* (Lanham, MD: Rowman & Littlefield, 2013), p. 181.

125. Randall E. Stross, *Bulls in the China Shop and Other Sino-American Business Encounters* (New York, NY: Pantheon Books, 1990).

126. Jim Mann, *Beijing Jeep: The Short, Unhappy Romance of American Business in China* (New York, NY: Simon & Schuster, 1989).

127. Freeman, "The Commercial and Economic Relationship," op. cit.

128. Craig Allen, "US–China Retrospective: Forty Years of Commercial Relations," in Anne F. Thurston (ed.), *Engaging China: Fifty Years of Sino-American Relations* (New York: Columbia University Press, 2021).

129. Jim McGregor, *One Billion Customers: Lessons from the Frontlines of Doing Business in China* (New York, NY: The Free Press, 2007).

130. Craig Allen, "Remarks to USCBC's Jubilee Gala," December 14, 2023.

131. Newly Purnell, "U.S. Business Confidence in China Drops to 24-Year Low," *Wall Street Journal*, September 19, 2023.

132. See AmCham China, "China Business Climate Survey Report," February 1, 2024, https://www.amchamchina.org/wp-content/uploads/2024/01/AmCham-China-2024-China-Business-Climate-Survey-Report.pdf, p. 41, p. 52.

133. Ibid., p. 10.

134. See US–China Business Council, 2023 Member Survey: https://www.uschina.org/sites/default/files/en-2023_member_survey.pdf.

135. Ibid., p. 2.

136. Ibid., p. 3.

137. Ibid., p. 22.

138. See "Starbucks Opens Its 6,000th Store in China," September 26, 2022, https://stories.starbucks.com/press/2022/starbucks-opens-its-6000th-store-in-china/#.

139. I am grateful to Ben Wasserstrom for this information: "The U.S. Business Community and China, 2012–2022," seminar paper, Elliott School of International Affairs, March 2022.

140. Ibid.

141. See Yang Jie and Aaron Tilley, "Apple's New Plan to Move Beyond China," *Wall Street Journal*, December 3–4, 2022; "The End of the China Affair," *The Economist*, October 29, 2022.

142. Meaghan Tobin, Alexandra Stevenson, and Tripp Mickle, "Souring on Apple in China," *The New York Times*, March 28, 2024.

143. "The Mind-Bending New Rules for Doing Business in China," *The Economist*, April 3, 2024.

144. See Mara Hvistendahl, Jack Ewing, and John Liu, "Musk's Reliance on China Draws Rising Scrutiny," *The New York Times*, March 28, 2024.

145. "The Half-Open Door," *The Economist*, February 17, 2024.

146. Cited by Fareed Zakaria in "Biden's Course Correction on China Is Smart and Important," *Washington Post*, April 21, 2023.

147. The Conference Board, "Confidence Among CEOs of Multinational Corporations Wanes as Economic Weakness Persists," https://www.conference-board.org/pdfdownload.cfm?masterProductID=49490.

148. Cited in Lingling Wei and Liza Lin, "The Cost of Doing Business with China? A $40,000 Dinner with Xi Jinping Might be Just the Start," *Wall Street Journal*, November 28, 2023.

149. See "Foreign Direct Investment to China Slumps to 30-Year Low," Bloomberg, February 18, 2024, https://www.bloomberg.com/news/articles/2024-02-18/foreign-direct-investment-into-china-slumps-to-worst-in-30-years?embedded-checkout=true.

150. Iori Kawate and Shunsuke Tabeta, "Foreign Direct Investment in China Falls to 30-Year Low," *Nikkei Asia*, February 19, 2024, https://asia.nikkei.com/Economy/Foreign-direct-investment-in-China-falls-to-30-year-low.

151. Macrotrends, "China: Foreign Direct Investment, 1979–2024," https://www.macrotrends.net/global-metrics/countries/CHN/china/foreign-direct-investment#:~:text=Data%20are%20in%20current%20U.S.,a%2035.22%25%20increase%20from%202019.

152. "Annual Inflow of Foreign Direct Investment (FDI) to China, 2012–2022," Statista: https://www.statista.com/statistics/1016973/china-foreign-direct-investment-inflows. Also see Jason Douglas, "Beijing Risks Loss of Investment," *Wall Street Journal*, May 4, 2023.

153. See, for example, Newley Purnell and Clarence Leong, "American Business Stalls in China," *Wall Street Journal*, March 27, 2024.

154. As cited in "Exit the Dragon: Ties Between Foreigners and China Keep Fraying," *The Economist*, September 30, 2023.

155. Thomas L. Friedman, "How China Lost America," *The New York Times*, November 1, 2022.

156. See https://data.worldbank.org/indicator/NE.CON.PRVT.ZS?locations=CN. https://www.statista.com/statistics/1197099/china-final-consumption-as-share-of-gdp.

157. Don Weinland, "The New Normal: Don't Expect Life to Get Easier for Foreign Firms Doing Business in China," *The Economist*, December 2023.

158. See the detailed discussion in Bethany Allen, *Beijing Rules: China's Quest for Global Influence* (London: John Murray, 2023), chapter 5.

159. See "Chinese Police Question Employees at Bain's Shanghai Office," *Financial Times*, April 26, 2023; Peter Humphrey, "Foreign Business Community in China Beware," *Politico*, April 5, 2023; Eliot Chen, "Beijing's Latest Crackdown Deepens Foreign Business's Confusion," *The Wire China*, May 14, 2023.

160. Chip Cutter, Elaine Yu, and Newly Purnell, "China Is Becoming a No-Go Zone for Executives," *Wall Street Journal*, October 6, 2023

161. See U.S. Department of State, "China Travel Advisory," https://travel.state.gov/content/travel/en/traveladvisories/traveladvisories/china-travel-advisory.html.

162. There are numerous media reports concerning each of these individual cases.

163. See Orville Schell, "Appeasement at the Cineplex," *New York Review of Books*, April 6, 2023; Isaac Stone Fish, *America Second: How America's Elites Are Making China Stronger* (London: Scribe Publications, 2022), chapter 5.

164. A lengthy exposé in *The Wire China* details the Greenbergs' longtime relationship with, and kowtowing to, Beijing. See Brent Crane, "Insuring Engagement," *The Wire China*, September 4, 2022.

165. For a description of Schwartzman's connections to China, including many fawning statements he has made about China and its leadership, see Peter Schweizer, *Red Handed: How American Elites Get Rich Helping China Win* (New York, NY: HarperCollins, 2022), pp. 122–130.

166. For a thorough exposé on Thornton, see John Pomfret, "The Thornton Touch," *The Wire China*, March 6, 2022.

167. See Zachary Smith, "DOJ Sues Casino Mogul and GOP Megadonor Steve Wynn to Register as Agent for China," Forbes, May 17, 2022. The suit was overturned by a federal judge on the basis that the DOJ could not compel individuals to register (individuals and entities must register on their own, although it could prosecute cases of transgressing FARA stipulations). See Stephen S. Hsu, "Judge Rejects DOJ Bid to Compel Steve Wynn to Register as China Agent," *Washington Post*, October 12, 2022.

168. See Weinland, "The New Normal," op. cit.; Cutter, Yu, and Purnell, "China Is Becoming a No-Go Zone for Executives," op. cit.

169. Among numerous articles, see Kate O'Keeffe, "New Chinese Law Raises Risks for American Firms in China, Officials Say," *Wall Street Journal*, June 30, 2023; Library of Congress, "China: Counterespionage Law Revised" September 21, 2023; Jill Goldenziel, "China's Anti-Espionage Law Raises Foreign Business Risk," *Forbes*, July 3, 2023; C. K. Tan and Shunsuke Tabeta, "China's Anti-Espionage Law Set to Politicize Business," *Nikkei Asia*, June 29, 2023; James Palmer, "China's Latest Data Restrictions Could Scare Off Investors: Broadening of Anti-Espionage law Alarms Businesses," *Foreign Policy*, May 2, 2023.

170. Goldenziel, ibid.

171. Lester Ross, "China's Espionage Law Updates Undercut Courting of Investors," *Nikkei Asia*, May 5, 2023.

172. See Daisuke Wakabayashi, Keith Bradsher, and Claire Fu, "China Expands Scope of 'State Secrets' Law in Security Push," *The New York Times*, February 28, 2024; Austin Ramzy, "China Expands State Secrets Law, Highlighting Risks for Foreign Businesses," *Wall Street Journal*, February 27, 2024; Laurie Chen, "China Broadens Law on State Security to Include 'Work Secrets,'" *Reuters*, February 28, 2024.

173. The Rhodium Group, *The Global Economic Disruptions from a Taiwan Conflict*, December 14, 2022.

174. Ibid.

175. Joshua Franklin, "US Bank Chiefs Warn of China Exit if Taiwan Is Attacked," *Financial Times*, September 21, 2022.

176. Cited in Cathy Chan, "Wall Street's Biggest Banks Face a Harsh Reality Check in China," Bloomberg, May 16, 2023.

177. See, for example, "Remarks by Secretary of the Treasury Janet L. Yellen on the U.S.–China Economic Relationship," Johns Hopkins School of Advanced International Studies, April 20, 2023, https://home.treasury.gov/news/press-releases/jy1425; "Remarks by Secretary of Treasury Janet L. Yellen on the U.S.–China Economic Relationship," US–China Business Council, December 14, 2023, https://home.treasury.gov/news/press-releases/jy1994.

178. Ibid.

179. European Commission, "Speech by President von der Leyen on EU–China Relations to the Mercator Institute for China Studies and the European Policy Center," March 30, 2023, https://ec.europa.eu/commission/presscorner/detail/en/speech_23_2063.

180. "Remarks by U.S. Secretary of Commerce Gina Raimondo on U.S. Competitiveness and the China Challenge," https://www.commerce.gov/news/speeches/2022/11/remarks-us-secretary-commerce-gina-raimondo-us-competitiveness-and-china.

181. Quoted in David Shepardson, "Commerce Chief Says US Firms Complain China Is 'Uninvestible,'" *Reuters*, August 29, 2023; David Ignatius, "Raimondo Finds a China Facing a Reality Check," *The Washington Post*, September 8, 2023.

182. Jason Douglas and Weilun Soon, "Foreign Firms Pull Billions in Earnings Out of China," *Wall Street Journal*, November 6, 2023.

183. David Lynch, "U.S.–China Economic Ties Continue to Fray, Despite Biden–Xi Meeting," *The Washington Post*, November 18, 2023.

184. Erin Griffith, "Silicon Valley Venture Capitalists Are Breaking Up with China," *The New York Times*, February 21, 2024.

185. CGTN, "Full Text of Xi Speech at Welcome Dinner in U.S.," https://news.cgtn.com/news/2023-11-17/Full-text-Xi-s-speech-at-welcome-dinner-in-U-S-1oMGfl69DxK/index.html.

186. The Editorial Board, "U.S. CEO's on the Chinese Menu," *Wall Street Journal*, November 17, 2023; Laura Silva Laughlin, "American CEO's Serve China's Xi a Too-Rich Desert," *Reuters*, November 17, 2023.

187. Quoted in Lingling Wei and Charles Hutzler, "Xi Asks U.S. Business Leaders to Help Ease Growing Tensions," *Wall Street Journal*, November 17, 2023.

188. For analyses of the pros and cons, and the potential costs of decoupling, see Daniel H. Rosen and Laruen Gloudeman, *Understanding US–China Decoupling: Macro Trends and Industry Prospects*, The Rhodium Group and U.S. Chamber of Commerce China Center, February 17, 2021; Charles W. Boustany Jr., and Aaron Friedberg, *Partial Disengagement: A New U.S. Strategy for Economic Competition with China* (Seattle, WA: National Bureau of Asian Research, November 2019).

189. See The White House, "Remarks by the National Security Advisor Jake Sullivan on Renewing American Economic Leadership at the Brookings Institution," https://www.whitehouse.gov/briefing-room/speeches-remarks/2023/04/27/remarks-by-national-security-advisor-jake-sullivan-on-renewing-american-economic-leadership-at-the-brookings-institution.

190. See Sun Yu, "US Private Funds Struggle to Cash Out from China," *Financial Times*, March 14, 2024.

191. James T. Areddy, "States Take on China in the Name of National Security," *Wall Street Journal*, April 26, 2024.

192. Hurubie Meko, Benjamin Okeskes, and Nicholas Fandos, "The Secrets of an Unassuming N.Y. Official Accused of Working for China," *The New York Times*, September 4, 2024.

193. Ed Pilkington, "China's Consul General in New York Reportedly Expelled," *Politico*, September 4, 2024, https://www.politico.com/news/2024/09/04/hochul-chinese-consul-general-00177319.

194. Ibid. China has *never* stated such an objective.

195. Such international united front work actually began in the 1930s–1940s at the CCP base area in Yenan. See James Reardon-Anderson, *Yenan and the Great Powers: The Origins of Chinese Communist Foreign Policy, 1944–1946* (New York, NY: Columbia University Press, 1980); Michael Hunt, *The Genesis of Chinese Communist Foreign Policy* (New York, NY: Columbia University Press, 1996); Lyman van Slyke, *Enemies and Friends: The United Front in Chinese Communist History* (Stanford, CA: Stanford University Press, 1967).

196. Mao Zedong, "The Chinese People Have Stood Up!" Opening Address to the First Plenary Session of the Chinese People's Political Consultative Congress, September 21, 1949, https://china.usc.edu/Mao-declares-founding-of-peoples-republic-of-china-chinese-people-have-stood-up.

197. In recent years, there has been a considerable amount of information uncovered and published about China's united front bureaucracy and "influence operations abroad." See, in particular, "Appendix 1: China's Influence Operations Bureaucracy," in Larry Diamond and Orville Schell (eds.), *China's Influence and American Interests Promoting Constructive Vigilance* (Stanford, CA: Hoover Institution Press, 2019).

198. Ibid., chapter 3.

199. See China General Chamber of Commerce-USA, "Mission, Vision, and Values," https://www.cgccusa.org/en/mission-vision-values; and ibid., chapter 7.

200. For a good description of these forums, see Emily de La Bruyère and Nathan Picarsic, *All Over the Map: The Chinese Communist Party's Subnational Interests in the United States* (Washington, DC: Foundation for Defense of Democracies, November 2021).

201. University of Southern California China scholar Erin Baggott Carter describes this phenomenon as "looking for Edgar Snow."

202. Diamond and Schell, *China's Influence and American Interests*, op. cit.

203. See, for example, U.S.–China Economic and Security Review Commission, *2023 Report to the Congress*, chapter 2, section 2, https://www.uscc.gov/sites/default/files/2023-11/2023_Annual_Report_to_Congress.pdf.

204. See "S.3405: Countering Corrupt Political (CCP) Influence Act," https://www.govtrack.us/congress/bills/118/s3405.

205. See Diamond and Schell, *China's Influence and American Interests* op. cit., chapter 6.

206. See US Department of State Global Engagement Center, *Special Report: How the People's Republic of China Seeks to Reshape the Global Information Environment* (2023); Sarah Cook, *Beijing's Global Megaphone: The Expansion of Chinese Communist Party Media Influence Since 2017* (Washington, DC: Freedom House Special Report 2020); David Shambaugh, "China's External Propaganda Work: Missions, Messengers, Mediums," Party Watch Annual Report 2018, https://docs.wixstatic.com/ugd/183fcc_e21fe3b7d14447bfaba30d3b6d6e3ac0.pdf.

207. See, for example, Tiffany Hsu and Steven Lee Myers, "China's Advancing Efforts to Influence the U.S. Election Raises Alarms," *The New York Times*, April 1, 2024; Tiffany Hsu, "A 'Spamoflage' Campaign Aims to Pump Up Voter Unrest," *The New York Times*, February 16, 2024; Steven Lee Myers, "China Uses Deceptive Methods to Sow Disinformation, U.S. Says," *The New York Times*, September 28, 2023; Dustin Volz, "China Aims Disinformation at U.S. Voters," *Wall Street Journal*, April 6, 2024. Spamoflage was first identified in 2019 and linked to an affiliate of China's Ministry of State Security. Meta (formerly Facebook) labeled Spamoflage as "the largest known cross-platform covert influence program in the world." Quoted in David Sanger, *New Cold Wars* (New York, NY: Crown Books, 2024), p. 345.

208. See U.S. Department of State, "Subnational Diplomacy Unit," https://www.state.gov/bureaus-offices/under-secretary-for-economic-growth-energy-and-the-environment/the-special-representative-for-subnational-diplomacy.

209. See No Author, "Xi Says China, U.S. Sister Cities Cooperation Fruitful," November 3, 2023, https://english.www.gov.cn/news/202311/03/content_WS6544894bc6d0868f4e8e0ebf.html.

210. A complete listing of sister cities can be found at "Sister Partnerships by Chinese Province," East-West Center, *China Matters for America Matters for China*, https://asiamattersforamerica.org/china/data/sister-partnerships/china.

211. Source: The Rhodium Group, "US–China Investment Hub," https://www.us-china-investment.org/fdi-data. All FDI data in this section comes from this source.
212. Visit California, "China Market Profile," https://industry.visitcalifornia.com/research/global-market-profiles-landing/china-market-profile.
213. Kyler A. Jaros, *State-Level US–China Relations at the Crossroads: Predicaments and Prospects for Subnational Engagement* (Washington, DC: Woodrow Wilson Center Kissinger Institute on US–China Relations, 2023), p. 81.
214. Kyle A. Jaros and Sara A. Newland, "Paradiplomacy in Hard Times: Cooperation and Confrontation in Subnational US–China Relations," cited in ibid.
215. "Federal Anti-China Sentiment Is Increasingly Seeping into State Laws," *The Hill*, April 28, 2023.
216. Grady McGregor, "Buying the Heartland," *The Wire China*, April 16, 2023.
217. Quoted from ibid.
218. "Now Showing in Local Theaters: State Legislatures Are Becoming Another Front in America's Clash with China," *The Economist*, June 3, 2023.
219. See Gregory S. Schneider and Laura Vozzella, "China Fuels Debate in Richmond After Youngkin Slams Door on Battery Plant," *The Washington Post*, February 20, 2023.
220. "Now Showing in Local Theaters," op. cit.
221. Ibid.; also see "Here Be Dragons," *The Economist*, January 27, 2024; Kristina Petersen and Anthony DeBarros, "Farmland Becomes Flashpoint in U.S.–China Relations," *Wall Street Journal*, February 6, 2023.
222. There are approximately 500,000 PRC passport-carrying citizens who are simultaneously US green-card holders. Source: CNN, February 14, 2023.
223. These are specified in McGregor, "Buying the Heartland," op. cit.
224. Ibid; and J. David Goodman, "How U.S.–China Tensions Could Affect Who Buys the House Next Door," *The New York Times*, February 7, 2023.
225. "Here Be Dragons," op. cit.
226. Ibid.
227. Petersen and DeBarros, "Farmland Becomes Flashpoint in U.S.–China Relations," op. cit.
228. Fatims Hussein, "US to Expand Control of Land Sales to Foreigners Near Military Sites," Associated Press, July 9, 2024.
229. Associated Press, "Amid Strained US Ties, China Finds Unlikely Friend in Utah," March 27, 2023; Thomas Kika, "China Using Mormon Church to Influence U.S. Politics, Investigation Finds," *Newsweek*, March 27, 2023.
230. As cited in the excellent report by Emily de La Bruyère and Nathan Picarsic, *All Over the Map: The Chinese Communist Party's Subnational Interests in the United States*, op. cit. Where individual governors fall on this spectrum is listed in this report, pp. 31–32.
231. The original survey, which goes well beyond cataloging governor's attitudes to include an extensive analysis of different American states' relations with the PRC, can be found at https://s3.documentcloud.org/documents/6779094/PRC-Think-Tank-Study-on-US-Governors-Attitudes.pdf.
232. The White House, "Remarks by Vice President Pence on the Administration's China Policy," The Hudson Institute, October 4, 2018, https://trumpwhitehouse.archives.gov/briefings-statements/remarks-vice-president-pence-administrations-policy-toward-china/.
233. Michael R. Pompeo, "U.S. States and the China Competition," National Governor's Association, February 8, 2020, https://2017-2021.state.gov/u-s-states-and-the-china-competition/.
234. See Christopher Wray, "Countering Threats Posed by the Chinese Government Inside the United States," January 31, 2022, https://www.fbi.gov/news/speeches/countering-threats-posed-by-the-chinese-government-inside-the-us-wray-013122.
235. See U.S. Department of Homeland Security Office of Intelligence and Analysis, *Homeland Threat Assessment 2024*, https://www.dhs.gov/sites/default/files/2023-09/23_0913_ia_23-333-ia_u_homeland-threat-assessment-2024_508C_V6_13Sep23.pdf.
236. See The National Counterintelligence and Security Center, *Safeguarding Our Future: Protecting Government and Business Leaders at the U.S. State and Local Level from People's Republic of China (PRC)Influence Operations (July 2022)*, https://www.dni.gov/files/NCSC/documents/SafeguardingOurFuture/PRC_Subnational_Influence-06-July-2022.pdf.
237. Jaros, *State-Level U.S.–China Relations at the Crossroads*, op. cit.

Chapter 8

1. Kurt M. Campbell and Jake Sullivan, "Competition Without Catastrophe: How America Can Both Challenge and Coexist with China," *Foreign Affairs* (August 1, 2019).
2. CBS, "60 Minutes," February 25, 2024, https://www.cbsnews.com/news/china-us-relationship-nicholas-burns-60-minutes/?intcid=CNR-01-0623.
3. See Gilbert Rozman, *The Chinese Debate About Soviet Socialism, 1978–1985* (Princeton, NJ: Princeton University Press, 1987).
4. David Engerman, *Know Your Enemy: The Rise and Fall of American Soviet Experts* (Oxford: Oxford University Press, 2009).
5. David McCourt, *The End of Engagement: America's China and Russia Experts and U.S. Strategy Since 1989* (New York, NY: Oxford University Press, 2024).
6. David Shambaugh, *Beautiful Imperialist: China Perceives America, 1972–1990* (Princeton, NJ: Princeton University Press, 1991).
7. Such as the RAND Corporation, CNA Corporation, and Center for Strategic and Budgetary Assessments.
8. Such as SAIC, Mitre Corporation, Centra Technology, Booz Allen Hamilton, CACI International, Leidos, the Eurasia Group, McKinsey & Co., and others.
9. Such as the National Defense University, National War College, US Army War College, Naval War College, and US Air War College.
10. Elizabeth N. Saunders, *The Insiders' Game: How Elites Make War and Peace* (Princeton, NJ: Princeton University Press, 2024); "Politics Can't Stop at the Water's Edge: The Right Way to Fight over Foreign Policy," *Foreign Affairs* (March/April 2024).
11. Elizabeth Saunders's presentation at Stanford University Center for International Security and Cooperation, May 2, 2024.
12. Campbell described these in an interview with David Sanger, diplomatic correspondent for *The New York Times*. See David Sanger, *New Cold Wars: China's Rise, Russia's Invasion, an America's Struggle to Defend the West* (New York: Crown Books, 2024), pp. 142–143.
13. It is unclear if this is Sanger's rendering or a verbatim quotation from Campbell. Ibid., p. 143.
14. Again, it is unclear if these were Campbell's words or Sanger's rendering of them.
15. Michael Pillsbury, *The Hundred Year Marathon: China's Secret Strategy to Replace America as the Global Superpower* (New York: St. Martin's Griffin, 2016);Bill Gertz, *Deceiving the Sky: Inside Communist China's Drive for Global Supremacy* (New York, NY: Encounter Books, 2021); Rush Doshi, *The Long Game: China's Grand Strategy to Displace American Order* (New York, NY: Oxford University Press, 2021); Robert Spalding, *War Without Rules: China's Playbook for Global Domination* (New York, NY: Penguin/Sentinel, 2022); Ian Easton, *The Final Struggle: Inside China's Global Strategy* (Manchester, UK: Eastbridge Books, 2022).
16. These include *Destined for War* (Allison), *Fake China Threat and Its Very Real Danger* (Solis-Mullen), *Understanding the China Threat* (Han and Thayer), *The Chinese Invasion Threat* (Easton), *America and the China Threat: From the End of History to the End of Empire* (Urio), *Bully of Asia: Why China's Dream Is the New Threat to World Order* (Mosher), *Trump vs. China: Facing America's Greatest Threat* (Gingrich), *Rise of the Red Dragon* (Sala), *Stealth War: How China Took Over While America's Elite Slept* (Spalding), *When China Attacks: A Warning to America* (Newsham), *America Second: How America's Elites Are Making China Stronger* (Fish), *Beijing Rules: How China Weaponized Its Economy to Confront the World* (Allen), *The Great US–China Tech War* (Chang), *Xi Jinping's China: The #1 Existential Threat to the USA* (Wilson), *The World Turned Upside Down: America, China, and the Struggle for Global Leadership* (Prestowitz), *China's Vision of Victory and Why America Must Win* (Ward), *Red Alert: How China's Growing Prosperity Threatens the American Way of Life* (Leeb and Dorsey), *You Will Be Assimilated: China's Plan to Sino-form the World* (Goldman), *The China Challenge: Standing Strong Against the Military, Economic, and Political Threats That Imperil America* (Dillon), *The Chinese Information War: Espionage, Cyberwar, Communications Control and Related Threats to United States Interests* (Poindexter).
17. Pillsbury, *The Hundred Year Marathon*, op. cit., p. 111.
18. Ibid., p. 115.
19. Ibid., p. 11.
20. The 36 Stratagems are battle scenarios. They are listed in Wikipedia, "Thirty-Six Strategems," https://en.wikipedia.org/wiki/Thirty-Six_Stratagems.

21. Ibid., p. 195.
22. For a Chinese review of Doshi's book see Zhou Wenxing, "Meiguo Baquan Sixiang Xia de Zhongguo 'Da Zhanlue'" [China's Grand Strategy Imagined by American Hegemony], *Meiguo Yanjiu*, No. 5 (2022).
23. Doshi, *The Long Game*, op. cit., p. 11.
24. Ibid., p. 14.
25. See U.S. Naval War College Faculty: Ian Easton, https://usnwc.edu/Faculty-and-Departments/Directory/Ian-Easton.
26. Robert Spalding, *Stealth War: How China Took Over While America's Elite Slept* (New York, NY: Portfolio/Penguin, 2019), pp. xvi–xvii.
27. See Robert G. Kaiser and Steven Mufson, "'Blue Team' Draws a Hard Line on Beijing," *The Washington Post*, February 22, 2000.
28. Parts of this section are drawn from my chapter "Parsing and Managing U.S.–China Competition," in Evan Medeiros (ed.), *Cold Rivals: The New Era of US-China Strategic Competition* (Washington, DC: Georgetown University Press, 2023).
29. See, for example, US House of Representatives Committee on Armed Services, Hearing on Strategic Competition with China, February 15, 2018; US Senate Committee on Armed Services, Hearing on the United States' Strategic Competition with China, June 8, 2021; US Senate Foreign Relations Committee, Hearing on Strategic Competition with China, March 17, 2021.
30. See Medeiros, *Cold Rivals: The New Era of US-China Strategic Competition*, op cit.; Elbridge A. Colby, *The Strategy of Denial: American Defense in an Age of Great Power Conflict* (New Haven, CT: Yale University Press, 2021); Clyde Prestowitz, *The World Turned Upside Down: America, China, and the Struggle for Global Leadership* (New Haven, CT: Yale University Press, 2021).
31. See, for example, Jonathan D. Moyer, Collin J. Meisel, Austin S. Matthews, David Bohl, and Mathew J. Burrows, *China–US Competition: Measuring Global Influence* (Washington, DC: The Atlantic Council, 2021); Michael Mazza, *Policies and Principles for Competition* (Washington, DC: American Enterprise Institute, 2023); Robert D. Blackwill, *Implementing Grand Strategy Toward China* (New York, NY: Council on Foreign Relations Special Report No. 85, 2020); Joseph S. Nye, Condoleezza Rice, and Nicholas Burns (eds.), *The Struggle for Power: U.S.–China Relations in the 21st Century* (Washington, DC: The Aspen Institute, 2020); Task Force on US China Policy, *Course Correction: Toward an Effective and Sustainable China Policy* (New York, NY: Asia Society Center on US–China Relations and UC-San Diego 21st Century China Center, 2019).
32. Christopher Paul et al., *A Guide to Extreme Competition with China* (Santa Monica, CA: The Rand Corporation, 2021); Michael Mazaar et al., *Understanding Influence in the Strategic Competition with China* (Santa Monica, CA: The Rand Corporation, 2021). Also see Andrew Scobell et al., *China's Grand Strategy: Trends, Trajectories, and Long-Term Competition* (Santa Monica, CA: The Rand Corporation, 2020).
33. The White House, *Indo-Pacific Strategy of the United States*, February 2022, p. 5.
34. David Shambaugh, "Sino-American Strategic Relations: From Partners to Competitors," *Survival*, Vol. 42, No. 1 (2000).
35. Harry Harding, "The United States and China: From Partners to Competitors in America's Eyes," in Medeiros, *Cold Rivals: The New Era of US–China Strategic Competition*, op. cit., p. 82.
36. See Nathan Levine, "A Clash of Worldviews: The United States and China Have Reached an Ideological Impasse," *Foreign Affairs* (August 30, 2023); Elizabeth Economy, "China's Alternative Order and What America Should Learn from It," *Foreign Affairs* (May/June 2024).
37. Michael R. Pompeo, "Communist China and the Free World's Future," Richard M. Nixon Presidential Library, July 23, 2020, https://trumpwhitehouse.archives.gov/briefings-statements/chinese-communist-partys-ideology-global-ambitions/; Robert O'Brien, "The Chinese Communist Party's Ideology and Global Ambitions," June 24, 2020, https://trumpwhitehouse.archives.gov/briefings-statements/chinese-communist-partys-ideology-global-ambitions/.
38. Matt Pottinger, "Beijing Targets American Business," *Wall Street Journal*, March 27–28, 2021.
39. Hal Brands and Zack Cooper, "U.S.–Chinese Rivalry Is a Battle Over Values: Great Power Competition Can't Be Won on Interests Alone," *Foreign Affairs* (March 16, 2021).
40. Cited in Matt Pottinger and Mike Gallagher, "No Substitute for Victory: America's Competition with China Must Be Won, Not Managed," *Foreign Affairs* (May/June 2024). The origin

of this quotation is unclear, although when I asked Pottinger directly he replied that it came from "an official [Chinese] document" (which he promised to send me but never did).

41. Ibid.

42. Quoted in Ken Moriyasu, "Calls for China Regime Change Are 'Reckless': Kurt Campbell," *Nikkei Asia*, June 13, 2024.

43. CBS, "60 Minutes," February 25, 2024, https://www.cbsnews.com/news/china-us-relationship-nicholas-burns-60-minutes/?intcid=CNR-01-0623.

44. See Peter Harrel, Elizabeth Rosenberg, and Edoardo Saravalle, *China's Use of Coercive Economic Measures* (Washington, DC: Center for New American Security, 2018); Alexander Holderness et al., *Expanding the Tool Kit to Counter China's Economic Coercion* (Washington, DC: Center for Strategic and International Studies, 2024).

45. See Emily Kilcrease and Michael Frazer, *Sanctions by the Numbers: SDN, CMIC, and Entity List Designations on China* (Washington, DC: Center for New American Security, 2023). Also see Emily Kilcrease, "America's China Strategy Has a Credibility Problem: A Muddled Approach to Economic Sanctions Won't Deter Beijing," *Foreign Affairs* (May 7, 2024).

46. See Helen Toner, "From Backwater to Near-Peer: Changing US Approaches Toward China as a Technological Competitor," in Medeiros, *Cold Rivals: The New Era of US–China Strategic Competition*, op. cit.

47. See Chris Miller, *Chip War: The Fight for the World's Most Critical Technology* (New York, NY: Scribner, 2022); Asia Society Center on US–China Relations and University of California, San Diego 21st Century China Center, *Meeting the China Challenge: A New American Strategy for Technology Competition*, November 2020, https://asiasociety.org/center-us-china-relations/meeting-china-challenge-new-american-strategy-technology-competition; Asia Society Center on US–China Relations and Hoover Institution, *Silicon Triangle: The United States, Taiwan, China, and Global Semiconductor Security*, May 2024, https://asiasociety.org/sites/default/files/2024-05/SiliconTriangle_full_240523.pdf.

48. See Congressional Research Service, *U.S. Export Controls and China*, March 24, 2022.

49. David Sanger, "Biden Issues New Order to Block Chinese Investment in Technology in the U.S.," *The New York Times*, September 15, 2022.

50. Paul Mozur, Ana Swanson, and Edward Wong, "U.S. Said to Plan New Limits on China's A.I. and Supercomputing Firms," *The New York Times*, October 3, 2022

51. Asa Finch, "U.S. Seeks to Further Restrict Cutting-Edge Chip Exports to China," *Wall Street Journal*, October 3, 2022.

52. The White House, "Remarks by National Security Advisor Jake Sullivan on Renewing American Economic Leadership," Brookings Institution, April 27, 2023, https://www.whitehouse.gov/briefing-room/speeches-remarks/2023/04/27/remarks-by-national-security-advisor-jake-sullivan-on-renewing-american-economic-leadership-at-the-brookings-institution/.

53. Among many excellent studies, see Avery Goldstein, "U.S.–China Interactions in Asia," in David Shambaugh (ed.), *Tangled Titans: The United States and China* (Lanham, MD: Rowman & Littlefield, 2013); Michael Swaine, *Creating a Stable Asia: An Agenda for a US–China Balance of Power* (Washington, DC: Carnegie Endowment for International Peace, 2016).

54. Keith Bradsher, "China's Leader, With Rare Bluntness, Blames U.S. Containment for China's Troubles," *The New York Times*, March 7, 2023.

55. See Colby, *The Strategy of Denial*, op. cit.

56. See, for example, Matt Pottinger (ed.), *The Boiling Moat: Urgent Steps to Defend Taiwan* (Stanford, CA: Hoover Institution Press, 2024).

57. See Murray Hiebert, *Under Beijing's Shadow: Southeast Asia's China Challenge* (Lanham, MD: Rowman & Littlefield, 2020); David Shambaugh, *Where Great Powers Meet: America & China in Southeast Asia* (New York, NY: Oxford University Press, 2021)

58. See Shambaugh, ibid.

59. Asia Society Working Group on Southeast Asia of the Task Force on US China Policy, *Prioritizing Southeast Asia in American China Strategy*), https://asiasociety.org/sites/default/files/2023-08/Prioritizing%20Southeast%20Asia%20in%20American%20China%20Policy%202.pdf.

60. See David Shambaugh, *China Goes Global: The Partial Power* (New York: Oxford University Press, 2013).

61. See, for example, Barbara Lippert and Volker Perthes (eds.), *Strategic Rivalry Between the United States and China: Causes, Trajectories and Implications for Europe* (Berlin: SWP, 2020);

European Think-Tank Network on China (ETNC), *Europe in the Face of U.S.–China Rivalry* (Madrid: Real Instituto Elcano, 2020).

62. See David Shambaugh and Dawn Murphy, "U.S.–China Interactions in the Middle East, Africa, Europe, and Latin America," in David Shambaugh (ed.), *Tangled Titans: The United States and China* (Lanham, MD: Rowman & Littlefield, 2013); and Ashley Tellis, Alison Szalwinski, Michael Wills (eds.), *Strategic Asia 2020: U.S–China Competition for Global Influence* (Seattle, WA: National Bureau of Asian Research, 2020).

63. This is a central argument in John Mearsheimer, *The Tragedy of Great Power Politics* (New York, NY: W. W. Norton, 2014).

64. For an analysis of these groupings in China's diplomacy, see Srikanth Kondapalli, "Regional Multilateralism with Chinese Characteristics," in David Shambaugh (ed.), *China and the World* (New York, NY: Oxford University Press, 2020).

65. See Dawn Murphy, *China's Rise in the Global South: The Middle East, Africa, and Beijing's Alternative World Order* (Stanford, CA: Stanford University Press, 2024); Joshua Eisenman and David Shinn, *China's Relations with Africa: A New Era of Strategic Engagement* (New York, NY: Columbia University Press, 2023).

66. See Rosemary Foot and Andrew Walter, *China, the United States, and Global Order* (Cambridge, MA: Cambridge University Press, 2010); and Rosemary Foot, "US–China Interactions in Global Governance and International Organizations," in Shambaugh, *Tangled Titans: The United States and China*, op. cit.

67. See David Shambaugh, "China and the Liberal World Order," in Nicholas Burns, Leah Bitounis, and Jonathon Price (eds.), *A World Turned Upside Down: Maintaining American Leadership in a Dangerous Age* (Washington, DC: The Aspen Institute, 2018).

68. Aspen Strategy Group, *The Struggle for Power: US–China Relations in the 21st Century* (Washington, DC: The Aspen Institute, 2020).

69. Anonymous, *The Longer Telegram: Toward a New American China Strategy* (Washington, DC: Atlantic Council, Scowcroft Center for Strategy and Security, 2021).

70. Brookings Institution, John L. Thornton China Center, *The Future of US Policy Toward China*, November 9, 2020.

71. Robert D. Blackwill, *Implementing Grand Strategy Toward China* (New York, NY: Council on Foreign Relations Special Report No. 85, January 2020).

72. Asia Society Center on US–China Relations and 21st Century China Center, University of California-San Diego, Task Force on U.S. China Policy, *Course Correction: Toward an Effective and Sustainable China Policy* (February 2019) and *China's New Direction: Challenges and Opportunities for U.S. Policy* (2021).

73. Medeiros, *Cold Rivals*, op. cit.

74. Evan S. Medeiros, "The Delusion of Peak China: America Can't Wish Away Its Toughest Challenger," *Foreign Affairs* (May/June 2024).

75. See Zachary Shore, *A Sense of the Enemy: The High-Stakes History of Reading Your Adversary's Mind* (New York, NY: Oxford University Press, 2014). Shore's book is well worth reading. Also see his article Zachary Shore "A Sense of the Enemy," *Joint Forces Quarterly*, No. 65 (April 2012).

76. Quoted in H. R. McMaster, *Battlegrounds: The Fight to Defend the Free World* (New York, NY: Harper, 2020), p. 16. Also see the interview with McMaster by David Barboza, "H. R. McMaster on Making Use of America's Strengths," *The Wire China*, September 27, 2020.

77. Among Whiting's most notable writings were Allen S. Whiting, *China Crosses the Yalu: The Decision to Enter the Korean War* (Stanford, CA: Stanford University Press, 1960); Allen S. Whiting, *The Chinese Calculus of Deterrence: India and Indochina* (Ann Arbor, MI: University of Michigan Press, 1981); Allen S. Whiting, "China's Use of Force: 1950–96 and Taiwan," *International Security* Vol. 26, No. 2 (Fall 2001).

78. McMaster defines "strategic narcissism" as "wishful thinking, mirror imaging, confirmation bias, and the belief that others will conform to a US developed 'script.'" McMaster, *Battlegrounds*, op. cit., p. 92.

79. Ibid., p. 92.

80. Ibid., p. 94.

81. Ibid., p. 98.

82. Ibid., pp. 130–131.

83. Ibid., p. 131.

84. See https://trumpwhitehouse.archives.gov/wp-content/uploads/2017/12/NSS-Final-12-18-2017-0905.pdf.

85. McMaster, *Battleground*, op. cit., pp. 130–131.

86. Thomas Fingar and David M. Lampton, "China's America Policy: Back to the Future," *The Washington Quarterly*, Vol. 46, No. 4 (Winter 2024).

87. Ibid., p. 46.

88. Ibid.

89. Ibid., p. 47.

90. Ibid., p. 55.

91. Ibid., p. 58.

92. Michael D. Swaine, Ezra F. Vogel, Paul Heer, J. Stapleton Roy, Rachel Esplin Odell, Mike Mochizuki, Avery Goldstein, and Alice Miller, "The Overreach of the China Hawks: Aggression Is the Wrong Response to Beijing," *Foreign Affairs* (October 23, 2020).

93. Aaron Friedberg, "An Answer to Aggression," *Foreign Affairs* (September/October 2020).

94. M. Taylor Fravel, J. Stapleton Roy, Michael D. Swaine, Susan A. Thornton, and Ezra F. Vogel, "China Is Not an Enemy," *Washington Post*, July 3, 2019

95. Swaine et al., "The Overreach of the China Hawks," op. cit.

96. Aaron Friedberg, "Friedberg Replies," *Foreign Affairs* (October 23, 2020).

97. Charles L. Glaser, "Time for a U.S.–China Grand Bargain: The Hard Choice Between Military Competition and Accommodation," *International Security*, Vol. 39, No. 4 (Spring 2015), pp. 49–90.

98. Ibid.

99. Ibid.

100. Charles W. Glaser, "Washington Is Avoiding the Tough Questions on Taiwan and China: The Case for Reconsidering U.S. Commitments in East Asia," *Foreign Affairs* (April 28, 2021).

101. Charles G. Glaser, "Assessing the Dangers of Conflict: The Sources and Consequences of Deepening US–China Competition," in Jacques deLisle and Avery Goldstein (eds.), *After Engagement: Dilemmas in U.S.–China Security Relations* (Washington, DC: Brookings Institution Press, 2021), pp. 70–71.

102. Among his many writings in this vein, see Hugh White, *The China Choice: Why We Should Share Power* (New York: Oxford University Press, 2013).

103. See, among his many writings, Kishore Mahbubani, *Has China Won? The Chinese Challenge to American Primacy* (New York: Public Affairs, 2022).

104. Ibid.

105. Among many of his articles on these themes, see Michael D. Swaine, "A Restraint Approach to US-China Relations: Reversing the Slide Towards Crisis and Conflict," Quincy Institute Paper No. 11 (2023): https://quincyinst.s3.amazonaws.com/wp-content/uploads/2023/04/17213105/QUINCY-PAPER-NO.-11-SWAINE-BACEVICH.pdf; Michael D. Swaine and Sarang Shidore, "A Restraint Recipe for America's Alliances and Security Partnerships," Quincy Institute Paper No. 37 (2022): https://quincyinst.s3.amazonaws.com/wp-content/uploads/2022/11/17213722/QUINCY-BRIEF-NO.-34-NOV-2022-SWAINE.pdf.

106. See Swaine et al., "The Overreach of the China Hawks," op. cit.; Fravel, Roy, Swaine, Thornton, and Vogel, "China Is Not an Enemy," op. cit.; Michael D. Swaine, "A Counterproductive Cold War with China," *Foreign Affairs* (March 2, 2018); Michael D. Swaine, "A Relationship Under Extreme Duress: US–China Relations at a Crossroads," The Carter Center, 2019, https://www.cartercenter.org/resources/pdfs/peace/china/china-program-2019/swaine.pdf.

107. See, for example, Michael D. Swaine, "The Worsening Taiwan Embroglio: An Urgent Need for Effective Crisis Management," *Quincy Institute Paper*, No. 34 (2022).

108. Jessica Chen Weiss, "The China Trap: U.S. Foreign Policy and the Perilous Logic of Zero-Sum Competition," *Foreign Affairs* (September/October 2022).

109. Ibid.

110. See Katrina Northrop, "Jessica Chen Weiss on Stepping Back from the Brink," *The Wire China*, October 9, 2022, https://www.thewirechina.com/2022/10/09/jessica-chen-weiss-on-stepping-back-from-the-brink/.

111. Heer's revised dissertation was subsequently published as Paul J. Heer, *Mr. X and the Pacific: George F. Kennan and American Policy in East Asia* (Ithaca, NY: Cornell University Press, 2018).

112. In the latter regard see, for example, Paul Heer, "Deconstructing the Bipartisan Consensus on the China Threat," *The National Interest*, March 16, 2023.

113. See, for example, Alex W. Palmer, "Paul Heer on the Danger of Overstating China's Ambitions," *The Wire China*, January 22, 2023.

114. Shore, *A Sense of the Enemy*, op. cit.

115. Paul Heer, "Condemning the Chinese Communist Party Is Not Enough," *The National Interest*, July 25, 2022.

116. Ibid.

117. Paul Heer, "Engagement with China Hasn't Failed, It Just Hasn't Succeeded Yet," *The National Interest*, July 14, 2022.

118. Heer, "Condemning the Chinese Communist Party Is Not Enough," op. cit.

119. Paul Heer, "What Is Really Driving Chinese Aggression?" *The National Interest*, February 11, 2022.

120. Paul Heer, "Rethinking U.S. Primacy in East Asia," *The National Interest*, January 8, 2019.

121. See Paul Heer, "Between Chinese Overreach and American Overreaction," *The National Interest*, November 15, 2022; "Understanding US–China Strategic Competition," *The National Interest*, October 20, 2020.

122. Paul Heer, "Washington's Willful Blind Spot on China," *The National Interest*, October 31, 2023.

123. Many of Orlins's speeches, interviews, and articles can be found at https://www.ncuscr.org/category/news.

124. Stephen Orlins, "How Joe Biden's America and China Can Turn the Page on a Rocky Relationship," *South China Morning Post*, January 21, 2021, https://www.scmp.com/comment/opinion/article/3117465/how-bidens-america-and-china-can-turn-page-rocky-relationship.

125. Verbatim notes I took at the dinner.

126. USCBC President Craig Allen's Remarks on the Jubilee Gala in Washington DC, https://www.uschina.org/advocacy/testimony-speeches/uscbc-president-craig-allen-remarks-jubilee-gala-washington-dc.

127. See, for example, "Evan Greenberg on US–China Economies," CSIS and Peterson Institute, 2021, https://www.youtube.com/watch?v=qjZyW43Y2QM.

128. https://www.reddit.com/r/tezos/comments/9lhtgq/a_fullpage_color_ad_in_the_national_edition_of/#.

129. "Open Letter to the Presidents of the United States and the People's Republic of China on the Need to Stabilize Bilateral Relations," *Wall Street Journal*, April 3, 2023.

130. Henry M. Paulson, "America's China Policy Is Not Working: The Dangers of a Broad Decoupling," *Foreign Affairs* (January 26, 2023).

131. See Bob Davis, "Stephen J. Hadley on Keeping China Relations on Track," *The Wire China*, April 2, 2023.

132. See Bob Davis, "Charlene Barshefsky on Why Engagement with China Is More Important Than Ever," *The Wire China*, May 8, 2022.

133. See, for example, David Barboza, "Stapleton Roy Asks What the US Wants from the China Relationship," *The Wire China*, July 25, 2021.

134. Susan A. Thornton. "Is American Diplomacy with China Dead?" *The Foreign Service Journal* (July/August 2019), p. 2, https://afsa.org/american-diplomacy-china-dead.

135. See Garrett O'Brien, "Susan Thornton on Escaping the Zero-Sum Mindset in U.S.–China Relations," *The Wire China*, August 28, 2022.

136. See Lampton's autobiography *Living U.S.–China Relations: From Cold War to Cold War* (Lanham, MD: Rowman & Littlefield, 2024).

137. "An Interview with David M. Lampton: Living U.S. China Relations," *U.S.–China Perception Monitor*, February 22, 2024.

138. "Dr. David Lampton on a Tipping Point in US–China Relations," (2015): https://www.youtube.com/watch?v=iecQMwXHCRk.

139. David M. Lampton, "The United States Should Seek Engagement Without Provocation of China," *East Asia Forum*, March 31, 2024.

140. Mel Gurtov, *Engaging China: Rebuilding Sino-American Relations* (Lanham, MD: Rowman & Littlefield, 2022).

141. Ibid., pp. 119–120.

142. "Remarks and Q&A by National Security Advisor Jake Sullivan on the Future of U.S.–China Relations," Council on Foreign Relations, January 30, 2024, https://www.whitehouse.gov/briefing-room/speeches-remarks/2024/01/30/remarks-and-qa-by-national-security-advisor-jake-sullivan-on-the-future-of-u-s-china-relations.

143. Kurt M. Campbell and Jake Sullivan, "Competition Without Catastrophe: How America Can Both Challenge and Coexist with China," *Foreign Affairs* (September/October 2019).

144. Bob Davis, "Nicholas Burns on Managing the Competition with China," *The Wire China*, June 4, 2023.

145. "C.V. Starr & Co. Annual Lecture on China: A Conversation with Nicholas Burns," Council on Foreign Relations, December 12, 2023, https://www.cfr.org/event/evolving-us-china-relationship-conversation-ambassador-nicholas-burns.

146. "A Conversation with US Ambassador to China R. Nicholas Burns on US–China Relations," Brookings Institution, December 15, 2023, https://www.brookings.edu/events/a-conversation-with-us-ambassador-to-china-r-nicholas-burns-on-us-china-relations.

147. See David Shambaugh, "Dealing with China: Tough Engagement and Managed Competition," *Asia Policy*, No. 23 (January 2017); David Shambaugh, "As the U.S. and China Wage a New Cold War, They Should Learn from the Last One," *Wall Street Journal*, July 31, 2020.

148. Michael McFaul, "Cold War Lessons and Fallacies for US–China Relations Today," *The Washington Quarterly* (Winter 2021); Condoleezza Rice and Niall Ferguson, "Cold Comfort," *Hoover Digest* (Winter 2024); "Niall Ferguson and Condoleezza Rice on the New Cold War," *The Economist*, November 13, 2023.

149. Pottinger and Gallagher, "No Substitute for Victory," op. cit.

150. Scott Kennedy, "U.S.–China Relations in 2024: Managing Competition Without Conflict," CSIS Commentary, January 3, 2024; Ryan Haas, "What America Wants from China: A Strategy to Keep Beijing Entangled in the World Order," *Foreign Affairs* (November/December 2023).

151. Ryan Haas, *Stronger: Adopting America's China Strategy in an Age of Competitive Interdependence* (New Haven, CT: Yale University Press, 2021).

152. Haas, "What America Wants from China," op. cit.

153. Kevin Rudd, *The Avoidable War: The Dangers of a Catastrophic Conflict Between the US and Xi Jinping's China* (New York: Public Affairs, 2022); "Short of War: How to Keep U.S.–Chinese Confrontation from Ending in Calamity," *Foreign Affairs* (March/April 2021).

154. Ibid., pp. 392–394.

155. See, for example, Bob Davis, "Kurt Campbell on Talking to China Again," *The Wire China*, July 16, 2023.

156. The White House, "Readout of President Joe Biden's Meeting with President Xi Jinping of the People's Republic of China," November 14, 2022, https://www.whitehouse.gov/briefing-room/statements-releases/2022/11/14/readout-of-president-joe-bidens-meeting-with-president-xi-jinping-of-the-peoples-republic-of-china/#:~:text=President%20Joseph%20R.,across%20a%20range%20of%20issues.

157. This is revealed and discussed in Sanger, *New Cold Wars*, op. cit., pp. 356–357.

158. Mike Gallagher, "Zombie Engagement with Beijing," *Wall Street Journal*, June 15, 2023.

159. Sanger, *New Cold Wars*, op. cit., p. 420.

160. Ibid., p. 421.

161. Office of the Spokesperson, US Department of State, "Deputy Secretary Campbell's Meeting with PRC Executive Vice Foreign Minister Ma Zhaoxu," May 31, 2024, https://www.state.gov/deputy-secretary-campbells-meeting-with-prc-executive-vice-foreign-minister-ma-zhaoxu.

162. Philip Zelikow and Condoleezza Rice, *To Build a Better World: Choices to End the Cold War and Create a Global Commonwealth* (New York, NY: Twelve Books, 2019), chapters 2–5

Chapter 9

1. Madeleine K. Albright, *Madam Secretary* (New York, NY: Miramax Books, 2003), p. 430.

2. Joseph S. Nye, "What Killed US–China Engagement?" *Taipei Times*, January 6, 2024, https://www.taipeitimes.com/News/editorials/archives/2024/01/06/2003811674.

3. David M. Lampton, *Living U.S.–China Relations: Cold War to Cold War* (Lanham, MD: Rowman & Littlefield, 2024).

4. See, for example,Gordon H. Chang, *Fateful Ties: A History of America's Preoccupation with China* (Cambridge, MA: Harvard University Press, 2015); Michael H. Hunt, *The Making of a Special Relationship: The United States and China to 1914* (New York, NY: Columbia University Press, 1985); Warren I. Cohen, *America's Response to China: A History of Sino-American Relations* (New York, NY: Columbia University Press, 2019); John Pomfret, *The Beautiful Country and the Middle Kingdom: America and China, 1776 to the Present* (New York, NY: Picador, 2017).

5. See Charles Krauthammer, "The Unipolar Moment," *Foreign Affairs* (January 1, 1990).

6. For a contrary view, see Evan S. Medeiros, "The Illusion of Peak China: America Can't Wish Away Its Toughest Challenger," *Foreign Affairs* (May/June 2024).

7. See Anne Applebaum, *Autocracy, Inc.: The Dictators Who Want to Run the World* (New York, NY: Random House, 2024).

8. See, for example, Robert D. Blackwill and Richard Fontaine, *No Limits? The China-Russia Relationship and U.S. Foreign Policy* (New York: Council on Foreign Relations Special Report No. 99, December 2024); Clara Fong and Lindsay Maizland, "China and Russia: Exploring Ties Between Two Authoritarian Powers," Council on Foreign Relations *Backgrounder*, March 20, 2024, https://www.cfr.org/backgrounder/china-russia-relationship-xi-putin-taiwan-ukraine; Bonnie Lin, "The China–Russia Axis Takes Shape," *Foreign Policy*, September 11, 2023, https://foreignpolicy.com/2023/09/11/china-russia-alliance-cooperation-brics-sco-economy-military-war-ukraine-putin-xi.

9. Elizabeth Economy, "China's Alternative Order, and What America Should Learn from It," *Foreign Affairs* (May/June 2024).

10. Although they do not include the five Asia-Pacific allies and Sweden, and Finland have since become members of NATO, see Natalie Armbruster and Benjamin H. Friedman, "Who Is an Ally and Why Does It Matter?" *Defense Priorities*, October 12, 2022, https://www.defensepriorities.org/explainers/who-is-an-ally-and-why-does-it-matter.

11. See Srikanth Kondapalli, "Regional Multilateralism with Chinese Characteristics," in David Shambaugh (ed.), *China & the World* (New York, NY: Oxford University Press, 2020).

12. Ryan Hass, *Stronger: Adapting America's China Strategy in an Age of Competitive Interdependence* (New Haven, CT: Yale University Press, 2021).

13. See the excellent study by Evan S. Medeiros, *The New Domestic Politics of U.S.–China Relations* (New York, NY: Asia Society Policy Institute Center for China Analysis, December 2023).

14. This section draws in part on my chapter David Shambaugh, "Towards a Smart China Strategy," in Leah Bitounis and Jonathon Price (eds.), *The Struggle for Power: US–China Relations in the 21st Century* (Washington, DC: The Aspen Institute, 2020) .

15. Hal Brands, *The Twilight Struggle: What the Cold War Teaches Us About Great Power Rivalry Today* (New Haven, CT: Yale University Press, 2022).

16. Kurt Campbell and Jake Sullivan, "Competition without Catastrophe: How America Can Both Challenge and Coexist with China," *Foreign Affairs* (August 1, 2019), p. 98.

17. See Gregg A. Brazinsky, *Winning the Third World: Sino-American Competition During the Cold War* (Chapel Hill, NC: University of North Carolina Press, 2017).

18. See Larry Diamond, *Ill Winds: Saving Democracy from Russian Rage, Chinese Ambition, and American Complacency* (New York, NY: Penguin, 2019).

19. See David Shambaugh, *China Goes Global: The Partial Power* (New York: Oxford University Press, 2013); David Shambaugh (ed.), *China & the World* (New York: Oxford University Press, 2020).

20. See Joseph Nye, "China Will Not Surpass America Anytime Soon," *Financial Times*, February 19, 2019.

21. See, for example, Asia Society Working Group on Southeast Asia of the Task Force on US China Policy, *Prioritizing Southeast Asia in American China Strategy*: https://asiasociety.org/sites/default/files/2023-08/Prioritizing%20Southeast%20Asia%20in%20American%20China%20Policy%202.pdf.

22. These data come from Brands, *The Twilight Struggle*, op. cit., p. 187.

23. See Anne Applebaum, "The New Propaganda War," *The Atlantic*, June 2024.

24. See Clive Hamilton and Mareike Ohlberg, *Hidden Hand: Exposing How the Chinese Communist Party Is Reshaping the World* (N.P.: One World Publishers, 2020); Sarah Cook, *The Implications for Democracy of China's Globalizing Media Influence*, Freedom House, 2019; Emily Feng, "China and the World: How Beijing Spreads the Message," *Financial Times*, July 12,

2018; Louisa Lim and Julia Bergin, "Inside China's Audacious Global Propaganda Campaign," *The Guardian*, December 7, 2018; David Shambaugh, "China's External Propaganda Work: Missions, Messengers, Mediums," *Party Watch 2018 Annual Report*, https://docs.wixstatic.com/ugd/183fcc_e21fe3b7d14447bfaba30d3b6d6e3ac0.pdf; David Shambaugh, "China's Soft Power Push: The Search for Respect," *Foreign Affairs* (July/August 2015); Daniel Wagner, "China Is Waging a Silent Media War for Global Influence," *The National Interest*, September 19, 2019; Marieke Ohlberg, *Testimony to the US–China Economic and Security Review Commission*, March 23, 2023, https://www.uscc.gov/sites/default/files/2023-03/Mareike_Ohlberg_Testimony.pdf.

25. "Fireside Chat with Condoleezza Rice and Robert M. Gates," Aspen Security Forum, July 19, 2024, https://www.youtube.com/watch?v=mlD9cvaPDy4&list=PL7fuyfNu8jfPTKp6PJ2yJugSfxXEDyEqM&index=30.

26. See US Department of State Global Engagement Center, *How the People's Republic of China Seeks to Reshape the Global Information Environment*, September 18, 2023, https://www.state.gov/gec-special-report-how-the-peoples-republic-of-china-seeks-to-reshape-the-global-information-environment.

27. The Atlantic Council has published a useful report with many practical suggestions for more effective efforts. See Kenton Thibout, *Effective US Government Strategies to Address China's Information Influence* (Washington, DC: Atlantic Council and DFRLab, 2024).

28. For a description of AMWG, see Brands, *The Twilight Struggle*, op. cit., pp. 189–190.

29. See Lara Jakes and Marc Tracy, "US Limits Chinese Staffs at News Agencies Controlled by Beijing," *The New York Times*, March 2, 2020; N.A., "China Banishes Journalists from *Wall Street Journal, New York Times*, and *Washington Post*," *Wall Street Journal*, March 18, 2020. Eighteen US journalists from these three flagship publications were expelled at the time. After the expulsions, only 39 Americans held journalist visas, while 100 Chinese were accredited in the United States.

30. See The Foreign Correspondents Club of China, *Covering China in 2021: Locked Down or Kicked Out*, https://fccchina.org/wp-content/uploads/2022/01/2021-FCCC-final.pdf.

31. See David C. Engerman, *Know Your Enemy: The Rise and Fall of America's Soviet Experts* (New York, NY: Oxford University Press, 2011); Brands, *The Twilight Struggle*, op. cit., chapters 7 and 8.

32. See David Shambaugh (ed.), *The American Study of Contemporary China* (Washington, DC: Woodrow Wilson Center Press, 1993); David Shambaugh, "The Evolution of American China Studies: Coming Full Circle?" *Journal of Contemporary China*, Vol. 33, No. 146 (March 2024).

33. For a detailed elaboration of this argument, see David Shambaugh, *China's Leaders: From Mao to Now* (Cambridge: Polity Press, 2023).

Appendix

1. Thomas L. Friedman, "How China Lost America," *The New York Times*, November 1, 2022.

2. For a description of CNKI see East View, *China National Knowledge Infrastructure (CKNI)*, https://www.eastview.com/resources/cnki-faq.

3. Interview at Stanford University, April 15, 2024.

4. All quotations in this paragraph are verbatim but anonymous. Seminar, Tsinghua University Institute of Strategic Studies, April 25, 2024.

5. See Yang Zhang, "Strategic Vigilance: Mao's 'Anti-Peaceful Evolution' Strategy and Policy Towards the United States, 1959–1976," *Journal of Cold War Studies*, Vol. 25, No. 2 (Spring 2023).

6. Cai Xia, "China–US Relations in the Eyes of the Chinese Communist Party," Hoover Institution China Global Sharp Power Project Occasional Paper, June 2021, https://www.hoover.org/sites/default/files/research/docs/xia_chinausrelations_web-ready.pdf.

7. See, for example, Tao Wenzhao, *Zhong-Mei Guanxi Shi* (Shanghai: Renmin chubanshe, 2023).

8. See, for example, Nai Zuzi, "Kelindun zhengfu dier renqi dui Hua de tiaozheng" [Adjustment of the Clinton Administration's China Policy in Its Second Term], *Xiandai Guoji Guanxi*, No. 8 (1997).

9. Ibid., p. 13.

10. Chu Shulong, "Mianxiang xin shijie de Zhong Mei guanxi zhanlue kuangjia" [The Strategic Framework of China–US Relations in the New Century], *Xiandai Guoji Guanxi*, No. 10 (1997).

11. Chen Jiamen, "Meiguo yingdui Zhongguo jueqi de zhanlue yuanze" [US Strategic Options for Coping with China's Rise], *Waijiao Pinglun*, No. 2 (2009), p. 47.

12. Zhang Yiting, "Kelindun de 'dui Hua jiechu' zhengce jiqi wendingxing" [Clinton's "China Engagement Policy" and Its Instability], *Waijiao Xueyuan Xuebao*, No. 1 (1997), p. 35.

13. Ibid.

14. Liang Gencheng, "Bian jiechu, bian ezhi" [Engagement on One Side, Containment on the Other], *Meiguo Yanjiu*, No. 2 (1996).

15. Niu Jun, "Lun Kelindun zhengfu diyi jiqi dui Hua zhengce de yanbian ji tedian" [The Elements and Evolution of the First Clinton Administration's Policy Toward China], *Meiguo Yanjiu*, No. 1 (1998).

16. Yang Jiemian, "Meiguo daxuan he Kelindun zhengfu tiaozheng dui Hua zhengce" [The US Election and the Clinton Administration's Adjustments to Its China Policy], *Meiguo Yanjiu*, No. 4 (1996).

17. See, for example, Zhao Pingan, Li Xuebao, and Gao Yuan, "Lengzhan hou Meiguo dui Hua zhengce de tiaozheng yu Zhong Mei guanxi de zouxiang" [Post Cold War US Policy Adjustments Toward China and the Direction of China–America Relations], *Waijiao Xueyuan Xuebao*, No. 3 (1996).

18. Li Shouyuan, "'Lengzhan sichao' yu zhanhou Meiguo de dui Hua zhengce" [The "Cold War Mentality" and Post-War American Policy Toward China], *Waijiao Xueyuan Xuebao*, No. 3 (1996), p. 21.

19. Ibid., p. 20.

20. Liu Jianfei, "Lengzhan hou Meiguo dui Hua zhengce zhong de yishixingtai yinsu" [The Ideological Factor in Post–Cold War American China Policy], *Xiandai Guoji Guanxi*, No. 8 (2002), pp. 13–14.

21. Wang Jisi, "'Ezhi' haishi 'Jiaowang'?" [Containment or Engagement?], *Meiguo Yanjiu*, No. 1 (1996).

22. Ibid., p. 2.

23. Zhu Feng, "'Zhongguo Jueqi' yu 'Zhongguo Weixie'" ["China Rise" and "China Threat"], *Meiguo Yanjiu*, No. 3 (2005).

24. See Yang Jiemian, "Dui xiao Bushi zhengfu dui Hua zhengce fenxi he sichao" [Observations and Reflections on the Little Bush Administration's China Policy], *Guoji Wenti Yanjiu*, No. 5 (2001); Fu Mengzi, "Meiguo dui Hua zhengce de zhanlue sichao" [American China Policy's Strategic Thinking], *Xiandai Guoji Guanxi*, No. 6 (2001).

25. See, for example, Zhang Ruizhuang, "Bushi dui Hua zhengce zhong de 'lan jun' yinying" [Shades of the "Blue Military" in Bush's China Policy], *Meiguo Yanjiu*, No. 1 (2002).

26. Wu Xinbo, "Shixi Bushi zhengfu dui Hua anquan zhengce de hexin gainian" [An Analysis of the Core Concepts of the Bush Administration's Security Policy Towards China], *Meiguo Yanjiu*, No. 4 (2007).

27. Author's meeting at CCP International Department, October 2, 2005, Beijing.

28. See, for example, Tao Wenzhao, "Jinrong weiji yu Zhong Mei guanxi" [The Financial Crisis and US–China Relations], *Heping yu Fazhan*, No. 4 (2009).

29. Xu Bu, "Meiguo 'shuailuo lun' yu dangqian guoji maodun goujian" [The "US Decline Debate" and Construction of the Current International Order], *Xiandai Guoji Guanxi*, No. 7 (2022).

30. Zhu Chenghu, "Jianlun Meiguo shili diwei de bianhua" [Some Thoughts on US National Power and Its Global Status], *Meiguo Yanjiu*, No. 2 (2012).

31. Chu Shulong, "Dui guanyu Meiguo de jige zhongda wenti de renzhi yu panduan" [Understanding and Judgments on Several Major Issues Concerning the United States], *Xiandai Guoji Guanxi*, No. 7 (2016).

32. Chu Shulong and Chen Songchuan, "Meiguo zhengzai zouxiang shuailuo ma?" [Is the United States Heading for Decline?], *Xiandai Guoji Guanxi*, No. 4 (2011).

33. Yuan Peng, "Zhong Mei guanxi xiang hechu qu?" [Where Are China–America Relations Headed?], *Waijiao Pinglun*, No. 2 (2010).

34. Zhu Feng, "Quanli zhuanyi lilun: Ba quanxing xianshizhuyi?" [The Power Transition Theory: Hegemonic Realism?], *Guoji Zhengzhi Yanjiu*, No. 3 (2006).

35. Yan Xuetong, "Dui Zhong Mei guanxi buwendingxing de fenxi" [Analysis of the Instability of China–US Relations], *Shijie Jingji yu Zhengzhi*, No. 12 (2010).

36. See Zhu Caihua, "Ezhi yu Hezuo: Hou weiji shidai Meiguo dui Hua jingji zhengce jiexi" [Containment and Cooperation: Analysis of US Economic Policy Towards China in the Post-Crisis Era], *Waijiao Pinglun*, No. 6 (2010).

37. Zhou Minkai, "Hou jinrong weiji duan Meiguo dui Hua guanxi xin dingwei yu Ya-Tai diqu anquan zhanlue tiaozheng" [Adjustments of US China Policy and Asia-Pacific Security Policy After the Financial Crisis], *Guoji Zhanwang*, No. 3 (2011).

38. Tao Wenzhao, "Ruhe kandai Meiguo de zhanlue tiaozheng" [How to View the Strategic Realignment of the United States?], *Meiguo Yanjiu*, No. 3 (2012).

39. Liu Jianfei, "Zhongguo waibu huanjing jianshe zhong de Zhong Mei guanxi" [China–US Relations in the Construction of China's External Environment], *Meiguo Yanjiu*, No. 5 (2014).

40. Xia Liping, "Meiguo de zhanlue zhongdian zhuanyi" [The Shift in Strategic Focus of the United States], *Meiguo Yanjiu*, No. 3 (2012).

41. See Robert Blackwill and Richard Fontaine, *Lost Decade: The US Pivot to Asia and the Rise of Chinese Power* (New York, NY: Oxford University Press, 2024).

42. See Liu Feitao, "Meiguo qianghua dui Hua jinzheng ji Zhong Mei guanxi de zoushi" [Intensification of US Competition with China and Trends in China–US Relations], *Guoji Wenti Yanjiu*, No. 1 (2016).

43. Li Haidong, "Dangqian Meiguo dui Hua zhengce de bianlun, xuanze yu zoushi fenxi" [Current Debates over US China Policy: Choices and Trends], *Meiguo Yanjiu*, No. 4 (2016).

44. Li attributes these views to Freeman on pp. 14–15.

45. Ibid., pp. 16–18.

46. Ibid., pp. 27–28.

47. CICIR is the 11th Bureau of the Ministry of State Security.

48. Diao Daming, "2016 nian daxuan yu Meiguo zhengzhi de songlai zouxiang" [The 2016 Elections and the Future Trends in American Politics], *Meiguo Yanjiu*, No. 6 (2016).

49. Wang Xi, "Tulangpu weihe dangxuan?" [Why Was It Possible for Trump to Win the Election?], *Meiguo Yanjiu*, No. 3 (2017), pp. 11–12. Professor Wang actually divided his time between Beijing University and the Indiana University of Pennsylvania, which lies in the heart of "Trump country" and he thus had firsthand exposure to the forces which he described in his article.

50. See Pan Yaling, "Meiguo zhengzhi wenhua de dangdai zhuanxing" [The Contemporary Transition in American Political Culture], *Meiguo Yanjiu*, No. 3 (2017). Pan is an Associate Research Fellow in the Center for American Studies at Fudan University in Shanghai.

51. Zhou Qi, "Zhengzhi jihua zheng zai rongna Meiguo de minzhu" [Political Polarization Is Eroding American Democracy], *Meiguo Yanjiu*, No. 2 (2022).

52. Jin Junda, "Tulangpu shidai Meiguo Gonghedang 'jianzhipai' de xingwei moshi fenxi" [An Analysis of the Republican 'Establishment Faction' in the Trump Era], *Meiguo Yanjiu*, No. 5 (2018). The author is the son of America specialist Jin Canrong of Renmin University and a PhD student at Boston University.

53. Zhang Yi, "Fenlie de Meiguo" [Divided America], *Meiguo Yanjiu*, No. 3 (2017).

54. Zhao Hai and Chen Zhan, "Meiguo jiyouji xinxi shengchan yu shehui dongyuan jizhi: Yi niming Q yundong weilie" [Information Production and the Social Mobilization Mechanism of the American Extreme Right: The Case of the QAnon Movement as an Example], *Meiguo Yanjiu*, No. 1 (2021).

55. Gai Hailong, "Meiguo zhengzhi zhong de 'shenceng guojia'" [The "Deep State" in American Politics], *Meiguo Yanjiu*, No. 3 (2022); Jie Dalei, "Meiguo de 'shenceng guojia': Xianshi yu misi" [The "Deep State" in America: Reality and Myth], *Meiguo Yanjiu*, No. 1 (2022); Zhang Yeliang, "'Jiegou xingzheng guo': Tulangpu baoshouzhuyi guonei zhengce de mubiao" ["Deconstruction of the Administrative State": The Goal of Trump's Conservative Domestic Agenda], *Meiguo Yanjiu*, No. 6 (2018).

56. "Tulangpu zhengfu neiwai zhengce pinhua" [Survey of Trump Government's Internal and External Policies], *Meiguo Yanjiu*, No. 3 (2017).

57. Da Wei, "Tulangpu zhengfu de dui Hua zhanlue qianjing: quedingxing yu bu quedingxing" [An Early Assessment of the Trump Administration's China Policy: Certainty and Uncertainty], *Meiguo Yanjiu*, No. 6 (2016).

58. Wang Wei, "Cong 'youshilun' dao 'youxianlun': lengzhanhou Meiguo duiwai zhengce sixiang de bianjin" [From "American Primacy" to "America First": Evolution of US Foreign Policy Thinking in the Post–Cold War Era], *Meiguo Yanjiu*, No. 5 (2018).

59. Jiang Fangfei, "Cong Oubama dao Tulangpu: Meiguo dui Hua 'duichong zhanlue' de yanbian" [From Obama to Trump: The Evolution of US "Hedging Strategy" Towards China], *Meiguo Yanjiu*, No. 4 (2018). Also see Liu Jianfei, "Xin shidai Zhongguo waijiao zhanlue zhong de Zhong Mei guanxi" [China–US Relations in China's Diplomatic Strategy in the New Era], *Meiguo Yanjiu*, No. 2 (2018).

60. Ni Feng, "Changgui yinsu feichanggui yinsu huihe: Meiguo dui Hua zhengce de zhibian" [Qualitative Change Caused by Regular and Irregular Factors: US China Policy Adjustment], *Xiandai Guoji Guanxi*, No. 7 (2018), p. 22.

61. Wu Xinbo, "Meiguo guonei zhengzhi shengtai bianhua ruhe zhongxing dui Hua zhengce" [How the Changing US Domestic Political Ecology Is Reshaping Its China Policy], *Meiguo Yanjiu*, No. 4 (2022).

62. Wei Zongyou, "Zhong Mei zhanlue jinzheng, Meiguo 'diwei jiaolu' yu Tulangpu zhengfu dui Hua zhanlue tiaozheng" [China–US Strategic Competition, Status Anxiety, and the Trump Administration's Strategic Adjustment Toward China], *Meiguo Yanjiu*, No. 4 (2018).

63. See, for example, Zhao Minghao, "Meiguo dui Hua zhanlue jinzheng de bianhua" [Intensification of US–China Competition], *Meiguo Yanjiu*, No. 4 (2020); Zhao Minghao, "Cong xin lengzhan lun kan Zhong Mei guanxi mianlin de zhuyao tiaozhan" [The New Cold War Narrative and New Challenges Facing China–US Relations], *Xiandai Guoji Guanxi*, No. 6 (2018); Xia Liping, "Lun xin shiqi Zhong Mei guanxi de zhonggou yu qiantu" [Reconfiguration and Prospects of China–US Relations in the New Era], *Guoji Zhanwang*, No. 3 (2019).

64. Zhang Zhaoxi, "Meiguo Gonghedang de dui Hua chaoqiang xingtai fenxi" [The Republican Party's Ultra-Tough Stance Toward China], *Xiandai Guoji Guanxi*, No. 8 (2021).

65. Chu Shulong and Xu Haina, "Meiguo dui Hua zhanlue ji Zhong Mei guanxi de genbenxing bianhua" [The Fundamental Change of America's China Strategy and Sino-US Relations], *Meiguo Yanjiu*, No. 6 (2021).

66. Yang Jiechi, "Dialogue with National Committee on US–China Relations," February 2, 2021.

67. Wang Jisi, "The Plot Against China? How Beijing Sees the New Washington Consensus," *Foreign Affairs* (July/August 2021).

68. Zhao Kejin, "'Liange Meiguo' yu Meiguo dui Hua zhengce zouxiang" ["Two Americas" and the Direction of US China Policy], *Xiandai Guoji Guanxi*, No. 12 (2020).

69. See, for example, Li Hengyang, "Baideng zhengfu dui Hua keji jingzhen zhanlue fenxi" [An Analysis of the Biden Administration's Strategy to Compete with China in Science and Technology], *Meiguo Yanjiu*, No. 5 (2021); Wei Zongyou, "Baideng zhengfu 'zhongchan jieji waijiao zhengce' yu Zhong Mei guanxi" [The Biden Administration's Foreign Policy for the Middle Class and China–US Relations], *Meiguo Yanjiu*, No. 4 (2021).

70. See the analyses in Ryan Hass, "China's Response to American-Led 'Containment and Suppression,'" *China Leadership Monitor*, No. 77 (Fall 2023); Joel Wuthnow and Elliot S. Ji, "Bolder Gambits, Same Challenges: Chinese Strategists Assess the Biden Administration's Indo-Pacific Strategy," ibid.

71. This impression derives from my meetings (in Washington, DC) with several visiting America specialists who were dispatched by Beijing—during the interval between Biden's electoral victory in November 2020 and his inauguration in January 2021—to try and anticipate what the new administration's China policy may be like. As some of these individuals knew that I had worked on the Biden campaign's China team and was being mentioned in the media at the time as a possible candidate for Ambassador to China, they felt it important to visit my office to gauge my views. I did my best to disabuse these visitors of the idea that the "old Engagement faction" would return to government and reengage with China.

72. Da Wei and Zhou Wuhua, "Hui dao weilai: 2020 nian Meiguo daxuan yu Zhong Mei guanxi de jiyu" [Back to the Future: The 2020 US General Election and the Opportunities for US–China Relations], *Meiguo Yanjiu*, No. 6 (2020).

73. Zhang Zhaoxi, "Ziyou yingpai yu Baideng zhengfu dui Hua zhanlue" [The Liberal Hawks and the Biden Government's China Strategy], *Xiandai Guoji Guanxi*, No. 8 (2022)

74. Ibid., pp. 37–38.

75. Wu Xinbo, "Duoluo Zhong Mei zhanlue jingzheng de xin changtai" [The New Normal of Deteriorating China–US Strategic Competition], *Guoji Wenti Yanjiu*, No. 2 (2022).

76. Ibid.

77. Xinhua News Agency, "His Excellency Xi Jinping, Galvanizing Our Peoples into a Strong Force for the Cause of US–China Friendship," San Francisco, November 15, 2023, https://www.mfa. gov.cn/eng/zxxx_662805/20231116_11181557.html.

78. "World Insights: Xi-Biden Summit Adds Stability to China–U.S. Ties," *Xinhua*, November 23, 2023.

79. "Raimondo's Remarks Expose Deep-Rooted Cold War Mentality: Foreign Minister," *Global Times*, December 4, 2023.

80. State Councilor and Foreign Minister Wang Yi, "The Right Way for China and the United States to Get Along in the New Era," Speech to The Asia Society, New York, November 22, 2022.

81. Wang Jisi et al., "Did America Get China Wrong? The Engagement Debate: A View from China," *Foreign Affairs* (June 14, 2018).

82. Wang Jisi, "The Plot Against China? How Beijing Sees the New Washington Consensus," *Foreign Affairs* (July/August 2021).

83. Ibid.

84. Wang Jisi, "America and China Are Not Yet in a Cold War, But They Must Not Wind Up in Something Worse," *Foreign Affairs* (November 23, 2023).

Index